Readings in Modern Philosophy
Volume II

Locke, Berkeley, Hume
and Associated Texts

Readings in Modern Philosophy
Volume II

Locke, Berkeley, Hume
and Associated Texts

Edited by
Roger Ariew
and
Eric Watkins

Hackett Publishing Company
Indianapolis/Cambridge

For David, Daniel, Christa, and Nicholas,
who we hope will find this anthology of use someday

Copyright © 2000 by Hackett Publishing Company, Inc.
All rights reserved
Printed in the United States of America

15 14 13 12   3 4 5 6 7

For further information, please address:
 Hackett Publishing Company, Inc.
 P.O. Box 44937
 Indianapolis, IN 46244-0937

www.hackettpublishing.com

Cover design by Abigail Coyle

Library of Congress Cataloging-in-Publication Data
Readings in modern philosophy / edited by Roger Ariew and Eric Watkins.
    p.   cm.
 Includes bibliographical references.
 Contents: v. 1. Descartes, Spinoza, Leibniz, and associated texts—v. 2. Locke,
Berkeley, Hume, and associated texts.
  ISBN 0-87220-535-5 (cloth: v. 1)—ISBN 0-87220-534-7 (paper: v. 1)—ISBN
0-87220-533-9 (cloth: v. 2)—ISBN 0-87220-532-0 (paper: v. 2)
  1. Philosophy, Modern. I. Ariew, Roger. II. Watkins, Eric, 1964–
  B791.M65 2000
  190–dc21   00-038860

ISBN-13: 978-0-87220-535-2 (cloth: v. 1)
ISBN-13: 978-0-87220-534-5 (pbk.: v. 1)
ISBN-13: 978-0-87220-533-8 (cloth: v. 2)
ISBN-13: 978-0-87220-532-1 (pbk.: v. 2)

CONTENTS

GENERAL INTRODUCTION

That John Locke, George Berkeley, and David Hume are of paramount importance to the history of modern European philosophy is generally agreed upon by historians of philosophy. The explanation of this judgment typically invokes a broader picture of modern philosophy, depicting two distinct camps: rationalists (Descartes, Spinoza, and Leibniz), who emphasize reason at the expense of the senses, and empiricists (Locke, Berkeley, and Hume), who emphasize the senses after rejecting innate ideas. This extremely rudimentary picture is often filled out as follows. After calling into doubt seemingly all beliefs (especially those based on the senses), René Descartes, the father of modern philosophy, attempts to ground all of our knowledge on innate ideas he discovers and rationally reflects on within himself, beginning with the idea he has of himself as a thinking thing (in the *cogito*). Accordingly, reason, by coming to a clear and distinct conception of its own ideas, attempts to establish knowledge about the world with the same kind of absolute certainty, precision, and necessity attainable in mathematics. While Baruch Spinoza and Gottfried Wilhelm Leibniz revise and even reject some of Descartes's fundamental principles, they both accept Descartes's "rationalist" approach of rejecting sensory ideas as inadequate or confused, in favor of innate ideas, which alone can be adequate or clear and distinct to reason. In this way, it is often claimed,

Spinoza and Leibniz carry Descartes's rationalist philosophy to its ultimate, logical conclusion.

Locke, by contrast, breaks with the rationalists' approach by rejecting innate ideas and by claiming instead that the content of all of our mental states or ideas must stem from experience, whether it be from sensation or reflection—a claim that more or less defines empiricism in this context. Locke rejects innate ideas, not only because he cannot find any ideas that enjoy universal assent, but also because he thinks that philosophers often talk about ideas without understanding clearly what meaning they have—an error encouraged by accepting innate ideas, since believing that an idea is innate precludes one from determining its true origin and thus its precise meaning. Since Locke rejects innate ideas, he views the proper task of philosophy as one of analyzing the precise meaning of the ideas we get from sensation and reflection and determining what we can come to know about the world purely on the basis of these ideas. Just as Spinoza and Leibniz follow Descartes's rationalist assumptions to their logical conclusions, so too, it is often claimed, Berkeley and especially Hume correct the inconsistencies in Locke's position, thus drawing out the proper consequences of Locke's empiricist approach. (Often Immanuel Kant is presented as the culminating figure of modern philosophy with his attempt at synthesizing the rationalist and empiricist traditions, though Kant, too, was in turn successively "corrected" by German Idealists, such as Fichte, Schelling, and Hegel.)

While the truth that underlies this very brief recounting of the places of Locke, Berkeley, and Hume in this history of modern philosophy might fully justify their prominence within this period, one can, we think, discern a much more interesting and significant picture of the importance of their philosophies by broadening one's view beyond the issue of whether one should accept or reject reason (or innate ideas), to include an account of their interests in other domains, such as science and religion.

Consider first the fact that Descartes accepts, whereas Locke rejects, the claim that matter is infinitely divisible. Descartes's claim that matter is infinitely divisible is based (at least in part) on his view that matter is simply extended substance and that because we have an innate idea of extension, we can see clearly and distinctly that it implies infinite divisibility. In short, Descartes's position on the infinite divisibility of matter would seem to be based on his doctrine of innate ideas insofar as our idea of extension is an innate idea. Since Locke rejects innate ideas, it is clear that such a justification would, in his eyes, be mistaken. However, concerns about innate ideas can be only part of the story. For even if Locke must reject Descartes's *justification* of the claim that matter is infinitely divisible, he need not immediately reject the claim itself (even if he would have to search for a new justification for it). It is clear that Locke is a corpuscularian (at least in part) because Boyle and Newton, that is, two of the most preeminent scientists of his day, presuppose corpuscularian principles in their scientific theories and Locke believes that, at least in principle, philosophy and science ought to be able to tell a single coherent story about the world. The importance of the scientific context is not, however, limited to Locke's acceptance of corpuscularianism; a similar explanation of the importance of the scientific context of the day could be developed for Locke's distinction between "primary" and "secondary" qualities as well as for his distinction between nominal and real essences.

Locke is not alone in having interests that extend beyond narrow epistemological issues. Consider also

Berkeley's and Hume's attitudes toward religion. One might think that the question of the meaning of the term "God" as well as the question of God's existence would be a straightforward matter for a strict empiricist. What empirical meaning can one ascribe to the idea of a perfect being endowed with infinite attributes (such as omnipotence, omniscience, and omnibenevolence)? And what empirical evidence does one have for thinking that such a being actually exists? Hume's account of our idea of God in §2 of the *Inquiry Concerning Human Understanding* develops an interesting answer to the former question, and Philo's forcefully argued position in Hume's *Dialogues on Natural Religion* famously expresses one very provocative empiricist response to the latter question (in the negative). Berkeley, by contrast, believes that even if one cannot have an idea of God, one can form a notion of God, and there is no doubt in Berkeley's mind that one can prove God's existence. In light of Hume's powerful arguments, one might suspect that Berkeley, as an Anglican priest, simply could not admit the true consequence of his own empiricist position with respect to God's existence. (Here we would have an especially clear-cut case of Hume's drawing out the logical conclusion of Locke's original empiricist assumptions.) However, it is crucial to note Hume's and Berkeley's different goals and thus different versions of empiricism. Hume is interested exclusively in the laws that govern the relations that exist between ideas in our mind and refuses to speculate on what outside the mind might cause the existence of our sensations. Berkeley, by contrast, is interested primarily in refuting materialists, atheists, and skeptics and, as a part of that project, is very interested in determining what the cause of our sensations could be. Matter, as something inert, cannot be their cause, and we must therefore take recourse to a mind (or spirit), which, when supplemented with further argument, turns out to be God. Thus, from a different point of view, it might seem that Berkeley's empiricism improves upon Hume's by being able to answer a question that Hume cannot, rather than Hume's correcting an inconsistency in Berkeley.

The point of these two brief examples is, we hope, clear. Locke, Berkeley, and Hume are important figures in the history of modern philosophy for *numerous* reasons, reasons that cannot be captured exhaustively in any simple story about a single topic, such as reason versus the senses (or innate ideas versus sensations). Their texts are complex and rich, displaying divergent interests and goals. What makes Locke, Berkeley, and Hume great philosophers and their texts significant philosophical works is the novel and sophisticated way in which they articulate their different interests and attempt to render coherent what would appear to be conflicting demands. Where we today share in their goals and interests, it is not impossible that they may help us to see more clearly truths that have been obscured over the centuries, and, where we do not, it can be instructive to see how we are different and to consider how we came to be so.

In order to allow our readers to understand the richness and complexity of the philosophies of Locke, Berkeley, and Hume, we have tried, as much as possible, to provide whole texts: for example, Berkeley's *Three Dialogues* and *Principles* and Hume's *Inquiry*. Given their considerable length, Locke's *Essay* as well as Hume's *Treatise* and *Dialogues* were excerpted. We have also attempted to surround these works with additional ones that would assist the reader in understanding the primary sources—for example, selections from Boyle, Bayle, and Reid help to put Locke and Hume in context. Of course, we have had to make many difficult choices; we hope we have supplied most, if not all, of the desired selections and have not cast off too many of our readers' favorites.

We have attempted to modernize and Americanize those primary texts originally written in English. Students who are typically given contemporary translations of foreign-language texts need not wade through seventeenth- or eighteenth-century English works just because they were originally written in English. We have replaced archaic words and expressions with their modern equivalents: *surface* for *superficies*, *up to now* or *previously* for *hitherto*, *admit* for *own*, *gladly*

or *inclined to* for *fain*, *endow* for *endue*, and so on—not to mention what we have done to *whereunto*, *therein*, *hark*, *hath*, and *doth*. Perhaps the greatest change has been the modernization of the punctuation; we have adopted an open style of punctuation. A modernization we did not undertake is the discarding of italics, the use of uppercase words for emphasis, mention, and so on. This early modern practice does not seem to be a significant bar to comprehension for twenty-first century students. We also did not attempt to render historical texts into gender-neutral language. Of course, some will inevitably feel that our modernization has been too extensive, while others might wish that we had made even greater emendations. We hope we have avoided both extremes, bearing in mind the needs of the readers for whom this anthology is intended.

This anthology is designed for the one semester or one quarter course often called "The Empiricists." It is a slightly revised and substantially expanded version of approximately the second third of our anthology, *Modern Philosophy*. We have omitted the selection from Malebranche but have included the whole of Berkeley's *Principles*, more selections from Book I of Hume's *Treatise*, a lengthy selection from his *Dialogues Concerning Natural Religion*, and a brief selection from Reid's *Inquiry into the Human Mind* and *Essays on the Intellectual Powers of Man*.[1]

We would like to thank Karl Ameriks, Bill Davis, Daniel Garber, Marjorie Grene, Patricia Kitcher, Nelson Lande, Joseph Pitt, Tad Schmaltz, and Kenneth Winkler for their many helpful suggestions concerning what selections to include. Finally, we wish to thank Deborah Wilkes at Hackett Publishing Company, who as usual has been tremendously helpful and supportive.

1. Footnotes inserted by the editors for the primary texts are in brackets.

1. LOCKE'S *ESSAY* AND ASSOCIATED TEXTS

John Locke (1632–1704) was a moral and political philosopher, philosopher of education, economic theorist, theological polemicist, medical doctor, and public servant. He was educated at Westminster School, 1647–52, and at Christ Church, Oxford, 1652–58 (Bachelor of Arts, 1656, and Master of Arts, 1658). He remained at Christ Church as student and tutor, spending many years studying medicine (Bachelor of Medicine, 1675). In the later 1660s he worked closely with Thomas Sydenham, a friend of Boyle, who was influenced by Descartes and Gassendi. In 1667 he moved to London to live with Anthony Ashley Cooper (later the first Earl of Shaftesbury), serving him as physician, secretary, and political adviser. In the 1670s and early 1680s Locke worked intermittently on philosophy but primarily assisted Shaftesbury and his circle on political matters. Shaftesbury died in exile in Holland in 1683; Locke also went into exile later that year. There he completed the *Essay Concerning Human Understanding*, begun in 1671. Locke was able to return to England in 1689, and the *Essay* was published at the end of 1690. Though not uncontroversial (especially important was a dispute with Edward Stillingfleet that began in 1697 and extended through a number of exchanges), it was an immediate success, appearing in four editions during Locke's lifetime, sometimes with significant revisions; a fifth edition, in preparation at the time of Locke's death, appeared posthumously in 1706.[1]

In his "Epistle to the Reader," which he appended to the *Essay*, Locke remarked that the *Essay* "was not meant for those who had already mastered this subject and made a thorough acquaintance with their own understandings," but for his "own information and the satisfaction of a few friends." He then related the history of the *Essay*, how he came to set about writing it: "five or six friends meeting at my chamber, and discoursing on a subject very remote from this, found themselves quickly at a standstill by the difficulties that arose on every side. After we had puzzled ourselves for a while without coming any nearer a resolution of those doubts which perplexed us, it came into my thoughts that we took a wrong course, and that

1. For more on Locke, see R. S. Woolhouse, *Locke* (Minneapolis: University of Minnesota Press, 1983); John W. Yolton, *Thinking Matter, Materialism in Eighteenth-Century Britain* (Minneapolis: University of Minnesota Press, 1983); Michael Ayers, *Locke*, 2 vols. (London: Routledge, 1991); and Vere Chappell, ed., *The Cambridge Companion to Locke* (Cambridge: Cambridge University Press, 1994).

before we set ourselves upon inquiries of that nature, it was necessary to examine our own abilities and see what objects our understandings were, or were not, fitted to deal with. This I proposed to the company, who all readily assented." The inquiry that Locke set out to conduct, then, was the limited one announced in his introduction: "to inquire into the origin, certainty, and extent of human knowledge, together with the grounds and degrees of belief, opinion, and assent;" Locke is thus in earnest when he says that he will "not at present meddle with the physical consideration of the mind," or trouble himself "to examine in what its essence consists." Locke's modest goals are also made explicit when, in the "Epistle to the Reader," he refers to himself as an under-laborer: "The commonwealth of learning is not at this time without master builders, whose mighty designs in advancing the sciences will leave lasting monuments to the admiration of posterity, but every one must not hope to be a Boyle or a Sydenham; and in an age that produces such masters as the great Huygens and the incomparable Mr. Newton, with some others of that strain, it is ambition enough to be employed as an under-laborer in clearing the ground a little, and removing some of the rubbish that lies in the way to knowledge." That statement, however modest it might have sounded, was surely also a reference to Descartes, who had announced that he would reform all of knowledge, sweeping it all away and starting again on new foundations.

Despite these modest pretensions, in the course of the *Essay*'s four books Locke developed an epistemology that is fundamentally distinct from that of Descartes and his other modern predecessors. While he shares Descartes's focus on ideas, he rejects Descartes's (and others') innate ideas (Book I: Of Innate Notions) in favor of experience. In particular, he claims that all of our ideas must ultimately stem from sensation and reflection (Book II: Of Ideas), where sensation includes any idea that we might get through one (or more) of our five senses and reflection is simply the act by which we turn back on our mind's own operations in thinking and willing. All complex ideas (such as those of substance, mode, and relation) are formed by combining or comparing in different ways the simple ideas gained from these two sources. The main task of Book II thus lies in showing how all meaningful ideas can be traced back to sensation and reflection. Along the way, Locke provides very insightful discussions of a number of fascinating topics such as the distinction between primary and secondary qualities (including a causal theory of perception), personal identity, free will, and causality (or power). What cannot be traced back to sensation and reflection is meaningless and likely stems from a misuse of language—Book III (Of Words). In this context Locke introduces a distinction between real and nominal essences, claiming that due to the limited nature of our access to the real or ultimate nature of substances, we must restrict ourselves to nominal essences, that is, what is directly connected with the name of an object. (For example, the nominal essence of gold is that of a yellow metal with a particular weight, as opposed to its real essence which, according to Locke, is unknown to us.) In Book IV (Of Knowledge and Opinion) Locke is finally in a position to determine what we can and cannot know, given the epistemological resources we have at our disposal. After defining knowledge as the perception of agreement or disagreement between our ideas, Locke restricts knowledge proper to intuition and demonstration, though he admits "sensitive knowledge" in a restricted way since it does go "beyond bare probability." Accordingly, we can have the following very limited kinds of knowledge: identity or diversity, relations of ideas, coexistence of our ideas, and real existence (but it must be noted that the only thing besides our ideas that we can know the real existence of is God).

Table of Contents (Selected):[2]

2. Approximately one third of the *Essay*.

Robert Boyle, *Of the Excellency and Grounds of the Corpuscular or Mechanical Philosophy* (1674)[1]

Robert Boyle (1627–91) was one of the foremost experimental natural philosophers of his day. He was educated at Eton and then given private lessons in Geneva. Around 1656 he settled in Oxford and became a leading member of a circle of experimentalists who later formed the Royal Society of London (in 1660), though he turned down the presidency of the Society in 1680 because of his religious scruples against oath-taking. He debated with Hobbes over the existence of the vacuum and the nature of the "spring" of the air, and with Spinoza over the interpretation of experiments. Boyle was a prolific author; among his many works are New Experiments Physico-Mechanicall, Touching the Spring of the Air *(1660), in which he reports the results of his experiments with an air-pump that he constructed;* The Sceptical Chymist *(1661), in which he rejects Aristotelian and Paracelsian theories of matter; and* Certain Physiological Essays *(1661), in which he announces his mechanical and corpuscularian philosophy. This philosophy, of course, is the topic of the following essay.[2]*

By embracing the corpuscular or mechanical philosophy, I am far from supposing with the Epicureans that atoms accidentally meeting in an infinite vacuum were able, of themselves, to produce a world and all its phenomena; nor do I suppose, when God had put into the whole mass of matter an invariable quantity of motion, he needed do no more to make the universe, the material parts being able by their own unguided motions to throw themselves into a regular system. The philosophy I plead for reaches only to purely corporeal things; and distinguishing between the first origin of things and the subsequent course of nature teaches that God indeed gave motion to matter, but that in the beginning he so guided the various motion of the parts of it as to contrive them into the world he designed they should compose, and established those rules of motion and that order among corporeal things which we call the laws of nature. Thus the universe being once framed by God, and the laws of motion settled and all upheld by his perpetual concourse and general providence, the same philosophy teaches that the phenomena of the world are physically produced by the mechanical properties of the parts of

1. [From *The Philosophical Works of the Honourable Robert Boyle, Abridged* . . . ed. Peter Shaw (London, 1725), 3 vols., English, modified.]

2. [For more on Boyle, see Peter Alexander, *Ideas, Qualities and Corpuscles: Locke and Boyle on the External World* (Cambridge: Cambridge University Press, 1985); Steve Shapin and

Simon Schaffer, *Leviathan and the Air Pump* (Princeton: Princeton University Press, 1985); and Rose-Mary Sargent, *The Diffident Naturalist: Robert Boyle and the Philosophy of Experiment* (Chicago: University of Chicago Press, 1995).]

matter, and that they operate upon one another according to mechanical laws. It is of this kind of corpuscular philosophy that I speak.

And the first thing that recommends it is the intelligibleness or clearness of its principles and explanations. Among the Peripatetics there are many intricate disputes about matter, privation, substantial forms, their eductions, etc. And the chemists are puzzled to give such definitions and accounts of their hypostatical principles, as are consistent with one another, and to some obvious phenomena; and much more dark and intricate are their doctrines about the Archeus, Astral Beings, and other odd notions,[3] which perhaps have in part occasioned the darkness and ambiguity of their expressions, that could not be very clear when the conceptions were obscure. And if the principles of the Aristotelians and chemists are thus obscure, it is not to be expected that the explications made by the help of such principles only should be intelligible. And, indeed, many of them are so general and slight, or otherwise so unsatisfactory, that, granting their principles, it is very hard to understand or admit their applications of them to particular phenomena. And, I think, even in some of the more ingenious and subtle of the Peripatetic discourses, the authors, upon their superficial and narrow theories, have acted more like painters than philosophers and only shown their skill in making men fancy they see castles, cities, and other structures, that appear solid, magnificent, and extensive, when the whole piece is superficial, artificially made up of colors, and comprised within a frame. But, as to the corpuscular philosophy, men do so easily understand one another's meaning when they talk of local motion, rest, magnitude, shape, order, situation, and contexture of material substances; and these principles afford such clear accounts of those things that are rightly deduced from them alone that even such Peripatetics or chemists as maintain other principles acquiesce in the explications made by these, when they can be had, and seek no further; though, perhaps, the effect is so admirable as to make it pass for that of a hidden form or an occult quality. Those very Aristotelians who believe the celestial bodies to be moved by intelligences have no recourse to any peculiar agency of theirs to account for eclipses; and we laugh at those East Indians who, to this day, go out in multitudes with some instruments to relieve the distressed luminary whose loss of light, they fancy, proceeds from some fainting fit, out of which it must be roused. For no intelligent man, whether chemist or Peripatetic, flies to his peculiar principles after he is informed that the moon is eclipsed by the interposition of the earth between her and it, and the sun by that of the moon between him and the earth. And when we see the image of a man cast into the air by a concave spherical mirror, though most men are amazed at it, and some suspect it to be no less than an effect of witchcraft, yet he who is skilled enough in catoptrics will, without consulting Aristotle or Paracelsus or flying to hypostatical principles or substantial forms, be satisfied that the phenomenon is produced by rays of light reflected and made to converge according to optical and mathematical laws.

I next observe that there cannot be fewer principles than the two grand ones of our philosophy, matter and motion; for matter alone, unless it is moved, is wholly inactive, and, while all the parts of a body continue in one state without motion, that body will not exercise any action or suffer any alteration, though it may, perhaps, modify the action of other bodies that move against it.

Nor can we conceive any principles more primary than matter and motion; for either both of them were immediately created by God, or, if matter is eternal, motion must either be produced by some immaterial supernatural agent or it must immediately flow, by way of emanation, from the nature of the matter it appertains to.

There cannot be any physical principles more simple than matter and motion, neither of them being resoluble into any other thing.

The next thing which recommends the corpuscular principles is their extensiveness. The genuine and necessary effect of the strong motion of one part of matter against another is either to drive it on in its entire bulk or to break and divide it into particles of a determinate motion, figure, size, posture, rest, order, or texture. The two first of these, for instance, are each of them capable of numerous varieties; for the figure of a portion of matter may either be one of the five regular geometrical figures, some determinate species of solid figures, or irregular, as the grains of sand, feathers, branches, files, etc. And,

---

3. [The "chemists" referred to are followers of Paracelsus and van Helmont; hypostatical principles are essential principles or elements, and the Archeus is a vital spirit responsible for chemical and physiological reactions.]

as the figure, so the motion of one of these particles may be exceedingly diversified, not only by the determination to a particular part of the world but by several other things, as by the almost infinitely different degrees of celerity, by the manner of its progression, with or without rotation, etc., and more yet by the line in which it moves, as circular, elliptical, parabolic, hyperbolic, spiral, etc. For, as later geometers have shown that these curves may be compounded of several motions, that is, described by a body whose motion is mixed and results from two or more simple motions; so, how many more curves may be made by new compositions and recompositions of motion is not easy to determine.

Now, since a single particle of matter, by virtue of only two mechanical properties that belong to it, may be diversified so many ways, what a vast number of variations may we suppose capable of being produced by the compositions and recompositions of myriads of single invisible corpuscles that may be contained and concreted in one small body, and each of them be endowed with more than two or three of the fertile universal principles above mentioned? And the aggregate of those corpuscles may be further diversified by the texture resulting from their convention into a body, which, as so made up, has its own magnitude, shape, pores, and many capacities of acting and suffering, upon account of the place it holds among other bodies in a world constituted like ours; so that, considering the numerous diversifications that compositions and recompositions may make of a small number, those who think the mechanical principles may serve, indeed, to account for the phenomena of some particular part of natural philosophy, as statics, the theory of planetary motions, etc., but prove inapplicable to all the phenomena of things corporeal, seem to imagine that by putting together the letters of the alphabet one may, indeed, make up all the words to be found in Euclid or Virgil, or in the Latin or English language, but that they can by no means supply words to all the books of a great library, much less to all the languages in the world.

There are other philosophers who, observing the great efficacy of magnitude, situation, motion, and connection in engines, are willing to allow those mechanical principles a great share in the operations of bodies of a sensible bulk and manifest mechanism and, therefore, to be usefully employed in accounting for the effects and phenomena of such bodies, though they will not admit that these principles can be applied to the hidden transactions among the minute particles of bodies and, therefore, think it necessary to refer these to what they call nature, substantial forms, real qualities, and the like unmechanical agents. But this is not necessary, for the mechanical properties of matter are to be found, and the laws of motion take place, not only in the great masses and the middle-sized lumps, but in the smallest fragments of matter—a less portion of it being as much a body as a greater must as necessarily as the other have its determinate bulk and figure. And whoever views sand through a good microscope will easily perceive that each minute grain has its own size and shape as well as a rock or a mountain. Thus too, when we let fall a large stone and a pebble from the top of a high building, they both move conformably to the laws of acceleration in heavy descending bodies, and the rules of motion are observed not only in cannon-bullets but in small shot; and the one strikes down a bird according to the same laws as the other batters a wall. And though nature works with much finer materials and employs more curious contrivances than art, yet an artist, according to the quantity of the matter he employs, the exigency of the design he undertakes, and the magnitude and shape of the instruments he uses, is able to make pieces of work of the same nature or kind, of extremely different bulks, where yet the like art, contrivance, and motion may be observed. Thus a smith who, with a hammer and other large instruments, can forge great bars or wedges out of masses of iron to make strong and ponderous chains to secure streets and gates may, with lesser instruments, make smaller nails and filings, almost as minute as dust, and with yet finer tools, make links wonderfully light and slender. And therefore, to say that though in natural bodies, whose bulk is manifest and their structure visible, the mechanical principles may be usefully admitted but are not to be extended to such portions of matter whose parts and texture are invisible, is like allowing that the laws of mechanism may take place in a town clock and not in a pocket watch, or, because the terraqueous globe is a vast magnetic body, one should affirm that magnetic laws are not to be expected manifest in a small spherical piece of lodestone; yet experience shows us that, notwithstanding the immense disproportion between these two spheres, the terella[4] as well as the earth has its poles, equator, and meridians, and in several other magnetic properties resembles the terrestrial globe.

When, to solve the phenomena of nature, agents are made use of which, though they involve no contradiction in their notions, as many think substantial forms and real qualities do, yet are such that we conceive not how they operate to produce effects — such agents I mean, as the soul of the world, the universal spirit, the plastic power, etc. — the curiosity of an inquisitive person who seeks not so much to know what is the general agent that produces a phenomenon, as by what means, and after what manner it is produced, is not satisfied hereby. Sennert and other physicians tell us of diseases which proceed from incantation; but surely, it is very trivial to a sober physician who comes to visit a patient reported to be bewitched, to hear only that the strange symptoms he meets with, and would have an account of, are produced by a witch or the devil; and he will never be satisfied with so short an answer if he can by any means reduce those extravagant symptoms to any more known and stated diseases; as epilepsies, convulsions, hysteric fits, etc., and if he cannot, he will confess his knowledge of this distemper to come far short of what might be expected and attained in other diseases, in which he thinks himself bound to search into the morbific matter, and will not be satisfied, until he can, probably, deduce from that, and the structure of the human body, and other concurring physical causes, the phenomena of the malady. And it would be of little satisfaction to one who desires to understand the causes of the phenomena in a watch and how it comes to point at and strike the hours to be told that a certain watchmaker so contrived it or, to him who would know the true causes of an echo, to be answered that it is a man, a vault, or a wood, that makes it.

I come now to consider that which I observe most alienates other sects from the mechanical philosophy, namely, a supposition that it pretends to have principles so universal and mathematical that no other physical hypothesis can be tolerated by it.

This I look upon as an easy, indeed, but an important mistake, for the mechanical principles are so universal and applicable to so many purposes that they are rather fitted to take in than to exclude any other hypothesis founded on nature. And such hypotheses, if prudently considered, will be found, as far as they have truth on their side, to be either legitimately deducible from the mechanical principles or fairly reconcilable to them. For such hypotheses will, probably, attempt to account for the phenomena of nature, either by the help of a determinate number of material ingredients, such as the *tria prima* of the chemists[5] or else by introducing some general agents, as the Platonic soul of the world and the universal spirit, asserted by some chemists, or by both these ways together.

Now, the chief thing that a philosopher should look after in explaining difficult phenomena is not so much what the agent is or does, as what changes are made in the patient to bring it to exhibit the phenomena proposed, and by what means, and after what manner those changes are effected. So that the mechanical philosopher being satisfied, one part of matter can act upon another only by virtue of local motion or its effects and consequences; he considers if the proposed agent is not intelligible and physical, it can never physically explain the phenomena, and if it is intelligible and physical, it will be reducible to matter and some or other of its universal properties. And the indefinite divisibility of matter, the wonderful efficacy of motion, and the almost infinite variety of coalitions and structures that may be made of minute and insensible corpuscles being duly weighed, why may not a philosopher think it possible to make out, by their help, the mechanical possibility of any corporeal agent, however subtle, diffused, or active, that can be solidly proved to have a real existence in nature? Though the Cartesians are mechanical philosophers, yet their subtle matter which the very name declares to be a corporeal substance is, for all I know, little less diffused through the universe, or less active in it than the universal spirit of some chemists, not to say the world soul of the Platonists. But whatever is the physical agent, whether it is inanimate or living, purely corporeal or united to an intellectual substance, the above mentioned changes

4. [A magnetic sphere or lodestone, described in William Gilbert's *De magnete* (1600).]

5. [The Paracelsian "elements" of salt, sulfur, and mercury.]

wrought in the body made to exhibit the phenomena may be brought about by the same or the like means, or after the same, or the like manner, as for instance, if corn is reduced to meal, the materials and shape of the millstones and their peculiar motion and adaptation will be much of the same kind; and, to be sure, the grains of corn will suffer various attritions and pulverizations in their passage to the form of meal, whether the corn is ground by a watermill, or a windmill, a horsemill, or a handmill, that is, a mill whose stones are turned by inanimate, by brute, or by rational agents. And if an angel himself should work a real change in the nature of a body, it is scarcely conceivable to men how he could do it without the assistance of local motion, since, if nothing were displaced or otherwise moved than before, it is hardly conceivable how it should be, in itself, different from what it was before.

But if the chemists or others who would deduce a complete natural philosophy from salt, sulfur, and mercury, or any determined number of ingredients of things, would well consider what they undertake, they might easily discover that the material parts of bodies can reach but to a few phenomena of nature, while these things are considered but as quiescent things; whence they would find themselves to suppose them active, and that things purely corporeal cannot but by means of local motion, and the effects that may result from it, be very variously shaped, sized, and combined parts of matter, so that the chemists must leave the greatest part of the phenomena of the universe unexplained by means of the ingredients of bodies, without taking in the mechanical and more comprehensive properties of matter, especially local motion. I willingly grant that salt, sulfur, and mercury, or some substances analogous to them, are obtainable by the action of the fire from a very great many bodies able to be dissipated here below. Nor do I deny that in explaining several phenomena of such bodies, it may be of use to a naturalist to know and consider that as sulfur, for instance, abounds in the body proposed, it may be, thence, probably argued that the qualities usually attending that principle, when predominant, may be also upon its account found in the body that so largely partakes of it. But, though chemical explications are sometimes the most obvious, yet they are not the most fundamental and satisfactory: for the chemical ingredient itself, whether sulfur or any other, must owe

its nature and other qualities to the union of insensible particles in a convenient size, shape, motion, or rest, and texture, all which are but mechanical properties of convening corpuscles. And this may be illustrated by what happens in artificial fireworks. For, though in most of those sorts made either for war or recreation, gun powder is a principal ingredient, and many of the phenomena may be derived from the greater or less proportion in which it enters the compositions, yet there may be fireworks made without gun powder, as appears by those of the ancient Greeks and Romans. And gun powder owes its aptness to fire, and to be exploded to the mechanical texture of more simple portions of matter, niter, charcoal, and sulfur. And sulfur itself, though it is mistaken for a hypostatical principle by many chemists, owes its inflammability to the union of still more simple and primary corpuscles, since chemists confess that it had an inflammable ingredient and experience shows that it very much abounds with an acid and uninflammable salt and is not destitute of a terrestrial part. It may, indeed, be here alleged that the productions of chemical analyses are simple bodies and, upon that account, irresoluble, but that several substances, which chemists call the salts, sulfurs, or mercuries of the bodies that afford them, are not simple and homogeneous is demonstrable. Nor is their not being easily dissipable or resoluble a clear proof of their not being made up of more primitive portions of matter. For compounded bodies may be as difficulty resoluble as most of those that chemists obtain by the fire: witness common greenglass, which is far more durable and irresoluble than many of those which pass for hypostatical substances. And some enamels will, for several times, even vitrify in the forge without losing their nature or often so much as their color, yet enamel consists of salt, powder of pebbles, or sand, and calcined tin, and, if not white, usually of some tinning metal or mineral. But however indestructible the chemical principles are supposed, several of the operations ascribed to them will never be made appear without the help of local motion; were it not for this, we can but little better solve the phenomena of many bodies by knowing what ingredients compose them than we can explain the operations of a watch by knowing of how many and of what metals, the balance, the wheels, the chain, and other parts consist, or than we can derive the operations of a windmill from barely knowing that it is made up of wood, stone, canvas, and iron. And here let me add that it would not at all overthrow the corpuscularian hypothesis, though, either by more exquisite purifications or by some other operations than the usual analysis by fire, it should appear that the material principles of mixed bodies are not the *tria prima* of the vulgar chemists, but either substances of another nature or fewer in number, or if it were true that the Helmontians had such a resolving menstruum as their master's alkahest[6], by which he affirms that he could reduce stones into salt of the same weight with the mineral, and bring both that salt and all other mixed and tangible bodies into insipid water. For whatever is the number or qualities of the chemical principles, if they really exist in nature, it may very possibly be shown that they are made up of insensible corpuscles of determinate bulks and shapes, and by the various coalitions and textures of such corpuscles, many material ingredients may be composed or made to result. But though the alkahestical reductions newly mentioned should be admitted, yet the mechanical principles might well be accommodated even to them. For the solidity, taste, etc., of salt may be fairly accounted for by the stiffness, sharpness, and other mechanical properties of the minute particles of which salt consists; and if, by a further action of the alkahest, the salt or any other solid body is reduced into insipid water, this also may be explained by the same principles, supposing a further comminution of its parts and such an attrition as wears off the edges and points that enabled them to strike briskly upon the organ of taste; for as to fluidity and firmness, they principally depend upon two of our grand principles, motion and rest. And it is certain that the agitation or rest and the looser contact or closer cohesion of the particles, is able to make the same portion of matter at one time a firm and at another a fluid body. So that, though future sagacity and industry of chemists should obtain from mixed bodies, homogeneous substances, different in number, nature, or both, from their vulgar salt, sulfur, and mercury, yet the corpuscular philosophy is so general and fertile as to be fairly reconcilable to such a discovery and also so useful that these new material principles will, as well as the old *tria prima*, stand in need of the more universal principles of the

corpuscularians, especially of local motion. And, indeed, whatever elements or ingredients men have pitched upon, yet if they do not take in the mechanical properties of matter, their principles are so deficient that I have observed both the materialists and chemists not only leave many things unexplained, to which their narrow principles will not extend, but even in the particulars they presume to give an account of, they either content themselves to assign such common and indefinite causes as are too general to be satisfactory, or, if they venture to give particular causes, they assign precarious or false ones, liable to be easily disproved by circumstance or instances to which their doctrines will not agree. The chemists, however, need not be frightened from acknowledging the prerogative of the mechanical philosophy, since that may be reconcilable with the truth of their own principles, so far as they agree with the phenomena they are applied to; for these more confined hypotheses may be subordinate to those more general and fertile principles, and there can be no ingredient assigned that has a real existence in nature but may be derived either immediately or by a row of compositions from the universal matter, modified by its mechanical properties. For if with the same bricks, differently put together and ranged, several bridges, vaults, houses, and other structures may be raised merely by a various contrivance of parts of the same kind, what a great variety of ingredients may be produced by nature from the various coalitions and contextures of corpuscles that need not be supposed, like bricks, all of the same size and shape, but to have, both in the one and the other, as great a variety as could be wished for? And the primary and minute concretions that belong to these ingredients may, without opposition from the mechanical philosophy, be supposed to have their particles so minute and strongly coherent that nature of herself scarce ever tears them asunder. Thus mercury and gold may be successively made to put on a multitude of disguises, and yet so retain their nature as to be reducible to their pristine forms.

From hence it is probable if, besides rational souls, there are any immaterial substances, such as the heavenly intelligences and the substantial forms of the Aristotelians that are regularly to be numbered among natural agents, their way of working being unknown to us, they can only help to constitute and effect things, but will

---

6. [A "resolving menstruum" is a solvent, and the "alkahest" is a universal solvent.]

very little help us to conceive how things are effected, so that, by whatever principles natural things are constituted, it is by the mechanical principles that their phenomena must be clearly explained. For instance, though we grant with the Aristotelians that the planets are made of a quintessential matter and moved by angels or immaterial intelligences, yet to explain the stations, progressions and retrogradations, and other phenomena of the planets, we must have recourse either to eccentrics, epicycles, etc., or to motions made in elliptical or other peculiar lines, and, in a word, to theories in which the motion, figure, situation, and other mathematical or mechanical properties are chiefly employed. But if the principles proposed are corporeal, they will then be fairly reducible or reconcilable to the mechanical principles, these being so general and fertile that, among real material things, there is none but may be derived from or reduced to them. And when the chemists shall show that mixed bodies owe their qualities to the predominance of any one of their three grand ingredients, the corpuscularians will show that the very qualities of this or that ingredient flow from its peculiar texture and the mechanical properties of the corpuscles that compose it. And to affirm that because the chemical furnaces afford a great number of uncommon productions and phenomena, that there are bodies or operations among purely corporeal things not derivable from or reconcilable to the principles of mechanical philosophy is to say, because there are many and various hymns, pavanes, threnodies, courantes, gavottes, sarabands, etc. in a music book, many of the tunes or notes have no dependence on the scale of music, or as if because excepting rhomboids, squares, pentagons, chiliagons, and numerous other polygons, one should affirm there are some rectilinear figures not reducible to triangles or that have properties which overthrow Euclid's doctrine of triangles and polygons.

I shall only add that as mechanical principles and explanations, where they can be had, are preferred by materialists themselves for their clearness, so the sagacity and industry of modern naturalists and mathematicians, having happily applied them to several of those difficult phenomena which before were referred to occult qualities, it is probable that when this philosophy is more scrutinized and further improved, it will be found applicable to the solution of still more phenomena of nature. And it is not always necessary that he who advances an hypothesis in astronomy, chemistry, anatomy, etc., be able, *a priori*, to prove it true or demonstratively to show that the other hypothesis proposed about the same subject must be false, for as Plato said that the world is God's epistle to mankind and might have added in his own way that it was written in mathematical characters, so, in the physical explanations of the parts of the system of the world, I think there is somewhat like what happens when men conjecturally frame several keys to read a letter written in ciphers. For though one man by his sagacity finds the right key, it will be very difficult for him either to prove, otherwise than by trial, that any particular word is not such as it is guessed to be by others according to their keys or to show *a priori* that theirs are to be rejected and his to be preferred, yet, if due trial being made, the key he proposes be found so agreeable to the characters of the letter as to enable one to understand them and make coherent sense of them, its suitableness to what it should decipher is, without either confutations or foreign positive proofs, alone sufficient to make it accepted as the right key of that cipher. Thus, in physical hypotheses, there are some that, without falling foul upon others, peaceably obtain the approbation of discerning men only by their fitness to solve the phenomena for which they were devised, without thwarting any known observation or law of nature; and therefore, if the mechanical philosophy shall continue to explain corporeal things, as it has of late, it is scarce to be doubted but that in time unprejudiced persons will think it sufficiently recommended by its being consistent with itself and applicable to so many phenomena of nature.

John Locke, *An Essay Concerning Human Understanding* (1690)[1]

Book I. Of Innate Notions. Chapter 1. *Introduction.*

1. *An inquiry into the understanding, pleasant and useful.* Since it is the *understanding* that sets man above the rest of sensible beings and gives him all the advantage and dominion he has over them, it is certainly a subject, even for its nobleness, worth our labor to inquire into. The understanding, like the eye, while it makes us see and perceive all other things, takes no notice of itself, and it requires art and pains to set it at a distance and make it its own object. But, whatever are the difficulties that lie in the way of this inquiry, whatever it is that keeps us so much in the dark to ourselves, I am sure that all the light we can let in upon our minds, all the acquaintance we can make with our own understandings, will not only be very pleasant, but bring us great advantage in directing our thoughts in the search of other things.

2. *Design.* This, therefore, being my *purpose* — to inquire into the origin, certainty, and extent of human knowledge, together with the grounds and degrees of belief, opinion, and assent — I shall not at present meddle with the physical consideration of the mind or trouble myself to examine in what its essence consists or by what motions of our spirits or alterations of our bodies we come to have any sensation by our organs or any *ideas* in our understandings and whether those *ideas* do in their formation, any or all of them, depend on matter or not. These are speculations which, however curious and entertaining, I shall decline, as lying out of my way in the design I am now upon. It shall suffice to my present purpose to consider the discerning faculties of a man as they are employed about the objects which they have to do with. And I shall imagine I have not wholly misemployed myself in the thoughts I shall have on this occasion, if in this historical, plain method, I can give any account of the ways by which our understandings come to attain those notions of things we have, and can set down any measures of the certainty of our knowledge, or the grounds of those persuasions which are to be found among men — so various, different, and wholly contradictory — and yet asserted somewhere or other with such assurance and confidence that he who shall take a view of the opinions of mankind, observe their opposition, and at the same time consider the fondness and devotion with which they are embraced, the resolution and eagerness with which they are maintained, may perhaps have reason to suspect that either there is no such thing as truth at all, or that mankind has no sufficient means to attain a certain knowledge of it.

1. [From *Works* (London, 1823), 10 vols., English, modified.]

3. *Method.* It is therefore worthwhile to search out the *bounds* between opinion and knowledge and examine by what measures, in things of which we have no certain knowledge, we ought to regulate our assent and moderate our persuasions. Toward that end I shall pursue this following method:

First, I shall inquire into the *origin* of those *ideas,* notions, or whatever else you please to call them, which a man observes and is conscious to himself he has in his mind and the ways by which the understanding comes to be furnished with them.

Secondly, I shall endeavor to show what *knowledge* the understanding has by those *ideas,* and the certainty, evidence, and extent of it.

Thirdly, I shall make some inquiry into the nature and grounds of *faith* or *opinion,* by which I mean that assent which we give to any proposition as true, of whose truth yet we have no certain knowledge; and here we shall have occasion to examine the reasons and degrees of *assent.*

4. *Useful to know the extent of our comprehension.* If by this inquiry into the nature of the understanding, I can discover the powers thereof, *how far* they reach, to what things they are in any degree proportionate, and where they fail us, I suppose it may be of use to prevail with the busy mind of man to be more cautious in meddling with things exceeding its comprehension, to stop when it is at the utmost extent of its tether, and to sit down in a quiet ignorance of those things which, upon examination, are found to be beyond the reach of our capacities. We should not then perhaps be so eager, out of an affectation of a universal knowledge, to raise questions and perplex ourselves and others with disputes about things to which our understandings are not suited, and of which we cannot frame in our minds any clear or distinct perceptions, or about which (as it has perhaps too often happened) we do not have any notions at all. If we can find out how far the understanding can extend its view, how far it has faculties to attain certainty, and in what cases it can only judge and guess, we may learn to content ourselves with what is attainable by us in this state. [. . .]

6. *Knowing the extent of our capacities will hinder us from useless curiosity, skepticism, and idleness.* When we know our own *strength,* we shall know better what to undertake with hopes of success. And when we have well surveyed the *powers* of our own minds and made some estimate what we may expect from them, we shall not be inclined either to sit still, and not set our thoughts on work at all in despair of knowing anything nor, on the other side, question everything and disclaim all knowledge, because some things are not to be understood. It is of great use to the sailor to know the length of his line, though he cannot fathom all the depths of the ocean with it. It is well he knows that it is long enough to reach the bottom at such places as are necessary to direct his voyage and caution him against running upon shoals that may ruin him. Our business here is not to know all things, but those which concern our conduct. If we can find out those measures by which a rational creature, put in that state in which man is in this world, may and ought to govern his opinions and actions depending thereon, we need not be troubled that some other things escape our knowledge.

7. *Occasion of this essay.* This was that which gave the first rise to this essay concerning the understanding. For I thought that the first step towards satisfying several inquiries, the mind of man was very apt to run into, was to take a survey of our own understandings, examine our own powers, and see to what things they were adapted. Until that was done, I suspected we began at the wrong end, and in vain sought for satisfaction in a quiet and sure possession of truths that most concerned us, while we let loose our thoughts into the vast ocean of *being,* as if all that boundless extent were the natural and undoubted possession of our understandings in which there was nothing exempt from its decisions or that escaped its comprehension. Thus men extending their inquiries beyond their capacities and letting their thoughts wander into those depths where they can find no sure footing, it is no wonder that they raise questions and multiply disputes, which, never coming to any clear resolution, are proper only to continue and increase their doubts and to confirm them at last in perfect skepticism; whereas, were the capacities of our understandings well considered, the extent of our knowledge once discovered, and the horizon found, which sets the bounds between the enlightened and dark parts of things, between what is and what is not comprehensi-

ble by us, men would perhaps with less scruple acqui-esce in the avowed ignorance of the one and employ their thoughts and discourse with more advantage and satisfaction in the other.

8. *What* idea *stands for.* This much I thought neces-sary to say concerning the occasion of this inquiry into human understanding. But, before I proceed on to what I have thought on this subject, I must here in the entrance beg pardon of my reader for the frequent use of the word *idea*, which he will find in the following treatise. It being that term, which, I think, serves best to stand for whatever is the object of the understanding when a man thinks, I have used it to express whatever is meant by *phantasm, notion, species*, or whatever it is which the mind can be employed about in thinking; and I could not avoid frequently using it.

I presume it will be easily granted me that there are such *ideas* in men's minds; everyone is conscious of them in himself, and men's words and actions will satisfy him that they are in others.

Our first inquiry then shall be how they come into the mind.

Chapter 2. No *Innate* Principles in The Mind, and Particularly No *Innate* Speculative Principles.

1. *The way shown how we come by any knowledge, sufficient to prove it not innate.* It is an established opinion among some men that there are in the under-standing certain *innate principles*; some primary no-tions [*koinai ennoiai*], characters, as it were, stamped upon the mind of man, which the soul receives in its very first being and brings into the world with it. It would be sufficient to convince unprejudiced readers of the falseness of this supposition, if I should only show (as I hope I shall in the following parts of this discourse) how men, barely by the use of their natural faculties, may attain to all the knowledge they have, without the help of any innate impressions, and may arrive at certainty without any such original notions or principles. For I imagine anyone will easily grant that it would be impertinent to suppose the *ideas* of colors innate in a creature to whom God has given sight and a power to receive them by the eyes

from external objects; and no less unreasonable would it be to attribute several truths to the impressions of nature and innate characters, when we may observe in ourselves faculties fit to attain as easy and certain knowledge of them as if they were originally im-printed on the mind.

But because a man is not permitted without cen-sure to follow his own thoughts in the search of truth when they lead him ever so little out of the common road, I shall set down the reasons that made me doubt of the truth of that opinion, as an excuse for my mistake, if I am in one, which I leave to be considered by those who, with me, dispose themselves to embrace truth wherever they find it.

2. *General assent the great argument.* There is noth-ing more commonly taken for granted than that there are certain principles, both *speculative* and *practical* (for they speak of both), universally agreed upon by all mankind, which, therefore, they argue, must nec-essarily be the constant impressions which the souls of men receive in their first beings, and which they bring into the world with them, as necessarily and really as they do any of their inherent faculties.

3. *Universal consent proves nothing innate.* This argument, drawn from *universal consent*, has this mis-fortune in it that, if it were true in matter of fact that there were certain truths in which all mankind agreed, it would not prove them innate, if there can be any other way shown how men may come to that universal agreement in the things they do consent in, which I presume may be done.

4. What is, is, *and*, it is impossible for the same thing to be, and not to be, *not universally assented to.* But, which is worse, this argument of universal consent, which is made use of to prove innate princi-ples, seems to me a demonstration that there are none such, because there are none to which all mankind give a universal assent. I shall begin with the specula-tive, and instance in those magnified principles of demonstration, "Whatever is, is," and "It is impossible for the same thing to be and not to be," which, of all others, I think have the most allowed title to innate. These have so settled a reputation of maxims univer-sally received that it will no doubt be thought strange if any one should seem to question it. But yet I take liberty to say that these propositions are so far from

having a universal assent that there is a great part of mankind to whom they are not so much as known.

5. *Not on the mind naturally imprinted, because not known to children, idiots, etc.* For, first, it is evident that all *children* and *idiots* do not have the least apprehension or thought of them. And the lack of that is enough to destroy that universal assent which must be the necessary concomitant of all innate truths, it seeming to me near a contradiction to say that there are truths imprinted on the soul which it does not perceive or understand—imprinting, if it signifies anything, being nothing else but the making certain truths to be perceived. For to imprint anything on the mind without the mind's perceiving it seems to me hardly intelligible. If therefore children and *idiots* have souls, have minds, with those impressions upon them, they must unavoidably perceive them, and necessarily know and assent to these truths. Since they do not, it is evident that there are no such impressions. For if they are not notions naturally imprinted, how can they be innate? And if they are notions imprinted, how can they be unknown? To say a notion is imprinted on the mind, and yet at the same time to say that the mind is ignorant of it and never yet took notice of it, is to make this impression nothing. No proposition can be said to be in the mind which it never yet knew, which it was never yet conscious of. For if any one may, then, by the same reason, all propositions that are true, and the mind is capable ever of assenting to, may be said to be in the mind and to be imprinted; since, if any one can be said to be in the mind, which it never yet knew, it must be only because it is capable of knowing it; and so the mind is [capable] of all truths it ever shall know. No, thus truths may be imprinted on the mind which it never did, nor ever shall know; for a man may live long and die at last in ignorance of many truths which his mind was capable of knowing, and that with certainty. So that if the capacity of knowing is the natural impression contended for, all the truths a man ever comes to know will, by this account, be every one of them innate; and this great point will amount to no more, but only to a very improper way of speaking, which, while it pretends to assert the contrary, says nothing different from those who deny innate principles. For nobody, I think, ever denied that the mind

was capable of knowing several truths. The capacity, they say, is innate, the knowledge acquired. But then to what end such contest for certain innate maxims? If truths can be imprinted on the understanding without being perceived, I can see no difference there can be between any truths the mind is capable of knowing in respect of their original. They must all be innate or all adventitious; in vain shall a man go about to distinguish them. He therefore who talks of innate notions in the understanding cannot (if he intends by this any distinct sort of truths) mean such truths to be in the understanding, as it never perceived, and is yet wholly ignorant of. For if these words (*to be in the understanding*) have any propriety, they signify to be understood, so that to be in the understanding and not to be understood, to be in the mind and never to be perceived, is all one as to say anything is and is not in the mind or understanding. If therefore these two propositions, "Whatever is, is" and "It is impossible for the same thing to be and not to be," are by nature imprinted, children cannot be ignorant of them; infants, and all that have souls, must necessarily have them in their understandings, know the truth of them, and assent to it.

6. *That men know them when they come to the use of reason answered.* To avoid this, it is usually answered that all men know and assent to them, *when they come to the use of reason*, and this is enough to prove them innate. I answer,

7. Doubtful expressions, that have scarcely any signification, go for clear reasons to those who, being prepossessed, do not take the pains to examine even what they themselves say. For to apply this answer with any tolerable sense to our present purpose, it must signify one of these two things: either that as soon as men come to the use of reason these supposed native inscriptions come to be known and observed by them; or else, that the use and exercise of men's reason assists them in the discovery of these principles, and certainly makes them known to them.

8. *If reason discovered them, that would not prove them innate.* If they mean that by the use of reason men may discover these principles, and that this is sufficient to prove them innate, their way of arguing will stand thus, namely, that, whatever truths reason can certainly discover to us and make us firmly assent

to, those are all naturally imprinted on the mind; since that universal assent, which is made the mark of them, amounts to no more but this—that by the use of reason we are capable to come to a certain knowledge of and assent to them, and, by this means, there will be no difference between the maxims of the mathematicians and theorems they deduce from them—all must be equally allowed innate, they being all discoveries made by the use of reason and truths that a rational creature may certainly come to know, if he applies his thoughts rightly that way.

9. *It is false that reason discovers them.* But how can these men think the *use of reason* necessary to discover principles that are supposed innate, when reason (if we may believe them) is nothing else but the faculty of deducing unknown truths from principles or propositions that are already known? That certainly can never be thought innate which we have need of reason to discover, unless, as I have said, we will have all the certain truths that reason ever teaches us to be innate. [. . .]

12. *The coming to the use of reason not the time we come to know these maxims.* If by knowing and assenting to them, *when we come to the use of reason,* is meant that this is the time when they come to be taken notice of by the mind, and that, as soon as children come to the use of reason they come also to know and assent to these maxims, this also is false and frivolous. *First,* it is false, because it is evident these maxims are not in the mind so early as the use of reason, and therefore the coming to the use of reason is falsely assigned as the time of their discovery. How many instances of the use of reason may we observe in children a long time before they have any knowledge of this maxim, "That it is impossible for the same thing to be and not to be"? And a great part of illiterate people and savages pass many years, even of their rational age, without ever thinking on this and the like general propositions. I grant, men do not come to the knowledge of these general and more abstract truths, which are thought innate, until they come to the use of reason; and I add, nor then neither. This is so because, until after they come to the use of reason, those general abstract *ideas* are not framed in the mind, about which those general maxims are which are mistaken for innate principles, but are

indeed discoveries made and verities introduced and brought into the mind by the same way, and discovered by the same steps, as several other propositions, which nobody was ever so extravagant as to suppose innate. [. . .]

14. *If coming to the use of reason were the time of their discovery, it would not prove them innate.* But, *secondly,* were it true that the precise time of their being known and assented to were when men come to the use of reason, neither would that prove them innate. This way of arguing is as frivolous as the supposition itself is false. For, by what kind of logic will it appear that any notion is originally by nature imprinted in the mind in its first constitution, because it comes first to be observed and assented to when a faculty of the mind, which has quite a distinct province, begins to exert itself? [. . .]

15. *The steps by which the mind attains several truths.* The senses at first let in particular *ideas,* and furnish the yet empty cabinet, and, the mind by degrees growing familiar with some of them, they are lodged in the memory, and names got to them. Afterwards, the mind proceeding further, abstracts them, and by degrees learns the use of general names. In this manner the mind comes to be furnished with *ideas* and language, the materials about which to exercise its discursive faculty. And the use of reason becomes daily more visible as these materials that give it employment increase. But though the having of general *ideas* and the use of general words and reason usually grow together, yet I do not see how this any way proves them innate. The knowledge of some truths, I confess, is very early in the mind, but in a way that shows them not to be innate. For, if we will observe, we shall find it still to be about *ideas,* not innate, but acquired—it being about those first which are imprinted by external things, with which infants have earliest to do, which make the most frequent impressions on their senses. In *ideas* thus got, the mind discovers that some agree and others differ, probably as soon as it has any use of memory, as soon as it is able to retain and perceive distinct *ideas.* But whether it is then, or not, this is certain, it does so long before it has the use of words or comes to that which we commonly call "the use of reason." For a child knows as certainly before it can speak the

difference between the *ideas* of sweet and bitter (i.e., that sweet is not bitter), as it knows afterwards (when it comes to speak) that wormwood and sugarplums are not the same thing. [. . .]

17. *Assenting as soon as proposed and understood does not prove them innate.* This evasion therefore of general assent when men come to the use of reason, failing as it does, and leaving no difference between those supposed innate and other truths that are afterwards acquired and learned, men have endeavored to secure a universal assent to those they call maxims by saying, they are *generally assented to as soon as proposed* and the terms they are proposed in understood; seeing all men, even children, as soon as they hear and understand the terms, assent to these propositions, they think it is sufficient to prove them innate. For, since men never fail, after they have once understood the words, to acknowledge them for undoubted truths, they would infer that certainly these propositions were first lodged in the understanding, which, without any teaching, the mind at the very first proposal immediately closes with and assents to, and after that never doubts again.

18. *If such an assent is a mark of innate, then, that one and two are equal to three, that sweetness is not bitterness, and a thousand the like, must be innate.* In answer to this I demand, "whether ready assent given to a proposition, *upon first hearing* and understanding the terms, is a certain mark of an innate principle?" If it is not, such a general assent is in vain urged as a proof of them; if it is said that it is a mark of innate, they must then allow all such propositions to be innate which are generally assented to as soon as heard, by which they will find themselves plentifully stored with innate principles. For, upon the same ground, namely, of assent at first hearing and understanding the terms, that men would have those maxims pass for innate, they must also admit several propositions about numbers to be innate; and thus, *that one and two are equal to three, that two and two are equal to four,* and a multitude of other like propositions in numbers that every body assents to at first hearing and understanding the terms, must have a place among these innate axioms. Nor is this the prerogative of numbers alone and propositions made

about several of them, but even natural philosophy and all the other sciences afford propositions which are sure to meet with assent as soon as they are understood. *That two bodies cannot be in the same place* is a truth that nobody any more sticks at than at these maxims, that "it is impossible for the same thing to be and not to be," that "white is not black," that "a square is not a circle," "that bitterness is not sweetness." [. . .] But since no proposition can be innate unless the *ideas* about which it is are innate, this will be to suppose all our *ideas* of colors, sounds, tastes, figure, etc., innate, than which there cannot be anything more opposite to reason and experience. Universal and ready assent upon hearing and understanding the terms is (I grant) a mark of self-evidence; but self-evidence, depending not on innate impressions, but on something else (as we shall show afterward), belongs to several propositions which nobody was yet so extravagant as to pretend to be innate.

19. *Such less general propositions known before these universal maxims.* Nor let it be said that those more particular self-evident propositions which are assented to at first hearing as *that one and two are equal to three, that green is not red,* etc., are received as the consequences of those more universal propositions which are looked on as innate principles, since anyone who will but take the pains to observe what passes in the understanding will certainly find that these, and the like less general propositions, are certainly known and firmly assented to by those who are utterly ignorant of those more general maxims; and so, being earlier in the mind than those (as they are called) first principles, cannot owe to them the assent with which they are received at first hearing. [. . .]

21. *These maxims not being known sometimes until proposed does not prove them innate.* But we have not yet done with *assenting to propositions at first hearing and understanding their terms.* It is fit we first take notice that this, instead of being a mark that they are innate, is a proof of the contrary, since it supposes that several who understand and know other things are ignorant of these principles until they are proposed to them, and that one may be unacquainted with these truths until he hears them from others. For, if they were innate, what need they be proposed in order to

gaining assent, when by being in the understanding by a natural and original impression (if there were any such) they could not but be known before? [. . .]

22. *Implicitly known before proposing signifies that the mind is capable of understanding them, or else signifies nothing.* If it is said, "The understanding has an *implicit knowledge* of these principles, but not an *explicit*, before this first hearing," (as they must who will say, "that they are in the understanding before they are known") it will be hard to conceive what is meant by a principle imprinted on the understanding implicitly, unless it is this, that the mind is capable of understanding and assenting firmly to such propositions. And thus all mathematical demonstrations as well as first principles must be received as native impressions on the mind. [. . .]

Book II. Of Ideas. Chapter 1. *Of* Ideas *in General, and Their Origin.*

1. Idea *is the object of thinking.* Every man being conscious to himself that he thinks, and that which his mind is applied about while thinking being the *ideas* that are there, it is past doubt that men have in their minds several *ideas* such as are those expressed by the words *whiteness, hardness, sweetness, thinking, motion, man, elephant, army, drunkenness,* and others. It is in the first place, then, to be inquired how he comes by them. I know it is a received doctrine that men have native *ideas* and original characters stamped upon their minds in their very first being. This opinion I have, at large, examined already, and I suppose what I have said in the foregoing book will be much more easily admitted when I have shown from where the understanding may get all the *ideas* it has and by what ways and degrees they may come into the mind—for which I shall appeal to everyone's own observation and experience.

2. *All ideas come from sensation or reflection.* Let us then suppose the mind to be, as we say, white paper, void of all characters, without any *ideas*. How does it come to be furnished? From where does it come by that vast store which the busy and boundless fancy of man has painted on it with an almost endless variety? From where does it have all the materials of

reason and knowledge? To this I answer, in one word, from *experience*; our knowledge is founded in all that, and from that it ultimately derives itself. Our observation employed either about *external sensible objects or about the internal operations of our minds, perceived and reflected on by ourselves, is that which supplies our understandings with all the materials of thinking.* These two are the fountains of knowledge from which all the *ideas* we have, or can naturally have, do spring.

3. *The objects of sensation one source of* ideas. First, *our senses,* conversant about particular sensible objects, do *convey into the mind* several distinct *perceptions* of things, according to those various ways in which those objects do affect them. And thus we come by those *ideas* we have of *yellow, white, heat, cold, soft, hard, bitter, sweet,* and all those which we call sensible qualities—which, when I say the senses convey into the mind, I mean, they from external objects convey into the mind what produces there those *perceptions*. This great source of most of the *ideas* we have, depending wholly upon our senses and derived by them to the understanding, I call SENSATION.

4. *The operations of our minds, the other source of them.* Secondly, the other fountain from which experience furnishes the understanding with *ideas* is the *perception of the operations of our own mind* within us, as it is employed about the *ideas* it has gotten—which operations, when the soul comes to reflect on and consider, do furnish the understanding with another set of *ideas*, which could not be had from things without. And such are *perception, thinking, doubting, believing, reasoning, knowing, willing,* and all the different actings of our own minds, which we, being conscious of and observing in ourselves, do from these receive into our understandings as distinct *ideas*, as we do from bodies affecting our senses. This source of *ideas* every man has wholly in himself; and though it is not sense, as having nothing to do with external objects, yet it is very like it, and might properly enough be called internal sense. But as I call the other *sensation*, so I call this REFLECTION, the *ideas* it affords being such only as the mind gets by reflecting on its own operations within itself. By REFLECTION then, in the following part of this

discourse, I would be understood to mean that notice which the mind takes of its own operations and the manner of them by reason of which there come to be *ideas* of these operations in the understanding. These two, I say, namely, external material things as the objects of SENSATION and the operations of our own minds within as the objects of REFLECTION, are to me the only origins from which all our *ideas* take their beginnings. The term *operations* here I use in a large sense, as comprehending not barely the actions of the mind about its *ideas*, but some sort of passions arising sometimes from them, such as is the satisfaction or uneasiness arising from any thought.

5. *All our* ideas *are of the one or the other of these.* The understanding seems to me not to have the least glimmering of any *ideas* which it does not receive from one of these two. *External objects furnish the mind with the* ideas *of sensible qualities*, which are all those different perceptions they produce in us. And the *mind furnishes the understanding with* ideas *of its own operations.*

These, when we have taken a full survey of them, and their several modes, combinations, and relations, we shall find to contain all our whole stock of *ideas*, and that we have nothing in our minds which did not come in one of these two ways. Let anyone examine his own thoughts and thoroughly search into his understanding—and then let him tell me whether all the original *ideas* he has there are any other than of the objects of his *senses*, or of the operations of his mind, considered as objects of his *reflection*—and however great a mass of knowledge he imagines to be lodged there, he will, upon taking a strict view, see that he *does not have any* idea *in his mind, but what one of these two have imprinted*, though perhaps with infinite variety compounded and enlarged by the understanding, as we shall see hereafter.

6. *Observable in children.* He who attentively considers the state of a *child* at his first coming into the world will have little reason to think him stored with plenty of *ideas* that are to be the matter of his future knowledge. It is by degrees he comes to be furnished with them. And though the *ideas* of obvious and familiar qualities imprint themselves before the memory begins to keep a register of time or order, yet it

is often so late before some unusual qualities come in the way that there are few men who cannot recollect the beginning of their acquaintance with them. And if it were worthwhile, no doubt a child might be so ordered as to have but a very few even of the ordinary *ideas* until he were grown up to a man. But all who are born into the world being surrounded with bodies that perpetually and diversely affect them, variety of *ideas*, whether care is taken of it or not, are imprinted on the minds of children. Light and colors are busy at hand everywhere when the eye is but open; sounds and some tangible qualities do not fail to solicit their proper senses and force an entrance to the mind; but yet, I think, it will be granted easily that if a child were kept in a place where he never saw any other but black and white until he were a man, he would have no more *ideas* of scarlet or green than he who from his childhood never tasted an oyster or a pineapple has of those particular relishes.

7. *Men are differently furnished with these, according to the different objects they converse with.* Men then come to be furnished with fewer or more simple *ideas* from without, according as the objects they converse with afford greater or less variety, and from the operations of their minds within, according as they more or less *reflect* on them. For though he who contemplates the operations of his mind cannot but have plain and clear *ideas* of them, yet, unless he turns his thoughts that way and considers them *attentively*, he will no more have clear and distinct *ideas* of all the *operations of his mind*, and all that may be observed in there, than he will have all the particular *ideas* of any landscape or of the parts and motions of a clock, who will not turn his eyes to it and with attention heed all the parts of it. The picture or clock may be so placed that they may come in his way every day, but yet he will have but a confused *idea* of all the parts they are made up of until he applies himself with attention to consider them each in particular.

8. Ideas *of reflection later, because they need attention.* And hence we see the reason why it is pretty late before most children get *ideas* of the operations of their own minds; and some do not have any very clear or perfect *ideas* of the greatest part of them all their lives, because, though they pass there continu-

ally, yet, like floating visions, they make not deep impressions enough to leave in their mind clear, distinct, lasting *ideas*, until the understanding turns inward upon itself, *reflects* on its own *operations*, and makes them the objects of its own contemplation. Children, when they come first into it, are surrounded with a world of new things, which, by a constant solicitation of their senses, draw the mind constantly to them, ready to take notice of new and apt to be delighted with the variety of changing objects. Thus the first years are usually employed and diverted in looking abroad. Men's business in them is to acquaint themselves with what is to be found without. And so growing up in a constant attention to outward sensation, [they] seldom make any considerable reflection on what passes within them until they come to be of riper years, and some scarcely ever at all.

9. *The soul begins to have* ideas *when it begins to perceive*. To ask *at what time a man has first any* ideas is to ask when he begins to perceive—having *ideas* and perception being the same thing. I know it is an opinion that the soul always thinks, and that it has the actual perception of *ideas* in itself constantly as long as it exists, and that actual thinking is as inseparable from the soul as actual extension is from the body—which if true, to inquire after the beginning of a man's *ideas* is the same as to inquire after the beginning of his soul. For by this account soul and its *ideas* as body and its extension will begin to exist both at the same time.

10. *The soul does not always think, for this wants proofs*. But whether the soul is supposed to exist antecedent to, or coeval with, or some time after the first rudiments of organization or the beginnings of life in the body, I leave to be disputed by those who have better thought of that matter. I confess myself to have one of those dull souls that does not perceive itself always to contemplate *ideas*; nor can conceive it any more necessary for the *soul always to think* than for the body always to move, the perception of *ideas* being (as I conceive) to the soul what motion is to the body—not its essence, but one of its operations. And therefore, though thinking is supposed never so much the proper action of the soul, yet it is not necessary to suppose that it should be always thinking, always in action; that perhaps is the privilege of the infinite author and preserver of things who never slumbers nor sleeps, but is not competent to any finite being, at least not to the soul of man. We know certainly by experience that we sometimes think—and from there draw this infallible consequence, that there is something in us that has a power to think—but whether that substance perpetually thinks or not, we can be no further assured than experience informs us. For to say that actual thinking is essential to the soul, and inseparable from it, is to beg what is in question and not to prove it by reason—which is necessary to be done, if it is not a self-evident proposition. But whether this, "that the soul always thinks," is a self-evident proposition that everybody assents to at first hearing, I appeal to mankind. It is doubted whether I thought at all last night or not; the question being about a matter of fact, it is begging it to bring, as a proof for it, an hypothesis, which is the very thing in dispute. In this way one may prove anything, and it is but supposing that all watches think while the balance beats; and it is sufficiently proved, and past doubt, that my watch thought all last night. But he who would not deceive himself ought to build his hypothesis on matter of fact, and make it out by sensible experience, and not presume on matter of fact, because of his hypothesis, that is, because he supposes it to be so. This way of proving amounts to this, that I must necessarily think all last night, because another supposes I always think, though I myself cannot perceive that I always do so.

But men in love with their opinions may not only suppose what is in question, but allege wrong matter of fact. How else could anyone make it an inference of mine that a thing is not, because we are not sensible of it in our sleep? I do not say there is no soul in a man because he is not sensible of it in his sleep. But I do say he cannot think at any time, waking or sleeping, without being sensible of it. Our being sensible of it is not necessary to anything but to our thoughts; and to them it is, and to them it always will be, necessary, until we can think without being conscious of it.

11. *It is not always conscious of it*. I grant that the soul in a waking man is never without thought because it is the condition of being awake. But whether sleeping without dreaming is not an affection of the

whole man, mind as well as body, may be worth a waking man's consideration, it being hard to conceive that anything should think and not be conscious of it. If the *soul* does *think in a sleeping man* without being conscious of it, I ask, whether during such thinking it has any pleasure or pain or is capable of happiness or misery? I am sure the man is not, no more than the bed or earth he lies on. For to be happy or miserable without being conscious of it seems to me utterly inconsistent and impossible. Or if it is possible that the soul can, while the body is sleeping, have its thinking, enjoyments, and concerns, its pleasures or pain, apart, which the man is not conscious of nor partakes in, it is certain that *Socrates* asleep and *Socrates* awake is not the same person. But his soul when he sleeps and *Socrates* the man, consisting of body and soul when he is waking, are two persons, since waking *Socrates* has no knowledge of, or concern for, that happiness or misery of his soul which it enjoys alone by itself while he sleeps, without perceiving anything of it, no more than he has for the happiness or misery of a man in the Indies whom he does not know. For if we take wholly away all consciousness of our actions and sensations, especially of pleasure and pain and the concern that accompanies it, it will be hard to know in what to place personal identity.

12. *If a sleeping man thinks without knowing it, the sleeping and waking man are two persons.* "The soul, during sound sleep, thinks," say these men. *While it thinks* and perceives, it is capable certainly of those of delight or trouble as well as any other perceptions, and *it must necessarily be conscious of its own perceptions.* But it has all this apart; the sleeping man, it is plain, is conscious of nothing of all this. Let us suppose then the soul of *Castor*, while he is sleeping, retired from his body—which is no impossible supposition for the men I have here to do with, who so liberally allow life without a thinking soul to all other animals. These men cannot then judge it impossible or a contradiction that the body should live without the soul, nor that the soul should subsist and think, or have perception, even perception of happiness or misery, without the body. Let us then, as I say, suppose the soul of *Castor* separated during his sleep from his body, to think apart. Let us suppose too, that it chooses

for its scene of thinking the body of another man, e.g., *Pollux*, who is sleeping without a soul. For if *Castor's* soul can think while *Castor* is asleep what *Castor* is never conscious of, it is no matter what place it chooses to think in. We have here then the bodies of two men with only one soul between them, which we will suppose to sleep and wake by turns; and the soul still thinking in the waking man, of which the sleeping man is never conscious, never has the least perception. I ask then, whether *Castor* and *Pollux*, thus, with only one soul between them, which thinks and perceives in one what the other is never conscious of nor is concerned for, are not two as distinct persons as *Castor* and *Hercules* or as *Socrates* and *Plato* were? And whether one of them might not be very happy and the other very miserable? Just by the same reason they make the soul and the man two persons who make the soul think apart what the man is not conscious of. For I suppose nobody will make identity of persons to consist in the soul's being united to the very same numerical particles of matter. For if that is necessary to identity, it will be impossible, in that constant flux of the particles of our bodies, that any man should be the same person two days or two moments together.

13. *Impossible to convince those who sleep without dreaming that they think.* Thus, I think, every drowsy nod shakes their doctrine, who teach that the soul is always thinking. Those, at least, who do at any time sleep without dreaming can never be convinced that their thoughts are sometimes busy for four hours without their knowing of it, and if they are taken in the very act, waked in the middle of that sleeping contemplation, can give no manner of account of it.

14. *That men dream without remembering it, in vain urged.* It will perhaps be said, "that the *soul* thinks even *in* the soundest *sleep, but the memory does not retain it.*" That the soul in a sleeping man should be this moment busy thinking, and the next moment in a waking man not remember nor be able to recollect one jot of all those thoughts, is very hard to be conceived and would need some better proof than bare assertion to make it be believed. For who can without any more ado, but being barely told so, imagine that the greatest part of men do, during all their lives, for several hours every day, think of some-

thing, which, if they were asked, even in the middle of these thoughts, they could remember nothing at all of? Most men, I think, pass a great part of their sleep without dreaming. I once knew a man who was bred a scholar and had no bad memory, who told me he had never dreamed in his life until he had that fever he was then newly recovered of, which was about the twenty-fifth or twenty-sixth year of his age. I suppose the world affords more such instances. At least everyone's acquaintance will furnish him with examples enough of such, as pass most of their nights without dreaming. [. . .]

19. *That a man should be busy in thinking, and yet not retain it the next moment, very improbable.* To suppose the soul to think and the man not to perceive it is, as has been said, to make two persons in one man. And if one considers well these men's way of speaking, one should be led into a suspicion that they do so. For they who tell us that the soul always thinks do never, that I remember, say that a man always thinks. Can the soul think and not the man? Or a man think and not be conscious of it? This perhaps would be suspected of *jargon* in others. If they say the man always thinks but is not always conscious of it, they may as well say his body is extended without having parts. For it is altogether as intelligible to say that a body is extended without parts as that anything *thinks without being conscious of it* or perceiving that it does so. They who talk thus may, with as much reason, if it is necessary to their hypothesis, say that a man is always hungry, but that he does not always feel it; whereas hunger consists in that very sensation, as thinking consists in being conscious that one thinks. If they say that a man is always conscious to himself of thinking, I ask how do they know it? Consciousness is the perception of what passes in a man's own mind. Can another man perceive that I am conscious of anything, when I perceive it not myself? No man's knowledge here can go beyond his experience. Wake a man out of a sound sleep, and ask him what he was that moment thinking of. If he himself is conscious of nothing he then thought on, he must be a notable diviner of thoughts that can assure him that he was thinking. May he not with more reason assure him he was not asleep? This is something beyond philosophy, and it cannot be less

than revelation that discovers to another thoughts in my mind when I can find none there myself; and they must necessarily have a penetrating sight who can certainly see that I think when I cannot perceive it myself and when I declare that I do not, and yet can see that dogs or elephants do not think when they give all the demonstration of it imaginable, except only telling us that they do so. This some may suspect to be a step beyond the Rosicrucians, it seeming easier to make one's self invisible to others than to make another's thoughts visible to me, which are not visible to himself. But it is but defining the soul to be "a substance that always thinks," and the business is done. If such definition is of any authority, I do not know what it can serve for but to make many men suspect that they have no souls at all, since they find a good part of their lives pass away without thinking. For no definitions that I know, no suppositions of any sect, are of force enough to destroy constant experience; and perhaps it is the affectation of knowing beyond what we perceive that makes so much useless dispute and noise in the world.

20. *No ideas but from sensation or reflection evident, if we observe children.* I see no reason, therefore, to believe that the *soul thinks before the senses have furnished it with* ideas to think on; and as those are increased and retained, so it comes by exercise to improve its faculty of thinking, in the several parts of it as well as afterwards, by compounding those *ideas* and reflecting on its own operations, [and so] it increases its stock as well as facility in remembering, imagining, reasoning, and other modes of thinking. [. . .]

23. If it shall be demanded then *when a man begins to have any* ideas, I think the true answer is, when he first has any *sensation.* For since there does not appear to be any *ideas* in the mind before the senses have conveyed any in, I conceive that *ideas* in the understanding are coeval with *sensation* — which is such an impression or motion made in some part of the body as produces some perception in the understanding. It is about these impressions made on our senses by outward objects that the mind seems first to employ itself in such operations as we call perception, remembering, consideration, reasoning, etc.

24. *The origin of all our knowledge.* In time, the mind comes to reflect on its own *operations* about

the *ideas* gotten by *sensation* and in this way stores itself with a new set of *ideas*, which I call *ideas* of reflection. These are the *impressions* that are made on our *senses* by outward objects that are extrinsic to the mind and its *own operations*, proceeding from powers intrinsic and proper to itself, which, when *reflected* on by itself, become also objects of its contemplation, and *are*, as I have said, *the origin of all knowledge*. Thus the first capacity of human intellect is that the mind is fitted to receive the impressions made on it either through the *senses* by outward objects or by its own operations when it *reflects* on them. This is the first step a man makes towards the discovery of anything and the groundwork on which to build all those notions which ever he shall have naturally in this world. All those sublime thoughts which tower above the clouds, and reach as high as heaven itself, take their rise and footing here. In all that great extent in which the mind wanders, in those remote speculations it may seem to be elevated with, it does not stir one jot beyond those *ideas* which *sense* or *reflection* have offered for its contemplation.

25. *In the reception of simple* ideas, *the understanding is most of all passive*. In this part the *understanding* is merely *passive*; and whether or not it will have these beginnings, and as it were materials of knowledge, is not in its own power. For the objects of our senses do, many of them, obtrude their particular *ideas* upon our minds whether we will or not; and the operations of our minds will not let us be without, at least some obscure notions of them. No man can be wholly ignorant of what he does when he thinks. These *simple ideas*, when offered to the mind, *the understanding can* no more refuse to have, nor alter, when they are imprinted, nor blot them out and make new ones itself than a mirror can refuse, alter, or obliterate the images or *ideas* which the objects set before it do produce there. As the bodies that surround us do diversely affect our organs, the mind is forced to receive the impressions and cannot avoid the perception of those *ideas* that are annexed to them.

Chapter 2. *Of Simple* Ideas.

1. *Uncompounded appearances*. The better to understand the nature, manner, and extent of our knowl-

edge, one thing is carefully to be observed concerning the *ideas* we have, and that is, that *some* of them are *simple*, and *some complex*.

Though the qualities that affect our senses are, in the things themselves, so united and blended that there is no separation, no distance between them, yet it is plain the *ideas* they produce in the mind enter by the senses simple and unmixed. For, though the sight and touch often take in from the same object at the same time different *ideas*—as a man sees at once motion and color, the hand feels softness and warmth in the same piece of wax—yet the simple *ideas* thus united in the same subject are as perfectly distinct as those that come in by different senses. The coldness and hardness which a man feels in a piece of *ice* being as distinct *ideas* in the mind as the smell and whiteness of a lily or as the taste of sugar and smell of a rose. And there is nothing can be plainer to a man than the clear and distinct perception he has of those simple *ideas*, which, being each in itself uncompounded, contains in it nothing but *one uniform appearance*, or conception, in the mind, and is not distinguishable into different *ideas*.

2. *The mind can neither make nor destroy them*. These simple *ideas*, the materials of all our knowledge, are suggested and furnished to the mind only by those two ways mentioned above, namely, *sensation* and *reflection*. When the understanding is once stored with these simple *ideas*, it has the power to repeat, compare, and unite them, even to an almost infinite variety, and so can make at pleasure new complex *ideas*. But it is not in the power of the most exalted wit or enlarged understanding, by any quickness or variety of thought, to invent or frame one new simple *idea* in the mind, not taken in by the ways before mentioned. Nor can any force of the understanding destroy those that are there. The dominion of man, in this little world of his own understanding, is much the same as it is in the great world of visible things—in which his power, however managed by art and skill, reaches no further than to compound and divide the materials that are made to his hand—but it can do nothing towards the making the least particle of new matter or destroying one atom of what is already in being. The same inability everyone will find in himself, who shall go about to fashion in his

understanding any simple *idea* not received in by his senses from external objects or by reflection from the operations of his own mind about them. I would have anyone try to fancy any taste which had never affected his palate, or *frame the* idea of a scent he had never smelt. And when he can do this, I will also conclude that a blind man has *ideas* of colors, and a deaf man true distinct notions of sounds.

3. This is the reason why, though we cannot believe it impossible to God to make a creature with other organs and more ways to convey into the understanding the notice of corporeal things than those five, as they are usually counted, which he has given to man; yet I think it is *not possible* for anyone *to imagine* any other *qualities* in bodies, however constituted, by which they can be taken notice of, besides sounds, tastes, smells, visible and tangible qualities. And had mankind been made but with four senses, the qualities, then, which are the objects of the fifth sense, had been as far from our notice, imagination, and conception, as now any *belonging to a sixth, seventh, or eighth sense* can possibly be. Whether yet, some other creatures in some other parts of this vast and stupendous universe, may not have this, will be a great presumption to deny. He who will not set himself proudly at the top of all things, but will consider the immensity of this fabric and the great variety that is to be found in this little and inconsiderable part of it which he has to do with, may be apt to think that in other mansions of it there may be other and different intelligent beings of whose faculties he has as little knowledge or apprehension as a worm shut up in one drawer of a cabinet has of the senses or understanding of a man — such variety and excellency being suitable to the wisdom and power of the maker. I have here followed the common opinion of man's having but five senses, though, perhaps, there may be justly counted more. But either supposition serves equally to my present purpose.

Chapter 3. *Of Ideas of One Sense.*

1. *As colors, of seeing; sounds, of hearing.* The better to conceive the *ideas* we receive from sensation, it may not be amiss for us to consider them in reference to the different ways by which they make their ap-

proaches to our minds and make themselves perceivable by us.

First, then, there are some which come into our minds *by one sense* only.

Secondly, there are others that convey themselves into the mind *by more senses than one.*

Thirdly, others that are had from *reflection* only.

Fourthly, there are some that make themselves [a] way and are suggested to the mind *by all the ways of sensation and reflection.*

We shall consider them apart under these several heads.

First, there are *some* ideas *which have admittance only through one sense,* which is peculiarly adapted to receive them. Thus light and colors, as white, red, yellow, blue, with their several degrees or shades and mixtures, as green, scarlet, purple, sea-green, and the rest, come in only by the eyes; all kinds of noises, sounds, and tones, only by the ears; the several tastes and smells, by the nose and palate. And if these organs, or the nerves which are the conduits to convey them from without to their audience in the brain, the mind's presence-room (as I may so call it), are any of them so disordered as not to perform their functions, they have no postern to be admitted by, no other way to bring themselves into view and be perceived by the understanding.

The most considerable of those belonging to the touch are heat and cold and solidity. All the rest, consisting almost wholly in the sensible configuration, as smooth and rough, or else more or less firm adhesion of the parts, as hard and soft, tough and brittle, are obvious enough.

2. *Few simple* ideas *have names.* I think it will be needless to enumerate all the particular *simple ideas* belonging to each sense. Nor indeed is it possible if we would, there being a great many *more* of them belonging to most of the senses *than we have names for.* The variety of smells, which are as many, almost, if not more, than species of bodies in the world, do most of them want names. Sweet and stinking commonly serve our turn for these *ideas,* which, in effect, is little more than to call them pleasing or displeasing, though the smell of a rose and violet, both sweet, are certainly very distinct *ideas.* Nor are the different tastes that we receive *ideas* of by our

palates much better provided with names. Sweet, bitter, sour, harsh, and salt are almost all the epithets we have to denominate that numberless variety of relishes, which are to be found distinct, not only in almost every sort of creatures, but all the different parts of the same plant, fruit, or animal. The same may be said of colors and sounds. I shall, therefore, in the account of simple *ideas* I am here giving, content myself to set down only such as are most material to our present purpose, or are in themselves less apt to be taken notice of, though they are very frequently the ingredients of our complex *ideas*, among which, I think, I may well account solidity— which therefore I shall treat of in the next chapter.

Chapter 4. *Of Solidity*.

1. *We receive this* idea *from touch*. The *idea* of *solidity* we receive by our touch. And it arises from the resistance which we find in body to the entrance of any other body into the place it possesses, until it has left it. There is no *idea* which we receive more constantly from sensation than *solidity*. Whether we move or rest, in whatever posture we are, we always feel something under us that supports us and hinders our further sinking downwards, and the bodies which we daily handle make us perceive that, while they remain between them, they do by an insurmountable force hinder the approach of the parts of our hands that press them. That which thus hinders the approach of two bodies, when they are moved one towards another, I call *solidity*. I will not dispute whether this acceptation of the word solid is nearer to its original signification than that which mathematicians use it in. It suffices that I think the common notion of solidity will allow, if not justify, this use of it, but if anyone thinks it better to call it *impenetrability*, he has my consent. Only, I have thought the term *solidity* the more proper to express this *idea*, not only because of its vulgar use in that sense, but also because it carries something more of positive in it than *impenetrability*, which is negative and is perhaps more a consequence of *solidity* than *solidity* itself. This, of all other, seems the *idea* most intimately connected with and essential to body, so as nowhere else to be found or imagined, but only in matter. And though

our senses take no notice of it but in masses of matter of a bulk sufficient to cause a sensation in us, yet the mind, having once gotten this *idea* from such grosser sensible bodies, traces it further, and considers it, as well as figure, in the most minute particle of matter that can exist, and finds it inseparably inherent in body, wherever or however modified.

2. *Solidity fills space*. This is the *idea* which belongs to body, by which we conceive it to *fill space*. The *idea* of which filling of space is that, where we imagine any space taken up by a solid substance, we conceive it so to possess it that it excludes all other solid substances and will forever hinder any other two bodies that move towards one another in a straight line from coming to touch one another, unless it removes from between them in a line not parallel to that which they move in. This *idea* of it the bodies which we ordinarily handle sufficiently furnish us with.

3. *Distinct from space*. This resistance, by which it keeps other bodies out of the space which it possesses, is so great that no force, however great, can surmount it. All the bodies in the world pressing a drop of water on all sides will never be able to overcome the resistance which it will make, soft as it is, to their approaching one another, until it is removed out of their way—by which our *idea* of *solidity* is *distinguished* both *from pure space*, which is capable neither of resistance nor motion, and from the ordinary *idea* of *hardness*. [. . .]

4. *From hardness. Solidity* is hereby also *differenced from hardness*, in that solidity consists in repletion, and so an utter exclusion of other bodies out of the space it possesses, but hardness in a firm cohesion of the parts of matter, making up masses of a sensible bulk, so that the whole does not easily change its figure. And, indeed, hard and soft are names that we give to things only in relation to the constitutions of our own bodies—that being generally called hard by us which will put us to pain sooner than change figure by the pressure of any part of our bodies, and that, on the contrary, soft which changes the situation of its parts upon an easy and unpainful touch. [. . .]

5. *On solidity depend impulse, resistance, and protrusion*. By this *idea* of solidity is the extension of body distinguished from the extension of space, the extension of body being nothing but the cohesion or

continuity of solid, separable, movable parts, and the extension of space the continuity of unsolid, inseparable, and immovable parts. *Upon the solidity of bodies* also *depend their mutual impulse, resistance, and protrusion.* Of pure space then, and solidity, there are several (among which I confess myself one) who persuade themselves they have clear and distinct *ideas*, and that they can think on space without anything in it that resists or is protruded by body. This is the *idea* of pure space, which they think they have as clear as any *idea* they can have of the extension of body. [. . .]

Chapter 5. *Of Simple* Ideas *by More Than One Sense.*

The *ideas* we get by more than one sense are of *space* or *extension*, *figure*, *rest*, and *motion*; for these make perceivable impressions, both on the eyes and touch, and we can receive and convey into our minds the *ideas* of the extension, figure, motion, and rest of bodies, both by seeing and feeling. But having occasion to speak more at large of these in another place, I here only enumerate them.

Chapter 6. *Of Simple* Ideas *of Reflection.*

1. *Simple* ideas *are the operations of the mind about its other* ideas. The mind receiving the *ideas* mentioned in the foregoing chapters from without, when it turns its view inward upon itself, and observes its own actions about those *ideas* it has, takes from this other *ideas* which are as capable to be the objects of its contemplation as any of those it received from foreign things.

2. The two great and principal actions of the mind which are most frequently considered and which are so frequent that everyone who pleases may take notice of them in himself are these two: *perception* or *thinking*; and *volition* or *willing*. The power of thinking is called the *understanding*, and the power of volition is called the *will*, and these two powers or abilities in the mind are denominated *faculties*. Of some of the modes of these simple *ideas* of reflection, such as are *remembrance*, *discerning*, *reasoning*, *judging*,

knowledge, *faith*, etc., I shall have occasion to speak hereafter.

Chapter 7. *Of Simple* Ideas *of Both Sensation and Reflection.*

1. *Pleasure and pain.* There are other simple *ideas* which convey themselves into the mind by all the ways of sensation and reflection, namely, *pleasure*, or *delight*, and its opposite, *pain*, or *uneasiness; power; existence; unity.*

2. *The* idea *of perception and* idea *of willing we have from reflection. Delight* or *uneasiness*, one or other of them, join themselves to almost all our *ideas* both of sensation and reflection. And there is scarcely any affection of our senses from without, any retired thought of our mind within, which is not able to produce in us *pleasure* or *pain*. By *pleasure* and *pain* I would be understood to signify whatever delights or molests us, whether it arises from the thoughts of our minds or anything operating on our bodies. For whether we call it satisfaction, delight, pleasure, happiness, etc., on the one side, or uneasiness, trouble, pain, torment, anguish, misery, etc., on the other, they are still but different degrees of the same thing and belong to the *ideas* of pleasure and pain, delight or uneasiness — which are the names I shall most commonly use for those two sorts of *ideas*. [. . .]

7. *Existence and unity. Existence* and *unity* are two other *ideas* that are suggested to the understanding by every object without and every *idea* within. When *ideas* are in our minds, we consider them as being actually there as well as we consider things to be actually without us — which is that they exist, or have *existence*. And whatever we can consider as one thing, whether a real being or *idea*, suggests to the understanding the *idea* of *unity*.

8. *Power. Power* also is another of those simple *ideas* which we receive from *sensation and reflection*. For observing in ourselves *that we can*, at pleasure, move several parts of our bodies which were at rest, the effects also that natural bodies are able to produce in one another, occurring every moment to our senses, we both these ways get the *idea* of power.

9. *Succession.* Besides these there is another *idea* which, though suggested by our senses, yet is more

constantly offered to us by what passes in our minds, and that is the *idea* of *succession*. For if we look immediately into ourselves and reflect on what is observable there, we shall find our *ideas* always, while we are awake or have any thought, passing in train, one going and another coming, without intermission.

10. *Simple* ideas *the materials of all our knowledge.* These, if they are not all, are at least (as I think) the most considerable of those *simple ideas* which the mind has and out of which is made all its other knowledge. All which it receives only by the two aforementioned ways of *sensation* and *reflection*.

Nor let anyone think these too narrow bounds for the capacious mind of man to expatiate in, which takes its flight further than the stars and cannot be confined by the limits of the world, that extends its thoughts often even beyond the utmost expansion of matter, and makes excursions into that incomprehensible *inane*. I grant all this, but desire anyone to assign any *simple idea* which is not *received from* one of *those inlets* before mentioned or any *complex idea* not *made out of those simple ones*. Nor will it be so strange to think these few simple *ideas* sufficient to employ the quickest thought or largest capacity and to furnish the materials of all that various knowledge and more various fancies and opinions of all mankind, if we consider how many words may be made out of the various composition of twenty-four letters — or if, going one step further, we will but reflect on the variety of combinations may be made with barely one of the above mentioned *ideas*, namely, number, whose stock is inexhaustible and truly infinite. And what a large and immense field does extension alone afford the mathematicians.

Chapter 8. *Other Considerations Concerning Simple* Ideas.

1. *Positive* ideas *from privative causes.* Concerning the simple *ideas* of sensation, it is to be considered that whatever is so constituted in nature as to be able, by affecting our senses, to cause any perception in the mind, does thereby produce in the understanding a simple *idea*; which, whatever is the external cause of it, when it comes to be taken notice of by our discerning faculty, it is by the mind looked on and considered there to be a real *positive idea* in the understanding, as much as any other whatsoever, though perhaps the cause of it is but a privation of the subject.

2. Thus the *ideas* of heat and cold, light and darkness, white and black, motion and rest, are equally clear and *positive ideas* in the mind, though perhaps some of *the causes* which produce them are barely *privations* in subjects from which our senses derive those *ideas*. These the understanding, in its view of them, considers all as distinct positive *ideas*, without taking notice of the causes that produce them — which is an inquiry not belonging to the *idea*, as it is in the understanding, but to the nature of the things existing without us. These are two very different things and carefully to be distinguished, it being one thing to perceive and know the *idea* of white or black and quite another to examine what kind of particles they must be, and how arranged in the surfaces, to make any object appear white or black.

3. A painter or dyer who never inquired into their causes has the *ideas* of white and black, and other colors, as clearly, perfectly, and distinctly in his understanding, and perhaps more distinctly, than the philosopher who has busied himself in considering their natures, and thinks he knows how far either of them is in its cause positive or privative; and the *idea of black* is no less *positive* in his mind than that of white, *however the cause* of that color in the external object may *be only a privation*.

4. If it were the design of my present undertaking to inquire into the natural causes and manner of perception, I should offer this as a reason *why a privative cause might*, in some cases at least, *produce a positive idea*, namely, that all sensation being produced in us only by different degrees and modes of motion in our animal spirits variously agitated by external objects, the abatement of any former motion must as necessarily produce a new sensation as the variation or increase of it, and so introduce a new *idea* which depends only on a different motion of the animal spirits in that organ.

5. But whether this is so or not, I will not here determine, but appeal to everyone's own experience whether the shadow of a man, though it consists of nothing but the absence of light (and the more the

absence of light is, the more discernible is the shadow), does not, when a man looks on it, cause as clear and positive *idea* in his mind as a man himself, though covered over with clear sunshine? And the picture of a shadow is a positive thing. Indeed we have *negative names* which do not stand directly for positive *ideas*, but for their absence, such as *insipid, silence, nihil*, etc., which words denote positive *ideas*—e.g., *taste, sound, being*—with a signification of their absence.

6. And thus one may truly be said to see darkness. For supposing a hole perfectly dark from which no light is reflected, it is certain one may see the figure of it or it may be painted. Or whether the ink I write with makes any other *idea* is a question. The privative causes I have here assigned of positive *ideas* are according to the common opinion, but in truth it will be hard to determine whether there are really any *ideas* from a privative cause, until it is determined *whether rest is any more a privation than motion*.

7. Ideas *in the mind, qualities in bodies*. To discover the nature of our *ideas* the better and to discourse of them intelligibly, it will be convenient to distinguish them as they are *ideas* or perceptions in our minds, and as they are modifications of matter in the bodies that cause such perceptions in us, so that we *may not* think (as perhaps usually is done) that they are exactly the images and *resemblances* of something inherent in the subject, most of those of sensation being in the mind no more the likeness of something existing without us than the names that stand for them are the likeness of our *ideas*, which yet upon hearing they are apt to excite in us.

8. Whatever the mind perceives in itself or is the immediate object of perception, thought, or understanding, that I call *idea*, and the power to produce any *idea* in our mind I call a *quality* of the subject in which that power is. Thus a snowball having the power to produce in us the *ideas* of *white, cold, and round*, the power to produce those *ideas* in us as they are in the snowball I call *qualities*; and as they are sensations or perceptions in our understandings I call them *ideas*; which *ideas* if I speak of sometimes as in the things themselves, I would be understood to mean those qualities in the objects which produce them in us.

9. *Primary and secondary qualities*. Qualities thus considered in bodies are, first such as are utterly inseparable from the body in whatever state it is; such as in all the alterations and changes it suffers, all the force can be used upon it, it constantly keeps; and such as sense constantly finds in every particle of matter which has bulk enough to be perceived and the mind finds inseparable from every particle of matter, though less than to make itself singly be perceived by our senses—e.g., take a grain of wheat, divide it into two parts, each part has still *solidity, extension, figure*, and *mobility*; divide it again, and it retains still the same qualities; and so divide it on until the parts become insensible, they must retain still each of them all those qualities. For division (which is all that a mill, or pestle, or any other body does upon another in reducing it to insensible parts) can never take away either solidity, extension, figure, or mobility from any body, but only makes two or more distinct separate masses of matter of that which was but one before. All which distinct masses reckoned as so many distinct bodies after division make a certain number. These I call *original* or *primary qualities* of body, which I think we may observe to produce simple *ideas* in us, namely, solidity, extension, figure, motion or rest, and number.

10. *Secondly*, such *qualities* which in truth are nothing in the objects themselves but powers to produce various sensations in us by their *primary qualities*—i.e., by the bulk, figure, texture, and motion of their insensible parts, as colors, sounds, tastes, etc.—these I call *secondary qualities*. To these might be added a third sort, which are allowed to be barely powers, though they are as much real qualities in the subject as those which I, to comply with the common way of speaking, call *qualities*, but for distinction, *secondary qualities*. For the power in fire to produce a new color or consistency in wax or clay, by its primary qualities, is as much a quality in fire as the power it has to produce in me a new *idea* or sensation of warmth or burning, which I did not feel before by the same primary qualities, namely, the bulk, texture, and motion of its insensible parts.

11. *How primary qualities produce their* ideas. The next thing to be considered is how *bodies* produce *ideas* in us, and that is manifestly *by impulse*, the only way which we can conceive bodies to operate in.

12. If then external objects are not united to our minds when they produce *ideas* in there, and yet we perceive *these original qualities* in such of them as singly fall under our senses, it is evident that some motion must be continued from there by our nerves, or animal spirits, by some parts of our bodies to the brains or the seat of sensation, there to *produce in our minds the particular* ideas *we have of them*. And since the extension, figure, number, and motion of bodies of an observable bigness may be perceived at a distance *by* the sight, it is evident some singly imperceptible bodies must come from them to the eyes, and thereby convey to the brain some *motion* which produces these *ideas* which we have of them in us.

13. *How secondary*. After the same manner that the *ideas* of these original qualities are produced in us, we may conceive that the *ideas of secondary qualities* are also *produced*, namely, *by the operation of insensible particles on our senses*. For it being manifest that there are bodies and good store of bodies, each of which are so small that we cannot, by any of our senses, discover either their bulk, figure, or motion as is evident in the particles of the air and water, and others extremely smaller than those, perhaps as much smaller than the particles of air and water as the particles of air and water are smaller than peas or hailstones. Let us suppose at present that the different motions and figures, bulk and number of such particles, affecting the several organs of our senses, produce in us those different sensations which we have from the colors and smells of bodies — e.g., that a violet, by the impulse of such insensible particles of matter of peculiar figures and bulks and in different degrees and modifications of their motions, causes the *ideas* of the blue color and sweet scent of that flower to be produced in our minds — it being no more impossible to conceive that God should annex such *ideas* to such motions with which they have no similitude than that he should annex the *idea* of pain to the motion of a piece of steel dividing our flesh with which that *idea* has no resemblance.

14. What I have said concerning *colors* and *smells* may be understood also of *tastes* and *sounds, and other the like sensible qualities* which, whatever reality we by mistake attribute to them, are in truth nothing in the objects themselves but powers to produce various sensations in us, and *depend on those primary qualities*, namely, bulk, figure, texture, and motion of parts, as I have said.

15. Ideas *of primary qualities are resemblances; of secondary, not.* From which I think it easy to draw this observation, that the *ideas of primary qualities* of bodies *are resemblances* of them, and their patterns do really exist in the bodies themselves, but the *ideas produced* in us *by* these *secondary qualities have no resemblance* of them at all. There is nothing like our *ideas* existing in the bodies themselves. They are, in the bodies we denominate from them, only a power to produce those sensations in us. And what is sweet, blue, or warm in *idea* is but the certain bulk, figure, and motion of the insensible parts in the bodies themselves which we call so.

16. *Flame* is denominated *hot* and *light; snow, white* and *cold*; and *manna, white* and *sweet*, from the *ideas* they produce in us. Which qualities are commonly thought to be the same in those bodies that those *ideas* are in us, the one the perfect resemblance of the other, as they are in a mirror, and it would by most men be judged very extravagant if one should say otherwise. And yet he who will consider that *the same fire* that, at one distance *produces* in us the sensation of *warmth*, does at a nearer approach produce in us the far different sensation of *pain*, ought to consider himself what reason he has to say that his *idea* of *warmth*, which was produced in him by the fire, is actually *in the fire*; and his *idea* of *pain*, which the same fire produced in him the same way, is *not* in the *fire*. Why are whiteness and coldness in snow, and pain not, when it produces the one and the other *idea* in us, and can do neither but by the bulk, figure, number, and motion of its solid parts?

17. The particular *bulk, number, figure, and motion of the parts of fire or snow are really in them*, whether anyone's senses perceive them or not. And therefore they may be called *real qualities*, because they really exist in those bodies. But *light, heat, whiteness*, or *coldness are no more really in them than sickness or pain is in* manna. Take away the sensation of them; let the eyes not see light, or colors, nor the ears hear sounds; let the palate not taste, nor the nose smell; and all colors, tastes, odors, and sounds as they are

such particular *ideas* vanish and cease, and are reduced to their causes, i.e., bulk, figure, and motion of parts.

18. A piece of *manna* of a sensible bulk is able to produce in us the *idea* of a round or square figure and, by being removed from one place to another, the *idea* of motion. This *idea* of motion represents it as it really is in the *manna* moving. A circle or square is the same, whether in *idea* or existence, in the mind or in the *manna*; and this both *motion and figure are really in the manna*, whether we take notice of them or not. This everybody is ready to agree to. Besides, *manna*, by the bulk, figure, texture, and motion of its parts, has a power to produce the sensations of sickness and sometimes of acute pains or gripings in us. That these *ideas* of *sickness and pain are not in the* manna, but effects of its operations on us, and are nowhere when we do not feel them, this also everyone readily agrees to. And yet men are hardly to be brought to think *that sweetness and whiteness are not really in manna*; which are but the effects of the operations of *manna* by the motion, size, and figure of its particles on the eyes and palate, as the pain and sickness caused by manna are confessedly nothing but the effects of its operations on the stomach and guts, by the size, motion, and figure of its insensible parts (for by nothing else can a body operate, as has been proved). As if it could not operate on the eyes and palate, and thereby produce in the mind particular distinct *ideas* which in itself it does not have, as well as we allow it can operate on the guts and stomach, and thereby produce distinct *ideas* which in itself it does not have—these *ideas* being all effects of the operations of *manna* on several parts of our bodies by the size, figure, number, and motion of its parts. Why those produced by the eyes and palate should rather be thought to be really in the manna than those produced by the stomach and guts, or why the pain and sickness, *ideas* that are the effect of *manna*, should be thought to be nowhere when they are not felt, and yet the sweetness and whiteness, effects of the same *manna* on other parts of the body by ways equally as unknown, should be thought to exist in the *manna* when they are not seen or tasted, would need some reason to explain.

19. Let us consider the red and white colors in *porphyry*. Hinder light from striking on it, and its colors vanish; it no longer produces any such *ideas* in us. Upon the return of light, it produces these appearances on us again. Can anyone think any real alterations are made in the *porphyry* by the presence or absence of light, and that those *ideas* of whiteness and redness are really in *porphyry* in the light, when it is plain *it has no color in the dark*? It has, indeed, such a configuration of particles, both night and day, as are apt, by the rays of light rebounding from some parts of that hard stone, to produce in us the *idea* of redness and from others the *idea* of whiteness; but whiteness or redness are not in it at any time but such a texture that has the power to produce such a sensation in us.

20. Pound an almond, and the clear white *color* will be altered into a dirty one and the sweet *taste* into an oily one. What real alteration can the beating of the pestle make in any body but an alteration of the *texture* of it?

21. *Ideas* being thus distinguished and understood, we may be able to give an account how the same water, at the same time, may produce the *idea* of cold by one hand and of heat by the other, whereas it is impossible that the same water, if those *ideas* were really in it, should at the same time be both hot and cold. For if we imagine *warmth*, as it is *in our hands*, to be *nothing but a certain sort and degree of motion in the minute particles of our nerves or animal spirits*, we may understand how it is possible that the same water may, at the same time, produce the sensations of heat in one hand and cold in the other; which yet figure never does that, never producing the *idea* of a square by one hand, which has produced the *idea* of a globe by another. But if the sensation of heat and cold are nothing but the increase or diminution of the motion of the minute parts of our bodies caused by the corpuscles of any other body, it is easy to be understood that, if that motion is greater in one hand than in the other, if a body is applied to the two hands, which has in its minute particles a greater motion than in those of one of the hands, and a less than in those of the other, it will increase the motion of the one hand and lessen it in the other, and so cause the different sensations of heat and cold that depend on it.

22. I have, in what just goes before, been engaged in physical inquiries a little further than perhaps I intended. But it being necessary to make the nature of sensation a little understood and to make the *difference between the qualities in bodies and the* ideas *produced by them in the mind* to be distinctly conceived, without which it would be impossible to discourse intelligibly of them, I hope I shall be pardoned this little excursion into natural philosophy, it being necessary in our present inquiry to distinguish the *primary* and *real qualities* of bodies which are always in them (namely, solidity, extension, figure, number, and motion, or rest, and are sometimes perceived by us, namely, when the bodies they are in are big enough singly to be discerned) from those *secondary* and *imputed qualities* which are but the powers of several combinations of those primary ones, when they operate without being distinctly discerned; by which we may also come to know what *ideas* are and what are not resemblances of something really existing in the bodies we denominate from them.

23. The *qualities* then that are in *bodies* rightly considered are of *three sorts*.

First, the *bulk, figure, number, situation*, and *motion, or rest* of their solid parts. Those are in them, whether we perceive them or not; and when they are of that size that we can discover them, we have by these an *idea* of the thing as it is in itself, as is plain in artificial things. These I call *primary qualities*.

Secondly, the *power* that is in any body *by* reason of *its* insensible *primary qualities* to operate after a peculiar manner on any of our senses and thereby *produce in us* the *different ideas* of several colors, sounds, smells, tastes, etc. These are usually called sensible qualities.

Thirdly, the *power* that is in any body *by* reason of the particular constitution of *its primary qualities to* make such a *change* in the *bulk, figure, texture, and motion of another body* as to make it operate on our senses differently from what it did before. Thus the sun has a power to make wax white, and fire to make lead fluid. These *are* usually called powers.

The first of these, as has been said, I think, may be properly called *real, original*, or *primary qualities*, because they are in the things themselves, whether

they are perceived or not. And upon their different modifications it is that the secondary qualities depend.

The other two are only powers to act differently upon other things, which powers result from the different modifications of those primary qualities.

24. *Reason of our mistake in this*. But though *the two latter sorts of qualities are powers barely* and nothing but powers, relating to several other bodies and resulting from the different modifications of the original qualities, yet they are generally otherwise thought of. For the *second sort*, namely, the powers to produce several *ideas* in us by our senses, *are looked upon as real qualities in the things* thus affecting us. But *the third sort are called and esteemed barely powers*—e.g., the *idea* of heat or light which we receive by our eyes or touch from the sun are commonly thought *real qualities*, existing in the sun, and something more than mere powers in it. But when we consider the sun in reference to wax which it melts or blanches, we look on the whiteness and softness produced in the wax, not as qualities in the sun, but effects produced by *powers* in it. Whereas, if rightly considered, these qualities of light and warmth, which are perceptions in me when I am warmed or enlightened by the sun, are no otherwise in the sun than the changes made in the wax, when it is blanched or melted, are in the sun. They are all of them equally powers in the sun, depending on its primary qualities, by which it is able, in the one case, so to alter the bulk, figure, texture, or motion of some of the insensible parts of my eyes or hands as thereby to produce in me the *idea* of light or heat, and in the other it is able so to alter the bulk, figure, texture, or motion of the insensible parts of the wax as to make them fit to produce in me the distinct *ideas* of white and fluid.

25. The reason *why the one is ordinarily taken for real qualities and the other only for bare powers* seems to be because the *ideas* we have of distinct colors, sounds, etc., containing nothing at all in them of bulk, figure, or motion, we are not apt to think them the effects of these primary qualities, which do not appear to our senses to operate in their production, and with which they do not have any apparent congruity or conceivable connection. Hence it is that we

are so ready to imagine that those *ideas* are the resemblances of something really existing in the objects themselves, since sensation discovers nothing of bulk, figure, or motion of parts in their production, nor can reason show how bodies, by their bulk, figure, and motion, should produce in the mind the *ideas* of blue or yellow, etc. But in the other case, in the operations of bodies changing the qualities one of another, we plainly discover that the quality produced has commonly no resemblance with anything in the thing producing it, for which reason we look on it as a bare effect of power. For though receiving the *idea* of heat or light from the sun, we are apt to think it is a perception and resemblance of such a quality in the sun, yet when we see wax, or a fair face, receive change of color from the sun, we cannot imagine that to be the reception or resemblance of anything in the sun, because we do not find those different colors in the sun itself. For our senses being able to observe a likeness or unlikeness of sensible qualities in two different external objects, we readily enough conclude the production of any sensible quality, in any subject, to be an effect of bare power and not the communication of any quality which was really in the efficient, when we find no such sensible quality in the thing that produced it. But our senses not being able to discover any unlikeness between the *idea* produced in us and the quality of the object producing it, we are apt to imagine that our *ideas* are resemblances of something in the objects and not the effects of certain powers placed in the modification of their primary qualities, with which primary qualities the *ideas* produced in us have no resemblance.

26. *Secondary qualities two-fold; first, immediately perceivable; secondly, mediately perceivable.* To conclude, besides those before-mentioned *primary qualities* in bodies, namely, bulk, figure, extension, number, and motion of their solid parts, all the rest by which we take notice of bodies and distinguish them one from another are nothing else but several powers in them depending on those primary qualities, by which they are fitted, either by immediately operating on our bodies to produce several different *ideas* in us, or else by operating on other bodies so to change their primary qualities as to render them capable of producing *ideas* in us different from what before they did. The former of these, I think, may be called *secondary qualities, immediately perceivable*. The latter, *secondary qualities, mediately perceivable*.

Chapter 9. *Of Perception.*

1. *It is the first simple* idea *of reflection. Perception*, as it is the first faculty of the mind exercised about our *ideas*; so it is the first and simplest *idea* we have from reflection, and is by some called thinking in general. Though thinking, in the propriety of the *English* tongue, signifies that sort of operation in the mind about its *ideas* in which the mind is active, where it, with some degree of voluntary attention, considers anything. For in bare naked *perception*, the mind is for the most part only passive. And what it perceives, it cannot avoid perceiving.

2. *Perception is only when the mind receives the impression. What perception is* everyone will know better by reflecting on what he does himself when he sees, hears, feels, etc., or thinks, than by any discourse of mine. Whoever reflects on what passes in his own mind cannot miss it. And if he does not reflect, all the words in the world cannot make him have any notion of it.

3. This is certain, that whatever alterations are made in the body, if they do not reach the mind, whatever impressions are made on the outward parts, if they are not taken notice of within, there is no perception. Fire may burn our bodies with no other effect than it does a billet, unless the motion is continued to the brain and there the sense of heat, or *idea* of pain, is produced in the mind—in what consists *actual perception*.

4. How often may a man observe in himself that while his mind is intently employed in the contemplation of some objects, and curiously surveying some *ideas* that are there, it takes no notice of impressions of sounding bodies made upon the organ of hearing, with the same alteration that uses to be for the producing the *idea* of sound? A sufficient impulse there may be on the organ, but, it not reaching the observation of the mind, there follows no perception. And though the motion that uses to produce the *idea* of sound

be made in the ear, yet no sound is heard. Want of sensation in this case is not through any defect in the organ, or that the man's ears are less affected than at other times when he does hear; but that which uses to produce the *idea*, though conveyed in by the usual organ, not being taken notice of in the understanding and so imprinting no *idea* in the mind, there follows no sensation — so *that wherever there is sense* or *perception, there some* idea *is actually produced and present in the understanding.*

5. *Children, though they have* ideas *in the womb, have none innate.* Therefore, I do not doubt but *children,* by the exercise of their senses about objects that affect them *in the womb, receive some few ideas* before they are born, as the unavoidable effects either of the bodies that surround them or else of those wants or diseases they suffer; among which (if one may conjecture concerning things not very capable of examination) I think the *ideas* of hunger and warmth are two, which probably are some of the first that children have, and which they scarcely ever part with again.

6. But though it is reasonable to imagine that *children* receive some *ideas* before they come into the world, yet these simple *ideas* are *far from* those *innate principles* which some contend for, and we above have rejected. These here mentioned, being the effects of sensation, are only from some affections of the body which happen to them there, and so depend on something exterior to the mind, not otherwise differing in their manner of production from other *ideas* derived from sense, but only in the precedence of time; whereas those innate principles are supposed to be quite of another nature, not coming into the mind by any accidental alterations in, or operations on the body, but, as it were, original characters impressed upon it in the very first moment of its being and constitution. [. . .]

8. Ideas *of sensation often changed by the judgment.* We are further to consider concerning perception that the *ideas we receive by sensation are often* in grown people *altered by the judgment* without our taking notice of it. When we set before our eyes a round globe of any uniform color — e.g., gold, alabaster, or jet — it is certain that the *idea* thereby imprinted in our mind is of a flat circle, variously shadowed,

with several degrees of light and brightness coming to our eyes. But we, having by use been accustomed to perceive what kind of appearance convex bodies are accustomed to make in us, what alterations are made in the reflections of light by the difference of the sensible figures of bodies, the judgment presently, by an habitual custom, alters the appearances into their causes, so that from that which is truly variety of shadow or color, collecting the figure, it makes it pass for a mark of figure and frames to itself the perception of a convex figure and a uniform color, when the *idea* we receive from this is only a plane variously colored, as is evident in painting. To which purpose I shall here insert a problem of that very ingenious and studious promoter of real knowledge, the learned and worthy Mr. *Molineaux,* which he was pleased to send me in a letter some months since; and it is this: *Suppose a man born blind and now adult, and taught by his touch to distinguish between a cube and a sphere of the same metal and nearly of the same bigness, so as to tell, when he felt one and the other, which is the cube, which the sphere. Suppose then the cube and sphere placed on a table and the blind man be made to see. Quaere, whether by his sight, before he touched them, he could now distinguish and tell which is the globe, which the cube?* To which the acute and judicious proposer answers: No. *For though he has obtained the experience of how a globe, how a cube affects his touch, yet he has not yet obtained the experience that what affects his touch so or so must affect his sight so or so. Or that a protuberant angle in the cube that pressed his hand unequally shall appear to his eye as it does in the cube.* I agree with this thinking gentleman, whom I am proud to call my friend, in his answer to this problem, and am of opinion that the blind man at first sight would not be able with certainty to say which was the globe, which the cube, while he only saw them, though he could unerringly name them by his touch and certainly distinguish them by the difference of their figures felt. [. . .]

11. *Perception puts the difference between animals and inferior beings.* This faculty of *perception* seems to me to be that which *puts the distinction between the animal kingdom and the inferior parts of nature.* For however vegetables have, many of them, some

degrees of motion, and, upon the different application of other bodies to them, do very briskly alter their figures and motions, and so have obtained the name of sensitive plants from a motion which has some resemblance to that which in animals follows upon sensation. Yet, I suppose, it is all bare mechanism, and no otherwise produced than the turning of a wild oat-beard by the insinuation of the particles of moisture, or the shortening of a rope by the affusion of water, all which is done without any sensation in the subject or the having or receiving any *ideas*.

12. *Perception*, I believe, is in some degree *in all sorts of animals*; though in some possibly the avenues provided by nature for the reception of sensations are so few, and the perception they are received with so obscure and dull, that it comes extremely short of the quickness and variety of sensation which is in other animals, but yet it is sufficient for, and wisely adapted to, the state and condition of that sort of animals who are thus made. [. . .]

Chapter 10. *Of Retention*.

1. *Contemplation*. The next faculty of the mind by which it makes a further progress towards knowledge is that which I call *retention*, or the keeping of those simple *ideas*, which from sensation or reflection it has received. This is done two ways: first, by keeping the *idea* which is brought into it, for some time, actually in view—which is called *contemplation*.

2. *Memory*. The other way of retention is the power to revive again in our minds those *ideas* which have disappeared after imprinting, or have been, as it were, laid aside out of sight, and thus we do when we conceive heat or light, yellow or sweet, the object being removed. This is *memory*, which is, as it were, the storehouse of our *ideas*. For the narrow mind of man not being capable of having many *ideas* under view and consideration at once, it was necessary to have a repository to lay up those *ideas* which at another time it might have use of. But our *ideas* being nothing but actual perceptions in the mind, which cease to be anything when there is no perception of them, this *laying up* of our *ideas* in the repository of the memory signifies no more but this, that the mind has a power in many cases to revive perceptions which

it has once had, with this additional perception annexed to them, that it has had them before. And in this sense it is that our *ideas* are said to be in our memories, when indeed they are actually nowhere, but only there is an ability in the mind when it will revive them again, and as it were paint them anew on itself, though some with more, some with less difficulty, some more lively, and others more obscurely. And thus it is by the assistance of this faculty that we are to have all those *ideas* in our understandings, which though we do not actually contemplate, yet we can bring in sight, and make appear again, and be the objects of our thoughts, without the help of those sensible qualities which first imprinted them there. [. . .]

Chapter 11. *Of Discerning, and Other Operations of the Mind*.

1. *No knowledge without it*. Another faculty we may take notice of in our minds is that of *discerning* and distinguishing between the several *ideas* it has. It is not enough to have a confused perception of something in general. Unless the mind had a distinct perception of different objects and their qualities, it would be capable of very little knowledge, though the bodies that affect us were as busy about us as they are now and the mind were continually employed in thinking. On this faculty of distinguishing one thing from another depends the *evidence and certainty* of several, even very general, propositions which have passed for innate truths, because men, overlooking the true cause why those propositions find universal assent, impute it wholly to native uniform impressions, whereas it in truth *depends upon this clear discerning faculty* of the mind by which it perceives two *ideas* to be the same, or different. [. . .]

4. *Comparing*. The comparing them one with another in respect of extent, degrees, time, place, or any other circumstances, is another operation of the mind about its *ideas*, and is that upon which depends all that large tribe of *ideas* comprehended under *relation*; which, of how vast an extent it is, I shall have occasion to consider hereafter.

6. *Compounding*. The next operation we may observe in the mind about its *ideas* is composition, by

which it puts together several of those simple ones it has received from sensation and reflection and combines them into complex ones. Under this of composition may be reckoned also that of enlarging, in which, though the composition does not so much appear as in more complex ones, yet it is nevertheless a putting several *ideas* together, though of the same kind. Thus by adding several units together we make the *idea* of a dozen, and putting together the repeated *ideas* of several perches we frame that of a furlong. [. . .]

8. *Naming.* When children have, by repeated sensations, got *ideas* fixed in their memories, they begin by degrees to learn the use of signs. And when they have gotten the skill to apply the organs of speech to the framing of articulate sounds, they begin to make *use of words* to signify their *ideas* to others. These verbal signs they sometimes borrow from others and sometimes make themselves, as one may observe among the new and unusual names children often give to things in the first use of language.

9. *Abstraction.* The use of words then being to stand as outward marks of our internal *ideas* and those *ideas* being taken from particular things, if every particular *idea* that we take in should have a distinct name, names must be endless. To prevent this, the mind makes the particular *ideas* received from particular objects become general, which is done by considering them as they are in the mind such appearances, separate from all other existences, and the circumstances of real existence, as time, place, or any other concomitant *ideas*. This is called abstraction, by which *ideas* taken from particular beings become general representatives of all of the same kind, and their names general names, applicable to whatever exists conformable to such abstract *ideas*. Such precise, naked appearances in the mind, without considering how, from where, or with what others they came there, the understanding lays up (with names commonly annexed to them) as the standards to rank real existences into sorts, as they agree with these patterns, and to *denominate* them accordingly. Thus the same color being observed today in chalk or snow which the mind yesterday received from milk, it considers that appearance alone, makes it a representative of all of that kind, and having given it the name *whiteness*, by that sound it signifies the same quality

wherever to be imagined or met with; and thus universals, whether *ideas* or terms, are made. [. . .]

17. *Dark room.* I pretend not to teach, but to inquire, and therefore cannot but confess here again that external and internal sensation are the only passages I can find of knowledge to the understanding. These alone, as far as I can discover, are the windows by which light is let into this *dark room*. For I think the *understanding* is not much unlike a closet wholly shut from light, with only some little openings left, to let in external visible resemblances or *ideas* of things without. Would the pictures coming into such a dark room but stay there and lie so orderly as to be found upon occasion, it would very much resemble the understanding of a man, in reference to all objects of sight and the *ideas* of them.

These are my guesses concerning the means by which the understanding comes to have and retain simple *ideas* and the modes of them with some other operations about them. I proceed now to examine some of these simple *ideas*, and their modes, a little more particularly.

Chapter 12. *Of Complex* Ideas.

1. *Made by the mind out of simple ones.* Up to now we have considered those *ideas* in the reception of which the mind is only passive, which are those simple ones received from *sensation* and *reflection* before mentioned, of which the mind cannot make one to itself, nor have any *idea* which does not wholly consist of them. But as the mind is wholly passive in the reception of all its simple *ideas*, so it exerts several acts of its own by which, out of its simple *ideas* as the materials and foundations of the rest, the others are framed. The acts of the mind, in which it exerts its power over its simple *ideas*, are chiefly these three: 1. Combining several simple *ideas* into one compound one, and thus all complex *ideas* are made. 2. The *second* is bringing two *ideas*, whether simple or complex, together and setting them by one another so as to take a view of them at once without uniting them into one—by which way it gets all its *ideas* of relations. 3. The *third* is separating them from all other *ideas* that accompany them in their real existence; this is called *abstraction*. And thus all its general

ideas are made. This shows man's power and its ways of operation to be much the same in the material and intellectual world. For the materials in both being such as he has no power over, either to make or destroy, all that man can do is either to unite them together, or to set them by one another, or wholly separate them. I shall here begin with the first of these in the consideration of complex *ideas* and come to the other two in their due places. As simple *ideas* are observed to exist in several combinations united together, so the mind has a power to consider several of them united together as one *idea*; and that not only as they are united in external objects, but as itself has joined them. Ideas thus made up of several simple ones put together I call *complex*—such as are *beauty, gratitude, a man, an army, the universe*—which, though complicated of various simple *ideas* or *complex ideas* made up of simple ones, yet are, when the mind pleases, considered each by itself as one entire thing and signified by one name.

2. *Made voluntarily*. In this faculty of repeating and joining together its *ideas*, the mind has great power in varying and multiplying the objects of its thoughts infinitely beyond what *sensation* or *reflection* furnishes it with, but all this still confined to those simple *ideas* which it received from those two sources and which are the ultimate materials of all its compositions. For simple *ideas* are all from things themselves, and of these *the mind can* have no more, nor other than what are suggested to it. It can have no other *ideas* of sensible qualities than what come from without by the senses, nor any *ideas* of other kind of operations of a thinking substance than what it finds in itself; but when it has once gotten these simple *ideas*, it is not confined barely to observation and what offers itself from without. It can, by its own power, put together those *ideas* it has and *make new complex ones* which it never received so united.

3. *Are either modes, substances, or relations.* Complex *ideas*, however compounded and decompounded, though their number is infinite and the variety endless, with which they fill and entertain the thoughts of men, yet I think they may be all reduced under these three heads: 1. *Modes*, 2. *Substances*, 3. *Relations*.

4. *Modes*. First, *modes* I call such complex *ideas* which, however compounded, do not contain in them the supposition of subsisting by themselves, but are considered as dependences on or affections of substances, such as are the *ideas* signified by the words *triangle, gratitude, murder*, etc. And if in this I use the word *mode* in somewhat a different sense from its ordinary signification, I beg pardon, it being unavoidable in discourses differing from the ordinary received notions either to make new words or to use old words in somewhat a new signification. The latter of which, in our present case, is perhaps the more tolerable of the two.

5. *Simple and mixed modes*. Of these modes, there are two sorts which deserve distinct consideration. First, there are some which are only variations or different combinations of the same simple *idea*, without the mixture of any other—as a dozen or score, which are nothing but the *ideas* of so many distinct units added together. And these I call *simple modes*, as being contained within the bounds of one simple *idea*. Secondly, there are others compounded of simple *ideas* of several kinds put together to make one complex one—e.g., *beauty*, consisting of a certain composition of color and figure causing delight to the beholder; *theft*, which being the concealed change of the possession of anything without the consent of the proprietor contains, as is visible, a combination of several *ideas* of several kinds. And these I call *mixed modes*.

6. *Substances single or collective*. Secondly, the *ideas* of *substances* are such combinations of simple *ideas* as are taken to represent distinct particular things subsisting by themselves, in which the supposed or confused *idea* of substance, such as it is, is always the first and chief. Thus if to substance is joined the simple *idea* of a certain dull whitish color, with certain degrees of weight, hardness, ductility, and fusibility, we have the *idea* of *lead* and a combination of the *ideas* of a certain sort of figure with the powers of motion. Thought and reasoning joined to substance make the ordinary *idea* of *a man*. Now of substances also there are two sorts of *ideas*: one of single substances, as they exist separately, as of *a man* or *a sheep*; the other of several of those put together, as an *army* of men or *flock* of sheep—which *collective* ideas *of* several *substances* thus put together are as

much each of them one single *idea* as that of a man or a unit.

7. *Relation*. Thirdly, the last sort of complex *ideas*, is that we call *relation*, which consists in the consideration and comparing one *idea* with another. Of these several kinds we shall treat in their order.

8. *The most abstruse* ideas *from the two sources*. If we will trace the progress of our minds and with attention observe how it repeats, adds together, and unites its simple *ideas* received from sensation or reflection, it will lead us further than at first perhaps we should have imagined. And, I believe, we shall find, if we warily observe the origins of our notions, that even *the most abstruse* ideas, however remote they may seem from sense or from any operations of our own minds, are yet only such as the understanding frames to itself, by repeating and joining together *ideas* that it had either from objects of sense or from its own operations about them. So that those even large *and abstract* ideas *are derived from sensation or reflection*, being no other than what the mind, by the ordinary use of its own faculties, employed about *ideas* received from objects of sense or from the operations it observes in itself about them, may and does attain unto. This I shall endeavor to show in the *ideas* we have of *space*, *time*, and *infinity*, and some few others that seem the most remote from those origins.

Chapter 13. *Of Simple Modes and, First, of the Simple Modes of Space.*

1. *Simple modes*. Though in the foregoing part I have often mentioned simple *ideas*, which are truly the materials of all our knowledge, yet having treated of them there rather in the way that they come into the mind than as distinguished from others more compounded, it will not be perhaps amiss to take a view of some of them again under this consideration and examine those different *modifications of the same* idea—which the mind either finds in things existing or is able to make within itself without the help of any extrinsic object or any foreign suggestion.

Those *modifications of any one simple* idea (which, as has been said, *I call simple modes*) are as perfectly different and distinct *ideas* in the mind as those of the greatest distance or contrariety. For the *idea* of

two is as distinct from that of *one* as *blueness* from *heat* or either of them from any number. And yet it is made up only of that simple *idea* of a unit repeated, and repetitions of this kind joined together make those distinct *simple modes*, of a *dozen*, a *gross*, a *million*.

2. Idea *of space*. I shall begin with the *simple idea of space*. I have showed above, chap. 4, that we get the *idea* of space both by our sight and touch; this, I think, is so evident that it would be as needless to go to prove that men perceive by their sight a distance between bodies of different colors, or between the parts of the same body, as that they see colors themselves; nor is it less obvious that they can do so in the dark by feeling and touch.

3. *Space and extension*. This space considered barely in length between any two beings without considering anything else between them is called *distance*; if considered in length, breadth, and thickness, I think it may be called *capacity*. The term extension is usually applied to it in whatever manner considered.

4. *Immensity*. Each different distance is a different modification of space, and *each* idea *of any different distance, or space, is a simple mode of this* idea. Men, for the use and by the custom of measuring, settle in their minds the *ideas* of certain stated lengths, such as are an *inch*, *foot*, *yard*, *fathom*, *mile*, *diameter of the earth*, etc., which are so many distinct *ideas* made up only of space. When any such stated lengths or measures of space are made familiar to men's thoughts, they can in their minds repeat them as often as they will without mixing or joining to them the *idea* of body or anything else, and frame to themselves the *ideas* of long, square, or cubic *feet*, *yards*, or *fathoms*, here among the bodies of the universe or else beyond the utmost bounds of all bodies; and by adding these still one to another, enlarge their *ideas* of space as much as they please. The power of repeating or doubling any *idea* we have of any distance and adding it to the former as often as we will, without being ever able to come to any stop or stint, let us enlarge it as much as we will, is that which gives us the *idea* of immensity.

5. *Figure*. There is another modification of this *idea*, which is nothing but the relation which the parts of the termination of extension, or circum-

scribed space, have among themselves. This the touch discovers in sensible bodies whose extremities come within our reach, and the eye takes both from bodies and colors whose boundaries are within its view, where observing how the extremities terminate either in straight lines which meet at discernible angles, or in crooked lines in which no angles can be perceived, by considering these as they relate to one another in all parts of the extremities of any body or space, it has that *idea* we call *figure*, which affords to the mind infinite variety. [. . .]

11. *Extension and body not the same.* There are some who would persuade us that *body and extension are the same thing*; but I would not suspect them of changing the signification of words, given that they have so severely condemned the philosophy of others because it has been placed too much in the uncertain meaning or deceitful obscurity of doubtful or insignificant terms. If therefore they mean by *body and extension the same* that other people do—namely, by *body*, something that is solid and extended, whose parts are separable and movable different ways, and by extension, only the space that lies between the extremities of those solid coherent parts, and which is possessed by them—they confound very different *ideas* one with another. For I appeal to every man's own thoughts whether the *idea* of space is not as distinct from that of solidity as it is from the *idea* of scarlet color? It is true, solidity cannot exist without extension. Neither can scarlet color exist without extension. But this does not hinder but that they are distinct *ideas*. Many *ideas* require others as necessary to their existence or conception, which yet are very distinct *ideas*. Motion can neither be, nor be conceived, without space, and yet motion is not space, nor space motion. Space can exist without it, and they are very distinct *ideas*; and so, I think, are those of space and solidity. Solidity is so inseparable an *idea* from body that upon that depends its filling of space, its contact, impulse, and communication of motion upon impulse. And if it is a reason to prove that spirit is different from body because thinking does not include the *idea* of extension in it, the same reason will be as valid, I suppose, to prove that *space is not body* because it does not include the *idea* of solidity in it—*space and solidity* being *as distinct ideas*

as thinking and extension and as wholly separable in the mind one from another. *Body* then and *extension*, it is evident, are two distinct *ideas*. For,

12. *First, extension* includes no solidity, nor resistance to the motion of *body*, as body does.

13. *Secondly,* the parts of pure space are inseparable one from the other, so that the continuity cannot be separated neither really nor mentally. For I demand of anyone to remove any part of it from another with which it is continued, even so much as in thought. To divide and separate actually is, as I think, by removing the parts one from another, to make two surfaces where before there was a continuity; and to divide mentally is to make in the mind two surfaces where before there was a continuity, and consider them as removed one from the other. This can only be done in things considered by the mind as capable of being separated—and by separation—of acquiring new distinct surfaces, which they then do not have but are capable of; but neither of these ways of separation, whether real or mental, is, as I think, compatible to pure *space*.

It is true, a man may consider so much of such a *space* as is answerable or commensurate to a foot without considering the rest—which is indeed a partial consideration, but not so much as mental separation, or division, since a man can no more mentally divide, without considering two surfaces separate one from the other, than he can actually divide, without making two surfaces disjoined one from the other. But a partial consideration is not separating. A man may consider light in the sun without its heat, or mobility in body without its extension, without thinking of their separation. One is only a partial consideration, terminating in one alone, and the other is a consideration of both as existing separately.

14. *Thirdly,* the parts of pure *space* are immovable, which follows from their inseparability, *motion* being nothing but change of distance between any two things. But this cannot be between parts that are inseparable, which therefore must necessarily be at perpetual rest one among another.

Thus the determined *idea* of simple *space* distinguishes it plainly and sufficiently from *body*, since its parts are inseparable, immovable, and without resistance to the motion of body. [. . .]

16. *Division of beings into bodies and spirits does not prove body and space the same.* Those who contend that *space and body* are *the same* bring this *dilemma*: either this *space* is something or nothing; if nothing is between two bodies, they must necessarily touch. If it is allowed to be something, they ask, whether it is body or spirit? To which I answer by another question: Who told them that there was, or could be, nothing but solid beings which could not think, and thinking beings that were not extended?—which is all they mean by the terms *body* and *spirit*.

17. *Substance, which we do not know, no proof against space without body.* If it is demanded (as usually it is) whether this *space* void of *body* is *substance* or *accident*, I shall readily answer, I do not know; nor shall be ashamed to own my ignorance, until they who ask show me a clear distinct *idea* of *substance*.

18. I endeavor as much as I can to deliver myself from those fallacies which we are apt to put upon ourselves by taking words for things. It does not help our ignorance to feign a knowledge where we have none, by making a noise with sounds without clear and distinct significations. Names made at pleasure neither alter the nature of things nor make us understand them but as they are signs of and stand for determined *ideas*. And I desire those who lay so much stress on the sound of these two syllables, *substance*, to consider whether applying it, as they do, to the infinite incomprehensible God, to finite spirits, and to body, it is in the same sense, and whether it stands for the same *idea*, when each of those three so different beings are called *substances*. If so, whether it will follow from this that God, spirits, and body, agreeing in the same common nature of *substance*, do not differ any otherwise than in a bare different modification of that *substance*, as a tree and a pebble being in the same sense body, and agreeing in the common nature of body, differ only in a bare modification of that common matter—which will be a very harsh doctrine. If they say that they apply it to God, finite spirit, and matter, in three different significations and that it stands for one *idea* when God is said to be a *substance*, for another when the soul is called *substance*, and for a third when body is called so; if the name *substance* stands for three several distinct *ideas*, they

would do well to make known those distinct *ideas*, or at least to give three distinct names to them, to prevent in so important a notion the confusion and errors that will naturally follow from the promiscuous use of so doubtful a term (which is so far from being suspected to have three distinct that in ordinary use it has scarcely one clear distinct signification). And if they can thus make three distinct *ideas* of *substance*, what hinders why another may not make a fourth?

19. *Substance and accidents of little use in philosophy.* They who first ran into the notion of *accidents*, as a sort of real beings that needed something to inhere in, were forced to find out the word *substance* to support them. Had the poor *Indian* philosopher (who imagined that the earth also wanted something to bear it up) but thought of this word *substance*, he did not need to have been troubled to find an elephant to support it and a tortoise to support his elephant. The word *substance* would have done it effectually. And he who inquired might have taken it for as good an answer from an *Indian* philosopher that *substance*, without knowing what it is, is that which supports the earth, as we take it for a sufficient answer and good doctrine from our *European* philosophers that substance, without knowing what it is, is that which supports *accidents*—so that of *substance*, we have no *idea* of what it is, but only a confused obscure one of what it does. [. . .]

21. A vacuum *beyond the utmost bounds of body.* But, to return to our *idea* of space, if *body* is not supposed infinite, which I think no one will affirm, I would ask, whether, if God placed a man at the extremity of corporeal beings, he could not stretch his hand beyond his body? If he could, then he would put his arm where there was before *space* without *body*; and if there he spread his fingers, there would still be *space* between them without *body*. If he could not stretch out his hand, it must be because of some external hindrance (for we suppose him alive, with such a power of moving the parts of his body that he has now, which is not in itself impossible, if God so pleased to have it, or at least it is not impossible for God so to move him); and then I ask, whether that which hinders his hand from moving outwards is substance or accident, something or nothing? And when they have resolved that, they will be able to

resolve themselves what that is, which is or may be between two bodies at a distance, that is not body and has no solidity. In the mean time, the argument is at least as good that where nothing hinders (as beyond the utmost bounds of all bodies) a *body* put in motion may move on, as where there is nothing between, there two bodies must necessarily touch; for pure *space* between is sufficient to take away the necessity of mutual contact, but bare *space* in the way is not sufficient to stop motion. The truth is, these men must either admit that they think body infinite, though they are loath to speak it out, or else affirm that *space* is not *body*. For I would gladly meet with that thinking man who can in his thoughts set any bounds to space more than he can to duration, or by thinking hope to arrive at the end of either. And therefore, if his *idea* of eternity is infinite, so is his *idea* of immensity; they are both finite or infinite alike.

22. *The power of annihilation proves a* vacuum. Further, those who assert the impossibility of *space* existing without *matter* must not only make body infinite, but must also deny a power in God to annihilate any part of matter. No one, I suppose, will deny that God can put an end to all motion that is in matter, and fix all the bodies of the universe in a perfect quiet and rest, and continue them so long as he pleases. Whoever, then, will allow that God can, during such a general rest, annihilate either this book or the body of him who reads it, must necessarily admit the possibility of a *vacuum*; for it is evident that the space that was filled by the parts of the annihilated body will still remain, and be a space without body. For the surrounding bodies being in perfect rest are a wall of adamant, and in that state make it a perfect impossibility for any other body to get into that space. And indeed the necessary motion of one particle of matter into the place from which another particle of matter is removed is but a consequence from the supposition of plenitude. This will therefore need some better proof than a supposed matter of fact which experiment can never make out, our own clear and distinct *ideas* plainly satisfying us that there is no necessary connection between *space* and *solidity*, since we can conceive the one without the other. And those who dispute for or against a *vacuum* do thereby confess they have distinct *ideas* of *vacuum*

and *plenum*—i.e., that they have an *idea* of extension void of solidity—though they deny its existence. Or else they dispute about nothing at all. For they who so much alter the signification of words as to call *extension, body*, and consequently make the whole essence of body to be nothing but pure extension without solidity, must talk absurdly whenever they speak of *vacuum*, since it is impossible for extension to be without extension. For *vacuum*, whether we affirm or deny its existence, signifies space without body, whose very existence no one can deny to be possible who will not make matter infinite and take from God a power to annihilate any particle of it.

23. *Motion proves a* vacuum. But not to go so far as beyond the utmost bounds of body in the universe, nor appeal to God's omnipotence to find a *vacuum*, the *motion* of bodies that are in our view and neighborhood seems to me plainly to evince it. For I desire anyone so to divide a solid body of any dimension he pleases as to make it possible for the solid parts to move up and down freely every way within the bounds of that surface, if there is not left in it a void space as big as the least part into which he has divided the said solid body. And if where the least particle of the body divided is as big as a mustard seed, a void space equal to the bulk of a mustard seed be requisite to make room for the free motion of the parts of the divided body within the bounds of its surface, where the particles of matter are 100,000,000 less than a mustard seed, there must also be a space void of solid matter as big as 100,000,000 part of a mustard seed; for if it hold in the one, it will hold in the other, and so on *in infinitum*. And let this void space be as little as it will, it destroys the hypothesis of *plenitude*. For if there can be a space void of body equal to the smallest separate particle of matter now existing in nature, it is still space without body, and makes as great a difference between space and body as if it were *mega chasma*, a distance as wide as any in nature. And, therefore, if we do not suppose the void space necessary to motion equal to the least parcel of the divided solid matter, but to 1/10 or 1/1000 of it, the same consequence will always follow of space without matter.

24. *The* ideas *of space and body distinct*. But the question being here "whether the *idea of space* or

extension is *the same with the idea of body*," it is not necessary to prove the real existence of a *vacuum*, but the *idea* of it, which it is plain men have when they inquire and dispute whether there is a *vacuum* or not. For if they did not have the *idea* of space without body, they could not make a question about its existence. And if their *idea* of body did not include in it something more than the bare *idea* of space, they could have no doubt about the plenitude of the world. And it would be as absurd to demand whether there were space without body as whether there were space without space, or body without body, since these were but different names of the same *idea*.

25. *Extension being inseparable from body, proves it not the same.* It is true the *idea* of *extension* joins itself so inseparably with all visible and most tangible qualities, that it suffers us to see no one, or feel very few external objects, without taking in impressions of extension too. This readiness of extension to make itself be taken notice of so constantly with other *ideas* has been the occasion, I guess, that some have made the whole essence of *body* to consist in extension; this is not much to be wondered at, since some have had their minds, by their eyes and touch (the busiest of all our senses), so filled with the *idea* of extension and, as it were, wholly possessed with it, that they allowed no existence to anything that did not have extension. I shall not now argue with those men who take the measure and possibility of all being only from their narrow and gross imaginations. But having here to do only with those who conclude the essence of body to be *extension* because they say they cannot imagine any sensible quality of any body without extension, I shall desire them to consider that had they reflected on their *ideas* of tastes and smells as much as on those of sight and touch—no, had they examined their *ideas* of hunger and thirst, and several other pains—they would have found that they included in them no *idea* of extension at all, which is but an affection of body, as well as the rest, discoverable by our senses, which are scarcely acute enough to look into the pure essences of things.

26. If those *ideas* which are constantly joined to all others must therefore be concluded to be the essence of those things which have constantly those *ideas* joined to them, and are inseparable from them,

then unity is without doubt the essence of everything. For there is not any object of sensation or reflection which does not carry with it the *idea* of one. But the weakness of this kind of argument we have already shown sufficiently.

27. Ideas *of space and solidity distinct.* To conclude, whatever men shall think concerning the existence of a *vacuum*, this is plain to me: that we have as clear an *idea of space distinct from solidity* as we have of solidity distinct from motion, or motion from space. We do not have any two more distinct *ideas*, and we can as easily conceive space without solidity as we can conceive body or space without motion, though it is never so certain that neither body nor motion can exist without space. [. . .]

Chapter 14. *Of Duration and Its Simple Modes.*

1. *Duration is fleeting extension.* There is another sort of distance or length the *idea* of which we do not get from the permanent parts of space, but from the fleeting and perpetually perishing parts of succession. This we call *duration*, the simple modes of which are any different lengths of it of which we have distinct *ideas*, as *hours, days, years*, etc., *time*, and *eternity*.

2. *Its* idea *from reflection on the train of our* ideas. The answer of a great man to one who asked what time was, "*Si non rogas intelligo*" (which amounts to this: the more I set myself to think of it, the less I understand it), might perhaps persuade one that time, which reveals all other things, is itself not to be discovered. *Duration, time*, and *eternity*, are, not without reason, thought to have something very abstruse in their nature. But however remote these may seem from our comprehension, yet if we trace them right to their origins, I do not doubt but one of those sources of all our knowledge, namely, *sensation* and *reflection*, will be able to furnish us with these *ideas*, as clear and distinct as many others which are thought much less obscure, and we shall find that the *idea* of eternity itself is derived from the same common origin with the rest of our *ideas*.

3. To understand *time* and *eternity* correctly, we ought with attention consider what *idea* it is we have of *duration* and how we came by it. It is evident to

anyone who will but observe what passes in his own mind that there is a train of *ideas* which constantly succeed one another in his understanding as long as he is awake. *Reflection* on these appearances of several *ideas* one after another in our minds is that which furnishes us with the *idea* of *succession*; and the distance between any parts of that succession, or between the appearance of any two *ideas* in our minds, is what we call *duration*. For while we are thinking, or while we receive successively several *ideas* in our minds, we know that we do exist; and so we call the existence, or the continuation of the existence of ourselves or anything else commensurate to the succession of any *ideas* in our minds, the *duration* of ourselves or any such other thing coexistent with our thinking. [. . .]

16. Ideas, *however made, include no sense of motion.* Whether these several *ideas* in a man's mind are made by certain motions, I will not here dispute. But this I am sure, that they include no *idea* of motion in their appearance; and if a man did not have the *idea* of motion otherwise, I think he would have none at all. This is enough to my present purpose and sufficiently shows that the notice we take of the *ideas* of our own minds, appearing there one after another, is that which gives us the *idea* of succession and duration, without which we should have no such *ideas* at all. It is not then *motion*, but the constant train of *ideas* in our minds while we are waking that furnishes us with the idea *of duration*, of which motion does not otherwise give us any perception than as it causes in our minds a constant succession of *ideas*, as I have shown before. And we have as clear an *idea* of succession and duration by the train of other *ideas* succeeding one another in our minds, without the *idea* of any motion, as by the train of *ideas* caused by the uninterrupted sensible change of distance between two bodies, which we have from motion. And therefore we should as well have the *idea* of duration were there no sense of motion at all.

17. *Time is duration set out by measures.* Having thus gotten the *idea* of duration, the next thing natural for the mind to do is to get some *measure of* this common *duration* by which it might judge of its different lengths and consider the distinct order in which several things exist, without which a great part of our knowledge would be confused and a great part

of history be rendered very useless. This consideration of duration, as set out by certain periods and marked by certain measures or *epochs*, is that, I think, which most properly we call *time*. [. . .]

27. *Eternity.* By the same means, therefore, and from the same origin that we come to have the *idea* of time, we have also that *idea* which we call *eternity*; namely, having gotten the *idea* of succession and duration by reflecting on the train of our own *ideas* caused in us either by the natural appearances of those *ideas* coming constantly of themselves into our waking thoughts, or else caused by external objects successively affecting our senses, and having from the revolutions of the sun gotten the *ideas* of certain lengths of duration, we can, in our thoughts, add such lengths of duration to one another as often as we please, and apply them, so added, to durations past or to come. And this we can continue to do on without bounds or limits, and proceed *in infinitum*, and apply thus the length of the annual motion of the sun to duration, supposed before the sun's, or any other motion had its being—which is no more difficult or absurd than to apply the notion I have of the moving of a shadow one hour today upon the sundial to the duration of something last night, e.g., the burning of a candle, which is now absolutely separate from all actual motion. And it is as impossible for the duration of that flame for an hour last night to coexist with any motion that now is, or forever shall be, as for any part of duration that was before the beginning of the world to coexist with the motion of the sun now. But yet this does not hinder, but that having the *idea* of the length of the motion of the shadow on a dial between the marks of two hours, I can as distinctly measure in my thoughts the duration of that candlelight last night as I can the duration of anything that does now exist. And it is no more than to think that, had the sun shone then on the dial, and moved after the same rate it does now, the shadow on the dial would have passed from one hour line to another while that flame of the candle lasted. [. . .]

31. And thus I think it is plain that *from those two fountains of all knowledge before mentioned, namely, reflection and sensation, we got the ideas of duration* and the measures of it.

For, *first,* by observing what passes in our minds,

how our *ideas* there in train constantly some vanish and others begin to appear, we come by the *idea* of *succession*.

Secondly, by observing a distance in the parts of this succession, we get the *idea* of *duration*.

Thirdly, by sensation observing certain appearances at certain regular and seeming equidistant periods, we get the *ideas* of certain lengths or *measures of duration* as minutes, hours, days, years, etc.

Fourthly, by being able to repeat those measures of time or *ideas* of stated length of duration in our minds, as often as we will, we can come to *imagine duration, where nothing does really endure or exist*; and thus we imagine tomorrow, next year, or seven years hence.

Fifthly, by being able to repeat *ideas* of any length of time, as of a minute, a year, or an age, as often as we will in our own thoughts, and adding them one to another, without ever coming to the end of such addition any nearer than we can to the end of number, to which we can always add, we come by the *idea* of *eternity*, as the future eternal duration of our souls as well as the eternity of that infinite Being which must necessarily have always existed.

Sixthly, by considering any part of infinite duration as set out by periodical measures, we come by the *idea* of what we call *time* in general.

Chapter 21. *Of Power*.

1. *This* idea *how got*. The mind being every day informed by the senses of the alteration of those simple *ideas* it observes in things without; and taking notice how one comes to an end and ceases to be and another begins to exist which was not before; reflecting also on what passes within itself and observing a constant change of its *ideas*, sometimes by the impression of outward objects on the senses and sometimes by the determination of its own choice; and concluding from what it has so constantly observed to have been that the like changes will for the future be made in the same things by like agents and, by the like ways, considers in one thing the possibility of having any of its simple *ideas* changed and in another the possibility of making that change; and so comes by that *idea* which we call *power*. Thus, we

say: fire has a *power* to melt gold—i.e., to destroy the consistency of its insensible parts, and consequently its hardness, and make it fluid—and gold has a *power* to be melted; that the sun has a *power* to blanch wax, and wax a *power* to be blanched by the sun, by which the yellowness is destroyed and whiteness made to exist in its room. In these and the like cases, the *power* we consider is in reference to the change of perceivable *ideas*. For we cannot observe any alteration to be made in, or operation upon anything, but by the observable change of its sensible *ideas*; nor conceive any alteration to be made, but by conceiving a change of some of its *ideas*.

2. *Power active and passive*. *Power*, thus considered, is two-fold, namely, as able to make or able to receive any change. The one may be called *active* and the other *passive power*. Whether matter is not wholly destitute of *active power*, as its author God is truly above all *passive power*; and whether the intermediate state of created spirits is not that alone which is capable of both *active* and *passive power*, may be worth consideration. I shall not now enter into that inquiry, my present business being not to search into the origin of power, but how we come by the *idea* of it. But since *active powers* make so great a part of our complex *ideas* of natural substances (as we shall see hereafter), and I mention them as such, according to common apprehension, yet they being not perhaps so truly *active powers* as our hasty thoughts are apt to represent them, I judge it not amiss, by this intimation, to direct our minds to the consideration of God and spirits for the clearest *idea* of *active powers*.

3. *Power includes relation*. I confess *power includes in it some kind of relation* (a relation to action or change), as, indeed, which of our *ideas*, of whatever kind, when attentively considered, does not? For, our *ideas* of extension, duration, and number, do they not all contain in them a secret relation of the parts? Figure and motion have something relative in them much more visibly. And sensible qualities, as colors and smells, etc., what are they but the *powers* of different bodies in relation to our perception, etc.? And if considered in the things themselves, do they not depend on the bulk, figure, texture, and motion of the parts? All which include some kind of relation in them. Our *idea*, therefore, of *power*, I think may

well have a place among other simple *ideas* and be considered as one of them, being one of those that make a principal ingredient in our complex *ideas* of substances, as we shall hereafter have occasion to observe.

4. *The clearest* idea *of active power had from spirit.* We are abundantly furnished with the *idea of passive power* by almost all sorts of sensible things. In most of them we cannot avoid observing their sensible qualities, no, their very substances, to be in a continual flux. And therefore with reason we look on them as liable still to the same change. Nor have we of *active power* (which is the more proper signification of the word *power*) fewer instances, since whatever change is observed, the mind must collect a power somewhere able to make that change as well as a possibility in the thing itself to receive it. But yet, if we will consider it attentively, bodies, by our senses, do not afford us so clear and distinct an *idea* of *active power* as we have from reflection on the operations of our minds. For all *power* relating to action, and there being but two sorts of action of which we have an *idea*, namely, thinking and motion, let us consider from where we have the clearest *ideas* of the *powers* which produce these actions. 1. Of thinking, body affords us no *idea* at all; it is only from reflection that we have that. 2. Neither have we from body any *idea* of the beginning of motion. A body at rest affords us no *idea* of any *active power* to move, and when it is set in motion itself, that motion is rather a passion than an action in it. For when the ball obeys the motion of a billiard stick, it is not any action of the ball, but bare passion. Also when by impulse it sets another ball in motion that lay in its way, it only communicates the motion it had received from another and loses in itself so much as the other received; this gives us but a very obscure *idea* of an *active power* of moving in body, while we observe it only to transfer but not produce any motion. For it is but a very obscure *idea* of *power* which does not reach the production of the action but the continuation of the passion. For so is motion in a body impelled by another, the continuation of the alteration made in it from rest to motion being little more an action, than the continuation of the alteration of its figure by the same blow is an action. The *idea* of the beginning

of motion we have only from reflection on what passes in ourselves, where we find by experience that barely by willing it, barely by a thought of the mind, we can move the parts of our bodies which were before at rest, so that it seems to me we have from the observation of the operation of bodies by our senses but a very imperfect obscure *idea* of *active power*, since they do not afford us any *idea* in themselves of the *power* to begin any action, either motion or thought. But if, from the impulse bodies are observed to make one upon another, anyone thinks he has a clear *idea* of *power*, it serves as well to my purpose, sensation being one of those ways by which the mind comes by its *ideas*. Only, I thought it worthwhile to consider here, by the way, whether the mind does not receive its *idea* of *active power* clearer from reflection on its own operations than it does from any external sensation.

5. *Will and understanding, two powers.* This, at least, I think evident, that we find in ourselves a *power* to begin or refrain, continue or end several actions of our minds and motions of our bodies, barely by a thought or preference of the mind, ordering, or as it were, commanding, the doing or not doing such or such a particular action. This *power* which the mind has, thus to order the consideration of any *idea* or the abstaining to consider it, or to prefer the motion of any part of the body to its rest, and *vice versa*, in any particular instance, is that which we call the *will*. The actual exercise of that power, by directing any particular action or its abstention, is that which we call *volition* or *willing*. The abstention of that action, consequent to such order or command of the mind, is called *voluntary*. And whatever action is performed without such a thought of the mind is called *involuntary*. The power of perception is that which we call the *understanding*. Perception, which we make the act of the understanding, is of three sorts: 1. The perception of *ideas* in our minds. 2. The perception of the signification of signs. 3. The perception of the connection or repugnance, agreement or disagreement, that there is between any of our *ideas*. All these are attributed to the *understanding*, or perceptive power, though it is the two latter only that use allows us to say we understand. [. . .]

7. *From where the* ideas *of liberty and necessity.* Everyone, I think, finds in himself a *power* to begin

or refrain, continue or put an end to several actions in himself. From the consideration of the extent of this power of the mind over the actions of the man, which everyone finds in himself, arise the *ideas* of *liberty* and *necessity*.

8. *Liberty, what.* All the actions that we have any *idea* of reducing themselves, as has been said, to these two, namely, thinking and motion, so far as a man has power to think or not to think, to move or not to move, according to the preference or direction of his own mind, so far is a man *free*. Wherever any performance or abstention is not equally in a man's power, wherever doing or not doing will not equally follow upon the preference of his mind directing it, there he is not *free*, though perhaps the action may be voluntary. So that the *idea* of *liberty* is the *idea* of a power in any agent to do or refrain any particular action, according to the determination or thought of the mind, by which either of them is preferred to the other. Where either of them is not in the power of the agent to be produced by him according to his *volition*, there he is not at *liberty*; that agent is under *necessity*. So that *liberty* cannot be where there is no thought, no volition, no will, but there may be thought, there may be will, there may be volition, where there is no *liberty*. [. . .]

10. *Does not belong to volition.* Again, suppose a man is carried while fast asleep into a room where a person is he longs to see and speak with, and is there locked fast in, beyond his power to get out; he awakes and is glad to find himself in so desirable company, which he stays willingly in, i.e., prefers his stay to going away. I ask, is not this stay voluntary? I think nobody will doubt it; and yet being locked fast in, it is evident he is not at liberty not to stay, he does not have freedom to be gone. So that *liberty is not an* idea *belonging to volition*, or preferring, but to the person having the power of doing, or abstaining to do, according as the mind shall choose or direct. Our *idea* of liberty reaches as far as that power, and no further. For wherever restraint comes to check that power, or compulsion takes away that indifference of ability on either side to act, or to refrain acting, there *liberty*, and our notion of it, presently ceases.

11. *Voluntary opposed to involuntary, not to necessary.* We have instances enough, and often more than

enough, in our own bodies. A man's heart beats, and the blood circulates, which it is not in his power by any thought or volition to stop; and therefore in respect to these motions, where rest does not depend on his choice, nor would follow the determination of his mind, if it should prefer it, he is not a *free agent.* Convulsive motions agitate his legs, so that though he *wills* it ever so much, he cannot by any power of his mind stop their motion (as in that odd disease called *chorea sancti Viti*) but he is perpetually dancing; he is not at liberty in this action, but under as much necessity of moving as a stone that falls or a tennis ball struck with a racket. On the other side, a palsy or the stocks hinder his legs from obeying the determination of his mind, if it would thereby transfer his body to another place. In all these there is want of *freedom*, though the sitting still even of a paralytic, while he prefers it to a removal, is truly voluntary. *Voluntary* then *is not opposed to necessary, but to involuntary.* For a man may prefer what he can do to what he cannot do — the state he is in to its absence or change — though necessity has made it in itself unalterable.

12. *Liberty, what.* As it is in the motions of the body, so it is in the thoughts of our minds: where anyone is such that we have power to take it up, or lay it by, according to the preference of the mind, there we are *at liberty*. A waking man, being under the necessity of having some *ideas* constantly in his mind, is not at *liberty* to think or not to think, no more than he is at *liberty* whether his body shall touch any other or not. But whether he will remove his contemplation from one *idea* to another is many times in his choice, and then he is in respect of his *ideas* as much at *liberty* as he is in respect of bodies he rests on; he can at pleasure remove himself from one to another. But yet some *ideas* to the mind, like some motions to the body, are such as in certain circumstances it cannot avoid, nor obtain their absence by the utmost effort it can use. A man on the rack is not at liberty to lay by the *idea* of pain and divert himself with other contemplations. And sometimes a boisterous passion hurries our thoughts, as a hurricane does our bodies, without leaving us the liberty of thinking on other things, which we would rather choose. But as soon as the mind regains the power

to stop or continue, begin or refrain any of these motions of the body without, or thoughts within, according as it thinks fit to prefer either to the other, we then consider the man as a *free agent* again. [. . .]

14. Liberty *does not belong to the will.* If this is so (as I imagine it is), I leave it to be considered whether it may not help to put an end to that long agitated, and I think, unreasonable, because unintelligible, question, namely, *whether man's will is free or not?* For if I am not mistaken, it follows from what I have said that the question itself is altogether improper; and it is as insignificant to ask whether man's *will* is free as to ask whether his sleep is swift or his virtue square, *liberty* being as little applicable to the *will* as swiftness of motion is to sleep or squareness to virtue. Everyone would laugh at the absurdity of such a question, as either of these. Because it is obvious that the modifications of motion do not belong to sleep, nor the difference of figure to virtue. And when anyone well considers it, I think he will as plainly perceive that *liberty*, which is but a power, belongs only to agents, and cannot be an attribute or modification of the *will*, which is also but a power. [. . .]

16. It is plain, then, that the *will* is nothing but one power or ability, and *freedom* another power or ability, so that to ask whether the *will has freedom* is to ask whether one power has another power, one ability another ability—a question at first sight too grossly absurd to make a dispute or need an answer. [. . .]

17. However, the *name faculty*, which men have given to this power called the *will*, and by which they have been led into a way of talking of the will as acting, may, by an appropriation that disguises its true sense, serve a little to palliate the absurdity, yet the *will* in truth signifies nothing but a power, or ability, to prefer or choose. And when the *will*, under the name of a *faculty*, is considered as it is, barely as an ability to do something, the absurdity in saying it is free, or not free, will easily discover itself. [. . .]

21. *But to the agent or man.* To return then to the inquiry about liberty, I think *the question is not proper, whether the will is free, but whether a man is free.* Thus, I think,

1. That so far as anyone can, by the direction or choice of his mind preferring the existence of any

action to the nonexistence of that action, and *vice versa*, make it exist or not exist, so far he is free. For if I can, by a thought directing the motion of my finger, make it move when it was at rest, or *vice versa*, it is evident that, in respect of that, I am free. And if I can, by a like thought of my mind, preferring one to the other, produce either words or silence, I am at liberty to speak or hold my peace. And as far as this power reaches, of acting or not acting, by the determination of his own thought preferring either, so far is a man *free*. For how can we think anyone freer than to have the power to do what he will? And so far as anyone can, by preferring any action to its not being, or rest to any action, produce that action or rest, so far can he do what he will. For such a preferring of action to its absence is the *willing* of it. And we can scarcely tell how to imagine any *being* freer than to be able to do what he *wills*. So that in respect of actions within the reach of such a power in him, a man seems as free as it is possible for freedom to make him.[. . .]

23. 2. That *willing* or *volition* being an action, and freedom consisting in a power of acting or not acting, *a man in respect of willing or the act of volition, when any action in his power is once proposed to his thoughts, as presently to be done, cannot be free.* The reason of this is very manifest. For, it being unavoidable that the action depending on his *will* should exist or not exist, and its existence or not existence following perfectly the determination and preference of his will, he cannot avoid willing the existence or not existence of that action, it is absolutely necessary that he *will* the one or the other, i.e., *prefer* the one to the other, since one of them must necessarily follow; and that which does follow follows by the choice and determination of his mind, that is, by his *willing it*; for if he did not *will* it, it would not be. So that in respect of the act of *willing*, a man in such a case is not free, liberty consisting in a power to act or not to act, which, in regard of volition, a man, upon such a proposal, does not have. For it is unavoidably necessary to prefer the doing or abstaining of an action in a man's power which is once so proposed to his thoughts. A man must necessarily *will* the one or the other of them, upon which preference or volition the action or its abstaining certainly follows and is truly

voluntary. But the act of volition, or preferring one of the two, being that which he cannot avoid, a man, in respect of that act of *willing*, is under a necessity, and so cannot be free, unless necessity and freedom can consist together and a man can be free and bound at once.

24. This then is evident, that, in all proposals of present action, *a man is not at liberty to will or not to will, because he cannot refrain willing*, liberty consisting in a power to act or to refrain acting, and in that only. For a man who sits still is said yet to be at liberty, because he can walk if he wills it. But if a man sitting still does not have a power to remove himself, he is not at liberty; so likewise a man falling down a precipice, though in motion, is not at liberty, because he cannot stop that motion if he would. This being so, it is plain that a man who is walking, to whom it is proposed to give off walking, is not at liberty whether he *will* determine himself to walk, or give off walking, or not. He must necessarily prefer one or the other of them, walking or not walking; and so it is in regard of all other actions in our power so proposed, which are the far greater number. For considering the vast number of voluntary actions that succeed one another every moment that we are awake in the course of our lives, there are but few of them that are thought on or proposed to the *will*, until the time they are to be done. And in all such actions, as I have shown, the mind in respect of *willing* does not have a power to act or not to act, in which consists liberty. The mind in that case does not have a power to refrain *willing*; it cannot avoid some determination concerning them. Let the consideration be as short, the thought as quick as it will, it either leaves the man in the state he was before thinking, or changes it, continues the action, or puts an end to it—by which it is manifest that it orders and directs one, in preference to or with neglect of the other, and thereby either the continuation or change becomes unavoidably voluntary.

25. *The will determined by something without it.* Since, then, it is plain that in most cases a man is not at liberty whether he will or not, the next thing demanded is *whether a man is at liberty to will which of the two he pleases, motion or rest?* This question

carries its absurdity so manifestly in itself that one might as a result sufficiently be convinced that liberty does not concern the will. For to ask whether a man is at liberty to will either motion or rest, speaking or silence, which he pleases, is to ask, whether a man can *will* what he *wills*, or be pleased with what he is pleased with? A question which, I think, needs no answer; and they who can make a question of it must suppose one will to determine the acts of another, and another to determine that, and so on *in infinitum*.

26. To avoid these and the like absurdities, nothing can be of greater use than to establish in our minds determined *ideas* of the things under consideration. If the *ideas* of liberty and volition were well fixed in the understandings and carried along with us in our minds, as they ought, through all the questions that are raised about them, I suppose a great part of the difficulties that perplex men's thoughts and entangle their understandings would be much easier resolved, and we should perceive where the confused signification of terms or where the nature of the thing caused the obscurity.

27. First then, it is carefully to be remembered that *freedom consists in the dependence of the existence or not existence of any action, upon our volition of it, and not in the dependence of any action or its contrary, on our preference*. A man standing on a cliff is at liberty to leap twenty yards downwards into the sea, not because he has a power to do the contrary action, which is to leap twenty yards upwards, for that he cannot do. But he is therefore free because he has a power to leap or not to leap. But if a greater force than his either holds him fast, or tumbles him down, he is no longer free in that case, because the doing or abstaining of that particular action is no longer in his power. He who is a close prisoner in a room twenty feet square, being at the north side of his chamber, is at liberty to walk twenty feet southward, because he can walk or not walk it, but is not, at the same time, at liberty to do the contrary, i.e., to walk twenty feet northward.

In this then consists freedom, namely, in our being able to act or not to act, according as we shall choose or will. [. . .]

30. *Will and desire must not be confounded.* But,

in the way to it, it will be necessary to premise that though I have above endeavored to express the act of volition by choosing, preferring, and the like terms that signify desire as well as volition, for want of other words to mark that act of the mind whose proper name is willing or volition, yet it being a very simple act, whoever desires to understand what it is will better find it by reflecting on his own mind and observing what it does when it wills, than by any variety of articulate sounds whatsoever. This caution of being careful not to be misled by expressions that do not enough keep up the difference between the will and several acts of the mind that are quite distinct from it, I think the more necessary, because I find the will often confounded with several of the affections, especially desire, and one put for the other — and that by men who would not willingly be thought not to have had very distinct notions of things and not to have written very clearly about them. This, I imagine, has been no small occasion of obscurity and mistake in this matter, and therefore is, as much as may be, to be avoided. For he who shall turn his thoughts inwards upon what passes in his mind when he *wills* shall see that the *will* or power of *volition* is conversant about nothing but that particular determination of the mind by which barely by a thought the mind endeavors to give rise, continuation, or stop, to any action which it takes to be in its power. This, well considered, plainly shows that the will is perfectly distinguished from *desire*, which in the very same action may have a quite contrary tendency from that which our *will* sets us upon. A man whom I cannot deny, may oblige me to use persuasions to another, which, at the same time I am speaking, I may wish may not prevail on him. In this case, it is plain the *will* and *desire* run counter. I will the action that tends one way, while my desire tends another, and that the direct contrary way. [. . .]

31. *Uneasiness determines the will.* To return then to the inquiry, *what is it that determines the will in regard to our actions?* And that, upon second thoughts, I am apt to imagine is not, as is generally supposed, the greater good in view, but some (and for the most part the most pressing) *uneasiness* a man is at present under. This is that which successively determines the

will and sets us upon those actions we perform. This *uneasiness* we may call, as it is, *desire*, which is an uneasiness of the mind for want of some absent good. [. . .]

35. *The greatest positive good does not determine the will, but uneasiness.* It seems so established and settled a maxim by the general consent of all mankind that good, the greater good, determines the will that I do not at all wonder that, when I first published my thoughts on this subject, I took it for granted; and I imagine that by a great many I shall be thought more excusable for having then done so, than that now I have ventured to recede from so received an opinion. But yet, upon a stricter inquiry, I am forced to conclude that *good*, the *greater good*, though apprehended and acknowledged to be so, does not determine the *will*, until our desire, raised proportionally to it, makes us *uneasy* in the want of it. Convince a man ever so much that plenty has its advantages over poverty, make him see and admit that the handsome conveniences of life are better than nasty penury, yet as long as he is content with the latter and finds no *uneasiness* in it, he does not move — his *will* never is determined to any action that shall bring him out of it. [. . .]

38. *Because all who allow the joys of heaven possible do not pursue them.* Were the *will* determined by the views of good, as it appears in contemplation greater or less to the understanding, which is the state of all absent good, and that which in the received opinion the *will* is supposed to move to, and to be moved by, I do not see how it could ever get loose from the infinite eternal joys of heaven, once proposed and considered as possible. [. . .]

This would be the state of the mind and regular tendency of the *will* in all its determinations, were it determined by that which is considered and in view the greater good; but that it is not so is visible in experience, the infinitely greatest confessed good being often neglected to satisfy the successive *uneasiness* of our desires pursuing trifles. [. . .]

41. *All desire happiness.* If it is further asked, what it is that moves *desire?* I answer, happiness, and that alone. *Happiness* and *misery* are the names of two extremes, the utmost bounds of which we do not

know; it is what "eye has not seen, ear has not heard, nor has it entered into the heart of man to conceive." But of some degrees of both we have very lively impressions, made by several instances of delight and joy on the one side and torment and sorrow on the other, which, for shortness' sake, I shall comprehend under the names of pleasure and pain, there being pleasure and pain of the mind as well as the body. "With him is fullness of joy and pleasure for evermore." Or, to speak truly, they are all of the mind, though some have their rise in the mind from thought, others in the body from certain modifications of motion.

42. *Happiness, what. Happiness*, then, in its full extent is the utmost pleasure we are capable of, and *misery*, the utmost pain, and the lowest degree of what can be called *happiness* is so much ease from all pain, and so much present pleasure as without which anyone cannot be content. Now because pleasure and pain are produced in us by the operation of certain objects, either on our minds or our bodies, and in different degrees, therefore what has an aptness to produce pleasure in us is that we call *good*, and what is apt to produce pain in us we call *evil*, for no other reason but for its aptness to produce pleasure and pain in us, in which consists our *happiness* and *misery*. Further, though what is apt to produce any degree of pleasure is in itself good, and what is apt to produce any degree of pain is evil, yet it often happens that we do not call it so when it comes in competition with a greater of its sort, because when they come in competition, the degrees also of pleasure and pain have justly a preference, so that if we will rightly estimate what we call *good* and *evil*, we shall find it lies much in comparison. For the cause of every less degree of pain as well as every greater degree of pleasure has the nature of *good*, and vice versa.

43. *What good is desired, what not.* Though this is that which is called *good* and *evil*, and all good is the proper object of *desire* in general, yet all good, even seen and confessed to be so, does not necessarily move every particular man's *desire*, but only that part, or so much of it as is considered and taken to make a necessary part of his happiness. All other good, however great in reality or appearance, does not excite a man's *desires*, who does not look on it to make a

part of that happiness with which he, in his present thoughts, can satisfy himself. Happiness, under this view, everyone constantly pursues and desires what makes any part of it. Other things acknowledged to be good, he can look upon without *desire*, pass by, and be content without. There is nobody, I think, so senseless as to deny that there is pleasure in knowledge. And for the pleasures of sense, they have too many followers to let it be questioned whether men are taken with them or not. Now let one man place his satisfaction in sensual pleasures, another in the delight of knowledge, though each of them cannot but confess there is great pleasure in what the other pursues, yet neither of them making the other's delight a part of his happiness, their *desires* are not moved, but each is satisfied without what the other enjoys, and so his will is not determined to the pursuit of it. But yet as soon as the studious man's hunger and thirst make him *uneasy*, he, whose *will* was never determined to any pursuit of good cheer, poignant sauces, delicious wine, by the pleasant taste he has found in them, is, by the uneasiness of hunger and thirst, presently determined to eating and drinking, though possibly with great indifference, what wholesome food comes in his way. And on the other side, the epicure buckles to study when shame or the desire to recommend himself to his mistress shall make him *uneasy* in the want of any sort of knowledge. Thus, however much men are in earnest and constant in pursuit of happiness, yet they may have a clear view of good, great and confessed good, without being concerned for it, or moved by it, if they think they can make up their happiness without it. Though, as to pain, that they are always concerned for. They can feel no *uneasiness* without being moved. And therefore being *uneasy* in the want of whatever is judged necessary to their happiness, as soon as any good appears to make a part of their portion of happiness, they begin to *desire* it.

44. *Why the greatest good is not always desired.* This, I think, anyone may observe in himself and others, that the *greater visible good* does not always raise men's *desires* in proportion to the greatness it appears and is acknowledged to have, though every little trouble moves us and sets us on work to get rid of it. The reason of which is evident from the nature

of our *happiness* and *misery* itself. All present pain, whatever it be, makes a part of our present *misery*; but all absent good does not at any time make a necessary part of our present *happiness*, nor the absence of it make a part of our *misery*. [. . .]

47. *The power to suspend the prosecution of any desire makes way for consideration.* There being in us a great many *uneasinesses* always soliciting and ready to determine the *will*, it is natural, as I have said, that the greatest and most pressing should determine the *will* to the next action, and so it does for the most part, but not always. For the mind, having in most cases, as is evident in experience, a power to *suspend* the execution and satisfaction of any of its desires, and so all, one after another, is at liberty to consider the objects of them, examine them on all sides, and weigh them with others. In this lies the liberty man has, and from the not using of it right comes all that variety of mistakes, errors, and faults which we run into in the conduct of our lives, and our endeavors after happiness, while we precipitate the determination of our *wills* and engage too soon before due *examination*. To prevent this, we have a power to *suspend* the prosecution of this or that desire, as everyone daily may experiment in himself. This seems to me the source of all liberty; in this seems to consist that which is (as I think improperly) called *free will*. For during this *suspension* of any desire, before the *will* is determined to action and the action (which follows that determination) done, we have opportunity to examine, view, and judge of the good or evil of what we are going to do, and when, upon due *examination*, we have judged, we have done our duty, all that we can or ought to do in pursuit of our happiness; and it is not a fault, but a perfection of our nature to desire, will, and act according to the last result of a fair *examination*. [. . .]

52. *The reason of it.* This is the hinge on which turns the *liberty* of intellectual beings, in their constant endeavors after and a steady prosecution of true felicity, that they can *suspend* this prosecution in particular cases until they have looked before them and informed themselves whether that particular thing, which is then proposed or desired, lie in the way to their main end and make a real part of that which is their greatest good. For the inclination and tendency of their nature to happiness is an obligation and motive to them, to take care not to mistake or miss it, and so necessarily puts them upon caution, deliberation, and wariness in the direction of their particular actions, which are the means to obtain it. Whatever necessity determines to the pursuit of real bliss, the same necessity with the same force establishes *suspense*, *deliberation*, and scrutiny of each successive desire, whether the satisfaction of it does not interfere with our true happiness and mislead us from it. This, as seems to me, is the great privilege of finite intellectual beings; and I desire it may be well-considered whether the great inlet and exercise of all the *liberty* men have, are capable of, or can be useful to them, and that on which depends the turn of their actions, does not lie in this, that they can *suspend* their desires, and stop them from determining their *wills* to any action, until they have duly and fairly *examined* the good and evil of it, insofar as the weight of the thing requires. This we are able to do, and when we have done it, we have done our duty, and all that is in our power, and indeed all that needs. For since the *will* supposes knowledge to guide its choice, all that we can do is to hold our *wills* undetermined until we have *examined* the good and evil of what we desire. What follows after that follows in a chain of consequences linked one to another, all depending on the last determination of the judgment which, whether it shall be upon a hasty and precipitate view, or upon a due and mature *examination*, is in our power, experience showing us that in most cases we are able to suspend the present satisfaction of any desire. [. . .]

72. Before I close this chapter, it may perhaps be to our purpose and help to give us clearer conceptions about *power*, if we make our thoughts take a little more exact survey of *action*. I have said above that we have *ideas* but of two sorts of *action*, namely, *motion* and *thinking*. These, in truth, though called and counted *actions*, yet if nearly considered, will not be found to be always perfectly so. For, if I am not mistaken, there are instances of both kinds which, upon due consideration, will be found rather *passions* than *actions*, and consequently so far the effects barely of passive powers in those subjects which yet on their accounts are thought *agents*. For in these instances,

the substance that has motion or thought receives the impression by which it is put into that *action* purely from without, and so acts merely by the capacity it has to receive such an impression from some external agent; and such a *power* is not properly an *active power*, but a mere passive capacity in the subject. Sometimes the substance or agent puts itself into *action* by its own power, and this is properly *active power*. Whatever modification a substance has by which it produces any effect that is called *action* — e.g., a solid substance by motion operates on, or alters the sensible *ideas* of another substance, and therefore this modification of motion we call action. But yet this motion in that solid substance is, when rightly considered, but a passion, if it received it only from some external agent, so that the *active power* of motion is in no substance which cannot begin motion in itself, or in another substance, when at rest. So likewise in *thinking*, a power to receive *ideas* or thoughts from the operation of any external substance is called a *power* of thinking. But this is but a *passive power* or capacity. But to be able to bring into view *ideas* out of sight at one's own choice, and to compare which of them one thinks fit, this is an *active power*. This reflection may be of some use to preserve us from mistakes about *powers* and *actions*, which grammar and the common frame of languages may be apt to lead us into, since what is signified by *verbs* that grammarians call *active* does not always signify *action* — e.g., this proposition: I see the moon, or a star, or I feel the heat of the sun, though expressed by a *verb active*, does not signify any *action* in me by which I operate on those substances, but only the reception of the *ideas* of light, roundness, and heat, in which I am not active, but barely passive, and cannot, in that position of my eyes or body, avoid receiving them. But when I turn my eyes another way, or remove my body out of the sunbeams, I am properly active; because of my own choice, by a power within myself, I put myself into that motion. Such an *action* is the product of *active power*.

73. And thus I have, in a short draught, given a view of our *original ideas*, from which all the rest are derived, and of which they are made up, which, if I would consider, as a philosopher, and examine on what causes they depend and of what they are made,

I believe they all might be reduced to these very few primary and original ones, namely: *extension*; *solidity*; *mobility*, or the power of being moved, which by our senses we receive from body; *perceptivity*, or the power of perception, or thinking; *motivity*, or the power of moving. These, by reflection, we receive from our minds. I crave leave to make use of these two new words to avoid the danger of being mistaken in the use of those which are equivocal. To these if we add *existence*, *duration*, *number*, which belong both to the one and the other, we have, perhaps, all the original *ideas* on which the rest depend. For by these, I imagine, might be explained the nature of colors, sounds, tastes, smells, and all other *ideas* we have, if we had but faculties acute enough to perceive the severally modified extensions and motions of these minute bodies, which produce those several sensations in us. But my present purpose being only to inquire into the knowledge the mind has of things by those *ideas* and appearances which *God* has fitted it to receive from them, and how the mind comes by that knowledge, rather than into their causes, or manner of production, I shall not, contrary to the design of this essay, set myself to inquire philosophically into the peculiar constitution of bodies, and the configuration of parts, by which they have the power to produce in us the *ideas* of their sensible qualities. I shall not enter any further into that disquisition, it sufficing to my purpose to observe that gold or saffron has a power to produce in us the *idea* of yellow, and snow or milk the *idea* of white, which we can only have by our sight, without examining the texture of the parts of those bodies or the particular figures or motion of the particles which rebound from them, to cause in us that particular sensation. Though when we go beyond the bare *ideas* in our minds, and would inquire into their causes, we cannot conceive anything else to be in any sensible object by which it produces different *ideas* in us, but the different bulk, figure, number, texture, and motion of its insensible parts.

Chapter 22. *Of Mixed Modes.*

1. *Mixed modes, what.* Having treated of *simple modes* in the foregoing chapters, and given several instances of some of the most considerable of them,

to show what they are, and how we come by them, we are now in the next place to consider those we call *mixed modes*. Such are the complex *ideas* we mark by the names *obligation, drunkenness*, a *lie*, etc., which, consisting of several combinations of simple *ideas* of different kinds, I have called *mixed modes*, to distinguish them from the more simple modes, which consist only of simple *ideas* of the same kind. These mixed modes being also such combinations of simple *ideas* as are not looked upon to be characteristic marks of any real beings that have a steady existence, but scattered and independent *ideas* put together by the mind, are thereby distinguished from the complex *ideas* of substances.

2. *Made by the mind.* That the mind, in respect of its simple *ideas*, is wholly passive, and receives them all from the existence and operations of things such as sensation or reflection offers them, without being able to make any one *idea*, experience shows us. But if we attentively consider these *ideas* I call *mixed modes* we are now speaking of, we shall find their origin quite different. *The mind* often *exercises an active power in making these* several *combinations*. For it being once furnished with simple *ideas*, it can put them together in several compositions, and so make a variety of complex *ideas*, without examining whether they exist so together in nature. And hence I think it is that these *ideas* are called *notions*, as if they had their origin and constant existence more in the thoughts of men than in the reality of things; and to form such *ideas*, it sufficed that the mind puts the parts of them together, and that they were consistent in the understanding, without considering whether they had any real being. Though I do not deny but several of them might be taken from observation, and the existence of several simple *ideas* so combined as they are put together in the understanding. For the man who first framed the *idea* of *hypocrisy* might have either taken it at first from the observation of one who made show of good qualities which he did not have, or else have framed that *idea* in his mind, without having any such pattern to fashion it by. For it is evident that in the beginning of languages and societies of men, several of those complex *ideas* which were consequent to the constitutions established among them must necessarily have been in the minds

of men before they existed anywhere else. And that many names that stood for such complex *ideas* were in use, and so those *ideas* framed before the combinations, they stood forever existed.

3. *Sometimes gotten by the explication of their names.* Indeed now that languages are made and abound with words standing for such combinations, *an usual way of getting these complex* ideas *is by the explication of those terms that stand for them.* For, consisting of a company of simple *ideas* combined, they may, by words standing for those simple *ideas*, be represented to the mind of one who understands those words, though that complex combination of simple *ideas* was never offered to his mind by the real existence of things. Thus a man may come to have the *idea* of *sacrilege* or *murder* by enumerating to him the simple *ideas* which these words stand for, without ever seeing either of them committed.

4. *The name ties the parts of the mixed modes into one* idea. Every *mixed mode* consisting of many distinct simple *ideas*, it seems reasonable to inquire "*From where it has its unity*, and how such a precise multitude comes to make but one *idea*, since that combination does not always exist together in nature?" To which I answer, it is plain it has its unity from an act of the mind combining those several simple *ideas* together, and considering them as one complex one, consisting of those parts, and the mark of this union, or that which is looked on generally to complete it, is one name given to that combination. For it is by their names that men commonly regulate their account of their distinct species of mixed modes, seldom allowing or considering any number of simple *ideas* to make one complex one, but such collections as there are names for. Thus, though the killing of an old man is as fit in nature to be united into one complex *idea*, as the killing [of] a man's father, yet there being no name standing precisely for the one as there is the name of *parricide* to mark the other, it is not taken for a particular complex *idea*, nor a distinct species of actions from that of killing a young man or any other man.

5. *The cause of making mixed modes.* If we should inquire a little further to see *what* it is that *occasions men to make several combinations of simple* ideas into distinct, and, as it were, settled *modes*, and neglect

others which, in the nature of things themselves, have as much an aptness to be combined and make distinct *ideas*, we shall find the reason of it to be the end of language; this being to mark or communicate men's thoughts to one another with all the dispatch that may be, they usually make such collections of *ideas* into complex modes and affix names to them as they have frequent use of in their way of living and conversation, leaving others, which they have but seldom an occasion to mention, loose and without names to tie them together; they rather choosing to enumerate (when they have need) such *ideas* as make them up by the particular names that stand for them than to trouble their memories by multiplying of complex *ideas* with names to them, which they seldom or never have any occasion to make use of. [. . .]

9. *How we get the* ideas *of mixed modes.* There are therefore *three ways by which we get these complex* ideas *of mixed modes:* 1. By experience and *observation* of things themselves. Thus by seeing two men wrestle or fence, we get the *idea* of wrestling or fencing. 2. By *invention,* or voluntary putting together of several simple *ideas* in our own minds. So he who first invented printing or etching had an *idea* of it in his mind before it ever existed. 3. Which is the most usual way, by *explaining the names* of actions we never saw or notions we cannot see; and by enumerating, and in this way, as it were, setting before our imaginations all those *ideas* which go to the making them up and are the constituent parts of them. For having by *sensation* and *reflection* stored our minds with simple *ideas*, and by use gotten the names that stand for them, we can by those means represent to another any complex *idea* we would have him conceive, so that it has in it no simple *ideas* but what he knows and has with us the same name for. For all our complex *ideas* are ultimately resolvable into simple *ideas*, of which they are compounded and originally made up, though perhaps their immediate ingredients, as I may so say, are also complex *ideas*. Thus the *mixed mode*, which the word *lie* stands for, is made of these simple *ideas*: 1. Articulate sounds. 2. Certain *ideas* in the mind of the speaker. 3. Those words the signs of those *ideas*. 4. Those signs put together by affirmation or negation, otherwise than the *ideas* they stand for are in the mind of the speaker.

I think I do not need go any further in the analysis of that complex *idea* we call a lie. What I have said is enough to show that it is made up of simple *ideas*. And it could not be but an offensive tediousness to my reader to trouble him with a more minute enumeration of every particular simple *idea* that goes to this complex one, which, from what has been said, he cannot but be able to make out to himself. The same may be done in all our complex *ideas* whatsoever, which, however compounded and decompounded, may at last be resolved into simple *ideas*, which are all the materials of knowledge or thought we have, or can have. Nor shall we have reason to fear that the mind is, as a result, stinted to too scanty a number of *ideas*, if we consider what an inexhaustible stock of simple modes number and figure alone afford us. How far then *mixed modes*, which admit of the various combinations of different simple *ideas* and their infinite modes, are from being few and scanty, we may easily imagine. So that before we have done, we shall see that nobody need be afraid he shall not have scope and compass enough for his thoughts to range in, though they are, as I pretend, confined only to simple *ideas* received from sensation or reflection, and their several combinations. [. . .]

11. *Several words seeming to signify action, signify but the effect. Power* being the source from which all action proceeds, the substances in which these powers are when they exert this power into act, are called *causes*, and the substances which then are produced, or the simple *ideas* which are introduced into any subject by the exerting of that power, are called *effects*. The *efficacy* by which the new substance or *idea* is produced is called, in the subject exerting that power, *action*; but in the subject in which any simple *idea* is changed or produced, it is called *passion*. This efficacy however various, and the effects almost infinite, yet we can, I think, conceive it in intellectual agents to be nothing else but modes of thinking and willing; in corporeal agents, nothing else but modifications of motion. I say, I think we cannot conceive it to be any other but these two. For whatever sort of action besides these produces any effects, I confess myself to have no notion nor *idea* of, and so it is quite remote from my thoughts, apprehensions, and knowledge, and as much in the dark to me as five

other senses, or as the *ideas* of colors to a blind man. And therefore *many words which seem to express some action* signify nothing of the action or *modus operandi* at all, *but* barely *the effect*, with some circumstances of the subject wrought on, or cause operating—e.g., creation, annihilation, contain in them no *idea* of the action or manner by which they are produced, but barely of the cause and the thing done. And when a countryman says the cold freezes water, though the word freezing seems to import some *action*, yet truly it signifies nothing but the effect, namely that water that was before fluid has become hard and consistent, without containing any *idea* of the action by which it is done.

12. *Mixed modes, made also of other* ideas. I think I shall not need to remark here that though power and action make the greatest part of mixed modes, marked by names, and familiar in the minds and mouths of men, yet other simple *ideas* and their several combinations are *not* excluded. Much less, I think, will it be *necessary for me* to enumerate all the mixed modes, which have been settled, with names to them; that would be to make a dictionary of the greatest part of the words made use of in divinity, ethics, law, and politics, and several other sciences. All that is requisite to my present design is to show what sort of *ideas* those are which I call *mixed modes*, how the mind comes by them, and that they are compositions made up of simple *ideas* gotten from sensation and reflection—which I suppose I have done.

Chapter 23. *Of Our Complex* Ideas *of Substances*.

1. Ideas *of substances, how made*. The mind being, as I have declared, furnished with a great number of the simple *ideas*, conveyed in by the *senses*, as they are found in exterior things, or by *reflection* on its own operations, takes notice also that a certain number of these simple *ideas* go constantly together, which, being presumed to belong to one thing, and words being suited to common apprehensions and made use of for quick dispatch, are called, so united in one subject, by one name. This, by inadvertence, we are apt afterward to talk of and consider as one simple *idea*, which

indeed is a complication of many *ideas* together, because, as I have said, not imagining how these simple *ideas* can subsist by themselves, we accustom ourselves to suppose some *substratum* in which they do subsist and from which they do result, which therefore we call *substance*.

2. *Our* idea *of substance in general*. Thus, if anyone will examine himself concerning his *notion of pure substance in general*, he will find he has no other *idea* of it at all, but only a supposition of he knows not what support of such qualities, which are capable of producing simple *ideas* in us—which qualities are commonly called *accidents*. If anyone should be asked what is the subject in which color or weight inheres, he would have nothing to say but the solid extended parts. And if he were demanded, what is it that solidity and extension adhere in, he would not be in a much better case than the *Indian* before mentioned who, saying that the world was supported by a great elephant, was asked what the elephant rested on—to which his answer was a great tortoise. But being again pressed to know what gave support to the broad-backed tortoise, replied, something he knew not what. And thus here, as in all other cases where we use words without having clear and distinct *ideas*, we talk like children who, being questioned what such a thing is which they do not know, readily give this satisfactory answer, that it is *something*; in truth this signifies no more, when so used either by children or men, but that they know not what; and that the thing they pretend to know and talk of is what they have no distinct *idea* of at all, and so are perfectly ignorant of it, and in the dark. The *idea* then we have, to which we give the general name substance, being nothing but the supposed but unknown support of those qualities we find existing, which we imagine cannot subsist, *"sine re substante,"* without something to support them, we call that support *substantia*; which, according to the true import of the word, is in plain English, *standing under* or *upholding*.

3. *Of the sorts of substances*. An obscure and relative *idea* of substance in general being thus made, we come to have the *ideas of particular sorts of substances*, by collecting such combinations of simple *ideas* as are, by experience and observation of men's senses,

taken notice of to exist together, and are therefore supposed to flow from the particular internal constitution or unknown essence of that substance. Thus we come to have the *ideas* of a man, horse, gold, water, etc., of which substances, whether anyone has any other clear *idea* further than of certain simple *ideas* coexistent together, I appeal to everyone's own experience. It is the ordinary qualities observable in iron or a diamond, put together that make the true complex *idea* of those substances, which a smith or a jeweler commonly knows better than a philosopher, who, whatever substantial forms he may talk of, has no other *idea* of those substances than what is framed by a collection of those simple *ideas* which are to be found in them; only we must take notice that our complex *ideas* of substances, besides all those simple *ideas* they are made up of, have always the confused *idea* of *something* to which they belong and in which they subsist. And therefore, when we speak of any sort of substance, we say it is a *thing* having such or such qualities. As body is a *thing* that is extended, figured, and capable of motion; spirit, a *thing* capable of thinking; and so hardness, friability, and power to draw iron, we say, are qualities to be found in a lodestone. These and the like fashions of speaking, intimate that the substance is supposed always *something* besides the extension, figure, solidity, motion, thinking, or other observable *ideas*, though we do not know what it is.

4. *No clear* idea *of substance in general*. Hence, when we talk or think of any particular sort of corporeal substances, as *horse*, *stone*, etc., though the *idea* we have of either of them is but the complication or collection of those several simple *ideas* of sensible qualities which we used to find united in the thing called *horse* or *stone*, yet because we cannot conceive how they should subsist alone, nor one in another, we suppose them existing in and supported by some common subject; *this support we denote by the name substance*, though it is certain we have no clear or distinct *idea* of that *thing* we suppose a support.

5. *As clear an* idea *of spirit as body*. The same thing happens concerning the operations of the mind, namely, thinking, reasoning, fearing, etc., which, we concluding not to subsist of themselves, nor apprehending how they can belong to body or be produced by it, we are apt to think these the actions of some other *substance*, which we call *spirit*; yet by this it is evident that having no other *idea* or notion of matter but *something* in which those many sensible qualities which affect our senses do subsist, by supposing a substance in which *thinking, knowing, doubting,* and a power of moving, etc., do subsist, *we have as clear a notion of the substance of spirit, as we have of body* — the one being supposed to be (without knowing what it is) the *substratum* to those simple *ideas* we have from without, and the other supposed (with a like ignorance of what it is) to be the *substratum* to those operations we experiment in ourselves within. It is plain then that the *idea* of corporeal *substance* in matter is as remote from our conceptions and apprehensions as that of spiritual *substance* or *spirit*; and therefore, from our not having any notion of the substance of spirit, we can no more conclude its nonexistence than we can, for the same reason, deny the existence of body, it being as rational to affirm there is no body because we have no clear and distinct *idea* of the *substance* of matter, as to say there is no spirit because we have no clear and distinct *idea* of the *substance* of a spirit.

6. *Of the sorts of substances*. Whatever, therefore, is the secret, abstract nature of *substance* in general, all *the* ideas *we have of particular distinct sorts of substances* are nothing but several combinations of simple *ideas*, coexisting in such, though unknown, cause of their union as makes the whole subsist of itself. It is by such combinations of simple *ideas* and nothing else that we represent particular sorts of *substances* to ourselves. Such are the *ideas* we have of their several species in our minds, and such only do we, by their specific names, signify to others, e.g., *man, horse, sun, water, iron*. Upon hearing these words, everyone who understands the language frames in his mind a combination of those several simple *ideas* which he has usually observed or fancied to exist together under that denomination; all this he supposes to rest in and be, as it were, adherent to that unknown common subject, which does not inhere in anything else. Though in the meantime it is manifest, and everyone upon inquiry into his own thoughts will find that he has no other *idea* of any *substance*, e.g., let it be *gold, horse, iron, man, vitriol, bread*, but what

he has barely of those sensible qualities which he supposes to inhere, with a supposition of such a *substratum* as gives, as it were, a support to those qualities or simple *ideas* which he has observed to exist united together. Thus the *idea* of the *sun*—what is it but an aggregate of those several simple *ideas*, bright, hot, roundish, having a constant regular motion, at a certain distance from us, and perhaps some other? As he who thinks and discourses of the *sun* has been more or less accurate in observing those sensible qualities, *ideas*, or properties, which are in that thing which he calls the sun.

7. *Powers a great part of our complex* ideas *of substances.* For he has the most perfect *idea* of any of the particular sorts of *substances* who has gathered and put together most of those simple *ideas* which do exist in it; among these are to be reckoned its active powers and passive capacities, which, though not simple *ideas*, yet in this respect for brevity's sake may conveniently enough be reckoned among them. Thus the power of drawing iron is one of the *ideas* of the complex one of that substance we call a *lodestone*; and a power to be so drawn is a part of the complex one we call *iron*—which powers pass for inherent qualities in those subjects. Because every *substance*, being as apt by the powers we observe in it to change some sensible qualities in other subjects as it is to produce in us those simple *ideas* which we receive immediately from it, does, by those new sensible qualities introduced into other subjects, discover to us those powers which do as a result mediately affect our senses as regularly as its sensible qualities do it immediately—e.g., we immediately by our senses perceive in *fire* its heat and color, which are, if rightly considered, nothing but powers in it to produce those *ideas* in us—we also by our senses perceive the color and brittleness of *charcoal*, by which we come by the knowledge of another power in fire, which it has to change the color and consistency of wood. By the former, fire immediately, by the latter, it mediately discovers to us these several powers, which therefore we look upon to be a part of the qualities of fire, and so make them a part of the complex *idea* of it. For all those powers that we take cognizance of, terminating only in the alteration of some sensible qualities in those subjects on which they operate, and so mak-

ing them exhibit to us new sensible *ideas*; therefore it is that I have reckoned these powers among the simple *ideas* which make the complex ones of the sorts of *substances*, though these powers, considered in themselves, are truly complex *ideas*. And in this looser sense I crave leave to be understood when I name any of these *potentialities among the simple ideas* which we recollect in our minds when we think *of particular substances*. For the powers that are severally in them are necessary to be considered, if we will have true distinct notions of the several sorts of substances.

8. *And why.* Nor are we to wonder that *powers make a great part of our complex* ideas *of substances*; since their secondary qualities are those which in most of them serve principally to distinguish substances one from another and commonly make a considerable part of the complex *idea* of the several sorts of them. For our senses failing us in the discovery of the bulk, texture, and figure of the minute parts of bodies, on which their real constitutions and differences depend, we are inclined to make use of their secondary qualities as the characteristic notes and marks by which to frame *ideas* of them in our minds and distinguish them one from another. All these secondary qualities, as has been shown, are nothing but bare powers. For the color and taste of *opium* are, as well as its soporific or anodyne virtues, mere powers depending on its primary qualities, by which it is fitted to produce different operations on different parts of our bodies.

9. *Three sorts of* ideas *make our complex ones of substances. The* ideas *that make our complex ones of corporeal substances* are of these three sorts. *First*, the *ideas* of the primary qualities of things, which are discovered by our senses, and are in them even when we do not perceive them—such are the bulk, figure, number, situation, and motion of the parts of bodies, which are really in them, whether we take notice of them or not. *Secondly*, the sensible secondary qualities, which, depending on these, are nothing but the powers those substances have to produce several *ideas* in us by our senses; these *ideas* are not in the things themselves otherwise than as anything is in its cause. *Thirdly*, the aptness we consider in any substance to give or receive such alterations of primary qualities, as that the substance so altered should produce in us

different *ideas* from what it did before; these are called active and passive powers. All these powers, as far as we have any notice or notion of them, terminate only in sensible simple *ideas*. For whatever alteration a *lodestone* has the power to make in the minute particles of iron, we should have no notion of any power it had at all to operate on iron, did not its sensible motion discover it. And I do not doubt but there are a thousand changes that bodies we daily handle have a power to cause in one another, which we never suspect, because they never appear in sensible effects.

10. *Powers make a great part of our complex* ideas *of substances*. Powers therefore justly *make a great part of our complex* ideas *of substances*. He who will examine his complex *idea* of gold will find several of its *ideas* that make it up to be only powers—as the power of being melted, but of not spending itself in the fire, of being dissolved in *aqua regia*, are *ideas* as necessary to make up our complex *idea* of gold as its color and weight, which, if duly considered, are also nothing but different powers. For to speak truly, yellowness is not actually in gold, but is a power in gold to produce that *idea* in us by our eyes, when placed in a due light; and the heat, which we cannot leave out of our *ideas* of the sun, is no more really in the sun than the white color it introduces into wax. These are both equally powers in the sun operating, by the motion and figure of its sensible parts, so on a man as to make him have the *idea* of heat, and so on wax as to make it capable to produce in a man the *idea* of white.

11. *The now secondary qualities of bodies would disappear, if we could discover the primary ones of their minute parts*. Had we senses acute enough to discern the minute particles of bodies and the real constitution on which their sensible qualities depend, I do not doubt but they would produce quite different *ideas* in us, and that which is now the yellow color of gold would then disappear, and instead of it we should see an admirable texture of parts of a certain size and figure. This, microscopes plainly discover to us; for what to our naked eyes produces a certain color is, by thus augmenting the acuteness of our senses, discovered to be quite a different thing; and the thus altering, as it were, the proportion of the bulk of the minute parts of a colored object to our

usual sight produces different *ideas* from what it did before. Thus sand or pounded glass, which is opaque and white to the naked eye, is pellucid in a microscope; and a hair seen this way loses its former color, and is in a great measure pellucid, with a mixture of some bright sparkling colors, such as appear from the refraction of diamonds and other pellucid bodies. Blood, to the naked eye, appears all red, but by a good microscope, in which its lesser parts appear, shows only some few globules of red swimming in a pellucid liquor. And how these red globules would appear, if glasses could be found that could yet magnify them a thousand or ten thousand times more, is uncertain.

12. *Our faculties of discovery suited to our state*. The infinitely wise contriver of us and all things about us has fitted our senses, faculties, and organs, to the conveniences of life and the business we have to do here. We are able, by our senses, to know and distinguish things, and to examine them so far as to apply them to our uses, and several ways to accommodate the exigencies of this life. We have insight enough into their admirable contrivances and wonderful effects to admire and magnify the wisdom, power, and goodness of their author. Such a knowledge as this, which is suited to our present condition, we do not want faculties to attain. But it does not appear that God intended we should have a perfect, clear, and adequate knowledge of them; that, perhaps, is not in the comprehension of any finite being. We are furnished with faculties (dull and weak as they are) to discover enough in the creatures to lead us to the knowledge of the Creator and the knowledge of our duty. And we are fitted well enough with abilities to provide for the conveniences of living. These are our business in this world. But were our senses altered and made much quicker and more acute, the appearance and outward scheme of things would have quite another face to us and, I am apt to think, would be inconsistent with our being, or at least well-being, in this part of the universe which we inhabit. He who considers how little our constitution is able to bear a remove into parts of this air not much higher than that we commonly breathe in will have reason to be satisfied that in this globe of earth allotted for our mansion, the all-wise Architect has suited our organs,

and the bodies that are to affect them, one to another. If our sense of hearing were but one thousand times quicker than it is, how would a perpetual noise distract us? And we should in the quietest retirement be less able to sleep or meditate than in the middle of a sea fight. No, if that most instructive of our senses, seeing, were in any man a thousand or a hundred thousand times more acute than it is by the best microscope, things several millions of times less than the smallest object of his sight now would then be visible to his naked eyes, and so he would come nearer to the discovery of the texture and motion of the minute parts of corporeal things, and in many of them probably get *ideas* of their internal constitutions. But then he would be in a quite different world from other people. Nothing would appear the same to him and others; the visible *ideas* of everything would be different. So that I doubt whether he and the rest of men could discourse concerning the objects of sight or have any communication about colors, their appearances being so wholly different. And perhaps such a quickness and tenderness of sight could not endure bright sunshine, or so much as open daylight, nor take in but a very small part of any object at once, and that, too, only at a very near distance. And if, by the help of such microscopic eyes (if I may so call them), a man could penetrate further than ordinary into the secret composition and radical texture of bodies, he would not make any great advantage by the change, if such an acute sight would not serve to conduct him to the market and exchange; if he could not see things he was to avoid, at a convenient distance, nor distinguish things he had to do with by those sensible qualities others do. [. . .]

14. *Complex* ideas *of substances.* But to return to the matter in hand, the *ideas* we have of substances and the ways we come by them, I say, our *specific* ideas *of substances* are nothing else but *a collection of a certain number of simple* ideas, *considered as united in one thing.* These *ideas* of substances, though they are commonly simple apprehensions, and the names of them simple terms, yet in effect are complex and compounded. Thus the *idea* which an Englishman signifies by the name *swan* is white color, long neck, red beak, black legs, and whole feet, and all these of a certain size, with a power of swimming in

the water and making a certain kind of noise. And perhaps, to a man who has long observed this kind of bird, some other properties which all terminate in sensible simple *ideas*, all united in one common subject.

15. Idea *of spiritual substances as clear as of bodily substances.* Besides the complex *ideas* we have of material sensible substances, of which I have last spoken, by the simple *ideas* we have taken from those operations of our own minds, which we experiment daily in ourselves, as thinking, understanding, willing, knowing, and power of beginning motion, etc., coexisting in some substance, we are able to frame *the complex* idea *of an immaterial spirit.* And thus, by putting together the *ideas* of thinking, perceiving, liberty, and power of moving themselves and other things, we have as clear a perception and notion of immaterial substances as we have of material. For putting together the *ideas* of thinking and willing, or the power of moving or quieting corporeal motion, joined to substance, of which we have no distinct *idea*, we have the *idea* of an immaterial spirit; and by putting together the *ideas* of coherent solid parts and a power of being moved, joined with substance, of which likewise we have no positive *idea*, we have the *idea* of matter. The one is as clear and distinct an *idea* as the other, the *idea* of thinking and moving a body being as clear and distinct *ideas* as the *ideas* of extension, solidity, and being moved. For our *idea* of substance is equally obscure, or none at all, in both; it is but a supposed I know not what, to support those *ideas* we call accidents. It is for want of reflection that we are apt to think that our senses show us nothing but material things. Every act of sensation, when duly considered, gives us an equal view of both parts of nature, the corporeal and spiritual. For while I know, by seeing or hearing, etc., that there is some corporeal being without me, the object of that sensation, I do more certainly know that there is some spiritual being within me that sees and hears. This, I must be convinced, cannot be the action of bare insensible matter, nor ever could be, without an immaterial thinking being.

16. No idea *of abstract substance.* By the complex *idea* of extended, figured, colored, and all other sensible qualities, which is all that we know of it, we are

as far from the *idea* of the substance of body as if we knew nothing at all. *Nor,* after all the acquaintance and familiarity which we imagine we *have* with matter and the many qualities *men* assure themselves they perceive and know in bodies, will it perhaps upon examination be found that they have any *more, or clearer, primary* ideas *belonging to body than they have belonging to immaterial spirit.*

17. *The cohesion of solid parts and impulse, the primary* ideas *of body. The primary* ideas *we have peculiar to body,* as contradistinguished to spirit, *are the cohesion of solid,* and consequently separable, *parts and a power of communicating motion by impulse.* These, I think, are the original *ideas* proper and peculiar to body, for figure is but the consequence of finite extension.

18. *Thinking and motivity the primary* ideas *of spirit.* The *ideas* we have belonging and *peculiar to spirit are thinking and will,* or a power of putting body into motion by thought, and which is consequent to it, liberty. For as body cannot but communicate its motion by impulse to another body which it meets with at rest, so the mind can put bodies into motion or refrain to do so, as it pleases. The *ideas* of existence, duration, and mobility are common to them both.

19. *Spirits capable of motion.* There is no reason why it should be thought strange that I make *mobility belong to spirit.* For having no other *idea* of motion but change of distance with other beings that are considered as at rest, and finding that spirits, as well as bodies, cannot operate but where they are, and that spirits do operate at several times in several places, I cannot but attribute change of place to all finite spirits (for of the infinite spirit I do not speak here). For my soul, being a real being as well as my body, is certainly as capable of changing distance with any other body or being as body itself—and so is capable of motion. And if a mathematician can consider a certain distance or a change of that distance between two points, one may certainly conceive a distance and a change of distance between two spirits, and so conceive their motion, their approach or removal, one from another.

20. Everyone finds in himself that his soul can think, will, and operate on his body in the place where that is, but cannot operate on a body or in a place a hundred miles distant from it. Nobody can imagine that his soul can think or move a body at *Oxford* while he is at *London,* and cannot but know that, being united to his body, it constantly changes place all the whole journey between *Oxford* and *London,* as the coach or horse does that carries him, and I think may be said to be truly all that while in motion. Or if that will not be allowed to afford us a clear *idea* enough of its motion, its being separated from the body in death, I think, will; for to consider it as going out of the body, or leaving it, and yet to have no *idea* of its motion, seems to me impossible. [. . .]

22. Idea *of soul and body compared.* Let us *compare* then our complex *idea* of an immaterial spirit with our complex *idea* of body, and see whether there is any more obscurity in one than in the other, and in which most. Our *idea* of body, as I think, is an extended solid substance, capable of communicating motion by impulse. And our *idea* of soul, as an immaterial spirit, is of a substance that thinks, and has a power of exciting motion in body, by willing or thought. These, I think, are *our complex* ideas *of soul and body, as contradistinguished*; and now let us examine which has most obscurity in it and difficulty to be apprehended. I know that people whose thoughts are immersed in matter, and have so subjected their minds to their senses that they seldom reflect on anything beyond them, are apt to say they cannot comprehend a thinking thing, which perhaps is true. But I affirm, when they consider it well, they can no more comprehend an extended thing.

23. *Cohesion of solid parts in body as hard to be conceived as thinking in a soul.* If anyone says he does not know what it is that thinks in him, he means he does not know what the substance is of that thinking thing. No more, say I, does he know what the substance is of that solid thing. Further, if he says he does not know how he thinks, I answer, neither does he know how he is extended, how the solid parts of body are united or cohere together to make extension. [. . .]

25. I allow it is usual for most people to wonder how anyone should find a difficulty in what they think they every day observe. Do we not see, will they be ready to say, the parts of bodies stick firmly together? Is there anything more common? And what doubt can

there be made of it? And the like, I say, concerning *thinking* and *voluntary motion*. Do we not every moment experiment it in ourselves, and, therefore, can it be doubted? The matter of fact is clear, I confess; but when we would a little nearer look into it and consider how it is done, there, I think, we are at a loss, both in the one and the other, and can as little understand how the parts of body cohere as how we ourselves perceive or move. I would have anyone intelligibly explain to me how the parts of gold or brass (that, but now in fusion, were as loose from one another as the particles of water or the sands of an hourglass) come in a few moments to be so united and adhere so strongly one to another that the utmost force of men's arms cannot separate them. A considering man will, I suppose, be here at a loss to satisfy his own or another man's understanding. [. . .]

28. *Communication of motion by impulse, or by thought, equally intelligible.* Another *idea* we have of body is the power of *communication of motion by impulse,* and of our souls, the power of *exciting motion by thought.* These *ideas,* the one of body, the other of our minds, every day's experience clearly furnishes us with. But if here again we inquire how this is done, we *are equally in the dark.* For to the communication of motion by impulse, in which as much motion is lost to one body as is gotten to the other, which is the most ordinary case, we can have no other conception but of the passing of motion out of one body into another. This, I think, is as obscure and inconceivable as how our minds move or stop our bodies by thought, which we every moment find they do. The increase of motion by impulse, which is observed or believed sometimes to happen, is yet harder to be understood. We have, by daily experience, clear evidence of motion produced both by impulse and by thought, but the manner how hardly comes within our comprehension. We are equally at a loss in both, so that, however we consider motion and its communication, either from body or spirit, the *idea* which belongs to spirit is at least as clear as that which belongs to body. And if we consider the active power of moving, or, as I may call it, *motivity,* it is much clearer in spirit than body, since two bodies placed by one another at rest will never afford us the *idea* of a power in the one to move the other but by a borrowed motion, whereas the mind every day affords us *ideas* of an active power of moving of bodies, and therefore it is worth our consideration whether active power is not the proper attribute of spirits, and passive power, of matter. Hence may be conjectured that created spirits are not totally separate from matter, because they are both active and passive. Pure spirit, namely, God, is only active; pure matter is only passive; those beings that are both active and passive we may judge to partake of both. [. . .]

30. Ideas *of body and spirit compared.* So that, in short, *the idea* we have *of spirit, compared with the idea* we have *of body,* stands thus: The substance of spirits is unknown to us, and so is the substance of body equally unknown to us. Two primary qualities or properties of body, namely, solid coherent parts and impulse, we have distinct clear *ideas* of. So, likewise, we know and have distinct clear *ideas* of two primary qualities or properties of spirit, namely, thinking and a power of action, i.e., a power of beginning or stopping several thoughts or motions. We have also the *ideas* of several qualities inherent in bodies and have the clear distinct *ideas* of them; these qualities are but the various modifications of the extension of cohering solid parts and their motion. We have likewise the *ideas* of the several modes of thinking, namely, believing, doubting, intending, fearing, hoping, all which are but the several modes of thinking. We have also the *ideas* of willing and moving the body consequent to it, and with the body itself, too; for, as has been shown, spirit is capable of motion.

31. *The notion of spirit involves no more difficulty in it than that of body.* Lastly, if this notion of immaterial spirit may have, perhaps, some difficulties in it not easily to be explained, we have therefore no more reason to deny or doubt the existence of such spirits than we have to deny or doubt the existence of body, because the notion of body is encumbered with some difficulties very hard, and perhaps impossible, to be explained or understood by us. For I would gladly have instanced anything in our notion of spirit more perplexed or nearer a contradiction, than the very notion of body includes in it. The divisibility *in infinitum* of any finite extension involving us, whether we grant or deny it, in consequences impossible to be explicated or made in our apprehensions consistent—

consequences that carry greater difficulty and more apparent absurdity than anything can follow from the notion of an immaterial knowing substance.

32. *We know nothing beyond our simple* ideas. Which we are not at all to wonder at since, we, having but some few superficial *ideas* of things discovered to us only by the senses from without or by the mind reflecting on what it experiments in itself within, have no knowledge beyond that, much less of the internal constitution and true nature of things, being destitute of faculties to attain it. And therefore experimenting and discovering in ourselves knowledge and the power of voluntary motion, as certainly as we experiment or discover in things without us the cohesion and separation of solid parts, which is the extension and motion of bodies, *we have as much reason to be satisfied with our notion of immaterial spirit as with our notion of body, and the existence of the one as well as the other.* For, it being no more a contradiction that thinking should exist separate and independent from solidity than it is a contradiction that solidity should exist separate and independent from thinking, they being both but simple *ideas*, independent one from another, and having as clear and distinct *ideas* in us of thinking as of solidity, I do not know why we may not as well allow a thinking thing without solidity, i.e., *immaterial*, to exist, as a solid thing without thinking, i.e., *matter*, to exist—especially since it is not harder to conceive how thinking should exist without matter than how matter should think. For whenever we would proceed beyond these simple *ideas* we have from sensation and reflection and dive further into the nature of things, we fall presently into darkness and obscurity, perplexity, and difficulties and can discover nothing further but our own blindness and ignorance. But whichever of these complex *ideas* is clearest, that of body or immaterial spirit, this is evident, that the simple *ideas* that make them up are no other than what we have received from sensation or reflection. And so is it of all our other *ideas* of substances, even of God himself.

33. Idea *of God.* For if we examine the *idea* we have of the incomprehensible supreme being, we shall find that we come by it the same way, and that the complex *ideas* we have both of God and separate spirits are made of the simple *ideas* we receive from reflection, e.g., having, from what we experiment in ourselves, gotten the *ideas* of existence and duration, of knowledge and power, of pleasure and happiness, and of several other qualities and powers, which it is better to have than to be without. When we would frame an *idea* the most suitable we can to the supreme being, we enlarge every one of these with our *idea* of infinity, and so putting them together make our complex *idea of God.* For that the mind has such a power of enlarging some of its *ideas*, received from sensation and reflection, has been already shown. [. . .]

37. *Recapitulation.* And thus we have seen *what kinds of* ideas *we have of substances of all kinds*, in what they consist, and how we came by them. From this, I think, it is very evident:

First, that all our *ideas* of the several sorts of substances are nothing but collections of simple *ideas*, with a supposition of something to which they belong and in which they subsist, though of this supposed something we have no clear distinct *idea* at all.

Secondly, that all the simple *ideas* that thus united in one common *substratum* make up our complex *ideas* of several sorts of substances are no other but such as we have received from *sensation* or *reflection*, so that even in those which we think we are most intimately acquainted with, and that come nearest the comprehension of, our most enlarged conceptions, we cannot go beyond those simple *ideas*. And even in those which seem most remote from all we have to do with, and do infinitely surpass anything we can perceive in ourselves by reflection, or discover by sensation in other things, we can attain to nothing but those simple *ideas*, which we originally received from sensation or reflection, as is evident in the complex *ideas* we have of angels and particularly of God himself.

Thirdly, that most of the simple *ideas* that make up our complex *ideas* of substances, when truly considered, are only powers, however we are apt to take them for positive qualities—e.g., the greatest part of the *ideas* that make our complex *idea of gold* are yellowness, great weight, ductility, fusibility, and solubility in *aqua regia*, etc., all united together in an unknown *substratum*. All these *ideas* are nothing else but so many relations to other substances, and are not really in the gold, considered barely in itself, though they depend on those real and primary qualities of its internal constitution by which it has a fitness differently to operate and be operated on by several other substances.

Chapter 27. *Of Identity and Diversity.*

1. *In what identity consists.* Another occasion the mind often takes of comparing is the very being of things, when, considering anything as existing at any determined time and place, we compare it with itself existing at another time, and upon it form the *ideas of identity* and *diversity.* When we see anything to be in any place in any instant of time, we are sure (be it what it will) that it is that very thing, and not another, which at that same time exists in another place, however like and indistinguishable it may be in all other respects. And in this consists *identity,* when the *ideas* it is attributed to vary not at all from what they were that moment in which we consider their former existence, and to which we compare the present. For we never finding, nor conceiving it possible, that two things of the same kind should exist in the same place at the same time, we rightly conclude that whatever exists anywhere at any time excludes all of the same kind and is there itself alone. When therefore we demand whether anything is the same or not, it refers always to something that existed such a time in such a place, which it was certain at that instant was the same with itself, and no other. From this it follows that one thing cannot have two beginnings of existence, nor two things one beginning, it being impossible for two things of the same kind to be or exist in the same instant in the very same place, or one and the same thing in different places. That, therefore, that had one beginning is the same thing; and that, which had a different beginning in time and place from that, is not the same, but diverse; that which has made the difficulty about this relation has been the little care and attention used in having precise notions of the things to which it is attributed.

2. *Identity of substances. Identity of modes.* We have the *ideas* but of three sorts of substances: 1. God. 2. Finite intelligences. 3. *Bodies.* First, God is without

beginning, eternal, unalterable, and everywhere, and, therefore, concerning his identity there can be no doubt. Secondly, finite spirits having had each its determinate time and place of beginning to exist, the relation to that time and place will always determine to each of them its identity, as long as it exists. Thirdly, the same will hold of every particle of matter, to which no addition or subtraction of matter being made, it is the same. For though these three sorts of substances, as we term them, do not exclude one another out of the same place, yet we cannot conceive but that they must necessarily each of them exclude any of the same kind out of the same place. Or else the notions and names of identity and diversity would be in vain, and there could be no such distinctions of substances or anything else, one from another. For example: could two bodies be in the same place at the same time, then those two parcels of matter must be one and the same, take them great or little. No, all bodies must be one and the same. For by the same reason that two particles of matter may be in one place, all bodies may be in one place, which, when it can be supposed, takes away the distinction of identity and diversity of one and more and renders it ridiculous. But it being a contradiction that two or more should be one, identity and diversity are relations and ways of comparing well-founded and of use to the understanding.

All other things being but modes or relations ultimately terminated in substances, the identity and diversity of each particular existence of them, too, will be by the same way determined. Only as to things whose existence is in succession, such as are the actions of finite beings, e.g., *motion* and *thought,* both which consist in a continued train of succession, concerning their diversity, there can be no question. Because, each perishing the moment it begins, they cannot exist in different times or in different places, as permanent beings can at different times exist in distant places; and therefore no motion or thought, considered as at different times, can be the same, each part of this having a different beginning of existence.

3. Principium individuationis. From what has been said, it is easy to discover what is so much inquired after, the *principium individuationis;* and that, it is plain, is existence itself, which determines a being of

any sort to a particular time and place, incommunicable to two beings of the same kind. This, though it seems easier to conceive in simple substances or modes, yet when reflected on, is not more difficult in compound ones, if care is taken to what it is applied—e.g., let us suppose an atom, i.e., a continued body under one immutable surface, existing in a determined time and place; it is evident that, considered in any instant of its existence, it is in that instant the same with itself. For, being at that instant what it is, and nothing else, it is the same, and so must continue as long as its existence is continued; for so long it will be the same, and no other. In like manner, if two or more atoms are joined together into the same mass, every one of those atoms will be the same, by the foregoing rule. And while they exist united together, the mass, consisting of the same atoms, must be the same mass or the same body, let the parts be ever so differently jumbled. But if one of these atoms is taken away or one new one added, it is no longer the same mass or the same body. In the state of living creatures, their identity does not depend on a mass of the same particles, but on something else. For in them the variation of great parcels of matter does not alter the identity. An oak growing from a plant to a great tree and then lopped is still the same oak; and a colt grown up to a horse, sometimes fat, sometimes lean, is all the while the same horse. Though in both these cases there may be a manifest change of the parts, so that truly they are not either of them the same masses of matter, though they are truly one of them the same oak and the other the same horse. The reason for this is that in these two cases, a mass of matter and a living body, *identity* is not applied to the same thing.

4. *Identity of vegetables*. We must therefore consider in what an oak differs from a mass of matter, and that seems to me to be in this, that the one is only the cohesion of particles of matter any how united, the other such a disposition of them as constitutes the parts of an oak, and such an organization of those parts as is fit to receive and distribute nourishment so as to continue and frame the wood, bark, and leaves, etc., of an oak, in which consists the vegetable life; that being then one plant which has such an organization of parts in one coherent body,

partaking of one common life, it continues to be the same plant as long as it partakes of the same life, though that life is communicated to new particles of matter vitally united to the living plant, in a like continued organization conformable to that sort of plants. For this organization, being at any one instant in any one collection of *matter*, is, in that particular concrete, distinguished from all other and is that individual life, which existing constantly from that moment both forwards and backwards, in the same continuity of insensibly succeeding parts united to the living body of the plant, it has that identity which makes the same plant, and all the parts of it, parts of the same plant during all the time that they exist united in that continued organization, which is fit to convey that common life to all the parts so united.

5. *Identity of animals*. The case is not so much different in *brutes*, but that anyone may hence see what makes an animal and continues it the same. Something we have like this in machines, and may serve to illustrate it. For example, what is a watch? It is plain it is nothing but a fit organization or construction of parts to a certain end, which, when a sufficient force is added to it, it is capable to attain. If we would suppose this machine one continued body, all whose organized parts were repaired, increased, or diminished by a constant addition or separation of insensible parts with one common life, we should have something very much like the body of an animal—with this difference, that in an animal, the fitness of the organization and the motion in which life consists begin together, the motion coming from within, but in machines, the force coming sensibly from without is often away when the organ is in order, and well-fitted to receive it.

6. *Identity of man*. This also shows in what the identity of the same *man* consists, namely, in nothing but a participation of the same continued life by constantly fleeting particles of matter in succession vitally united to the same organized body. He who shall place the *identity* of man in anything else but, like that of other animals, in one fitly organized body, taken in any one instant, and from this continued under one organization of life in several successively fleeting particles of matter united to it, will find it hard to make an *embryo* one of years, mad and sober,

the same man, by any supposition that will not make it possible for *Seth, Ismael, Socrates, Pilate, St. Austin,* and *Caesar Borgia* to be the same man. For if the *identity* of soul alone makes the same man, and there is nothing in the nature of matter why the same individual spirit may not be united to different bodies, it will be possible that those men living in distant ages, and of different tempers, may have been the same man. This way of speaking must be, from a very strange use of the word *man,* applied to an *idea* out of which body and shape are excluded. And that way of speaking would agree yet worse with the notions of those philosophers who allow of transmigration and are of the opinion that the souls of men may, for their miscarriages, be thrust into the bodies of beasts as fit habitations, with organs suited to the satisfaction of their brutal inclinations. But yet I think nobody, could he be sure that the soul of *Heliogabalus* were in one of his hogs, would yet say that hog were a *man* or *Heliogabalus.*

7. *Identity suited to the* idea. It is not, therefore, unity of substance that comprehends all sorts of *identity* or will determine it in every case. But to conceive and judge of it correctly, we must consider what *idea* the word it is applied to stands for, it being one thing to be the same *substance,* another the same *man,* and a third the same *person,* if *person, man,* and *substance* are three names standing for three different *ideas;* for such as is the *idea* belonging to that name, such must be the *identity.* This, if it had been a little more carefully attended to, would possibly have prevented a great deal of that confusion which often occurs about this matter, with no small seeming difficulties, especially concerning *personal identity,* which therefore we shall in the next place a little consider.

8. *Same man.* An animal is a living organized body; and consequently the same animal, as we have observed, is the same continued life communicated to different particles of matter as they happen successively to be united to that organized living body. And whatever is talked of other definitions, ingenuous observation puts it past doubt that the *idea* in our minds, of which the sound *man* in our mouths is the sign, is nothing else but of an animal of such a certain form. Since I think I may be confident that whoever should see a creature of his own shape and make,

though it had no more reason all its life than a *cat* or a *parrot,* would call him still a *man;* or whoever should hear a *cat* or a *parrot* discourse, reason, and philosophize would call or think it nothing but a *cat* or a *parrot* and say the one was a dull, irrational *man,* and the other a very intelligent rational *parrot.* [. . .] For I presume it is not the *idea* of a thinking or rational being alone that makes the *idea* of a man in most people's sense, but of a body, so and so shaped, joined to it. And if that is the *idea* of a man, the same successive body not shifted all at once must, as well as the same immaterial spirit, go to the making of the same man.

9. *Personal identity.* This being premised, to find in what *personal identity* consists, we must consider what *person* stands for; this, I think, is a thinking intelligent being that has reason and reflection and can consider itself as itself, the same thinking thing in different times and places, which it does only by that consciousness which is inseparable from thinking and, as it seems to me, essential to it—it being impossible for anyone to perceive without perceiving that he does perceive. When we see, hear, smell, taste, feel, meditate, or will anything, we know that we do so. Thus it is always as to our present sensations and perceptions. And by this everyone is to himself that which he calls *self;* it not being considered in this case whether the same *self* is continued in the same or diverse substances. For since consciousness always accompanies thinking, and it is that which makes everyone to be what he calls *self* and thereby distinguishes himself from all other thinking things, in this alone consists *personal identity,* i.e., the sameness of a rational being. And as far as this consciousness can be extended backwards to any past action or thought, so far reaches the identity of that *person;* it is the same *self* now it was then, and it is by the same *self* with this present one that now reflects on it that that action was done.

10. *Consciousness makes personal identity.* But it is further inquired whether it is the same identical substance. This few would think they had reason to doubt of if these perceptions, with their consciousness, always remained present in the mind, by means of which the same thinking thing would be always consciously present and, as would be thought,

evidently the same to itself. But that which seems to make the difficulty is this, that this consciousness, being interrupted always by forgetfulness, there being no moment of our lives in which we have the whole train of all our past actions before our eyes in one view, but even the best memories losing the sight of one part while they are viewing another, and we sometimes, and that the greatest part of our lives, not reflecting on our past selves, being intent on our present thoughts, and in sound sleep having no thoughts at all, or at least none with that consciousness which remarks our waking thoughts. I say, in all these cases, our consciousness being interrupted, and we losing the sight of our past *selves*, doubts are raised whether we are the same thinking thing, i.e., the same substance or not. This, however reasonable or unreasonable, does not concern *personal identity* at all, the question being what makes the same *person*, and not whether it is the same identical substance which always thinks in the same *person*; which in this case does not matter at all — different substances by the same consciousness (where they do partake in it) being united into one person, as well as different bodies by the same life are united into one animal whose *identity* is preserved in that change of sub-stances by the unity of one continued life. For it being the same consciousness that makes a man be himself to himself, *personal identity* depends on that only, whether it is annexed solely to one individual substance or can be continued in a succession of several substances. For as far as any intelligent being can repeat the *idea* of any past action with the same consciousness it had of it at first, and with the same consciousness it has of any present action, so far it is the same *personal self*. For it is by the consciousness it has of its present thoughts and actions that it is *self* to *itself* now, and so will be the same *self* as far as the same consciousness can extend to actions past or to come, and would be by distance of time or change of substance no more two *persons* than a man is two men by wearing other clothes today than he did yesterday, with a long or a short sleep between. The same consciousness uniting those distant actions into the same *person*, whatever substances contributed to their production.

11. *Personal identity in change of substances.* That

this is so, we have some kind of evidence in our very bodies, all whose particles, while vitally united to this same thinking conscious self so that we feel when they are touched and are affected by, and conscious of, good or harm that happens to them, are a part of our*selves*; i.e., of our thinking conscious *self*. Thus the limbs of his body are to everyone a part of *himself*; he sympathizes and is concerned for them. Cut off a hand and thereby separate it from that consciousness he had of its heat, cold, and other affections, and it is then no longer a part of that which is *himself*, any more than the remotest part of matter. Thus we see the *substance* of which *personal self* consisted at one time may be varied at another without the change of personal *identity*, there being no question about the same person, though the limbs which but now were a part of it are cut off.

12. *Whether in the change of thinking substances.* But the question is, "Whether if the same substance which thinks is changed, it can be the same person, or, remaining the same, it can be different persons?"

And to this I answer: First, this can be no question at all to those who place thought in a purely material animal constitution, void of an immaterial substance. For whether their supposition is true or not, it is plain they conceive personal identity preserved in something else than identity of substance, as animal identity is preserved in identity of life and not of substance. And therefore those who place thinking in an immaterial substance only, before they can come to deal with these men, must show why personal identity cannot be preserved in the change of immate-rial substances, or variety of particular immaterial substances, as well as animal identity is preserved in the change of material substances, or variety of particular bodies. Unless they will say it is one imma-terial spirit that makes the same life in brutes, as it is one immaterial spirit that makes the same person in men, which the *Cartesians*, at least, will not admit for fear of making brutes thinking things, too.

13. But next, as to the first part of the question, "Whether if the same thinking substance (supposing immaterial substances only to think) is changed, it can be the same person?" I answer that cannot be resolved but by those who know what kind of sub-stances they are that do think and whether the con-

sciousness of past actions can be transferred from one thinking substance to another. I grant, were the same consciousness the same individual action, it could not. But it being a present representation of a past action, why it may not be possible that that may be represented to the mind to have been which really never was, will remain to be shown. And therefore how far the consciousness of past actions is annexed to any individual agent, so that another cannot possibly have it, will be hard for us to determine until we know what kind of action it is that cannot be done without a reflex act of perception accompanying it, and how performed by thinking substances, who cannot think without being conscious of it. But that which we call the *same consciousness*, not being the same individual act, why one intellectual substance may not have represented to it, as done by itself, what it never did, and was perhaps done by some other agent—why, I say, such a representation may not possibly be without reality of matter of fact, as well as several representations in dreams are, which yet while dreaming we take for true, will be difficult to conclude from the nature of things. And that it never is so, will by us, until we have clearer views of the nature of thinking substances, be best resolved into the goodness of God, who, as far as the happiness or misery of any of his sensible creatures is concerned in it, will not by a fatal error of theirs transfer from one to another that consciousness which draws reward or punishment with it. How far this may be an argument against those who would place thinking in a system of fleeting animal spirits, I leave to be considered. But yet to return to the question before us, it must be allowed that if the same consciousness (which, as has been shown, is quite a different thing from the same numerical figure or motion in body) can be transferred from one thinking substance to another, it will be possible that two thinking substances may make but one person. For the same consciousness being preserved, whether in the same or different substances, the personal identity is preserved.

14. As to the second part of the question, "Whether the same immaterial substance remaining, there may be two distinct persons?"—this question seems to me to be built on this, whether the same immaterial being, being conscious of the action of its past duration, may be wholly stripped of all the consciousness of its past existence and lose it beyond the power of ever retrieving it again, and so, as it were, beginning a new account from a new period, have a consciousness that cannot reach beyond this new state? All those who hold preexistence are evidently of this mind, since they allow the soul to have no remaining consciousness of what it did in that preexistent state, either wholly separate from body or informing any other body; and if they should not, it is plain [that] experience would be against them. Thus, personal identity reaching no further than consciousness reaches, a preexistent spirit not having continued so many ages in a state of silence must necessarily make different persons. Suppose a Christian, *Platonist*, or *Pythagorean* should, upon God's having ended all his works of creation the seventh day, think his soul has existed ever since, and should imagine it has revolved in several human bodies, as I once met with one who was persuaded his had been the soul of *Socrates* (how reasonably I will not dispute; this I know, that in the post he filled, which was no inconsiderable one, he passed for a very rational man, and the press has shown that he did not want parts or learning); would anyone say that he, being not conscious of any of *Socrates's* actions or thoughts, could be the same person with *Socrates*? Let anyone reflect upon himself and conclude that he has in himself an immaterial spirit, which is that which thinks in him, and in the constant change of his body keeps him the same, and is that which he calls himself. Let him also suppose it to be the same soul that was in *Nestor* or *Thersites* at the siege of *Troy* (for souls being, as far as we know anything of them, in their nature indifferent to any parcel of matter, the supposition has no apparent absurdity in it), which it may have been, as well as it is now the soul of any other man. But he now having no consciousness of any of the actions either of *Nestor* or *Thersites*, does or can he conceive himself the same person with either of them? Can he be concerned in either of their actions, attribute them to himself, or think them his own more than the actions of any other men that ever existed? Thus, this consciousness not reaching to any of the actions of either of those men, he is no more one self with

either of them than if the soul or immaterial spirit that now informs him had been created and began to exist when it began to inform his present body, though it were ever so true that the same spirit that informed *Nestor's* or *Thersites's* body was numerically the same that now informs his. For this would no more make him the same person with *Nestor* than if some of the particles of matter that were once a part of *Nestor* were now a part of this man—the same immaterial substance, without the same consciousness, no more making the same person by being united to any body than the same particle of matter, without consciousness united to any body, makes the same person. But let him once find himself conscious of any of the actions of *Nestor*, he then finds himself the same person with *Nestor*.

15. And thus we may be able, without any difficulty, to conceive the same person at the resurrection, though in a body not exactly in make or parts the same which he had here, the same consciousness going along with the soul that inhabits it. But yet the soul alone, in the change of bodies, would scarcely to anyone but to him who makes the soul the *man* be enough to make the same *man*. For should the soul of a prince, carrying with it the consciousness of the prince's past life, enter and inform the body of a cobbler, as soon as deserted by his own soul, everyone sees he would be the same person with the prince, accountable only for the prince's actions. But who would say it was the same man? The body too goes to the making the man, and would, I guess, to everybody determine the man in this case, in which the soul, with all its princely thoughts about it, would not make another man. But he would be the same cobbler to everyone besides himself. I know that, in the ordinary way of speaking, the same person and the same man stand for one and the same thing. And indeed everyone will always have a liberty to speak as he pleases, and to apply what articulate sounds to what *ideas* he thinks fit and change them as often as he pleases. But yet when we will inquire what makes the same *spirit, man,* or *person,* we must fix the *ideas* of *spirit, man,* or *person* in our minds; and having resolved with ourselves what we mean by them, it will not be hard to determine in either of them, or the like, when it is the *same* and when not.

16. *Consciousness makes the same person.* But though the same immaterial substance or soul does not alone, wherever it is and in whatever state, make the same man, yet it is plain [that] consciousness, as far as ever it can be extended, should it be to ages past, unites existences and actions very remote in time into the same person, as well as it does the existences and actions of the immediately preceding moment, so that whatever has the consciousness of present and past actions is the same person to whom they both belong. Had I the same consciousness that I saw the ark and *Noah's* flood as that I saw an overflowing of the *Thames* last winter, or as that I write now, I could no more doubt that I who write this now, that saw the *Thames* overflowed last winter and that viewed the flood at the general deluge, was the same *self*—place that *self* in what substance you please—than that I who write this am the same *myself* now while I write (whether I consist of all the same substance, material or immaterial, or no) that I was yesterday. For as to this point of being the same *self,* it does not matter whether this present *self* is made up of the same or other substances, I being as much concerned and as justly accountable for any action that was done a thousand years since, appropriated to me now by this self-consciousness, as I am for what I did the last moment.

17. *Self depends on consciousness. Self* is that conscious thinking thing, whatever substance made up of (whether spiritual or material, simple or compounded, it matters not), which is sensible, or conscious of pleasure and pain, capable of happiness or misery, and so is concerned for it*self,* as far as that consciousness extends. Thus everyone finds that, while comprehended under that consciousness, the little finger is as much a part of him*self* as what is most so. Upon separation of this little finger, should this consciousness go along with the little finger and leave the rest of the body, it is evident the little finger would be the *person,* the *same person*; and self then would have nothing to do with the rest of the body. As in this case it is the consciousness that goes along with the substance, when one part is separate from another, which makes the same *person* and constitutes this inseparable *self,* so it is in reference to substances remote in time; that with which the *consciousness* of

this present thinking thing can join itself makes the same *person*, and is one *self* with it and with nothing else, and so attributes to it*self* and owns all the actions of that thing as its own, as far as that consciousness reaches, and no further—as everyone who reflects will perceive.

18. *Objects of reward and punishment.* In this *personal identity* is founded all the right and justice of reward and punishment; happiness and misery being that for which everyone is concerned for *himself*, and not mattering what becomes of any substance not joined to or affected with that consciousness. For as it is evident in the instance I gave but now, if the consciousness went along with the little finger when it was cut off, that would be the same *self* which was concerned for the whole body yesterday as making part of it*self*, whose actions then it cannot but admit as its own now. Though if the same body should still live, and immediately, from the separation of the little finger, have its own peculiar consciousness, of which the little finger knew nothing, it would not at all be concerned for it, as a part of itself, or could own any of its actions or have any of them imputed to him.

19. This may show us in what *personal identity* consists, not in the identity of substance, but, as I have said, in the identity of *consciousness*; in which, if *Socrates* and the present mayor of *Queenborough* agree, they are the same person. If the same *Socrates* waking and sleeping do not partake of the same *consciousness*, *Socrates* waking and sleeping is not the same person. And to punish *Socrates* waking for what sleeping *Socrates* thought and waking *Socrates* was never conscious of would be no more of right than to punish one twin for what his twin brother did, of which he knew nothing, because their outsides were so like that they could not be distinguished; for such twins have been seen.

20. But yet possibly it will still be objected, suppose I wholly lose the memory of some parts of my life beyond a possibility of retrieving them, so that perhaps I shall never be conscious of them again, yet am I not the same person that did those actions, had those thoughts that I once was conscious of, though I have now forgot them? To which I answer that we must here take notice what the word *I* is applied to, which, in this case, is the man only. And the same man

being presumed to be the same person, I is easily here supposed to stand also for the same person. But if it is possible for the same man to have distinct incommunicable consciousness at different times, it is past doubt the same man would at different times make different persons, which, we see, is the sense of mankind in the solemnest declaration of their opinions, human laws not punishing the *mad man* for the *sober man's* actions, nor the *sober man* for what the *mad man* did, by that means making them two persons. This is somewhat explained by our way of speaking in *English*, when we say such a one *is not himself*, or is *beside himself*; in which phrases it is insinuated, as if those who now, or at least first, used them, thought that *self* was changed, the *self*-same person was no longer in that man.

21. *Difference between identity of man and person.* But yet it is hard to conceive that *Socrates*, the same individual man, should be two persons. To help us a little in this, we must consider what is meant by *Socrates*, or the same individual *man*.

First, it must be either the same individual, immaterial, thinking substance—in short, the same numerical soul, and nothing else.

Secondly, or the same animal, without any regard to an immaterial soul.

Thirdly, or the same immaterial spirit united to the same animal.

Now take which of these suppositions you please, it is impossible to make personal identity to consist in anything but consciousness or reach any further than that does.

For, by the first of them, it must be allowed possible that a man born of different women and in distant times may be the same man. A way of speaking, which whoever admits must allow it possible for the same man to be two distinct persons, as any two who have lived in different ages without the knowledge of one another's thoughts.

By the second and thirdly, *Socrates* in this life and after it, cannot be the same man any way but by the same consciousness; and so making *human identity* to consist in the same thing in which we place *personal identity*, there will be no difficulty to allow the same man to be the same person. But then they who place *human identity* in consciousness only, and not in something else, must consider how they will make the infant *Socrates* the same man with *Socrates* after the resurrection. But whatever to some men makes a *man*, and consequently the same individual man, in what perhaps few are agreed, personal identity can by us be placed in nothing but consciousness (which is that alone which makes what we call *self*) without involving us in great absurdities.

22. But is not a man drunk and sober the same person? Why else is he punished for the fact he commits when drunk, though he is never afterwards conscious of it? Just as much the same person as a man who walks and does other things in his sleep is the same person and is answerable for any mischief he shall do in it. Human laws punish both, with a justice suitable to their way of knowledge, because in these cases they cannot distinguish certainly what is real, what counterfeit. And so the ignorance in drunkenness or sleep is not admitted as a plea. For though punishment is annexed to personality, and personality to consciousness, and the drunkard perhaps is not conscious of what he did, yet human judicatures justly punish him, because the fact is proved against him, but want of consciousness cannot be proved for him. But in the great day in which the secrets of all hearts shall be laid open, it may be reasonable to think, no one shall be made to answer for what he knows nothing of, but shall receive his doom, his conscience accusing or excusing him.

23. *Consciousness alone makes self.* Nothing but consciousness can unite remote existences into the same person; the identity of substance will not do it, for whatever substance there is, however framed, without consciousness there is no person. And a carcass may be a person, as well as any sort of substance be so, without consciousness.

Could we suppose two distinct incommunicable consciousnesses acting [in] the same body, the one constantly by day, the other by night, and, on the other side, the same consciousness acting by intervals [in] two distinct bodies? I ask, in the first case, whether the *day* and the *night man* would not be two as distinct persons as *Socrates* and *Plato?* And whether, in the second case, there would not be one person in two distinct bodies, as much as one man is the same in

two distinct clothings? Nor is it at all material to say that this same and this distinct *consciousness*, in the cases above mentioned, is owing to the same and distinct immaterial substances, bringing it with them to those bodies, which, whether true or not, alters not the case, since it is evident the *personal identity* would equally be determined by the consciousness, whether that consciousness were annexed to some individual immaterial substance or not. For, granting that the thinking substance in man must be necessarily supposed immaterial, it is evident that immaterial thinking thing may sometimes part with its past consciousness and be restored to it again, as appears in the forgetfulness men often have of their past actions. And the mind many times recovers the memory of a past consciousness which it had lost for twenty years together. Make these intervals of memory and forgetfulness take their turns regularly by day and night, and you have two persons with the same immaterial spirit, as much as in the former instance two persons with the same body. Thus, *self* is not determined by identity or diversity of substance, which it cannot be sure of but only by identity of consciousness.

24. Indeed it may conceive the substance of which it is now made up to have existed formerly, united in the same conscious being. But consciousness removed that substance is no more it*self*, or makes no more a part of it than any other substance, as is evident in the instance we have already given of a limb cut off, of whose heat, or cold, or other affections, having no longer any consciousness, it is no more of a man's self than any other matter of the universe. In like manner it will be in reference to any immaterial substance, which is void of that consciousness by which I am my*self* to my*self*. If there is any part of its existence which I cannot upon recollection join with that present consciousness by which I am now my*self*, it is in that part of its existence no more my*self* than any other immaterial being. For whatever any substance has thought or done which I cannot recollect and by my consciousness make my own thought and action, it will no more belong to me, whether a part of me thought or did it, than if it had been thought or done by any other immaterial being anywhere existing.

25. I agree, the more probable opinion is that this consciousness is annexed to, and the affection of, one individual immaterial substance.

But let men, according to their diverse hypotheses, resolve of that as they please; this every intelligent being, sensible of happiness or misery, must grant: that there is something that is *himself* that he is concerned for and would have happy; that this *self* has existed in a continued duration more than one instant, and therefore it is possible may exist, as it has done, months and years to come without any certain bounds to be set to its duration, and may be the same *self*, by the same consciousness continued on for the future. And thus, by this consciousness he finds himself to be the *same self* which did such or such an action some years since by which he comes to be happy or miserable now. In all which account of *self*, the same numerical substance is not considered as making the same *self* but the same continued consciousness in which several substances may have been united and again separated from it, which, while they continued in a vital union with that in which this consciousness then resided, made a part of that same *self*. Thus any part of our bodies, vitally united to that which is conscious in us, makes a part of our*selves*. But upon separation from the vital union by which that consciousness is communicated, that which a moment since was part of our*selves* is now no more so than a part of another man's *self* is a part of me, and it is not impossible but in a little time may become a real part of another person. And so we have the same numerical substance become a part of two different persons and the same person preserved under the change of various substances. Could we suppose any spirit wholly stripped of all its memory or consciousness of past actions, as we find our minds always are of a great part of ours, and sometimes of them all, the union or separation of such a spiritual substance would make no variation of personal identity any more than that of any particle of matter does. Any substance vitally united to the present thinking being is a part of that very *same self* which now is. Anything united to it by a consciousness of former actions makes also a part of the *same self*, which is the same both then and now.

26. *Person a forensic term.* Person, as I take it, is the name for this *self*. Wherever a man finds what he calls *himself*, there I think another may say is the same *person*. It is a forensic term appropriating actions and their merit, and so belongs only to intelligent agents capable of a law and happiness and misery. This personality extends *itself* beyond present existence to what is past only by consciousness, by which it becomes concerned and accountable, owns, and imputes to its*elf* past actions, just upon the same ground and for the same reason that it does the present. All this is founded in a concern for happiness, the unavoidable concomitant of consciousness, that which is conscious of pleasure and pain, desiring that that *self* that is conscious should be happy. And therefore whatever past actions it cannot reconcile or appropriate to that present *self* by consciousness, it can be no more concerned in than if they had never been done. And to receive pleasure or pain, i.e., reward or punishment, on the account of any such action is all one as to be made happy or miserable in its first being, without any demerit at all. For supposing a man punished now for what he had done in another life, of which he could be made to have no consciousness at all, what difference is there between that punishment and being created miserable? And therefore, conformable to this, the apostle tells us that at the great day, when everyone shall *"receive according to his doings, the secrets of all hearts shall be laid open."* The sentence shall be justified by the consciousness all persons shall have that they *themselves*, in whatever bodies they appear or whatever substances that consciousness adheres to, are the *same* who committed those actions and deserve that punishment for them.

27. I am apt enough to think I have, in treating of this subject, made some suppositions that will look strange to some readers, and possibly they are so in themselves. But yet, I think, they are such as are pardonable in this ignorance we are in of the nature of that thinking thing that is in us, and which we look on as our*selves*. Did we know what it was or how it was tied to a certain system of fleeting animal spirits; or whether it could or could not perform its operations of thinking and memory out of a body organized as

ours is; and whether it has pleased God that no one such spirit shall ever be united to any but one such body, upon the right constitution of whose organs its memory should depend, we might see the absurdity of some of those suppositions I have made. But taking, as we ordinarily now do (in the dark concerning these matters), the soul of a man for an immaterial substance, independent from matter and indifferent alike to it all, there can from the nature of things be no absurdity at all to suppose that the same soul may, at different times, be united to different bodies, and with them make up, for that time, one man — as well as we suppose a part of a sheep's body yesterday should be a part of a man's body tomorrow, and in that union make a vital part of *Meliboeus* himself, as well as it did of his ram.

28. *The difficulty from ill use of names.* To conclude: Whatever substance begins to exist, it must, during its existence, necessarily be the same. Whatever compositions of substances begin to exist, during the union of those substances the concrete must be the same. Whatever mode begins to exist, during its existence it is the same. And so if the composition is of distinct substances and different modes, the same rule holds. By this it will appear that the difficulty or obscurity that has been about this matter rather rises from the names ill-used than from any obscurity in things themselves. For whatever makes the specific *idea* to which the name is applied, if that *idea* is steadily kept to, the distinction of anything into the same and diverse will easily be conceived, and there can arise no doubt about it.

29. *Continued existence makes identity.* For supposing a rational spirit is the *idea* of a *man*, it is easy to know what is the *same man*; namely, the *same spirit*, whether separate or in a body, will be the *same man*. Supposing a rational spirit vitally united to a body of a certain conformation of parts to make a *man*, while that rational spirit, with that vital conformation of parts, though continued in a fleeting successive body, remains, it will be the same man. But if to anyone the *idea* of a *man* is but the vital union of parts in a certain shape, as long as that vital union and shape remain, in a concrete not otherwise the same, but by a continued succession of fleeting particles, it will be the same *man*. For whatever is the composition of

which the complex *idea* is made, whenever existence makes it one particular thing under any denomination, the same existence, continued, preserves it the same individual under the same denomination.

Book III. Of Words. Chapter 3. *Of General Terms.*

1. *The greatest part of words general.* All things that exist being particulars, it may perhaps be thought reasonable that words, which ought to be conformed to things, should be so too — I mean in their signification; but yet we find the quite contrary. The far *greatest part of words* that make all languages *are general terms*, which has not been the effect of neglect or chance, but of reason and necessity.

2. *For every particular thing to have a name is impossible.* First, it is impossible that every particular thing should have a distinct peculiar name. For the signification and use of words depending on that connection which the mind makes between its *ideas* and the sounds it uses as signs of them, it is necessary, in the application of names to things, that the mind should have distinct *ideas* of the things, and retain also the particular name that belongs to every one, with its peculiar appropriation to that *idea*. But it is beyond the power of human capacity to frame and retain distinct *ideas* of all the particular things we meet with: Every bird and beast men saw, every tree and plant that affected the senses, could not find a place in the most capacious understanding. If it is looked on as an instance of a prodigious memory that some generals have been able to call every soldier in their army by his proper name, we may easily find a reason why men have never attempted to give names to each sheep in their flock or crow that flies over their heads, much less to call every leaf of plants or grain of sand that came in their way by a peculiar name.

3. *And useless. Secondly,* if it were possible, *it would yet be useless* because it would not serve to the chief end of language. Men would in vain heap up names of particular things that would not serve them to communicate their thoughts. Men learn names and use them in talk with others only that they may be understood; this is then only done when, by use or

consent, the sound I make by the organs of speech excites in another man's mind who hears it the *idea* I apply it to in mine when I speak it. This cannot be done by names applied to particular things of which, I alone having the *ideas* in my mind, the names of them could not be significant or intelligible to another who was not acquainted with all those very particular things which had fallen under my notice.

4. Thirdly, but yet, granting this also feasible (which I think is not), yet *a distinct name for every particular thing would not be of any great use for the improvement of knowledge*, which, though founded in particular things, enlarges itself by general views to which things reduced into sorts under general names, are properly subservient. [. . .]

6. *How general words are made*. The next thing to be considered is *how general words come to be made*. For since all things that exist are only particulars, how do we come by general terms, or where do we find those general natures they are supposed to stand for? Words become general by being made the signs of general *ideas*; and *ideas* become general by separating from them the circumstances of time and place and any other *ideas* that may determine them to this or that particular existence. By this way of abstraction they are made capable of representing more individuals than one; each of these, having in it a conformity to that abstract *idea*, is (as we call it) of that sort.

7. But to deduce this a little more distinctly, it will not perhaps be amiss to trace our notions and names from their beginning and observe by what degrees we proceed and by what steps we enlarge our *ideas* from our first infancy. There is nothing more evident than that the *ideas* of the persons children converse with (to instance in them alone) are like the persons themselves, only particular. The *ideas* of the nurse and the mother are well framed in their minds and, like pictures of them there, represent only those individuals. The names they first gave to them are confined to these individuals, and the names of *nurse* and *mamma* the child uses determine themselves to those persons. Afterwards, when time and a larger acquaintance have made them observe that there are a great many other things in the world that, in some common agreements of shape and several other qualities, resemble their father and mother and those per-

sons they have been used to, they frame an *idea* which they find those many particulars do partake in; and to that they give, with others, the name *man*, for example. And *thus they come to have a general name* and a general *idea*. They make nothing new in this, but only leave out of the complex *idea* they had of *Peter* and *James*, *Mary* and *Jane*, that which is peculiar to each, and retain only what is common to them all.

8. By the same way that they come by the general name and *idea* of *man*, they easily *advance to more general names and notions*. For, observing that several things that differ from their *idea* of *man* and [that] cannot therefore be comprehended under that name have yet certain qualities in which they agree with *man*, by retaining only those qualities and uniting them into one *idea*, they have again another and more general *idea* to which, having given a name, they make a term of a more comprehensive extension; this new *idea* is made, not by any new addition, but only as before, by leaving out the shape and some other properties signified by the name *man* and retaining only a body with life, sense, and spontaneous motion, comprehended under the name *animal*.

9. *General natures are nothing but abstract ideas*. That this is the way *by which men first formed general* ideas *and general names to them*, I think, is so evident that there needs no other proof of it but the considering of a man's self or others and the ordinary proceedings of their minds in knowledge. And he who thinks general natures or notions are anything else but such abstract and partial *ideas* of more complex ones, taken at first from particular existences, will, I fear, be at a loss where to find them. For let any one reflect and then tell me, in what does his *idea* of *man* differ from that of *Peter* and *Paul*, or his *idea* of *horse* from that of *Bucephalus*, but in the leaving out something that is peculiar to each individual and retaining so much of those particular complex *ideas* of several particular existences as they are found to agree in? Of the complex *ideas* signified by the names *man* and *horse*, leaving out but those particulars in which they differ and retaining only those in which they agree, and of those making a new distinct complex *idea* and giving the name *animal* to it, one has a more general term that comprehends with man several other creatures. Leave out of the *idea* of *animal*, sense and

spontaneous motion—and the remaining complex *idea*, made up of the remaining simple ones of body, life, and nourishment, becomes a more general one, under the more comprehensive term *vivens*. And not to dwell longer upon this particular so evident in itself, by the same way the mind proceeds to *body*, *substance*, and at last to *being, thing*, and such universal terms which stand for any of our *ideas* whatsoever. To conclude, this whole *mystery* of *genera* and *species*, which make such a noise in the schools and are with justice so little regarded out of them, is nothing else but abstract *ideas*, more or less comprehensive, with names annexed to them. In all this, it is constant and invariable that every more general term stands for such an *idea* and is but a part of any of those contained under it.

10. *Why the* genus *is ordinarily of use in definitions.* This may show us the reason *why, in the defining of words*, which is nothing but declaring their significations, *we make use of the genus* or next general word that comprehends it. This is not out of necessity, but only to save the labor of enumerating the several simple *ideas* which the next general word or genus stands for, or, perhaps, sometimes the shame of not being able to do it. But though defining by *genus* and *differentia* (I beg permission to use these terms of art, though originally Latin, since they most properly suit those notions they are applied to) I say, though defining by the *genus* is the shortest way, yet I think it may be doubted whether it is the best. This I am sure, it is not the only [way], and so not absolutely necessary. For, definition being nothing but making another understand by words what *idea* the term defined stands for, a definition is best made by enumerating those simple *ideas* that are combined in the signification of the term defined; and if, instead of such an enumeration, men have accustomed themselves to use the next general term, it has not been out of necessity or for greater clearness, but for quickness and dispatch sake. For I think that, to one who desired to know what *idea* the word man stood for, if it should be said that man was a solid extended substance having life, sense, spontaneous motion, and the faculty of reasoning, I do not doubt but the meaning of the term man would be as well understood, and the *idea*

it stands for be at least as clearly made known as when it is defined to be a rational animal, which, by the several definitions of *animal, vivens*, and *corpus*, resolves itself into those enumerated *ideas*. I have, in explaining the term *man*, followed here the ordinary definition of the schools, which, though perhaps not the most exact, yet serves well enough to my present purpose. And one may, in this instance, see what gave occasion to the rule that a definition must consist of *genus* and *differentia*; and it suffices to show us the little necessity there is of such a rule, or advantage in the strict observing of it. For definitions, as has been said, being only the explaining of one word by several others so that the meaning or *idea* it stands for may be certainly known; languages are not always so made according to the rules of logic that every term can have its signification exactly and clearly expressed by two others. Experience sufficiently satisfies us to the contrary: or else those who have made this rule have done ill, that they have given us so few definitions conformable to it. But of definitions more in the next chapter.

11. *General and universal are creatures of the understanding.* To return to general words, it is plain, by what has been said, that *general and universal* do not belong to the real existence of things, but are the *inventions and creatures of the understanding*, made by it for its own use, *and concern only signs*, whether words or *ideas*. Words are general, as has been said, when used for signs of general *ideas*, and so are applicable indifferently to many particular things, and *ideas* are general when they are set up as the representatives of many particular things; but universality does not belong to things themselves, which are all of them particular in their existence, even those words and *ideas* which in their signification are general. When therefore we quit particulars, the generals that rest are only creatures of our own making, their general nature being nothing but the capacity they are put into by the understanding of signifying or representing many particulars. For the signification they have is nothing but a relation that, by the mind of man, is added to them.

12. *Abstract* ideas *are the essences of the* genera *and* species. The next thing, therefore, to be considered

is *what kind of signification it is that general words have*. For as it is evident that they do not signify barely one particular thing—for then they would not be general terms but proper names—so on the other side it is as evident they do not signify a plurality, for man and men would then signify the same, and the distinction of numbers (as the grammarians call them) would be superfluous and useless. That then which general words signify is a sort of things, and each of them does that by being a sign of an abstract *idea* in the mind, to which *idea*, as things existing are found to agree, so they come to be ranked under that name, or, which is all one, be of that sort. In this way it is evident that the *essences of* the *sorts, or* (if the Latin word pleases better) *species* of things, are nothing else but these abstract *ideas*. For the having the essence of any species being that which makes anything to be of that species, and the conformity to the *idea* to which the name is annexed being that which gives a right to that name, the having the essence and the having that conformity must necessarily be the same thing, since to be of any species and to have a right to the name of that species is all one. As for example, to be a *man*, or of the species *man*, and to have right to the name *man* is the same thing. Again, to be a *man*, or of the species *man*, and have the essence of a *man* is the same thing. Now since nothing can be a *man* or have a right to the name *man* but what has a conformity to the abstract *idea* the name *man* stands for, nor anything be a man or have a right to the species *man* but what has the essence of that species, it follows that the abstract *idea* for which the name stands and the essence of the species is one and the same. From this it is easy to observe that the essences of the sorts of things and, consequently, the sorting of things is the workmanship of the understanding that abstracts and makes those general *ideas*.

13. *They are the workmanship of the understanding but have their foundation in the similitude of things.* I would not here be thought to forget, much less to deny, that nature in the production of things makes several of them alike. There is nothing more obvious, especially in the races of animals and all things propagated by seed. But yet I think we may say the *sorting*

of them under names *is the workmanship of the understanding, taking occasion from the similitude* it observes among them to make abstract general *ideas* and set them up in the mind, with names annexed to them as patterns or forms (for in that sense the word form has a very proper signification) to which, as particular things existing are found to agree, so they come to be of that species, have that denomination, or are put into that *class*. For when we say, this is a man, that a horse; this justice, that cruelty; this a watch, that a jack; what else do we but rank things under different specific names, as agreeing to those abstract *ideas* of which we have made those names the signs? And what are the essences of those species set out and marked by names, but those abstract *ideas* in the mind which are, as it were, the bonds between particular things that exist and the names they are to be ranked under? And when general names have any connection with particular beings, these abstract *ideas* are the medium that unites them, so that the essences of species, as distinguished and denominated by us, neither are nor can be anything but these precise abstract *ideas* we have in our minds. And therefore the supposed real essences of substances, if different from our abstract *ideas*, cannot be the essences of the species we rank things into. For two species may be one as rationally as two different essences be the essence of one species; and I demand what are the alterations which may or may not be made in a *horse* or *lead* without making either of them to be of another species? In determining the species of things by our abstract *ideas*, this is easy to resolve; but if anyone will regulate himself here by supposed real essences, he will, I suppose, be at a loss; and he will never be able to know when anything precisely ceases to be of the species of a *horse* or *lead*. [. . .]

15. *Real and nominal essence.* But since the essences of things are thought by some (and not without reason) to be wholly unknown, it may not be amiss to consider the *several significations of the word essence*.

First, essence may be taken for the very being of anything, by which it is what it is. And thus the real internal, but generally, in substances, unknown, constitution of things, on which their discoverable qualities depend, may be called their *essence*. This is the proper original signification of the word, as is evident from the formation of it, *essentia*, in its primary notation, signifying properly *being*. And in this sense it is still used when we speak of the *essence* of particular things without giving them any name.

Secondly, the learning and disputes of the schools having been much busied about *genus* and *species*, the word *essence* has almost lost its primary signification, and, instead of the real constitution of things, has been almost wholly applied to the artificial constitution of *genus* and *species*. It is true there is ordinarily supposed a real constitution of the sorts of things, and it is past doubt there must be some real constitution on which any collection of simple *ideas* coexisting must depend. But it being evident that things are ranked under names into sorts or *species* only as they agree to certain abstract *ideas* to which we have annexed those names, the *essence* of each *genus*, or sort, comes to be nothing but that abstract *idea* which the general, or *sortal* (if I may have leave so to call it from *sort*, as I do *general* from *genus*) name stands for. And this we shall find to be that which the word *essence* imports in its most familiar use. These two sorts of *essences*, I suppose, may not unfitly be termed, the one the *real*, the other *nominal essence*.

16. *Constant connection between the name and nominal essence.* Between the nominal essence and the name there is so *near a connection* that the name of any sort of things cannot be attributed to any particular being but what has this *essence*, by which it answers that abstract *idea* of which that name is the sign.

17. *Supposition that species are distinguished by their real essences useless.* Concerning the real essences of corporeal substances (to mention these only) there are, if I am not mistaken, two opinions. The one is of those who, using the word *essence* for they know not what, suppose a certain number of those essences, according to which all natural things are made and in which they do exactly every one of them partake, and so become, of this or that *species*. The other and more rational opinion is of those who look on all natural things to have a real, but unknown constitution of their insensible parts, from which flow those sensible qualities which serve us to distinguish them one from another, according as we have occa-

sion to rank them into sorts under common denominations. The former of these opinions, which supposes these *essences* as a certain number of forms or molds in which all natural things that exist are cast and do equally partake, has, I imagine, very much perplexed the knowledge of natural things. The frequent productions of monsters, in all the species of animals and of changelings and other strange issues of human birth, carry with them difficulties not possible to consist with this *hypothesis*, since it is as impossible that two things partaking exactly of the same real *essence* should have different properties as that two figures partaking of the same real *essence* of a circle should have different properties. But were there no other reason against it, yet the *supposition of essences that cannot be known* and the making of them nevertheless to be that which distinguishes the species of things is so wholly useless and unserviceable to any part of our knowledge that that alone were sufficient to make us lay it by and content ourselves with such essences of the sorts or species of things as come within the reach of our knowledge. When seriously considered, this will be found, as I have said, to be nothing else but those abstract complex *ideas* to which we have annexed distinct general names.

18. *Real and nominal essence the same in simple* ideas *and modes, different in substances.* Essences being thus distinguished into *nominal and real*, we may further observe that, in the species of *simple* ideas *and modes*, they *are always the same* but in *substances always quite different*. Thus a figure including a space between three lines is the real as well as nominal *essence* of a triangle, it being not only the abstract *idea* to which the general name is annexed but the very *essentia* or being of the thing itself, that foundation from which all its properties flow and to which they are all inseparably annexed. But it is far otherwise concerning that parcel of matter which makes the ring on my finger, in which these two essences are apparently different. For it is the real constitution of its insensible parts on which depend all those properties of color, weight, fusibility, fixedness, etc. which are to be found in it, which constitution we know not, and so having no particular *idea* of, have no name that is the sign of it. But yet it is its color, weight, fusibility, fixedness, etc. which makes it to be

gold, or gives it a right to that name, which is therefore its nominal *essence*. Since nothing can be called *gold* but what has a conformity of qualities to that abstract complex *idea* to which that name is annexed. But this distinction of *essences* belonging particularly to substances, we shall, when we come to consider their names, have an occasion to treat of more fully. [. . .]

Chapter 6. *Of the Names of Substances.*

1. *The common names of substances stand for sorts.* The common names of substances, as well as other general terms, *stand for sorts*, which is nothing else but the being made signs of such complex *ideas* in which several particular substances do or might agree, by virtue of which they are capable of being comprehended in one common conception and signified by one name. I say do or might agree; for though there is but one sun existing in the world, yet the *idea* of it being abstracted so that more substances (if there were several) might each agree in it, it is as much a sort as if there were as many suns as there are stars. They do not lack their reasons who think there are, and that each fixed star would answer the *idea* the name *sun* stands for, to one who was placed in a due distance—which, by the way, may show us how much the sorts or, if you please, *genera* and *species* of things (for those Latin terms signify to me no more than the English word *sort*) depend on such collections of *ideas* as men have made, and not on the real nature of things, since it is not impossible but that, in propriety of speech, that might be a sun to one which is a star to another.

2. *The essence of each sort is the abstract idea.* The measure and boundary of each sort, or species, by which it is constituted that particular sort and distinguished from others, are what we call its *essence*, which is nothing but that *abstract* idea *to which the name is annexed*, so that every thing contained in that *idea* is essential to that sort. This, though it is all the *essence* of natural substances that we know, or by which we distinguish them into sorts, yet I call it by a peculiar name, the *nominal essence*, to distinguish it from the real constitution of substances, upon which depends this *nominal essence* and all the properties of that sort; this therefore, as has been said, may be

called the *real essence*: e.g., the *nominal essence* of *gold* is that complex *idea* the word *gold* stands for—let it be, for instance, a body yellow, of a certain weight, malleable, fusible, and fixed. But the *real essence* is the constitution of the insensible parts of that body on which those qualities and all the other properties of *gold* depend. How far these two are different, though they are both called *essence*, is obvious at first sight to discover.

3. *The nominal and real essence different.* For, though perhaps voluntary motion with sense and reason joined to a body of a certain shape is the complex *idea* to which I and others, annex the name *man*, and so is the *nominal essence* of the *species* so called, yet nobody will say that complex *idea* is the *real essence* and source of all those operations which are to be found in any individual of that sort. The foundation of all those qualities which are the ingredients of our complex *idea* is something quite different; and had we such a knowledge of that constitution of *man* from which his faculties of moving, sensation, and reasoning, and other powers flow, and on which his so regular shape depends, as it is possible angels have and it is certain his Maker has, we should have a quite other *idea* of his *essence* than what now is contained in our definition of that species, be it what it will; and our *idea* of any individual *man* would be as far different from what it is now as is his who knows all the springs and wheels and other contrivances within of the famous clock at *Strasbourg*, from that which a gazing countryman has for it who barely sees the motion of the hand, and hears the clock strike, and observes only some of the outward appearances.

4. *Nothing essential to individuals.* That *essence*, in the ordinary use of the word, relates to *sorts*—and that it is considered in particular beings no further than as they are ranked into *sorts*—appears from hence: that, take but away the abstract *ideas* by which we sort individuals, and rank them under common names, and then the thought of anything *essential* to any of them instantly vanishes; we have no notion of the one without the other; which plainly shows their relation. It is necessary for me to be as I am—God and nature has made me so; but there is nothing I have [that] is essential to me. An accident or disease may very much alter my color or shape; a fever or

fall may take away my reason or memory or both; and an apoplexy leave neither sense nor understanding, no, nor life. Other creatures of my shape may be made with more and better or fewer and worse faculties than I have; and others may have reason and sense in a shape and body very different from mine. None of these are essential to the one or the other or to any individual whatever until the mind refers it to some sort or *species* of things; and then presently, according to the abstract *idea* of that sort, something is found *essential*. Let any one examine his own thoughts, and he will find that as soon as he supposes or speaks of *essential*, the consideration of some *species* or the complex *idea* signified by some general name comes into his mind; and it is in reference to that, that this or that quality is said to be *essential*. So that if it is asked whether it is *essential* to me or any other particular corporeal being to have reason, I say no; no more than it is *essential* to this white thing I write on to have words in it. But if that particular being is to be counted of the sort *man* and to have the name *man* given it, then reason is *essential* to it, supposing reason to be a part of the complex *idea* the name *man* stands for—as it is *essential* to this thing I write on to contain words, if I will give it the name *treatise* and rank it under that *species*. So that *essential and not essential relate only to our abstract* ideas *and the names annexed to them*, which amounts to no more than this, that whatever particular thing does not have in it those qualities which are contained in the abstract *idea* which any general term stands for cannot be ranked under that *species* nor be called by that name, since that abstract *idea* is the very *essence* of that *species*.

5. Thus, if the *idea* of *body* with some people is bare extension or space, then solidity is not *essential* to body. If others make the *idea* to which they give the name *body* to be solidity and extension, then solidity is essential to *body*. That, therefore, and *that alone* is considered as *essential which makes a part of the complex* idea *the name of a sort stands for*, without which no particular thing can be reckoned of that sort nor be entitled to that name. Should there be found a parcel of matter that had all the other qualities that are in *iron* but lacked obedience to the lodestone and would neither be drawn by it nor re-

ceive direction from it, would any one question whether it wanted anything *essential?* It would be absurd to ask whether a thing really existing wanted anything *essential* to it. Or could it be demanded whether this made an *essential* or *specific* difference or not, since we have no other measure of *essential* or *specific* but our abstract *ideas?* And to talk of specific differences in nature without reference to general *ideas* and names is to talk unintelligibly. For I would ask anyone what is sufficient to make an essential difference in nature between any two particular beings without any regard had to some abstract *idea* which is looked upon as the essence and standard of a *species?* All such patterns and standards being quite laid aside, particular beings, considered barely in themselves, will be found to have all their qualities equally *essential;* and everything in each individual will be *essential* to it or, which is more, nothing at all. For though it may be reasonable to ask whether obeying the magnet is *essential* to *iron*, yet, I think, it is very improper and insignificant to ask whether it is *essential* to the particular parcel of matter I cut my pen with, without considering it under the name *iron* or as being of a certain *species*. And if, as has been said, our abstract *ideas* which have names annexed to them, are the boundaries of *species*, nothing can be *essential* but what is contained in those *ideas*.

6. It is true, I have often mentioned a *real essence*, distinct in substances from those abstract *ideas* of them which I call their *nominal essence*. By this *real essence* I mean the real constitution of anything, which is the foundation of all those properties that are combined in, and are constantly found to coexist with the *nominal essence*—that particular constitution which everything has within itself, without any relation to anything without it. But *essence*, even in this sense, *relates to a sort* and supposes a *species:* for being that real constitution on which the properties depend, it necessarily supposes a sort of things, properties belonging only to *species* and not to individuals; e.g., supposing the nominal essence of *gold* to be a body of such a peculiar color and weight, with malleability and fusibility, the real essence is that constitution of the parts of matter on which these qualities and their union depend and is also the foundation of its solubility in *aqua regia* and other properties accompanying

that complex *idea*. Here are *essences* and *properties*, but all upon supposition of a sort or general abstract *idea*, which is considered as immutable; but there is no individual parcel of matter to which any of these qualities are so annexed as to be *essential* to it or inseparable from it. That which is *essential* belongs to it as a condition by which it is of this or that sort; but take away the consideration of its being ranked under the name of some abstract *idea*, and then there is nothing necessary to it, nothing inseparable from it. Indeed, as to the *real essences* of substances, we only suppose their being, without precisely knowing what they are; but that which annexes them still to the *species* is the nominal essence of which they are the supposed foundation and cause.

7. *The nominal essence bounds the species.* The next thing to be considered is, by which of those essences it is that *substances are determined into* sorts, or *species*; and that, it is evident, is *by the nominal essence.* For it is that alone that the name, which is the mark of the sort, signifies. It is impossible therefore that anything should determine the sorts of things which we rank under general names, but that *idea* which that name is designed as a mark for, which is that, as has been shown, which we call *nominal essence.* Why do we say, this is a *horse*, that a *mule*; this is an *animal*, that an *herb*? How does any particular thing come to be of this or that sort, but because it has that nominal essence or, which is all one, agrees to that abstract *idea* that name is annexed to? And I desire anyone but to reflect on his own thoughts, when he hears or speaks any of those or other names of substances, to know what sort of *essences* they stand for.

8. And that the *species of things to us are nothing but the ranking them under distinct names, according to the complex* ideas *in us,* and not according to precise, distinct, real essences in them, is plain from this, that we find many of the individuals that are ranked into one sort, called by one common name, and so received as being of one *species*, have yet qualities depending on their real constitutions, as far different one from another as from others from which they are accounted to differ *specifically.* [. . .]

9. *Not the real essence, which we do not know.* Nor indeed *can we* rank and *sort things* and consequently

(which is the end of sorting) denominate them *by their real essences*, because we do not know them. Our faculties carry us no further towards the knowledge and distinction of substances than a collection of those sensible *ideas* which we observe in them—which, however, made with the greatest diligence and exactness we are capable of, yet is more remote from the true internal constitution from which those qualities flow than, as I said, a countryman's *idea* is from the inward contrivance of that famous clock at *Strasbourg*, of which he only sees the outward figure and motions. There is not so contemptible a plant or animal that does not confound the most enlarged understanding. Though the familiar use of things about us take off our wonder, yet it does not cure our ignorance. When we come to examine the stones we tread on or the iron we daily handle, we presently find we do not know their make and can give no reason of the different qualities we find in them. It is evident the internal constitution, on which their properties depend, is unknown to us. For, to go no further than the grossest and most obvious we can imagine among them, what is that texture of parts, that real essence, that makes lead and antimony fusible, wood and stones not? What makes lead and iron malleable, antimony and stones not? And yet how infinitely these come short of the fine contrivances and inconceivable real essences of plants or animals, everyone knows. The workmanship of the all-wise and powerful God in the great fabric of the universe and every part of it further exceeds the capacity and comprehension of the most inquisitive and intelligent man than the best contrivance of the most ingenious man does the conceptions of the most ignorant of rational creatures. Therefore, we in vain pretend to range things into sorts and dispose them into certain classes, under names, *by their real essences*, that are so far from our discovery or comprehension. [. . .]

12. *There are probably numberless species of spirits.* It is not impossible to conceive nor repugnant to reason that there may be many *species of spirits*, as much separated and diversified one from another by distinct properties of which we have no *ideas* as the *species* of sensible things are distinguished one from another by qualities which we know and observe in them. That there should be more *species* of intelligent

creatures above us than there are of sensible and material below us is probable to me from this: that in all the visible corporeal world we see no chasms or gaps. All quite down from us the descent is by easy steps and a continued series of things that in each remove differ very little one from the other. There are fishes that have wings and are not strangers to the airy region; and there are some birds that are inhabitants of the water whose blood is cold as fishes, and their flesh so like in taste that the scrupulous are allowed them on fish-days. There are animals so near of kin both to birds and beasts that they are in the middle between both. Amphibious animals link the terrestrial and aquatic together, seals live at land and sea, and porpoises have the warm blood and entrails of a hog, not to mention what is confidently reported of mermaids or seamen. There are some brutes that seem to have as much knowledge and reason, as some that are called men; and the animal and vegetable kingdoms are so nearly joined that, if you will take the lowest of one and the highest of the other, there will scarcely be perceived any great difference between them, and so on, until we come to the lowest and the most inorganic parts of matter, we shall find everywhere that the several *species* are linked together, and differ but in almost insensible degrees. [. . .]

14. *Difficulties against a certain number of real essences.* To distinguish substantial beings into *species*, according to the usual supposition that there are certain precise *essences* or *forms* of things by which all the individuals existing are by nature distinguished into *species*, these things are necessary:

15. *First*, to be assured that nature, in the production of things, always designs them to partake of certain regulated established *essences*, which are to be the models of all things to be produced. This, in that crude sense it is usually proposed, would need some better explication before it can fully be assented to.

16. *Secondly*, it would be necessary to know whether nature always attains that essence it designs in the production of things. The irregular and monstrous births that in various sorts of animals have been observed will always give us reason to doubt of one or both of these.

17. *Thirdly*, it ought to be determined whether those we call *monsters* are really a distinct *species*,

according to the scholastic notion of the word *species*; since it is certain that everything that exists has its particular constitution. And yet we find that some of these monstrous productions have few or none of those qualities which are supposed to result from and accompany the *essence* of that *species* from which they derive their origins and to which, by their descent, they seem to belong.

18. *Fourthly*, the *real essences* of those things which we distinguish into *species*, and as so distinguished, we name, ought to be known; i.e., we ought to have *ideas* of them. But since we are ignorant in these four points, *the supposed real essences of things do not stand us in stead for the distinguishing substances into species.*

19. *Our nominal essences of substances, not perfect collections of properties. Fifthly*, the only imaginable help in this case would be that, having framed perfect complex *ideas* of the *properties* of things flowing from their different real essences, we should distinguish them into *species* by them. But neither can this be done; for, being ignorant of the real essence itself, it is impossible to know all those properties that flow from it and are so annexed to it that, any one of them being away, we may certainly conclude that that essence is not there, and so the thing is not of that *species*. [. . .]

26. *Therefore very various and uncertain.* Since then it is evident that we sort and name substances by their *nominal* and not by their real *essences*, the next thing to be considered is how and by whom these essences come to be made. As to the latter, it is evident they *are made by the mind* and not by nature; for were they nature's workmanship, they could not be so various and different in several men as experience tells us they are. For if we will examine it, we shall not find the nominal essence of any one *species* of substances in all men the same—no, not of that which of all others we are the most intimately acquainted with. [. . .]

28. *But not so arbitrary as mixed modes.* But though these *nominal essences of substances* are made by the mind, they are *not yet made so arbitrarily as those of mixed modes*. To the making of any nominal essence, it is necessary, *first*, that the *ideas* of which it consists have such a union as to make but one *idea*, however

compounded. *Secondly*, that the particular *idea* so united be exactly the same, neither more nor less. For if two abstract complex *ideas* differ either in number or sorts of their component parts, they make two different, and not one and the same, essence. In the first of these, the mind, in making its complex *ideas* of substances, only follows nature and puts none together which are not supposed to have a union in nature. Nobody joins the voice of a sheep with the shape of a horse, nor the color of lead with the weight and fixedness of gold to be the complex *ideas* of any real substances unless he has a mind to fill his head with chimeras and his discourse with unintelligible words. Men, observing certain qualities always joined and existing together, copied nature in this, and of *ideas* so united made their complex ones of substances. For though men may make what complex *ideas* they please and give what names to them they will, yet if they will be understood when they speak of things really existing, they must in some degree conform their *ideas* to the things they would speak of; or else men's language will be like that of *Babel*; and every man's words, being intelligible only to himself, would no longer serve to conversation and the ordinary affairs of life if the *ideas* they stand for are not some way answering the common appearances and agreement of substances as they really exist.

29. *Though very imperfect.* Secondly, though the mind of man, *in making* its *complex* ideas *of substances*, never puts any together that do not really or are not supposed to coexist, and so it truly borrows that union from nature, yet the number it combines *depends upon the various care, industry, or fancy of him that makes it*. Men generally content themselves with some few sensible obvious qualities, and often, if not always, leave out others as material and as firmly united as those that they take. [. . .]

32. *The more general our ideas are, the more incomplete and partial they are.* If the *number of simple* ideas *that make the nominal essence* of the lowest *species*, or first sorting, of individuals *depends on the mind* of man variously collecting them, it is much more evident that they do so in the more comprehensive *classes* which, by the masters of logic, are called *genera*. These are complex *ideas* designedly imperfect; and it is visible at first sight that several of those qualities that are to be found in the things themselves are purposely left out of *generical ideas*. For, as the mind, to make general *ideas* comprehending several particulars, leaves out those of time, and place, and such other that make them incommunicable to more than one individual, so to make other yet more general *ideas* that may comprehend different sorts, it leaves out those qualities that distinguish them and puts into its new collection only such *ideas* as are common to several sorts. [. . .]

36. *Though nature makes the similitude.* This then, in short, is the case: *Nature makes many particular things which do agree* one with another in many sensible qualities and probably, too, in their internal frame and constitution; but it is not this real essence that distinguishes them into *species*; it is *men* who, taking occasion from the qualities they find united in them and in which they observe often several individuals to agree, *range them into sorts in order to their naming* for the convenience of comprehensive signs; under these individuals, according to their conformity to this or that abstract *idea*, come to be ranked as under ensigns: so that this is of the blue, that the red regiment; this is a man, that a drill; and in this, I think, consists the whole business of *genus* and *species*. [. . .]

Book IV. Of Knowledge and Opinion. Chapter 1. *Of Knowledge in General.*

1. *Our knowledge conversant about our* ideas. Since the *mind* in all its thoughts and reasonings has no other immediate object but its own *ideas*, which it alone does or can contemplate, it is evident that our knowledge is only conversant about them.

2. *Knowledge is the perception of the agreement or disagreement of two* ideas. *Knowledge* then seems to me to be nothing but *the perception of the connection and agreement, or disagreement and repugnance, of any of our ideas*. In this alone it consists. Where this perception is, there is knowledge, and where it is not, there, though we may fancy, guess, or believe, yet we always come short of knowledge. For when we know that *white is not black*, what do we else but perceive that these two *ideas* do not agree? When we possess ourselves with the utmost security of the demonstration that the *three angles of a triangle are equal to*

two right ones, what do we more but perceive that equality to two right ones does necessarily agree to, and is inseparable from, the three angles of a triangle?

3. *This agreement fourfold.* But to understand a little more distinctly in what this agreement or disagreement consists, I think we may reduce it all to these four sorts.

1. *Identity* or *diversity*.

2. *Relation*.

3. *Coexistence* or *necessary connection*.

4. *Real existence*.

4. *First, of identity or diversity. First,* as to the first sort of agreement or disagreement, namely, *identity* or *diversity*. It is the first act of the mind, when it has any sentiments or *ideas* at all, to perceive its *ideas*; and so far as it perceives them, to know each what it is and in this way also to perceive their difference and that one is not another. This is so absolutely necessary that without it there could be no knowledge, no reasoning, no imagination, no distinct thoughts at all. By this, the mind clearly and infallibly perceives each *idea* to agree with itself and to be what it is, and all distinct *ideas* to disagree, i.e., the one not to be the other. And this it does without pains, labor, or deduction, but at first view, by its natural power of perception and distinction. And though men of art have reduced this into those general rules, "*What is, is,*" *and* "*It is impossible for the same thing to be and not to be,*" for ready application in all cases in which there may be occasion to reflect on it, yet it is certain that the first exercise of this faculty is about particular *ideas*. A man infallibly knows, as soon as ever he has them in his mind, that the *ideas* he calls *white* and *round* are the very *ideas* they are, and that they are not other *ideas* which he calls *red* or *square*. Nor can any maxim or proposition in the world make him know it clearer or surer than he did before and without any such general rule. This then is the first agreement or disagreement which the mind perceives in its *ideas*, which it always perceives at first sight. And if there ever happens to be any doubt about it, it will always be found to be about the names, and not the *ideas* themselves, whose identity and diversity will always

be perceived as soon and clearly as the *ideas* themselves are; nor can it possibly be otherwise.

5. *Secondly, relation. Secondly,* the next sort of agreement or disagreement the mind perceives in any of its *ideas* may, I think, be called *relative* and is nothing but *the perception of the relation between any two ideas,* of whatever kind, whether substances, modes, or any other. For since all distinct *ideas* must eternally be known not to be the same, and so be universally and constantly denied one of another, there could be no room for any positive knowledge at all if we could not perceive any relation between our *ideas* and find out the agreement or disagreement they have one with another in several ways the mind takes of comparing them.

6. *Thirdly, of coexistence. Thirdly,* the third sort of agreement or disagreement to be found in our *ideas*, which the perception of the mind is employed about, is *coexistence*, or *non-coexistence* in the same subject, and this belongs particularly to substances. Thus when we pronounce concerning *gold* that it is fixed, our knowledge of this truth amounts to no more but this, that fixedness, or a power to remain in the fire unconsumed, is an *idea* that always accompanies, and is joined with that particular sort of yellowness, weight, fusibility, malleableness, and solubility in *aqua regia*, which make our complex *idea*, signified by the word *gold*.

7. *Fourthly, of real existence. Fourthly,* the fourth and last sort is that of *actual real existence* agreeing to any *idea*. Within these four sorts of agreement or disagreement is, I suppose, contained all the knowledge we have or are capable of. For all the inquiries we can make concerning any of our *ideas*, all that we know or can affirm concerning any of them is that it is or is not the same with some other; that it does or does not always coexist with some other *idea* in the same subject; that it has this or that relation with some other *idea*; or that it has a real existence without the mind. Thus "*blue is not yellow*" is of identity. "*Two triangles upon equal bases between two parallels are equal*" is of relation. "*Iron is susceptible of magnetic impressions*" is of coexistence. "*God is*" is of real existence. Though identity and coexistence are truly nothing but relations, yet they are such peculiar ways of agreement or disagreement of our *ideas*

that they deserve well to be considered as distinct heads and not under relation in general, since they are so different grounds of affirmation and negation, as will easily appear to anyone who will but reflect on what is said in several places of this essay. I should now proceed to examine the several degrees of our knowledge, but that it is necessary first to consider the different acceptations of the word *knowledge*.

8. *Knowledge actual or habitual.* There are several ways in which the mind is possessed of truth, each of which is called *knowledge*.

1. There is *actual knowledge*, which is the present view the mind has of the agreement or disagreement of any of its *ideas* or of the relation they have one to another.

2. A man is said to know any proposition which, having been once laid before his thoughts, he evidently perceived the agreement or disagreement of the *ideas* of which it consists and so lodged it in his memory that whenever that proposition comes again to be reflected on, he, without doubt or hesitation, embraces the right side, assents to, and is certain of the truth of it. This, I think, one may call *habitual knowledge*. And thus a man may be said to know all those truths which are lodged in his memory by a foregoing clear and full perception, of which the mind is assured past doubt as often as it has occasion to reflect on them. For our finite understandings being able to think clearly and distinctly but on one thing at once, if men had no knowledge of any more than what they actually thought on, they would all be very ignorant; and he who knew most would know but one truth, that being all he was able to think on at one time.

9. *Habitual knowledge twofold.* Of habitual knowledge there are also, vulgarly speaking, two degrees.

First, the one is of *such truths laid up in the memory as, whenever they occur to the mind, it actually perceives the relation between those ideas*. And this is in all those truths of which we have an *intuitive knowledge*, where the *ideas* themselves, by an immediate view, discover their agreement or disagreement one with another.

Secondly, the other is of *such truths of which the mind having been convinced, it retains the memory of the conviction without the proofs*. Thus a man who remembers certainly that he once perceived the demonstration that the three angles of a triangle are equal to two right ones is certain that he knows it, because he cannot doubt the truth of it. In his adherence to a truth where the demonstration by which it was at first known is forgot—though a man may be thought rather to believe his memory than really to know, and this way of entertaining a truth seemed formerly to me like something between opinion and knowledge, a sort of assurance which exceeds bare belief, for that relies on the testimony of another—yet upon a due examination I find it does not come short of perfect certainty and is in effect true knowledge; that which is apt to mislead our first thoughts into a mistake in this matter is that the agreement or disagreement of the *ideas* in this case is not perceived, as it was at first, by an actual view of all the intermediate *ideas* by which the agreement or disagreement of those in the proposition was at first perceived, but by other intermediate *ideas* that show the agreement or disagreement of the *ideas* contained in the proposition whose certainty we remember. For example, in this proposition that "the three angles of a triangle are equal to two right ones," one who has seen and clearly perceived the demonstration of this truth knows it to be true when that demonstration is gone out of his mind, so that at present it is not actually in view and possibly cannot be recollected. But he knows it in a different way from what he did before. The agreement of the two *ideas* joined in that proposition is perceived, but it is by the intervention of other *ideas* than those which at first produced that perception. He remembers, i.e., he knows (for remembrance is but the reviving of some past knowledge), that he was once certain of the truth of this proposition, that the three angles of a triangle are equal to two right ones. The immutability of the same relations between the same immutable things is now the *idea* that shows him that if the three angles of a triangle were once equal to two right ones, they will always be equal to two right ones. And hence he comes to be certain that what was once true in the case is always true; what *ideas* once agreed will always agree; and consequently what he once knew to be true, he will always know to be true as long as he can remember that he once knew it. Upon this ground it is that particular demonstrations in mathematics afford general knowledge. If, then, the perception that the same *ideas* will eternally have the same habitudes and relations is not a sufficient ground of knowledge, there could be no knowledge of general propositions in mathematics, for no mathematical demonstration would be any other than particular. And when a man had demonstrated any proposition concerning one triangle or circle, his knowledge would not reach beyond that particular diagram. If he would extend it further, he must renew his demonstration in another instance before he could know it to be true in another like triangle, and so on. By these means one could never come to the knowledge of any general propositions. Nobody, I think, can deny that Mr. *Newton* certainly knows any proposition that he now at any time reads in his book to be true, though he does not have in actual view that admirable chain of intermediate *ideas* by which he at first discovered it to be true. Such a memory as that, able to retain such a train of particulars, may be well thought beyond the reach of human faculties, when the very discovery, perception, and laying together that wonderful connection of *ideas* is found to surpass most readers' *comprehension*. But yet it is evident the author himself knows the proposition to be true, remembering he once saw the connection of those *ideas*, as certainly as he knows such a man wounded another, remembering that he saw him run him through. But because the memory is not always so clear as actual perception and does in all men more or less decay in length of time, this, among other differences, is one which shows that *demonstrative knowledge* is much more imperfect than *intuitive*, as we shall see in the following chapter.

Chapter 2. *Of the Degrees of Our Knowledge.*

1. *Intuitive.* All our knowledge consisting, as I have said, in the view the mind has of its own *ideas*, which is the utmost light and greatest certainty we, with our

faculties and in our way of knowledge, are capable of, it may not be amiss to consider a little the degrees of its evidence. The different clearness of our knowledge seems to me to lie in the different way of perception the mind has of the agreement or disagreement of any of its *ideas*. For if we will reflect on our own ways of thinking, we shall find that sometimes the mind perceives the agreement or disagreement of two *ideas* immediately by themselves, without the intervention of any other. And this, I think, we may call *intuitive knowledge*. For in this the mind is at no pains of proving or examining, but perceives the truth, as the eye does light, only by being directed towards it. Thus the mind perceives that *white* is not *black*, that a *circle* is not a *triangle*, that *three* are more than *two* and equal to *one* and *two*. Such kinds of truths the mind perceives at the first sight of the *ideas* together, by bare *intuition*, without the intervention of any other *idea*; and this kind of knowledge is the clearest and most certain that human frailty is capable of. This part of knowledge is irresistible and, like bright sunshine, forces itself immediately to be perceived as soon as ever the mind turns its view that way, and leaves no room for hesitation, doubt, or examination, but the mind is presently filled with the clear light of it. It is on this *intuition* that depends all the certainty and evidence of all our knowledge; this certainty everyone finds to be so great that he cannot imagine and therefore not require a greater. For a man cannot conceive himself capable of a greater certainty than to know that any *idea* in his mind is such as he perceives it to be, and that two *ideas* in which he perceives a difference are different and not precisely the same. He who demands a greater certainty than this, demands he knows not what and shows only that he has a mind to be a skeptic without being able to be so. Certainty depends so wholly on this intuition, that in the next degree of *knowledge*, which I call *demonstrative*, this intuition is necessary in all the connections of the intermediate *ideas*, without which we cannot attain knowledge and certainty.

2. *Demonstrative.* The next degree of knowledge is where the mind perceives the agreement or disagreement of any *ideas*, but not immediately. Though wherever the mind perceives the agreement or disagreement of any of its *ideas*, there is certain knowl-

edge; yet it does not always happen that the mind sees that agreement or disagreement which there is between them even where it is discoverable and in that case remains in ignorance and at most gets no further than a probable conjecture. The reason why the mind cannot always perceive presently the agreement or disagreement of two *ideas* is because those *ideas,* concerning whose agreement or disagreement the inquiry is made, cannot by the mind be so put together as to show it. In this case then, when the mind cannot so bring its *ideas* together as by their immediate comparison and as it were juxtaposition or application one to another to perceive their agreement or disagreement, it is inclined, by the intervention of other *ideas* (one or more, as it happens), to discover the agreement or disagreement which it searches; and this is that which we call *reasoning.* Thus the mind, being willing to know the agreement or disagreement in bigness between the three angles of a triangle and two right ones, cannot, by an immediate view and comparing them, do it, because the three angles of a triangle cannot be brought at once and be compared with any other one or two angles; and so of this the mind has no immediate, no intuitive knowledge. In this case the mind is inclined to find out some other angles to which the three angles of a triangle have an equality, and, finding those equal to two right ones, comes to know their equality to two right ones.

3. *Depends on proofs.* Those intervening *ideas* which serve to show the agreement of any two others are called *proofs;* and where the agreement or disagreement is by this means plainly and clearly perceived, it is called *demonstration,* it being *shown* to the understanding, and the mind made to see that it is so. A quickness in the mind to find out these intermediate *ideas* (that shall discover the agreement or disagreement of any other) and to apply them right is, I suppose, that which is called *sagacity.*

4. *But not so easy.* This knowledge by intervening proofs, though it is certain, yet the evidence of it is *not* altogether *so clear* and bright, nor the assent so ready, *as* in *intuitive* knowledge. For though in *dem-onstration* the mind does at last perceive the agreement or disagreement of the *ideas* it considers, yet it is not without pains and attention. There must be

more than one transient view to find it. A steady application and pursuit are required to this discovery. And there must be a progression by steps and degrees before the mind can in this way arrive at certainty and come to perceive the agreement or repugnance between two *ideas* that need proofs and the use of reason to show it.

5. *Not without precedent doubt.* Another difference between intuitive and demonstrative knowledge is that though in the latter all doubt is removed when by the intervention of the intermediate *ideas* the agreement or disagreement is perceived, yet before the demonstration there was a doubt, which in intuitive knowledge cannot happen to the mind that has its faculty of perception left to a degree capable of distinct *ideas,* no more than it can be a doubt to the eye (that can distinctly see white and black) whether this ink and this paper are all of a color. If there is sight in the eyes, it will at first glimpse, without hesitation, perceive the words printed on this paper different from the color of the paper. And so if the mind has the faculty of distinct perception, it will perceive the agreement or disagreement of those *ideas* that produce intuitive knowledge. If the eye has lost the faculty of seeing or the mind of perceiving, we in vain inquire after the quickness of sight in one or clearness of perception in the other.

6. *Not so clear.* It is true the perception produced by *demonstration* is also very clear, yet it is often with a great abatement of that evident luster and full assurance that always accompany that which I call *intuitive;* like a face reflected by several mirrors one to another, where as long as it retains the similitude and agreement with the object, it produces a knowledge; but it is still in every successive reflection, with a lessening of that perfect clearness and distinctness which is in the first; until at last, after many removes, it has a great mixture of dimness and is not at first sight so knowable, especially to weak eyes. Thus it is with knowledge made out by a long train of proof.

7. *Each step must have intuitive evidence.* Now, *in every step reason makes in demonstrative knowledge, there is an intuitive knowledge* of that agreement or disagreement it seeks with the next intermediate *idea* which it uses as a proof; for if it were not so, that yet would need a proof, since without the perception of

such agreement or disagreement there is no knowledge produced. If it is perceived by itself, it is intuitive knowledge. If it cannot be perceived by itself, there is need of some intervening *idea*, as a common measure, to show their agreement or disagreement. By this it is plain that every step in reasoning that produces knowledge has intuitive certainty, which, when the mind perceives, there is no more required but to remember it, to make the agreement or disagreement of the *ideas* concerning which we inquire visible and certain. So that to make anything a *demonstration* it is necessary to perceive the immediate agreement of the intervening *ideas*, by which the agreement or disagreement of the two *ideas* under examination (of which the one is always the first and the other the last in the account) is found. This intuitive perception of the agreement or disagreement of the intermediate *ideas* in each step and progression of the *demonstration* must also be carried exactly in the mind, and a man must be sure that no part is left out—which because in long deductions and the use of many proofs the memory does not always so readily and exactly retain; therefore it comes to pass that this is more imperfect than intuitive knowledge, and men embrace often falsehood for demonstrations. [. . .]

9. *Demonstration not limited to quantity*. It has been generally taken for granted that mathematics alone is capable of demonstrative certainty; but to have such an agreement or disagreement as may intuitively be perceived, being, as I imagine, not the privilege of the *ideas* of *number, extension,* and *figure* alone, it may possibly be the want of due method and application in us, and not of sufficient evidence in things, that demonstration has been thought to have so little to do in other parts of knowledge and been scarcely so much as aimed at by any but mathematicians. For whatever *ideas* we have in which the mind can perceive the immediate agreement or disagreement that is between them, there the mind is capable of intuitive knowledge; and where it can perceive the agreement or disagreement of any two *ideas* by an intuitive perception of the agreement or disagreement they have with any intermediate *ideas*, there the mind is capable of demonstration, which is not limited to *ideas* of extension, figure, number, and their modes.

10. *Why it has been so thought*. The reason why it has been generally sought for and supposed to be only in those, I imagine, has been not only the general usefulness of those sciences, but because, in comparing their equality or excess, the modes of numbers have every the least difference very clear and perceivable; and though in extension every the least excess is not so perceptible, yet the mind has found out ways to examine and discover demonstratively the just equality of two angles, or extensions, or figures. And both these, i.e., numbers and figures, can be set down by visible and lasting marks in which the *ideas* under consideration are perfectly determined, which for the most part they are not where they are marked only by names and words.

11. But in other simple *ideas*, whose modes and differences are made and counted by degrees and not quantity, we have not so nice and accurate a distinction of their differences as to perceive, or find ways to measure, their just equality, or the least differences. For those other simple *ideas*, being appearances of sensations produced in us by the size, figure, number, and motion of minute corpuscles singly insensible, their different degrees also depend upon the variation of some or of all those causes which, since it cannot be observed by us in particles of matter of which each is too subtle to be perceived, it is impossible for us to have any exact measures of the different degrees of these simple *ideas*. [. . .]

13. Not knowing therefore what number of particles, nor what motion of them, is fit to produce any precise degree of *whiteness*, we cannot demonstrate the certain equality of any two degrees of *whiteness*; because we have no certain standard to measure them by nor means to distinguish every the least real difference, the only help we have being from our senses, which in this point fail us. But where the difference is so great as to produce in the mind clearly distinct *ideas* whose differences can be perfectly retained, there these *ideas* or colors, as we see in different kinds, as blue and red, are as capable of demonstration as *ideas* of number and extension. What I have here said of *whiteness* and colors, I think, holds true in all secondary qualities and their modes.

14. *Sensitive knowledge of particular existence*. These two, namely, intuition and demonstration, are

the degrees of our knowledge; whatever comes short of one of these, with whatever assurance embraced, is but faith or opinion but not knowledge, at least in all general truths. There is, indeed, another *perception* of the mind, employed about *the particular existence of finite beings* without us, which, going beyond bare probability and yet not reaching perfectly to either of the foregoing degrees of certainty, passes under the name of knowledge. There can be nothing more certain than that the *idea* we receive from an external object is in our minds; this is intuitive knowledge. But whether there is anything more than barely that *idea* in our minds, whether we can certainly infer from this the existence of anything without us which corresponds to that *idea*, is that of which some men think there may be a question made; because men may have such *ideas* in their minds when no such thing exists, no such object affects their senses. But yet here, I think, we are provided with an evidence that puts us past doubting. For I ask anyone, whether he is not invincibly conscious to himself of a different perception when he looks on the sun by day and thinks on it by night—when he actually tastes worm-wood, or smells a rose, or only thinks on that savor or odor? We as plainly find the difference there is between any *idea* revived in our minds by our own memory and actually coming into our minds by our senses, as we do between any two distinct *ideas*. If anyone says a dream may do the same thing, and all these *ideas* may be produced in us without any external objects, he may please to dream that I make him this answer: 1. That it is no great matter whether I remove his scruple or not; where all is but dream, reasoning and arguments are of no use, truth and knowledge nothing. 2. That I believe he will allow a very manifest difference between dreaming of being in the fire and being actually in it. But yet if he is resolved to appear so skeptical as to maintain that what I call being actually in the fire is nothing but a dream and that we cannot thereby certainly know that any such thing as fire actually exists without us, I answer that we certainly find that pleasure or pain follows upon the application of certain objects to us whose existence we perceive, or dream that we perceive, by our senses; this certainty is as great as our happiness or misery, beyond which we have no

concern to know or to be. Thus, I think, we may add to the two former sorts of *knowledge* this also, of the existence of particular external objects by that perception and consciousness we have of the actual entrance of *ideas* from them, and allow these *three degrees of knowledge*, namely, *intuitive, demonstrative, and sensitive*, in each of which there are different degrees and ways of evidence and certainty.

15. *Knowledge not always clear, where the* ideas *are so.* But since our knowledge is founded on and employed about our *ideas* only, will it not follow from this that it is conformable to our *ideas*; and that where our *ideas* are clear and distinct or obscure and confused our knowledge will be so too? To which I answer, no. For our knowledge consisting in the perception of the agreement or disagreement of any two *ideas*, its clearness or obscurity consists in the clearness or obscurity of that perception and not in the clearness or obscurity of the *ideas* themselves—e.g., a man who has as clear *ideas* of the angles of a triangle and of equality to two right ones as any mathematician in the world may yet have but a very obscure perception of their agreement and so have but a very obscure knowledge of it. But *ideas* which, by reason of their obscurity or otherwise, are confused cannot produce any clear or distinct knowledge, because, as far as any *ideas* are confused, so far the mind cannot perceive clearly whether they agree or disagree. Or to express the same thing in a way less apt to be misunderstood: he who has not determined *ideas* to the words he uses cannot make propositions of them of whose truth he can be certain.

Chapter 3. *Of the Extent of Human Knowledge.*

1. *First, no further than we have* ideas. Knowledge, as has been said, lying in the perception of the agreement or disagreement of any of our *ideas*, it follows from hence that *First*, we can have *knowledge* no further than we have *ideas*.

2. *Secondly, no further than we can perceive their agreement or disagreement. Secondly*, that we can have no *knowledge* further than we can have perceptions of that agreement or disagreement which perception being: 1. either by *intuition*, or the immediate

comparing any two *ideas*; or, 2. by *reason*, examining the agreement or disagreement of two *ideas*, by the intervention of some others; or, 3. by *sensation*, perceiving the existence of particular things. Hence it also follows:

3. *Thirdly, intuitive knowledge does not extend itself to all the relations of all our* ideas. *Thirdly*, that we cannot have an *intuitive knowledge* that shall extend itself to all our *ideas* and all that we would know about them because we cannot examine and perceive all the relations they have one to another by *juxta*position, or an immediate comparison one with another. Thus having the *ideas* of an obtuse and an acute angled triangle, both drawn from equal bases and between parallels, I can, by intuitive knowledge, perceive the one not to be the other but cannot that way know whether they are equal or not because their agreement or disagreement in equality can never be perceived by an immediate comparing them. The difference of figure makes their parts incapable of an exact immediate application; and therefore there is need of some intervening qualities to measure them by, which is demonstration or rational knowledge.

4. *Fourthly, nor demonstrative knowledge.* Fourthly, it follows also from what is above observed that our *rational knowledge* cannot reach to the whole extent of our *ideas* because between two different *ideas* we would examine, we cannot always find such *mediums* as we can connect one to another with an intuitive knowledge in all the parts of the deduction; and wherever that fails, we come short of knowledge and demonstration.

5. *Fifthly, sensitive knowledge, narrower than either.* Fifthly, *sensitive knowledge* reaching no further than the existence of things actually present to our senses is yet much narrower than either of the former.

6. *Sixthly, our knowledge therefore narrower than our* ideas. From all [of] which it is evident that *the extent of our knowledge* comes not only short of the reality of things, but even of the extent of our own *ideas*. Though our knowledge is limited to our *ideas* and cannot exceed them either in extent or perfection, and though these are very narrow bounds, in respect of the extent of all being, and far short of what we may justly imagine to be in some even created understandings, not tied down to the dull and narrow infor-

mation, is to be received from some few and not very acute ways of perception, such as are our senses, yet it would be well with us if our knowledge were but as large as our *ideas*, and there were not many doubts and inquiries concerning the *ideas* we have, of which we are not, nor I believe ever shall be, in this world, resolved. Nevertheless I do not question but that human knowledge, under the present circumstances of our beings and constitutions, may be carried much further than it has been up to now, if men would sincerely and with freedom of mind employ all that industry and labor of thought in improving the means of discovering truth which they do for the coloring or support of falsehood to maintain a system, interest, or party they are once engaged in. But yet, after all, I think I may, without injury to human perfection, be confident that our knowledge would never reach to all we might desire to know concerning those *ideas* we have, nor be able to surmount all the difficulties and resolve all the questions that might arise concerning any of them. We have the *ideas* of a *square*, a *circle*, and *equality*, and yet, perhaps, shall never be able to find a circle equal to a square and certainly know that it is so. We have the *ideas* of *matter* and *thinking* but possibly shall never be able to know whether any mere material being thinks or not, it being impossible for us, by the contemplation of our own *ideas*, without revelation, to discover whether omnipotence has not given to some systems of matter fitly disposed, a power to perceive and think, or else joined and fixed to matter so disposed, a thinking immaterial substance—it being in respect of our notions not much more remote from our comprehension to conceive that God can, if he pleases, superadd to matter a faculty of thinking, than that he should superadd to it another substance with a faculty of thinking, since we do not know in what thinking consists, nor to what sort of substances the Almighty has been pleased to give that power, which cannot be in any created being but merely by the good pleasure and bounty of the Creator. For I see no contradiction in it that the first eternal thinking Being or omnipotent Spirit should, if he pleased, give to certain systems of created senseless matter, put together as he thinks fit, some degrees of sense, perception, and thought, though as I think I have proved, *lib. iv.*, chap. 10, sec. 14, etc., it is no less than a contradiction to suppose matter (which is evidently, in its own nature, void of sense and thought) should be that eternal first-thinking Being. What certainty of knowledge can anyone have that some perceptions, such as, e.g., pleasure and pain, should not be in some bodies themselves after a certain manner modified and moved, as well as that they should be in an immaterial substance upon the motion of the parts of body? Body, as far as we can conceive, being able only to strike and affect body, and motion, according to the utmost reach of our *ideas*, being able to produce nothing but motion; so that when we allow it to produce pleasure or pain, or the *idea* of a color or sound, we are inclined to quit our reason, go beyond our *ideas*, and attribute it wholly to the good pleasure of our Maker. For since we must allow he has annexed effects to motion which we can no way conceive motion able to produce, what reason have we to conclude that he could not order them as well to be produced in a subject we cannot conceive capable of them, as well as in a subject we cannot conceive the motion of matter can any way operate upon? I do not say this that I would any way lessen the belief of the soul's immateriality. I am not here speaking of probability, but knowledge; and I think not only that it becomes the modesty of philosophy not to pronounce magisterially where we want that evidence that can produce knowledge, but also that it is of use to us to discern how far our knowledge does reach, for the state we are at present in not being that of vision, we must in many things content ourselves with faith and probability; and in the present question about the immateriality of the soul, if our faculties cannot arrive at demonstrative certainty, we need not think it strange. All the great ends of morality and religion are well enough secured without philosophical proofs of the soul's immateriality, since it is evident that he who made us at the beginning to subsist here, sensible intelligent beings, and for several years continued us in such a state, can and will restore us to the like state of sensibility in another world and make us capable there to receive the retribution he has designed to men according to their doings in this life. And therefore it is not of such mighty necessity to determine one way or the other, as some over-zealous for or against the immateriality of the soul have been ready to make the world believe. Who, either on the one side indulging too much their thoughts, immersed altogether in matter, can allow no existence to what is not material. Or who, on the other side not finding *cogitation* within the natural powers of matter examined over and over again by the utmost intention of mind, have the confidence to conclude that omnipotence itself cannot give perception and thought to a substance which has the modification of solidity. He who considers how hardly sensation is, in our thoughts, reconcilable to extended matter, or existence to anything that has no extension at all, will confess that he is very far from certainly knowing what his soul is. It is a point which seems to me to be put out of the reach of our knowledge. And he who will give himself leave to consider freely and look into the dark and intricate part of each hypothesis will scarcely find his reason able to determine him fixedly for or against the soul's materiality. Since on whichever side he views it, either as an unextended substance or as a thinking extended matter, the difficulty to conceive either will, while either alone is in his thoughts, still drive him to the contrary side — an unfair way which some men take with themselves who, because of the inconceivableness of something they find in one, throw themselves violently into the contrary hypothesis, though altogether as unintelligible to an unbiased understanding. This serves not only to show the weakness and the scantiness of our knowledge, but the insignificant triumph of such sort of arguments, which, drawn from our own views, may satisfy us that we can find no certainty on one side of the question, but do not at all thereby help us to truth by running into the opposite opinion, which, on examination, will be found clogged with equal difficulties. For what safety, what advantage to anyone is it for the avoiding the seeming absurdities and, to him, insurmountable rubs he meets with in one opinion, to take refuge in the contrary, which is built on something altogether as inexplicable and as far remote from his comprehension? It is past controversy that we have in us something that thinks; our very doubts about what it is confirm the certainty of its being, though we must content ourselves in the ignorance of what *kind* of being it is. And it is in vain to go about to be skeptical in this, as it is unreasonable in most other cases to be positive against the being of anything because we cannot comprehend its nature. For I would gladly know what substance exists that does not have something in it which manifestly baffles our understandings. Other spirits who see and know the nature and inward constitution of things, how much must they exceed us in knowledge? To which if we add larger comprehension, which enables them at one glance to see the connection and agreement of very many *ideas* and readily supplies to them the intermediate proofs, which we, by single and slow steps and long poring in the dark, hardly at last find out, and are often ready to forget one before we have hunted out another. We may guess at some part of the happiness of superior ranks of spirits, who have a quicker and more penetrating sight as well as a larger field of knowledge. But to return to the argument in hand, our *knowledge*, I say, is not only limited to the paucity and imperfections of the *ideas* we have and which we employ it about, but even comes short of that too. But how far it reaches, let us now inquire.

7. *How far our knowledge reaches.* The affirmations or negations we make concerning the *ideas* we have may, as I have before intimated in general, be reduced to these four sorts, namely, identity, coexistence, relation, and real existence. I shall examine how far our knowledge extends in each of these.

8. *First, our knowledge of identity and diversity, as far as our* ideas. *First, as to identity and diversity,* in this way of agreement or disagreement of our *ideas, our intuitive knowledge is as far extended as our ideas* themselves; and there can be no *idea* in the mind which it does not presently, by an intuitive knowledge, perceive to be what it is and to be different from any other.

9. *Secondly, of coexistence, a very little way.* Secondly, *as to* the second sort, which is *the agreement or disagreement* of our *ideas in coexistence,* in this our knowledge is very short, though in this consists the greatest and most material part of our knowledge concerning substances. For our *ideas* of the species of substances being, as I have showed, nothing but certain collections of simple *ideas* united in one subject and so coexisting together: e.g., our *idea* of *flame* is a body hot, luminous, and moving upward; of *gold,*

a body heavy to a certain degree, yellow, malleable, and fusible. These, or some such complex *ideas* as these in men's minds, stand for these two names of the different substances, *flame* and *gold*. When we would know anything further concerning these or any other sort of substances, what do we inquire but what other qualities or power these substances have or have not? This is nothing else but to know what other simple *ideas* do or do not coexist with those that make up that complex *idea*.

10. *Because the connection between most simple* ideas *is unknown*. This, however weighty and considerable a part of human science, is yet very narrow and scarcely any at all. The reason of which is that the simple *ideas* of which our complex *ideas* of substances are made up, are, for the most part, such as carry with them in their own nature no visible necessary connection or inconsistency with any other simple *ideas* whose coexistence with them we would inform ourselves about.

11. *Especially of secondary qualities*. The *ideas* that our complex ones of substances are made up of, and about which our knowledge concerning substances is most employed, are those of their *secondary qualities*. These depending all (as has been shown) upon the primary qualities of their minute and insensible parts, or, if not upon them, upon something yet more remote from our comprehension, it is impossible we should know which have a necessary union or inconsistency one with another. For not knowing the root they spring from, not knowing what size, figure, and texture of parts they are, on which depend and from which result those qualities which make our complex *idea* of *gold*, it is impossible we should know what other qualities result from or are incompatible with the same constitution of the insensible parts of gold and so consequently must always coexist with that complex *idea* we have of it or else are *inconsistent* with it.

12. *And further, because all connection between any secondary and primary qualities is undiscoverable*. Besides this ignorance of the primary qualities of the insensible parts of bodies on which depend all their secondary qualities, there is yet another and more incurable part of ignorance which sets us more remote from a certain knowledge of the *coexistence* or *in-*

coexistence (if I may so say) of different *ideas* in the same subject, and that is that there is no discoverable connection between any *secondary quality and those primary qualities* which it depends on.

13. That the size, figure, and motion of one body should cause a change in the size, figure, and motion of another body is not beyond our conception. The separation of the parts of one body upon the intrusion of another and the change from rest to motion upon impulse, these and the like seem to have some *connection* one with another. And if we knew these primary qualities of bodies, we might have reason to hope we might be able to know a great deal more of these operations of them one upon another. But our minds not being able to discover any *connection* between these primary qualities of bodies and the sensations that are produced in us by them, we can never be able to establish certain and undoubted rules of the consequence or *coexistence* of any secondary qualities, though we could discover the size, figure, or motion of those invisible parts which immediately produce them. We are so far from knowing what figure, size, or motion of parts produce a yellow color, a sweet taste, or a sharp sound, that we can by no means conceive how any *size, figure,* or *motion* of any particles can possibly produce in us the *idea* of any *color, taste,* or *sound* whatsoever; there is no conceivable *connection* between the one and the other.

14. In vain, therefore, shall we endeavor to discover by our *ideas* (the only true way of certain and universal knowledge) what other *ideas* are to be found constantly joined with that of our complex *idea* of any substance. Since we neither know the real constitution of the minute parts on which their qualities do depend, nor, did we know them, could we discover any necessary *connection* between them and any of the *secondary qualities*; which is necessary to be done before we can certainly know their *necessary coexistence*. So that, let our complex *idea* of any species of substances be what it will, we can hardly, from the simple *ideas* contained in it, certainly determine the necessary coexistence of any other quality whatsoever. Our knowledge in all these inquiries reaches very little further than our experience. Indeed, some few of the primary qualities have a necessary dependence and visible connection one with another, as figure necessarily supposes extension. Receiving or communicating motion by impulse supposes solidity. But though these and perhaps some others of our *ideas* have, yet there are so *few* of them that have a *visible connection* one with another, that we can by intuition or demonstration discover the coexistence of very few of the qualities that are to be found united in substances. And we are left only to the assistance of our senses to make known to us what qualities they contain. For of all the qualities that are *coexistent* in any subject, without this dependence and evident connection of their *ideas* one with another, we cannot know certainly any two to *coexist* any further than experience, by our senses, informs us. Thus, though we see the yellow color and, upon trial, find the weight, malleableness, fusibility, and fixedness that are united in a piece of gold, yet because no one of these *ideas* has any evident *dependence* or necessary connection with the other, we cannot certainly know that where any four of these are, the fifth will be there also, however highly probable it may be, because the highest probability amounts not to certainty, without which there can be no true knowledge. For this *coexistence* can be no further known than it is perceived; and it cannot be perceived but either in particular subjects, by the observation of our senses, or in general, by the necessary *connection* of the *ideas* themselves.

15. *Of repugnance to coexist, larger. As to the incompatibility* or *repugnance to coexistence*, we may know that any subject may have of each sort of primary qualities, but one particular at once: e.g., each particular extension, figure, number of parts, motion, excludes all other of each kind. The like also is certain of all sensible *ideas* peculiar to each sense, for whatever of each kind is present in any subject excludes all others of that sort: e.g., no one subject can have two smells or two colors at the same time. To this perhaps will be said, has not an opal, or the infusion of *lignum nephriticum,* two colors at the same time? To which I answer that these bodies, to eyes differently placed, may at the same time afford different colors. But I take liberty also to say that to eyes differently placed, it is different parts of the object that reflect the particles of light. And therefore it is not the same part of the object, and so not the very same subject,

which at the same time appears both yellow and azure. For it is as impossible that the very same particle of any body should at the same time differently modify or reflect the rays of light as that it should have two different figures and textures at the same time.

16. *Of the coexistence of powers, a very little way.* But *as to the powers of substances* to change the sensible qualities of other bodies, which make a great part of our inquiries about them and is no inconsiderable branch of our knowledge, I doubt as to these whether *our knowledge reaches* much further than our experience or whether we can come to the discovery of most of these powers and be certain that they are in any subject by the connection with any of those *ideas* which to us make its essence. Because the active and passive powers of bodies and their ways of operating, consisting in a texture and motion of parts which we cannot by any means come to discover, it is but in very few cases we can be able to perceive their dependence on, or repugnance to, any of those *ideas* which make our complex one of that sort of things. I have here instanced in the corpuscularian hypothesis as that which is thought to go furthest in an intelligible explication of those qualities of bodies; and I fear the weakness of human understanding is scarcely able to substitute another which will afford us a fuller and clearer discovery of the necessary connection and *coexistence* of the powers which are to be observed united in several sorts of them. This at least is certain, that whichever hypothesis is clearest and truest (for of that it is not my business to determine), our knowledge concerning corporeal substances will be very little advanced by any of them until we are made to see what qualities and powers of bodies have a *necessary connection or repugnance* one with another—which in the present state of philosophy, I think, we know but to a very small degree. And I doubt whether with those faculties we have we shall ever be able to carry our general knowledge (I say not particular experience) in this part much further. Experience is that which in this part we must depend on. And it is to be wished that it would be more improved. We find the advantages [that] some men's generous pains have [in] this way brought to the stock of natural knowledge. And if others, especially the philosophers by fire, who pretend to it, had been so wary in their

observations and sincere in their reports as those who call themselves philosophers ought to have been, our acquaintance with the bodies here about us and our insight into their powers and operations had been yet much greater.

17. *Of the spirits yet narrower.* If we are at a loss in respect of the powers and operations of bodies, I think it is easy to conclude, *we are much more in the dark in reference to spirits*; of which we naturally have no *ideas* but what we draw from that of our own by reflecting on the operations of our own souls within us as far as they can come within our observation. But how inconsiderable a rank the spirits that inhabit our bodies hold among those various and possibly innumerable kinds of nobler beings, and how far short they come of the endowments and perfections of cherubims and seraphims and infinite sorts of spirits above us, is what, by a transient hint in another place, I have offered to my reader's consideration.

18. *Thirdly, of other relations, it is not easy to say how far. Morality capable of demonstration.* As to the third sort of our knowledge, namely, the *agreement or disagreement of any of our* ideas *in any other relation*, this, as it is the largest field of our knowledge, so it is hard to determine how far it may extend. Because the advances that are made in this part of knowledge, depending on our sagacity in finding intermediate *ideas* that may show the *relations* and *habitudes* of *ideas* whose coexistence is not considered, it is a hard matter to tell when we are at an end of such discoveries and when reason has all the helps it is capable of for the finding of proofs or examining the agreement or disagreement of remote *ideas*. They who are ignorant of *algebra* cannot imagine the wonders in this kind are to be done by it. And what further improvements and helps, advantageous to other parts of knowledge, the sagacious mind of man may yet find out, it is not easy to determine. This, at least, I believe, that the *ideas* of quantity are not those alone that are capable of demonstration and knowledge, and that other and perhaps more useful parts of contemplation would afford us certainty if vices, passions, and domineering interest did not oppose or menace such endeavors.

The *idea* of a supreme being, infinite in power, goodness, and wisdom, whose workmanship we are and on whom we depend, and the *idea* of our selves as understanding rational creatures, being such as are clear in us, would, I suppose, if duly considered and pursued, afford such foundations of our duty and rules of action as might place *morality among the sciences capable of demonstration;* in which I do not doubt but from self-evident propositions by necessary consequences as incontestable as those in mathematics, the measures of right and wrong might be made out to anyone who will apply himself with the same indifference and attention to the one as he does to the other of these sciences. The *relation* of other *modes* may certainly be perceived as well as those of number and extension. And I cannot see why they should not also be capable of demonstration if due methods were thought on to examine or pursue their agreement or disagreement. "*Where there is no property, there is no injustice,*" is a proposition as certain as any demonstration in *Euclid.* For the *idea* of *property* being a right to anything, and the *idea* to which the name *injustice* is given being the invasion or violation of that right, it is evident that, these *ideas* being thus established and these names annexed to them, I can as certainly know this proposition to be true as that a triangle has three angles equal to two right ones. Again, "*No government allows absolute liberty.*" The *idea* of government being the establishment of society upon certain rules or laws which require conformity to them, and the *idea* of absolute liberty being for anyone to do whatever he pleases, I am as capable of being certain of the truth of this proposition as of any in the mathematics.

19. *Two things have made moral ideas thought incapable of demonstration. Their complexity and want of sensible representations.* That which in this respect has given the advantage to the *ideas* of quantity and made them thought more capable of certainty and demonstration is:

First, that they can be set down and represented by sensible marks, which have a greater and nearer correspondence with them than any words or sounds whatsoever. Diagrams drawn on paper are copies of the *ideas* in the mind and not liable to the uncertainty that words carry in their signification. An angle, circle, or square drawn in lines lies open to the view and cannot be mistaken. It remains unchangeable and

may at leisure be considered and examined, and the demonstration be revised, and all the parts of it may be gone over more than once without any danger of the least change in the *ideas.* This cannot be thus done in *moral ideas;* we have no sensible marks that resemble them by which we can set them down; we have nothing but words to express them by, which though when written they remain the same, yet the *ideas* they stand for may change in the same man; and it is very seldom that they are not different in different persons.

Secondly, another thing that makes the greater difficulty in *ethics* is that *moral ideas* are commonly more complex than those of the figures ordinarily considered in mathematics. From this these two inconveniences follow: *first,* that their names are of more uncertain signification, the precise collection of simple *ideas* they stand for not being so easily agreed on, and so the sign that is used for them in communication always, and in thinking often, does not steadily carry with it the same *idea,* upon which the same disorder, confusion, and error follow as would if a man, going to demonstrate something of an heptagon, should in the diagram he took to do it leave out one of the angles, or by oversight make the figure with one angle more than the name ordinarily imported or he intended it should when at first he thought of his demonstration. This often happens and is hardly avoidable in very complex moral *ideas,* where the same name being retained, one angle, i.e., one simple *idea,* is left out or put in the complex one (still called by the same name) more at one time than another. *Secondly,* from the complexity of these moral *ideas* there follows another inconvenience, namely, that the mind cannot easily retain those precise combinations so exactly and perfectly as is necessary in the examination of the habitudes and correspondences, agreements, or disagreements of several of them one with another, especially where it is to be judged of by long deductions and the intervention of several other complex *ideas* to show the agreement or disagreement of two remote ones.

The great help against this which mathematicians find in diagrams and figures which remain unalterable in their drafts is very apparent, and the memory would often have great difficulty otherwise to retain them so exactly while the mind went over the parts of them step by step to examine their several correspondences. And though in casting up a long sum either in addition, multiplication, or division, every part is only a progression of the mind taking a view of its own *ideas* and considering their agreement or disagreement; and the resolution of the question is nothing but the result of the whole, made up of such particulars of which the mind has a clear perception. Yet without setting down the several parts by marks whose precise significations are known and by marks that last and remain in view when the memory had let them go, it would be almost impossible to carry so many different *ideas* in the mind without confounding or letting slip some parts of the reckoning and thereby making all our reasonings about it useless. In which case the ciphers or marks help not the mind at all to perceive the agreement of any two or more numbers, their equalities or proportions; that the mind has only by intuition of its own *ideas* of the numbers themselves. But the numerical characters are helps to the memory to record and retain the several *ideas* about which the demonstration is made by which a man may know how far his intuitive knowledge, in surveying several of the particulars, has proceeded; that so he may without confusion go on to what is yet unknown and at last have in one view before him the result of all his perceptions and reasonings.

20. *Remedies of those difficulties.* One part of *these disadvantages* in moral *ideas*, which has made them be thought not capable of demonstration, may in a good measure be *remedied* by definitions, setting down that collection of simple *ideas* which every term shall stand for, and then using the terms steadily and constantly for that precise collection. And what methods algebra or something of that kind may hereafter suggest to remove the other difficulties, it is not easy to foretell. Confident I am that if men would, in the same method and with the same indifference, search after moral as they do mathematical truths, they would find them have a stronger connection one with another and a more necessary consequence from our clear and distinct *ideas*, and to come nearer perfect demonstration than is commonly imagined. [. . .]

21. *Fourthly, of real existence we have an intuitive knowledge of our own, demonstrative of God's, sensible of some few other things.* As to the fourth sort of our knowledge, namely, *of the real actual existence* of things, we have an intuitive knowledge of our own *existence*; and a demonstrative knowledge of the *existence* of a God; of the *existence* of anything else, we have no other but a sensitive knowledge which does not extend beyond the objects present to our senses.

22. *Our ignorance great.* Our knowledge being so narrow as I have shown, it will perhaps give us some light into the present state of our minds if we look a little into the dark side and take a view of *our ignorance*, which, being infinitely larger than our knowledge, may serve much to the quieting of disputes and improvement of useful knowledge. If, discovering how far we have clear and distinct *ideas*, we confine our thoughts within the contemplation of those things that are within the reach of our understandings and do not launch out into that abyss of darkness (where we do not have eyes to see, nor faculties to perceive anything) out of a presumption that nothing is beyond our comprehension, we need not go far to be satisfied of the folly of such a conceit. He who knows anything knows this in the first place, that he does not need to seek long for instances of his ignorance. The meanest and most obvious things that come in our way have dark sides that the quickest sight cannot penetrate into. The clearest and most enlarged understandings of thinking men find themselves puzzled, and at a loss, in every particle of matter. We shall the less wonder to find it so when we consider the *causes of our ignorance*, which, from what has been said, I suppose, will be found to be these three:

First, want of *ideas*.

Secondly, want of a discoverable connection between the *ideas* we have.

Thirdly, want of tracing and examining our *ideas*.

23. *First, one cause of it, want of ideas, either such as we have no conception of or such as particularly we have not.* First, there are some things, and those not a few, that we are ignorant of for *want of ideas*.

First, all the simple *ideas* we have are confined (as I have shown) to those we receive from corporeal objects by sensation and from the operations of our own minds as the objects of reflection. But how much these few and narrow inlets are disproportionate to the vast whole extent of all beings will not be hard to persuade those who are not so foolish as to think their span the measure of all things. What other simple *ideas* it is possible the creatures in other parts of the universe may have by the assistance of senses and faculties more or more perfect than we have or different from ours, it is not for us to determine. But to say or think there are no such because we conceive nothing of them, is no better an argument than if a blind man should be positive in it that there was no such thing as sight and colors because he had no manner of *idea* of any such thing nor could by any means frame to himself any notions about seeing. [. . .]

24. *Because of their remoteness. Secondly,* another great cause of ignorance is the *want of* ideas *we are capable of.* As the want of *ideas* which our faculties are not able to give us shuts us wholly from those views of things which it is reasonable to think other beings more perfect than we have, of which we know nothing, so the want of *ideas* I now speak of keeps us in ignorance of things we conceive capable of being known to us. *Bulk, figure,* and *motion* we have *ideas* of. But though we are not without *ideas* of these primary qualities of bodies in general, yet not knowing what is the particular *bulk, figure,* and *motion* of the greatest part of the bodies of the universe, we are ignorant of the several powers, efficacies, and ways of operation by which the effects, which we daily see, are produced. These are hidden from us, in some things by being *too remote and* in others by being too *minute.* When we consider the vast distance of the known and visible parts of the world and the reasons we have to think that what lies within our ken is but a small part of the universe, we shall then discover a huge abyss of ignorance. What are the particular fabrics of the great masses of matter which make up the whole stupendous frame of corporeal beings, how far they are extended, what is their motion and how continued or communicated, and what influence they have one upon another, are contemplations that, at first glimpse, our thoughts lose themselves in. If we narrow our contemplations and confine our thoughts to this little canton, I mean this system of our sun and the grosser masses of matter that visibly move about it, what several sorts of vegetables, ani-

mals, and intellectual corporeal beings, infinitely different from those of our little spot of earth, may there probably be in the other planets, to the knowledge of which, even of their outward figures and parts, we can no way attain while we are confined to this earth, there being no natural means, either by sensation or reflection, to convey their certain *ideas* into our minds? They are out of the reach of those inlets of all our knowledge. And what sorts of furniture and inhabitants those mansions contain in them, we cannot so much as guess, much less have clear and distinct *ideas* of them.

25. *Because of their minuteness.* If a great, no, far the greatest part of the several ranks of *bodies* in the universe escape our notice by their remoteness, there are others that are no less concealed from us by their *minuteness.* These insensible corpuscles being the active parts of matter and the great instruments of nature on which depend not only all their secondary qualities but also most of their natural operations, our want of precise distinct *ideas* of their primary qualities keeps us in an incurable ignorance of what we desire to know about them. I do not doubt but if we could discover the figure, size, texture, and motion of the minute constituent parts of any two bodies, we should know without trial several of their operations one upon another, as we do now the properties of a square or a triangle. Did we know the mechanical affections of the particles of *rhubarb, hemlock, opium,* and a *man*; as a watchmaker does those of a watch by which it performs its operations, and of a file which, by rubbing on them, will alter the figure of any of the wheels, we should be able to tell beforehand that *rhubarb* will purge, *hemlock* kill, and *opium* make a man sleep, as well as a watchmaker can that a little piece of paper laid on the balance will keep the watch from going until it is removed, or that, some small part of it being rubbed by a file, the machine would quite lose its motion and the watch go no more. The dissolving of silver in *aqua fortis,* and gold in *aqua regia,* and not vice versa, would be then perhaps no more difficult to know than it is to a smith to understand why the turning of one key will open a lock, and not the turning of another. But while we are destitute of senses acute enough to discover the minute particles of bodies and to give us *ideas* of their

mechanical affections, we must be content to be ignorant of their properties and ways of operation; nor can we be assured about them any further than some few trials we make are able to reach. But whether they will succeed again another time we cannot be certain. This hinders our certain knowledge of universal truths concerning natural bodies; and our reason carries us here very little beyond particular matter of fact.

26. *Hence no science of bodies.* And therefore I am apt to doubt that, however far human industry may advance useful and *experimental* philosophy *in physical things, scientific* will still be out of our reach, because we want perfect and adequate *ideas* of those very bodies which are nearest to us and most under our command. Those which we have ranked into classes under names and we think ourselves best acquainted with, we have but very imperfect and incomplete *ideas* of. Distinct *ideas* of the several sorts of bodies that fall under the examination of our senses perhaps we may have. But adequate *ideas*, I suspect, we do not have of anyone among them. And though the former of these will serve us for common use and discourse, yet while we want the latter, we are not capable of *scientific knowledge*; nor shall ever be able to discover general, instructive, unquestionable truths concerning them. *Certainty* and *demonstration* are things we must not, in these matters, pretend to. By the color, figure, taste, and smell, and other sensible qualities, we have as clear and distinct *ideas* of sage and hemlock as we have of a circle and a triangle. But having no *ideas* of the particular primary qualities of the minute parts of either of these plants, nor of other bodies which we would apply them to, we cannot tell what effects they will produce; nor when we see those effects can we so much as guess, much less know, their manner of production. [. . .]

28. *Secondly, want of a discoverable connection between* ideas *we have. Secondly,* what a small part of the substantial beings that are in the universe the want of *ideas* leaves open to our knowledge, we have seen. In the next place, another cause of ignorance, of no less moment, is a want of a *discoverable connection* between those *ideas* we have. For wherever we want that, we are utterly incapable of universal and certain knowledge and are, in the former case, left only to

observation and experiment, which, how narrow and confined it is, how far from general knowledge, we need not be told. I shall give some few instances of this cause of our ignorance and so leave it. It is evident that the bulk, figure, and motion of several bodies about us produce in us several sensations, as of colors, sounds, tastes, smells, pleasure and pain, etc. These mechanical affections of bodies having no affinity at all with those *ideas* they produce in us (there being no conceivable connection between any impulse of any sort of body and any perception of a color or smell which we find in our minds), we can have no distinct knowledge of such operations beyond our experience and can reason no otherwise about them than as effects produced by the appointment of an infinitely wise agent which perfectly surpass our comprehensions. As the *ideas* of sensible secondary qualities which we have in our minds can by us be no way deduced from bodily causes, nor any correspondence or connection be found between them and those primary qualities which (experience shows us) produce them in us, so on the other side, the operation of our minds upon our bodies is as inconceivable. How any thought should produce a motion in body is as remote from the nature of our *ideas* as how any body should produce any thought in the mind; that it is so, if experience did not convince us, the consideration of the things themselves would never be able in the least to discover to us. These, and the like, though they have a constant and regular connection in the ordinary course of things, yet that connection being not discoverable in the *ideas* themselves, which, appearing to have no necessary dependence one on another, we can attribute their connection to nothing else but the arbitrary determination of that all-wise agent who has made them to be and to operate as they do, in a way wholly above our weak understandings to conceive.

29. *Instances.* In some of our *ideas* there are certain relations, habitudes, and connections so visibly included in the nature of the *ideas* themselves that we cannot conceive them separable from them by any power whatsoever. And in these only we are capable of certain and universal knowledge. Thus the *idea* of a right-lined triangle necessarily carries with it an equality of its angles to two right ones. Nor can we

conceive this relation, this connection of these two *ideas*, to be possibly mutable or to depend on any arbitrary power which of choice made it thus or could make it otherwise. But the coherence and continuity of the parts of matter, the production of sensation in us of colors and sounds, etc., by impulse and motion—no, the original rules and communication of motion being such that we can discover no natural connection with any *ideas* we have in them—we cannot but ascribe them to the arbitrary will and good pleasure of the wise architect. I need not, I think, here mention the resurrection of the dead, the future state of this globe of earth, and such other things which are by everyone acknowledged to depend wholly on the determination of a free agent. The things that, as far as our observation reaches, we constantly find to proceed regularly, we may conclude do act by a law set them, but yet by a law that we know not. Though causes work steadily in this and effects constantly flow from them, yet their *connections* and *dependencies* being not discoverable in our *ideas*, we can have but an experimental knowledge of them. From all this it is easy to perceive what a darkness we are involved in, how little it is of being, and the things that are that we are capable to know. And therefore we shall do no injury to our knowledge when we modestly think with ourselves that we are so far from being able to comprehend the whole nature of the universe and all the things contained in it that we are not capable of a philosophical knowledge of the bodies that are about us and make a part of us. Concerning their secondary qualities, powers, and operations, we can have no universal certainty. Several effects come every day within the notice of our senses, of which we have so far *sensitive knowledge*; but the causes, manner, and certainty of their production, for the two foregoing reasons, we must be content to be very ignorant of. In these we can go no further than particular experience informs us of matter of fact and, by analogy, to guess what effects the like bodies are, upon other trials, like to produce. But as to a perfect *science* of natural bodies (not to mention spiritual beings) we are, I think, so far from being capable of any such thing that I conclude it lost labor to seek after it.

30. *Thirdly, want of tracing our* ideas. Thirdly, where we have adequate *ideas*, and where there is a certain and discoverable connection between them, yet we are often ignorant, for want of *tracing* those *ideas* which we have, or may have, and for want of finding out those intermediate *ideas* which may show us what habitude of agreement or disagreement they have one with another. And thus many are ignorant of mathematical truths, not out of any imperfection of their faculties or uncertainty in the things themselves, but for lack of application in acquiring, examining, and by due ways comparing those *ideas*; that which has most contributed to hinder the due *tracing* of our *ideas* and finding out their relations and agreements or disagreements one with another has been, I suppose, the ill use of *words*. It is impossible that men should ever truly seek or certainly discover the agreement or disagreement of *ideas* themselves, while their thoughts flutter about or stick only in sounds of doubtful and uncertain significations. Mathematicians, abstracting their thoughts from names and accustoming themselves to set before their minds the *ideas* themselves that they would consider, and not sounds instead of them, have avoided by these means a great part of that perplexity, puddering, and confusion which has so much hindered men's progress in other parts of knowledge. For while they stick in words of undetermined and uncertain signification, they are unable to distinguish true from false, certain from probable, consistent from inconsistent in their own opinions. This having been the fate or misfortune of a great part of men of letters, the increase brought into the stock of real knowledge has been very little in proportion to the schools, disputes, and writings the world has been filled with, while students, being lost in the great wood of words, did not know where they were, how far their discoveries were advanced, or what was wanting in their own or the general stock of knowledge. Had men, in the discoveries of the material, done as they have in those of the intellectual world, [that is,] involved all in the obscurity of uncertain and doubtful ways of talking, [then] volumes written of navigation and voyages, theories and stories of zones and tides multiplied and disputed, no, ships built and fleets sent out would never have taught us the way beyond the line, and the Antipodes would be still as much unknown as when it was declared

heresy to hold there were any. But having spoken sufficiently of words and the ill or careless use that is commonly made of them, I shall not say anything more of it here.

31. *Extent in respect of universality.* Up to now we have examined the *extent* of our knowledge in respect of the several sorts of beings that are. There is another *extent of it in respect of universality* which will also deserve to be considered; and in this regard, our knowledge follows the nature of our *ideas.* If the *ideas* are abstract whose agreement or disagreement we perceive, our knowledge is universal. For what is known of such general *ideas* will be true of every particular thing in whom that essence, i.e., that abstract *idea,* is to be found, and what is once known of such *ideas* will be perpetually and forever true, so that as to all general knowledge we must search and find it only in our minds, and it is only the examining of our own *ideas* that furnishes us with that. Truths belonging to essences of things (that is, to abstract *ideas*) are eternal and are to be found out by the contemplation only of those essences, as the existence of things is to be known only from experience. But having more to say of this in the chapters where I shall speak of general and real knowledge, this may here suffice as to the universality of our knowledge in general.

Chapter 4. *Of the Reality of Knowledge.*

1. *Objection, knowledge placed in* ideas *may be all bare vision.* I do not doubt but my reader by this time may be apt to think that I have been all this while only building a castle in the air, and be ready to say to me, "To what purpose all this stir? Knowledge, you say, is only the perception of the agreement or disagreement of our own *ideas.* But who knows what those *ideas* may be? Is there anything so extravagant as the imaginations of men's brains? Where is the head that has no *chimeras* in it? Or if there is a sober and a wise man, what difference will there be, by your rules, between his knowledge and that of the most extravagant fancy in the world? They both have their *ideas* and perceive their agreement and disagreement one with another. If there is any difference between them, the advantage will be on the warm-headed man's side as having the more *ideas,* and the more lively. And so, by your rules, he will be the more knowing. If it is true that all knowledge lies only in the perception of the agreement or disagreement of our own *ideas,* the visions of an enthusiast and the reasonings of a sober man will be equally certain. It is no matter how things are; so a man observes but the agreement of his own imaginations and talks conformably, it is all truth, all certainty. Such castles in the air will be as strongholds of truth as the demonstrations of *Euclid.* That a harpy is not a centaur is by this way as certain knowledge, and as much a truth, as that a square is not a circle.

But *of what use is all this fine knowledge of men's own imaginations* to a man who inquires after the reality of things? It does not matter what men's fancies are, it is the knowledge of things that is only to be prized. It is this alone gives a value to our reasonings and preference to one man's knowledge over another's that it is of things as they really are, and not of dreams and fancies.

2. *Answer. Not so, where* ideas *agree with things.* To which I answer that if our knowledge of our *ideas* terminate in them and reach no further where there is something further intended, our most serious thoughts will be of little more use than the reveries of a crazy brain and the truths built upon this of no more weight than the discourses of a man who sees things clearly in a dream and with great assurance utters them. But, I hope, before I have done, to make it evident that this way of certainty, by the knowledge of our own *ideas,* goes a little further than bare imagination. And I believe it will appear that all the certainty of general truths a man has lies in nothing else.

3. It is evident the mind does not know things immediately, but only by the intervention of the *ideas* it has of them. *Our knowledge* therefore is *real* only so far as there is a conformity between our *ideas* and the reality of things. But what shall be here the criterion? How shall the mind, when it perceives nothing but its own *ideas,* know that they agree with things themselves? This, though it seems not to want difficulty, yet, I think, there are two sorts of *ideas* that we may be assured, agree with things.

4. *As, first, all simple* ideas *do. First,* the first are simple *ideas,* which since the mind, as has been

shown, can by no means make to itself, must necessarily be the product of things operating on the mind in a natural way, and producing in there those perceptions which by the wisdom and will of our maker they are ordained and adapted to. From which it follows that *simple* ideas *are not fictions* of our fancies but the natural and regular productions of things without us really operating upon us, and so carry with them all the conformity which is intended or which our state requires. For they represent to us things under those appearances which they are fitted to produce in us, by which we are enabled to distinguish the sorts of particular substances, to discern the states they are in, and so to take them for our necessities and apply them to our uses. Thus the *idea* of whiteness or bitterness, as it is in the mind, exactly answering that power which is in any body to produce it there, has all the real conformity it can or ought to have with things without us. And this conformity between our simple *ideas* and the existence of things is sufficient for real knowledge.

5. *Secondly, all complex* ideas, *except of substances.* Secondly, all our complex ideas, *except those of substances,* being *archetypes* of the mind's own making, not intended to be the copies of anything nor referred to the existence of anything, as to their origins, *cannot want any conformity necessary to real knowledge.* For that which is not designed to represent anything but itself can never be capable of a wrong representation nor mislead us from the true apprehension of anything by its dislikeness to it; and such, excepting those of substances, are all our complex *ideas,* which, as I have shown in another place, are combinations of *ideas* which the mind, by its free choice, puts together without considering any connection they have in nature. And hence it is, that in all these sorts the *ideas* themselves are considered as the archetypes, and things no otherwise regarded but as they are conformable to them. So that we cannot but be infallibly certain that all the knowledge we attain concerning these *ideas* is real, and reaches things themselves, because in all our thoughts, reasonings, and discourses of this kind, we intend things no further than as they are conformable to our *ideas.* So that in these we cannot miss of a certain and undoubted reality.

6. *Hence the reality of mathematical knowledge.* I do not doubt but it will be easily granted that the *knowledge* we have of *mathematical truths* is not only certain, but *real knowledge* and not the bare empty vision of vain insignificant *chimeras* of the brain. And yet, if we will consider, we shall find that it is only of our own *ideas.* The mathematician considers the truth and properties belonging to a rectangle or circle only as they are in *idea* in his own mind. For it is possible he never found either of them existing mathematically, i.e., precisely true, in his life. But yet the knowledge he has of any truths or properties belonging to a circle or any other mathematical figure is nevertheless true and certain, even of real things existing, because real things are no further concerned, nor intended to be meant by any such propositions, than as things really agree to those *archetypes* in his mind. Is it true of the *idea* of a *triangle* that its three angles are equal to two right ones? It is true also of a *triangle* wherever it really exists. Whatever other figure exists that is not exactly answerable to that *idea* of a *triangle* in his mind is not at all concerned in that proposition. And therefore he is certain all his knowledge concerning such *ideas* is real knowledge, because intending things no further than they agree with those his *ideas,* he is sure [that] what he knows concerning those figures when they have barely an *ideal existence* in his mind will hold true of them also when they have real existence in matter, his consideration being barely of those figures which are the same, wherever or however they exist.

7. *And of moral.* And hence it follows that *moral knowledge* is as *capable of real certainty* as mathematics. For certainty being but the perception of the agreement or disagreement of our *ideas*; and demonstration nothing but the perception of such agreement by the intervention of other *ideas* or mediums; our moral *ideas* as well as mathematical, being archetypes themselves, and so adequate and complete *ideas*; all the agreement or disagreement which we shall find in them will produce real knowledge, as well as in mathematical figures.

8. *Existence not required to make it real.* For the attaining of knowledge and certainty, it is requisite that we have determined *ideas,* and to make our knowledge *real,* it is requisite that the *ideas* answer their *archetypes.* Nor let it be wondered that I place

the certainty of our knowledge in the consideration of our *ideas*, with so little care and regard (as it may seem) to the real existence of things. Since most of those discourses which take up the thoughts and engage the disputes of those who pretend to make it their business to inquire after truth and certainty, will, I presume, upon examination be found to be *general propositions* and notions in which existence is not at all concerned. All the discourses of the mathematicians about the squaring of a circle, conic sections, or any other part of mathematics, *do not concern* the *existence* of any of those figures, but their demonstrations, which depend on their *ideas*, are the same whether there is any square or circle existing in the world or not. In the same manner the truth and certainty of *moral* discourses abstract from the lives of men, and the existence of those virtues in the world of which they treat. Nor are *Tully's* offices less true because there is nobody in the world who exactly practices his rules and lives up to that pattern of a virtuous man which he has given us and which existed nowhere when he wrote, but in *idea*. If it is true in speculation, i.e., in *idea*, that *murder deserves death*, it will also be true in reality of any action that exists conformable to that *idea of murder*. [...]

11. Ideas *of substances have their archetypes without us. Thirdly*, there is another sort of *complex ideas* which, being referred to *archetypes* without us, may differ from them, and so our knowledge about them may come short of being real. Such are our *ideas* of substances, which, consisting of a collection of simple *ideas* supposed taken from the works of nature, may yet vary from them by having more or different *ideas* united in them than are to be found united in the things themselves. From this it comes to pass that they may, and often do, fail of being exactly conformable to things themselves.

12. So *far as they agree with those so far our knowledge concerning them is real*. I say then that to have *ideas* of *substances* which, by being conformable to things, may afford us real knowledge, it is not enough, as in modes, to put together such *ideas* as have no inconsistency, though they did never before so exist: e.g., the *ideas* of *sacrilege* or *perjury*, etc., were as real and true *ideas* before as after the existence of any such fact. But *our ideas of substances*, being supposed copies and referred to *archetypes* without us, must still be taken from something that does or has existed; they must not consist of *ideas* put together at the pleasure of our thoughts, without any real pattern they were taken from, though we can perceive no inconsistency in such a combination. The reason of this is because we, knowing not what real constitution it is of substances on which our simple *ideas* depend, and which really is the cause of the strict union of some of them one with another and the exclusion of others, there are very few of them that we can be sure are or are not inconsistent in nature any further than experience and sensible observation reach. In this, therefore, is founded the *reality* of our knowledge concerning *substances*, that all our complex *ideas* of them must be such, and such only, as are made up of such simple ones as have been discovered to coexist in nature. And our *ideas*, being thus true, though not, perhaps, very exact copies, are yet the subjects of *real* (as far as we have any) *knowledge* of them—which (as has been already shown) will not be found to reach very far; but so far as it does, it will still be *real knowledge*. [...]

Chapter 10. *Of Our Knowledge of the Existence of a God.*

1. *We are capable of knowing certainly that there is a God.* Though God has given us no innate *ideas* of himself, though he has stamped no original characters on our minds in which we may read his being, yet having furnished us with those faculties our minds are endowed with, he has not left himself without witness, since we have sense, perception, and reason, and cannot want a clear proof of him as long as we carry ourselves about us. Nor can we justly complain of our ignorance in this great point, since he has so plentifully provided us with the means to discover and know him, so far as is necessary, to the end of our being, and the great importance of our happiness. But though this is the most obvious truth that reason discovers, and though its evidence is (if I am not mistaken) equal to mathematical certainty, yet it requires thought and attention and the mind must apply itself to a regular deduction of it from some part of our intuitive knowledge, or else we shall be as uncer-

tain and ignorant of this as of other propositions which are in themselves capable of clear demonstration. To show, therefore, that we are capable of *knowing*, i.e., *being certain that there is a* God and how we may come by this certainty, I think we need go no further than ourselves and that undoubted knowledge we have of our own existence.

2. *Man knows that he himself is.* I think it is beyond question that *man has a clear idea of his own being;* he knows certainly he exists and that he is something. He who can doubt whether he is anything or not, I do not speak to, no more than I would argue with pure nothing or endeavor to convince nonentity that it were something. If anyone pretends to be so skeptical as to deny his own existence (for really to doubt of it is manifestly impossible), let him for me enjoy his beloved happiness of being nothing, until hunger or some other pain convinces him of the contrary. This then, I think, I may take for a truth which everyone's certain knowledge assures him of beyond the liberty of doubting, namely, that he is something that actually exists.

3. *He knows also that nothing cannot produce a being, therefore something eternal.* In the next place, man knows by an intuitive certainty that bare *nothing can no more produce any real being than it can be equal to two right angles.* If a man does not know that nonentity, or the absence of all being, cannot be equal to two right angles, it is impossible he should know any demonstration in *Euclid.* If, therefore, we know there is some real being, and that nonentity cannot produce any real being, it is an evident demonstration that from eternity there has been something, since what was not from eternity had a beginning and what had a beginning must be produced by something else.

4. That *eternal Being must be most powerful.* Next, it is evident that what had its being and beginning from another must also have all that which is in and belongs to its being from another too. All the powers it has must be owing to and received from the same source. This eternal source, then, of all being must also be the source and origin of all power; and *so this eternal Being must be also the most powerful.*

5. *And most knowing.* Again, a man finds in himself *perception* and *knowledge.* We have then gotten one

step further, and we are certain now that there is not only some being, but some knowing intelligent being in the world.

There was a time, then, when there was no knowing being and when knowledge began to be; or else there has been also *a knowing being from eternity.* If it is said, there was a time when no being had any knowledge, when that eternal being was void of all understanding, I reply that then it was impossible there should ever have been any knowledge—it being as impossible that things wholly void of knowledge and operating blindly and without any perception, should produce a knowing being, as it is impossible that a triangle should make itself three angles bigger than two right ones. For it is as repugnant to the *idea* of senseless matter that it should put into itself, sense, perception, and knowledge, as it is repugnant to the *idea* of a triangle that it should put into itself greater angles than two right ones.

6. *And therefore God.* Thus from the consideration of ourselves and what we infallibly find in our own constitutions, our reason leads us to the knowledge of this certain and evident truth that *there is an eternal, most powerful, and most knowing being,* which, whether anyone will please to call *God,* it matters not. The thing is evident, and from this *idea* duly considered will easily be deduced all those other attributes which we ought to ascribe to this eternal being. If, nevertheless, anyone should be found so senselessly arrogant as to suppose man alone knowing and wise but yet the product of mere ignorance and chance, and that all the rest of the universe acted only by that blind haphazard, I shall leave with him that very rational and emphatic rebuke of *Tully,* I. ii. *De Leg.,* to be considered at his leisure. "What can be more sillily arrogant and misbecoming than for a man to think that he has a mind and understanding in him, but yet in all the universe besides there is no such thing? Or that those things which with the utmost stretch of his reason he can scarcely comprehend should be moved and managed without any reason at all?" [. . .]

From what has been said, it is plain to me we have a more certain knowledge of the existence of a God than of anything our senses have not immediately discovered to us. No, I presume I may say that we more certainly know that there is a God than that there is anything else without us. When I say we *know*, I mean there is such a knowledge within our reach which we cannot miss if we will but apply our minds to that as we do to several other inquiries.

7. *Our* idea *of a most perfect Being not the sole proof of a God. How far the* idea *of a most perfect Being* which a man may frame in his mind does or does not prove *the existence of a* God, I will not here examine. For in the different make of men's tempers and application of their thoughts, some arguments prevail more on one, and some on another, for the confirmation of the same truth. But yet, I think, this I may say, that it is an ill way of establishing this truth and silencing atheists to lay the whole stress of so important a point as this upon that sole foundation and take some men's having that *idea* of God in their minds (for it is evident some men have none, and some worse than none, and the most very different) for the only proof of a deity. And, out of an over-fondness of that darling invention, dismiss, or at least endeavor to invalidate, all other arguments and forbid us to listen to those proofs as being weak or fallacious which our own existence and the sensible parts of the universe offer so clearly and cogently to our thoughts that I deem it impossible for a considering man to withstand them. For I judge it as certain and clear a truth as can anywhere be delivered that *"the invisible things of* God *are clearly seen from the creation of the world, being understood by the things that are made, even his eternal power and Godhead"* [Romans 1.20] — though our own being furnishes us, as I have shown, with an evident and incontestable proof of a deity, and I believe nobody can avoid the cogency of it who will but as carefully attend to it as to any other demonstration of so many parts. Yet this being so fundamental a truth and of that consequence that all religion and genuine morality depend on it, I do not doubt but I shall be forgiven by my reader if I go over some parts of this argument again and enlarge a little more upon them.

8. *Something from eternity.* There is no truth more evident than that *something* must be *from eternity.* I never yet heard of anyone so unreasonable or that could suppose so manifest a contradiction as a time in which there was perfectly nothing, this being of all absurdities the greatest, to imagine that pure nothing, the perfect negation and absence of all beings, should ever produce any real existence.

It being then unavoidable for all rational creatures to conclude that something has existed from eternity, let us next see what kind of thing that must be.

9. *Two sorts of beings, cogitative and incogitative.* There are but two sorts of beings in the world that man knows or conceives.

First, such as are purely material, without sense, perception, or thought, as the clippings of our beards and parings of our nails.

Secondly, sensible, thinking, perceiving beings, such as we find ourselves to be, which, if you please, we will hereafter call *cogitative and incogitative beings,* which, to our present purpose if for nothing else are perhaps better terms than material and immaterial.

10. *Incogitative being cannot produce a cogitative.* If, then, there must be something eternal, let us see what sort of being it must be. And to that it is very obvious to reason that it must necessarily be a *cogitative* being. For it is as impossible to conceive that ever bare incogitative matter should produce a thinking intelligent being as that nothing should of itself produce matter. Let us suppose any parcel of matter eternal, great or small, we shall find it, in itself, able to produce nothing. For example, let us suppose the matter of the next pebble we meet with eternal closely united and the parts firmly at rest together; if there were no other being in the world, must it not eternally remain so, a dead inactive lump? Is it possible to conceive it can add motion to itself, being purely matter, or produce anything? Matter then, by its own strength, cannot produce in itself so much as motion. The motion it has must also be from eternity, or else be produced and added to matter by some other being more powerful than matter — matter, as is evident, not having power to produce motion in itself. But let us suppose motion eternal, too; yet matter, *incogitative matter* and motion, whatever changes it might produce of figure and bulk, *could never produce thought.* Knowledge will still be as far beyond the power of motion and matter to produce as matter is beyond the power of *nothing* or *nonentity* to produce. And I appeal to everyone's own thoughts, whether he

cannot as easily conceive matter produced by *nothing*, as thought to be produced by pure matter, when, before, there was no such thing as thought or an intelligent being existing? Divide matter into as minute parts as you will (which we are apt to imagine a sort of spiritualizing or making a thinking thing of it) vary the figure and motion of it as much as you please—a globe, cube, cone, prism, cylinder, etc., whose diameters are but 1,000,000th part of a gry,[2] will operate not otherwise upon other bodies of proportional bulk than those of an inch or foot diameter—and you may as rationally expect to produce sense, thought, and knowledge, by putting together, in a certain figure and motion, gross particles of matter, as by those that are the very minutest that do anywhere exist. They knock, impel, and resist one another, just as the greater do; and that is all they can do. So that if we will suppose nothing first, or eternal, *matter* can never begin to be. If we suppose bare matter, without *motion*, eternal motion can never begin to be. If we suppose only matter and motion first, or eternal, *thought* can never begin to be. For it is impossible to conceive that matter, either with or without motion, could have originally in and from itself sense, perception, and knowledge; as is evident from hence that then sense, perception, and knowledge must be a property eternally inseparable from matter and every particle of it. Not to add that though our general or specific conception of matter makes us speak of it as one thing, yet really all matter is not one individual thing, neither is there any such thing existing as one material being, or one single body that we know or can conceive. And, therefore, if matter were the eternal first cogitative being, there would not be one eternal infinite cogitative being, but an infinite number of eternal finite cogitative beings, independent one of another, of limited force and distinct thoughts, which could never produce that order, harmony, and beauty which are to be found in nature. Since therefore whatever is the first eternal *being* must necessarily be cogitative, and whatever is first of all things must necessarily contain in it and actually have, at least, all the perfections that can ever after exist, nor can it ever give to another

any perfection that it has not either actually in itself, or at least in a higher degree, it necessarily follows that the first eternal being cannot be matter.

11. *Therefore there has been an eternal Wisdom.* If therefore it is evident that *something* necessarily must *exist from eternity*, it is also as evident that *that something must* necessarily *be a cogitative being*. For it is as impossible that incogitative matter should produce a cogitative being, as that nothing, or the negation of all being, should produce a positive being or matter.

12. Though this discovery of the *necessary existence of an eternal mind* does sufficiently lead us into the knowledge of God, since it will hence follow that all other knowing beings that have a beginning must depend on him, and have no other ways of knowledge or extent of power than what he gives them; and therefore if he made those, he made also the less excellent pieces of this universe, all inanimate beings, by which his *omniscience*, *power*, and *providence* will be established and all his other attributes necessarily follow. Yet to clear up this a little further, we will see what doubts can be raised against it.

13. *Whether material or not.* First, perhaps it will be said that though it is as clear as demonstration can make it that there must be an eternal being, and that being must also be knowing, yet it does not follow but that thinking being may also be material. Let it be so; it equally still follows that there is a God. For if there is an eternal, omniscient, omnipotent being, it is certain that there is a God, whether you imagine that Being to be material or not. But in this, I suppose, lies the danger and deceit of that supposition. There being no way to avoid the demonstration that there is an eternal knowing being, men, devoted to matter, would willingly have it granted that this knowing being is material, and then, letting slide out of their minds, or the discourse, the demonstration by which an eternal knowing being was proved necessarily to exist, would argue all to be matter, and so deny a God, that is, an eternal cogitative being—by which means, they are so far from establishing that they destroy their own hypothesis. For if there can be, in their opinion, eternal matter without any eternal cogitative being, they manifestly separate matter and thinking and suppose no necessary connection of the one with the other and so establish the necessity of

2. [A "gry" is one hundredth of an inch.]

an eternal spirit, but not of matter, since it has been proved already that an eternal cogitative being is unavoidably to be granted. Now if thinking and matter may be separated, *the eternal existence of matter will not follow from the eternal existence of a cogitative being,* and they suppose it to no purpose.

14. *Not material, first, because every particle of matter is not cogitative.* But now let us see how they can satisfy themselves or others that this *eternal thinking being* is *material.*

First, I would ask them, whether they imagine that all matter, *every particle of matter, thinks?* This, I suppose, they will scarcely say, since then there would be as many eternal thinking beings as there are particles of matter, and so an infinity of gods. And yet if they will not allow matter as matter, that is, every particle of matter to be cogitative as well as extended, they will have as hard a task to make out to their own reasons a cogitative being out of incogitative particles, as an extended being out of unextended parts, if I may so speak.

15. *Secondly, one particle alone of matter cannot be cogitative. Secondly,* if all matter does not think, I next ask "whether it is *only one atom that does so?"* This has as many absurdities as the other, for then this atom of matter must be alone eternal or not. If this alone is eternal, then this alone, by its powerful thought or will, made all the rest of matter. And so we have the creation of matter by a powerful thought, which is what the materialists stick at. For if they suppose one single thinking atom to have produced all the rest of matter, they cannot ascribe that preeminence to it upon any other account than that of its thinking, the only supposed difference. But allow it to be by some other way which is above our conception, it must still be creation, and these men must give up their great maxim, *"ex nihilo nil fit."* If it is said that all the rest of matter is equally eternal as that thinking atom, it will be to say anything at pleasure, though ever so absurd, for to suppose all matter eternal, and yet one small particle in knowledge and power infinitely above all the rest, is without any the least appearance of reason to frame an hypothesis. Every particle of matter as matter is capable of all the same figures and motions of any other; and I

challenge anyone, in his thoughts, to add anything else to one above another.

16. *Thirdly, a system of incogitative matter cannot be cogitative.* If then neither one peculiar atom alone can be this eternal thinking being, nor all matter as matter, i.e., every particle of matter can be [this eternal thinking being], it only remains that it is *some certain system of matter* duly put together that is this *thinking eternal being.* This is that which, I imagine, is that notion which men are most apt to have of God, who would have him a material being, as most readily suggested to them by the ordinary conceit they have of themselves and other men, which they take to be material thinking beings. But this imagination, however more natural, is no less absurd than the other. For to suppose the eternal thinking being to be nothing else but a composition of particles of matter, each of which is incogitative, is to ascribe all the wisdom and knowledge of that eternal being only to the *juxtaposition* of parts—than which nothing can be more absurd. For unthinking particles of matter, however put together, can have nothing thereby added to them but a new relation of position, which it is impossible should give thought and knowledge to them.

17. *Whether in motion or at rest.* But further, this *corporeal system* either has all its parts at rest or it is a certain motion of the parts in which its thinking consists. If it is perfectly at rest, it is but one lump and so can have no privileges above one atom.

If it is the motion of its parts on which its thinking depends, all the thoughts there must be unavoidably accidental and limited, since all the particles that by motion cause thought, being each of them in itself without any thought, cannot regulate its own motions, much less be regulated by the thought of the whole; since that thought is not the cause of motion (for then it must be antecedent to it, and so without it) but the consequence of it, by means of which freedom, power, choice, and all rational and wise thinking or acting will be quite taken away. So that such a thinking being will be no better nor wiser than pure blind matter, since to resolve all into the accidental unguided motions of blind matter, or into thought depending on unguided motions of blind matter, is the same thing—not to mention the narrowness of such thoughts and knowledge that must depend on the motion of such parts. But there needs no enumeration of any more absurdities and impossibilities in this hypothesis (however full of them it be) than that before mentioned, since let this thinking system be all or a part of the matter of the universe, it is impossible that any one particle should either know its own or the motion of any other particle, or [that] the whole know the motion of every particle and so regulate its own thoughts or motions or indeed have any thought resulting from such motion.

18. *Matter not coeternal with an eternal Mind.* Others would have *matter* be *eternal*, notwithstanding that they allow an eternal cogitative immaterial being. This, though it does not take away the being of a God, yet, since it denies one and the first great piece of his workmanship, the creation, let us consider it a little. *Matter* must be allowed eternal. Why? Because you cannot conceive how it can be made out of nothing. Why do you not also think yourself eternal? You will answer, perhaps, because about twenty or forty years since, you began to be. But if I ask you, what is that *you* which began then to be, you can scarcely tell me. The matter of which you are made did not begin then to be, for if it did, then it is not eternal. But it began to be put together in such a fashion and frame as makes up your body; but yet that frame of particles is not you; it does not make that thinking thing you are (for I have now to do with one who allows an eternal immaterial thinking being, but would have unthinking matter eternal too); therefore when did that thinking thing begin to be? If it did never begin to be, then have you always been a thinking thing from eternity—the absurdity of which I need not confute until I meet with one who is so void of understanding as to admit it. If therefore you can allow a thinking thing to be made out of nothing (as all things that are not eternal must be), why also can you not allow it possible for a material being to be made out of nothing by an equal power, but that you have the experience of the one in view and not of the other? Though, when well considered, creation of a spirit will be found to require no less power than the creation of matter. No, possibly, if we would

emancipate ourselves from vulgar notions, and raise our thoughts as far as they would reach, to a closer contemplation of things, we might be able to aim at some dim and seeming conception how matter might at first be made and begin to exist by the power of that eternal first being. But to give beginning and being to a spirit would be found a more inconceivable effect of omnipotent power. But, this being what would perhaps lead us too far from the notions on which the philosophy now in the world is built, it would not be pardonable to deviate so far from them, or to inquire, so far as grammar itself would authorize, if the common settled opinion opposes it, especially in this place where the received doctrine serves well enough to our present purpose and leaves this past doubt that the creation or beginning of any one substance out of nothing, being once admitted, the creation of all other but the Creator himself, may, with the same ease, be supposed.

19. But, you will say, is it not impossible to admit of the *making anything out of nothing*, since we cannot possibly conceive it? I answer, No, because it is not reasonable to deny the power of an infinite being, because we cannot comprehend its operations. We do not deny other effects upon this ground, because we cannot possibly conceive the manner of their production. We cannot conceive how anything but impulse of body can move body, and yet that is not a reason sufficient to make us deny it possible, against the constant experience we have of it in ourselves in all our voluntary motions which are produced in us only by the free action or thought of our own minds and are not, nor can be, the effects of the impulse or determination of the motion of blind matter in or upon our own bodies; for then it could not be in our power or choice to alter it. For example: My right hand writes, while my left hand is still. What causes rest in one, and motion in the other? Nothing but my will, a thought of my mind; my thought only changing, the right hand rests and the left hand moves. This is matter of fact which cannot be denied. Explain this, and make it intelligible, and then the next step will be to understand creation. For the giving a new determination to the motion of the animal spirits (which some make use of to explain voluntary

motion) does not clear the difficulty one jot—to alter the determination of motion being, in this case, no easier nor less than to give motion itself, since the new determination given to the animal spirits must be either immediately by thought or by some other body put in their way by thought, which was not in their way before and so must owe its motion to thought, either of which leaves voluntary motion as unintelligible as it was before. In the meantime it is an overvaluing ourselves to reduce all to the narrow measure of our capacities and to conclude all things impossible to be done whose manner of doing exceeds our comprehension. This is to make our comprehension infinite or God finite, when what he can do is limited to what we can conceive of it. If you do not understand the operations of your own finite mind, that thinking thing within you, do not deem it strange that you cannot comprehend the operations of that eternal infinite mind, who made and governs all things and whom the heaven of heavens cannot contain.

Chapter 11. *Of Our Knowledge of the Existence of Other Things.*

1. *Is to be had only by sensation.* The knowledge of our own being we have by intuition. The existence of a God, reason clearly makes known to us, as has been shown.

The *knowledge of the existence* of any other thing, we can have only by *sensation*. For there being no necessary connection of *real existence* with any *idea* a man has in his memory, nor of any other existence but that of God with the existence of any particular man, no particular man can know the *existence* of any other being but only when, by actual operating upon him, it makes itself perceived by him. For the having the *idea* of anything in our mind no more proves the existence of that thing than the picture of a man evidences his being in the world, or the visions of a dream make, by this means, a true history.

2. *Instance: whiteness of this paper.* It is therefore the actual receiving of *ideas* from without that gives us notice of the *existence* of other things and makes us know that something does exist at that time without us which causes that *idea* in us, though perhaps we

neither know nor consider how it does it. For it does not take, from the certainty of our senses and the *ideas* we receive by them, that we do not know the manner in which they are produced—e.g., while I write this, I have, by the paper affecting my eyes, that *idea* produced in my mind, which, whatever object causes, I call *white*; by this I know that that quality or accident (i.e., whose appearance before my eyes always causes that *idea*) does really exist and has a being without me. And of this the greatest assurance I can possibly have and to which my faculties can attain, is the testimony of my eyes, which are the proper and sole judges of this thing whose testimony I have reason to rely on as so certain that I can no more doubt, while I write this, that I see white and black and that something really exists that causes that sensation in me, than that I write or move my hand—which is a certainty as great as human nature is capable of, concerning the existence of anything but a man's self alone and of God.

3. *This, though not so certain as demonstration, yet may be called knowledge, and proves the existence of things without us. The notice we have by our senses of the existing of things without* us, though it is not altogether so certain as our intuitive knowledge or the deductions of our reason employed about the clear abstract *ideas* of our own minds, yet it is an assurance that *deserves the name of knowledge.* If we persuade ourselves that our faculties act and inform us right concerning the existence of those objects that affect them, it cannot pass for an ill-grounded confidence. For I think nobody can, in earnest, be so skeptical as to be uncertain of the existence of those things which he sees and feels. At least, he who can doubt so far (whatever he may have with his own thoughts) will never have any controversy with me, since he can never be sure I say anything contrary to his own opinion. As to myself, I think God has given me assurance enough of the existence of things without me, since by their different application I can produce in myself both pleasure and pain, which is one great concern of my present state. This is certain: The confidence that our faculties do not deceive us in this is the greatest assurance we are capable of, concerning the existence of material beings. For we cannot act [on] anything but by our faculties, nor

talk of knowledge itself, but by the help of those faculties which are fitted to apprehend even what knowledge is. But besides the assurance we have from our senses themselves that they do not err in the information they give us of the existence of things without us, when they are affected by them, we are further confirmed in this assurance by other concurrent reasons.

4. *First, because we cannot have them but by the inlets of the senses. First,* it is plain those perceptions are produced in us by exterior causes affecting our senses, because *those who want the organs of any sense never can have the* ideas *belonging to that sense* produced in their minds. This is too evident to be doubted. And therefore we cannot but be assured that they come in by the organs of that sense and no other way. The organs themselves, it is plain, do not produce them, for then the eyes of a man in the dark would produce colors and his nose smell roses in the winter. But we see nobody gets the relish of a pineapple until he goes to the *Indies,* where it is, and tastes it.

5. *Secondly, because an idea from actual sensation and another from memory are very distinct perceptions. Secondly,* because *sometimes I find that I cannot avoid the having those* ideas *produced in my mind.* For though, when my eyes are shut, or windows fast, I can at pleasure recall to my mind the *ideas* of *light,* or the *sun,* which former sensations had lodged in my memory; so I can at pleasure lay by that *idea* and take into my view that of the *smell* of a rose or *taste* of sugar. But, if I turn my eyes at noon towards the sun, I cannot avoid the *ideas* which the light or sun then produces in me, so that there is a manifest difference between the *ideas* laid up in my memory (over which, if they were there only, I should have constantly the same power to dispose of them and lay them by at pleasure), and those which force themselves upon me and I cannot avoid having. And therefore it must necessarily be some exterior cause, and the brisk acting of some objects without me whose efficacy I cannot resist, that produces those *ideas* in my mind, whether I will or not. Besides, there is nobody who does not perceive the difference in himself between contemplating the sun, as he has the *idea* of it in his memory, and actually looking upon it; of which two his perception is so distinct that

few of his *ideas* are more distinguishable one from another. And therefore he has certain knowledge that they are not both memory, or the actions of his mind, and fancies only within him, but that actual seeing has a cause without.

6. *Thirdly, pleasure or pain, which accompanies actual sensation, does not accompany the returning of those* ideas without *the external objects. Thirdly,* add to this that *many of those* ideas *are produced in us with pain which afterwards we remember without the least offense.* Thus the pain of heat or cold, when the *idea* of it is revived in our minds, gives us no disturbance, which, when felt, was very troublesome and is again when actually repeated. This is occasioned by the disorder the external object causes in our bodies when applied to it. And we remember the pains of *hunger, thirst,* or the *headache,* without any pain at all, which would either never disturb us or else constantly do it as often as we thought of it, were there nothing more but *ideas* floating in our minds and appearances entertaining our fancies without the real existence of things affecting us from abroad. The same may be said of pleasure accompanying several actual sensations. And though mathematical demonstration does not depend upon sense, yet the examining them by diagrams gives great credit to the evidence of our sight and seems to give it a certainty approaching to that of demonstration itself. For it would be very strange that a man should allow it for an undeniable truth, that two angles of a figure, which he measures by lines and angles of a diagram, should be bigger one than the other, and yet doubt of the existence of those lines and angles which, by looking on, he makes use of to measure that by.

7. *Fourthly, our senses assist one another's testimony of the existence of outward things. Fourthly,* our *senses* in many cases bear *witness* to the truth of each other's report concerning the existence of sensible things without us. He who sees a *fire* may, if he doubts whether it is anything more than a bare fancy, feel it, too, and be convinced by putting his hand in it, which certainly could never be put into such exquisite pain by a bare *idea* or phantom unless the pain is a fancy, too. This yet he cannot, when the burn is well, by raising the *idea* of it, bring upon himself again.

Thus I see, while I write this, I can change the

appearance of the paper, and, by designing the letters, tell beforehand what new *idea* it shall exhibit the very next moment by barely drawing my pen over it. This will neither appear (let me fancy as much as I will) if my hands stand still or, though I move my pen, if my eyes are shut. Nor, when those characters are once made on the paper, can I choose afterwards, but see them as they are, that is, have the *ideas* of such letters as I have made. From where it is manifest that they are not barely the sport and play of my own imagination, when I find that the characters that were made at the pleasure of my own thoughts do not obey them nor yet cease to be whenever I shall fancy it, but continue to affect my senses constantly and regularly according to the figures I made them. To this, if we will add that the sight of those shall, from another man, draw such sounds as I beforehand design they shall stand for, there will be little reason left to doubt that those words I write do really exist without me when they cause a long series of regular sounds to affect my ears, which could not be the effect of my imagination, nor could my memory retain them in that order.

8. *This certainty is as great as our condition needs.* But yet, if, after all this, anyone will be so skeptical as to distrust his senses and affirm that all we see and hear, feel and taste, think and do during our whole being is but the series and deluding appearances of a long dream of which there is no reality and, therefore, will question the existence of all things or our knowledge of anything, I must desire him to consider that, if all is a dream, then he does but dream that he makes the question, and so it does not much matter that a waking man should answer him. But yet, if he pleases, he may dream that I make him this answer, that *the certainty of* things existing *in rerum natura*, when we have *the testimony of our senses* for it, is not only *as great* as our frame can attain to, but *as our condition needs.* For our faculties being suited not to the full extent of being, nor to a perfect, clear, comprehensive knowledge of things free from all doubt and scruple, but to the preservation of us in whom they are and accommodated to the use of life, they serve to our purpose well enough if they will but give us certain notice of those things which are convenient or inconvenient to us. For he who sees

a candle burning and has experimented the force of its flame by putting his finger in it will little doubt that this is something existing without him which does him harm and puts him to great pain. This is assurance enough, when no man requires greater certainty to govern his actions by, than what is as certain as his actions themselves. And if our dreamer pleases to try whether the glowing heat of a glass furnace is barely a wandering imagination in a drowsy man's fancy, by putting his hand into it, he may perhaps be wakened into a certainty greater than he could wish, that it is something more than bare imagination. Thus this evidence is as great as we can desire, being as certain to us as our pleasure or pain, i.e., happiness or misery; beyond which we have no concern, either of knowing or being. Such an assurance of the existence of things without us is sufficient to direct us in the attaining the good and avoiding the evil which is caused by them; this is the important concern we have of being made acquainted with them.

9. *But reaches no further than actual sensation.* Finally, then, when our senses do actually convey into our understandings any *idea*, we cannot but be satisfied that there does something at that time really exist without us which does affect our senses and, by them, give notice of itself to our apprehensive faculties and actually produce that *idea* which we then perceive. And we cannot so far distrust their testimony as to doubt that such collections of simple *ideas* as we have observed by our senses to be united together do really exist together. But *this knowledge extends as far as the present testimony of our senses*, employed about particular objects that do then affect them, *and no further.* For if I saw such a collection of simple *ideas*, as is accustomed to be called *man*, existing together one minute ago, and am now alone, I cannot be certain that the same man exists now, since there is no necessary connection of his existence a minute ago with his existence now. By a thousand ways he may cease to be, since I had the testimony of my senses for his existence. And if I cannot be certain that the man I saw last today is now in being, I can less be certain that he is so who has been longer removed from my senses and I have not seen since yesterday, or since the last year; and much less can

I be certain of the existence of men that I never saw. And therefore, though it is highly probable that millions of men do now exist, yet while I am alone writing this I do not have that certainty of it which we strictly call knowledge, though the great likelihood of it puts me past doubt, and it is reasonable for me to do several things upon the confidence that there are men (and men also of my acquaintance, with whom I have to do) now in the world. But this is but probability, not knowledge.

10. *Folly to expect demonstration in everything.* By means of which yet we may observe how foolish and vain a thing it is for a man of a narrow knowledge, who, having reason given him to judge of the different evidence and probability of things and to be swayed accordingly—how *vain*, I say, it is *to expect demonstration* and certainty *in things not capable of it,* and refuse assent to very rational propositions, and act contrary to very plain and clear truths because they cannot be made out so evident as to surmount even the least (I will not say reason, but) pretense of doubting. He who in the ordinary affairs of life would admit of nothing but direct plain demonstration would be sure of nothing in this world but of perishing quickly. The wholesomeness of his meat or drink would not give him reason to venture on it. And I would gladly know what it is he could do upon such grounds as are capable of no doubt, no objection.

11. *Past existence is known by memory.* As when our senses are actually employed about any object, we do know that it does exist, so *by our memory* we may be assured that previously things that affected our senses have existed. And thus *we have knowledge of the past existence* of several things of which, our senses having informed us, our memories still retain the *ideas*; and of this we are past all doubt so long as we remember well. But this knowledge also reaches no further than our senses have formerly assured us. Thus, seeing water at this instant, it is an unquestionable truth to me that water does exist. And remembering that I saw it yesterday, it will also be always true and, as long as my memory retains it, always an undoubted proposition to me that water did exist the 10th of *July*, 1688, as it will also be equally true that a certain number of very fine colors did exist which at the same time I saw upon a bubble of that water.

But, being now quite out of sight both of the water and bubbles, too, it is no more certainly known to me that the water does now exist than that the bubbles or colors in there do so, it being no more necessary that water should exist today because it existed yesterday, than that the colors or bubbles exist today because they existed yesterday, though it is exceedingly much more probable, because water has been observed to continue long in existence, but bubbles and the colors on them quickly cease to be.

12. *The existence of spirits not knowable.* What *ideas* we have of spirits and how we come by them, I have already shown. But though we have those *ideas* in our minds and know we have them there, the having the *ideas* of spirits does not make us *know* that any such things do exist without us or *that there are any finite spirits* or any other spiritual beings but the Eternal God. We have ground from revelation and several other reasons to believe with assurance that there are such creatures. But, our senses not being able to discover them, we want the means of knowing their particular existences. For we can no more know that there are finite spirits really existing, by the *idea* we have of such beings in our minds, than, by the *ideas* anyone has of fairies or centaurs, he can come to know that things answering those *ideas* do really exist.

And, therefore, concerning the existence of finite spirits as well as several other things, we must content ourselves with the evidence of faith; but universal certain propositions concerning this matter are beyond our reach. For however true it may be, e.g., that all the intelligent spirits that God ever created do still exist, yet it can never make a part of our certain knowledge. These and the like propositions we may assent to as highly probable but are not, I fear, in this state, capable of knowing. We are not then to put others upon demonstrating nor ourselves upon search of universal certainty in all those matters in which we are not capable of any other knowledge but what our senses give us in this or that particular.

13. *Particular propositions concerning existence are knowable.* By which it appears that there are two sorts of *propositions:* 1. There is one sort of propositions *concerning* the *existence* of anything answerable to such an *idea*—as, having the *idea* of an *elephant, phoenix, motion,* or an *angel* in my mind, the first

and natural inquiry is, whether such a thing does anywhere exist? And this knowledge is only of *particulars*. No existence of anything without us, but only of God, can certainly be known further than our senses inform us. 2. There is another sort of *propositions* in which is expressed the agreement or disagreement of our abstract *ideas* and their dependence on one another. Such propositions may be *universal* and certain. So, having the *idea* of God and myself, of fear and obedience, I cannot but be sure that God is to be feared and obeyed by me, and this proposition will be certain concerning *man* in general, if I have made an abstract *idea* of such a species of which I am one particular. But yet this proposition, however certain, that men ought to fear and obey God, does not prove to me the existence of men in the world, but will be true of all such creatures, whenever they do exist. Which *certainty* of such general propositions depends on the agreement or disagreement to be discovered in those abstract *ideas*.

14. *And general propositions concerning abstract* ideas. In the former case, our knowledge is the consequence of the existence of things producing *ideas* in our minds by our senses. In the latter, knowledge is the consequence of the *ideas* (be they what they will) that are in our minds, producing there general certain propositions. Many of these are called *eternal truths* (*aeternae veritates*), and all of them, indeed, are so, not from being written, all or any of them, in the minds of all men, or that they were, any of them, propositions in anyone's mind until he, having gotten the abstract *ideas*, joined or separated them by affirmation or negation. But wherever we can suppose such a creature as *man* is endowed with such faculties and, by this means, furnished with such *ideas* as we have, we must conclude he must necessarily, when he applies his thoughts to the consideration of his *ideas*, know the truth of certain propositions that will arise from the agreement or disagreement which he will perceive in his own *ideas*. Such propositions are therefore called *eternal truths*, not because they are eternal propositions actually formed and antecedent to the understanding that at any time makes them, nor because they are imprinted on the mind from any patterns that are anywhere out of the mind and existed before. But because, being once made about

abstract *ideas*, so as to be true, they will, whenever they can be supposed to be made again at any time past or to come, by a mind having those *ideas*, always actually be true. For names being supposed to stand perpetually for the same *ideas*, and the same *ideas* having immutably the same habitudes one to another, propositions concerning any abstract *ideas* that are once true must necessarily be *eternal verities*.

Chapter 15. *Of Probability*.

1. *Probability is the appearance of agreement upon fallible proofs*. As demonstration is the showing the agreement or disagreement of two *ideas* by the intervention of one or more proofs which have a constant, immutable, and visible connection one with another, so *probability* is nothing but the appearance of such an agreement or disagreement by the intervention of proofs whose connection is not constant and immutable, or at least is not perceived to be so, but is, or appears for the most part to be so, and is enough to induce the mind to *judge* the proposition to be true or false, rather than the contrary. For example, in the demonstration of it, a man perceives the certain immutable connection [that] there is of equality between the three angles of a *triangle* and those intermediate ones which are made use of to show their equality to two right ones; and so, by an intuitive knowledge of the agreement or disagreement of the intermediate *ideas* in each step of the progress, the whole series is continued with an evidence which clearly shows the agreement or disagreement of those three angles in equality to two right ones. And thus he has certain knowledge that it is so. But another man, who never took the pains to observe the demonstration, hearing a mathematician, a man of credit, affirm the three angles of a triangle to be equal to two right ones, *assents* to it, i.e., receives it for true. In this case the foundation of his assent is the probability of the thing, the proof being such as for the most part carries truth with it; the man on whose testimony he receives it not being accustomed to affirm anything contrary to or besides his knowledge, especially in matters of this kind. So that that which causes his assent to this proposition, that the three angles of a triangle are equal to two right ones, that which makes him take

these *ideas* to agree without knowing them to do so, is the accustomed veracity of the speaker in other cases, or his supposed veracity in this.

2. *It is to supply the want of knowledge.* Our knowledge, as has been shown, being very narrow, and we not happy enough to find certain truth in everything which we have occasion to consider, most of the propositions we think, reason, discourse — no, act upon — are such as we cannot have undoubted knowledge of their truth; yet some of them border so near upon certainty that we make no doubt at all about them, but *assent* to them as firmly, and act according to that assent as resolutely as if they were infallibly demonstrated and that our knowledge of them was perfect and certain. But there being degrees in this from the very neighborhood of certainty and demonstration, quite down to improbability and unlikeness, even to the confines of impossibility, and also degrees of *assent* from full assurance and confidence, quite down to *conjecture*, *doubt*, and *distrust*, I shall come now (having, as I think, found out the bounds of human knowledge and certainty) in the next place to consider *the several degrees and grounds of probability, and assent or faith.*

3. *Being that which makes us presume things to be true, before we know them to be so.* Probability is likeliness to be true, the very notation of the word signifying such a proposition for which there are arguments or proofs to make it pass or be received for true. The entertainment the mind gives this sort of propositions is called *belief*, *assent*, or *opinion*, which is the admitting or receiving any proposition for true upon arguments or proofs that are found to persuade us to receive it as true, without certain knowledge that it is so. And in this lies the *difference between probability* and *certainty*, *faith* and *knowledge*, that in all the parts of knowledge there is intuition; each immediate *idea*, each step, has its visible and certain connection; in belief, not so. That which makes me believe is something extraneous to the thing I believe, something not evidently joined on both sides to, and so not manifestly showing the agreement or disagreement of those *ideas* that are under consideration.

4. *The grounds of probability are two: conformity with our own experience or the testimony of others' experience.* Probability then, being to supply the de-

fect of our knowledge and to guide us where that fails, is always conversant about propositions of which we have no certainty, but only some inducements to receive them for true. The *grounds of it* are, in short, these two following:

First, the conformity of anything with our own knowledge, observation, and experience.

Secondly, the testimony of others, vouching their observation and experience. In the testimony of others is to be considered: 1. The number. 2. The integrity. 3. The skill of the witnesses. 4. The design of the author, where it is a testimony out of a book cited. 5. The consistency of the parts, and circumstances of the relation. 6. Contrary testimonies.

5. *In this, all the arguments pro and con ought to be examined before we come to a judgment.* Probability wanting that intuitive evidence which infallibly determines the understanding and produces certain knowledge, *the mind, if it will proceed rationally, ought to examine all the grounds of probability* and see how they make more or less *for or against* any proposition, before it assents to or dissents from it, and upon a due balancing the whole, reject or receive it, with a more or less firm assent, proportionally to the preponderance of the greater grounds of probability on one side or the other. For example:

If I myself see a man walk on the ice, it is past *probability*; it is knowledge. But if another tells me he saw a man in *England*, in the midst of a sharp winter, walk upon water hardened with cold, this has so great conformity with what is usually observed to happen that I am disposed by the nature of the thing itself to assent to it, unless some manifest suspicion attend the relation of that matter of fact. But if the same thing is told to one born between the tropics, who never saw nor heard of any such thing before, there the whole probability relies on testimony; and as the relators are more in number, and of more credit, and have no interest to speak contrary to the truth, so that matter of fact is likely to find more or less belief. Though to a man whose experience has always been quite contrary, and who has never heard of anything like it, the most untainted credit of a witness will scarcely be able to find belief. As it happened to a Dutch ambassador who, entertaining the King of *Siam* with the particularities of *Holland*, which he was inquisitive after, among other things told him that the water in his country would sometimes in cold weather be so hard that men walked upon it, and that it would bear an elephant if he were there—to which the king replied, "Up to now I have believed the strange things you have told me, because I look upon you as a sober fair man, but now I am sure you lie." [...]

Chapter 16. *Of the Degrees of Assent.*

1. *Our assent ought to be regulated by the grounds of probability.* We have laid down the grounds of probability in the foregoing chapter; as they are the foundations on which our *assent* is built, so are they also the measure by which its several degrees are, or ought to be, *regulated:* Only we are to take notice that, whatever grounds of probability there may be, they yet operate no further on the mind which searches after truth and endeavors to judge right, than they appear, at least, in the first judgment or search that the mind makes. I confess, in the opinions men have and firmly stick to, in the world, their assent is not always from an actual view of the reasons that at first prevailed with them, it being in many cases almost impossible, and, in most, very hard, even for those who have very admirable memories, to retain all the proofs which, upon a due examination, made them embrace that side of the question. It suffices that they have once with care and fairness sifted the matter as far as they could, and that they have searched into all the particulars that they could imagine to give any light to the question, and, with the best of their skill, cast up the account upon the whole evidence; and thus, having once found on which side the probability appeared to them, after as full and exact an inquiry as they can make, they lay up the conclusion in their memories as a truth they have discovered; and for the future they remain satisfied with the testimony of their memories, that this is the opinion that, by the proofs they have once seen of it, deserves such a *degree* of their *assent* as they afford it. [...]

3. *The ill consequence of the remembrance that we once saw ground for such a degree of assent, if our former judgment were not rightly made.* I cannot but admit that men's *sticking to* their *past judgment* and adhering firmly to conclusions formerly made is often the cause of great obstinacy in error and mistake. But the fault is not that they rely on their memories for what they have before well judged, but because they judged before they had well examined. [...] Who almost is there who has the leisure, patience, and means to collect together all the proofs concerning most of the opinions he has, so as safely to conclude that he has a clear and full view, and that there is no more to be alleged for his better information? And yet we are forced to determine ourselves on the one side or other. The conduct of our lives and the management of our great concerns will not bear delay; for those depend, for the most part, on the determination of our judgment in points in which we are not capable of certain and demonstrative knowledge, and in which it is necessary for us to embrace the one side or the other.

4. *The right use of it is mutual charity and forbearance.* Since therefore it is unavoidable to the greatest part of men, if not all, to have several *opinions*, without certain and indubitable proofs of their truth; and it carries too great an imputation of ignorance, lightness, or folly, for men to quit and renounce their former tenets presently upon the offer of an argument, which they cannot immediately answer and show the insufficiency of; it would, I think, become all men to maintain *peace*, and the common offices of humanity *and friendship, in the diversity of opinions*, since we cannot reasonably expect that anyone should readily and obsequiously quit his own opinion and embrace ours, with a blind resignation to an authority which the understanding of man does not acknowledge. [...] For where is the man who has incontestable evidence of the truth of all that he holds or of the falsehood of all he condemns or can say that he has examined to the bottom all his own or other men's opinions? The necessity of believing without knowledge, no, often upon very slight grounds, in this fleeting state of action and blindness we are in, should make us more busy and careful to inform ourselves than constrain others. At least those who have not thoroughly examined to the bottom all their own tenets must confess they are unfit to prescribe to others; and are unreasonable in imposing that as truth

on other men's belief which they themselves have not searched into, nor weighed the arguments of probability on which they should receive or reject it. [. . .]

5. *Probability is either of matter of fact or speculation.* But to return to the grounds of assent and the several degrees of it, we are to take notice that the propositions we receive upon inducements of *probability* are *of two sorts:* either concerning some particular existence, or, as it is usually termed, matter of fact, which, falling under observation, is capable of human testimony; or else concerning things which, being beyond the discovery of our senses, are not capable of any such testimony.

6. *The concurrent experience of all other men with ours produces assurance approaching to knowledge.* Concerning the *first* of these, namely, *particular matter of fact.*

First, where any particular thing, consonant to the constant observation of ourselves and others in the like case, comes attested by the concurrent reports of all that mention it, we receive it as easily, and build as firmly upon it, as if it were certain knowledge; and we reason and act upon this with as little doubt, as if it were perfect demonstration. Thus, if all Englishmen who have occasion to mention it should affirm that it froze in England the last winter, or that there were swallows seen there in the summer, I think a man could almost as little doubt of it as that seven and four are eleven. The first, therefore, and *highest degree of probability* is when the general consent of all men, in all ages, as far as it can be known, concurs with a man's constant and never failing experience in like cases to confirm the truth of any particular matter of fact attested by fair witnesses; such are all the stated constitutions and properties of bodies and the regular proceedings of causes and effects in the ordinary course of nature. This we call an argument from the nature of things themselves. For what our own and other men's constant observation has found always to be after the same manner, that we with reason conclude to be the effect of steady and regular causes, though they do not come within the reach of our knowledge. Thus, that fire warmed a man, made lead fluid, and changed the color or consistency in wood or charcoal, that iron sunk in water and swam in quicksilver, these and the like propositions about

particular facts, being agreeable to our constant experience, as often as we have to do with these matters, and being generally spoken of (when mentioned by others) as things found constantly to be so, and therefore not so much as controverted by anybody, we are put past doubt that a relation affirming any such thing to have been, or any predication that it will happen again in the same manner, is very true. These *probabilities* rise so near to *certainty* that they govern our thoughts as absolutely, and influence all our actions as fully, as the most evident demonstration, and in what concerns us we make little or no difference between them and certain knowledge. Our belief, thus grounded, rises to *assurance.*

7. *Unquestionable testimony and experience for the most part produce confidence. Secondly, the next degree of probability* is, when I find by my own experience and the agreement of all others that mention it, a thing to be for the most part so and that the particular instance of it is attested by many and undoubted witnesses, e.g., history giving us such an account of men in all ages, and my own experience, as far as I had an opportunity to observe, confirming it, that most men prefer their private advantage to the public; if all historians who write of *Tiberius* say that *Tiberius* did so, it is extremely probable. And in this case, our assent has a sufficient foundation to raise itself to a degree which we may call *confidence.*

8. *Fair testimony, and the nature of the thing indifferent, produces also confident belief. Thirdly,* in things that happen indifferently, as that a bird should fly this or that way, that it should thunder on a man's right or left hand, etc., when any particular matter of fact is vouched by the concurrent testimony of unsuspected witnesses, there our assent is also unavoidable. Thus, that there is such a city in *Italy* as *Rome*; that, about one thousand seven hundred years ago, there lived in it a man called *Julius Caesar*; that he was a general, and that he won a battle against another, called *Pompey*: This, though in the nature of the thing there is nothing for nor against it, yet being related by historians of credit and contradicted by no one writer, a man cannot avoid believing it, and can as little doubt of it as he does of the being and actions of his own acquaintance of which he himself is a witness.

9. *Experience and testimonies clashing, infinitely vary the degrees of probability*. Thus far the matter goes easy enough. Probability upon such grounds carries so much evidence with it that it naturally determines the judgment and leaves us as little liberty to believe, or disbelieve, as a demonstration does, whether we will know, or be ignorant. The difficulty is, when testimonies contradict common experience and the reports of history and witnesses clash with the ordinary course of nature or with one another; there it is, where diligence, attention, and exactness are required to form a right judgment and to proportion the *assent* to the different evidence and probability of the thing which rises and falls according as those two foundations of credibility, namely, common observation in like cases and particular testimonies in that particular instance, favor or contradict it. These are liable to so great variety of contrary observations, circumstances, reports, different qualifications, tempers, designs, oversights, etc., of the reporters that it is impossible to reduce to precise rules the various degrees in which men give their assent. This only may be said in general, that as the arguments and proofs *pro* and *con*, upon due examination, nicely weighing every particular circumstance, shall to anyone appear, upon the whole matter, in a greater or less degree to preponderate on either side; so they are fitted to produce in the mind such different entertainments as we call *belief, conjecture, guess, doubt, wavering, distrust, disbelief*, etc.

10. *Traditional testimonies, the further removed, the less their proof*. This is what concerns assent in matters in which testimony is made use of; concerning which, I think, it may not be amiss to take notice of a rule observed in the law of England, which is, that though the attested copy of a record be good proof, yet the copy of a copy ever so well attested, and by ever so credible witnesses, will not be admitted as a proof in judicature. This is so generally approved as reasonable and suited to the wisdom and caution to be used in our inquiry after material truths that I never yet heard of anyone that blamed it. This practice, if it be allowable in the decisions of right and wrong, carries this observation along with it, namely, that any testimony, the further off it is from the original truth, the less force and proof it has. The being and existence of the thing itself is what I call the original truth. A credible man vouching his knowledge of it is a good proof; but if another equally credible does witness it from his report, the testimony is weaker; and a third that attests the hearsay of a hearsay is yet less considerable. So that *in traditional truths, each remove weakens the force of the proof*, and the more hands the tradition has successively passed through, the less strength and evidence does it receive from them. This I thought necessary to be taken notice of, because I find among some men the quite contrary commonly practiced, who look on opinions to gain force by growing older; and what a thousand years since would not, to a rational man contemporary with the first voucher, have appeared at all probable, is now urged as certain beyond all question, only because several have since, from him, said it one after another. Upon this ground, propositions, evidently false or doubtful enough in their first beginning, come, by an inverted rule of probability, to pass for authentic truths; and those which found or deserved little credit from the mouths of their first authors are thought to grow venerable by age and are urged as undeniable.

11. *Yet history is of great use*. I would not be thought here to lessen the credit and use of *history*: It is all the light we have in many cases, and we receive from it a great part of the useful truths we have, with a convincing evidence. I think nothing more valuable than the records of antiquity; I wish we had more of them, and more uncorrupted. But this truth itself forces me to say that no *probability* can arise higher than its first origin. [. . .]

12. *In things which sense cannot discover, analogy is the great rule of probability*. The probabilities we have mentioned up to now are only such as concern matter of fact, and such things as are capable of observation and testimony. There remains that other sort, *concerning* which men entertain opinions with variety of assent, though the *things* are such *that, not falling under the reach of our senses, they are not capable of testimony*. Such are: 1. The existence, nature, and operations of finite immaterial beings without us; as spirits, angels, devils, etc., or the existence of material beings which, either for their smallness in themselves, or remoteness from us, our senses cannot take notice of, as whether there are any plants,

animals, and intelligent inhabitants in the planets and other mansions of the vast universe. 2. Concerning the manner of operation in most parts of the works of nature, in which, though we see the sensible effects, yet their causes are unknown, and we do not perceive the ways and manner how they are produced. We see animals are generated, nourished, and move; the lodestone draws iron; and the parts of a candle, successively melting, turn into flame, and give us both light and heat. These and the like effects we see and know, but the causes that operate, and the manner they are produced in, we can only guess and probably conjecture. For these and the like, not coming within the scrutiny of human senses, cannot be examined by them or be attested by anybody and therefore can appear more or less probable only as they more or less agree to truths that are established in our minds and as they hold proportion to other parts of our knowledge and observation. Analogy in these matters is the only help we have, and it is from that alone we draw all our grounds of probability. Thus, observing that the bare rubbing of two bodies violently one upon another produces heat and, very often, fire itself, we have reason to think that what we call heat and fire consists in a violent agitation of the imperceptible minute parts of the burning matter. Observing likewise that the different refractions of pellucid bodies produce in our eyes the different appearances of several colors, and also that the different ranging and laying the superficial parts of several bodies, as of velvet, watered silk, etc., do the like, we think it probable that the color and shining of bodies are in them nothing but the different arrangement and refraction of their minute and insensible parts. Thus, finding, in all parts of the creation that fall under human observation, that there is a gradual connection of one with another, without any great or discernible gaps between, in all that great variety of things we see in the world which are so closely linked together that, in the several ranks of beings, it is not easy to discover the bounds between them, we have reason to be persuaded that by such gentle steps things ascend upwards in degrees of perfection. It is a hard matter to say where sensible and rational begin and where insensible and irrational end; and who is there quick-sighted enough to determine precisely which is the

lowest species of living things and which the first of those which have no life? Things, as far as we can observe, lessen and augment, as the quantity does in a regular cone, where, though there is a manifest odds between the bigness of the diameter at a remote distance, yet the difference between the upper and under, where they touch one another, is hardly discernible. The difference is exceeding great between some men and some animals; but if we will compare the understanding and abilities of some men and some brutes, we shall find so little difference that it will be hard to say that that of the man is either clearer or larger. Observing, I say, such gradual and gentle descents downwards in those parts of the creation that are beneath man, the rule of analogy may make it probable that it is so also in things above us and our observation, and that there are several ranks of intelligent beings, excelling us in several degrees of perfection, ascending upwards towards the infinite perfection of the Creator, by gentle steps and differences that are every one at no great distance from the next to it. This sort of probability, which is the best conduct of rational experiments and the rise of hypothesis, has also its use and influence; and a wary reasoning from analogy leads us often into the discovery of truths and useful productions which would otherwise lie concealed.

13. *One case where contrary experience lessens not the testimony.* Though the common experience and the ordinary course of things have justly a mighty influence on the minds of men, to make them give or refuse credit to anything proposed to their belief, yet there is one case in which the strangeness of the fact does not lessen the assent to a fair testimony given of it. For where such supernatural events are suitable to ends aimed at by him who has the power to change the course of nature, there, under such circumstances, they may be the fitter to procure belief, by how much the more they are beyond or contrary to ordinary observation. This is the proper case of *miracles*, which, well attested, do not only find credit themselves but give it also to other truths, which need such confirmation.

14. *The bare testimony of revelation is the highest certainty.* Besides those we have mentioned up to now, there is one sort of propositions that challenge

the highest degree of our assent upon bare testimony, whether the thing proposed agree or disagree with common experience, and the ordinary course of things, or not. The reason of this is because the testimony is of such a one as cannot deceive nor be deceived, and that is of God himself. This carries with it an assurance beyond doubt, evidence beyond exception. This is called by a peculiar name, *revelation*; and our assent to it, faith, which as absolutely determines our minds, and as perfectly excludes all wavering, as our knowledge itself; and we may as well doubt of our own being as we can whether any revelation from God is true. So that faith is a settled and sure principle of assent and assurance and leaves no manner of room for doubt or hesitation. Only we must be sure that it be a divine revelation and that we understand it right; else we shall expose ourselves to all the extravagance of enthusiasm and all the error of wrong principles if we have faith and assurance in what is not divine revelation. And therefore, in those cases, our assent can be rationally no higher than the evidence of its being a revelation, and that this is the meaning of the expressions it is delivered in. If the evidence of its being a revelation, or that this is its true sense, is only on probable proofs, our assent can reach no higher than an assurance or diffidence, arising from the more or less apparent probability of the proofs. But of faith, and the precedence it ought to have before other arguments of persuasion, I shall speak more afterward, where I treat of it as it is ordinarily placed, in contradistinction to reason, though in truth it is nothing else but an assent founded on the highest reason.

G. W. Leibniz, Preface to the *New Essays* (1703–5)[1]

Since the *Essays on the Understanding*, published by an illustrious Englishman, is one of the finest and most esteemed works of our age, I resolved to comment on it, insofar as I had given sufficient thought for some time to the same subject and to most of the matters touched upon there; I thought that this would be a good opportunity to publish something entitled *New Essays on the Understanding* and to procure a more favorable reception for my thoughts by putting them in such good company. I further thought that I might profit from someone else's work, not only to make my task easier (since, in fact, it is easier to follow the thread of a good author than to work out everything anew), but also to add something to what he has given us, which is always easier than starting from the beginning. It is true that I often hold an opinion different from his, but far from denying on that account the merit of this famous writer, I bear witness to it by showing in what and why, I differ from his view, when I deem it necessary to prevent his authority from prevailing against reason on some important points.

In fact, although the author of the *Essay* says a thousand fine things of which I approve, our systems are very different. His bears more relation to Aristotle's and mine to Plato's, although we both differ in many ways from the doctrines of these two ancients. He is more popular, while I am forced at times to be a little more esoteric and abstract, which is not an advantage to me, especially when writing in a living language. However, I believe that by making two characters speak, one of whom presents the views of the author of the *Essay*, while the other adds my observations, the parallel will be more to the liking of the reader than some dry remarks, whose reading would have to be interrupted at every moment by the necessity of having to return to the author's book in order to understand mine. Nevertheless, it would be good to compare our writings from time to time, and to judge his views by his work alone, even though I have usually retained his expressions. It is true that the constraint of having to follow the thread of someone else's discourse in making my remarks has meant that

1. [Translated from the French by R. Ariew and D. Garber in G. W. Leibniz, *Philosophical Essays* (Indianapolis: Hackett Publishing Company, 1989). Leibniz became acquainted with the outline of John Locke's *Essay Concerning Human Understanding* before it was actually published, through an abstract of the book, written by Locke, translated into French, and published in Le Clerc's *Bibliothèque Universelle* (1688). Leibniz read the *Essay* in English, after it was published in 1690, and sent some criticisms of it to Locke through Thomas Burnet (ca. 1635–1715) and Lady Masham (1658–1708). When, in 1700, Pierre Coste's French translation of the *Essay* was published, Leibniz was able to make a thorough study of it; he planned to publish his critique under the title *New Essays on the Understanding*. Locke died in 1704, and Leibniz abandoned his project to publish the work.]

I could not think of capturing the charm of which the dialogue is capable, but I hope that the content will make up for the defect in style.

Our differences are about subjects of some importance. There is the question about whether the soul in itself is completely empty like tablets upon which nothing has been written [*tabula rasa*], as Aristotle and the author of the *Essay* maintain, and whether everything inscribed on it comes solely from the senses and from experience, or whether the soul contains from the beginning the source [*principe*] of several notions and doctrines, which external objects awaken only on certain occasions, as I believe with Plato and even with the Schoolmen, and with all those who find this meaning in the passage of St. Paul (Romans 2:15) where he states that the law of God is written in our hearts. The Stoics call these principles *Prolepses*, that is, fundamental assumptions, or what is taken as agreed in advance. Mathematicians call them *common notions*, [*koinai ennoiai*]. Modern philosophers give them other fine names, and Julius Scaliger in particular called them the seeds of eternity, and also *zopyra*, meaning living fires, or flashes of light hidden inside us but made to appear through the contact of the senses, like sparks that can be struck from a steel. And it is not unreasonable to believe that these flashes reveal something divine and eternal, something that especially appears in necessary truths. This raises another question, namely, whether all truths depend upon experience, that is, upon induction and instances, or whether some of them have another foundation. For if some occurrences can be foreseen before they have been tested, it is obvious that we contribute something of our own here. Although the senses are necessary for all our actual knowledge, they are not sufficient to give us all of it, since the senses never give us anything but instances, that is, particular or individual truths. Now all the instances confirming a general truth, however numerous they may be, are not sufficient to establish the universal necessity of that same truth, for it does not follow that what has happened before will always happen in the same way. For example, the Greeks, Romans, and all other people of the earth have always observed that before the passage of twenty-four hours, day changes into night and night into day. But they would have been mistaken if they had believed that the same rule is observed everywhere, since the contrary was observed during a visit to Nova Zembla. And anyone who believed that this is a necessary and eternal truth, at least in our climate, would also be mistaken, since we must recognize that the earth and even the sun do not exist necessarily, and that there may be a time when this beautiful star will no longer exist, at least in its present form, and neither will its whole system. As a result it appears that necessary truths, such as we find in pure mathematics and particularly in arithmetic and geometry, must have principles whose proof does not depend on instances nor, consequently, on the testimony of the senses, although without the senses it would never occur to us to think of them. This is a distinction that should be noted carefully, and it is one Euclid understood so well that he proves by reason things that are sufficiently evident through experience and sensible images. Logic, together with metaphysics and morals, of which the one shapes natural theology and the other natural jurisprudence, are full of such truths, and consequently, their proof can only arise from internal principles, which are called innate. It is true that we must not imagine that we can read these eternal laws of reason in the soul from an open book, as the edict of the praetor can be read from his tablet without effort and scrutiny. But it is enough that they can be discovered in us by dint of attention; the senses furnish occasions for this, and the success of experiments also serves to confirm reason, a bit like empirical trials help us avoid errors of calculation in arithmetic when the reasoning is long. Also, it is in this respect that human knowledge differs from that of beasts. Beasts are purely empirical and are guided solely by instances, for, as far as we are able to judge, they never manage to form necessary propositions, whereas man is capable of demonstrative knowledge [*sciences demonstratives*]. In this, the faculty beasts have for drawing consequences is inferior to the reason humans have. The consequences beasts draw are just like those of simple empirics,[2] who claim that what has happened will happen again in a case where

2. [The Empirics were a sect of physicians before Galen (ca. A.D. 150). In later times, the epithet "Empiric" was given to physicians who despised theoretical study and trusted tradition and their own experience.]

what strikes them is similar, without being able to determine whether the same reasons are at work. This is what makes it so easy for men to capture beasts, and so easy for simple empirics to make mistakes. Not even people made skillful by age and experience are exempt from this when they rely too much on their past experiences. This has happened to several people in civil and military affairs, since they do not take sufficiently into consideration the fact that the world changes and that men have become more skillful in finding thousands of new tricks, unlike the stags and hares of today, who have not become any more clever than those of yesterday. The consequences beasts draw are only a shadow of reasoning; that is, they are only connections of imagination, transitions from one image to another; for, when a new situation appears similar to the preceding one, they expect to find again what was previously joined to it, as though things were linked in fact, just because their images are linked in the memory. It is, indeed, true that reason ordinarily counsels us to expect that we will find in the future that which conforms to our long experience of the past; but this is not, on that account, a necessary and infallible truth, and it can fail us when we least expect it, when the reasons which have maintained it change. This is why the wisest people do not rely on it to such an extent that they do not try to probe into the reason for what happens (if that is possible), so as to judge when exceptions must be made. For only reason is capable of establishing sure rules and of providing what uncertain rules lack by formulating exceptions to them, and lastly, capable of finding connections that are certain in the compulsion [*force*] of necessary consequences. This often provides a way of foreseeing an occurrence without having to experience the sensible links between images, which the beasts are reduced to doing. Thus what justifies the internal principles of necessary truths also distinguishes humans from beasts.

Perhaps our able author will not entirely disagree with my opinion. For after having devoted his whole first book to rejecting innate illumination, understood in a certain way, he admits, however, at the beginning of the second book and in what follows, that the ideas which do not originate in sensation come from reflection. Now, reflection is nothing other than attention to what is within us, and the senses do not give

us what we already bring with us. Given this, can anyone deny that there is a great deal innate in our mind, since we are innate to ourselves, so to speak, and since we have within ourselves being, unity, substance, duration, change, action, perception, pleasure, and a thousand other objects of our intellectual ideas? And since these objects are immediate and always present to our understanding (though they may not always be perceived consciously [*apperçus*] on account of our distractions and our needs), why should it be surprising that we say that these ideas, and everything that depends upon them, are innate in us? I have also used the comparison with a block of veined marble, rather than a completely uniform block of marble, or an empty tablet, that is, what the philosophers call a *tabula rasa*. For if the soul were like these empty tablets, truths would be in us as the shape of Hercules is in a block of marble, when the marble is completely indifferent to receiving this shape or another. But if the stone had veins which marked out the shape of Hercules rather than other shapes, then that block would be more determined with respect to that shape and Hercules would be as though innate in it in some sense, even though some labor would be required for these veins to be exposed and polished into clarity by the removal of everything that prevents them from appearing. This is how ideas and truths are innate in us, as natural inclinations, dispositions, habits, or potentialities [*virtualités*] are, and not as actions are, although these potentialities are always accompanied by some corresponding, though often insensible, actions.

Our able author seems to claim that there is nothing *potential* [*virtuel*] in us, and even nothing that we are not always actually conscious of perceiving [*appercevions*]. But he cannot hold this in all strictness; otherwise his position would be too paradoxical, since, again, acquired habits and the contents of our memory are not always consciously perceived [*apperçues*] and do not even always come to our aid when needed, though often we easily recall them to mind when some trivial occasion reminds us of them, as when we need only the beginning of a song to make us remember the rest. He also limits his thesis in other places, saying that there is nothing in us that we did not at least previously perceive consciously [*apperçu*]. But no one can guarantee by reason alone

how far back our past and perhaps forgotten apperceptions can go, especially in view of the Platonists' doctrine of reminiscence, which, fabulous though it is,
is not at all incompatible with pure reason. Furthermore, why must it be that everything is acquired by
apperceptions of external things and that nothing can
be unearthed from within ourselves? Is our soul in
itself so empty that, without images borrowed from
the outside, it is nothing? This is not, I am convinced,
a view our judicious author could approve. Where
could one find some tablets which do not have a
certain amount of variety in themselves? Will we ever
see a perfectly homogeneous and uniform surface?
Then why could we not also provide ourselves some
object of thought from our own depths, when we are
willing to dig there? Thus I am led to believe that,
fundamentally, his view on this point is no different
from mine, or rather from the common view, insofar
as he recognizes two sources of our knowledge, the
senses and reflection.

I do not know whether it will be as easy to reconcile
him with me and with the Cartesians when he maintains that the mind does not always think, and in
particular, that it is without perception during dream-
less sleep, and when he objects that since bodies can
be without motion, souls can just as well be without
thought. But here I reply somewhat differently from
what is customary. For I maintain that a substance
cannot naturally be without action, and that there is
never even any body without motion. Experience
already supports me, and to be convinced of this, one
need only consult the book of the illustrious Mr.
Boyle against absolute rest.[3] But I believe that reason
also supports this, and it is one of the proofs I use
for refuting atoms. Moreover, there are a thousand
indications that allow us to judge that at every moment there is an infinity of perceptions in us, but
without apperception and without reflection — that is,
changes in the soul itself, which we do not consciously
perceive [*appercevons*], because these impressions are
either too small or too numerous, or too homogeneous, in the sense that they have nothing sufficiently
distinct in themselves; but combined with others, they
do have their effect and make themselves felt in the

assemblage, at least confusedly. It is in this way that
custom makes us ignore the motion of a mill or of a
waterfall, after we have lived nearby for some time.
It is not that this motion ceases to strike our organs
and that there is nothing corresponding to it in the
soul, on account of the harmony of the soul and the
body, but that the impressions in the soul and in the
body, lacking the appeal of novelty, are not sufficiently
strong to attract our attention and memory, which are
applied only to more demanding objects. All attention
requires memory, and when we are not alerted, so
to speak, to pay heed to some of our own present
perceptions, we let them pass without reflection and
without even noticing them. But if someone alerts
us to them right away and makes us take note, for
example, of some noise we have just heard, we remember it, and we consciously perceive that we just
had some sensation of it. Thus there were perceptions
that we did not consciously perceive right away, the
apperception in this case arising only after an interval,
however brief. In order better to recognize [*juger*]
these tiny perceptions [*petites perceptions*] that cannot
be distinguished in a crowd, I usually make use of
the example of the roar or noise of the sea that strikes
us when we are at the shore. In order to hear this
noise as we do, we must hear the parts that make up
this whole; that is, we must hear the noise of each
wave, even though each of these small noises is known
only in the confused assemblage of all the others,
and would not be noticed if the wave making it were
the only one. For we must be slightly affected by
the motion of this wave, and we must have some
perception of each of these noises, however small
they may be; otherwise we would not have the noise of
a hundred thousand waves, since a hundred thousand
nothings cannot make something. Moreover, we
never sleep so soundly that we do not have some
weak and confused sensation, and we would never
be awakened by the greatest noise in the world if we
did not have some perception of its beginning, small
as it might be, just as we could never break a rope
by the greatest effort in the world, unless it were
stretched and strained slightly by the least efforts, even
though the slight extension they produce is not apparent.

These tiny perceptions are therefore more effectual
than one thinks. They make up this I-know-not-what,

---

3. [Robert Boyle, *Discourse about the Absolute Rest in Bodies*
(London, 1669).]

those flavors, those images of the sensory qualities, clear in the aggregate but confused in their parts; they make up those impressions the surrounding bodies make on us, which involve the infinite, and this connection that each being has with the rest of the universe. It can even be said that as a result of these tiny perceptions, the present is filled with the future and laden with the past, that everything conspires together (*sympnoia panta*, as Hippocrates said), and that eyes as piercing as those of God could read the whole sequence of the universe in the smallest of substances.

The things that are, the things that have been, and the things that will soon be brought in by the future.[4]

These insensible perceptions also indicate and constitute the individual, which is individuated [*caractérise*] by the traces which these perceptions preserve of its previous states, connecting it up with his present state. They can be known by a superior mind, even when the individual himself does not sense them, that is, when he no longer has an explicit memory of them. But these perceptions even provide a way of recovering the memory, as needed, through periodic unfoldings which may occur one day. That is why death might only be a state of sleep, and might not even remain one, insofar as the perceptions merely cease to be sufficiently distinct and, in animals, are reduced to a state of confusion which suspends apperception, but which cannot last forever; I shall not speak here of man, who ought to have great prerogatives in this matter in order to retain his personality.

It is also by means of these insensible perceptions that I explain the marvelous pre-established harmony between the soul and the body, and also between all the monads or simple substances, which takes the place of that untenable influence of the one on the others, and which, in the judgment of the author of the finest of dictionaries,[5] raises the greatness of divine perfections beyond anything ever conceived before. After this I would add little if I said that it is these tiny perceptions which determine us in many situations without our thinking of them, and which deceive the common people by giving the appearance of an *indifference of equilibrium*, as if it made no difference to us, for example, whether we turned right or left. Nor is it necessary for me to point out here, as I've done in the book itself,[6] that they cause this uneasiness, which I show to consist in something that differs from pain only as the small differs from the great, and yet which often brings about our desire and even our pleasure by giving it a kind of spice. The insensible parts of our sensible perceptions also bring about a relation between those perceptions of color, heat, and other sensible qualities, and the motions in bodies that correspond to them. But the Cartesians and our author, penetrating though he is, think of the perceptions we have of these qualities as arbitrary, that is, as if God had given them to the soul according to his good pleasure without having regard to any essential relation between perceptions and their objects, a view which surprises me and seems to me unworthy of the wisdom of the author of things, who does nothing without harmony and reason.

In short, *insensible perceptions* have as much use in philosophy of mind [*Pneumatique*] as corpuscles do in physics; and it is equally unreasonable to reject the one as the other under the pretext that they are beyond the reach of the senses. Nothing takes place all at once, and it is one of the greatest and best verified maxims that *nature never makes leaps*; this is what I called the *law of continuity* when I once spoke about this in the *Nouvelles de la république des lettres*,[7] and this law is of considerable use in physics. It entails that one always passes from the small to the large and back again through what lies between, both in degrees and in parts, and that a motion never arises immediately from rest nor is it reduced to rest except through a lesser motion, just as we never manage to pass through any line or length before having passed through a shorter one. But until now, those who have given the laws of motion have not observed this law, believing that a body can instantaneously receive a motion opposite to the previous motion. All this can

---

4. [Virgil, *Georgics* IV 393.]
5. [Pierre Bayle. The reference is to Bayle's discussion of Leibniz in notes H and L to the article "Rorarius" in his *Dictionary*. Bayle's point is that Leibniz's pre-established harmony puts implausibly severe demands on God's power.]

6. [In the *New Essays* II.23.]
7. [The reference is to "A Letter of Mr. Leibniz on a General Principle Useful in Explaining the Laws of Nature . . .", which appeared in the July 1687 issue of the *Nouvelles*.]

allow us to judge that noticeable perceptions arise by degrees from ones too small to be noticed. To judge otherwise is to know little of the immense subtlety of things, which always and everywhere involves an actual infinity.

I have also noticed that because of insensible variations, two individual things cannot be perfectly alike and must always differ in something over and above number. This puts an end to the empty tablets of the soul, a soul without thought, a substance without action, void space, atoms, and even particles in matter not actually divided, complete uniformity in a part of time, place, or matter, the perfect globes of the second element that derive from the perfect original cubes, and a thousand other fictions of philosophers which arise from their incomplete notions. These are things that the nature of things does not allow, things that are allowed to pass because of our ignorance and lack of attention; they cannot be tolerated unless we limit them to being abstractions of the mind, which protests that it does not deny the things it sets aside, but only judges that they need not enter into consideration at present. If we thought in earnest that things we do not consciously perceive [*s'apperçoit*] are not in the soul or in the body, we would fail in philosophy as in politics, by neglecting the *mikron*, imperceptible changes. But an abstraction is not an error, provided we know that what we are ignoring is really there. This is similar to what mathematicians do when they talk about the perfect lines they propose to us, uniform motions and other regular effects, although *matter* (that is, the mixture of the effects of the surrounding infinity) always provides some exception. We proceed in this way in order to distinguish various considerations and, as far as is possible, to reduce effects to their reasons, and foresee some of their consequences. For the more careful we are not to neglect any consideration we can subject to rules [*reguler*], the more closely practice corresponds to theory. But only the supreme reason, which nothing escapes, can distinctly understand the whole infinite, all the reasons, and all the consequences. With respect to infinities, we can only know them confusedly, but at least we can distinctly know that they exist; otherwise we would be very poor judges of the beauty and greatness of the universe, just as we would also be unable to develop a good physics which explains the nature of things in general, and still less a good philosophy of mind [*Pneumatique*], which includes the knowledge of God, of souls, and of simple substances in general.

This knowledge of insensible perceptions also serves to explain why and how two souls of the same species, whether human or otherwise, never leave the hands of the creator perfectly alike, and why and how each of them always has its original relation to the point of view it will have in the universe. But this already follows from what I pointed out previously about two individuals, namely that the *difference* between them is always *more than numerical*. There is another significant point on which I must differ, not only from the opinion of our author, but also from those of most of the moderns. I hold with most of the ancients that all spiritual beings [*génies*], all souls, all simple created substances, are always joined to a body, and that souls are never completely separated from bodies. I have *a priori* reasons for this, but this doctrine will be found to have the further advantage that it resolves all the philosophical difficulties about the state of souls, their perpetual conservation, their immortality, and their operation. Since the difference between one of their states and another is never, nor has it ever been anything but the difference between the more and the less sensible, between the more and the less perfect (or the other way around), the past or future state of souls is just as explicable as their present one. The slightest reflection is sufficient to show that this is reasonable, and that a leap from one state to an infinitely different one cannot be natural. I am surprised that the schools, by needlessly abandoning nature, have been willing to readily plunge into enormous difficulties, and thus to give free thinkers [*esprits forts*] an opportunity for their apparent triumphs. The arguments of the free thinkers collapse all at once with this explanation of things, in which it is no more difficult to conceive the preservation of souls (or rather, on my view, of the animal), than it is to conceive the change from caterpillar to butterfly and the preservation of thought in sleep, to which Jesus Christ has divinely compared death.[8] Also, I have already said that no sleep can last forever; but it will have less duration or almost no duration at all in the case of rational souls, which are always

8. [John 11:11.]

destined to remain the persons [*personnage*] they were in the city of God, and consequently, to retain their memory, so that they can be better able to receive rewards and punishments. I further add that, in general, no disordering of its visible organs is capable of bringing things in the animal to the point of complete confusion, or to destroy all its organs, and to deprive the soul of the whole of its organic body and of the ineradicable remains of all its preceding traces. But the ease with which people have abandoned the ancient doctrine that angels have subtle bodies (a doctrine which has been confused with the corporality of angels), the introduction of the allegedly separated intelligences among created things (to which the intelligences that rotated Aristotle's heavens have contributed much), and finally the poorly understood opinion some have held that we cannot retain the souls of beasts without falling into metempsychosis, all these in my opinion have resulted in the neglect of the natural way of explaining the preservation of the soul. This has done great harm to natural religion, and has led many to believe that our immortality is nothing but a miraculous grace of God. Our celebrated author speaks with some doubt about this, as I will soon point out. But I wish that all who are of this opinion discussed it as wisely and as sincerely as he does. For it is to be feared that several who speak of immortality through grace merely do so in order to preserve appearances, and are at bottom not very far from those Averroists and certain pernicious Quietists who imagine an absorption and reunion of the soul with the ocean of divinity, a notion whose impossibility is clearly shown by my system alone, perhaps.

It seems, moreover, that we also disagree about matter, insofar as the author judges that the void is necessary for motion, since he believes that the small parts of matter are rigid. I admit that if matter were composed of such parts, motion in a plenum would be impossible; it would be as if a room were filled with a quantity of little pebbles without containing the least empty place. But I cannot grant this assumption, for which there seems to be no reason, even though this able author goes so far as to believe that the rigidity or the cohesion of the small parts constitutes the essence of bodies. Rather, we should conceive of space as filled with matter that was originally fluid, matter capable of any division, and indeed,

actually subjected to division and subdivision to infinity, but with this difference, however, that it is unequally divisible and unequally divided in different places because of the motions there, motions which are already more or less harmonious. This brings it about that it has rigidity as well as fluidity everywhere, and that no body is hard or fluid to the ultimate degree, that is, that no atom has insuperable hardness, nor is any mass entirely indifferent to division. The order of nature, and particularly the law of continuity, also destroys both alternatives equally well.

I have also shown that *cohesion*, which is not itself an effect of impulsion or motion, would cause *traction*, properly speaking. For if there were an originally rigid body, an Epicurean atom, for example, which had a part projecting in the form of a hook (since we can imagine atoms in all sorts of shapes), this hook when pushed would pull with it the rest of the atom, that is to say, the part not pushed and not falling within the line of the impulse. However, our able author is himself opposed to those philosophical tractions, like the ones formerly attributed to the fear of the void, and he reduces them to impulses, maintaining with the moderns that one part of matter operates on another only by pushing against it from close by. I think that they are right about this, because otherwise the operation would not be intelligible at all.

I must not, however, conceal the fact that I have noticed a kind of retraction on this point on the part of our excellent author, and I cannot refrain from praising his modest sincerity about it, just as I have admired his penetrating insight on other occasions. His retraction occurs on page 408 of the reply to the second letter of the late Bishop of Worcester, printed in 1699. There, in order to justify the view he maintained against this learned prelate, namely that matter is capable of thought, he says among other things: "*It is true,*" I say "*that bodies operate by impulse and nothing else*" (*Essay*, Book II, chap. 8, sec. 11). "*And so I thought when I writ it, and can yet conceive no other way of their operation. But I am since convinced by the judicious Mr. Newton's incomparable book, that it is too bold a presumption to limit God's power, [in this point,] by our narrow conceptions. The gravitation of matter towards matter, by ways inconceivable to me, is not only a demonstration that God can, if he pleases, put into bodies powers and ways of operation, above what can be derived from our idea of body or can be explained by what we know of matter, but also an unquestionable [and everywhere visible] instance, that he has actually done so. And therefore, in the next edition of my book I shall take care to have that passage rectified.*"[9] I find in the French version of this book, which was no doubt taken from the latest editions, that sec. 11 reads thus: *It is manifest, at least insofar as we can conceive it, that it is by impulse and nothing else that bodies operate one upon another, it being impossible to conceive that body should operate on what it does not touch, which is all one to imagine that it can operate where it is not.*[10]

I can only praise the modest piety of our famous author, who recognizes that God can do what goes beyond our understanding, and thus, that there may be inconceivable mysteries in the articles of faith. But I would not want us to be obliged to appeal to miracles in the ordinary course of nature, and to admit absolutely inexplicable powers and operations there. Otherwise, on the strength of what God can do, we would grant too much license to bad philosophers, allowing them those *centripetal virtues* or those *immediate attractions* at a distance, without it being possible to make them intelligible; I do not see what would prevent our Scholastics from saying that everything happens simply through faculties and from maintaining their intentional species, which go from objects to us and find a way of entering our souls. If this is acceptable, *What I said could not be will now happen.*[11] So it seems to me that our author, judicious as he is, is here going rather too much from one extreme to the other. He raises difficulties about the operations of *souls*, when it is merely a matter of admitting what is not *sensible*, while here he grants *bodies* what is not even *intelligible*, allowing them powers and actions

beyond everything which, in my opinion, a created mind could do or understand; for he grants them attraction, even at great distances, without limitation to any sphere of activity, and he does so in order to maintain a view which is no less inexplicable, namely the possibility of matter thinking in the natural order of things.[12]

The question he is discussing with the noted prelate who had attacked him is whether *matter can think.* Since this is an important point, and an important point for the present work as well, I cannot avoid going into it a bit, and taking account of their debate. I shall represent the substance of their dispute and take the liberty of saying what I think of it. The late Bishop of Worcester [Edward Stillingfleet], fearing (but without great cause, in my opinion) that the author's doctrine of ideas was subject to some abuses prejudicial to the Christian faith, undertook to examine some aspects of it in his *Vindication of the Doctrine of the Trinity.* He first gives this excellent writer his due, by recognizing that the writer judges that the existence of the mind is as certain as that of the body, even though as regards these substances, the one is as little known as the other. He then asks (pp. 241 seqq.) how reflection could assure us of the existence of the mind if God can give matter the faculty of thinking, as our author believes (Book IV, chap. 3, [sec. 6]) since, as a consequence, the way of ideas, which should serve to discriminate what can belong to the soul or to the body, would become useless. However, it was said in Book II of the *Essay on the Understanding* (chap. 23, sec. 15, 27, 28), that the operations of the soul provide us with the idea of the mind, and that the understanding, together with the will, makes this idea as intelligible to us as the nature of body is made intelligible by solidity and impulse. Here is how our author replies to this in his First Letter (pp. 65 seqq.): [[*I think that I have proved that there is a spiritual substance in us. For*]] *we experi-*

---

9. [*Works* III, 467–68. The two passages in the brackets were omitted in Leibniz's French translation of Locke's text. In addition, Locke talks of "my narrow conceptions" rather than "our narrow conceptions."]

10. [Leibniz is referring here to Pierre Coste's translation, *Essai Philosophique Concernant l'Entendement Humain.* Published in 1700, the same year as the important 4th edition of the *Essay*, it represents an intermediate stage between the 3rd and 4th editions.]

11. [Ovid, *Tristia*, I.7.7.]

12. [In his notes for the preface, Leibniz wrote: "The philosophy of the author destroys what appears to me to be the most important thing, that the soul is imperishable, whereas on his view there must be a miracle for it to endure. This is directly opposed to the Platonic philosophy joined to that of Democritus and Aristotle, such as mine is." *Sämtliche Schriften und Briefe* (Darmstadt and Leipzig, 1923–) VI, 6, 48.]

ment in ourselves thinking. *The idea of this action, or mode of thinking, is inconsistent with the idea of self-subsistence, and therefore has a necessary connection with a support or subject of inhesion: the idea of that support is what we call substance. . . . The general idea of substance being the same everywhere, the modification of thinking, or the power of thinking, joined to it, makes it a spirit, without considering what other modification it has, as whether it has the modification of solidity or not. As, on the other side, substance, that has the modification of solidity, is matter, whether it has the modification of thinking or no. And therefore, if your lordship means by a spiritual, an immaterial substance, I grant I have not proved, nor upon my principles, can it be proved [. . .] that there is an immaterial substance in us [. . . .] Though I presume, what I have said about the supposition of a system of matter [. . .]* (Book IV, chap. 10, sec. 16) *(which there demonstrates that God is immaterial) will prove it in the highest degree probable, that the thinking substance in us is immaterial. . . .* [[*Yet I have shown* (adds the author, p. 68)]] *that all the great ends of religion and morality are secured . . . by the immortality of the soul, without a necessary supposition that the soul is immaterial.*[13]

In his *Reply* to this letter, to show that our author was of another opinion when he wrote Book II of the *Essay*, the learned Bishop quotes (p. 51) the following passage (Book II, chap. 23, sec. 15), where it is said that *by the simple ideas we have taken from those operations of our own minds [. . .] we are able to frame the complex idea of spirit. And thus, by putting together the ideas of thinking, perceiving, liberty, and power of moving our bodies, we have as clear a [. . .] notion of immaterial substances as we have of material.*[14] He further cites other passages to show that the author opposed mind to body. He says (p. 54) that the end of religion and morality is better secured by proving that the soul is immortal by its very nature, that is, immaterial. He further cites this passage (p. 70), that *all the ideas we have of particular, distinct sorts of*

substances *are nothing but several combinations of simple ideas,*[15] and that, consequently, the author believed that the idea of thinking and willing results in a substance different from that given by the idea of solidity and impulse. And he says that in sec. 17 the author remarks that the latter ideas constitute the body as opposed to the mind.

The Bishop of Worcester could have added that from the fact that the general idea of substance is in body and in mind, it does not follow that their differences are *modifications* of a single thing, as our author just said in the passage I cited from his *First Letter*. We must distinguish between modifications and attributes. The faculties of having perception and of acting, as well as extension, and solidity, are attributes, or perpetual and principal predicates; but thought, impetuosity, shapes, and motions are modifications of these attributes. Moreover, we must distinguish between the physical (or real) genus and logical (or ideal) genus. The things of the same physical genus, or those which are *homogeneous*, are of the same matter, so to speak, and can often be changed from one into another by changing their modifications, like circles and squares. But two heterogeneous things can have a common logical genus, and then their *differences* are neither simple accidental modifications of a single subject, nor of a single metaphysical or physical matter. Thus time and space are quite heterogeneous things, and we would be wrong to imagine some common real subject I-know-not-what which had only continuous quantity in general and whose modifications resulted in time or space. Yet their common logical genus is continuous quantity. Someone might perhaps make fun of these philosophical distinctions between two genera, the one only logical and the other real, and between two matters, the one physical — that of bodies — and the other only metaphysical or general, as if someone were to say that two parts of space are of the same matter or that two hours are also of the same matter as one another. Yet these distinctions concern not only terms, but also things themselves, and seem to be particularly relevant here, where their confusion has given rise to a false conclusion. These two genera have a common

---

13. [*Works* III, 33–34. Passages in double brackets are transitional phrases added by Leibniz.]
14. [In Locke, it was "themselves" rather than "our bodies." In later editions Leibniz added "immaterial" to spirit.]

15. [*Essay*, II.23.6.]

notion, and the notion of real genus is common to both sets of matters, so that their genealogy would be as follows:

GENUS
{
the merely *logical*, distinguished by simple *differences*

the *real*, that is, MATTER, where differences are *modifications*
}
{
the merely *metaphysical*, in which there is homogeneity

the *physical*, in which there is a solid, homogeneous mass
}

I have not seen the author's *Second Letter* to the bishop; the *Reply* that the prelate makes to it hardly touches the point about the thinking of matter. But our author's *Reply* to this *Second Reply* returns to it. *God* (he says, nearly in these words, page 397) *adds the qualities and perfections that please him to the essence of matter; to some parts [he adds] simple motion, to plants vegetation, and to animals sensation. Those who agree with me so far exclaim against me as soon as I go a step further and say that God may give to matter thought, reason, and volition — as if this would destroy the essence of matter. But to prove this assertion they advance that thought or reason is not included in the essence of matter; this proves nothing since motion and life are not included in it either. They also advance that we cannot conceive that matter can think; but our conception is not the measure of God's power.*[16] After this he quotes the example of the attraction of matter (p. 99, but especially p. 408), in which he speaks of the gravitation of matter toward matter, attributed to Mr. Newton, in the words I quoted above, admitting that we can never conceive how this happens. This is, in fact, a return to occult qualities or, what is more, to inexplicable qualities. He adds (p. 401) that nothing is more apt to favor the skeptics than denying what we don't understand, and (p. 402) that we do not even conceive how the soul thinks. He holds (p. 403) that since the two substances, material and immaterial, can be conceived in their bare essence without any activity, it is up to God to give the power of thinking to the one or to the other. And he wants to take advantage of his adversary's view, which grants sensation to beasts,

16. [This is a paraphrase of *Works* III 460–61.]

but does not grant them any immaterial substance. He claims that freedom, self-consciousness (p. 408), and the power of making abstractions can be given to matter, not as matter, but as enriched by divine power. Finally he reports (p. 434) the observation of a traveler as eminent and judicious as Mr. de la Loubere that the pagans of the East know of the immortality of the soul without being able to understand its immateriality.

With regard to all this I will note, before coming to the explanation of my opinion, that it is certain that matter is as little capable of producing sensation mechanically as it is of producing reason, as our author agrees. Furthermore, I note, indeed, that I recognize that we are not allowed to deny what we do not understand, though I add that we have the right to deny (at least in the order of nature) what is absolutely unintelligible and inexplicable. I also maintain that substances (material or immaterial) cannot be conceived in their bare essence without activity, and that activity is of the essence of substance in general. And finally, I maintain that the conception of creatures is not the measure of God's power, but that their conceptivity, or ability [*force*] to conceive, is the measure of nature's power; everything in conformity with the natural order can be conceived or understood by some creature.

Those who understand my system will judge that I will not be in complete agreement with either of these two excellent authors, whose dispute, however, is very instructive. But to explain myself distinctly, one must above all take into account that the modifications which can come naturally or without miracle to a single subject must come to it from the limitations or variations of a real genus or of an original nature, constant and absolute. For this is how in philosophy we distinguish the modes of an absolute being from the being itself; for example, we know that magnitude, shape, and motion are obviously limitations and variations of corporeal nature. For it is clear how a limitation of extension produces shapes, and that the change which takes place there is nothing but motion. And every time we find some quality in a subject, we ought to think that, if we understood the nature of this subject and of this quality, we would understand how this quality could result from that nature. Thus in the order of nature (setting miracles aside) God does not arbitrarily give these or those qualities indifferently to substances; he never gives them any but those which are natural to them, that is to say, those that can be derived from their nature as explicable modifications. Thus we can judge that matter does not naturally have the attraction mentioned above, and does not of itself move on a curved path, because it is not possible to conceive how this takes place, that is to say, it is not possible to explain it mechanically, whereas that which is natural should be capable of becoming distinctly conceivable, if we were admitted into the secrets of things. This distinction between what is natural and explicable and what is inexplicable and miraculous removes all the difficulties: If we were to reject it, we would uphold something worse than occult qualities, and in doing so we would renounce philosophy and reason, and throw open refuges for ignorance and idleness through a hollow system, a system which admits not only that there are qualities we do not understand (of which there are only too many) but also that there are some qualities that the greatest mind could not understand, even if God provided him with every possible advantage, that is, qualities that would be either miraculous or without rhyme or reason. And it would indeed be without rhyme or reason that God should ordinarily perform miracles, so that this do-nothing hypothesis would equally destroy philosophy, which searches for reasons, and the divine wisdom, which provides them.

As for the question of thinking, it is certain—and our author recognizes in more than one place—that thinking cannot be an intelligible modification of matter, that is, that a sensing or thinking being is not a mechanical thing like a watch or a windmill, in the sense that we could conceive of magnitudes, shapes, and motions whose mechanical conjunction could produce something thinking, and even sensing, in a mass in which there was nothing of the kind, that would likewise cease to be if the mechanism got out of order. Thus it is not natural for matter to sense and to think, and there are only two ways in which it could do so. One of these would be for God to join to it a substance to which thought is natural, and the other would be for God to endow it with

thought miraculously. In this, then, I agree entirely with the Cartesians, except that I extend the view to beasts as well, and believe that they have sensation and souls which are, properly speaking, immaterial and as imperishable as the atoms of Democritus or Gassendi. But the Cartesians, who are confused about the souls of beasts, and do not know what to do with them if they are preserved (since it did not occur to them that the animal might be preserved in a reduced form), have been forced to deny them even sensation, contrary to all appearances, and contrary to the judgment of mankind. But if someone said that God, at very least, can add this faculty of thinking to a mechanism properly prepared, I would answer that if this occurred, and if God added this faculty to matter without at the same time endowing it with a substance that was the subject in which this same faculty inhered (as I conceive it), that is, without adding an immaterial soul there, then matter would have to be raised miraculously so as to be capable of receiving a power of which it is not capable naturally, just as some Scholastics claim that God raises fire to the point of giving it the power directly to burn minds separated from matter, which would be a miracle, pure and simple. It is enough that we can maintain that matter thinks only if we attribute to it either an imperishable soul, or else a miracle, and thus, that the immortality of our souls follows from what is natural, since we could then hold that they are destroyed only by miracle, whether by exalting matter or by annihilating the soul. For we know, of course, that the power of God could make our souls mortal, even though they may be immaterial (or immortal by nature alone), since he is capable of annihilating them.

Now the truth of the immateriality of the soul is undoubtedly important. For it is infinitely more useful to religion and morality, especially in our days (when many people have scant respect for revelation by itself or for miracles), to show that souls are naturally immortal, and that it would be a miracle if they were not, than it would be to maintain that our souls must naturally die, and that it is due to a miraculous grace, based solely on God's promise, that they do not die. Moreover, we have known for a long time that those who wished to destroy natural religion, and reduce everything to revelation, as if reason taught us nothing about it, have been held suspect, and not always without reason. But our author is not of their number. He maintains a demonstration of God's existence and he attributes to the immateriality of the soul *a probability of the highest degree*, which may consequently pass for a *moral certainty*, so that I imagine that, having as much sincerity as penetration, he might quite well come to agree with the doctrine I have just expounded, a doctrine fundamental in every reasonable philosophy. For otherwise, I do not see how we can prevent ourselves from falling back into a fanatical philosophy, such as the *Mosaic philosophy* of Fludd, which saves all phenomena by attributing them immediately and miraculously to God, or into a barbaric philosophy, like that of certain philosophers and physicians of former days, who still savored of the barbarism of their own age, and who today are justly despised. They saved the appearances by explicitly fabricating suitable occult qualities or faculties, which were thought to be like little demons or spirits able to do what was required of them without any fuss, just as if pocket watches told time by some faculty of clockness without the need of wheels, or mills crushed grain by a fractive faculty without the need of anything like millstones. As for the difficulty many people have had in conceiving an immaterial substance, it soon ceases (at least in large part) when one no longer requires substances separated from matter; I hold, in fact, that such substances have never existed naturally among created things.

2. BERKELEY'S *PRINCIPLES*, *THREE DIALOGUES*, AND *ON MOTION*

George Berkeley was born in Kilkenny, Ireland, in 1685 and attended Kilkenny College from 1696 to 1700 and then Trinity College, Dublin, earning his B.A. in 1704 and his M.A. in 1707; he was then elected a Fellow of Trinity College. An ordained Anglican priest, he traveled first to London in 1713, where Swift presented him at Court and introduced him to Pope, Gay, Addison, and Steele, and then to France and Italy (1713–14 and again 1716–20). In 1728, after marrying Anne Foster, he sailed to Newport, Rhode Island, in hopes of founding a college in Bermuda to train the sons of mainland colonists and native Americans in religion and the useful arts. After several years of waiting for funds that were promised but never sent, he returned to England in 1731. In 1734 he became Anglican Bishop of Cloyne (in southern Ireland) and remained there until he retired to Oxford in 1752. He died a year later. Throughout the course of his career, he worked in a wide variety of areas of natural philosophy, including optics, mathematics, and physics as well as epistemology and metaphysics. Specifically, he published *An Essay towards a New Theory of Vision* in 1709, *A Treatise concerning the Principles of Human Knowledge* in 1710, *Three Dialogues between Hylas and Philonous* in 1713, *On Motion* in 1721, *Alciphron: or the Minute Philosopher* in 1732, *The Theory of Vision, or Visual Language Vindicated and Explained* in 1733, *The Analyst* in 1734, and *Siris* in 1744.[1]

While the literary form of Berkeley's two best-known philosophical works, namely the *Principles* and *Three Dialogues*, are very different, the doctrines presented in each are virtually identical. The *Principles* begins with a straightforward statement of Berkeley's main principles (in the Introduction and in §§1–33 of Part I) and is followed by discussions of possible objections one might make to these principles (§§34–84) and of how to understand their consequences (§§85–156), while the *Three Dialogues* takes the form

---

1. For more on Berkeley, see Ian C. Tipton, *Berkeley: The Philosophy of Immaterialism* (London: Methuen, 1974); Robert Merrihew Adams, "Berkeley's 'Notion' of Spiritual Substance," *Archiv für Geschichte der Philosophie* 55 (1973), pp. 47–69; Kenneth Winkler, *Berkeley: An Interpretation* (Oxford: Oxford University Press, 1989); and Margaret Atherton, *Berkeley's Revolution in Vision* (Ithaca: Cornell University Press, 1990).

of a spirited debate between Hylas, who attempts to articulate and defend a position that accepts material substance, and Philonaus, who represents Berkeley's own idealistic position.

The doctrine for which Berkeley is best known is his thesis that *esse est percipi aut percipere*, that is, to be is to be perceived or to perceive. In other words, the only things that exist, according to Berkeley, are ideas and the minds (or immaterial spirits) that have them. Most importantly, in both works he argues at length against independently existing material substance (of the sort that Locke accepted, albeit as "something I know not what" that underlies an object's properties and that causes one's ideas of it). The general thrust of Berkeley's argument is that we can have no intelligible (i.e., non-contradictory) conception of such a substance, and even if we could form such a conception, we could have no reason (or evidence) for believing that such a substance existed. Such a substance cannot be conceived, because it is contradictory to talk of conceiving of a thing that is unconceived. (Material substance must be "unconceived" insofar as, by definition, it exists independently of any mind.) Even if we could form an idea of such a substance, we have no reason to accept that such a substance exists, since all we ever directly perceive are our ideas as opposed to material substance. Plus, it is admitted by all that our perceptions could be what they are even if no material substance existed at all (e.g., if God caused us to have all the ideas we have). In fact, Berkeley claims important advantages for his theory. For example, it eliminates the problem of skepticism, since one need not worry about whether one's ideas correspond to an external reality (given that external reality is being denied). He also thinks that matter is the main support for atheism and fatalism. Accordingly, rejecting matter takes away support from doctrines that are, in his eyes, dangerous.

One can also see how Berkeley is influenced by and reacts to both Locke and Malebranche. While he seems to agree with Locke's broadly empiricist framework (according to which experience, as opposed to innate ideas, forms the basis for all ideas), he rejects Locke's distinction between primary and secondary qualities. At least part of Locke's motive

for drawing the distinction was to show that the ideas we have of at least some qualities, namely secondary qualities (such as color, taste, sound, etc.), do not imply the existence of those qualities in the object on the grounds that they are not required to explain what occurs in these objects (since the primary qualities such as bulk, figure, number, and motion are supposed to suffice for such explanations). Obviously, Berkeley is sympathetic to arguments showing that our ideas of certain properties do not imply the existence of these properties in the object. However, since Berkeley rejects not just secondary qualities, but material substances altogether, he must also reject the primary qualities that are alleged to inhere in them. To this end, he develops many of Locke's arguments against secondary qualities in such a way that they apply to primary qualities as well. In effect, he shows that there is no distinction between our ideas of primary and secondary qualities and thus that a rejection of the one implies a rejection of the other. Of course, without either primary or secondary qualities, there is no content to our notion of material substances.

Given that Berkeley rejects material substances, it is clear that they cannot be used to explain the perceptions that minds have. So what can? What causes me to sense this book in front of me, given that the book does not exist independently of me? Berkeley's answer is God. At this point, Berkeley's position might appear to be very close to Malebranche's. Malebranche rejects all causation at the level of finite substances, insisting that God alone is a real cause. This general doctrine then implies that it is God, rather than any finite substance (whether material or immaterial), who creates ideas. Malebranche famously develops his epistemology on this basis, claiming that we can have knowledge of objects only through a vision in God, that is, by participating in God's ideas. Obviously, Berkeley is sympathetic to Malebranche's idea that God rather any material substance causes our ideas of objects (as well as to Malebranche's view of self-consciousness, according to which the mind is aware of itself immediately, i.e., not by way of ideas). Berkeley's *On Motion*, in particular, can be read as developing the implications of this Malebranchean thesis for physics. However, Berkeley does not accept Malebranche's theory of the vision in God. For according to Berkeley, "it is evident that the things I perceive are my own ideas," not God's.

The point is often made against Berkeley's idealism (e.g., by his contemporary, Samuel Johnson) that it cannot account for our commonsense view of the world: If there are no material substances, no matter or material object that exists independently of me, then the stone that I see in front of me would not hurt my foot in the least, were I to kick it; after all, the stone is merely an idea. However, Berkeley argues that this objection is misplaced. Although the stone is nothing beyond the idea I have, that in no way precludes the pain that I have when I kick it. For the pain, too, is nothing more than an idea. This response follows from Berkeley's more general advice to think with the learned, but speak with the vulgar. For Berkeley thinks that idealism does not force one to change the way one speaks, though it may force one to change what one understands by what one says; one can say that the stone exists (and that I would hurt my foot if I decided to kick it), but one should not understand this to mean that the stone exists independently of the mind.

George Berkeley, A *Treatise Concerning the Principles of Human Knowledge* (1710)[1]

Preface

What I *make public here has, after a long and scrupulous inquiry, seemed to me evidently true and not unuseful to be known — particularly to those who are tainted with skepticism or want a demonstration of the existence and immateriality of God or the natural immortality of the soul. Whether it is so or not, I am content the reader should impartially examine, since I do not think myself any further concerned for the success of what I have written than as it is agreeable to truth. But to the end this may not suffer, I make it my request that the reader suspend his judgment until he has, at least, once read the whole through with that degree of attention and thought which the subject matter shall seem to deserve. For as there are some passages that, taken by themselves, are very liable to gross misinterpretation (nor could it be remedied), and to be charged with most absurd consequences, which, nevertheless, upon an entire perusal will appear not to follow from them; so likewise, though the whole should be read over, yet if this is done transiently, it is very probable my sense may be mistaken, but to a thinking reader, I flatter myself, it will be throughout*

clear and obvious. As for the characters of novelty and singularity, which some of the following notions may seem to bear, it is, I hope, needless to make any apology on that account. He must surely be either very weak or very little acquainted with the sciences, who shall reject a truth that is capable of demonstration for no other reason but because it is newly known and contrary to the prejudices of mankind. This much I thought fit to premise in order to prevent, if possible, the hasty censures of a sort of men who are too apt to condemn an opinion before they rightly comprehend it.

Introduction

1. Philosophy being nothing else but the study of wisdom and truth, it may with reason be expected that those who have spent most time and pains in it should enjoy a greater calm and serenity of mind, a greater clearness and evidence of knowledge, and be less disturbed with doubts and difficulties than other men. Yet so it is, we see the illiterate bulk of mankind, who walk the high road of plain, common sense and are governed by the dictates of nature, for the most part easy and undisturbed. To them nothing that is familiar appears unaccountable or difficult to comprehend. They do not complain of any want of evidence in their senses, and are out of all danger of

1. [From *The Works of George Berkeley*, ed. G. N. Wright (London, 1843), 2 vols., English, modified.]

becoming *skeptics*. But no sooner do we depart from sense and instinct to follow the light of a superior principle, to reason, meditate, and reflect on the nature of things, but a thousand scruples spring up in our minds concerning those things which before we seemed fully to comprehend. Prejudices and errors of sense do from all parts discover themselves to our view, and, endeavoring to correct these by reason, we are insensibly drawn into uncouth paradoxes, difficulties, and inconsistencies, which multiply and grow upon us as we advance in speculation, until at length, having wandered through many intricate mazes, we find ourselves just where we were, or, which is worse, sit down in a forlorn skepticism.

2. The cause of this is thought to be the obscurity of things or the natural weakness and imperfection of our understandings. It is said the faculties we have are few and those designed by nature for the support and comfort (pleasure) of life and not to penetrate into the inward essence and constitution of things. Besides, the mind of man being finite, when it treats of things which partake of infinity, it is not to be wondered at if it runs into absurdities and contradictions out of which it is impossible it should ever extricate itself, it being of the nature of infinite not to be comprehended by that which is finite.

3. But, perhaps, we may be too partial to ourselves in placing the fault originally in our faculties and not rather in the wrong use we make of them. It is a hard thing to suppose that right deductions from true principles should ever end in consequences which cannot be maintained or made consistent. We should believe that God has dealt more bountifully with the sons of men than to give them a strong desire for that knowledge which he had placed quite out of their reach. This would not be agreeable to the accustomed indulgent methods of Providence, which, whatever appetites it may have implanted in the creatures, does usually furnish them with such means as, if rightly made use of, will not fail to satisfy them. Upon the whole I am inclined to think that the far greater part, if not all, of those difficulties which have up to now amused philosophers and blocked up the way to knowledge are entirely owing to ourselves—that we have first raised a dust and then complain we cannot see.

4. My purpose, therefore, is to try if I can discover what those principles are which have introduced all that doubtfulness and uncertainty, those absurdities and contradictions, into the several sects of philosophy, inasmuch as the wisest men have thought our ignorance incurable, conceiving it to arise from the natural dullness and limitation of our faculties. And surely it is a work well deserving our pains to make a strict inquiry concerning the first principles of *human knowledge*, to sift and examine them on all sides, especially since there may be some grounds to suspect that those obstacles and difficulties which stay and embarrass the mind in its search after truth do not spring from any darkness and intricacy in the objects or natural defect in the understanding so much as from false principles which have been insisted on and might have been avoided.

5. However difficult and discouraging this attempt may seem when I consider how many great and extraordinary men have gone before me in the same designs, yet I am not without some hopes upon the consideration that the largest views are not always the clearest and that he who is shortsighted will be obliged to draw the object nearer and may, perhaps, by a close and narrow survey discern that which had escaped far better eyes.

6. In order to prepare the mind of the reader for the easier conceiving what follows, it is proper to premise somewhat, by way of introduction, concerning the nature and abuse of language. But unraveling this matter leads me in some measure to anticipate my design by taking notice of what seems to have had a chief part in rendering speculation intricate and perplexed and to have occasioned innumerable errors and difficulties in almost all parts of knowledge. And that is the opinion that the mind has a power of framing *abstract ideas* or notions of things. He who is not a perfect stranger to the writings and disputes of philosophers must necessarily acknowledge that no small part of them are spent about abstract ideas. These are in a more especial manner thought to be the object of those sciences which go by the name of *logic* and *metaphysics* and of all that which passes under the notion of the most abstracted and sublime learning, in all of which one shall scarce find any question handled in such a manner as does not

suppose their existence in the mind and that it is well acquainted with them.

7. It is agreed on all hands that the qualities or modes of things never do really exist each of them apart by itself and separated from all others, but are mixed, as it were, and blended together, several in the same object. But we are told the mind, being able to consider each quality singly or abstracted from those other qualities with which it is united, does by that means frame abstract ideas to itself. For example, there is perceived by sight an object extended, colored, and moved; this mixed or compound idea the mind resolving into its simple constituent parts, and viewing each by itself, exclusive of the rest, does frame the abstract ideas of extension, color, and motion. Not that it is possible for color or motion to exist without extension, but only that the mind can frame to itself by *abstraction* the idea of color exclusive of extension and of motion exclusive of both color and extension.

8. Again, the mind having observed that, in the particular extensions perceived by sense, there is something common and alike in all, and some other things peculiar as this or that figure or magnitude, which distinguish them one from another, it considers apart or singles out by itself that which is common, making thereof a most abstract idea of extension which is neither line, surface, nor solid, nor has any figure or magnitude, but is an idea entirely prescinded from all these. So likewise the mind, by leaving out of the particular colors perceived by sense that which distinguishes them one from another and retaining that only which is common to all, makes an idea of color in abstract which is neither red, nor blue, nor white, nor any other determinate color. And, in like manner, by considering motion abstractly not only from the body moved, but likewise from the figure it describes and all particular directions and velocities, the abstract idea of motion is framed—which equally corresponds to all particular motions whatsoever that may be perceived by sense.

9. And as the mind frames to itself abstract ideas of qualities or modes, so it does, by the same precision or mental separation, attain abstract ideas of the more compounded beings, which include several coexistent qualities. For example, the mind, having observed that *Peter, James,* and *John* resemble each other in certain common agreements of shape and other qualities, leaves out of the complex or compounded idea it has of *Peter, James,* and any other particular man that which is peculiar to each, retaining only what is common to all, and so makes an abstract idea in which all the particulars equally partake, abstracting entirely from and cutting off all those circumstances and differences which might determine it to any particular existence. And after this manner it is said we come by the abstract idea of *man* or, if you please, humanity or human nature, in which it is true there is included color, because there is no man but has some color; but then it can be neither white, nor black, nor any particular color, because there is no one particular color in which all men partake. So likewise there is included stature, but then it is neither tall stature nor short stature, nor yet middle stature, but something abstracted from all these. And so of the rest. Moreover, there being a great variety of other creatures that partake in some parts, but not all, of the complex idea of *man,* the mind, leaving out those parts which are peculiar to men and retaining those only which are common to all the living creatures, frames the idea of *animal,* which abstracts not only from all particular men, but also all birds, beasts, fishes, and insects. The constituent parts of the abstract idea of animal are body, life, sense, and spontaneous motion. By *body* is meant body without any particular shape or figure, there being no one shape or figure common to all animals without covering either of hair or feathers, or scales, etc., nor yet naked—hair, feathers, scales, and nakedness being the distinguishing properties of particular animals, and, for that reason, left out of the *abstract idea.* Upon the same account the spontaneous motion must be neither walking, nor flying, nor creeping; it is nevertheless a motion, but what that motion is, it is not easy to conceive.

10. Whether others have this wonderful faculty of *abstracting their ideas,* they best can tell; for myself, I find indeed I have a faculty of imagining, or representing to myself the ideas of those particular things I have perceived and of variously compounding and dividing them. I can imagine a man with two heads or the upper parts of a man joined to the body of a

horse. I can consider the hand, the eye, the nose, each by itself abstracted or separated from the rest of the body. But then whatever hand or eye I imagine, it must have some particular shape and color. Likewise the idea of man that I frame to myself must be either of a white or a black or a tawny, a straight or a crooked, a tall or a short or a middle-sized man. I cannot by any effort of thought conceive the abstract idea above described. And it is equally impossible for me to form the abstract idea of motion distinct from the body moving and which is neither swift nor slow, curvilinear nor rectilinear; and the like may be said of all other abstract general ideas whatsoever. To be plain, I admit myself able to abstract in one sense, as when I consider some particular parts or qualities separated from others with which, though they are united in some object, yet it is possible they may really exist without them. But I deny that I can abstract one from another or conceive separately those qualities which it is impossible should exist so separated or that I can frame a general notion by abstracting from particulars in the manner aforesaid — which two last are the proper meanings of *abstraction*. And there are grounds to think most men will acknowledge themselves to be in my case. The generality of men which are simple and illiterate never pretend to *abstract notions*. It is said they are difficult and not to be attained without pains and study. We may therefore reasonably conclude that if there are such, they are confined only to the learned.

11. I proceed to examine what can be alleged in defense of the doctrine of abstraction and try if I can discover what it is that inclines the men of speculation to embrace an opinion so remote from common sense as that seems to be. There has been a late deservedly esteemed philosopher who, no doubt, has given it very much countenance by seeming to think that having abstract general ideas is what puts the widest difference in point of understanding between man and beast.[2] "The having of general ideas," he says, "is that which puts a perfect distinction between man and brutes, and is an excellency which the faculties of brutes do by no means attain unto. For it is evident we observe no footsteps in them of making use of

general signs for universal ideas, from which we have reason to imagine that they do not have the faculty of *abstracting* or making general ideas, since they have no use of words or any other general signs." And a little after: "Therefore, I think, we may suppose that it is in this that the species of brutes are discriminated from men, and it is that proper difference in which they are wholly separated, and which at last widens to so wide a distance. For if they have any ideas at all, and are not bare machines (as some would have them), we cannot deny them to have some reason. It seems as evident to me that they do some of them in certain instances reason as that they have sense, but it is only in particular ideas, just as they receive them from their senses. They are the best of them tied up within those narrow bounds, and have not (as I think) the faculty to enlarge them by any kind of *abstraction*." *Essay on Human Understanding* II, chap. 9, sec. 10, 11. I readily agree with this learned author that the faculties of brutes can by no means attain to *abstraction*. But then if this is made the distinguishing property of that sort of animals, I fear a great many of those that pass for men must be reckoned into their number. The reason that is here assigned why we have no grounds to think brutes have abstract general ideas is that we observe in them no use of words or any other general signs, which is built on this supposition, namely, that the making use of words implies the having general ideas. From this it follows that men who use language are able to abstract or generalize their ideas. That this is the sense and argument of the author will further appear by his answering the question he puts in another place. "Since all things that exist are only particulars, how do we come by general terms?" His answer is, "Words become general by being made the signs of general ideas." *Essay on Human Understanding* III, chap. 3, sec. 6. But to this I cannot assent, for it seems that a word becomes general by being made the sign, not of an abstract general idea, but of several particular ideas, any one of which it indifferently suggests to the mind. For example, when it is said *the change of motion is proportional to the impressed force*, or that *whatever has extension is divisible*, these propositions are to be understood of motion and extension in general, and nevertheless it will not follow that they

2. [Berkeley is referring to Locke.]

suggest to my thoughts an idea of motion without a body moved or any determinate direction and velocity, or that I must conceive an abstract general idea of extension which is neither line, surface, nor solid, neither great nor small, black, white, nor red, nor of any other determinate color. It is only implied that whatever motion I consider, whether it is swift or slow, perpendicular, horizontal, or oblique, or in whatever object, the axiom concerning it holds equally true. As does the other of every particular extension, it does not matter whether line, surface, or solid, whether of this or that magnitude or figure.

12. By observing how ideas become general, we may the better judge how words are made so. And here it is to be noted that I do not deny absolutely there are general ideas, but only that there are any *abstract general ideas,* for, in the passages above quoted, in which there is mention of general ideas, it is always supposed that they are formed by abstraction, after the manner set forth in sec. 8 and 9. Now, if we will annex a meaning to our words and speak only of what we can conceive, I believe we shall acknowledge that an idea, which considered in itself is particular, becomes general by being made to represent or stand for all other particular ideas of the same sort. To make this plain by an example, suppose a geometrician is demonstrating the method of cutting a line in two equal parts. He draws, for instance, a black line of an inch in length; this, which in itself is a particular line, is nevertheless with regard to its signification general, since, as it is used there, it represents all particular lines whatsoever, so that what is demonstrated of it is demonstrated of all lines or, in other words, of a line in general. And as that particular line becomes general by being made a sign, so the name *line,* which, taken absolutely is particular, by being a sign is made general. And as the former owes its generality not to its being the sign of an abstract or general line, but of all particular right lines that may possibly exist, so the latter must be thought to derive its generality from the same cause, namely, the various particular lines which it indifferently denotes.

13. To give the reader a yet clearer view of the nature of abstract ideas and the uses they are thought necessary to, I shall add one more passage out of the *Essay on Human Understanding,* which is as follows. "*Abstract ideas* are not so obvious or easy to children or the yet unexercised mind as particular ones. If they seem so to grown men, it is only because by constant and familiar use they are made so. For when we nicely reflect upon them, we shall find that general ideas are fictions and contrivances of the mind that carry difficulty with them, and do not so easily offer themselves as we are apt to imagine. For example, does it not require some pains and skill to form the general idea of a triangle (which is yet none of the most abstract, comprehensive, and difficult)? For it must be neither oblique nor rectangle, neither equilateral, isosceles, nor scalene, but *all and none* of these at once. In effect, it is something imperfect that cannot exist, an idea in which some parts of several different and *inconsistent* ideas are put together. It is true the mind in this imperfect state has need of such ideas, and makes all the haste to them it can for the convenience of communication and enlargement of knowledge, to both which it is naturally very much inclined. But yet one has reason to suspect such ideas are marks of our imperfection. At least this is enough to show that the most abstract and general ideas are not those that the mind is first and most easily acquainted with, nor such as its earliest knowledge is conversant about." IV, chap. 7, sec. 9. If any man has the faculty of framing in his mind such an idea of a triangle as is here described, it is in vain to pretend to dispute him out of it, nor would I go about it. All I desire is that the reader would fully and certainly inform himself whether he has such an idea or not. And this, I think, can be no hard task for anyone to perform. What is more easy than for anyone to look a little into his own thoughts and there try whether he has, or can attain to have, an idea that shall correspond with the description that is here given of the general idea of a triangle, which is *neither oblique, nor rectangle, equilateral, isosceles, nor scalene, but all and none of these at once?*

14. Much is here said of the difficulty that abstract ideas carry with them and the pains and skill requisite to the forming them. And it is on all hands agreed that there is need of great toil and labor of the mind to emancipate our thoughts from particular objects and raise them to those sublime speculations that are

conversant about abstract ideas, from all of which the natural consequence should seem to be that so difficult a thing as the forming abstract ideas was not necessary for *communication*, which is so easy and familiar to all sorts of men. But, we are told, if they seem obvious and easy to grown men, *it is only because by constant and familiar use they are made so.* Now I would gladly know at what time it is men are employed in surmounting that difficulty and furnishing themselves with those necessary helps for discourse. It cannot be when they are grown up, for then it seems they are not conscious of any such pains-taking; it remains, therefore, to be the business of their childhood. And surely the great and multiplied labor of framing abstract notions will be found a hard task for that tender age. Is it not a hard thing to imagine that a couple of children cannot chatter together about their sugarplums, and rattles, and the rest of their little trinkets, until they have first tacked together countless inconsistencies and so framed in their minds *abstract general ideas* and annexed them to every common name they make use of?

15. Nor do I think them a whit more needful for the *enlargement of knowledge* than for *communication*. It is, I know, a point much insisted on, that all knowledge and demonstration are about universal notions, to which I fully agree, but then it does not appear to me that those notions are formed by *abstraction* in the manner premised; *universality*, so far as I can comprehend, not consisting in the absolute, positive nature or conception of anything, but in the relation it bears to the particulars signified or represented by it, by virtue of which it is the case that things, names, or notions, being in their own nature *particular*, are rendered *universal*. Thus, when I demonstrate any proposition concerning triangles, it is to be supposed that I have in view the universal idea of a triangle, which ought not be understood as if I could frame an idea of a triangle which was neither equilateral, nor scalene, nor isosceles, but only that the particular triangle I consider—whether of this or that sort it does not matter—does equally stand for and represent all rectilinear triangles whatsoever, and is in that sense *universal*. All this seems very plain and not to include any difficulty in it.

16. But here it will be demanded how we can know any proposition to be true of all particular triangles, except we have first seen it demonstrated of the abstract idea of a triangle which equally agrees to all? For, because a property may be demonstrated to agree to some one particular triangle, it will not then follow that it equally belongs to any other triangle which in all respects is not the same with it. For example, having demonstrated that the three angles of an isosceles rectangular triangle are equal to two right ones, I cannot therefore conclude this affection agrees to all other triangles which have neither a right angle nor two equal sides. It seems therefore that to be certain this proposition is universally true we must either make a particular demonstration for every particular triangle, which is impossible, or once and for all demonstrate it of the *abstract idea of a triangle*, in which all the particulars do indifferently partake and by which they are all equally represented. To which I answer that, though the idea I have in view while I make the demonstration is, for instance, that of an isosceles rectangular triangle whose sides are of a determinate length, I may nevertheless be certain it extends to all other rectilinear triangles of whatever sort or bigness—and that because neither the right angle, nor the equality, nor determinate length of the sides are at all concerned in the demonstration. It is true the diagram I have in view includes all these particulars, but then there is not the least mention made of them in the proof of the proposition. It is not said the three angles are equal to two right ones because one of them is a right angle or because the sides comprehending it are of the same length. This sufficiently shows that the right angle might have been oblique and the sides unequal, and for all that the demonstration has held good. And for this reason it is that I conclude that to be true of any obliquangular or scalene which I had demonstrated of a particular right-angled, isosceles triangle, and not because I demonstrated the proposition of the abstract idea of a triangle. And here it must be acknowledged that a man may consider a figure merely as triangular, without attending to the particular qualities of the angles or relations of the sides. So far he may abstract, but this will never prove that he can frame an abstract general inconsistent idea of a triangle. In like manner we may consider *Peter* insofar as he is a man or insofar

as he is an animal without framing the aforementioned abstract idea either of man or of animal inasmuch as all that is perceived is not considered.

17. It would be an endless as well as a useless thing to trace the *schoolmen,* those great masters of abstraction, through all the manifold, inextricable labyrinths of error and dispute which their doctrine of abstract natures and notions seems to have led them into. What bickerings and controversies and what a learned dust has been raised about those matters, and what mighty advantage has been derived to mankind from this, are things at this day too clearly known to need being insisted on. And it had been well if the ill effects of that doctrine were confined to those only who make the most avowed profession of it. When men consider the great pains, industry, and parts that have, for so many ages, been laid out on the cultivation and advancement of the sciences, and that, notwithstanding all this, the far greater part of them remain full of darkness and uncertainty, and disputes that are likely never to have an end, and even those that are thought to be supported by the most clear and cogent demonstrations, contain in them paradoxes which are perfectly irreconcilable to the understandings of men, and that, taking all together, a small portion of them does supply any real benefit to mankind otherwise than by being an innocent diversion and amusement—I say, the consideration of all this is apt to throw them into a despondency and perfect contempt of all study. But this may perhaps cease, upon a view of the false principles that have obtained in the world, among all of which there is none, I think, has a more wide influence over the thoughts of speculative men than this of abstract general ideas.

18. I come now to consider the *source* of this prevailing notion, and that seems to me to be language. And surely nothing of less extent than reason itself could have been the source of an opinion so universally received. The truth of this appears as from other reasons so also from the plain confession of the ablest patrons of abstract ideas, who acknowledge that they are made in order to naming—from which it is a clear consequence that if there had been no such thing as speech or universal signs, there never had been any thought of abstraction. See book III, chap. 6, sec. 39, and elsewhere, of the *Essay on Human Understanding.* Let us therefore examine the manner in which words have contributed to the origin of that mistake. First, then, it is thought that every name has, or ought to have, only one precise and settled signification, which inclines men to think there are certain *abstract determinate ideas* which constitute the true and only immediate signification of each general name. And that it is by the mediation of these abstract ideas that a general name comes to signify any particular thing. Whereas, in truth, there is no such thing as one precise and definite signification annexed to any general name, they all signifying indifferently a great number of particular ideas—all of which does evidently follow from what has been already said and will clearly appear to anyone by a little reflection. To this it will be objected that every name that has a definition is thereby restrained to one certain signification. For example, a *triangle* is defined to be a *plain surface comprehended by three right lines,* by which that name is limited to denote one certain idea and no other. To this I answer that in the definition it is not said whether the surface is great or small, black or white, nor whether the sides are long or short, equal or unequal, nor with what angles they are inclined to each other, in all of which there may be great variety, and consequently there is no one settled idea which limits the signification of the word *triangle.* It is one thing to keep a name constantly to the same definition and another to make it stand everywhere for the same idea—the one is necessary, the other useless and impracticable.

19. Secondly, but to give a further account how words came to produce the doctrine of abstract ideas, it must be observed that it is a received opinion that language has no other end but the communicating of our ideas and that every significant name stands for an idea. This being so, and it being in addition certain that names which yet are not thought altogether insignificant do not always mark out particular conceivable ideas, it is straightway concluded that they stand for abstract notions. That there are many names in use among speculative men which do not always suggest to others determinate particular ideas is what nobody will deny. And a little attention will discover that it is not necessary (even in the strictest reasonings) that significant names which stand for

ideas should, every time they are used, excite in the understanding the ideas they are made to stand for—in reading and discoursing, names being for the most part used as letters are in *algebra*, in which, though a particular quantity is marked by each letter, yet to proceed right it is not requisite that in every step each letter suggest to your thoughts that particular quantity it was appointed to stand for.

20. Besides, the communicating of ideas marked by words is not the chief and only end of language, as is commonly supposed. There are other ends such as the raising of some passion, the exciting to or deterring from an action, the putting the mind in some particular disposition—to which the former is in many cases barely subservient, and sometimes entirely omitted, when these can be obtained without it, as I think does not infrequently happen in the familiar use of language. I entreat the reader to reflect with himself and see if it does not often happen either in hearing or reading a discourse that the passions of fear, love, hatred, admiration, disdain, and the like, arise immediately in his mind upon the perception of certain words without any ideas coming between. At first, indeed, the words might have occasioned ideas that were fit to produce those emotions; but, if I am not mistaken, it will be found that when language is once grown familiar, the hearing of the sounds or sight of the characters is often immediately attended with those passions which at first were accustomed to be produced by the intervention of ideas that are now quite omitted. May we not, for example, be affected with the promise of a *good thing*, though we do not have an idea of what it is? Or is not being threatened with danger sufficient to excite a dread, though we do not think of any particular evil likely to befall us, nor yet frame to ourselves an idea of danger in abstract? If anyone shall join ever so little reflection of his own to what has been said, I believe it will evidently appear to him that general names are often used in the propriety of language without the speaker's designing them for marks of ideas in his own which he would have them raise in the mind of the hearer. Even proper names themselves do not seem always spoken with a design to bring into our view the ideas of those individuals that are supposed to be marked by them. For example, when a school-

man tells me "Aristotle has said it," all I conceive he means by it is to dispose me to embrace his opinion with the deference and submission which custom has annexed to that name. And this effect may be so instantly produced in the minds of those who are accustomed to resign their judgment to the authority of that philosopher, as it is impossible any idea either of his person, writings, or reputation should go before. Innumerable examples of this kind may be given, but why should I insist on those things which everyone's experience will, I do not doubt, plentifully suggest unto him?

21. We have, I think, shown the impossibility of *abstract ideas*. We have considered what has been said for them by their ablest patrons, and endeavored to show they are of no use for those ends to which they are thought necessary. And lastly, we have traced them to the source from which they flow, which appears to be language. It cannot be denied that words are of excellent use in that by their means all that stock of knowledge which has been purchased by the joint labors of inquisitive men in all ages and nations may be drawn into the view and made the possession of one single person. But at the same time it must be admitted that most parts of knowledge have been strangely perplexed and darkened by the abuse of words and general ways of speech in which they are delivered. Since, therefore, words are so apt to impose on the understanding whatever ideas I consider, I shall endeavor to take them bare and naked into my view, keeping out of my thoughts, so far as I am able, those names which long and constant use has so strictly united with them—from which I may expect to derive the following advantages:

22. First, I shall be sure to get clear of all controversies purely verbal—the springing up of which weeds in almost all the sciences has been a main hindrance to the growth of true and sound knowledge. Secondly, this seems to be a sure way to extricate myself out of that fine and subtle net of *abstract ideas* which has so miserably perplexed and entangled the minds of men; and that with this peculiar circumstance, that by how much the finer and more curious was the wit of any man, by so much the deeper was he like to be ensnared and faster held there. Thirdly, so long as I confine my thoughts to my own ideas divested

of words, I do not see how I can be easily mistaken. The objects I consider I clearly and adequately know. I cannot be deceived in thinking I have an idea which I do not have. It is not possible for me to imagine that any of my own ideas are alike or unlike that are not truly so. To discern the agreements or disagreements that are between my ideas, to see what ideas are included in any compound idea and what not, there is nothing more requisite than an attentive perception of what passes in my own understanding.

23. But the attainment of all these advantages does presuppose an entire deliverance from the deception of words, which I dare hardly promise myself—so difficult a thing it is to dissolve a union so early begun and confirmed by so long a habit as that between words and ideas. This difficulty seems to have been very much increased by the doctrine of *abstraction*. For so long as men thought abstract ideas were annexed to their words, it does not seem strange that they should use words for ideas, it being found an impracticable thing to lay aside the word and retain the abstract idea in the mind, which in itself was perfectly inconceivable. This seems to me the principal cause why those men who have so emphatically recommended to others the laying aside all use of words in their meditations and contemplating their bare ideas have yet failed to perform it themselves. Of late many have been very sensible of the absurd opinions and insignificant disputes which grow out of the abuse of words. And in order to remedy these evils they advise well that we attend to the ideas signified and draw off our attention from the words which signify them. But however good this advice may be they have given others, it is plain they could not have a due regard to it themselves so long as they thought the only immediate use of words was to signify ideas and that the immediate signification of every general name was a *determinate, abstract idea*.

24. But, these being known to be mistakes, a man may with greater ease prevent his being imposed on by words. He who knows he has no other than *particular* ideas will not puzzle himself in vain to find out and conceive the *abstract* idea annexed to any name. And he who knows names do not always stand for ideas will spare himself the labor of looking for ideas where there are none to be had. It is, therefore, to

be wished that everyone would use his utmost endeavors to obtain a clear view of the ideas he would consider, separating from them all that dress and encumbrance of words which so much contribute to blind the judgment and divide the attention. In vain do we extend our view into the heavens and pry into the entrails of the earth, in vain do we consult the writings of learned men and trace the dark footsteps of antiquity; we need only draw the curtain of words to behold the fairest tree of knowledge, whose fruit is excellent and within the reach of our hand.

25. Unless we take care to clear the first principles of knowledge from the embarrassment and delusion of words, we may make infinite reasonings upon them to no purpose; we may draw consequences from consequences and be never the wiser. The further we go, we shall only lose ourselves the more irrecoverably and be the deeper entangled in difficulties and mistakes. Whoever, therefore, designs to read the following sheets, I entreat him to make my words the occasion of his own thinking and endeavor to attain the same train of thoughts in reading that I had in writing them. By this means it will be easy for him to discover the truth or falsity of what I say. He will be out of all danger of being deceived by my words and I do not see how he can be led into an error by considering his own naked, undisguised ideas.

Part I

1. It is evident to anyone who takes a survey of the objects of human knowledge that they are either ideas actually imprinted on the senses or else such as are perceived by attending to the passions and operations of the mind or, lastly, ideas formed by help of memory and imagination, either compounding, dividing, or barely representing those originally perceived in the aforesaid ways. By sight I have the ideas of light and colors with their several degrees and variations. By touch I perceive, for example, hard and soft, heat and cold, motion and resistance, and of all these more and less either as to quantity or degree. Smelling furnishes me with odors, the palate with tastes, and hearing conveys sounds to the mind in all their variety of tone and composition. And as several of these are observed to accompany each other, they come to be

marked by one name, and so to be reputed as one thing. Thus, for example, a certain color, taste, smell, figure, and consistency having been observed to go together are accounted one distinct thing and signified by the name *apple*. Other collections of ideas constitute a stone, a tree, a book, and the like sensible things—which, as they are pleasing or disagreeable, excite the passions of love, hatred, joy, grief, and so forth.

2. But, besides all that endless variety of ideas or objects of knowledge, there is likewise something which knows or perceives them and exercises various operations as willing, imagining, remembering about them. This perceiving, active being is what I call *mind*, *spirit*, *soul*, or *myself*, by which words I do not denote any one of my ideas, but a thing entirely distinct from them, in which they exist or, which is the same thing, by which they are perceived—for the existence of an idea consists in being perceived.

3. That neither our thoughts, nor passions, nor ideas formed by the imagination exist without the mind is what everybody will allow. And (to me) it seems no less evident that the various sensations or ideas imprinted on the sense, however blended or combined together (that is, whatever objects they compose), cannot exist otherwise than in a mind perceiving them. I think an intuitive knowledge may be obtained of this by anyone who shall attend to what is meant by the term *exist* when applied to sensible things. The table I write on, I say, exists; that is, I see and feel it; and if I were out of my study I should say it existed—meaning by that that if I was in my study I might perceive it, or that some other spirit actually does perceive it. There was an odor; that is, it was smelled; there was a sound, that is to say, it was heard; a color or figure, and it was perceived by sight or touch. This is all that I can understand by these and the like expressions. For as to what is said of the absolute existence of unthinking things, without any relation to their being perceived, that seems perfectly unintelligible. Their *esse* is *percipi*, nor is it possible they should have any existence out of the minds or thinking things which perceive them.

4. It is indeed an opinion strangely prevailing among men that houses, mountains, rivers, and, in a word, sensible objects have an existence, natural or real, distinct from their being perceived by the understanding. But with however great an assurance and acquiescence this principle may be entertained in the world, yet whoever shall find in his heart to call it in question may, if I am not mistaken, perceive it to involve a manifest contradiction. For what are the aforementioned objects but the things we perceive by sense? And what do we perceive besides our own ideas or sensations? And is it not plainly repugnant that any one of these or any combination of them should exist unperceived?

5. If we thoroughly examine this tenet, it will, perhaps, be found at bottom to depend on the doctrine of *abstract ideas*. For can there be a nicer strain of abstraction than to distinguish the existence of sensible objects from their being perceived, so as to conceive them existing unperceived? Light and colors, heat and cold, extension and figures—in a word, the things we see and feel—what are they but so many sensations, notions, ideas, or impressions on the sense? And is it possible to separate, even in thought, any of these from perception? For my part I might as easily divide a thing from itself. I may indeed divide in my thoughts or conceive apart from each other those things which, perhaps, I never perceived by sense so divided. Thus I imagine the trunk of a human body without the limbs or conceive the smell of a rose without thinking of the rose itself. So far I will not deny I can abstract, if that may properly be called *abstraction* which extends only to the conceiving separately such objects as it is possible may really exist or be actually perceived asunder. But my conceiving or imagining power does not extend beyond the possibility of real existence or perception. Hence, as it is impossible for me to see or feel anything without an actual sensation of that thing, so is it impossible for me to conceive in my thoughts any sensible thing or object distinct from the sensation or perception of it. In truth, the object and the sensation are the same thing and cannot therefore be abstracted from each other.

6. Some truths are so near and obvious to the mind that a man need only open his eyes to see them. Such I take this important one to be, namely, that all the choir of heaven and furniture of the earth, in a word, all those bodies which compose the mighty frame of

the world, do not have any subsistence without a mind—that their being [*esse*] is to be perceived or known, that consequently so long as they are not actually perceived by me or do not exist in my mind or that of any other created spirit, they must either have no existence at all or else subsist in the mind of some eternal spirit—it being perfectly unintelligible and involving all the absurdity of abstraction to attribute to any single part of them an existence independent of a spirit. To be convinced of this, the reader need only reflect and try to separate in his own thoughts the being of a sensible thing from its being perceived.

7. From what has been said it follows there is not any other substance than *spirit,* or that which perceives. But for the fuller proof of this point, let it be considered the sensible qualities are color, figure, motion, smell, taste, and qualities of a similar kind— that is, the ideas perceived by sense. Now for an idea to exist in an unperceiving thing is a manifest contradiction, for to have an idea is all one as to perceive; that, therefore, in which color, figure, and the like qualities exist must perceive them; hence it is clear there can be no unthinking substance or *substratum* of those ideas.

8. But, you say, though the ideas themselves do not exist without the mind, yet there may be things like them of which they are copies or resemblances, which things exist without the mind in an unthinking substance. I answer, an idea can be like nothing but an idea; a color or figure can be like nothing but another color or figure. If we look but ever so little into our thoughts, we shall find it impossible for us to conceive a likeness except only between our ideas. Again, I ask whether those supposed originals or external things of which our ideas are the pictures or representations are themselves perceivable or not? If they are, then they are ideas and we have gained our point; but if you say they are not, I appeal to anyone whether it makes sense to assert a color is like something which is invisible; hard or soft, like something which is intangible; and so of the rest.

9. There are some who make a distinction between *primary* and *secondary* qualities. By the former they mean extension, figure, motion, rest, solidity or impenetrability, and number; by the latter they denote all other sensible qualities, as colors, sounds, tastes, and so forth. The ideas we have of these they acknowledge not to be the resemblances of anything existing without the mind or unperceived, but they will have our ideas of the primary qualities to be patterns or images of things which exist without the mind, in an unthinking substance which they call matter. By matter, therefore, we are to understand an inert, senseless substance, in which extension, figure, and motion do actually subsist. But it is evident from what we have already shown that extension, figure, and motion are only ideas existing in the mind, and that an idea can be like nothing but another idea, and that consequently neither they nor their archetypes can exist in an unperceiving substance. Hence it is plain that the very notion of what is called matter, or corporeal substance, involves a contradiction in it.[3]

10. Those who assert that figure, motion, and the rest of the primary or original qualities do exist without the mind in unthinking substances do at the same time acknowledge that colors, sounds, heat, cold, and secondary qualities of a similar kind do not—which they tell us are sensations existing in the mind alone that depend on and are occasioned by the different size, texture, and motion of the minute particles of matter. This they take for an undoubted truth which they can demonstrate beyond all exception. Now, if it is certain that those original qualities are inseparably united with the other sensible qualities and not, even in thought, capable of being abstracted from them, it plainly follows that they exist only in the mind. But I desire anyone to reflect and try whether he can, by any abstraction of thought, conceive the extension and motion of a body without all other sensible qualities. For my own part, I see evidently that it is not in my power to frame an idea of a body extended and moved, but I must in addition give it some color or other sensible quality which is acknowledged to exist only in the mind. In short, extension, figure, and

3. Inasmuch as I should not think it necessary to spend more time in exposing its absurdity. But because the tenet of the existence of matter seems to have taken so deep a root in the minds of philosophers, and draws after it so many ill consequences, I choose rather to be thought prolix and tedious than omit anything that might conduce to the full discovery and extirpation of that prejudice.

motion, abstracted from all other qualities, are inconceivable. Where, therefore, the other sensible qualities are, these must be also, namely, in the mind and nowhere else.

11. Again, *great* and *small*, *swift* and *slow*, are allowed to exist nowhere without the mind, being entirely relative, and changing as the frame or position of the organs of sense varies. The extension, therefore, which exists without the mind is neither great nor small, the motion neither swift nor slow—that is, they are nothing at all. But, you say, they are extension in general and motion in general; thus we see how much the tenet of extended, movable substances existing without the mind depends on that strange doctrine of *abstract ideas*. And here I cannot but remark how nearly the vague and indeterminate description of matter or corporeal substance which the modern philosophers are run into by their own principles resembles that antiquated and so much ridiculed notion of *materia prima*, to be met with in *Aristotle* and his followers. Without extension, solidity cannot be conceived; since, therefore, it has been shown that extension exists not in an unthinking substance, the same must also be true of solidity.

12. That number is entirely the creature of the mind, even though the other qualities are allowed to exist without, will be evident to whoever considers that the same thing bears a different denomination of number as the mind views it with different respects. Thus, the same extension is one, or three, or thirty-six, according as the mind considers it with reference to a yard, a foot, or an inch. Number is so visibly relative and dependent on men's understanding that it is strange to think how anyone should give it an absolute existence without the mind. We say one book, one page, one line; all these are equally units, though some contain several of the others. And in each instance it is plain the unit relates to some particular combination of ideas arbitrarily put together by the mind.

13. Unity, I know, some will have to be a simple or uncompounded idea accompanying all other ideas into the mind. That I have any such idea answering the word *unity* I do not find; and if I had, I think I could not miss finding it; on the contrary, it should be the most familiar to my understanding, since it is said to accompany all other ideas and to be perceived by all the ways of sensation and reflection. To say no more, it is an *abstract idea*.

14. I shall further add that, after the same manner as modern philosophers prove certain sensible qualities to have no existence in matter, or without the mind, the same thing may be likewise proved of all other sensible qualities whatsoever. Thus, for instance, it is said that heat and cold are affections only of the mind and not at all patterns of real beings, existing in the corporeal substances which excite them, for that the same body which appears cold to one hand seems warm to another. Now, why may we not as well argue that figure and extension are not patterns or resemblances of qualities existing in matter, because to the same eye at different stations, or eyes of a different texture at the same station, they appear various and cannot, therefore, be the images of anything settled and determinate without the mind? Again, it is proved that sweetness is not really in the said thing, because, the thing remaining unaltered, the sweetness is changed into bitter as in case of a fever or otherwise vitiated palate. Is it not as reasonable to say that motion is not without the mind, since, if the succession of ideas in the mind becomes swifter, the motion, it is acknowledged, shall appear slower without any alteration in any external object?

15. In short, let anyone consider those arguments which are thought manifestly to prove that colors and tastes exist only in the mind, and he shall find they may with equal force be brought to prove the same thing of extension, figure, and motion. Though it must be confessed this method of arguing does not so much prove that there is no extension or color in an outward object as that we do not know by sense which is the true extension or color of the object. But the previous arguments plainly show it to be impossible that any color or extension at all, or other sensible quality whatsoever, should exist in an unthinking subject without the mind or, in truth, that there should be any such thing as an outward object.

16. But let us examine a little the received opinion. It is said extension is a mode or accident of matter, and that matter is the *substratum* that supports it. Now I desire that you would explain what is meant by matter's *supporting* extension; you say, I have no

idea of matter and, therefore, cannot explain it. I answer, though you have no positive, yet if you have any meaning at all, you must at least have a relative idea of matter; though you do not know what it is, yet you must be supposed to know what relation it bears to accidents, and what is meant by its supporting them. It is evident *support* cannot here be taken in its usual or literal sense, as when we say that pillars support a building; in what sense therefore must it be taken?

17. If we inquire into what the most accurate philosophers declare themselves to mean by *material substance*, we shall find them acknowledge they have no other meaning annexed to those sounds but the idea of being in general together with the relative notion of its supporting accidents. The general idea of being appears to me the most abstract and incomprehensible of all others; and as for its supporting accidents, this, as we have just now observed, cannot be understood in the common sense of those words; it must, therefore, be taken in some other sense, but what that is they do not explain. So that when I consider the two parts or branches which make the signification of the words *material substance*, I am convinced there is no distinct meaning annexed to them. But why should we trouble ourselves any further in discussing this material *substratum* or support of figure and motion and other sensible qualities? Does it not suppose they have an existence without the mind? And is not this a direct repugnance and altogether inconceivable?

18. But though it is possible that solid, figured, movable substances may exist without the mind corresponding to the ideas we have of bodies, yet how is it possible for us to know this? Either we must know it by sense or by reason. As for our senses, by them we have knowledge only of our sensations, ideas, or those things that are immediately perceived by sense, call them what you will; but they do not inform us that things exist without the mind, or unperceived, like those which are perceived. This the materialists themselves acknowledge. It remains, therefore, that if we have any knowledge at all of external things, it must be by reason, inferring their existence from what is immediately perceived by sense. But what reason can induce us to believe the existence of bodies with-

out the mind from what we perceive, since the very patrons of matter themselves do not pretend there is any necessary connection between them and our ideas? I say it is granted on all hands (and what happens in dreams, frenzies, and the like, puts it beyond dispute) that it is possible we might be affected with all the ideas we have now, though no bodies resembling them existed without. Hence it is evident the supposition of external bodies is not necessary for the producing our ideas, since it is granted they are produced sometimes and might possibly be produced always in the same order we see them in at present without their concurrence.

19. But though we might possibly have all our sensations without them, yet perhaps it may be thought easier to conceive and explain the manner of their production by supposing external bodies in their likeness rather than otherwise; and so it might be at least probable there are such things as bodies that excite their ideas in our minds. But neither can this be said, for though we give the materialists their external bodies, they by their own confession are never the nearer knowing how our ideas are produced, since they admit themselves unable to comprehend in what manner body can act upon spirit or how it is possible it should imprint any idea in the mind. Hence it is evident the production of ideas or sensations in our minds can be no reason why we should suppose matter or corporeal substances, since that is acknowledged to remain equally inexplicable with or without this supposition. If, therefore, it were possible for bodies to exist without the mind, yet to hold they do so must necessarily be a very precarious opinion, since it is to suppose, without any reason at all that God has created innumerable beings that are entirely useless and serve to no manner of purpose.

20. In short, if there were external bodies, it is impossible we should ever come to know it; and if there were not, we might have the very same reasons to think there were that we have now. Suppose— what no one can deny possible—an intelligence, without the help of external bodies, to be affected with the same train of sensations or ideas that you are, imprinted in the same order and with like vividness in his mind. I ask whether that intelligence does not have all the reason to believe the existence of corporeal

substances, represented by his ideas and exciting them in his mind, that you can possibly have for believing the same thing? Of this there can be no question—this one consideration is enough to make any reasonable person suspect the strength of whatever arguments he may think himself to have for the existence of bodies without the mind.

21. Were it necessary to add any further proof against the existence of matter after what has been said, I could instance several of those errors and difficulties (not to mention impieties) which have sprung from that tenet. It has occasioned countless controversies and disputes in philosophy, and not a few of greater moment in religion. But I shall not enter into the detail of them in this place as well because I think arguments *a posteriori* are unnecessary for confirming what has been, if I am not mistaken, sufficiently demonstrated *a priori*, as because I shall find occasion to say something about them below.

22. I am afraid I have given cause to think me needlessly prolix in handling this subject. For to what purpose is it to dilate on that which may be demonstrated with the utmost evidence in a line or two to anyone who is capable of the least reflection? It is but looking into your own thoughts and so trying whether you can conceive it possible for a sound, or figure, or motion, or color, to exist without the mind or unperceived. This easy trial may make you see that what you contend for is a downright contradiction. Inasmuch as I am content to put the whole upon this issue, if you can but conceive it possible for one extended, movable substance, or in general, for any one idea, or anything like an idea, to exist otherwise than in a mind perceiving it, I shall readily give up the cause; and as for all that *compages*[4] of external bodies which you contend for, I shall grant you its existence, though you cannot either give me any reason why you believe it exists or assign any use to it when it is supposed to exist. I say the bare possibility of your opinion's being true shall pass for an argument that it is so.

23. But, you say, surely there is nothing easier than to imagine trees, for instance, in a park or books

4. [Wholes formed by the juncture of parts, frameworks or systems of conjoined parts, or complex structures.]

existing in a closet and nobody nearby to perceive them. I answer: you may so, there is no difficulty in it; but what is all this, I beseech you, more than framing in your mind certain ideas which you call *books* and *trees* and at the same time omitting to frame the idea of anyone that may perceive them? But do not you yourself perceive or think of them all the while? This, therefore, is nothing to the purpose; it only shows you have the power of imagining or forming ideas in your mind, but it does not show that you can conceive it possible that the objects of your thought may exist without the mind. To make this out, it is necessary that you conceive them existing unconceived or unthought of, which is a manifest repugnance. When we do our utmost to conceive the existence of external bodies, we are all the while only contemplating our own ideas. But the mind, taking no notice of itself, is deluded to think it can and does conceive bodies existing unthought of or without the mind, though at the same time they are apprehended by or exist in itself. A little attention will discover to anyone the truth and evidence of what is said here and make it unnecessary to insist on any other proofs against the existence of material substance.

24. It is very obvious, upon the least inquiry into our own thoughts, to know whether it is possible for us to understand what is meant by the *absolute existence of sensible objects in themselves or without the mind*. To me it is evident those words mark out either a direct contradiction or else nothing at all. And to convince others of this, I know no readier or fairer way than to entreat they would calmly attend to their own thoughts; and if by this attention the emptiness or repugnance of those expressions does appear, surely nothing more is requisite for their conviction. It is on this, therefore, that I insist, namely, that "the absolute existence of unthinking things" are words without a meaning or which include a contradiction. This is what I repeat and inculcate, and earnestly recommend to the attentive thoughts of the reader.

25. All our ideas, sensations, or the things which we perceive, by whatever names they may be distinguished, are visibly inactive—there is nothing of power or agency included in them. So that one idea or object of thought cannot produce or make any

alteration in another. To be satisfied of the truth of this, there is nothing else requisite but a bare observation of our ideas. For since they and every part of them exist only in the mind, it follows that there is nothing in them but what is perceived. But whoever shall attend to his ideas, whether of sense or reflection, will not perceive in them any power or activity; there is, therefore, no such thing contained in them. A little attention will discover to us that the very being of an idea implies passiveness and inertness in it, inasmuch as it is impossible for an idea to do anything or, strictly speaking, to be the cause of anything; neither can it be the resemblance or pattern of any active being, as is evident from sec. 8. From this it plainly follows that extension, figure, and motion cannot be the cause of our sensations. To say, therefore, that these are the effects of powers resulting from the configuration, number, motion, and size of corpuscles must certainly be false.

26. We perceive a continual succession of ideas; some are excited anew, others are changed or totally disappear. There is, therefore, some cause of these ideas on which they depend and which produces and changes them. That this cause cannot be any quality or idea or combination of ideas is clear from the preceding section. It must, therefore, be a substance; but it has been shown that there is no corporeal or material substance. It remains, therefore, that the cause of ideas is an incorporeal active substance or spirit.

27. A spirit is one simple, undivided, active being; as it perceives ideas it is called the *understanding,* and as it produces or otherwise operates about them it is called the *will*. Hence there can be no idea formed of a soul or spirit; for all ideas whatever, being passive and inert (see sec. 25), they cannot represent unto us, by way of image or likeness, that which acts. A little attention will make it plain to anyone that to have an idea which shall be like that active principle of motion and change of ideas is absolutely impossible. Such is the nature of *spirit*, or that which acts, that it cannot be of itself perceived but only by the effects which it produces. If any man shall doubt of the truth of what is here delivered, let him but reflect and try if he can frame the idea of any power or active

being, and whether he has ideas of two principal powers marked by the names *will* and *understanding,* distinct from each other as well as from a third idea of substance or being in general, with a relative notion of its supporting or being the subject of the aforesaid powers—which is signified by the name *soul* or *spirit*. This is what some hold; but, so far as I can see, the words *will, soul, spirit* do not stand for different ideas or, in truth, for any idea at all, but for something which is very different from ideas, and which, being an agent, cannot be like or represented by any idea whatsoever—though it must be admitted at the same time that we have some notion of soul, spirit, and the operations of the mind, such as willing, loving, hating, inasmuch as we know or understand the meaning of those words.

28. I find I can excite ideas in my mind at pleasure and vary and shift the scene as often as I think fit. It is no more than willing, and straightway this or that idea arises in my fancy; and by the same power it is obliterated and makes way for another. This making and unmaking of ideas does very properly denominate the mind active. This much is certain and grounded on experience, but when we talk of unthinking agents or of exciting ideas exclusive of volition, we only amuse ourselves with words.

29. But whatever power I may have over my own thoughts, I find the ideas actually perceived by sense do not have a like dependence on my will. When in broad daylight I open my eyes, it is not in my power to choose whether I shall see or not, or to determine what particular objects shall present themselves to my view; and so likewise as to the hearing and other senses—the ideas imprinted on them are not creatures of my will. There is, therefore, some other will or spirit that produces them.

30. The ideas of sense are more strong, lively, and distinct than those of the imagination; they have likewise a steadiness, order, and coherence and are not excited at random as those which are the effects of human wills often are, but in a regular train or series, the admirable connection of which sufficiently testifies to the wisdom and benevolence of its author. Now the set rules or established methods in which the mind we depend on excites in us the ideas of

sense are called the *laws of nature*; and these we learn by experience, which teaches us that such and such ideas are attended with such and such other ideas in the ordinary course of things.

31. This gives us a sort of foresight which enables us to regulate our actions for the benefit of life. And without this we should be eternally at a loss; we could not know how to do anything that might procure us the least pleasure or remove the least pain of sense. That food nourishes, sleep refreshes, and fire warms us; that to sow in the seedtime is the way to reap in the harvest; and, in general, that to obtain such or such ends, such or such means are conducive—all this we know, not by discovering any necessary connection between our ideas, but only by the observation of the settled laws of nature, without which we should be all in uncertainty and confusion, and a grown man would no more know how to manage himself in the affairs of life than an infant just born.

32. And yet this consistent, uniform working which so evidently displays the goodness and wisdom of that governing Spirit whose will constitutes the laws of nature is so far from leading our thoughts to him that it rather sends them wandering after second causes. For when we perceive certain ideas of sense constantly followed by other ideas and we know this is not of our own doing, we immediately attribute power and agency to the ideas themselves and make one the cause of another, than which nothing can be more absurd and unintelligible. Thus, for example, having observed that when we perceive by sight a certain round luminous figure, we at the same time perceive by touch the idea or sensation called *heat*, we do conclude from this the sun to be the cause of heat. And in like manner perceiving the motion and collision of bodies to be attended with sound, we are inclined to think the latter an effect of the former.

33. The ideas imprinted on the senses by the author of nature are called *real things*; and those excited in the imagination, being less regular, vivid, and constant, are more properly termed *ideas*, or *images of things* which they copy and represent. But then our sensations, be they never so vivid and distinct, are nevertheless *ideas*; that is, they exist in the mind or are perceived by it as truly as the ideas of its own

framing. The ideas of sense are allowed to have more reality in them, that is, to be more strong, orderly, and coherent than the creatures of the mind, but this is no argument that they exist without the mind. They are also less dependent on the spirit, or thinking substance which perceives them in that they are excited by the will of another and more powerful spirit, yet still they are *ideas*; and certainly no *idea*, whether faint or strong, can exist otherwise than in a mind perceiving it.

34. Before we proceed any further, it is necessary to spend some time in answering objections which may probably be made against the principles laid down so far. In doing this, if I seem too prolix to those of quick apprehensions, I hope it may be pardoned, since all men do not equally apprehend things of this nature; and I am willing to be understood by everyone. *First*, then, it will be objected that, by the foregoing principles, all that is real and substantial in nature is banished out of the world, and instead of this a chimerical scheme of *ideas* takes place. All things that exist, exist only in the mind, that is, they are purely notional. What therefore becomes of the sun, moon, and stars? What must we think of houses, rivers, mountains, trees, stones—no, even of our own bodies? Are all these but so many chimeras and illusions on the fancy? To all this and whatever else of the same sort may be objected, I answer that by the principles premised we are not deprived of any one thing in nature. Whatever we see, feel, hear, or any way conceive or understand remains as secure as ever, and is as real as ever. There is a *rerum natura*, and the distinction between realities and chimeras retains its full force. This is evident from sec. 29, 30, and 33, where we have shown what is meant by *real things* in opposition to *chimeras*, or ideas of our own framing; but then they both equally exist in the mind, and in that sense are like *ideas*.

35. I do not argue against the existence of any one thing that we can apprehend either by sense or reflection. That the things I see with my eyes and touch with my hands do exist, really exist, I do not question in the least. The only thing whose existence we deny is that which philosophers call matter or corporeal substance. And in doing this, there is no

damage done to the rest of mankind, who, I dare say, will never miss it. The atheist indeed will want the color of an empty name to support his impiety, and the philosophers may possibly find that they have lost a great handle for trifling and disputation.

36. If any man thinks this detracts from the existence or reality of things, he is very far from understanding what has been premised in the plainest terms I could think of. Take here an abstract of what has been said. There are spiritual substances, minds, or human souls, which will or excite ideas in themselves at pleasure, but these are faint, weak, and unsteady in respect of others they perceive by sense, which, being impressed upon them according to certain rules or laws of nature, speak themselves the effects of a mind more powerful and wise than human spirits. These latter are said to have more *reality* in them than the former—by which is meant that they are affecting, orderly, and distinct, and that they are not fictions of the mind perceiving them. And in this sense, the sun that I see by day is the real sun, and that which I imagine by night is the idea of the former. In the sense here given of *reality*, it is evident that every vegetable, star, mineral, and in general each part of the mundane system is as much a *real being* by our principles as by any other. Whether others mean anything by the term *reality* different from what I do, I entreat them to look into their own thoughts and see.

37. It will be urged that this much at least is true, namely that we take away all corporeal substances. To this my answer is that if the word *substance* is taken in the vulgar sense for a combination of sensible qualities, such as extension, solidity, weight, and the like, this we cannot be accused of taking away. But if it is taken in a philosophic sense for the support of accidents or qualities without the mind, then, indeed, I acknowledge that we take it away—if one may be said to take away that which never had any existence, not even in the imagination.

38. But, you say, it sounds very harsh to say we eat and drink ideas and are clothed with ideas. I acknowledge it does so, the word *idea* not being used in common discourse to signify the several combinations of sensible qualities which are called *things*;

and it is certain that any expression which varies from the familiar use of language will seem harsh and ridiculous. But this does not concern the truth of the proposition, which in other words is no more than to say we are fed and clothed with those things which we perceive immediately by our senses. The hardness or softness, the color, taste, warmth, figure, and such like qualities, which combined together constitute the several sorts of victuals and apparel, have been shown to exist only in the mind that perceives them; and this is all that is meant by calling them *ideas*. This word, if it was as ordinarily used as *thing*, would sound no harsher nor more ridiculous than it. I am not for disputing about the propriety but the truth of the expression. If therefore you agree with me that we eat, and drink, and are clad with the immediate objects of sense, which cannot exist unperceived or without the mind, I shall readily grant it is more proper or conformable to custom that they should be called things rather than ideas.

39. If it is demanded why I make use of the word *idea* and do not rather, in compliance with custom, call them *things*, I answer I do it for two reasons: first, because the term *thing*, in contradistinction to *idea*, is generally supposed to denote somewhat existing without the mind; second, because *thing* has a more comprehensive signification than *idea*, including spirits, or thinking things, as well as ideas. Since, therefore, the objects of sense exist only in the mind and are withal thoughtless and inactive, I chose to mark them by the word *idea*, which implies those properties.

40. But, say what we can, someone perhaps may be apt to reply that he will still believe his senses, and never suffer any arguments, however plausible, to prevail over the certainty of them. Be it so, assert the evidence of sense as high as you please, we are willing to do the same. That what I see, hear, and feel does exist, that is to say, is perceived by me, I no more doubt than I do of my own being. But I do not see how the testimony of sense can be alleged as a proof for the existence of anything which is not perceived by sense. We are not for having any man turn *skeptic*, and disbelieve his senses; on the contrary, we give them all the stress and assurance imaginable;

nor are there any principles more opposite to skepticism than those we have laid down, as shall be hereafter clearly shown.

41. *Secondly*, it will be objected that there is a great difference between real fire, for instance, and the idea of fire, between dreaming or imagining one's self burned and actually being so: this and the like may be urged in opposition to our tenets. To all which the answer is evident from what has been already said, and I shall only add in this place that if real fire is very different from the idea of fire, so also is the real pain that it occasions very different from the idea of the same pain; and yet nobody will pretend that real pain either is, or can possibly be, in an unperceiving thing or without the mind, any more than its idea.

42. *Thirdly*, it will be objected that we see things actually without or at a distance from us, and which consequently do not exist in the mind, it being absurd that those things which are seen at the distance of several miles should be as near to us as our own thoughts. In answer to this, I desire it may be considered that in a dream we do often perceive things as existing at a great distance off, and yet, for all that, those things are acknowledged to have their existence only in the mind.

43. But for the fuller clearing of this point, it may be worthwhile to consider how it is that we perceive distance and things placed at a distance by sight. For that we should in truth see external space, and bodies actually existing in it, some nearer, others further off, seems to carry with it some opposition to what has been said of their existing nowhere without the mind. The consideration of this difficulty it was that gave birth to my *Essay Towards a New Theory of Vision*, which was published not long since. Wherein it is shown that *distance*, or outness, is neither immediately of itself perceived by sight nor yet apprehended or judged of by lines and angles, or anything that has a necessary connection with it, but that it is only suggested to our thoughts by certain visible ideas and sensations attending vision, which in their own nature have no manner of similitude or relation, either with distance or things placed at a distance. But, by a connection taught us by experience, they come to signify and suggest them to us after the same manner

that words of any language suggest the ideas they are made to stand for. Insomuch that a man born blind and afterwards made to see, would not, at first sight, think the things he saw to be without his mind, or at any distance from him. See sec. 41 of the aforementioned treatise.

44. The ideas of sight and touch make two species, entirely distinct and heterogeneous. The former are marks and prognostics of the latter. That the proper objects of sight neither exist without the mind nor are the images of external things was shown even in that treatise. Though throughout the same, the contrary is supposed true of tangible objects—not that to suppose that vulgar error was necessary for establishing the notions laid down there, but because it was beside my purpose to examine and refute it in a discourse concerning *vision*. So that in strict truth the ideas of sight, when we apprehend by them distance and things placed at a distance, do not suggest or mark out to us things actually existing at a distance, but only admonish us what ideas of touch will be imprinted in our minds at such and such distances of time, and in consequence of such or such actions. It is, I say, evident from what has been said in the foregoing parts of this treatise, and in sec. 147 and elsewhere of the *Essay Concerning Vision*, that visible ideas are the language by which the governing Spirit, on whom we depend, informs us what tangible ideas he is about to imprint upon us, in case we excite this or that motion in our own bodies. But for a fuller information in this point, I refer to the essay itself.

45. *Fourthly*, it will be objected that from the foregoing principles it follows that things are every moment annihilated and created anew. The objects of sense exist only when they are perceived: The trees therefore are in the garden, or the chairs in the parlor, no longer than while there is somebody by to perceive them. Upon shutting my eyes, all the furniture in the room is reduced to nothing, and barely upon opening them it is again created. In answer to all which, I refer the reader to what has been said in sec. 3, 4, etc., and desire he will consider whether he means anything by the actual existence of an idea, distinct from its being perceived. For my part, after the nicest inquiry I could make, I am not able to discover that

anything else is meant by those words. And I once more entreat the reader to sound his own thoughts, and not suffer himself to be imposed on by words. If he can conceive it possible either for his ideas or their archetypes to exist without being perceived, then I give up the cause: But if he cannot, he will acknowledge it is unreasonable for him to stand up in defense of he knows not what, and pretend to charge on me as an absurdity the not assenting to those propositions which at bottom have no meaning in them.

46. It will not be amiss to observe how far the received principles of philosophy are themselves chargeable with those pretended absurdities. It is thought strangely absurd that upon closing my eyelids all the visible objects around me should be reduced to nothing; and yet is not this what philosophers commonly acknowledge when they agree on all hands that light and colors, which alone are the proper and immediate objects of sight, are mere sensations that exist no longer than they are perceived? Again, it may to some perhaps seem very incredible that things should be every moment creating; yet this very notion is commonly taught in the Schools. For the *Schoolmen,* though they acknowledge the existence of matter, and that the whole mundane fabric is framed out of it, are nevertheless of the opinion that it cannot subsist without the divine conservation, which by them is expounded to be a continual creation.

47. Further, a little thought will discover to us that though we allow the existence of matter or corporeal substance, yet it will unavoidably follow from the principles which are now generally admitted that the particular bodies, of whatever kind, do none of them exist while they are not perceived. For it is evident from sec. 11 and the following sections that the matter philosophers contend for is an incomprehensible somewhat, which has none of those particular qualities whereby the bodies falling under our senses are distinguished one from another. But to make this more plain, it must be remarked that the infinite divisibility of matter is now universally allowed, at least by the most approved and considerable philosophers, who, on the received principles, demonstrate it beyond all exception. Hence it follows that there is an infinite number of parts in each particle of

matter which are not perceived by sense. The reason, therefore, that any particular body seems to be of a finite magnitude, or exhibits only a finite number of parts to sense, is not because it contains no more, since in itself it contains an infinite number of parts, but because the sense is not acute enough to discern them. In proportion, therefore, as the sense is rendered more acute, it perceives a greater number of parts in the object; that is, the object appears greater, and its figure varies, those parts in its extremities which were before unperceivable appearing now to bound it in very different lines and angles from those perceived by a more obtuse sense. And, at length, after various changes of size and shape, when the sense becomes infinitely acute, the body shall seem infinite. During all which, there is no alteration in the body, but only in the sense. Each body, therefore, considered in itself, is infinitely extended and consequently void of all shape or figure. From which it follows that, though we should grant the existence of matter to be ever so certain, yet it is withal as certain, the materialists themselves are by their own principles forced to acknowledge that neither the particular bodies perceived by sense nor anything like them exist without the mind. Matter, I say, and each particle thereof, is, according to them, infinite and shapeless, and it is the mind that frames all that variety of bodies which compose the visible world, any one whereof does not exist longer than it is perceived.

48. If we consider it, the objection proposed in sec. 45 will not be found reasonably charged on the principles we have premised, so as in truth to make any objection at all against our notions. For though we hold, indeed, the objects of sense to be nothing else but ideas which cannot exist unperceived, yet we may not hence conclude they have no existence, except only while they are perceived by us, since there may be some other spirit that perceives them, though we do not. Wherever bodies are said to have no existence without the mind, I would not be understood to mean this or that particular mind, but all minds whatsoever. It does not therefore follow from the foregoing principles that bodies are annihilated and created every moment or exist not at all during the intervals between our perception in them.

49. *Fifthly*, it may perhaps be objected that if extension and figure exist only in the mind, it follows that the mind is extended and figured, since extension is a mode or attribute which (to speak with the schools) is predicated of the subject in which it exists. I answer: Those qualities are in the mind only as they are perceived by it that is, not by way of *mode* or *attribute*, but only by way of *idea*; and it no more follows that the soul or mind is extended because extension exists in it alone than it does that it is red or blue because those colors are on all hands acknowledged to exist in it and nowhere else. As to what philosophers say of subject and mode, that seems very groundless and unintelligible. For instance, in this proposition, a die is hard, extended, and square; they will have it that the word *die* denotes a subject or substance, distinct from the hardness, extension, and figure which are predicated of it and in which they exist. This I cannot comprehend: To me a die seems to be nothing distinct from those things which are termed its modes or accidents. And to say a die is hard, extended, and square is not to attribute those qualities to a subject distinct from and supporting them, but only an explication of the meaning of the word *die*.

50. *Sixthly*, you will say there have been a great many things explained by matter and motion: Take away these and you destroy the whole corpuscular philosophy and undermine those mechanical principles which have been applied with so much success to account for the *phenomena*. In short, whatever advances have been made either by ancient or modern philosophers in the study of nature do all proceed on the supposition that corporeal substance or matter does really exist. To this I answer that there is not any one *phenomenon* explained on that supposition which may not as well be explained without it, as might easily be made appear by an induction of particulars. To explain the *phenomena* is all one as to show why upon such and such occasions we are affected with such and such ideas. But how matter should operate on a spirit, or produce any idea in it, is what no philosopher will pretend to explain. It is therefore evident that there can be no use of matter in natural philosophy. Besides, they who attempt to account for things do it not by corporeal substance, but by figure,

motion, and other qualities, which are in truth no more than mere ideas, and therefore cannot be the cause of anything, as has been already shown. See sec. 25.

51. *Seventhly*, it will upon this be demanded whether it does not seem absurd to take away natural causes and ascribe everything to the immediate operation of spirits? We must no longer say upon these principles that fire heats, or water cools, but that a spirit heats, and so forth. Would not a man be deservedly laughed at who should talk after this manner? I answer: He would so; in such things we ought to *think with the learned and speak with the vulgar*. They who to demonstration are convinced of the truth of the Copernican system do nevertheless say the sun rises, the sun sets, or comes to the meridian; and if they affected a contrary style in common talk, it would without doubt appear very ridiculous. A little reflection on what is here said will make it manifest that the common use of language would receive no manner of alteration or disturbance from the admission of our tenets.

52. In the ordinary affairs of life, any phrases may be retained so long as they excite in us proper sentiments, or dispositions to act in such a manner as is necessary for our well-being, however false they may be, if taken in a strict and speculative sense. No, this is unavoidable, since propriety being regulated by custom, language is suited to the received opinions, which are not always the truest. Hence it is impossible, even in the most rigid philosophic reasonings, so far to alter the bent and genius of the tongue we speak as never to give a handle for cavillers to pretend difficulties and inconsistencies. But a fair and ingenuous reader will collect the sense from the scope and tenor and connection of a discourse, making allowances for those inaccurate modes of speech which use has made inevitable.

53. As to the opinion that there are no corporeal causes, this has been maintained up to now by some of the Schoolmen, as it is of late by others among the modern philosophers who, though they allow matter to exist, yet will have God alone to be the immediate efficient cause of all things. These man saw that among all the objects of sense, there was

none which had any power or activity included in it and that, by consequence, this was likewise true of whatever bodies they supposed to exist without the mind, like unto the immediate objects of sense. But then that they should suppose an innumerable multitude of created beings, which they acknowledge are not capable of producing any one effect in nature, and which therefore are made to no manner of purpose, since God might have done everything as well without them; this I say, though we should allow it possible, must yet be a very unaccountable and extravagant supposition.

54. In the *eighth* place, the universal concurrent assent of mankind may be thought by some an invincible argument in behalf of matter, or the existence of external things. Must we suppose the whole world to be mistaken? If so, what cause can be assigned of so widespread and predominant an error? I answer, first, that upon a narrow inquiry, it will not perhaps be found so many as is imagined do really believe the existence of matter or things without the mind. Strictly speaking, to believe that which involves a contradiction, or has no meaning in it, is impossible: and whether the foregoing expressions are not of that sort, I refer it to the impartial examination of the reader. In one sense, indeed, men may be said to believe that matter exists, that is, they act as if the immediate cause of their sensations, which affects them every moment and is so nearly present to them, were some senseless, unthinking being. But that they should clearly apprehend any meaning marked by those words and form thereof a settled speculative opinion is what I am not able to conceive. This is not the only instance wherein men impose upon themselves by imagining they believe those propositions they have often heard, though at bottom they have no meaning in them.

55. But secondly, though we should grant a notion to be ever so universally and steadfastly adhered to, yet this is but a weak argument of its truth to whoever considers what a vast number of prejudices and false opinions are everywhere embraced with the utmost tenaciousness by the unreflecting (which are the far greater) part of mankind. There was a time when the antipodes and motion of the earth were looked upon as monstrous absurdities, even by men of learning:

and if it is considered what a small proportion they bear to the rest of mankind, we shall find that, at this day, those notions have gained but a very inconsiderable footing in the world.

56. But it is demanded that we assign a cause of this prejudice and account for its obtaining in the world. To this I answer that men knowing they perceived several ideas of which they themselves were not the authors, as not being excited from within nor depending on the operation of their wills, this made them maintain that those ideas or objects of perception had an existence independent of, and without, the mind, without ever dreaming that a contradiction was involved in those words. But philosophers having plainly seen that the immediate objects of perception do not exist without the mind, they in some degree corrected the mistake of the vulgar, but at the same time run into another which seems no less absurd, namely, that there are certain objects really existing without the mind, or having a subsistence distinct from being perceived, of which our ideas are only images or resemblances, imprinted by those objects on the mind. And this notion of the philosophers owes its origin to the same cause with the former, namely, their being conscious that they were not the authors of their own sensations, which they evidently knew were imprinted from without and which therefore must have some cause distinct from the minds on which they are imprinted.

57. But why they should suppose the ideas of sense to be excited in us by things in their likeness, and not rather have recourse to *spirit* which alone can act may be accounted for, first, because they were not aware of the repugnancy there is in supposing things like unto our ideas existing without, as well as attributing to them power or activity. Secondly, because the supreme spirit, which excites those ideas in our minds, is not marked out and limited to our view by any particular finite collection of sensible ideas, as human agents are by their size, complexion, limbs, and motions. And thirdly, because his operations are regular and uniform. Whenever the course of nature is interrupted by a miracle, men are ready to admit the presence of a superior agent. But when we see things go on in the ordinary course, they do not excite in us any reflection; their order and

concatenation, though it is an argument of the greatest wisdom, power, and goodness in their creator, is yet so constant and familiar to us that we do not think them the immediate effects of a *free spirit*: especially since inconstancy and mutability in acting, though it is an imperfection, is looked on as a mark of *freedom*.

58. *Tenthly*, it will be objected that the notions we advance are inconsistent with several sound truths in philosophy and mathematics. For example, the motion of the earth is now universally admitted by astronomers as a truth grounded on the clearest and most convincing reasons; but on the foregoing principles, there can be no such thing. For motion being only an idea, it follows that if it is not perceived, it does not exist; but the motion of the earth is not perceived by sense. I answer: That tenet, if rightly understood, will be found to agree with the principles we have premised; for the question, whether the earth moves or not, amounts in reality to no more than this, namely, whether we have reason to conclude from what has been observed by astronomers that if we were placed in such and such circumstances, and such or such a position and distance, both from the earth and sun, we should perceive the former to move among the choir of the planets and appearing in all respects like one of them: and this, by the established rules of nature which we have no reason to mistrust, is reasonably collected from the phenomena.

59. We may, from the experience we have had of the train and succession of ideas in our minds, often make, I will not say uncertain conjectures, but sure and well-grounded predictions, concerning the ideas we shall be affected with, pursuant to a great train of actions, and be enabled to pass a right judgment of what would have appeared to us, in case we were in circumstances very different from those we are in at present. Herein consists the knowledge of nature, which may preserve its use and certainty very consistently with what has been said. It will be easy to apply this to whatever objections of the like sort may be drawn from the magnitude of the stars, or any other discoveries in astronomy or nature.

60. In the *eleventh* place, it will be demanded to what purpose serves that curious organization of plants and the admirable mechanism in the parts of animals? Might not vegetables grow, and shoot forth leaves and blossoms, and animals perform all their motions as well without as with all that variety of internal parts so elegantly contrived and put together, which, being ideas, have nothing powerful or operative in them nor have any necessary connection with the effects ascribed to them? If it is a spirit that immediately produces every effect by a *fiat*, or act of his will, we must think all that is fine and artificial in the works, whether of man or nature, to be made in vain. By this doctrine, though an artist has made the spring and wheels, and every movement of a watch, and adjusted them in such a manner as he knew would produce the motions he designed; yet he must think all this done to no purpose, and that it is an intelligence which directs the index, and points to the hour of the day. If so, why may not the intelligence do it, without his being at the pains of making the movements and putting them together? Why does not an empty case serve as well as another? And how does it come to pass that whenever there is any fault in the going of a watch, there is some corresponding disorder to be found in the movements, which being mended by a skillful hand, all is right again? The like may be said of all the clockwork of nature, great part whereof is so wonderfully fine and subtle as scarcely to be discerned by the best microscope. In short it will be asked, how upon our principles any tolerable account can be given, or any final cause assigned of an innumerable multitude of bodies and machines framed with the most exquisite art, which in the common philosophy have very apposite uses assigned them, and serve to explain abundance of phenomena.

61. To all which I answer, first, that though there were some difficulties relating to the administration of providence, and the uses by it assigned to the several parts of nature, which I could not solve by the foregoing principles, yet this objection could be of small weight against the truth and certainty of those things which may be proved *a priori*, with the utmost evidence. Secondly, but neither are the received principles free from the like difficulties; for it may still be demanded to what end God should take those round-about methods of effecting things by instruments and machines, which no one can deny might have been effected by the mere command of his will,

without all that *apparatus:* no, (thirdly,) if we narrowly consider it, we shall find the objection may be retorted with greater force on those who hold the existence of those machines without the mind; for it has been made evident that solidity, bulk, figure, motion, and the like, have no *activity* or *efficacy* in them so as to be capable of producing any one effect in nature. See sec. 25. Whoever therefore supposes them to exist (allowing the supposition possible) when they are not perceived, does it manifestly to no purpose, since the only use that is assigned to them, as they exist unperceived, is that they produce those perceivable effects, which in truth cannot be ascribed to anything but spirit.

62. But to come nearer the difficulty, it must be observed that though the fabrication of all those parts and organs is not absolutely necessary to the producing of any effect, yet it is necessary to the producing of things in a constant, regular way, according to the laws of nature. There are certain general laws that run through the whole chain of natural effects—these are learned by the observation and study of nature and are by men applied as well to the framing artificial things for the use and ornament of life as to the explaining the various *phenomena*—which explication consists only in showing the conformity any particular phenomenon has to the general laws of nature or, which is the same thing, in discovering the *uniformity* there is in the production of natural effects, as will be evident to whoever shall attend to the several instances in which philosophers pretend to account for appearances. That there is a great and conspicuous use in these regular constant methods of working observed by the supreme agent has been shown in sec. 31. And it is no less visible that a particular size, figure, motion, and disposition of parts are necessary, though not absolutely to the producing of any effect, yet to producing it according to the standing mechanical laws of nature. Thus, for instance, it cannot be denied that God, or the intelligence which sustains and rules the ordinary course of things, might, if he were minded to produce a miracle, cause all the motions on the dial-plate of a watch, though nobody had ever made the movements, and put them in it; but yet if he will act agreeably to the rules of mechanism, by him for wise ends established and

maintained in the creation, it is necessary that those actions of the watchmaker whereby he makes the movements and rightly adjusts them precede the production of the aforesaid motions, as also that any disorder in them is attended with the perception of some corresponding disorder in the movements which, being once corrected, all is right again.

63. It may indeed on some occasions be necessary that the author of nature display his overruling power in producing some appearance out of his ordinary series of things. Such exceptions from the general rules of nature are proper to surprise and awe men into an acknowledgment of the divine being, but then they are to be used but seldom, otherwise there is a plain reason why they should fail of that effect. Besides, God seems to choose the convincing our reason of his attributes by the works of nature, which discover so much harmony and contrivance in their make and are such plain indications of wisdom and beneficence in their author, rather than to astonish us into a belief of his being by anomalous and surprising events.

64. To set this matter in a clearer light, I shall observe that what has been objected in sec. 60 amounts in reality to no more than this: Ideas are not any how and at random produced, there being a certain order and connection between them, like to that of cause and effect; there are also several combinations of them, made in a very regular and artificial manner, which seem like so many instruments in the hand of nature that being hid, as it were, behind the scenes, have a secret operation in producing those appearances which are seen on the theatre of the world, being themselves discernible only to the curious eye of the philosopher. But since one idea cannot be the cause of another, to what purpose is that connection? And since those instruments, being barely *inefficacious perceptions* in the mind, are not subservient to the production of natural effects, it is demanded why they are made, or, in other words, what reason can be assigned why God should make us, upon a close inspection into his works, behold so great variety of ideas, so artfully laid together, and so much according to rule, it not being credible that he would be at the expense (if one may so speak) of all that art and regularity to no purpose?

65. To all which my answer is, first, that the connec-

tion of ideas does not imply the relation of *cause* and *effect*, but only of a mark or *sign* with the thing *signified*. The fire I see is not the cause of the pain I suffer upon my approaching it, but the mark that forewarns me of it. In like manner, the noise that I hear is not the effect of this or that motion or collision of the ambient bodies, but the sign thereof. Secondly, the reason why ideas are formed into machines, that is, artificial and regular combinations, is the same with that for combining letters into words. That a few original ideas may be made to signify a great number of effects and actions, it is necessary they are variously combined together and, to the end their use is permanent and universal, these combinations must be made by *rule* and with *wise contrivance*. By this means abundance of information is conveyed unto us concerning what we are to expect from such and such actions, and what methods are proper to be taken for the exciting such and such ideas—which in effect is all that I conceive to be distinctly meant when it is said that by discerning the figure, texture, and mechanism of the inward parts of bodies, whether natural or artificial, we may attain to know the several uses and properties depending thereon or the nature of the thing.

66. Hence it is evident that those things which, under the notion of a cause cooperating or concurring to the production of effects, are altogether inexplicable, and run us into great absurdities, may be very naturally explained, and have a proper and obvious use assigned them, when they are considered only as marks or signs for our information. And it is the searching after, and endeavoring to understand, those signs (this language, if I may so call it) instituted by the author of nature that ought to be the employment of the natural philosopher, and not the pretending to explain things by corporeal causes, which doctrine seems to have too much estranged the minds of men from that active principle, that supreme and wise spirit, "in whom we live, move, and have our being."

67. In the *twelfth* place, it may perhaps be objected that though it is clear from what has been said that there can be no such thing as an inert, senseless, extended, solid, figured, movable substance, existing without the mind, such as philosophers describe matter: yet if any man shall leave out of his idea of *matter*,

the positive ideas of extension, figure, solidity, and motion, and say that he means only by that word an inert senseless substance that exists without the mind, or unperceived, which is the occasion of our ideas, or at the presence whereof God is pleased to excite ideas in us: it does not appear, but that matter taken in this sense may possibly exist. In answer to which I say, first, that it seems no less absurd to suppose a substance without accidents than it is to suppose accidents without a substance. But secondly, though we should grant this unknown substance may possibly exist, yet where can it be supposed to be? That it does not exist in the mind is agreed, and that it does not exist in place is no less certain, since all (place or) extension exists only in the mind, as has been already proved. It remains therefore that it exists nowhere at all.

68. Let us examine a little the description that is here given us of *matter*. It neither acts, nor perceives, nor is perceived—for this is all that is meant by saying it is an inert, senseless, unknown substance—which is a definition entirely made up of negatives, excepting only the relative notion of its standing under or supporting: but then it must be observed that it *supports* nothing at all; and how nearly this comes to the description of a *nonentity*, I desire may be considered. But, you say, it is the *unknown occasion*, at the presence of which ideas are excited in us by the will of God. Now I would gladly know how anything can be present to us which is neither perceivable by sense nor reflection, nor capable of producing any idea in our minds, nor is at all extended, nor has any form, nor exists in any place. The words *to be present*, when thus applied, must necessarily be taken in some abstract and strange meaning, and which I am not able to comprehend.

69. Again, let us examine what is meant by *occasion*; so far as I can gather from the common use of language, that word signifies either the agent which produces any effect or else something that is observed to accompany or go before it in the ordinary course of things. But when it is applied to matter as above described, it can be taken in neither of those senses. For matter is said to be passive and inert, and so cannot be an agent or efficient cause. It is also unperceivable, as being devoid of all sensible qualities, and

so cannot be the occasion of our perceptions in the latter sense: as when the burning of my finger is said to be the occasion of the pain that attends it. What therefore can be meant by calling matter an *occasion?* This term is either used in no sense at all or else in some sense very distant from its received signification.

70. You will perhaps say that matter, though it is not perceived by us, is nevertheless perceived by God, to whom it is the occasion of exciting ideas in our minds. For, you say, since we observe our sensations to be imprinted in an orderly and constant manner, it is but reasonable to suppose there are certain constant and regular occasions of their being produced. That is to say that there are certain permanent and distinct parcels of matter, corresponding to our ideas, which, though they do not excite them in our minds or in any way immediately affect us, as being altogether passive and unperceivable to us, they are nevertheless to God, by whom they are perceived, as it were so many occasions to remind him when and what ideas to imprint on our minds: that so things may go on in a constant, uniform manner.

71. In answer to this I observe that as the notion of matter is here stated, the question is no longer concerning the existence of a thing distinct from *spirit* and *idea,* from perceiving and being perceived: but whether there are not certain ideas, of I know not what sort, in the mind of God, which are so many marks or notes that direct him how to produce sensations in our minds, in a constant and regular method: much after the same manner as a musician is directed by the notes of music to produce that harmonious train and composition of sound which is called a *tune,* though they who hear the music do not perceive the notes, and may be entirely ignorant of them. But this notion of matter[5] seems too extravagant to deserve a confutation. Besides, it is in effect no objection against what we have advanced, namely, that there is no senseless, unperceived *substance.*

72. If we follow the light of reason, we shall, from the constant, uniform method of our sensations, collect the goodness and wisdom of the spirit who excites them in our minds. But this is all that I can see

reasonably concluded from thence. To me, I say, it is evident that the being of a *spirit infinitely wise, good, and powerful* is abundantly sufficient to explain all the appearances of nature. But as for *inert, senseless matter,* nothing that I perceive has any the least connection with it or leads to the thoughts of it. And I would gladly see anyone explain any the meanest *phenomenon* in nature by it or show any manner of reason, though in the lowest rank of probability, that he can have for its existence, or even make any tolerable sense or meaning of that supposition. For as to its being an occasion, we have, I think, evidently shown that, with regard to us, it is no occasion: It remains therefore that it must be, if at all, the occasion to God of exciting ideas in us; and what this amounts to, we have just now seen.

73. It is worthwhile to reflect a little on the motives which induced men to suppose the existence of *material substance,* that so having observed the gradual ceasing and expiration of those motives or reasons, we may proportionally withdraw the assent that was grounded on them. First, therefore, it was thought that color, figure, motion, and the rest of the sensible qualities or accidents did really exist without the mind; and for this reason, it seemed needful to suppose some unthinking *substratum* or substance wherein they did exist, since they could not be conceived to exist by themselves. Afterwards, (secondly) in process of time, men being convinced that colors, sounds, and the rest of the sensible secondary qualities had no existence without the mind, they stripped this *substratum* or material substance of those qualities, leaving only the primary ones, figure, motion, and such like, which they still conceived to exist without the mind, and consequently to stand in need of a material support. But it having been shown that none, even of these, can possibly exist otherwise than in a spirit or mind which perceives them, it follows that we have no longer any reason to suppose the being of *matter.* No, that it is utterly impossible there should be any such thing, so long as that word is taken to denote an *unthinking substratum* of qualities or accidents, wherein they exist without the mind.

74. But though it is allowed by the *materialists* themselves that matter was thought of only for the sake of supporting accidents and the reason entirely

5. [1710 edition: (Which, after all, is the only intelligible one that I can pick from what is said of unknown occasions.)]

ceasing, one might expect the mind should naturally, and without any reluctance at all, quit the belief of what was solely grounded on it. Yet the prejudice is riveted so deeply in our thoughts that we can scarce tell how to part with it and are therefore inclined, since the *thing* itself is indefensible, at least to retain the *name*; which we apply to I know not what abstracted and indefinite notions of *being* or *occasion*, though without any show of reason, at least so far as I can see. For what is there on our part or what do we perceive among all the ideas, sensations, notions which are imprinted on our minds either by sense or reflection from which may be inferred the existence of an inert, thoughtless, unperceived occasion? And on the other hand, on the part of an *all-sufficient spirit*, what can there be that should make us believe or even suspect he is *directed* by an inert occasion to excite ideas in our minds?

75. It is a very extraordinary instance of the force of prejudice and much to be lamented that the mind of man retains so great a fondness, against all the evidence of reason, for a stupid, thoughtless *somewhat*, by the interposition whereof it would, as it were, screen itself from the providence of God and remove him further off from the affairs of the world. But though we do the utmost we can to secure the belief of *matter*, though, when reason forsakes us, we endeavor to support our opinion on the bare possibility of the thing, and though we indulge ourselves in the full scope of an imagination not regulated by reason to make out that poor *possibility*, yet the upshot of all is that there are certain *unknown ideas* in the mind of God; for this, if anything, is all that I conceive to be meant by occasion with regard to God. And this, at the bottom, is no longer contending for the *thing*, but for the *name*.

76. Whether, therefore, there are such ideas in the mind of God and whether they may be called by the name *matter*, I shall not dispute. But if you stick to the notion of an unthinking substance or support of extension, motion, and other sensible qualities, then to me it is most evidently impossible there should be any such thing. Since it is a plain repugnancy that those qualities should exist in or be supported by an unperceiving substance.

77. But, you say, though it is granted that there is no thoughtless support of extension and the other qualities or accidents which we perceive, yet there may, perhaps, be some inert unperceiving substance or *substratum* of some other qualities as incomprehensible to us as colors are to a man born blind, because we have not a sense adapted to them. But if we had a new sense, we should possibly no more doubt of their existence than a blind man made to see does of the existence of light and colors. I answer, first, if what you mean by the word *matter* is only the unknown support of unknown qualities, it is no matter whether there is such a thing or not, since it in no way concerns us, and I do not see the advantage there is in disputing about we know not *what*, and we know not *why*.

78. But secondly, if we had a new sense, it could only furnish us with new ideas or sensations, and then we should have the same reason against their existing in an unperceiving substance that has been already offered with relation to figure, motion, color, and the like. Qualities, as has been shown, are nothing else but *sensations* or *ideas*, which exist only in a *mind* perceiving them, and this is true not only of the ideas we are acquainted with at present, but likewise of all possible ideas whatsoever.

79. But, you will insist, what if I have no reason to believe the existence of matter, what if I can assign any use to it or explain anything by it or even conceive what is meant by that word? Yet still it is no contradiction to say that matter exists and that this matter is *in general* a *substance* or *occasion of ideas*; though, indeed, to go about to unfold the meaning or adhere to any particular explication of those words may be attended with great difficulties. I answer, when words are used without a meaning, you may put them together as you please without danger of running into a contradiction. You may say, for example, that *twice two* is equal to *seven*, so long as you declare you do not take the words of that proposition in their usual acceptation, but for marks of you know not what. And, by the same reason, you may say there is an inert, thoughtless substance without accidents, which is the occasion of our ideas. And we shall understand just as much by one proposition as the other.

80. In the *last* place, you will say, what if we give up the cause of material substance and assert that

matter is an unknown *somewhat,* neither substance nor accident, spirit nor idea, inert, thoughtless, indivisible, immovable, unextended, existing in no place? For, you say, whatever may be urged against *substance,* or *occasion,* or any other positive or relative notion of matter, has no place at all, so long as this *negative* definition of matter is adhered to. I answer, you may, if so it shall seem good, use the word *matter* in the same sense that other men use *nothing* and so make those terms convertible in your style. For after all, this is what appears to me to be the result of that definition, the parts whereof when I consider with attention, either collectively or separate from each other, I do not find that there is any kind of effect or impression made on my mind different from what is excited by the term *nothing.*

81. You will reply perhaps that in the aforesaid definition is included, what does sufficiently distinguish it from nothing, the positive, abstract idea of *quiddity, entity,* or *existence.* I admit indeed that those who pretend to the faculty of framing abstract general ideas do talk as if they had such an idea which is, say they, the most abstract and general notion of all that is to me the most incomprehensible of all others. That there are a great variety of spirits of different orders and capacities whose faculties, both in number and extent, are far exceeding those the author of my being has bestowed on me, I see no reason to deny. And for me to pretend to determine by my own few, stinted, narrow inlets of perception what ideas the inexhaustible power of the supreme spirit may imprint upon them, were certainly the utmost folly and presumption. Since there may be, for all that I know, innumerable sorts of ideas or sensations as different from one another and from all that I have perceived as colors are from sounds. But however ready I may be to acknowledge the scantiness of my comprehension with regard to the endless variety of spirits and ideas that might possibly exist, yet for anyone to pretend to a notion of entity or existence, *abstracted* from *spirit* and *idea,* from perceiving and being perceived, is, I suspect, a downright repugnancy and trifling with words. It remains that we consider the objections which may possibly be made on the part of religion.

82. Some there are who think that though the arguments for the real existence of bodies, which are drawn from reason, are allowed not to amount to demonstration, yet (first) the holy scriptures are so clear in the point as will sufficiently convince every good Christian that bodies do really exist and are something more than mere ideas, there being in holy writ innumerable facts related which evidently suppose the reality of timber, and stone, mountains, and rivers, and cities, and human bodies. To which I answer that no sort of writings whatever, sacred or profane, which use those and the like words in the vulgar acceptation, or so as to have a meaning in them, are in danger of having their truth called in question by our doctrine. That all those things do really exist, that there are bodies, even corporeal substances, when taken in the vulgar sense, has been shown to be agreeable to our principles, and the difference between *things* and *ideas, realities* and *chimeras,* has been distinctly explained. And I do not think that either what philosophers call matter or the existence of objects without the mind is anywhere mentioned in scripture.

83. Again, whether there are or are not external things, it is agreed on all hands that the proper use of words is the marking our conceptions or things only as they are known and perceived by us; whence it plainly follows that in the tenets we have laid down there is nothing inconsistent with the right use and significance of *language,* and that discourse of whatever kind, so far as it is intelligible, remains undisturbed. But all this seems so manifest from what has been set forth in the premises that it is needless to insist any further on it.

84. But, (secondly) it will be urged that miracles do, at least, lose much of their stress and import by our principles. What must we think of Moses' rod, was it not *really* turned into a serpent or was there only a change of *ideas* in the minds of the spectators? And can it be supposed that our Savior did no more at the marriage-feast in Cana than impose on the sight and smell and taste of the guests so as to create in them the appearance or idea only of wine? The same may be said of all other miracles, which, in consequence of the foregoing principles, must be looked upon only as so many cheats, or illusions of fancy. To this I reply that the rod was changed into a real serpent and the water into real wine. That this

does not, in the least, contradict what I have elsewhere said, will be evident from sec. 24, 35. But this business of *real* and *imaginary* has been already so plainly and fully explained and so often referred to and the difficulties about it are so easily answered from what has gone before that it were an affront to the reader's understanding to resume the explication of it in this place. I shall only observe that if at table all who were present should see and smell and taste and drink wine, and find the effects of it, with me there could be no doubt of its reality. So that at bottom, the scruple concerning real miracles has no place at all on ours, but only on the received principles, and, consequently, makes rather for, than against, what has been said.

85. Having done with the objections, which I endeavored to propose in the clearest light, and given them all the force and weight I could, we proceed in the next place to take a view of our tenets in their consequences. Some of these appear at first sight as that several difficult and obscure questions on which abundance of speculation has been thrown away are entirely banished from philosophy. Whether corporeal substance can think? Whether matter is infinitely divisible? And how it operates on spirit? These and the like inquiries have given infinite amusement to philosophers in all ages. But, depending on the existence of *matter*, they have no longer any place on our principles. There are many other advantages with regard to *religion* as well as to the *sciences*, which it is easy for anyone to deduce from what has been premised. But this will appear more plainly in the sequel.

86. From the principles we have laid down, it follows that human knowledge may naturally be reduced to two heads: that of *ideas* and that of *spirits*. Of each of these I shall treat in order. And *first*, as to ideas or unthinking things, our knowledge of these has been very much obscured and confounded and we have been led into very dangerous errors by supposing a twofold existence of the objects of sense, the one *intelligible*, or in the mind, the other *real* and without the mind, whereby unthinking things are thought to have a natural subsistence of their own, distinct from being perceived by spirits. This, which, if I am not mistaken, has been shown to be a most

groundless and absurd notion, is the very root of *skepticism*; for so long as men thought that real things subsisted without the mind and that their knowledge was only so far forth *real* as it was conformable to *real things*, it follows they could not be certain that they had any real knowledge at all. For how can it be known that the things which are perceived are conformable to those which are not perceived, or exist without the mind?

87. Color, figure, motion, extension, and the like, considered only as so many *sensations* in the mind, are perfectly known, there being nothing in them which is not perceived. But if they are looked on as notes or images, referred to *things* or *archetypes* existing without the mind, then we are all involved in *skepticism*. We see only the appearances and not the real qualities of things. What may be the extension, figure, or motion of anything really and absolutely, or in itself, it is impossible for us to know, but only the proportion or the relation they bear to our senses. Things remaining the same, our ideas vary, and which of them, or even whether any of them at all represent the true quality really existing in the thing, it is out of our reach to determine. So that, for all we know, all we see, hear, and feel may be only phantom and vain chimera and not at all agree with the real things, existing in *rerum natura*. All this skepticism follows from our supposing a difference between *things* and *ideas* and that the former have a subsistence without the mind, or unperceived. It were easy to dilate on this subject and show how the arguments urged by *skeptics* in all ages depend on the supposition of external objects.[6]

88. So long as we attribute a real existence to unthinking things, distinct from their being perceived, it is not only impossible for us to know with evidence the nature of any real unthinking being, but even that it exists. Hence it is that we see philosophers distrust their senses and doubt of the existence of heaven and earth, of everything they see or feel, even of their own bodies. And after all their labor and struggle of thought, they are forced to admit that we cannot attain to any self-evident or demonstrative

6. [1710 edition: "But this is too obvious to need being insisted on."]

knowledge of the existence of sensible things. But all this doubtfulness, which so bewilders and confounds the mind and makes *philosophy* ridiculous in the eyes of the world, vanishes if we annex a meaning to our words and do not amuse ourselves with the terms *absolute, external, exist,* and such like, signifying we know not what. I can as well doubt of my own being, as of the being of those things which I actually perceive by sense, it being a manifest contradiction that any sensible object should be immediately perceived by sight or touch, and, at the same time, have no existence in nature, since the very *existence* of an unthinking being consists in *being perceived.*

89. Nothing seems of more importance towards erecting a firm system of sound and real knowledge, which may be proof against the assaults of *skepticism,* than to lay the beginning in a distinct explication of what is meant by *thing, reality, existence:* for in vain shall we dispute concerning the real existence of things or pretend to any knowledge thereof so long as we have not fixed the meaning of those words. *Thing* or *being* is the most general name of all; it comprehends under it two kinds, entirely distinct and heterogeneous and which have nothing common but the name, namely, *spirits* and *ideas.* The former are *active, indivisible* (incorruptible) *substances,* the latter are *inert, fleeting,* (perishable passions,) or *dependent beings,* which subsist not by themselves, but are supported by or exist in minds or spiritual substances. [We comprehend our own existence by inward feeling or reflection and that of other spirits by reason. We may be said to have some knowledge or notion of our own minds, of spirits and active beings, whereof, in a strict sense, we have no ideas. In like manner we know and have a notion of relations between things or ideas, which relations are distinct from the ideas or things related, inasmuch as the latter may be perceived by us without our perceiving the former. To me it seems that *ideas, spirits,* and *relations* are all, in their respective kinds, the object of human knowledge and subject of discourse, and that the term *idea* would be improperly extended to signify everything we know or have any notion of.][7]

7. [The bracketed section does not appear in the edition of 1710.]

90. Ideas imprinted on the senses are real things, or do really exist; this we do not deny, but we deny they can subsist without the minds which perceive them or that they are resemblances of any archetypes existing without the mind, since the very being of a sensation or idea consists in being perceived, and an idea can be like nothing but an idea. Again, the things perceived by sense may be termed *external* with regard to their origin, in that they are not generated from within, by the mind itself, but imprinted by a spirit distinct from that which perceives them. Sensible objects may likewise be said to be without the mind in another sense, namely, when they exist in some other mind. Thus, when I shut my eyes, the things I saw may still exist, but it must be in another mind.

91. It were a mistake to think that what is here said derogates in the least from the reality of things. It is acknowledged on the received principles that extension, motion, and, in a word, all sensible qualities have need of a support, as not being able to subsist by themselves. But the objects perceived by sense are allowed to be nothing but combinations of those qualities and, consequently, cannot subsist by themselves. Thus far it is agreed on all hands. So that in denying the things perceived by sense an existence independent of a substance or support wherein they may exist, we detract nothing from the received opinion of their *reality* and are guilty of no innovation in that respect. All the difference is that according to us the unthinking beings perceived by sense have no existence distinct from being perceived and cannot therefore exist in any other substance than those unextended, indivisible substances, or *spirits,* which act and think and perceive them, whereas philosophers vulgarly hold that the sensible qualities exist in an inert, extended, unperceiving substance, which they call *matter,* to which they attribute a natural subsistence, exterior to all thinking beings, or distinct from being perceived by any mind whatsoever, even the eternal mind of the Creator, wherein they suppose only ideas of the corporeal substances created by him, if indeed they allow them to be at all created.

92. For as we have shown the doctrine of matter, or corporeal substance, to have been the main pillar and support of *skepticism,* so likewise upon the same foundation have been raised all the impious schemes

of *atheism* and irreligion. No, so great a difficulty has it been thought to conceive matter produced out of nothing that the most celebrated among the ancient philosophers, even of these who maintained the being of a God, have thought matter to be uncreated and coeternal with him. How great a friend *material substance* has been to *atheists* in all ages, were needless to relate. All their monstrous systems have so visible and necessary a dependence on it that when this corner-stone is once removed, the whole fabric cannot choose but fall to the ground; insomuch that it is no longer worthwhile to bestow a particular consideration on the absurdities of every wretched sect of *atheists*.

93. That impious and profane persons should readily fall in with those systems which favor their inclinations, by deriding immaterial substance and supposing the soul to be divisible and subject to corruption as the body; which exclude all freedom, intelligence, and design from the formation of things and instead thereof make a self-existent, stupid, unthinking substance the root and origin of all beings. That they should hearken to those who deny a Providence, or inspection of a superior mind over the affairs of the world, attributing the whole series of events either to blind chance or fatal necessity, arising from the impulse of one body on another. All this is very natural. And on the other hand, when men of better principles observe the enemies of religion lay so great a stress on *unthinking matter*, and all of them use so much industry and artifice to reduce everything to it; I think they should rejoice to see them deprived of their grand support and driven from that only fortress, without which your Epicureans, Hobbesians, and the like, have not even the shadow of a pretence, but become the most cheap and easy triumph in the world.

94. The existence of matter, or bodies unperceived, has not only been the main support of *atheists* and *fatalists*, but on the same principle does *idolatry* likewise in all its various forms depend. Did men but consider that the sun, moon, and stars, and every other object of the senses are only so many sensations in their minds, which have no other existence but barely being perceived, doubtless they would never fall down and worship their own *ideas*; but rather

address their homage to that eternal invisible Mind which produces and sustains all things.

95. The same absurd principle, by mingling itself with the articles of our faith, has occasioned no small difficulties to Christians. For example, about the *resurrection*, how many scruples and objections have been raised by Socinians and others? But do not the most plausible of them depend on the supposition that a body is denominated the same, with regard not to the form or that which is perceived by sense, but the material substance which remains the same under several forms? Take away this *material substance*, about the identity whereof all the dispute is, and mean by *body* what every plain ordinary person means by that word, namely, that which is immediately seen and felt, which is only a combination of sensible qualities, or ideas, and then their most unanswerable objections come to nothing.

96. Matter being once expelled out of nature drags with it so many skeptical and impious notions, such an incredible number of disputes and puzzling questions which have been thorns in the sides of theologians as well as philosophers and made so much fruitless work for mankind, that if the arguments we have produced against it are not found equal to demonstration (as to me they evidently seem), yet I am sure all friends to knowledge, peace, and religion have reason to wish they were.

97. Beside the external existence of the objects of perception, another great source of errors and difficulties, with regard to ideal knowledge, is the doctrine of *abstract ideas* such as it has been set forth in the introduction. The plainest things in the world, those we are most intimately acquainted with and perfectly know, when they are considered in an abstract way, appear strangely difficult and incomprehensible. Time, place, and motion, taken in particular or concrete, are what everybody knows; but having passed through the hands of a metaphysician, they become too abstract and fine to be apprehended by men of ordinary sense. Bid your servant meet you at such a *time*, in such a *place*, and he shall never stay to deliberate on the meaning of those words: in conceiving that particular time and place or the motion by which he is to get there, he finds not the least difficulty. But if *time* is taken, exclusive of all those

particular actions and ideas that diversify the day, merely for the continuation of existence or duration in abstract, then it will perhaps perplex even a philosopher to comprehend it.

98. Whenever I attempt to frame a simple idea of *time*, abstracted from the succession of ideas in my mind, which flows uniformly and is participated by all beings, I am lost and embroiled in inextricable difficulties. I have no notion of it at all, only I hear others say it is infinitely divisible and speak of it in such a manner as leads me to entertain odd thoughts of my existence; since that doctrine lays one under an absolute necessity of thinking either that he passes away innumerable ages without a thought, or else that he is annihilated every moment of his life: both which seem equally absurd. Time therefore being nothing, abstracted from the succession of ideas in our minds, it follows that the duration of any finite spirit must be estimated by the number of ideas or actions succeeding each other in that spirit or mind. Hence it is a plain consequence that the soul always thinks: and in truth, whoever shall go about to divide in his thoughts, or abstract the *existence* of a spirit from its *cogitation*, will, I believe, find it no easy task.

99. So likewise, when we attempt to abstract extension and motion from all other qualities and consider them by themselves, we presently lose sight of them and run into great extravagancies.[8] All which depend on a twofold abstraction: first, it is supposed that extension, for example, may be abstracted from all other sensible qualities; and secondly that the entity of extension may be abstracted from its being perceived. But whoever shall reflect and take care to understand what he says, will, if I am not mistaken, acknowledge that all sensible qualities are alike *sensations*, and alike *real*; that where the extension is, there is the color, too, namely, in his mind, and that their archetypes can exist only in some other *mind*: and that the objects of sense are nothing but those sensations combined, blended, or (if one may so speak) concreted together; none of all which can be supposed to exist unperceived.

100. What it is for a man to be happy, or an object of good, everyone may think he knows. But to frame an abstract idea of *happiness*, prescinded from all particular pleasure, or of *goodness*, [prescinded] from everything that is good, this is what few can pretend to. So, likewise, a man may be just and virtuous without having precise ideas of *justice* and *virtue*. The opinion that those and the like words stand for general notions abstracted from all particular persons and actions seems to have rendered morality difficult and the study thereof of less use to mankind. And in effect,[9] the doctrine of *abstraction* has not a little contributed towards spoiling the most useful parts of knowledge.

101. The two great provinces of speculative science, conversant about ideas received from sense and their relations, are *natural philosophy* and *mathematics*; with regard to each of these I shall make some observations. And first, I shall say somewhat of natural philosophy. On this subject it is that the *skeptics* triumph: All that stock of arguments they produce to depreciate our faculties, and make mankind appear ignorant and low, are drawn principally from this head, namely, that we are under an invincible blindness as to the *true* and *real* nature of things. This they exaggerate and love to enlarge on. We are miserably bantered, they say, by our senses, and amused only with the outside and show of things. The real essence, the internal qualities, and constitution of every meanest object is hidden from our view; something there is in every drop of water, every grain of sand, which it is beyond the power of human understanding to fathom or comprehend. But it is evident from what has been shown that all this complaint is groundless and that we are influenced by false principles to that degree as to mistrust our senses and think we know nothing of those things which we perfectly comprehend.

102. One great inducement to our pronouncing ourselves ignorant of the nature of things is the current

---

8. [1710 edition: "Hence spring those odd paradoxes that the fire is not hot, nor the wall white, etc., or that heat and color are in the objects, nothing but figure and motion."]

9. [1710 edition: "One may make great progress in school ethics without ever being the wiser or better man for it or knowing how to behave himself, in the affairs of life, more to the advantage of himself or his neighbors than he did before. This hint may suffice to let anyone see that."]

opinion that everything includes within itself the cause of its properties: or that there is in each object an inward essence, which is the source from where its discernible qualities flow and on which they depend. Some have pretended to account for appearances by occult qualities, but of late they are mostly resolved into mechanical causes, namely, the figure, motion, weight, and such like qualities of insensible particles; whereas in truth there is no other agent or efficient cause than *spirit*, it being evident that motion, as well as all other *ideas*, is perfectly inert. See sec. 25. Hence, to endeavor to explain the production of colors or sounds by figure, motion, magnitude, and the like, must necessarily be labor in vain. And accordingly, we see the attempts of that kind are not at all satisfactory. Which may be said, in general, of those instances wherein one idea or quality is assigned for the cause of another. I need not say how many *hypotheses* and speculations are left out and how much the study of nature is abridged by this doctrine.

103. The great mechanical principle now in vogue is *attraction*. That a stone falls to the earth or the sea swells towards the moon may to some appear sufficiently explained thereby. But how are we enlightened by being told this is done by attraction? Is it that that word signifies the manner of the tendency, and that it is by the mutual drawing of bodies instead of their being impelled or protruded towards each other? But nothing is determined of the manner or action, and it may as truly (for all we know) be termed *impulse*, or *protrusion*, as *attraction*. Again, the parts of steel we see cohere firmly together, and this also is accounted for by attraction; but in this, as in the other instances, I do not perceive that anything is signified besides the effect itself; for, as to the manner of the action whereby it is produced or the cause which produces it, these are not so much as aimed at.

104. Indeed, if we take a view of the several *phenomena* and compare them together, we may observe some likeness and conformity between them. For example, in the falling of a stone to the ground, in the rising of the sea towards the moon, in cohesion and crystallization, there is something alike, namely a union or mutual approach of bodies. So that any one of these or the like *phenomena* may not seem strange or surprising to a man who has nicely observed and compared the effects of nature. For that only is thought so which is uncommon, or a thing by itself, and out of the ordinary course of our observation. That bodies should tend towards the center of the earth is not thought strange, because it is what we perceive every moment of our lives. But that they should have a like gravitation towards the center of the moon may seem odd and unaccountable to most men, because it is discerned only in the tides. But a philosopher, whose thoughts take in a larger compass of nature, having observed a certain similitude of appearances in the heavens as well as the earth that argue innumerable bodies to have a mutual tendency towards each other which he denotes by the general name *attraction*, whatever can be reduced to that he thinks justly accounted for. Thus he explains the tides by the attraction of the terraqueous globe towards the moon, which to him does not appear odd or anomalous, but only a particular example of a general rule or law of nature.

105. If therefore we consider the difference there is between natural philosophers and other men with regard to their knowledge of the *phenomena*, we shall find it consists, not in a more exact knowledge of the efficient cause that produces them, for that can be no other than the *will of a spirit*, but only in a greater largeness of comprehension whereby analogies, harmonies, and agreements are discovered in the works of nature and the particular effects explained, that is, reduced to general rules (see sec. 62), which rules, grounded on the analogy and uniformness observed in the production of natural effects, are most agreeable and sought after by the mind; for that they extend our prospect beyond what is present and near to us and enable us to make very probable conjectures, touching things that may have happened at very great distances of time and place, as well as to predict things to come; which sort of endeavor towards omniscience is much affected by the mind.

106. But we should proceed warily in such things, for we are apt to lay too great a stress on analogies and, to the prejudice of truth, humor that eagerness of the mind whereby it is carried to extend its knowledge into general theorems. For example, gravitation, or mutual attraction, because it appears in many instances, some are straightway for pronouncing

universal; and that to *attract and be attracted by every other body is an essential quality inherent in all bodies whatsoever.* Whereas it appears the fixed stars have no such tendency towards each other; and so far is that gravitation from being *essential* to bodies that in some instances a quite contrary principle seems to show itself, as in the perpendicular growth of plants and the elasticity of the air. There is nothing necessary or essential in the case, but it depends entirely on the will of the *governing spirit,* who causes certain bodies to cleave together, or tend towards each other, according to various laws, while he keeps others at a fixed distance; and to some he gives a quite contrary tendency to fly asunder, just as he sees convenient.

107. After what has been premised, I think we may lay down the following conclusions. First, it is plain philosophers amuse themselves in vain, when they inquire for any natural efficient cause distinct from a *mind* or *spirit.* Secondly, considering the whole creation is the workmanship of a *wise and good agent,* it should seem to become philosophers to employ their thoughts (contrary to what some hold) about the final causes of things; and I must confess, I see no reason why pointing out the various ends to which natural things are adapted and for which they were originally, with unspeakable wisdom, contrived, should not be thought one good way of accounting for them and altogether worthy a philosopher. Thirdly, from what has been premised, no reason can be drawn why the history of nature should not still be studied and observations and experiments made, which, that they are of use to mankind and enable us to draw any general conclusions, is not the result of any immutable habitudes, or relations between things themselves, but only of God's goodness and kindness to men in the administration of the world. See sec. 30, 31. Fourthly, by a diligent observation of the *phenomena* within our view, we may discover the general laws of nature and from them deduce the other *phenomena.* I do not say *demonstrate,* for all deductions of that kind depend on a supposition that the Author of nature always operates uniformly and in a constant observance of those rules we take for principles, which we cannot evidently know.

108. Those men who frame general rules from the *phenomena* and afterwards derive the *phenomena*

from those rules seem to consider signs rather than causes. A man may well understand natural signs without knowing their analogy or being able to say by what rule a thing is so or so.[10] And as it is very possible to write improperly through too strict an observance of general grammar rules: so in arguing from general rules of nature, it is not impossible we may extend the analogy too far and by that means run into mistakes.

109. As in reading other books, a wise man will choose to fix his thoughts on the sense and apply it to use, rather than lay them out in grammatical remarks on the language; so in perusing the volume of nature, it seems beneath the dignity of the mind to affect an exactness in reducing each particular *phenomenon* to general rules or showing how it follows from them. We should propose to ourselves nobler views, such as to recreate and exalt the mind, with a prospect of the beauty, order, extent, and variety of natural things: hence, by proper inferences, to enlarge our notions of the grandeur, wisdom, and beneficence of the Creator: and lastly, to make the several parts of the creation, so far as in us lies, subservient to the ends they were designed for, God's glory, and the sustentation and comfort of ourselves and fellow-creatures.

110. The best key for the aforesaid analogy, or natural science, will be easily acknowledged to be a certain celebrated treatise of *mechanics:*[11] in the

---

10. [In the edition of 1710, sec. 108 begins as follows: "It appears from sec. 66 that the steady, consistent methods of nature may not unfitly be styled the language of its Author, by which he discovers his attributes to our view and directs us how to act for the convenience and felicity of life. And to me, those men who frame general rules from the phenomena and afterwards derive the phenomena from those rules seem to be grammarians and their art the grammar of nature. Two ways there are of learning a language, either by rule or by practice. A man may be well read in the language of nature without understanding the grammar of it or being able to say by what rule a thing is so or so."]

11. [This section is much altered and abridged from the edition of 1710, in which the beginning is given as follows: "The best grammar of the kind we are speaking of will be easily acknowledged to be a treatise of Mechanics, demonstrated and applied to nature by a philosopher of a neighboring nation, whom all the world admire. I shall not take upon me to make remarks on that extraordinary person: only some things he has advanced so directly opposite to the doctrine we have previously

entrance of which justly admired treatise, time, space, and motion are distinguished into *absolute* and *relative*, *true* and *apparent*, *mathematical* and *vulgar*: which distinction, as it is at large explained by the author, does suppose those quantities to have an existence without the mind: and that they are ordinarily conceived with relation to sensible things, to which nevertheless, in their own nature, they bear no relation at all.

111. As for *time*, as it is there taken in an absolute or abstracted sense, for the duration or perseverance of the existence of things, I have nothing more to add concerning it, after what has been already said on that subject, sec. 97, 98. For the rest, this celebrated author holds there is an *absolute space*, which, being unperceivable to sense, remains in itself similar and immovable: and relative space to be the measure thereof, which being movable and defined by its situation in respect of sensible bodies is vulgarly taken for immovable space. *Place* he defines to be that part of space which is occupied by any body. And according as the space is absolute or relative, so also is the place. *Absolute motion* is said to be the translation of a body from absolute place to absolute place, as relative motion is from one relative place to another. And because the parts of absolute space do not fall under our senses, instead of them we are obliged to use their sensible measures and so define both place and motion with respect to bodies which we regard as immovable. But it is said that in philosophical matters we must abstract from our senses, since it may be that none of those bodies which seem to be quiescent are truly so, and the same thing which is moved relatively may be really at rest. As likewise one and the same body may be in relative rest and motion or even moved with contrary relative motions at the same time, according as its place is variously defined. All which ambiguity is to be found in the apparent motions, but not at all in the true or absolute, which should therefore be alone regarded in philosophy. And the true, we are told, are distinguished from apparent or relative motions by the following proper-

ties. First, in true or absolute motion, all parts which preserve the same position with respect to the whole partake of the motions of the whole. Secondly, the place being moved, that which is placed therein is also moved, so that a body moving in a place which is in motion does participate the motion of its place. Thirdly, true motion is never generated or changed otherwise than by force impressed on the body itself. Fourthly, true motion is always changed by force impressed on the body moved. Fifthly, in circular motion barely relative, there is no centrifugal force, which nevertheless in that which is true or absolute is proportional to the quantity of motion.

112. But notwithstanding what has been said, it does not appear to me that there can be any motion other than *relative*, so that to conceive motion, there must be at least conceived two bodies, whereof the distance or position in regard to each other is varied. Hence if there was one only body in being, it could not possibly be moved. This seems evident in that the idea I have of motion does necessarily include relation.[12]

113. But though in every motion it is necessary to conceive more bodies than one, yet it may be that one only is moved, namely that on which the force causing the change of distance is impressed, or in other words that to which the action is applied. For however some may define relative motion, so as to term that body *moved* which changes its distance from some other body, whether the force or action causing that change were applied to it, or not: yet as relative motion is that which is perceived by sense and regarded in the ordinary affairs of life, it should seem that every man of common sense knows what it is as well as the best philosopher: now I ask anyone, whether in this sense of motion as he walks along the streets, the stones he passes over may be said to *move*, because they change distance with his feet? To me it seems that though motion includes a relation of one thing to another, yet it is not necessary that each term of the relation is denominated from it. As

---

laid down that we should be wanting in the regard due to the authority of so great a man, did we not take some notice of them."]

12. [1710 edition: "This to me seems very evident, in that the idea I have of motion does necessarily involve relation in it. Whether others can conceive it otherwise, a little attention may satisfy them."]

a man may think of somewhat which does not think, so a body may be moved to or from another body, which is not therefore itself in motion.[13]

114. As the place happens to be variously defined, the motion which is related to it varies. A man in a ship may be said to be quiescent with relation to the sides of the vessel and yet move with relation to the land. Or he may move eastward in respect of the one and westward in respect of the other. In the common affairs of life, men never go beyond the earth to define the place of any body: and what is quiescent in respect of that is accounted *absolutely* to be so. But philosophers, who have a greater extent of thought and more just notions of the system of things, discover even the earth itself to be moved. In order therefore to fix their notions, they seem to conceive the corporeal world as finite and the utmost unmoved walls or shell thereof to be the place whereby they estimate true motions. If we sound our own conceptions, I believe we may find all the absolute motion we can frame an idea of to be at bottom no other than relative motion thus defined. For as has been already observed, absolute motion exclusive of all external relation is incomprehensible; and to this kind of relative motion all the above-mentioned properties, causes, and effects ascribed to absolute motion, will, if I am not mistaken, be found to agree. As to what is said of the centrifugal force, namely, that it does not at all belong to circular relative motion, I do not see how this follows from the experiment which is brought to prove it. See *Philosophiae Naturalis Principia Mathematica,* in Schol. Def. 8. For the water in the vessel, at that time wherein it is said to have the greatest relative circular motion, has, I think, no motion at all; as is plain from the foregoing section.

115. For to denominate a body *moved,* it is requisite, first, that it changes its distance or situation with regard to some other body: and secondly, that the force or action occasioning that change is applied to it. If either of these is wanting, I do not think that, agreeable to the sense of mankind or the propriety of language, a body can be said to be in motion. I grant indeed that it is possible for us to think a body

which we see change its distance from some other, to be moved, though it have no force applied to it, (in which sense there may be apparent motion,) but then it is because the force causing the change of distance is imagined by us to be applied or impressed on that body thought to move. Which indeed shows we are capable of mistaking a thing to be in motion which is not, and that is all.[14]

116. From what has been said, it follows that the philosophical consideration of motion does not imply the being of an *absolute space,* distinct from that which is perceived by sense and related to bodies—which that it cannot exist without the mind is clear upon the same principles that demonstrate the like of all other objects of sense. And perhaps, if we inquire narrowly, we shall find we cannot even frame an idea of *pure space* exclusive of all body. This, I must confess, seems impossible, as being a most abstract idea. When I excite a motion in some part of my body, if it is free or without resistance, I say there is *space;* but if I find a resistance, then I say there is *body,* and, in proportion as the resistance to motion is lesser or greater, I say the space is more or less *pure.* So that when I speak of pure or empty space, it is not to be supposed that the word *space* stands for an idea distinct from or conceivable without body and motion. Though indeed we are apt to think every noun substantive stands for a distinct idea that may be separated from all others, which has occasioned infinite mistakes. When therefore supposing all the world to be annihilated besides my own body, I say

13. [1710 edition: "I mean relative motion, for other I am not able conceive."]

14. [The edition of 1710 continues, "But does not prove that, in the common acceptation of motion, a body is moved merely because it changes distance from another; since as soon as we are undeceived and find that the moving force was not communicated to it, we no longer hold it to be moved. So on the other hand, when only one body, the parts whereof preserve a given position between themselves, is imagined to exist, there are some who think that it can be moved all manner of ways, though without any change of distance or situation to any other bodies, which we should not deny, if they meant only that it might have an impressed force which, upon the bare creation of other bodies, would produce a motion of some certain quantity and determination. But that an actual motion (distinct from the impressed force, or power productive of change of place, in case there were bodies present whereby to define it) can exist in such a single body, I must confess I am not able to comprehend."]

there still remains *pure space*; thereby nothing else is meant, but only that I conceive it possible for the limbs of my body to be moved on all sides without the least resistance, but if that too were annihilated, then there could be no motion and consequently no space. Some perhaps may think the sense of seeing does furnish them with the idea of pure space; but it is plain from what we have elsewhere shown that the ideas of space and distance are not obtained by that sense. See the *Essay Concerning Vision*.

117. What is here laid down seems to put an end to all those disputes and difficulties which have sprung up among the learned concerning the nature of *pure space*. But the chief advantage arising from it is that we are freed from that dangerous *dilemma* to which several who have employed their thoughts on this subject imagine themselves reduced, namely, of thinking either that real space is God or else that there is something beside God which is eternal, uncreated, infinite, indivisible, immutable. Both which may justly be thought pernicious and absurd notions. It is certain that not a few theologians, as well as philosophers of great note, have, from the difficulty they found in conceiving either limits or annihilation of space, concluded it must be *divine*. And some of late have set themselves particularly to show that the incommunicable attributes of God agree to it. Which doctrine, however unworthy it may seem of the divine nature, yet I do not see how we can get clear of it, so long as we adhere to the received opinions.

118. Until now [the discussion has been] of natural philosophy; we come now to make some inquiry concerning that other great branch of speculative knowledge, namely, *mathematics*. These, however celebrated they may be for their clearness and certainty of demonstration, which is hardly anywhere else to be found, cannot nevertheless be supposed altogether free from mistakes, if in their principles there lurks some secret error, which is common to the professors of those sciences with the rest of mankind. Mathematicians, though they deduce their theorems from a great height of evidence, yet their first principles are limited by the consideration of quantity; and they do not ascend into any inquiry concerning those transcendental maxims which influence all the particular sciences, each part of which, mathematics not ex-

cepted, does consequently participate of the errors involved in them. That the principles laid down by mathematicians are true and their way of deduction from those principles clear and incontestable, we do not deny. But we hold there may be certain erroneous maxims of greater extent than the object of mathematics and for that reason not expressly mentioned, though tacitly supposed throughout the whole progress of that science; and that the ill effects of those secret, unexamined errors are diffused through all the branches thereof. To be plain, we suspect the mathematicians are, as well as other men, concerned in the errors arising from the doctrine of abstract general ideas and the existence of objects without the mind.

119. *Arithmetic* has been thought to have for its object abstract ideas of *number*. Of which to understand the properties and mutual habitudes is supposed no mean part of speculative knowledge. The opinion of the pure and intellectual nature of numbers in abstract has made them in esteem with those philosophers who seem to have affected an uncommon fineness and elevation of thought. It has set a price on the most trifling numerical speculations, which in practice are of no use but serve only for amusement, and has therefore so far infected the minds of some that they have dreamt of mighty *mysteries* involved in numbers and attempted the explication of natural things by them. But if we inquire into our own thoughts and consider what has been premised, we may perhaps entertain a low opinion of those high flights and abstractions and look on all inquiries about numbers only as so many *difficiles nugae*, so far as they are not subservient to practice and promote the benefit of life.

120. Unity in abstract we have considered before, in sec. 13, from which and what has been said in the Introduction it plainly follows there is not any such idea. But number being defined a *collection of units*, we may conclude that if there is no such thing as unity or unit in abstract, there are no ideas of number in abstract denoted by the numeral names and figures. The theories, therefore, in arithmetic, if they are abstracted from the names and figures, as likewise from all use and practice as well as from the particular things numbered, can be supposed to have nothing

at all for their object. Hence we may see how entirely the science of numbers is subordinate to practice and how jejune and trifling it becomes when considered as a matter of mere speculation.

121. However since there may be some who, deluded by the specious show of discovering abstracted verities, waste their time in arithmetical theorems and problems which have not any use; it will not be amiss if we more fully consider and expose the vanity of that pretence, and this will plainly appear, by taking a view of arithmetic in its infancy and observing what it was that originally put men on the study of that science and to what scope they directed it. It is natural to think that at first men, for ease of memory and help of computation, made use of counters or, in writing, of single strokes, points, or the like, each of which was made to signify a unit that is some one thing of whatever kind they had occasion to reckon. Afterwards they found out the more compendious ways of making one character stand in place of several strokes or points. And lastly, the notation of the Arabians or Indians came into use, wherein, by the repetition of a few characters or figures and varying the signification of each figure according to the place it obtains, all numbers may be most aptly expressed, which seems to have been done in imitation of language so that an exact analogy is observed between the notation by figures and names, the nine simple figures, answering the nine first numeral names and places in the former, corresponding to denominations in the latter. And agreeably to those conditions of the simple and local value of figures were contrived methods of finding, from the given figures or marks of the parts, what figures, and how placed, are proper to denote the whole, or vice versa. And having found the sought figures, the same rule or analogy being observed throughout, it is easy to read them into words; and so the number becomes perfectly known. For then the number of any particular things is said to be known when we know the names or figures (with their due arrangement) that according to the standing analogy belong to them. For these signs being known, we can, by the operations of arithmetic, know the signs of any part of the particular sums signified by them; and thus computing in signs (because of the connection established between them

and the distinct multitudes of things, of which one is taken for a unit), we may be able rightly to sum up, divide, and proportion the things themselves that we intend to number.

122. In *arithmetic*, therefore, we regard not the *things* but the *signs*, which nevertheless are not regarded for their own sake, but because they direct us how to act with relation to things and dispose rightly of them. Now agreeably to what we have before observed of words in general (sec. 19, Introduction), it happens here likewise that abstract ideas are thought to be signified by numeral names or characters, while they do not suggest ideas of particular things to our minds. I shall not at present enter into a more particular dissertation on this subject, but only observe that it is evident from what has been said that those things which pass for abstract truths and theorems concerning numbers are, in reality, conversant about no object distinct from particular numerable things, except only names and characters, which originally came to be considered on no other account but their being *signs*, or capable to represent aptly whatever particular things men had need to compute. Whence it follows that to study them for their own sake would be just as wise and to as good purpose, as if a man, neglecting the true use or original intention and subservience of language, should spend his time in impertinent criticisms upon words or purely verbal reasonings and controversies.

123. From numbers we proceed to speak of *extension*, which, considered as relative, is the object of geometry. The *infinite* divisibility of *finite* extension, though it is not expressly laid down either as an axiom or theorem in the elements of that science, yet is throughout the same every where supposed and thought to have so inseparable and essential a connection with the principles and demonstrations in geometry that mathematicians never admit it into doubt or make the least question of it. And as this notion is the source from whence do spring all those amusing geometrical paradoxes which have such a direct repugnancy to the plain common sense of mankind and are admitted with so much reluctance into a mind not yet debauched by learning, so is it the principal occasion of all that nice and extreme subtlety which renders the study of *mathematics* so diffi-

cult and tedious. Hence, if we can make it appear that no finite extension contains innumerable parts or is infinitely divisible, it follows that we shall at once clear the science of geometry from a great number of difficulties and contradictions which have ever been esteemed a reproach to human reason and withal make the attainment thereof a business of much less time and pains than it has been previously.

124. Every particular finite extension which may possibly be the object of our thought, is an *idea* existing only in the mind, and consequently each part thereof must be perceived. If therefore I cannot perceive innumerable parts in any finite extension that I consider, it is certain that they are not contained in it, but it is evident that I cannot distinguish innumerable parts in any particular line, surface, or solid, which I either perceive by sense or figure to myself in my mind; wherefore I conclude they are not contained in it. Nothing can be plainer to me than that the extensions I have in view are no other than my own ideas and it is no less plain that I cannot resolve any one of my ideas into an infinite number of other ideas, that is, that they are not infinitely divisible. If by *finite extension* is meant something distinct from a finite idea, I declare I do not know what that is and so cannot affirm or deny anything of it. But if the terms *extension, parts,* and the like are taken in any sense conceivable, that is, for ideas, then to say a finite quantity or extension consists of parts infinite in number is so manifest a contradiction that everyone at first sight acknowledges it to be so. And it is impossible it should ever gain the assent of any reasonable creature who is not brought to it by gentle and slow degrees, as a converted gentile to the belief of *transubstantiation.* Ancient and rooted prejudices do often pass into principles, and those propositions which once obtain the force and credit of a *principle* are not only themselves, but likewise whatever is deducible from them, thought privileged from all examination. And there is no absurdity so gross which by this means the mind of man may not be prepared to swallow.

125. He whose understanding is prepossessed with the doctrine of abstract general ideas may be persuaded that (whatever is thought of the ideas of sense) extension in *abstract* is infinitely divisible. And one who thinks the objects of sense exist without the mind will perhaps in virtue thereof be brought to admit that a line but an inch long may contain innumerable parts really existing, though too small to be discerned. These errors are grafted in the minds of geometricians as well as of other men and have a like influence on their reasonings; and it were no difficult thing to show how the arguments from geometry, made use of to support the infinite divisibility of extension, are bottomed on them. At present we shall only observe in general whence it is that the mathematicians are all so fond and tenacious of this doctrine.

126. It has been observed in another place that the theorems and demonstrations in geometry are conversant about universal ideas: sec. 15, Introduction. Where it is explained in what sense this ought to be understood, namely, that the particular lines and figures included in the diagram are supposed to stand for innumerable others of different sizes — or in other words, the geometer considers them abstracting from their magnitude, which does not imply that he forms an abstract idea, but only that he cares not what the particular magnitude is, whether great or small, but looks on that as a thing indifferent to the demonstration — hence it follows that a line in the scheme, but an inch long, must be spoken of as though it contained ten thousand parts, since it is regarded not in itself, but as it is universal; and it is universal only in its signification, whereby it represents innumerable lines greater than itself, in which may be distinguished ten thousand parts or more, though there may not be above an inch in it. After this manner the properties of the lines signified are (by a very usual figure) transferred to the sign, and thence through mistake thought to appertain to it considered in its own nature.

127. Because there is no number of parts so great but it is possible there may be a line containing more, the inch-line is said to contain parts more than any assignable number, which is true, not of the inch taken absolutely, but only for the things signified by it. But men not retaining that distinction in their thoughts slide into a belief that the small particular line described on paper contains in itself parts innumerable. There is no such thing as the ten-thousandth part of an *inch*; but there is of a *mile* or *diameter of*

the earth, which may be signified by that inch. When therefore I delineate a triangle on paper and take one side not above an inch, for example, in length to be the *radius,* this I consider as divided into ten thousand or a hundred thousand parts or more. For though the ten-thousandth part of that line, considered in itself, is nothing at all, and consequently may be neglected without any error or inconvenience, yet these described lines being only marks standing for greater quantities, whereof it may be the ten-thousandth part is very considerable, it follows that to prevent notable errors in practice, the *radius* must be taken of ten thousand parts or more.

128. From what has been said, the reason is plain why, to the end any theorem may become universal in its use, it is necessary we speak of the lines described on paper as though they contained parts which really they do not. In doing of which, if we examine the matter thoroughly, we shall perhaps discover that we cannot conceive an inch itself as consisting of, or being divisible into a thousand parts, but only some other line which is far greater than an inch and represented by it. And that when we say a line is *infinitely divisible,* we must mean a line which is *infinitely great.* What we have here observed seems to be the chief cause why to suppose the infinite divisibility of finite extension has been thought necessary in geometry.

129. The several absurdities and contradictions which flowed from this false principle might, one would think, have been esteemed so many demonstrations against it. But by I know not what *logic,* it is held that proofs *a posteriori* are not to be admitted against propositions relating to infinity. As though it were not impossible even for an infinite mind to reconcile contradictions. Or as if anything absurd and repugnant could have a necessary connection with truth or flow from it. But whoever considers the weakness of this pretence will think it was contrived on purpose to humor the laziness of the mind which had rather acquiesce in an indolent skepticism than be at the pains to go through with a severe examination of those principles it has ever embraced for true.

130. Of late, the speculations about infinites have run so high and grown to such strange notions as have occasioned no small scruples and disputes among the geometers of the present age. Some there are of great note who, not content with holding that finite lines may be divided into an infinite number of parts, do yet further maintain that each of those infinitesimals is itself subdivisible into an infinity of other parts, or infinitesimals of a second order, and so on *ad infinitum.* These, I say, assert there are infinitesimals of infinitesimals of infinitesimals, without ever coming to an end. So that according to them an inch does not barely contain an infinite number of parts, but an infinity of an infinity of an infinity *ad infinitum* of parts. Others there are who hold all orders of infinitesimals below the first to be nothing at all, thinking it with good reason absurd to imagine there is any positive quantity or part of extension which, though multiplied infinitely, can ever equal the smallest given extension. And yet, on the other hand, it seems no less absurd to think the square, cube, or other power of a positive real root should itself be nothing at all; which they who hold infinitesimals of the first order, denying all of the subsequent orders, are obliged to maintain.

131. Have we not therefore reason to conclude that they are *both* in the wrong and that there is in effect no such thing as parts infinitely small or an infinite number of parts contained in any finite quantity? But you will say that if this doctrine obtains, it will follow that the very foundations of geometry are destroyed and those great men who have raised that science to so astonishing a height have been all the while building a castle in the air. To this it may be replied that whatever is useful in geometry and promotes the benefit of human life does still remain firm and unshaken on our principles. That science, considered as practical, will rather receive advantage than any prejudice from what has been said. But to set this in a due light may be the subject of a distinct inquiry. For the rest, though it should follow that some of the more intricate and subtle parts of *speculative mathematics* may be pared off without any prejudice to truth, yet I do not see what damage will be thence derived to mankind. On the contrary, it were highly to be wished that men of great abilities and obstinate application would draw off their thoughts from those amusements

and employ them in the study of such things as lie nearer the concerns of life or have a more direct influence on the manners.

132. If it is said that several theorems undoubtedly true are discovered by methods in which infinitesimals are made use of, which could never have been if their existence included a contradiction in it, I answer that upon a thorough examination it will not be found that in any instance it is necessary to make use of or conceive infinitesimal parts of finite lines, or even quantities less than the *minimum sensibile*; no, it will be evident this is never done, it being impossible.[15]

133. By what we have premised, it is plain that very numerous and important errors have taken their rise from those false principles which were impugned in the foregoing parts of this treatise. And the opposites of those erroneous tenets at the same time appear to be most fruitful principles from whence do flow innumerable consequences highly advantageous to true philosophy as well as to religion. Particularly, *matter, or the absolute existence of corporeal objects*, has been shown to be that wherein the most avowed and pernicious enemies of all knowledge, whether human or divine, have ever placed their chief strength and confidence. And surely, if by distinguishing the real existence of unthinking things from their being perceived and allowing them a substance of their own out of the minds of spirits, no one thing is explained in nature; but on the contrary a great many inexplicable difficulties arise: if the supposition of matter is barely precarious, as not being grounded on so much as one single reason: if its consequences cannot endure the light of examination and free inquiry, but screen themselves under the dark and general pretense of

infinites being incomprehensible: if withal the removal of this *matter* is not attended with the least evil consequence, if it is not even missed in the world, but everything as well, no much easier conceived without it: if lastly, both *skeptics* and *atheists* are forever silenced upon supposing only spirits and ideas, and this scheme of things is perfectly agreeable both to *reason* and *religion*: I think we may expect it should be admitted and firmly embraced, though it were proposed only as a *hypothesis*, and the existence of matter had been allowed possible, which yet I think we have evidently demonstrated that it is not.

134. True it is that in consequence of the foregoing principles, several disputes and speculations which are esteemed no mean parts of learning are rejected as useless. But however great a prejudice against our notions this may give to those who have already been deeply engaged and made large advances in studies of that nature, yet by others, we hope it will not be thought any just ground of dislike to the principles and tenets herein laid down that they abridge the labor of study and make human sciences more clear, compendious, and attainable than they were before.

135. Having dispatched what we intended to say concerning the knowledge of *ideas*, the method we proposed leads us, in the next place, to treat of *spirits*, with regard to which, perhaps human knowledge is not so deficient as is vulgarly imagined. The great reason that is assigned for our being thought ignorant of the nature of spirits is our not having an idea of it. But surely it ought not to be looked on as a defect in a human understanding that it does not perceive the idea of *spirit*, if it is manifestly impossible there should be any such *idea*. And this, if I am not mistaken, has been demonstrated in sec. 27—to which I shall here add that a spirit has been shown to be the only substance or support wherein the unthinking beings or ideas can exist, but that this *substance* which supports or perceives ideas should itself be an *idea*, or like an *idea*, is evidently absurd.

136. It will perhaps be said that we want a sense (as some have imagined) proper to know substances withal which, if we had, we might know our own soul as we do a triangle. To this I answer that in case we had a new sense bestowed upon us, we could only

15. [The following passage is added in the edition of 1710: "And whatever mathematicians may think of fluxions or the differential calculus and the like, a little reflection will show them that in working by those methods, they do not conceive or imagine lines or surfaces less than what are perceivable to sense. They may, indeed, call those little and almost insensible quantities infinitesimals or infinitesimals of infinitesimals, if they please; but at bottom this is all, they being in truth finite, nor does the solution of problems require supposing any other. But this will be more clearly made out hereafter."]

receive thereby some new sensations or ideas of sense. But I believe nobody will say that what he means by the terms *soul* and *substance* is only some particular sort of idea or sensation. We may therefore infer that all things duly considered, it is not more reasonable to think our faculties defective, in that they do not furnish us with an idea of spirit or active thinking substance, than it would be if we should blame them for not being able to comprehend a *round square*.

137. From the opinion that spirits are to be known after the manner of an idea or sensation have risen many absurd and heterodox tenets and much skepticism about the nature of the soul. It is even probable that this opinion may have produced a doubt in some about whether they had any soul at all distinct from their body, since upon inquiry they could not find they had an idea of it. That an *idea*, which is inactive, and the existence whereof consists in being perceived, should be the image or likeness of an agent subsisting by itself seems to need no other refutation than barely attending to what is meant by those words. But perhaps you will say that though an *idea* cannot resemble a *spirit* in its thinking, acting, or subsisting by itself, yet it may in some other respects, and it is not necessary that an idea or image is in all respects like the original.

138. I answer: If it does not in those mentioned, it is impossible it should represent it in any other thing. Do but leave out the power of willing, thinking, and perceiving ideas and there remains nothing else wherein the idea can be like a spirit. For by the word *spirit* we mean only that which thinks, wills, and perceives; this, and this alone, constitutes the signification of that term. If, therefore, it is impossible that any degree of those powers should be represented in an idea, it is evident there can be no idea of a spirit.

139. But it will be objected that if there is no idea signified by the terms *soul, spirit,* and *substance,* they are wholly insignificant, or have no meaning in them. I answer: Those words do mean or signify a real thing, which is neither an idea nor like an idea, but that which perceives ideas and wills and reasons about them. What I am myself, that which I denote by the term *I,* is the same with what is meant by *soul* or *spiritual substance.* If it is said that this is only quarrelling at a word, and that since the immediate significa-

tions of other names are, by common consent, called *ideas,* no reason can be assigned why that which is signified by the name *spirit* or *soul* may not partake in the same appellation. I answer that all the unthinking objects of the mind agree in that they are entirely passive and their existence consists only in being perceived, whereas a soul or spirit is an active being whose existence consists not in being perceived, but in perceiving ideas and thinking. It is therefore necessary, in order to prevent equivocation and confounding natures perfectly disagreeing and unlike, that we distinguish between *spirit* and *idea.* See sec. 27.

140. In a large sense indeed, we may be said to have an idea or rather a notion of *spirit,* that is, we understand the meaning of the word, otherwise we could not affirm or deny anything of it. Moreover, as we conceive the ideas that are in the minds of other spirits by means of our own, which we suppose to be resemblances of them, so we know other spirits by means of our own soul, which in that sense is the image or idea of them, it having a like respect to other spirits that blueness or heat by me perceived has to those ideas perceived by another.

141.[16] It must not be supposed that they who assert the natural immortality of the soul are of the opinion that it is absolutely incapable of annihilation, even by the infinite power of the Creator who first gave it being, but only that it is not liable to be broken or dissolved by the ordinary laws of nature or motion. They, indeed, who hold the soul of man to be only a thin vital flame or system of animal spirits, make it perishing and corruptible as the body, since there is nothing more easily dissipated than such a being, which it is naturally impossible should survive the ruin of the tabernacle in which it is enclosed. And this notion has been greedily embraced and cherished by the worst part of mankind as the most effectual antidote against all impressions of virtue and religion. But it has been made evident that bodies, of whatever frame or texture, are barely passive ideas in the mind, which is more distant and heterogeneous from them

---

16. [Original edition: "The natural immortality of the soul is a necessary consequence of the foregoing doctrine, but before we attempt to prove that, it is fit that we explain the meaning of that tenet."]

than light is from darkness. We have shown that the soul is indivisible, incorporeal, unextended, and it is consequently incorruptible. Nothing can be plainer than that the motions, changes, decays, and dissolutions which we hourly see befall natural bodies (and which is what we mean by the *course of nature*) cannot possibly affect an active, simple, uncompounded substance; such a being therefore is indissoluble by the force of nature, that is to say, *the soul of man is naturally immortal*.

142. After what has been said, it is I suppose plain that our souls are not to be known in the same manner as senseless, inactive objects, or by way of *idea*. *Spirits* and *ideas* are things so wholly different that when we say *they exist, they are known*, or the like, these words must not be thought to signify anything common to both natures. There is nothing alike or common in them, and to expect that by any multiplication or enlargement of our faculties we may be enabled to know a spirit as we do a triangle seems as absurd as if we should hope *to see a sound*. This is inculcated because I imagine it may be of moment towards clearing several important questions and preventing some very dangerous errors concerning the nature of the soul. We may not, I think, strictly be said to have an idea of an active being or of an action, although we may be said to have a notion of them. I have some knowledge or notion of my mind and its acts about ideas, inasmuch as I know or understand what is meant by those words. What I know, that I have some notion of. I will not say that the terms *idea* and *notion* may not be used convertibly, if the world will have it so. But yet it conduces to clearness and propriety that we distinguish things very different by different names. It is also to be remarked that, all relations including an act of the mind, we cannot so properly be said to have an idea, but rather a notion of the relations or habitudes between things. But if, in the modern way, the word *idea* is extended to spirits and relations and acts, this is, after all, an affair of verbal concern.

143. It will not be amiss to add that the doctrine of *abstract ideas* has had no small share in rendering those sciences intricate and obscure which are particularly conversant about spiritual things. Men have imagined they could frame abstract notions of the powers and acts of the mind, and consider them prescinded from the mind or spirit itself as well as from their respective objects and effects. Hence a great number of dark and ambiguous terms, presumed to stand for abstract notions, have been introduced into metaphysics and morality and from these have grown infinite distractions and disputes among the learned.

144. But nothing seems more to have contributed towards engaging men in controversies and mistakes with regard to the nature and operations of the mind than being used to speak of those things in terms borrowed from sensible ideas. For example, the will is termed the *motion* of the soul; this infuses a belief that the mind of man is as a ball in motion, impelled and determined by the objects of sense as necessarily as that is by the stroke of a racket. Hence arise endless scruples and errors of dangerous consequence in morality. All which, I do not doubt, may be cleared and truth appear plain, uniform, and consistent, could but philosophers be prevailed on to retire into themselves and attentively consider their own meaning.

145. From what has been said, it is plain that we cannot know the existence of other spirits otherwise than by their operations or the ideas by them excited in us. I perceive several motions, changes, and combinations of ideas that inform me there are certain particular agents like myself, which accompany them and concur in their production. Hence the knowledge I have of other spirits is not immediate, as is the knowledge of my ideas; but depending on the intervention of ideas, referred by me to agents or spirits distinct from myself as effects or concomitant signs.

146. But though there are some things which convince us human agents are concerned in producing them, yet it is evident to everyone that those things which are called the works of nature, that is, the far greater part of the ideas or sensations perceived by us are not produced by or dependent on the wills of men. There is therefore some other spirit that causes them, since it is repugnant that they should subsist by themselves. See sec. 29. But if we attentively consider the constant regularity, order, and concatenation of natural things, the surprising magnificence, beauty, and perfection of the larger, and the exquisite contrivance of the smaller parts of the creation,

together with the exact harmony and correspondence of the whole, but, above all, the never enough admired laws of pain and pleasure, and the instincts or natural inclinations, appetites, and passions of animals, I say if we consider all these things and at the same time attend to the meaning and import of the attributes, one, eternal, infinitely wise, good, and perfect, we shall clearly perceive that they belong to the aforesaid spirit, *who works all in all,* and *by whom all things consist.*

147. Hence it is evident that God is known as certainly and immediately as any other mind or spirit whatsoever, distinct from ourselves. We may even assert that the existence of God is far more evidently perceived than the existence of men, because the effects of nature are infinitely more numerous and considerable than those ascribed to human agents. There is not any one mark that denotes a man, or effect produced by him, which does not more strongly evince the being of that Spirit who is the *Author of Nature.* For it is evident that in affecting other persons, the will of man has no other object than barely the motion of the limbs of his body; but that such a motion should be attended by or excite any idea in the mind of another depends wholly on the will of the Creator. He alone it is who, *upholding all things by the word of his power,* maintains that intercourse between spirits whereby they are able to perceive the existence of each other. And yet this pure and clear light which enlightens everyone is itself invisible.[17]

148. It seems to be a general pretence of the unthinking herd that they cannot *see* God. Could we but see him, say they, as we see a man, we should believe that he is and, believing, obey his commands. But, alas, we need only open our eyes to see the sovereign Lord of all things with a more full and clear view than we do any one of our fellow creatures. Not that I imagine we see God (as some will have it) by a direct and immediate view, or see corporeal things, not by themselves, but by seeing that which represents them in the essence of God, which doctrine is, I must confess, to me incomprehensible. But I shall explain my meaning. A human spirit or person is not per-

ceived by sense as not being an idea; when therefore we see the color, size, figure, and motions of a man, we perceive only certain sensations or ideas excited in our own minds, and these being exhibited to our view in sundry distinct collections, serve to mark out unto us the existence of finite and created spirits like ourselves. Hence it is plain, we do not see a man, if by *man* is meant that which lives, moves, perceives, and thinks as we do, but only such a certain collection of ideas as directs us to think there is a distinct principle of thought and motion like to ourselves, accompanying and represented by it. And, after the same manner, we see God; all the difference is that, whereas some one finite and narrow assemblage of ideas denotes a particular human mind, wherever we direct our view, we do at all times and in all places perceive manifest tokens of the divinity, everything we see, hear, feel, or anywise perceive by sense being a sign or effect of the power of God, as is our perception of those very motions which are produced by men.

149. It is therefore plain that nothing can be more evident to anyone who is capable of the least reflection than the existence of God, or a Spirit who is intimately present to our minds, producing in them all that variety of ideas or sensations which continually affect us, on whom we have an absolute and entire dependence, in short, *in whom we live, and move, and have our being.* That the discovery of this great truth, which lies so near and obvious to the mind, should be attained to by the reason of so very few is a sad instance of the stupidity and inattention of men, who, though they are surrounded with such clear manifestations of the Deity, are yet so little affected by them that they seem, as it were, blinded with excess of light.

150. But you will say: Has nature no share in the production of natural things, and must they be all ascribed to the immediate and sole operation of God? I answer: If by *nature* is meant only the visible *series* of effects or sensations imprinted on our minds according to certain fixed and general laws, then it is plain that nature taken in this sense cannot produce anything at all. But if by *nature* is meant some being distinct from God as well as from the laws of nature and things perceived by sense, I must confess that word is to me an empty sound, without any intelligible meaning annexed to it. Nature in this acceptation is

17. [Original edition continues: "to the greatest part of mankind."]

a vain *chimera* introduced by those heathens who had no just notions of the omnipresence and infinite perfection of God. But it is more unaccountable that it should be received among Christians professing belief in the holy scriptures, which constantly ascribe those effects to the immediate hand of God that heathen philosophers are wont to impute to nature. "The Lord, he causeth the vapors to ascend; he maketh lightnings with rain; he bringeth forth the wind out of his treasures," Jer. X. 13. "He turneth the shadow of death into the morning, and maketh the day dark with night," Amos V. 8. "He visiteth the earth, and maketh it soft with showers; he blesseth the springing thereof, and crowneth the year with his goodness, so that the pastures are clothed with flocks, and the valleys are covered over with corn." See Psalm LXV. But notwithstanding that this is the constant language of scripture, yet we have I know not what aversion from believing that God concerns himself so nearly in our affairs. Gladly would we suppose him at a great distance off and substitute some blind unthinking deputy in his stead, though (if we may believe St. Paul) he is "not far from every one of us."

151. It will, I do not doubt, be objected that the slow and gradual methods observed in the production of natural things do not seem to have for their cause the immediate hand of an *almighty agent*. Besides, monsters, untimely births, fruits blasted in the blossom, rains falling in desert places, miseries incident to human life are so many arguments that the whole frame of nature is not immediately actuated and superintended by a spirit of infinite wisdom and goodness. But the answer to this objection is in a good measure plain from sec. 62, it being visible that the aforesaid methods of nature are absolutely necessary, in order to [be] working by the most simple and general rules and after a steady and consistent manner, which argues both the *wisdom* and *goodness* of God.[18] Such is the artificial contrivance of this mighty machine of nature that while its motions and various phenomena strike on our senses, the hand which

actuates the whole is itself unperceivable to men of flesh and blood. "Verily," says the prophet, "thou art a God that hidest thyself," Isaiah XLV. 15. But though God conceal himself from the eyes of the *sensual* and *lazy*, who will not be at the least expense of thought, yet to an unbiased and attentive mind nothing can be more plainly legible than the intimate presence of an *all-wise Spirit*, who fashions, regulates, and sustains the whole system of being. (Secondly,) it is clear from what we have elsewhere observed that the operating according to general and stated laws is so necessary for our guidance in the affairs of life and letting us into the secret of nature that without it, all reach and compass of thought, all human sagacity and design could serve to no manner of purpose, it were even impossible there should be any such faculties or powers in the mind. See sec. 31. Which one consideration abundantly outbalances whatever particular inconveniences may thence arise.

152. We should further consider that the very blemishes and defects of nature are not without their use in that they make an agreeable sort of variety and augment the beauty of the rest of the creation, as shades in a picture serve to set off the brighter and more enlightened parts. We would likewise do well to examine whether our taxing the waste of seeds and embryos and accidental destruction of plants and animals before they come to full maturity, as an imprudence in the author of nature, is not the effect of prejudice contracted by our familiarity with impotent and saving mortals. In man, indeed, a thrifty management of those things which he cannot procure without much pains and industry may be esteemed *wisdom*. But we must not imagine that the inexplicably fine machine of an animal or vegetable costs the great Creator any more pains or trouble in its production than a pebble does, nothing being more evident than that an omnipotent spirit can indifferently produce everything by a mere *fiat* or act of his will. Hence it is plain that the splendid profusion of natural things should not be interpreted as weakness or prodigality in the agent who produces them, but rather be looked on as an argument of the riches of his power.

153. As for the mixture of pain or uneasiness which is in the world, pursuant to the general laws of nature and the actions of finite imperfect spirits, this, in the

18. [1710 edition: "(First) For it does hence follow that the finger of God is not so conspicuous to the resolved and careless sinner, which gives him an opportunity to harden in his impiety, and grow ripe for vengeance. See sec. 57."]

state we are in at present, is indispensably necessary to our well-being. But our prospects are too narrow: we take, for instance, the idea of some one particular pain into our thoughts and account it *evil*; whereas if we enlarge our view so as to comprehend the various ends, connections, and dependencies of things, on what occasions and in what proportions we are affected with pain and pleasure, the nature of human freedom, and the design with which we are put into the world, we shall be forced to acknowledge that those particular things which considered in themselves appear to be *evil* have the nature of *good* when considered as linked with the whole system of beings.

154. From what has been said, it will be manifest to any considering person that it is merely for want of attention and comprehensiveness of mind that there are any favorers of *atheism* or the *Manichean heresy* to be found. Little and unreflecting souls may indeed burlesque the works of Providence, the beauty and order of which they have not capacity or will not be at the pains to comprehend. But those who are masters of any justness and extent of thought, and are withal used to reflect, can never sufficiently admire the divine traces of wisdom and goodness that shine throughout the economy of nature. But what truth is there which shines so strongly on the mind that by an aversion of thought, a willful shutting of the eyes, we may not escape seeing it? Is it therefore to be wondered at if the generality of men, who are ever intent on business or pleasure and little used to fix or open the eye of their mind, should not have all that conviction and evidence of the being of God which might be expected in reasonable creatures?

155. We should rather wonder that men can be found so stupid as to neglect, than that neglecting they should be unconvinced of such an evident and momentous truth. And yet it is to be feared that too many of parts and leisure who live in Christian countries are merely through a supine and dreadful negligence sunk into a sort of *atheism*. Since it is downright impossible that a soul pierced and enlightened with a thorough sense of the omnipresence, holiness, and justice of that *Almighty Spirit* should persist in a remorseless violation of his laws. We ought therefore earnestly to meditate and dwell on those important points; that so we may attain conviction without all scruple that *the eyes of the Lord are in every place beholding the evil and the good; that he is with us and keepeth us in all places whither we go, and giveth us bread to eat, and raiment to put on;* that he is present and conscious to our innermost thoughts; and that we have a most absolute and immediate dependence on him. A clear view of which great truths cannot choose but fill our heart with an awful circumspection and holy fear, which is the strongest incentive to *virtue* and the best guard against *vice*.

156. For after all, what deserves the first place in our studies is the consideration of *God* and our *duty;* which to promote, as it was the main drift and design of my labors, so shall I esteem them altogether useless and ineffectual if by what I have said I cannot inspire my readers with a pious sense of the presence of God: and having shown the falseness or vanity of those barren speculations which make the chief employment of learned men, the better dispose them to reverence and embrace the salutary truths of the gospel, which to know and to practice is the highest perfection of human nature.

George Berkeley, *Three Dialogues between Hylas and Philonous, in Opposition to Skeptics and Atheists* (1713)[1]

The Preface

Though it seems the general opinion of the world, no less than the design of nature and providence, that the end of speculation is practice or the improvement and regulation of our lives and actions, yet those who are most addicted to speculative studies seem as generally of another mind. And, indeed, if we consider the pains that have been taken to perplex the plainest things—that distrust of the senses, those doubts and scruples, those abstractions and refinements that occur in the very entrance of the sciences—it will not seem strange that men of leisure and curiosity should lay themselves out in fruitless disquisitions without descending to the practical parts of life or informing themselves in the more necessary and important parts of knowledge.

Upon the common principles of philosophers, we are not assured of the existence of things from their being perceived. And we are taught to distinguish their real nature from that which falls under our senses. Hence arise *skepticism* and *paradoxes*. It is not enough that we see and feel, that we taste and smell a thing. Its true nature, its absolute external entity, is still concealed. For, though it is the fiction of our own brain, we have made it inaccessible to all our faculties. Sense is fallacious, reason defective. We spend our lives in doubting of those things which other men evidently know and believing those things which they laugh at and despise.

In order, therefore, to divert the busy mind of man from vain researches, it seemed necessary to inquire into the source of its perplexities and, if possible, to lay down such principles as by an easy solution of them together with their own native evidence may at once recommend themselves for genuine to the mind and rescue it from those endless pursuits it is engaged in. This, with a plain demonstration of the immediate providence of an all-seeing God and the natural immortality of the soul, should seem the readiest preparation as well as the strongest motive to the study and practice of virtue.

This design I proposed in the First Part of a Treatise concerning the *Principles of Human Knowledge*, published in the year 1710. But before I proceed to publish the Second Part,[2] I thought it requisite to treat more clearly and fully of certain principles laid down

---

1. [From *The Works of George Berkeley*, ed. G. N. Wright (London, 1843), 2 vols., English, modified.]

2. [A few years later, while traveling in Italy, Berkeley lost his partly written draft of the Second Part of the *Principles*. He never rewrote or finished it.]

in the First, and to place them in a new light, which is the business of the following *Dialogues*.

In this treatise, which does not presuppose in the reader any knowledge of what was contained in the former, it has been my aim to introduce the notions I advance into the mind in the most easy and familiar manner, especially because they carry with them a great opposition to the prejudices of philosophers, which have so far prevailed against the common sense and natural notions of mankind.

If the principles which I here endeavor to propagate are admitted for true, the consequences which, I think, evidently flow from them are that *atheism* and *skepticism* will be utterly destroyed, many intricate points made plain, great difficulties solved, several useless parts of science retrenched, speculation referred to practice, and men reduced from paradoxes to common sense.

And although it may perhaps seem an uneasy reflection to some that when they have taken a circuit through so many refined and unvulgar notions they should at last come to think like other men, yet I think that this return to the simple dictates of nature after having wandered through the wild mazes of philosophy is not unpleasant. It is like coming home from a long voyage—a man reflects with pleasure on the many difficulties and perplexities he has passed through, sets his heart at ease, and enjoys himself with more satisfaction for the future.

As it was my intention to convince *skeptics* and *infidels* by reason, so it has been my endeavor strictly to observe the most rigid laws of reasoning. And, to an impartial reader, I hope, it will be manifest that the sublime notion of a God and the comfortable expectation of immortality do naturally arise from a close and methodical application of thought whatever may be the result of that loose, rambling way, not altogether improperly termed *freethinking* by certain libertines in thought who can no more endure the restraints of *logic* than those of *religion* or *government*.

It will perhaps be objected to my design that so far as it tends to ease the mind of difficult and useless inquiries it can affect only a few speculative persons; but if, by their speculations rightly laced, the study

of morality and the law of nature were brought more into fashion among men of parts and genius, the discouragements that draw to *skepticism* removed, the measures of right and wrong accurately defined, and the principles of natural religion reduced into regular systems, as artfully disposed and clearly connected as those of some other sciences, then there are grounds to think these effects would not only have a gradual influence in repairing the too much defaced sense of virtue in the world, but also, by showing that such parts of revelation as lie within the reach of human inquiry are most agreeable to right reason, it would dispose all prudent, unprejudiced persons to a modest and wary treatment of those sacred mysteries which are above the comprehension of our faculties.

It remains that I desire the reader to withhold his censure of these *Dialogues* until he has read them through. Otherwise he may lay them aside in a mistake of their design or on account of difficulties or objections which he would find answered in the sequel. A treatise of this nature would require to be once read over coherently in order to comprehend its design, the proofs, solution of difficulties, and the connection and disposition of its parts. If it is thought to deserve a second reading, this, I imagine, will make the entire scheme very plain—especially if recourse is had to an Essay I wrote some years since upon *Vision*,[3] and the *Treatise Concerning the Principles of Human Knowledge*. There various notions advanced in these *Dialogues* are further pursued or placed in different lights, and other points handled which naturally tend to confirm and illustrate them.

The First Dialogue

Philonous. Good morning, Hylas; I did not expect to find you up so early.

Hylas. It is indeed something unusual, but my thoughts were so taken up with a subject I was discoursing of last night that, finding I could not sleep, I resolved to rise and take a turn in the garden.

Phil. It happened well to let you see what innocent and agreeable pleasures you lose every morning. Can

3. [*An Essay towards a New Theory of Vision* (1709).]

there be a pleasanter time of the day, or a more delightful season of the year? That purple sky, those wild but sweet notes of birds, the fragrant bloom upon the trees and flowers, the gentle influence of the rising sun, these and a thousand nameless beauties of nature inspire the soul with secret transports; its faculties too being at this time fresh and lively are fit for these meditations which the solitude of a garden and tranquillity of the morning naturally dispose us to. But I am afraid I interrupt your thoughts, for you seemed very intent on something.

Hyl. It is true, I was, and shall be obliged to you if you will permit me to go on in the same vein; not that I would by any means deprive myself of your company, for my thoughts always flow more easily in conversation with a friend than when I am alone, but my request is that you would allow me to impart my reflections to you.

Phil. With all my heart, it is what I should have requested myself if you had not prevented me.

Hyl. I was considering the odd fate of those men who have in all ages, through an affectation of being distinguished from the vulgar — or some unaccountable turn of thought — pretended either to believe nothing at all or to believe the most extravagant things in the world. This, however, might be borne if their paradoxes and skepticism did not draw after them some consequences of general disadvantage to mankind. But the mischief lies here, that when men of less leisure see them who are supposed to have spent their whole time in the pursuits of knowledge, professing an entire ignorance of all things or advancing such notions as are repugnant to plain and commonly received principles, they will be tempted to entertain suspicions concerning the most important truths which they had up to now held sacred and unquestionable.

Phil. I entirely agree with you as to the ill tendency of the affected doubts of some philosophers and fantastic conceits of others. I am even so far gone of late in this way of thinking that I have discarded several of the sublime notions I had got in their schools for vulgar opinions. And I give it you on my word, since this revolt from metaphysical notions to the plain dictates of nature and common sense, I find my understanding strangely enlightened so that I can now easily comprehend a great many things which before were all mystery and riddle.

Hyl. I am glad to find there was nothing in the accounts I heard of you.

Phil. Pray, what were those?

Hyl. You were represented in last night's conversation as one who maintained the most extravagant opinion that ever entered into the mind of man, namely, that there is no such thing as *material substance* in the world.

Phil. That there is no such thing as what philosophers call *material substance*, I am seriously persuaded, but if I were made to see anything absurd or skeptical in this, I should then have the same reason to renounce this that I imagine I have now to reject the contrary opinion.

Hyl. What! Can anything be more fantastic, more repugnant to common sense, or a more manifest piece of skepticism than to believe there is no such thing as *matter*?

Phil. Softly, good Hylas. What if it should prove that you, who hold there is, are by virtue of that opinion a greater skeptic and maintain more paradoxes and repugnancies to common sense than I who believe no such thing?

Hyl. You may as soon persuade me the part is greater than the whole as that, in order to avoid absurdity and skepticism, I should ever be obliged to give up my opinion in this point.

Phil. Well then, are you content to admit that opinion for true which upon examination shall appear most agreeable to common sense and remote from skepticism?

Hyl. With all my heart. Since you are for raising disputes about the plainest things in nature, I am content for once to hear what you have to say.

Phil. Pray, Hylas, what do you mean by a *skeptic*?

Hyl. I mean what all men mean, one that doubts of everything.

Phil. He, then, who entertains no doubt concerning some particular point, with regard to that point, cannot be thought a *skeptic*.

Hyl. I agree with you.

Phil. Whether doubting consists in embracing the affirmative or negative side of a question?

Hyl. In neither; for whoever understands English cannot but know that *doubting* signifies a suspense between both.

Phil. He, then, who denies any point can no more be said to doubt of it than he who affirms it with the same degree of assurance.

Hyl. True.

Phil. And, consequently, in this case his denial is no more to be esteemed *skeptical* than the other.

Hyl. I acknowledge it.

Phil. How does it come to pass, then, Hylas, that you pronounce me a *skeptic,* because I deny what you affirm, namely, the existence of matter? Since, for all you can tell, I am as peremptory in my denial as you in your affirmation.

Hyl. Hold on, Philonous, I have been a little out in my definition, but every false step a man makes in discourse is not to be insisted on. I said, indeed, that a *skeptic* was one who doubted of everything, but I should have added: or who denies the reality and truth of things.

Phil. What things? Do you mean the principles and theorems of sciences? But these you know are universal intellectual notions and consequently independent of matter; the denial of this therefore does not imply denying them.

Hyl. I grant it. But are there no other things? What do you think of distrusting the senses, of denying the real existence of sensible things or pretending to know nothing of them? Is not this sufficient to call a man a *skeptic?*

Phil. Shall we therefore examine which of us it is that denies the reality of sensible things or professes the greatest ignorance of them, since, if I take you rightly, he is to be esteemed the greatest *skeptic?*

Hyl. That is what I desire.

Phil. What do you mean by sensible things?

Hyl. Those things which are perceived by the senses. Can you imagine that I mean anything else?

Phil. Pardon me, Hylas, if I am desirous clearly to apprehend your notions, since this may much shorten our inquiry. Allow me then to ask you this further question. Are those things only perceived by the senses which are perceived immediately? Or may those things properly be said to be *sensible* which are

perceived mediately or not without the intervention of others?

Hyl. I do not sufficiently understand you.

Phil. In reading a book, what I immediately perceive are the letters, but mediately, or by means of these, are suggested to my mind the notions of God, virtue, truth, etc. Now that the letters are truly sensible things, or perceived by sense, there is no doubt; but I would like to know whether you take the things suggested by them to be so too.

Hyl. No, certainly, it would be absurd to think *God* or *virtue* sensible things, though they may be signified and suggested to the mind by sensible marks with which they have an arbitrary connection.

Phil. It seems then, that by *sensible things* you mean those only which can be perceived immediately by sense.

Hyl. Right.

Phil. Does it not follow from this that though I see one part of the sky red, and another blue, and that my reason does then evidently conclude there must be some cause of that diversity of colors, yet that cause cannot be said to be a sensible thing or perceived by the sense of seeing?

Hyl. It does.

Phil. In like manner, though I hear a variety of sounds, yet I cannot be said to hear the causes of those sounds.

Hyl. You cannot.

Phil. And when by my touch I perceive a thing to be hot and heavy, I cannot say with any truth or propriety that I feel the cause of its heat or weight.

Hyl. To prevent any more questions of this kind, I tell you once and for all that by *sensible things* I mean those only which are perceived by sense and that, in truth, the senses perceive nothing which they do not perceive immediately, for they make no inferences. The deducing, therefore, of causes or occasions from effects and appearances which alone are perceived by sense entirely relates to reason.

Phil. This point then is agreed between us—that *sensible things are those only which are immediately perceived by sense.* You will further inform me whether we immediately perceive by sight anything besides light, and colors, and figures; or by hearing anything but sounds; by the palate, anything besides tastes; by the smell, besides odors; or by the touch, more than tangible qualities.

Hyl. We do not.

Phil. It seems, therefore, that if you take away all sensible qualities, there remains nothing sensible.

Hyl. I grant it.

Phil. Sensible things, therefore, are nothing else but so many sensible qualities or combinations of sensible qualities.

Hyl. Nothing else.

Phil. Heat, then, is a sensible thing.

Hyl. Certainly.

Phil. Does the reality of sensible things consist in being perceived? Or, is it something distinct from their being perceived and that bears no relation to the mind?

Hyl. To *exist* is one thing, and to be *perceived* is another.

Phil. I speak with regard to sensible things only; and of these I ask whether by their real existence you mean a subsistence exterior to the mind and distinct from their being perceived?

Hyl. I mean a real absolute being, distinct from and without any relation to their being perceived.

Phil. Heat, therefore, if it is allowed a real being, must exist without the mind.

Hyl. It must.

Phil. Tell me, Hylas, is this real existence equally compatible to all degrees of heat which we perceive, or is there any reason why we should attribute it to some and deny it others? And if there is, pray let me know that reason.

Hyl. Whatever degree of heat we perceive by sense, we may be sure the same exists in the object that occasions it.

Phil. What! The greatest as well as the least?

Hyl. I tell you, the reason is plainly the same in respect of both: They are both perceived by sense; no, the greater degree of heat is more sensibly perceived and, consequently, if there is any difference, we are more certain of its real existence than we can be of the reality of a lesser degree.

Phil. But is not the most vehement and intense degree of heat a very great pain?

Hyl. No one can deny it.

Phil. And is any unperceiving thing capable of pain or pleasure?

Hyl. No, certainly.

Phil. Is your material substance a senseless being or a being endowed with sense and perception?

Hyl. It is senseless without doubt.

Phil. It cannot, therefore, be the subject of pain.

Hyl. By no means.

Phil. Nor, consequently, of the greatest heat perceived by sense, since you acknowledge this to be no small pain.

Hyl. I grant it.

Phil. What shall we say then of your external object; is it a material substance or not?

Hyl. It is a material substance with the sensible qualities inhering in it.

Phil. How, then, can a great heat exist in it, since you admit it cannot in a material substance? I desire you would clear this point.

Hyl. Hold on, Philonous, I fear I was wrong in yielding intense heat to be a pain. It should seem rather that pain is something distinct from heat and the consequence or effect of it.

Phil. Upon putting your hand near the fire, do you perceive one simple uniform sensation or two distinct sensations?

Hyl. But one simple sensation.

Phil. Is not the heat immediately perceived?

Hyl. It is.

Phil. And the pain?

Hyl. True.

Phil. Seeing, therefore, they are both immediately perceived at the same time and the fire affects you only with one simple or uncompounded idea, it follows that this same simple idea is both the intense heat immediately perceived and the pain, and, consequently, that the intense heat immediately perceived is nothing distinct from a particular sort of pain.

Hyl. It seems so.

Phil. Again, try in your thoughts, Hylas, if you can conceive a vehement sensation to be without pain or pleasure.

Hyl. I cannot.

Phil. Or can you frame to yourself an idea of

sensible pain or pleasure in general, abstracted from every particular idea of heat, cold, tastes, smells, etc.?

Hyl. I do not find that I can.

Phil. Does it not therefore follow that sensible pain is nothing distinct from those sensations or ideas in an intense degree? ·

Hyl. It is undeniable, and, to speak the truth, I begin to suspect a very great heat cannot exist but in a mind perceiving it.

Phil. What! Are you then in that *skeptical* state of suspense between affirming and denying?

Hyl. I think I may be positive in the point. A very violent and painful heat cannot exist without the mind.

Phil. It does not, therefore, according to you, have any real being.

Hyl. I admit it.

Phil. Is it therefore certain that there is no body in nature really hot?

Hyl. I have not denied there is any real heat in bodies. I only say there is no such thing as an intense real heat.

Phil. But did you not say before that all degrees of heat were equally real or, if there was any difference, that the greater would be more undoubtedly real than the lesser?

Hyl. True, but it was because I did not then consider the ground there is for distinguishing between them which I now plainly see. And it is this: Because intense heat is nothing else but a particular kind of painful sensation and pain cannot exist but in a perceiving being, it follows that no intense heat can really exist in an unperceiving corporeal substance. But this is no reason why we should deny heat in an inferior degree to exist in such a substance.

Phil. But how shall we be able to discern those degrees of heat which exist only in the mind from those which exist without it?

Hyl. That is no difficult matter. You know the least pain cannot exist unperceived; therefore, whatever degree of heat is a pain exists only in the mind. But as for all other degrees of heat, nothing obliges us to think the same of them.

Phil. I think you granted before that no unperceiving being was capable of pleasure any more than of pain.

Hyl. I did.

Phil. And is not warmth, or a more gentle degree of heat than what causes uneasiness, a pleasure?

Hyl. What then?

Phil. Consequently, it cannot exist without the mind in any unperceiving substance or body.

Hyl. So it seems.

Phil. Since, therefore, those degrees of heat that are not painful, as well as those that are, can exist only in a thinking substance, may we not conclude that external bodies are absolutely incapable of any degree of heat whatsoever?

Hyl. On second thought, I do not think it so evident that warmth is a pleasure as that a great degree of heat is a pain.

Phil. I do not pretend that warmth is as great a pleasure as heat is a pain. But if you grant it to be even a small pleasure, it serves to make good my conclusion.

Hyl. I could rather call it an *indolence*. It seems to be nothing more than a privation of both pain and pleasure. And that such a quality or state as this may agree to an unthinking substance, I hope you will not deny.

Phil. If you are resolved to maintain that warmth, or a gentle degree of heat, is no pleasure, I do not know how to convince you otherwise than by appealing to your own sense. But what do you think of cold?

Hyl. The same that I do of heat. An intense degree of cold is a pain, for to feel a very great cold is to perceive a great uneasiness; it cannot, therefore, exist without the mind, but a lesser degree of cold may, as well as a lesser degree of heat.

Phil. Those bodies, therefore, upon whose application to our own we perceive a moderate degree of heat must be concluded to have a moderate degree of heat or warmth in them; and those upon whose application we feel a like degree of cold must be thought to have cold in them.

Hyl. They must.

Phil. Can any doctrine be true that necessarily leads a man into an absurdity?

Hyl. Without doubt it cannot.

Phil. Is it not an absurdity to think that the same thing should be at the same time both cold and warm?

Hyl. It is.

Phil. Suppose now one of your hands hot, and the other cold, and that they are both at once put into the same vessel of water in an intermediate state; will not the water seem cold to one hand and warm to the other?

Hyl. It will.

Phil. Ought we not, therefore, by your principles conclude: It is really both cold and warm at the same time, that is, according to your own concession, believe an absurdity?

Hyl. I confess it seems so.

Phil. Consequently, the principles themselves are false, since you have granted that no true principle leads to an absurdity.

Hyl. But, after all, can anything be more absurd than to say *there is no heat in the fire*?

Phil. To make the point still clearer, tell me whether in two cases exactly alike we ought not make the same judgment?

Hyl. We ought.

Phil. When a pin pricks your finger, does it not rend and divide the fibers of your flesh?

Hyl. It does.

Phil. And when a coal burns your finger, does it do so any more?

Hyl. It does not.

Phil. Since, therefore, you neither judge the sensation itself occasioned by the pin, nor anything like it, to be in the pin, you should not, conformably to what you have now granted, judge the sensation occasioned by the fire, or anything like it, to be in the fire.

Hyl. Well, since it must be so, I am content to yield this point and acknowledge that heat and cold are only sensations existing in our minds, but there still remain qualities enough to secure the reality of external things.

Phil. But what will you say, Hylas, if it shall appear that the case is the same with regard to all other sensible qualities and that they can no more be supposed to exist without the mind than heat and cold?

Hyl. Then indeed you will have done something to the purpose, but that is what I despair of seeing proved.

Phil. Let us examine them in order. What think you of tastes—do they exist without the mind or not?

Hyl. Can any man in his senses doubt whether sugar is sweet or wormwood bitter?

Phil. Inform me, Hylas. Is a sweet taste a particular kind of pleasure or pleasant sensation, or is it not?

Hyl. It is.

Phil. And is not bitterness some kind of uneasiness or pain?

Hyl. I grant it.

Phil. If, therefore, sugar and wormwood are unthinking corporeal substances existing without the mind, how can sweetness and bitterness, that is, pleasure and pain, agree to them?

Hyl. Hold on, Philonous, I now see what deluded me all this time. You asked whether heat and cold, sweetness and bitterness, were not particular sorts of pleasure and pain—to which I answered simply that they were. Whereas I should have distinguished thus: Those qualities, as perceived by us, are pleasures or pains, but not as existing in the external objects. We must not, therefore, conclude absolutely that there is no heat in the fire or sweetness in the sugar, but only that heat or sweetness, as perceived by us, is not in the fire or sugar. What do you say to this?

Phil. I say it is nothing to the purpose. Our discourse proceeded altogether concerning sensible things, which you defined to be the things we *immediately perceive by our senses*. Therefore, whatever other qualities you speak of as distinct from these, I know nothing of them, nor do they at all belong to the point in dispute. You may indeed pretend to have discovered certain qualities which you do not perceive and assert those insensible qualities exist in fire and sugar. But what use can be made of this to your present purpose, I am at a loss to conceive. Tell me then once more—do you acknowledge that heat and cold, sweetness and bitterness (meaning those qualities which are perceived by the senses), do not exist without the mind?

Hyl. I see it is to no purpose to hold out, so I give up the cause as to those mentioned qualities. Though I profess it sounds odd to say that sugar is not sweet.

Phil. But for your further satisfaction, take this along with you: That which at other times seems sweet shall, to a distempered palate, appear bitter. And nothing can be plainer than that various persons perceive different tastes in the same food, since that which one man delights in, another abhors. And how could this be, if the taste was something really inherent in the food?

Hyl. I acknowledge I do not know how.

Phil. In the next place, odors are to be considered. And with regard to these, I would gladly know whether what has been said of tastes does not exactly agree to them? Are they not so many pleasing or displeasing sensations?

Hyl. They are.

Phil. Can you then conceive it possible that they should exist in an unperceiving thing?

Hyl. I cannot.

Phil. Or can you imagine that filth and garbage affect those brute animals that feed on them out of choice with the same smells which we perceive in them?

Hyl. By no means.

Phil. May we not, therefore, conclude of smells, as of the other aforementioned qualities, that they cannot exist in any but a perceiving substance or mind?

Hyl. I think so.

Phil. Then as to sounds, what must we think of them—are they accidents really inherent in external bodies or not?

Hyl. That they do not inhere in the sonorous bodies is plain from this: because a bell struck in the exhausted receiver of an air pump sends forth no sound. The air, therefore, must be thought the subject of sound.

Phil. What reason is there for that, Hylas?

Hyl. Because, when any motion is raised in the air, we perceive a greater or lesser sound in proportion to the air's motion, but without some motion in the air we never hear any sound at all.

Phil. And granting that we never hear a sound but when some motion is produced in the air, yet I do not see how you can infer from this that the sound itself is in the air.

Hyl. It is this very motion in the external air that produces in the mind the sensation of *sound.* For striking on the drum of the ear, it causes a vibration, which, being communicated to the brain by the auditory nerves, then affects the soul with the sensation called sound.

Phil. What! Is sound then a sensation?

Hyl. I tell you, as perceived by us, it is a particular sensation in the mind.

Phil. And can any sensation exist without the mind?

Hyl. No, certainly.

Phil. How then can sound, being a sensation, exist in the air if by the air you mean a senseless substance existing without the mind.

Hyl. You must distinguish, Philonous, between sound as it is perceived by us and as it is in itself, or (which is the same thing) between the sound we immediately perceive and that which exists without us. The former, indeed, is a particular kind of sensation, but the latter is merely a vibrational or undulatory motion in the air.

Phil. I thought I had already obviated that distinction by the answer I gave when you were applying it in a like case before. But, to say no more of that, are you sure then that sound is really nothing but motion?

Hyl. I am.

Phil. Whatever therefore agrees to real sound may with truth be attributed to motion.

Hyl. It may.

Phil. It is then good sense to speak of *motion* as of a thing that is *loud, sweet, acute,* or *grave.*

Hyl. I see you are resolved not to understand me. Is it not evident those accidents or modes belong only to sensible sound, or *sound* in the common meaning of the word, but not to *sound* in the real and philosophic sense, which, as I just now told you, is nothing but a certain motion of the air?

Phil. It seems then there are two sorts of sound, the one vulgar, or that which is heard, the other philosophical and real.

Hyl. Even so.

Phil. And the latter consists in motion.

Hyl. I told you so before.

Phil. Tell me, Hylas, to which of the senses do you think the idea of motion belongs—to the hearing?

Hyl. No, certainly, but to the sight and touch.

Phil. It should follow, then, that according to you, real sounds may possibly be *seen* or *felt,* but never *heard.*

Hyl. Look, Philonous, you may if you please make a jest of my opinion, but that will not alter the truth of things. I admit, indeed, the inferences you draw me into sound something odd, but common language, you know, is framed by and for the use of the vulgar. We must not therefore wonder if expressions adapted to exact philosophic notions seem uncouth and out of the way.

Phil. Is it come to that? I assure you, I imagine myself to have gained no small point, since you make so light of departing from common phrases and opinions, it being a main part of our inquiry to examine whose notions are widest of the common road and most repugnant to the general sense of the world. But can you think it no more than a philosophical paradox to say that *real sounds are never heard* and that the idea of them is obtained by some other sense. And is there nothing in this contrary to nature and the truth of things?

Hyl. To deal ingenuously, I do not like it. And after the concessions already made, I had as well grant that sounds, too, have no real being without the mind.

Phil. And I hope you will make no difficulty to acknowledge the same of colors.

Hyl. Pardon me, the case of colors is very different. Can anything be plainer than that we see them on the objects?

Phil. The objects you speak of are, I suppose, corporeal substances existing without the mind.

Hyl. They are.

Phil. And have true and real colors inhering in them?

Hyl. Each visible object has that color which we see in it.

Phil. How! Is there anything visible but what we perceive by sight?

Hyl. There is not.

Phil. And do we perceive anything by sense which we do not perceive immediately?

Hyl. How often must I be obliged to repeat the same thing? I tell you, we do not.

Phil. Have patience, good Hylas, and tell me once more whether there is anything immediately perceived by the senses except sensible qualities. I know you asserted there was not, but I would now be informed whether you still persist in the same opinion.

Hyl. I do.

Phil. Pray, is your corporeal substance either a sensible quality or made up of sensible qualities?

Hyl. What a question that is! Who ever thought it was?

Phil. My reason for asking was because in saying *each visible object has that color which we see in it,* you make visible objects be corporeal substances, which implies either that corporeal substances are sensible qualities or else that there is something besides sensible qualities perceived by sight; but as this point was formerly agreed between us and is still maintained by you, it is a clear consequence that your corporeal substance is nothing distinct from sensible qualities.

Hyl. You may draw as many absurd consequences as you please and endeavor to perplex the plainest things, but you shall never persuade me out of my senses. I clearly understand my own meaning.

Phil. I wish you would make me understand it too. But since you are unwilling to have your notion of corporeal substance examined, I shall urge that point no further. Only be pleased to let me know whether the same colors which we see exist in external bodies or some other.

Hyl. The very same.

Phil. What! Are then the beautiful red and purple we see on yonder clouds really in them? Or do you imagine they have in themselves any other form than that of a dark mist or vapor?

Hyl. I must admit, Philonous, those colors are not really in the clouds as they seem to be at this distance. They are only apparent colors.

Phil. Apparent call you them? How shall we distinguish these apparent colors from real?

Hyl. Very easily. Those are to be thought apparent which, appearing only at a distance, vanish upon a nearer approach.

Phil. And those, I suppose, are to be thought real which are discovered by the most near and exact survey.

Hyl. Right.

Phil. Is the nearest and most exact survey made by the help of a microscope or by the naked eye?

Hyl. By a microscope, doubtless.

Phil. But a microscope often discovers colors in an object different from those perceived by the unassisted sight. And in case we had microscopes magnifying to any assigned degree, it is certain that no object whatsoever viewed through them would appear in the same color which it exhibits to the naked eye.

Hyl. And what will you conclude from all this? You cannot argue that there are really and naturally no colors on objects because they may be altered or made to vanish by artificial managements.

Phil. I think it may evidently be concluded from your own concessions that all the colors we see with our naked eyes are only apparent as those on the clouds, since they vanish upon a more close and accurate inspection, which is afforded us by a microscope. Then as to what you say by way of prevention, I ask you whether the real and natural state of an object is better discovered by a very sharp and piercing sight or by one which is less sharp.

Hyl. By the former without doubt.

Phil. Is it not plain from *Dioptrics* that microscopes make the sight more penetrating and represent objects as they would appear to the eye, in case it were naturally endowed with a most exquisite sharpness?

Hyl. It is.

Phil. Consequently, the microscopic representation is to be thought that which best sets forth the real nature of the thing or what it is in itself. The colors therefore perceived by it are more genuine and real than those perceived otherwise.

Hyl. I confess there is something in what you say.

Phil. Besides, it is not only possible but manifest that there actually are animals whose eyes are by nature framed to perceive those things which by reason of their minuteness escape our sight. What do you think of those inconceivably small animals perceived by glasses? Must we suppose they are all stark blind? Or, in case they see, can it be imagined their sight does not have the same use in preserving their bodies from injuries which appears in that of all other animals? And if it does, is it not evident they must see particles less than their own bodies, which will present them with a far different view in each object from that which strikes our senses? Even our own eyes do not always represent objects to us after the same manner. With *jaundice,* everyone knows that all things seem yellow. Is it not therefore highly probable that those animals in whose eyes we discern a very different texture from that of ours and whose bodies abound with different humors do not see the

same colors in every object that we do? From all of which, should it not seem to follow that all colors are equally apparent and that none of those which we perceive are really inherent in any outward object?

Hyl. It should.

Phil. The point will be past all doubt if you consider that in case colors were real properties or affections inherent in external bodies, they could admit of no alteration without some change made in the very bodies themselves. But is it not evident from what has been said that upon the use of microscopes, upon a change happening in the humors of the eye or a variation of distance without any manner of real alteration in the thing itself, the colors of any object are either changed or totally disappear? No, all other circumstances remaining the same, change but the situation of some objects and they shall present different colors to the eye. The same thing happens upon viewing an object in various degrees of light. And what is more known than that the same bodies appear differently colored by candlelight from what they do in the open day? Add to these the experiment of a prism which, separating the heterogeneous rays of light, alters the color of any object and will cause the whitest to appear of a deep blue or red to the naked eye. And now tell me whether you are still of the opinion that every body has its true, real color inhering in it; and if you think it has, I would gladly know further from you what certain distance and position of the object, what peculiar texture and formation of the eye, what degree or kind of light is necessary for ascertaining that true color and distinguishing it from apparent ones.

Hyl. I admit myself entirely satisfied that they are all equally apparent and that there is no such thing as color really inhering in external bodies, but that it is altogether in the light. And what confirms me in this opinion is that, in proportion to the light, colors are still more or less vivid, and if there is no light, then there are no colors perceived. Besides, allowing there are colors on external objects, yet how is it possible for us to perceive them? For no external body affects the mind unless it acts first on our organs of sense. But the only action of bodies is motion, and motion cannot be communicated otherwise than by impulse. A distant object, therefore, cannot act on the eye, nor consequently make itself or its properties perceivable to the soul. From this it plainly follows that it is immediately some contiguous substance which, operating on the eye, occasions a perception of colors—and such is light.

Phil. How! Is light then a substance?

Hyl. I tell you, Philonous, external light is nothing but a thin fluid substance whose minute particles, being agitated with a brisk motion and in various manners reflected from the different surfaces of outward objects to the eyes, communicate different motions to the optic nerves which, being propagated to the brain, cause various impressions in it; and these are attended with the sensations of red, blue, yellow, etc.

Phil. It seems, then, the light does no more than shake the optic nerves.

Hyl. Nothing else.

Phil. And, consequent to each particular motion of the nerves, the mind is affected with a sensation which is some particular color.

Hyl. Right.

Phil. And these sensations have no existence without the mind.

Hyl. They do not.

Phil. How then do you affirm that colors are in the light, since by light you understand a corporeal substance external to the mind?

Hyl. Light and colors, as immediately perceived by us, I grant cannot exist without the mind. But in themselves they are only the motions and configurations of certain insensible particles of matter.

Phil. Colors then, in the vulgar sense, or taken for the immediate objects of sight, cannot agree to any but a perceiving substance.

Hyl. That is what I say.

Phil. Well then, since you give up the point as to those sensible qualities which are alone thought colors by all mankind besides, you may hold what you please with regard to those invisible ones of the philosophers. It is not my business to dispute about them; only I would advise you to envision yourself, whether, considering the inquiry we are upon, it would be prudent for you to affirm: *The red and blue which we see are not real colors, but certain unknown motions and figures which no man ever did or can see are truly*

so. Are not these shocking notions, and are not they subject to as many ridiculous inferences as those you were obliged to renounce before in the case of sounds?

Hyl. I frankly admit, Philonous, that it is in vain to stand out any longer. Colors, sounds, tastes, in a word, all those termed *secondary qualities* have certainly no existence without the mind. But by this acknowledgment I must not be supposed to derogate anything from the reality of matter or external objects, seeing it is no more than several philosophers maintain who, nevertheless, are the furthest imaginable from denying matter. For the clearer understanding of this, you must know sensible qualities are by philosophers divided into *primary* and *secondary*. The former are extension, figure, solidity, gravity, motion, and rest. And these they hold exist really in bodies. The latter are those above enumerated or, briefly, all sensible qualities besides the primary which they assert are only so many sensations or ideas existing nowhere but in the mind. But all this, I do not doubt, you are already apprised of. For my part, I have been a long time sensible there was such an opinion current among philosophers, but was never thoroughly convinced of its truth until now.

Phil. You are still, then, of the opinion that extension and figures are inherent in external unthinking substances.

Hyl. I am.

Phil. But what if the same arguments which are brought against secondary qualities will hold proof against these also?

Hyl. Why, then I shall be obliged to think they, too, exist only in the mind.

Phil. Is it your opinion that the very figure and extension which you perceive by sense exist in the outward object or material substance?

Hyl. It is.

Phil. Have all other animals as good grounds to think the same of the figure and extension which they see and feel?

Hyl. Without doubt, if they have any thought at all.

Phil. Answer me, Hylas. Do you think the senses were bestowed upon all animals for their preservation and well being in life? Or were they given to men alone for this end?

Hyl. I make no question but they have the same use in all other animals.

Phil. If so, is it not necessary they should be enabled by them to perceive their own limbs and those bodies which are capable of harming them?

Hyl. Certainly.

Phil. A mite therefore must be supposed to see his own foot, and things equal or even less than it, as bodies of some considerable dimension, though at the same time they appear to you scarce discernible or at best as so many visible points.

Hyl. I cannot deny it.

Phil. And to creatures less than the mite they will seem yet larger.

Hyl. They will.

Phil. To the extent that what you can hardly discern will to another extremely minute animal appear as some huge mountain.

Hyl. All this I grant.

Phil. Can one and the same thing be at the same time in itself of different dimensions?

Hyl. That would be absurd to imagine.

Phil. But from what you have laid down it follows that both the extension perceived by you and that perceived by the mite itself, as likewise all those perceived by lesser animals, are each of them the true extension of the mite's foot—that is to say, by your own principles you are led into an absurdity.

Hyl. There seems to be some difficulty in the point.

Phil. Again, have you not acknowledged that no real inherent property of any object can be changed without some change in the thing itself?

Hyl. I have.

Phil. But as we approach to or recede from an object, the visible extension varies, being at one distance ten or a hundred times greater than at another. Does it not therefore follow from this, likewise, that it is not really inherent in the object?

Hyl. I admit I am at a loss what to think.

Phil. Your judgment will soon be determined if you will venture to think as freely concerning this quality as you have done concerning the rest. Was it not admitted as a good argument that neither heat nor cold was in the water because it seemed warm to one hand and cold to the other?

Hyl. It was.

Phil. Is it not the very same reasoning to conclude there is no extension or figure in an object because to one eye it shall seem little, smooth, and round, when at the same time it appears to the other great, uneven, and angular?

Hyl. The very same. But does this latter fact ever happen?

Phil. You may at any time make the experiment by looking with one eye bare and with the other through a microscope.

Hyl. I do not know how to maintain it, and yet I am loath to give up *extension*; I see so many odd consequences following upon such a concession.

Phil. Odd, you say? After the concessions already made, I hope you will stick at nothing for its oddness. But on the other hand should it not seem very odd if the general reasoning which includes all other sensible qualities did not also include extension? If it is allowed that no idea nor anything like an idea can exist in an unperceiving substance, then surely it follows that no figure or mode of extension which we can either perceive or imagine or have any idea of can be really inherent in matter—not to mention the peculiar difficulty there must be in conceiving a material substance, prior to and distinct from extension, to be the *substratum* of extension. Whatever the sensible quality is, figure, or sound, or color, it seems equally impossible it should subsist in that which does not perceive it.

Hyl. I give up the point for the present, reserving still a right to retract my opinion, in case I shall hereafter discover any false step in my progress to it.

Phil. That is a right you cannot be denied. Figures and extension being dispatched, we proceed next to *motion.* Can a real motion in any external body be at the same time both very swift and very slow?

Hyl. It cannot.

Phil. Is not the motion of a body swift in a reciprocal proportion to the time it takes up in describing any given space? Thus a body that describes a mile in an hour moves three times faster than it would in case it described only a mile in three hours.

Hyl. I agree with you.

Phil. And is not time measured by the succession of ideas in our minds?

Hyl. It is.

Phil. And is it not possible ideas should succeed one another twice as fast in your mind as they do in mine or in that of some spirit of another kind?

Hyl. I admit it.

Phil. Consequently, the same body may to another seem to perform its motion over any space in half the time that it does to you. And the same reasoning will hold as to any other proportion—that is to say, according to your principles (since the motions perceived are both really in the object) it is possible one and the same body shall be really moved the same way at once, both very swift and very slow. How is this consistent either with common sense or with what you just now granted?

Hyl. I have nothing to say to it.

Phil. Then as for *solidity*, either you do not mean any sensible quality by that word and so it is besides our inquiry or, if you do, it must be either hardness or resistance. But both the one and the other are plainly relative to our senses, it being evident that what seems hard to one animal may appear soft to another who has greater force and firmness of limbs. Nor is it less plain that the resistance I feel is not in the body.

Hyl. I admit the very sensation of resistance, which is all you immediately perceive, is not in the *body*, but the cause of that sensation is.

Phil. But the causes of our sensations are not things immediately perceived, and, therefore, not sensible. This point I thought had been already determined.

Hyl. I admit it was, but you will pardon me if I seem a little embarrassed; I do not know how to quit my old notions.

Phil. To help you out, do but consider that if extension is once acknowledged to have no existence without the mind, the same must necessarily be granted of motion, solidity, and gravity, since they all evidently suppose extension. It is therefore superfluous to inquire particularly concerning each of them. In denying extension, you have denied them all to have any real existence.

Hyl. I wonder, Philonous, if what you say is true, why those philosophers who deny the secondary qualities any real existence should yet attribute it to the primary. If there is no difference between them, how can this be accounted for?

Phil. It is not my business to account for every opinion of the philosophers. But among other reasons which may be assigned for this, it seems probable that pleasure and pain, being annexed to the former rather than the latter, may be one. Heat and cold, tastes and smells, have something more vividly pleasing or disagreeable than the ideas of extension, figure, and motion affect us with. And it being too visibly absurd to hold that pain or pleasure can be in an unperceiving substance, men are more easily weaned from believing the external existence of the secondary than the primary qualities. You will be satisfied there is something in this if you recollect the difference you made between an intense and more moderate degree of heat, allowing the one a real existence while you denied it to the other. But after all, there is no rational ground for that distinction, for surely an indifferent sensation is as truly *a sensation* as one more pleasing or painful and, consequently, should not any more than they be supposed to exist in an unthinking subject.

Hyl. It has just come into my head, Philonous, that I have somewhere heard of a distinction between absolute and sensible extension. Now, though it is acknowledged that great and small, consisting merely in the relation which other extended beings have to the parts of our own bodies, do not really inhere in the substances themselves, yet nothing obliges us to hold the same with regard to *absolute extension*, which is something abstracted from *great* and *small*, from this or that particular magnitude or figure. So likewise as to motion, *swift* and *slow* are altogether relative to the succession of ideas in our own minds. But it does not follow, because those modifications of motion do not exist without the mind, that absolute motion abstracted from them therefore does not.

Phil. Pray what is it that distinguishes one motion or one part of extension from another? Is it not something sensible, as some degree of swiftness or slowness, some certain magnitude or figure peculiar to each?

Hyl. I think so.

Phil. These qualities, therefore, stripped of all sensible properties, are without all specific and numerical differences, as the schools call them.

Hyl. They are.

Phil. That is to say, they are extension in general and motion in general.

Hyl. Let it be so.

Phil. But it is a universally received maxim that *everything which exists is particular.* How, then, can motion in general or extension in general exist in any corporeal substance?

Hyl. I will take time to solve your difficulty.

Phil. But I think the point may be speedily decided. Without doubt you can tell whether you are able to frame this or that idea. Now I am content to put our dispute on this issue. If you can frame in your thoughts a distinct abstract idea of motion or extension, divested of all those sensible modes as swift and slow, great and small, round and square, and the like which are acknowledged to exist only in the mind I will then yield the point you contend for. But if you cannot, it will be unreasonable on your side to insist any longer upon what you have no notion of.

Hyl. To confess ingenuously, I cannot.

Phil. Can you even separate the ideas of extension and motion from the ideas of all those qualities which they who make the distinction term *secondary?*

Hyl. What! Is it not an easy matter to consider extension and motion by themselves, abstracted from all other sensible qualities? Pray how do the mathematicians treat of them?

Phil. I acknowledge, Hylas, it is not difficult to form general propositions and reasonings about those qualities without mentioning any other and in this sense to consider or treat of them abstractly. But how does it follow that, because I can pronounce the word *motion* by itself, I can form the idea of it in my mind exclusive of body? Or because theorems may be made of extension and figures without any mention of *great* or *small* or any other sensible mode or quality, that therefore it is possible such an abstract idea of extension, without any particular size or figure or sensible quality, should be distinctly formed and apprehended by the mind? Mathematicians treat of quantity, without regarding what other sensible qualities it is attended with, as being altogether indifferent to their demonstrations. But when, laying aside the words, they contemplate the bare ideas, I believe you will find they are not the pure abstracted ideas of extension.

Hyl. But what do you say to *pure intellect?* May not abstracted ideas be framed by that faculty?

Phil. Since I cannot frame abstract ideas at all, it is plain I cannot frame them by the help of *pure intellect,* whatever faculty you understand by those words. Besides, not to inquire into the nature of pure intellect and its spiritual objects, as *virtue, reason, God,* or the like—this much seems manifest—that sensible things are only to be perceived by sense or represented by the imagination. Figures, therefore, and extension, being originally perceived by sense, do not belong to pure intellect. But for your further satisfaction, try, if you can, [to] frame the idea of any figure abstracted from all particularities of size or even from other sensible qualities.

Hyl. Let me think a little—I do not find that I can.

Phil. And can you think it possible that what implies a repugnance in its conception should really exist in nature?

Hyl. By no means.

Phil. Since, therefore, it is impossible even for the mind to disunite the ideas of extension and motion from all other sensible qualities, does it not follow that where the one exists, there necessarily the other exists likewise?

Hyl. It should seem so.

Phil. Consequently, the very same arguments which you admitted as conclusive against the secondary qualities are without any further application of force against the primary, too. Besides, if you will trust your senses, is it not plain all sensible qualities coexist or appear to them as being in the same place? Do they ever represent a motion, or figure, as being divested of all other visible and tangible qualities?

Hyl. You need say no more on this head. I am free to admit, if there is no secret error or oversight in our proceedings up to now, that all sensible qualities are alike to be denied existence without the mind. But my fear is that I have been too liberal in my former concessions or overlooked some fallacy or other. In short, I did not take time to think.

Phil. For that matter, Hylas, you may take what time you please in reviewing the progress of our inquiry. You are at liberty to recover any slips you might have made or offer whatever you have omitted which makes for your first opinion.

Hyl. One great oversight I take to be this: that I did not sufficiently distinguish the *object* from the *sensation*. Now though this latter may not exist without the mind, yet it will not follow from this that the former cannot.

Phil. What object do you mean? The object of the senses?

Hyl. The same.

Phil. It is then immediately perceived?

Hyl. Right.

Phil. Make me understand the difference between what is immediately perceived and a sensation.

Hyl. The sensation I take to be an act of the mind perceiving, besides which there is something perceived, and this I call the *object*. For example, there is red and yellow on that tulip. But then the act of perceiving those colors is in me only, and not in the tulip.

Phil. What tulip do you speak of? Is it that which you see?

Hyl. The same.

Phil. And what do you see besides color, figure, and extension?

Hyl. Nothing.

Phil. What you would say then is, that the red and yellow are coexistent with the extension; is it not?

Hyl. That is not all. I would say they have a real existence without the mind in some unthinking substance.

Phil. That the colors are really in the tulip, which I see, is manifest. Neither can it be denied that this tulip may exist independent of your mind or mine; but that any immediate object of the senses, that is, any idea or combination of ideas, should exist in an unthinking substance or exterior to all minds is in itself an evident contradiction. Nor can I imagine how this follows from what you said just now, namely, that the red and yellow were on the tulip *you saw*, since you do not pretend to see that unthinking substance.

Hyl. You have an artful way, Philonous, of diverting our inquiry from the subject.

Phil. I see you have no mind to be pressed that way. To return, then, to your distinction between *sensation* and *object*; if I take you right, you distinguish in every perception two things, the one an action of the mind, the other not.

Hyl. True.

Phil. And this action cannot exist in or belong to any unthinking thing, but whatever besides is implied in a perception, may.

Hyl. That is my meaning.

Phil. So that if there was a perception without any act of the mind, it was possible such a perception should exist in an unthinking substance.

Hyl. I grant it. But it is impossible there should be such a perception.

Phil. When is the mind said to be active?

Hyl. When it produces, puts an end to, or changes anything.

Phil. Can the mind produce, discontinue, or change anything but by an act of the will?

Hyl. It cannot.

Phil. The mind therefore is to be accounted active in its perceptions, insofar as volition is included in them.

Hyl. It is.

Phil. In plucking this flower I am active, because I do it by the motion of my hand, which was consequent upon my volition—so likewise in applying it to my nose. But is either of these smelling?

Hyl. No.

Phil. I act too in drawing the air through my nose, because my breathing so, rather than otherwise, is the effect of my volition. But neither can this be called *smelling*, for if it were, I should smell every time I breathed in that manner.

Hyl. True.

Phil. Smelling, then, is somewhat consequent to all this.

Hyl. It is.

Phil. But I do not find my will concerned any further. Whatever more there is, as that I perceive such a particular smell or any smell at all, this is independent of my will and I am altogether passive in this. Do you find it otherwise with you, Hylas?

Hyl. No, the very same.

Phil. Then as to seeing, is it not in your power to open your eyes or keep them shut, to turn them this or that way?

Hyl. Without doubt.

Phil. But does it in like manner depend on your will that, in looking on this flower, you perceive *white* rather than any other color? Or directing your open eyes towards that part of the heaven beyond, can you avoid seeing the sun? Or is light or darkness the effect of your volition?

Hyl. No, certainly.

Phil. You are then in these respects altogether passive.

Hyl. I am.

Phil. Tell me now, whether *seeing* consists in perceiving light and colors, or in opening and turning the eyes?

Hyl. Without doubt, in the former.

Phil. Since, therefore, you are, in the very perception of light and colors, altogether passive, what has become of that action you were speaking of as an ingredient in every sensation? And does it not follow from your own concessions that the perception of light and colors, including no action in it, may exist in an unperceiving substance? And is this not a plain contradiction?

Hyl. I do not know what to think of it.

Phil. Besides, since you distinguish the *active* and *passive* in every perception, you must do it in that of pain. But how is it possible that pain—let it be as little active as you please—should exist in an unperceiving substance? In short, do but consider the point and then confess ingenuously whether light and colors, tastes, sounds, etc., are not all equally passions or sensations in the soul. You may indeed call them *external objects* and give them in words what subsistence you please. But examine your own thoughts and then tell me whether it is not as I say?

Hyl. I acknowledge, Philonous, that upon a fair observation of what passes in my mind, I can discover nothing else but that I am a thinking being, affected with variety of sensations; neither is it possible to conceive how a sensation should exist in an unperceiving substance. But then, on the other hand, when I look on sensible things in a different view, considering them as so many modes and qualities, I find it necessary to suppose a material *substratum,* without which they cannot be conceived to exist.

Phil. Material substratum call you it? Pray, by which of your senses did you become acquainted with that being?

Hyl. It is not itself sensible, its modes and qualities only being perceived by the senses.

Phil. I presume, then, it was by reflection and reason you obtained the idea of it.

Hyl. I do not pretend to any proper positive idea of it. However, I conclude it exists, because qualities cannot be conceived to exist without a support.

Phil. It seems then you have only a relative notion of it, or that you conceive it not otherwise than by conceiving the relation it bears to sensible qualities.

Hyl. Right.

Phil. Be pleased, therefore, to let me know in what that relation consists.

Hyl. Is it not sufficiently expressed in the term *substratum,* or *substance?*

Phil. If so, the word *substratum* should import that it is spread under the sensible qualities or accidents.

Hyl. True.

Phil. And consequently under extension.

Hyl. I admit it.

Phil. It is therefore somewhat in its own nature entirely distinct from extension.

Hyl. I tell you, extension is only a mode, and matter is something that supports modes. And is it not evident the thing supported is different from the thing supporting?

Phil. So that something distinct from and exclusive of extension is supposed to be the *substratum* of extension.

Hyl. Just so.

Phil. Answer me, Hylas. Can a thing be spread without extension? Or is not the idea of extension necessarily included in *spreading?*

Hyl. It is.

Phil. Whatever, therefore, you suppose spread under anything must have in itself an extension distinct from the extension of that thing under which it is spread.

Hyl. It must.

Phil. Consequently, every corporeal substance being the *substratum* of extension must have in itself another extension by which it is qualified to be a *substratum,* and so on to infinity. And I ask whether this is not absurd in itself and repugnant to what you granted just now, namely, that the *substratum* was something distinct from and exclusive of extension.

Hyl. Yes, but, Philonous, you take me wrong. I do not mean that matter is *spread* in a gross literal sense under extension. The word *substratum* is used only to express in general the same thing with *substance*.

Phil. Well then, let us examine the relation implied in the term *substance*. Is it not that it stands under accidents?

Hyl. The very same.

Phil. But that one thing may stand under or support another, must it not be extended?

Hyl. It must.

Phil. Is not, therefore, this supposition liable to the same absurdity with the former?

Hyl. You still take things in a strict literal sense; that is not fair, Philonous.

Phil. I am not for imposing any sense on your words; you are at liberty to explain them as you please. Only I beseech you, make me understand something by them. You tell me matter supports or stands under accidents. How? Is it as your legs support your body?

Hyl. No; that is the literal sense.

Phil. Pray let me know any sense, literal or not literal, that you understand it in. How long must I wait for an answer, Hylas?

Hyl. I declare I do not know what to say. I once thought I understood well enough what was meant by matter's supporting accidents. But now, the more I think on it, the less can I comprehend it; in short, I find that I know nothing of it.

Phil. It seems then you have no idea at all, neither relative nor positive, of matter; you know neither what it is in itself nor what relation it bears to accidents.

Hyl. I acknowledge it.

Phil. And yet you asserted that you could not conceive how qualities or accidents should really exist without conceiving at the same time a material support of them.

Hyl. I did.

Phil. That is to say, when you conceive the real existence of qualities, you do in addition conceive something which you cannot conceive.

Hyl. It was wrong, I admit. But still I fear there is some fallacy or other. Pray what do you think of this? It has just come into my head that the ground of all our mistake lies in your treating of each quality by itself. Now, I grant that each quality cannot singly subsist without the mind. Color cannot exist without extension, neither can figure without some other sensible quality. But as the several qualities united or blended together form entire sensible things, nothing hinders why such things may not be supposed to exist without the mind.

Phil. Either, Hylas, you are jesting or have a very bad memory. Though indeed we went through all the qualities by name one after another, yet my arguments, or rather your concessions, nowhere tended to prove that the secondary qualities did not subsist each alone by itself, but that they were not *at all* without the mind. Indeed, in treating of figure and motion, we concluded they could not exist without the mind because it was impossible even in thought to separate them from all secondary qualities so as to conceive them existing by themselves. But then this was not the only argument made use of upon that occasion. But (to pass by all that has been said up to now and reckon it for nothing, if you will have it so) I am content to put the whole upon this issue. If you can conceive it possible for any mixture or combination of qualities or any sensible object whatever to exist without the mind, then I will grant it actually to be so.

Hyl. If it comes to that, the point will soon be decided. What is more easy than to conceive a tree or house existing by itself, independent of, and unperceived by any mind whatsoever? I do at this present time conceive them existing after that manner.

Phil. What are you saying, Hylas—can you see a thing which is at the same time unseen?

Hyl. No, that would be a contradiction.

Phil. Is it not as great a contradiction to talk of *conceiving* a thing which is *unconceived*?

Hyl. It is.

Phil. The tree or house, therefore, which you think of is conceived by you.

Hyl. How should it be otherwise?

Phil. And what is conceived is surely in the mind.

Hyl. Without question, that which is conceived is in the mind.

Phil. How then did you come to say you conceived a house or tree existing independent and out of all minds whatsoever?

Hyl. That was, I admit, an oversight; but stay, let

me consider what led me into it. It is a pleasant mistake enough. As I was thinking of a tree in a solitary place where no one was present to see it, I thought that was to conceive a tree as existing unperceived or unthought of, not considering that I myself conceived it all the while. But now I plainly see that all I can do is to frame ideas in my own mind. I may indeed conceive in my own thoughts the idea of a tree, or a house, or a mountain, but that is all. And this is far from proving that I can conceive them *existing out of the minds of all spirits*.

Phil. You acknowledge then that you cannot possibly conceive how any one corporeal sensible thing should exist otherwise than in a mind.

Hyl. I do.

Phil. And yet you will earnestly contend for the truth of that which you cannot so much as conceive.

Hyl. I profess I do not know what to think, but still some scruples remain with me. Is it not certain I see things at a distance? Do we not perceive the stars and moon, for example, to be a great way off? Is this not, I say, manifest to the senses?

Phil. Do you not in a dream, too, perceive those or the like objects?

Hyl. I do.

Phil. And do they not then have the same appearance of being distant?

Hyl. They have.

Phil. But you do not then conclude the apparitions in a dream to be without the mind?

Hyl. By no means.

Phil. You ought not therefore conclude that sensible objects are without the mind, from their appearance or manner in which they are perceived.

Hyl. I acknowledge it. But does not my sense deceive me in those cases?

Phil. By no means. Of the idea or thing which you immediately perceive, neither sense nor reason informs you that it actually exists without the mind. By sense you only know that you are affected with such certain sensations of light and colors, etc. And these you will not say are without the mind.

Hyl. True, but besides all that, do you not think the sight suggests something of *outness* or *distance*?

Phil. Upon approaching a distant object, do the visible size and figure change perpetually or do they appear the same at all distances?

Hyl. They are in a continual change.

Phil. Sight, therefore, does not suggest, or in any way inform you, that the visible object you immediately perceive exists at a distance or will be perceived when you advance further onward, there being a continued series of visible objects succeeding each other during the whole time of your approach.

Hyl. It does not; but still I know, upon seeing an object, what object I shall perceive after having passed over a certain distance—no matter whether it be exactly the same or no—there is still something of distance suggested in the case.

Phil. Good Hylas, do but reflect a little on the point and then tell me whether there is any more in it than this: From the ideas you actually perceive by sight, you have, by experience, learned to collect what other ideas you will (according to the standing order of nature) be affected with, after such a certain succession of time and motion.

Hyl. Upon the whole, I take it to be nothing else.

Phil. Now is it not plain that if we suppose a man born blind was suddenly made to see, he could at first have no experience of what may be suggested by sight?

Hyl. It is.

Phil. He would not then, according to you, have any notion of distance annexed to the things he saw; but would take them for a new set of sensations existing only in his mind.

Hyl. It is undeniable.

Phil. But to make it still more plain: is not *distance* a line turned endwise to the eye?

Hyl. It is.

Phil. And can a line so situated be perceived by sight?

Hyl. It cannot.

Phil. Does it not therefore follow that distance is not properly and immediately perceived by sight?

Hyl. It should seem so.

Phil. Again, is it your opinion that colors are at a distance?

Hyl. It must be acknowledged they are only in the mind.

Phil. But do not colors appear to the eye as coexisting in the same place with extension and figures?

Hyl. They do.

Phil. How can you then conclude from sight that figures exist without, when you acknowledge colors do not, the sensible appearance being the very same with regard to both?

Hyl. I do not know what to answer.

Phil. But allowing that distance was truly and immediately perceived by the mind, yet it would not then follow it existed out of the mind. For whatever is immediately perceived is an idea; and can any idea exist out of the mind?

Hyl. To suppose that would be absurd, but inform me, Philonous, can we perceive or know nothing besides our ideas?

Phil. As for the rational deducing of causes from effects, that is beside our inquiry. And by the senses you can best tell whether you perceive anything which is not immediately perceived. And I ask you whether the things immediately perceived are other than your own sensations or ideas? You have, indeed, more than once, in the course of this conversation, declared yourself on those points; but you seem, by this last question, to have departed from what you then thought.

Hyl. To speak the truth, Philonous, I think there are two kinds of objects, the one perceived immediately, which are likewise called ideas, the other are real things or external objects perceived by the mediation of ideas, which are their images and representations. Now I admit ideas do not exist without the mind, but the latter sort of object does. I am sorry I did not think of this distinction sooner; it would probably have cut short your discourse.

Phil. Are those external objects perceived by sense or by some other faculty?

Hyl. They are perceived by sense.

Phil. How! Is there anything perceived by sense which is not immediately perceived?

Hyl. Yes, Philonous, in some sort there is. For example, when I look on a picture or statue of Julius Caesar, I may be said, after a manner, to perceive him (though not immediately) by my senses.

Phil. It seems then you will have our ideas, which alone are immediately perceived, to be pictures of external things, and that these also are perceived by sense inasmuch as they have a conformity or resemblance to our ideas.

Hyl. That is my meaning.

Phil. And in the same way that Julius Caesar, in himself invisible, is nevertheless perceived by sight; real things, in themselves imperceptible, are perceived by sense.

Hyl. In the very same.

Phil. Tell me, Hylas, when you behold the picture of Julius Caesar, do you see with your eyes any more than some colors and figures, with a certain symmetry and composition of the whole?

Hyl. Nothing else.

Phil. And would not a man who had never known anything of Julius Caesar see as much?

Hyl. He would.

Phil. Consequently, he has his sight and the use of it in as perfect a degree as you.

Hyl. I agree with you.

Phil. From where does it come then that your thoughts are directed to the Roman emperor and his are not? This cannot proceed from the sensations or ideas of sense by you then perceived, since you acknowledge you have no advantage over him in that respect. It should seem therefore to proceed from reason and memory, should it not?

Hyl. It should.

Phil. Consequently, it will not follow from that instance that anything is perceived by sense which is not immediately perceived. Though I grant we may in one meaning be said to perceive sensible things mediately by sense, that is, when, from a frequently perceived connection, the immediate perception of ideas by one sense suggests to the mind others, perhaps belonging to another sense, which are accustomed to be connected with them. For instance, when I hear a coach drive along the streets, immediately I perceive only the sound; but, from the experience I have had that such a sound is connected with a coach, I am said to hear the coach. It is nevertheless evident that, in truth and strictness, nothing can be *heard* but *sound,* and the coach is not then properly perceived by sense, but suggested from experience. So likewise when we are said to see a red-hot bar of iron, the solidity and heat of the iron are not the objects of sight, but suggested to the imagination by the color and figure which are properly perceived by that sense. In short, those things alone are actually and strictly perceived by any sense which would have been perceived in case that same sense had then been first conferred on us. As for other things, it is plain they are only suggested to the mind by experience grounded on former perceptions. But to return to your comparison of Caesar's picture, it is plain, if you keep to that, you must hold that the real things or archetypes of our ideas are not perceived by sense, but by some internal faculty of the soul as reason or memory. I would therefore gladly know what arguments you can draw from reason for the existence of what you call *real things* or *material objects*, or whether you remember to have seen them formerly as they are in themselves, or if you have heard or read of anyone who did.

Hyl. I see, Philonous, you are disposed to raillery, but that will never convince me.

Phil. My aim is only to learn from you the way to come at the knowledge of *material beings*. Whatever we perceive is perceived either immediately or mediately, by sense, or by reason and reflection. But as you have excluded sense, pray show me what reason you have to believe their existence, or what *medium* you can possibly make use of to prove it, either to mine or your own understanding.

Hyl. To deal ingenuously, Philonous, now that I consider the point, I do not find I can give you any good reason for it. But this much seems pretty plain — that it is at least possible such things may really exist, and as long as there is no absurdity in supposing them, I am resolved to believe as I did, until you bring good reasons to the contrary.

Phil. What! Has it come to this, that you only believe the existence of material objects and that your belief is founded barely on the possibility of its being true? Then you will have me bring reasons against it, though another would think it reasonable the proof should lie on him who holds the affirmative. And after all, this very point which you are now resolved to maintain without any reason is, in effect, what you have more than once during this discourse seen good

reason to give up. But to pass over all this — if I understand you rightly, you say our ideas do not exist without the mind, but that they are copies, images, or representations of certain originals that do.

Hyl. You take me right.

Phil. They are then like external things.

Hyl. They are.

Phil. Have those things a stable and permanent nature independent of our senses, or are they in a perpetual change upon our producing any motions in our bodies, suspending, exerting, or altering our faculties or organs of sense.

Hyl. Real things, it is plain, have a fixed and real nature, which remains the same, notwithstanding any change in our senses or in the posture and motion of our bodies, which indeed may affect the ideas in our minds, but it would be absurd to think they had the same effect on things existing without the mind.

Phil. How then is it possible that things perpetually fleeting and variable as our ideas should be copies or images of anything fixed and constant? Or, in other words, since all sensible qualities, as size, figure, color, etc., that is, our ideas, are continually changing upon every alteration in the distance, medium, or instruments of sensation, how can any determinate material objects be properly represented or painted forth by several distinct things, each of which is so different from and unlike the rest? Or if you say it resembles some one only of our ideas, how shall we be able to distinguish the true copy from all the false ones?

Hyl. I profess, Philonous, I am at a loss. I do not know what to say to this.

Phil. But neither is this all. Which are material objects in themselves — perceptible or imperceptible?

Hyl. Properly and immediately nothing can be perceived but ideas. All material things, therefore, are in themselves insensible and to be perceived only by their ideas.

Phil. Ideas then are sensible, and their archetypes or originals insensible.

Hyl. Right.

Phil. But how can that which is sensible be like that which is insensible? Can a real thing in itself *invisible* be like a *color*; or a real thing which is not *audible* be like a *sound*? In a word, can anything be like a sensation or idea but another sensation or idea?

Hyl. I must admit, I think not.

Phil. Is it possible there should be any doubt in the point? Do you not perfectly know your own ideas?

Hyl. I know them perfectly, since what I do not perceive or know can be no part of my idea.

Phil. Consider, therefore, and examine them, and then tell me if there is anything in them which can exist without the mind or if you can conceive anything like them existing without the mind.

Hyl. Upon inquiry, I find it is impossible for me to conceive or understand how anything but an idea can be like an idea. And it is most evident that *no idea can exist without the mind*.

Phil. You are, therefore, by your principles forced to deny the reality of sensible things, since you made it to consist in an absolute existence exterior to the mind. That is to say, you are a downright *skeptic*. So I have gained my point, which was to show your principles led to skepticism.

Hyl. For the present I am, if not entirely convinced, at least silenced.

Phil. I would gladly know what more you would require in order to have a perfect conviction. Have you not had the liberty of explaining yourself all manner of ways? Were any little slips in discourse laid hold and insisted on? Or were you not allowed to retract or reinforce anything you had offered, as best served your purpose? Has not everything you could say been heard and examined with all the fairness imaginable? In a word, have you not in every point been convinced out of your own mouth? And if you can at present discover any flaw in any of your former concessions, or think of any remaining subterfuge, any new distinction, color, or comment whatsoever, why do you not produce it?

Hyl. A little patience, Philonous. I am at present so amazed to see myself ensnared and, as it were, imprisoned in the labyrinths you have drawn me into that on the sudden it cannot be expected I should find my way out. You must give me time to look about me and recollect myself.

Phil. Listen, is not this the college bell?

Hyl. It rings for prayers.

Phil. We will go in then, if you please, and meet here again tomorrow morning. In the meantime you may employ your thoughts on this morning's discourse and try if you can find any fallacy in it or invent any new means to extricate yourself.

Hyl. Agreed.

The Second Dialogue

Hylas. I beg your pardon, Philonous, for not meeting you sooner. All this morning my head was so filled with our late conversation that I had not leisure to think of the time of the day or, indeed, of anything else.

Philonous. I am glad you were so intent upon it, in hopes if there were any mistakes in your concessions or fallacies in my reasonings from them, you will now discover them to me.

Hyl. I assure you, I have done nothing ever since I saw you but search after mistakes and fallacies— and, with that view, have minutely examined the whole series of yesterday's discourse—but all in vain, for the notions it led me into, upon review, appear still more clear and evident, and the more I consider them, the more irresistibly do they force my assent.

Phil. And is this not, you think, a sign that they are genuine, that they proceed from nature and are conformable to right reason? Truth and beauty are in this alike, that the strictest survey sets them both off to advantage. While the false luster of error and disguise cannot endure being reviewed or too nearly inspected.

Hyl. I admit there is a great deal in what you say. Nor can anyone be more entirely satisfied of the truth of those odd consequences so long as I have in view the reasonings that lead to them. But when these are out of my thoughts, there seems, on the other hand, something so satisfactory, so natural and intelligible in the modern way of explaining things, that I profess I do not know how to reject it.

Phil. I do not know what way you mean.

Hyl. I mean the way of accounting for our sensations or ideas.

Phil. How is that?

Hyl. It is supposed the soul makes her residence in some part of the brain from which the nerves take their rise and are thus extended to all parts of the body and that outward objects, by the different impressions they make on the organs of sense, communicate certain vibrational motions to the nerves and, these being filled with spirits, propagate them to the brain or seat of the soul, which, according to the various impressions or traces thereby made in the brain, is variously affected with ideas.

Phil. And do you call this an explication of the manner whereby we are affected with ideas?

Hyl. Why not, Philonous? Have you anything to object against it?

Phil. I would first know whether I rightly understand your hypothesis. You make certain traces in the brain to be the causes or occasions of our ideas. Pray tell me whether by the *brain* you mean any sensible thing?

Hyl. What else do you think I could mean?

Phil. Sensible things are all immediately perceivable; and those things which are immediately perceivable are ideas; and these exist only in the mind. This much you have, if I am not mistaken, long since agreed to.

Hyl. I do not deny it.

Phil. The brain therefore you speak of, being a sensible thing, exists only in the mind. Now, I would gladly know whether you think it reasonable to suppose that one idea or thing existing in the mind occasions all other ideas. And if you think so, pray how do you account for the origin of that primary idea or brain itself?

Hyl. I do not explain the origin of our ideas by that brain which is perceivable to sense, this being itself only a combination of sensible ideas, but by another which I imagine.

Phil. But are not things imagined as truly *in the mind* as things perceived?

Hyl. I must confess they are.

Phil. It comes, therefore, to the same thing, and you have been all this while accounting for ideas by certain motions or impressions in the brain, that is, by some alterations in an idea—whether sensible or imaginable, it does not matter.

Hyl. I begin to suspect my hypothesis.

Phil. Beside spirits, all that we know or conceive are our own ideas. When, therefore, you say all ideas are occasioned by impressions in the brain, do you conceive this brain or not? If you do, then you talk of ideas imprinted in an idea causing that same idea, which is absurd. If you do not conceive it, you talk unintelligibly instead of forming a reasonable hypothesis.

Hyl. I now clearly see it was a mere dream. There is nothing in it.

Phil. You need not be much concerned at it; for, after all, this way of explaining things, as you called it, could never have satisfied any reasonable man. What connection is there between a motion in the nerves and the sensations of sound or color in the mind? Or how is it possible these should be the effect of that?

Hyl. But I could never think it had so little in it as now it seems to have.

Phil. Well then, are you at length satisfied that no sensible things have a real existence and that you are in truth a thoroughgoing *skeptic?*

Hyl. It is too plain to be denied.

Phil. Look! Are not the fields covered with a delightful greenery? Is there not something in the woods and groves, in the rivers and clear springs, that soothes, that delights, that transports the soul? At the prospect of the wide and deep ocean, or some huge mountain whose top is lost in the clouds, or of an old gloomy forest, are not our minds filled with a pleasing horror? Even in rocks and deserts, is there not an agreeable wildness? How sincere a pleasure is it to behold the natural beauties of the earth! To preserve and renew our relish for them, is not the veil of night alternately drawn over her face, and does she not change her dress with the seasons? How aptly are the elements disposed! What variety and use in the meanest production of nature! What delicacy, what beauty, what contrivance in animal and vegetable bodies! How exquisitely are all things suited as well to their particular ends as to constitute opposite parts of the whole! And while they mutually aid and support, do they not also set off and illustrate each other! Raise now your thoughts from this ball of earth to all those glorious luminaries that adorn the high arch of heaven. The motion and situation of the planets, are they not admirable for use and order? Were those (miscalled *erratic*) globes ever known to stray in their repeated journeys through the pathless void? Do they not measure areas round the sun ever proportioned to the times? So fixed, so immutable, are the laws by which the unseen Author of nature actuates the universe. How vivid and radiant is the luster of the fixed stars! How magnificent and rich that negligent profusion with which they appear to be scattered throughout the whole azure vault! Yet if you take the telescope, it brings into your sight a new host of stars that escape the naked eye. Here they seem contiguous and minute, but to a nearer view immense orbs of light at various distances, far sunk in the abyss of space. Now you must call imagination to your aid. The feeble narrow sense cannot ascertain innumerable worlds revolving round the central fires and, in those worlds, the energy of an all-perfect mind displayed in endless forms. But neither sense nor imagination is big enough to comprehend the boundless extent with all its glittering furniture. Though the laboring mind exerts and strains each power to its utmost reach, there still stands out ungrasped an immeasurable surplus. Yet all the vast bodies that compose this mighty frame, however distant and remote, are by some secret mechanism, some divine art and force, linked in a mutual dependence and intercourse with each other, even with this earth, which was almost slipped from my thoughts and lost in the crowd of worlds. Is not the whole system immense, beautiful, glorious beyond expression and beyond thought? What treatment then do those philosophers deserve who would deprive these noble and delightful scenes of all reality? How should those principles be entertained that lead us to think all the visible beauty of the creation a false imaginary glare? To be plain, can you expect this skepticism of yours will not be thought extravagantly absurd by all men of sense?

Hyl. Other men may think as they please, but for your part you have nothing to reproach me with. My comfort is, you are as much a skeptic as I am.

Phil. There, Hylas, I must beg leave to differ from you.

Hyl. What! Have you all along agreed to the premises, and do you now deny the conclusion and leave me to maintain these paradoxes which you led me into by myself? This surely is not fair.

Phil. I deny that I agreed with you in those notions that led to skepticism. You indeed said the reality of sensible things consisted in an *absolute existence* out of the minds of spirits or distinct from their being perceived. And, pursuant to this notion of reality, you are obliged to deny sensible things any real existence; that is, according to your own definition, you profess yourself a *skeptic*. But I neither said nor thought the reality of sensible things was to be defined after that manner. To me it is evident, for the reasons you allow of, that sensible things cannot exist otherwise than in a mind or spirit. From this I conclude, not that they have no real existence, but that, seeing they do not depend on my thought, and have an existence distinct from being perceived by me, *there must be some other mind in which they exist*. As sure, therefore, as the sensible world really exists, so sure is there an infinite, omnipresent Spirit who contains and supports it.

Hyl. What! This is no more than I and all Christians hold—no, and all others too who believe there is a God and that he knows and comprehends all things.

Phil. Yes, but here lies the difference. Men commonly believe that all things are known or perceived by God because they believe the being of a God, whereas I, on the other side, immediately and necessarily conclude the being of a God because all sensible things must be perceived by him.

Hyl. But so long as we all believe the same thing, what matter is it how we come by that belief?

Phil. But neither do we agree in the same opinion. For philosophers, though they acknowledge all corporeal beings to be perceived by God, yet they attribute to them an absolute subsistence distinct from their being perceived by any mind whatever, which I do not. Besides, is there no difference between saying *there is a God, therefore he perceives all things*, and saying *sensible things do really exist—and if they really exist, they are necessarily perceived by an infinite mind—therefore there is an infinite mind, or God?* This furnishes you with a direct and immediate demonstration, from a most evident principle, of the *being of a God*. Theologians and philosophers had proved beyond all controversy, from the beauty and usefulness of the several parts of the creation, that it was the workmanship of God. But that—setting aside all help of astronomy and natural philosophy, all contemplation of the contrivance, order, and adjustment of things—an infinite mind should be necessarily inferred from the bare existence of the sensible world is an advantage peculiar to them only who have made this easy reflection: that the sensible world is that which we perceive by our several senses; and that nothing is perceived by the senses besides ideas; and that no idea or archetype of an idea can exist otherwise than in a mind. You may now, without any laborious search into the sciences, without any subtlety of reason or tedious length of discourse, oppose and baffle the most strenuous advocate for atheism. Those miserable refuges, whether in an eternal succession of unthinking causes and effects or in a fortuitous concourse of atoms—those wild imaginations of Vanini, Hobbes, and Spinoza, in a word, the whole system of atheism—is it not entirely overthrown by this single reflection on the repugnance included in supposing the whole or any part, even the most rude and shapeless of the visible world, to exist without a mind? Let anyone of those abettors of impiety but look into his own thoughts and there try if he can conceive how so much as a rock, a desert, a chaos, or confused jumble of atoms, how anything at all, either sensible or imaginable, can exist independent of a mind, and he need go no further to be convinced of his folly. Can anything be fairer than to put a dispute on such an issue and leave it to a man himself to see if he can conceive, even in thought, what he holds to be true in fact, and to allow it a real existence from a notion?

Hyl. It cannot be denied, there is something highly serviceable to religion in what you advance. But do you not think it looks very like a notion entertained by some eminent moderns, of *seeing all things in God*?

Phil. I would gladly know that opinion; pray explain it to me.

Hyl. They conceive that the soul, being immaterial, is incapable of being united with material things so as to perceive them in themselves, but that she perceives them by her union with the substance of God, which, being spiritual, is therefore purely intelligible or capable of being the immediate object of a spirit's thought. Besides, the divine essence contains in it perfections correspondent to each created being, and which are, for that reason, proper to exhibit or represent them to the mind.

Phil. I do not understand how our ideas, which are things altogether passive and inert, can be the essence or any part (or like any part) of the essence

or substance of God, who is an impassive, indivisible, purely active being. Many more difficulties and objections occur at first view against this hypothesis, but I shall only add that it is liable to all the absurdities of the common hypotheses in making a created world exist otherwise than in the mind of a spirit. Besides all which, it has this peculiar to itself, that it makes that material world serve to no purpose. And if it passes for a good argument against other hypotheses in the sciences that they suppose nature or the Divine Wisdom to make something in vain or do by tedious round-about methods what might have been performed in a much more easy and compendious way, what shall we think of that hypothesis which supposes the whole world made in vain?

Hyl. But what do you say, are not you, too, of the opinion that we see all things in God? If I am not mistaken, what you advance comes near it.

Phil. Few men think, yet all will have opinions. Hence men's opinions are superficial and confused. It is nothing strange that tenets which in themselves are ever so different should nevertheless be confounded with each other by those who do not consider them attentively. I shall not therefore be surprised if some men imagine that I run into the enthusiasm of Malebranche, though in truth I am very remote from it. He builds on the most abstract general ideas, which I entirely disclaim. He asserts an absolute external world, which I deny. He maintains that we are deceived by our senses and do not know the real natures or the true forms and figures of extended beings—to all of which I hold the direct contrary. So that, upon the whole, there are no principles more fundamentally opposite than his and mine. It must be admitted I entirely agree with what the Holy Scripture says that "in God we live, and move, and have our being" (Acts 17:28). But that we see things in his essence, after the manner above set forth, I am far from believing. Take here in brief my meaning. It is evident that the things I perceive are my own ideas and that no idea can exist unless it be in a mind. Nor is it less plain that these ideas, or things perceived by me, either themselves or their archetypes, exist independently of my mind, since I do not know myself to be their author, it being out of my power to determine at pleasure what particular ideas I shall be affected with upon opening my eyes or ears. They must therefore exist in some other mind, whose will it is they should be exhibited to me. The things, I say, immediately perceived, are ideas or sensations, call them which you will. But how can any idea or sensation exist in, or be produced by, anything but a mind or spirit? This indeed is inconceivable, and to assert that which is inconceivable is to talk nonsense, is it not?

Hyl. Without doubt.

Phil. But, on the other hand, it is very conceivable that they should exist in and be produced by a spirit, since this is no more than I daily experience in myself—inasmuch as I perceive numberless ideas and, by an act of my will, can form a great variety of them and raise them up in my imagination, though it must be confessed, these creatures of the fancy are not altogether so distinct, so strong, vivid, and permanent, as those perceived by my senses, which latter are called *real things*. From all which I conclude *there is a mind which affects me every moment with all the sensible impressions I perceive*. And from the variety, order, and manner of these, I conclude the author of them to be *wise, powerful, and good beyond comprehension*. Mark it well: I do not say I see things by perceiving that which represents them in the intelligible substance of God. This I do not understand; but I say the things perceived by me are known by the understanding and produced by the will of an infinite Spirit. And is not all this most plain and evident? Is there any more in it than what a little observation of our own minds, and that which passes in them, not only enables us to conceive but also obliges us to acknowledge?

Hyl. I think I understand you very clearly and admit the proof you give of a Deity seems no less evident than it is surprising. But allowing that God is the supreme and universal cause of all things, yet may not there be still a third nature besides spirits and ideas? May we not admit a subordinate and limited cause of our ideas? In a word, may there not for all that be *matter*?

Phil. How often must I inculcate the same thing? You allow the things immediately perceived by sense to exist nowhere without the mind, but there is nothing perceived by sense which is not perceived immediately. Therefore, there is nothing sensible that exists without the mind. The matter, therefore, which you still insist on is something intelligible, I suppose, something that may be discovered by reason and not by sense.

Hyl. You are in the right.

Phil. Pray let me know what reasoning your belief of matter is grounded on, and what this matter is in your present sense of it.

Hyl. I find myself affected with various ideas of which I know I am not the cause; neither are they the cause of themselves or of one another, or capable of subsisting by themselves, as being altogether inactive, fleeting, dependent beings. They have therefore some cause distinct from me and them, of which I pretend to know no more than that it is *the cause of my ideas*. And this thing, whatever it is, I call matter.

Phil. Tell me, Hylas, has everyone a liberty to change the current proper signification annexed to a common name in any language? For example, suppose a traveler should tell you that in a certain country men might pass unhurt through the fire, and, upon explaining himself, you found he meant by the word *fire* that which others call *water*, or if he should assert there are trees which walk upon two legs, meaning men by the term *trees*. Would you think this reasonable?

Hyl. No, I should think it very absurd. Common custom is the standard of propriety in language. And for any man to affect speaking improperly is to pervert the use of speech and can never serve to a better purpose than to protract and multiply disputes where there is no difference in opinion.

Phil. And does not *matter*, in the common current meaning of the word, signify an extended, solid, movable, unthinking, inactive substance?

Hyl. It does.

Phil. And has it not been made evident that no such substance can possibly exist? And though it should be allowed to exist, yet how can that which is *inactive* be a *cause* or that which is *unthinking* be a *cause of thought*? You may, indeed, if you please, annex to the word *matter* a contrary meaning to what is vulgarly received and tell me you understand by it an unextended, thinking, active being which is the cause of our ideas. But what else is this than to play with words and run into that very fault you just now condemned with so much reason? I do by no means find fault with your reasoning, in that you collect a cause from the *phenomena,* but I deny that the cause deducible by reason can properly be termed matter.

Hyl. There is indeed something in what you say. But I am afraid you do not thoroughly comprehend my meaning. I would by no means be thought to deny that God, or an infinite spirit, is the supreme cause of all things. All I contend for is that subordinate to the supreme agent there is a cause of a limited and inferior nature which concurs in the production of our ideas, not by any act of will or spiritual efficiency, but by that kind of action which belongs to matter, namely *motion.*

Phil. I find you are at every turn relapsing into your old exploded conceit of a movable and consequently an extended substance existing without the mind. What! Have you already forgot you were convinced, or are you willing I should repeat what has been said on that head? In truth this is not fair dealing in you still to suppose the being of that which you have so often acknowledged to have no being. But not to insist further on what has been so largely handled, I ask whether all your ideas are not perfectly passive and inert, including nothing of action in them?

Hyl. They are.

Phil. And are sensible qualities anything else but ideas?

Hyl. How often have I acknowledged that they are not?

Phil. But is not motion a sensible quality?

Hyl. It is.

Phil. Consequently, it is no action.

Hyl. I agree with you. And, indeed, it is very plain that when I stir my finger, it remains passive, but my will which produced the motion is active.

Phil. Now I desire to know, in the first place, whether motion being allowed to be no action, you can conceive any action besides volition; and, in the second place, whether to say something and conceive nothing is not to talk nonsense; and, lastly, whether having considered the premises, you do not perceive that to suppose any efficient or active cause of our ideas other than *spirit* is highly absurd and unreasonable?

Hyl. I give up the point entirely. But though matter may not be a cause, yet what hinders its being an *instrument* subservient to the supreme agent in the production of our ideas?

Phil. An instrument, you say; pray what may be the figure, springs, wheels, and motions of that instrument?

Hyl. Those I pretend to determine nothing of, both the substance and its qualities being entirely unknown to me.

Phil. What? You are then of the opinion, it is made up of unknown parts, that it has unknown motions, and an unknown shape.

Hyl. I do not believe it has any figure or motion at all, being already convinced that no sensible qualities can exist in an unperceiving substance.

Phil. But what notion is it possible to frame of an instrument void of all sensible qualities, even extension itself?

Hyl. I do not pretend to have any notion of it.

Phil. And what reason do you have to think this unknown, this inconceivable somewhat does exist? Is it that you imagine God cannot act as well without it or that you find by experience the use of some such thing when you form ideas in your own mind?

Hyl. You are always teasing me for reasons of my belief. Pray, what reasons do you have not to believe it?

Phil. It is to me a sufficient reason not to believe the existence of anything if I see no reason for believing it. But, not to insist on reasons for believing, you will not so much as let me know what it is you would have me believe, since you say you have no manner of notion of it. After all, let me entreat you to consider whether it is like a philosopher, or even like a man of common sense, to pretend to believe you do not know what and you do not know why.

Hyl. Hold on, Philonous. When I tell you matter is an *instrument,* I do not mean altogether nothing. It is true, I do not know the particular kind of instrument, but, however, I have some notion of *instrument in general,* which I apply to it.

Phil. But what if it should prove that there is something, even in the most general notion of *instrument,* as taken in a distinct sense from *cause,* which makes the use of it inconsistent with the divine attributes?

Hyl. Make that appear, and I shall give up the point.

Phil. What do you mean by the general nature or notion of *instrument*?

Hyl. That which is common to all particular instruments composes the general notion.

Phil. Is it not common to all instruments that they are applied to the doing those things only which cannot be performed by the mere act of our wills? Thus, for instance, I never use an instrument to move my finger because it is done by a volition. But I should use one if I were to remove part of a rock or tear up a tree by the roots. Are you of the same mind? Or can you show any example where an instrument is made use of in producing an effect immediately depending on the will of the agent?

Hyl. I admit I cannot.

Phil. How, therefore, can you suppose that an all-perfect Spirit, on whose will all things have an absolute and immediate dependence, should need an instrument in his operations or, not needing it, make use of it? Thus it seems to me that you are obliged to admit the use of a lifeless, inactive instrument to be incompatible with the infinite perfection of God—that is, by your own confession to give up the point.

Hyl. It does not readily occur what I can answer you.

Phil. But I think you should be ready to admit the truth when it has been fairly proved to you. We, indeed, who are beings of finite powers, are forced to make use of instruments. And the use of an instrument shows the agent to be limited by rules of another's prescription and that he cannot obtain his end but in such a way and by such conditions. From this it seems a clear consequence that the supreme unlimited agent uses no tool or instrument at all. The will of an omnipotent Spirit is no sooner exerted than executed, without the application of means which, if they are employed by inferior agents, it is not upon account of any real efficacy that is in them or necessary aptitude to produce any effect, but merely in compliance with the laws of nature or those conditions prescribed to them by the first cause, who is himself above all limitation or prescription whatsoever.

Hyl. I will no longer maintain that matter is an instrument. However, I would not be understood to give up its existence either, since, notwithstanding what has been said, it may still be an *occasion*.

Phil. How many shapes is your matter to take? Or how often must it be proved not to exist before you are content to part with it? But to say no more of this (though by all the laws of disputation I may justly blame you for so frequently changing the signification of the principal term) I would gladly know what you mean by affirming that matter is an occasion, having already denied it to be a cause. And when you have shown in what sense you understand *occasion*, pray, in the next place, be pleased to show me what reason induces you to believe there is such an occasion of our ideas.

Hyl. As to the first point: By *occasion*, I mean an inactive, unthinking being, at the presence of which God excites ideas in our minds.

Phil. And what may be the nature of that inactive, unthinking being?

Hyl. I know nothing of its nature.

Phil. Proceed then to the second point and assign some reason why we should allow an existence to this inactive, unthinking, unknown thing.

Hyl. When we see ideas produced in our minds after an orderly and constant manner, it is natural to think they have some fixed and regular occasions at the presence of which they are excited.

Phil. You acknowledge then God alone to be the cause of our ideas and that he causes them at the presence of those occasions.

Hyl. That is my opinion.

Phil. Those things which you say are present to God, without doubt he perceives.

Hyl. Certainly. Otherwise they could not be to him an occasion of acting.

Phil. Not to insist now on your making sense of this hypothesis or answering all the puzzling questions and difficulties it is liable to: I only ask whether the order and regularity observable in the series of our ideas or the course of nature are not sufficiently accounted for by the wisdom and power of God, and whether it does not derogate from those attributes to suppose he is influenced, directed, or put in mind, when and how he is to act, by any unthinking substance. And, lastly, whether in case I granted all you contend for, it would make anything to your purpose, it not being easy to conceive how the external or absolute existence of an unthinking substance, distinct from its being perceived, can be inferred from my allowing that there are certain things perceived by the mind of God which are to him the occasion of producing ideas in us.

Hyl. I am perfectly at a loss what to think, this notion of *occasion* seeming now altogether as groundless as the rest.

Phil. Do you not at length perceive that in all these different meanings of *matter*, you have been only supposing you do not know what, for no manner of reason, and to no kind of use?

Hyl. I freely admit myself less fond of my notions since they have been so accurately examined. But still, I think I have some confused perception that there is such a thing as *matter*.

Phil. Either you perceive the being of matter immediately or mediately. If immediately, pray inform me by which of the senses you perceive it. If mediately, let me know by what reasoning it is inferred from those things which you perceive immediately. So much for the perception. Then for the matter itself, I ask whether it is object, *substratum*, cause, instrument, or occasion? You have already pleaded for each of these, shifting your notions and making matter to appear sometimes in one shape, then in another. And what you have offered has been disapproved and rejected by yourself. If you have anything new to advance, I would gladly hear it.

Hyl. I think I have already offered all I had to say on those heads. I am at a loss what more to urge.

Phil. And yet you are loath to part with your old prejudice. But to make you quit it more easily, I desire that, besides what has been suggested up to now, you will further consider whether, upon the supposition that matter exists, you can possibly conceive how you should be affected by it? Or, supposing it did not exist, whether it is not evident you might for all that be affected with the same ideas you now are, and consequently have the very same reasons to believe its existence that you now can have?

Hyl. I acknowledge it is possible we might perceive all things just as we do now, though there was no matter in the world; neither can I conceive, if there is matter, how it should produce any idea in our minds. And I do further grant you have entirely satisfied me that it is impossible there should be such a thing as matter in any of the foregoing senses. But still I cannot help supposing that there is *matter* in some sense or other. What that is I do not indeed pretend to determine.

Phil. I do not expect you should define exactly the nature of that unknown being. Only be pleased to tell me whether it is a substance, and if so, whether you can suppose a substance without accidents, or in case you suppose it to have accidents or qualities, I desire you will let me know what those qualities are, at least what is meant by matter's supporting them.

Hyl. We have already argued on those points. I have no more to say to them. But to prevent any further questions, let me tell you, I at present understand by *matter* neither substance nor accident, thinking nor extended being, neither cause, instrument, nor occasion, but something entirely unknown, distinct from all these.

Phil. It seems then you include in your present notion of matter nothing but the general abstract of idea of *entity*.

Hyl. Nothing else, save only that I superadd to this general idea the negation of all those particular things, qualities, or ideas that I perceive, imagine, or in any way apprehend.

Phil. Pray where do you suppose this unknown matter to exist?

Hyl. Oh Philonous! Now you think you have entangled me; for if I say it exists in place, then you will infer that it exists in the mind, since it is agreed that place or extension exists only in the mind, but I am not ashamed to admit my ignorance. I do not know where it exists; only I am sure it does not exist in place. There is a negative answer for you and you must expect no other to all the questions you put for the future about matter.

Phil. Since you will not tell me where it exists, be pleased to inform me after what manner you suppose it to exist or what you mean by its existence.

Hyl. It neither thinks nor acts, neither perceives, nor is perceived.

Phil. But what is there positive in your abstracted notion of its existence?

Hyl. Upon a nice observation, I do not find I have any positive notion or meaning at all. I tell you again I am not ashamed to admit my ignorance. I do not know what is meant by its *existence* or how it exists.

Phil. Continue, good Hylas, to act the same ingenuous part and tell me sincerely whether you can frame a distinct idea of entity in general, prescinded from and exclusive of all thinking and corporeal beings, all particular things whatsoever.

Hyl. Hold on, let me think a little—I profess, Philonous, I do not find that I can. At first glance I thought I had some dilute and airy notion of pure entity in abstract, but upon closer attention it has quite vanished out of sight. The more I think on it, the more am I confirmed in my prudent resolution of giving none but negative answers and not pretending to the least degree of any positive knowledge or conception of matter, its *where*, its *how*, its *entity*, or anything belonging to it.

Phil. When, therefore, you speak of the existence of matter, you do not have any notion in your mind.

Hyl. None at all.

Phil. Pray tell me if the case does not stand thus: at first, from a belief in material substance, you would have it that the immediate objects existed without the mind; then, that they are archetypes; then causes; next instruments; then occasions; lastly, *something in general*, which being interpreted proves *nothing*. So matter comes to nothing. What do you think, Hylas? Is not this a fair summary of your whole proceeding?

Hyl. Be that as it will, yet I still insist upon it that our not being able to conceive a thing is no argument against its existence.

Phil. That from a cause, effect, operation, sign, or other circumstance, there may reasonably be inferred the existence of a thing not immediately perceived, and that it would be absurd for any man to argue against the existence of that thing from his having no direct and positive notion of it, I freely admit. But where there is nothing of all this; where neither reason nor revelation induces us to believe the existence of a thing; where we have not even a relative notion of it; where an abstraction is made from perceiving and being perceived, from spirit and idea; lastly, where there is not so much as the most inadequate or faint idea pretended to, I will not, indeed, then conclude against the reality of any notion or existence of anything, but my inference shall be that you mean nothing at all, that you imply words to no manner of purpose, without any design or signification whatsoever. And I leave it to you to consider how mere jargon should be treated.

Hyl. To deal frankly with you, Philonous, your arguments seem in themselves unanswerable, but they do not have so great an effect on me as to produce that entire conviction, that hearty acquiescence which attends demonstration. I find myself still relapsing into an obscure surmise of I do not know what—*matter*.

Phil. But are you not sensible, Hylas, that two things must concur to take away all scruple and work a plenary assent in the mind? Let a visible object be set in never so clear a light, yet, if there is any imperfection in the sight, or if the eye is not directed towards it, it will not be distinctly seen. And though a demonstration be never so well grounded and fairly proposed, yet, if there is in addition a stain of prejudice or a wrong bias on the understanding, can it be expected on a sudden to perceive clearly and adhere firmly to the truth? No, there is need of time and pains; the attention must be awakened and detained by a frequent repetition of the same thing placed often in the same, often in different lights. I have said it already, and find I must still repeat and inculcate, that it is an unaccountable license you take in pretending to maintain you do not know what, you do not know for what reason, you do not know to what purpose. Can this be paralleled in any art or science, any sect or profession of men? Or is there anything so barefacedly groundless and unreasonable to be met with even in the lowest of common conversation? But perhaps you will still say, matter may exist, though at the same time you neither know what is meant by *matter*, nor by its *existence*. This indeed is surprising, and the more so because it is altogether voluntary, you not being led to it by any one reason; for I challenge you to show me that thing in nature which needs matter to explain or account for it.

Hyl. The reality of things cannot be maintained without supposing the existence of matter. And is not this, you think, a good reason why I should be earnest in its defense?

Phil. The reality of things! What things, sensible or intelligible?

Hyl. Sensible things.

Phil. My glove, for example?

Hyl. That or any other thing perceived by the senses.

Phil. But to fix on some particular thing, is it not a sufficient evidence to me of the existence of this *glove* that I see it, and feel it, and wear it? Or if this will not do, how is it possible I should be assured of the reality of this thing which I actually see in this place by supposing that some unknown thing which I never did or can see exists after an unknown manner, in an unknown place, or in no place at all? How can the supposed reality of that which is intangible be a proof that anything tangible really exists? Or of that which is invisible, that any visible thing, or in general of anything which is imperceptible, that a perceptible exists? Do but explain this and I shall think nothing too hard for you.

Hyl. Upon the whole, I am content to admit the existence of matter is highly improbable; but the direct and absolute impossibility of it does not appear to me.

Phil. But granting matter to be possible, yet, upon that account merely, it can have no more claim to existence than a golden mountain or a centaur.

Hyl. I acknowledge it, but still you do not deny it is possible; and that which is possible, for all you know, may actually exist.

Phil. I deny it to be possible, and have, if I am not mistaken, evidently proved from your own concessions that it is not. In the common meaning of the word *matter,* is there any more implied than an extended, solid, figured, movable substance, existing without the mind? And have not you acknowledged over and over that you have seen evident reason for denying the possibility of such a substance?

Hyl. True, but that is only one sense of the term *matter.*

Phil. But is it not the only proper genuine received sense? And if matter in such a sense is proved impossible, may it not be thought with good grounds absolutely impossible? How else could anything be proved impossible? Or indeed how could there be any proof at all one way or the other to a man who takes the liberty to unsettle and change the common signification of words?

Hyl. I thought philosophers might be allowed to speak more accurately than the vulgar and were not always confined to the common meaning of a term.

Phil. But this now mentioned is the common received sense among philosophers themselves. But not to insist on that, have you not been allowed to take matter in what sense you pleased? And have you not used this privilege in the utmost extent, sometimes entirely changing, at others leaving out or putting into the definition of it whatever for the present best served your design, contrary to all the known rules of reason and logic? And has not this shifting, unfair method of yours spun out our dispute to an unnecessary length, matter having been particularly examined and by your own confession refuted in each of those senses? And can any more be required to prove the absolute impossibility of a thing than the proving it impossible in every particular sense that either you or anyone else understands it in?

Hyl. But I am not so thoroughly satisfied that you have proved the impossibility of matter in the last most obscure, abstracted, and indefinite sense.

Phil. When is a thing shown to be impossible?

Hyl. When a repugnance is demonstrated between the ideas comprehended in its definition.

Phil. But where there are no ideas, there no repugnance can be demonstrated between ideas.

Hyl. I agree with you.

Phil. Now, in that which you call the obscure, indefinite sense of the word matter, it is plain, by your own confession, there was included no idea at all, no sense except an unknown sense, which is the same thing as none. You are not, therefore, to expect I should prove a repugnance between ideas where there are no ideas, or the impossibility of matter taken in an *unknown* sense—that is, no sense at all. My business was only to show you meant *nothing,* and this you were brought to admit. So that in all your various senses, you have been shown either to mean nothing at all or, if anything, an absurdity. And if this is not sufficient to prove the impossibility of a thing, I desire you will let me know what is.

Hyl. I acknowledge you have proved that matter is impossible; nor do I see what more can be said in defense of it. But, at the same time that I give up this, I suspect all my other notions. For surely none could be more seemingly evident than this once was, and yet it now seems as false and absurd as ever it did true before. But I think we have discussed the point sufficiently for the present. The remaining part of the day I would willingly spend in running over in my thoughts the several heads of this morning's conversation and tomorrow shall be glad to meet you here again about the same time.

Phil. I will not fail to attend you.

The Third Dialogue

Philonous. Tell me, Hylas, what are the fruits of yesterday's meditation? Has it confirmed you in the same mind you were in at parting? Or have you since seen cause to change your opinion?

Hylas. Truly my opinion is that all our opinions are alike vain and uncertain. What we approve today, we condemn tomorrow. We keep a stir about knowledge and spend our lives in the pursuit of it, when, alas, we know nothing all the while; nor do I think it possible for us ever to know anything in this life. Our faculties are too narrow and too few. Nature certainly never intended us for speculation.

Phil. What! You say we can know nothing, Hylas?

Hyl. There is not that single thing in the world of which we can know the real nature, or what it is in itself.

Phil. Will you tell me I do not really know what fire or water is?

Hyl. You may indeed know that fire appears hot and water fluid, but this is no more than knowing what sensations are produced in your own mind upon the application of fire and water to your organs of sense. Their internal constitution, their true and real nature, you are utterly in the dark as to *that*.

Phil. Do I not know this to be a real stone that I stand on and that which I see before my eyes to be a real tree?

Hyl. Know? No, it is impossible you or any man alive should know it. All you know is that you have such a certain idea or appearance in your own mind. But what is this to the real tree or stone? I tell you that color, figure, and hardness which you perceive

are not the real natures of those things or in the least like them. The same may be said of all other real things or corporeal substances which compose the world. They have, none of them, anything in themselves like those sensible qualities perceived by us. We should not, therefore, pretend to affirm or know anything of them as they are in their own nature.

Phil. But surely, Hylas, I can distinguish gold, for example, from iron, and how could this be, if I knew not what either truly was?

Hyl. Believe me, Philonous, you can only distinguish between your own ideas. That yellowness, that weight, and other sensible qualities, do you think they are really in the gold? They are only relative to the senses and have no absolute existence in nature. And in pretending to distinguish the species of real things by the appearances in your mind, you may perhaps act as wisely as he who should conclude two men were of a different species because their clothes were not of the same color.

Phil. It seems, then, we are altogether put off with the appearances of things, and those false ones too. The very meat I eat and the cloth I wear have nothing in them like what I see and feel.

Hyl. Even so.

Phil. But is it not strange the whole world should be thus imposed on and so foolish as to believe their senses? And yet I do not know how it is, but men eat, and drink, and sleep, and perform all the offices of life as comfortably and conveniently as if they really knew the things they are conversant about.

Hyl. They do so, but you know ordinary practice does not require a nicety of speculative knowledge. Hence the vulgar retain their mistakes and, for all that, make a shift to bustle through the affairs of life. But philosophers know better things.

Phil. You mean, they know that they *know nothing*.

Hyl. That is the very top and perfection of human knowledge.

Phil. But are you all this while in earnest, Hylas; and are you seriously persuaded that you know nothing real in the world? Suppose you are going to write, would you not call for pen, ink, and paper, like another man; and do you not know what it is you call for?

Hyl. How often must I tell you that I do not know the real nature of any one thing in the universe? I may, indeed, upon occasion, make use of pen, ink, and paper. But what any one of them is in its own true nature, I declare positively I do not know. And the same is true with regard to every other corporeal thing. And, what is more, we are not only ignorant of the true and real nature of things, but even of their existence. It cannot be denied that we perceive such certain appearances or ideas; but it cannot be concluded from this that bodies really exist. No, now I think on it, I must, agreeably to my former concessions, further declare that it is impossible any real corporeal thing should exist in nature.

Phil. You amaze me. Was anything ever more wild and extravagant than the notions you now maintain, and is it not evident you are led into all these extravagances by the belief of *material substance?* This makes you dream of those unknown natures in everything. It is this which occasions your distinguishing between the reality and sensible appearances of things. It is to this you are indebted for being ignorant of what everybody else knows perfectly well. Nor is this all: you are not only ignorant of the true nature of everything, but you do not know whether anything really exists or whether there are any true natures at all. For as much as you attribute to your material beings an absolute or external existence in which you suppose their reality consists and, as you are forced in the end to acknowledge such an existence means either a direct repugnance or nothing at all, it follows that you are obliged to pull down your own hypothesis of material substance and positively to deny the real existence of any part of the universe. And so you are plunged into the deepest and most deplorable *skepticism* that ever man was. Tell me, Hylas, is it not as I say?

Hyl. I agree with you. *Material substance* was no more than an hypothesis, and a false and groundless one too. I will no longer spend my breath in defense of it. But whatever hypothesis you advance, or whatever scheme of things you introduce in its stead, I do not doubt it will appear every whit as false; let me but be allowed to question you upon it. That is, allow me to serve you in your own kind and I warrant it shall conduct you through as many perplexities and contradictions to the very same state of skepticism that I myself am in at present.

Phil. I assure you, Hylas, I do not pretend to frame any hypothesis at all. I am of a vulgar cast, simple enough to believe my senses and leave things as I find them. To be plain, it is my opinion that the real things are those very things I see and feel and perceive by my senses. These I know, and, finding they answer all the necessities and purposes of life, have no reason to be solicitous about any other unknown beings. A piece of sensible bread, for instance, would stay my stomach better than ten thousand times as much of that insensible, unintelligible, real bread you speak of. It is likewise my opinion that colors and other sensible qualities are in the objects. I cannot for my life help thinking that snow is white and fire hot. You indeed, who by *snow* and *fire* mean certain external, unperceived, unperceiving substances, are in the right to deny whiteness or heat to be affections inherent in them. But I, who understand by those words the things I see and feel, am obliged to think like other folks. And as I am no skeptic with regard to the nature of things, so neither am I as to their existence. That a thing should be really perceived by my senses and at the same time not really exist is to me a plain contradiction, since I cannot prescind or abstract, even in thought, the existence of a sensible thing from its being perceived. Wood, stones, fire, water, flesh, iron, and the like things which I name and discourse of are things that I know. And I should not have known them but that I perceived them by my senses; and things perceived by the senses are immediately perceived; and things immediately perceived are ideas; and ideas cannot exist without the mind; their existence, therefore, consists in being perceived; when, therefore, they are actually perceived, there can be no doubt of their existence. Away then with all that skepticism, all those ridiculous philosophical doubts. What a jest is it for a philosopher to question the existence of sensible things until he has it proved to him from the veracity of God or to pretend our knowledge in this point falls short of intuition or demonstration! I might as well doubt of my own being as of the being of those things I actually see and feel.

Hyl. Not so fast, Philonous; you say you cannot conceive how sensible things should exist without the mind. Do you not?

Phil. I do.

Hyl. Supposing you were annihilated, cannot you conceive it possible that things perceivable by sense may still exist?

Phil. I can; but then it must be in another mind. When I deny sensible things an existence out of the mind, I do not mean my mind in particular, but all minds. Now it is plain they have an existence exterior to my mind, since I find them by experience to be independent of it. There is, therefore, some other mind in which they exist during the intervals between the times of my perceiving them, as likewise they did before my birth and would do after my supposed annihilation. And as the same is true with regard to all other finite created spirits, it necessarily follows there is an *omnipresent, eternal Mind* which knows and comprehends all things, and exhibits them to our view in such a manner and according to such rules as he himself has ordained and are by us termed the *laws of nature.*

Hyl. Answer me, Philonous. Are all our ideas perfectly inert beings? Or do they have any agency included in them?

Phil. They are altogether passive and inert.

Hyl. And is not God an agent, a being purely active?

Phil. I acknowledge it.

Hyl. No idea, therefore, can be like or represent the nature of God.

Phil. It cannot.

Hyl. Since, therefore, you have no idea of the mind of God, how can you conceive it possible that things should exist in his mind? Or, if you can conceive the mind of God without having an idea of it, why may I not be allowed to conceive the existence of matter, notwithstanding that I have no idea of it?

Phil. As to your first question, I admit I have properly no idea, either of God or any other spirit; for these, being active, cannot be represented by things perfectly inert as our ideas are. I do nevertheless know that I, who am a spirit or thinking substance, exist as certainly as I know my ideas exist. Further, I know what I mean by the terms *I* and *myself*; and I know this immediately, or intuitively, though I do not perceive it as I perceive a triangle, a color, or a sound. The mind, spirit, or soul is that indivisible, unextended thing, which thinks, acts, and perceives. I say *indivisible*, because unextended and *unextended*, because ex-

tended, figured, movable things are ideas; and that which perceives ideas, which thinks and wills, is plainly itself no idea, nor like an idea. Ideas are things inactive and perceived, and spirits a sort of beings altogether different from them. I do not therefore say my soul is an idea or like an idea. However, taking the word *idea* in a large sense, my soul may be said to furnish me with an idea, that is, an image or likeness of God, though indeed extremely inadequate. For all the notion I have of God is obtained by reflecting on my own soul, heightening its powers and removing its imperfections. I have, therefore, though not an inactive idea, yet in myself some sort of an active thinking image of the Deity. And though I do not perceive him by sense, yet I have a notion of him or know him by reflection and reasoning. My own mind and my own ideas I have an immediate knowledge of and, by the help of these, do mediately apprehend the possibility of the existence of other spirits and ideas. Further, from my own being and from the dependency I find in myself and my ideas, I do by an act of reason necessarily infer the existence of a God and of all created things in the mind of God. So much for your first question. For the second, I suppose by this time you can answer it yourself. For you neither perceive matter objectively, as you do an inactive being or idea, nor know it, as you do yourself, by a reflective act—neither do you mediately apprehend it by similitude of the one or the other, nor yet collect it by reasoning from that which you know immediately—all of which makes the case of *matter* widely different from that of the *Deity*.

Hyl. You say your own soul supplies you with some sort of an idea or image of God. But at the same time you acknowledge you have, properly speaking, no idea of your own soul. You even affirm that spirits are a sort of beings altogether different from ideas, consequently, that no idea can be like a spirit. We have, therefore, no idea of any spirit. You admit nevertheless that there is spiritual substance, although you have no idea of it, while you deny there can be such a thing as material substance, because you have no notion or idea of it. Is this fair dealing? To act consistently, you must either admit matter or reject spirit. What do you say to this?

Phil. I say, in the first place, that I do not deny the

existence of material substance merely because I have no notion of it, but because the notion of it is inconsistent or, in other words, because it is repugnant that there should be a notion of it. Many things, for all I know, may exist of which neither I nor any other man has or can have any idea or notion whatsoever. But then those things must be possible; that is, nothing inconsistent must be included in their definition. I say, secondly, that, although we believe things to exist which we do not perceive, yet we may not believe that any particular thing exists without some reason for such belief, but I have no reason for believing the existence of matter. I have no immediate intuition of this; neither can I mediately from my sensations, ideas, notions, actions, or passions infer an unthinking, unperceiving, inactive substance, either by probable deduction or necessary consequence, whereas the being of myself, that is, my own soul, mind, or thinking principle, I evidently know by reflection. You will forgive me if I repeat the same things in answer to the same objections. In the very notion or definition of material substance, there is included a manifest repugnance and inconsistency. But this cannot be said of the notion of spirit. That ideas should exist in what does not perceive, or be produced by what does not act, is repugnant. But it is no repugnance to say that a perceiving thing should be the subject of ideas or an active thing the cause of them. It is granted we have neither an immediate evidence nor a demonstrative knowledge of the existence of other finite spirits, but it will not then follow that such spirits are on a foot with material substances, if to suppose the one is inconsistent and it is not inconsistent to suppose the other; if the one can be inferred by no argument, and there is a probability for the other; if we see signs and effects indicating distinct finite agents like ourselves, and see no sign or symptom whatever that leads to a rational belief of matter. I say, lastly, that I have a notion of spirit, though I do not have, strictly speaking, an idea of it. I do not perceive it as an idea or by means of an idea, but know it by reflection.

Hyl. Notwithstanding all you have said, it seems to me that, according to your own way of thinking, and in consequence of your own principles, it should follow that you are only a system of floating ideas without any substance to support them. Words are not to be used without a meaning. And as there is no more meaning in spiritual substance than in material substance, the one is to be exploded as well as the other.

Phil. How often must I repeat that I know or am conscious of my own being and that I myself am not my ideas, but something else, a thinking, active principle that perceives, knows, wills, and operates about ideas? I know that I, one and the same self, perceive both colors and sounds; that a color cannot perceive a sound nor a sound a color; that I am therefore one individual principle, distinct from color and sound and, for the same reason, from all other sensible things and inert ideas. But I am not in like manner conscious of either the existence or essence of matter. On the contrary, I know that nothing inconsistent can exist and that the existence of matter implies an inconsistency. Further, I know what I mean when I affirm that there is a spiritual substance or support of ideas, that is, that a spirit knows and perceives ideas. But I do not know what is meant when it is said that an unperceiving substance has inherent in it and supports either ideas or the archetypes of ideas. There is, therefore, upon the whole no parity of case between spirit and matter.

Hyl. I admit myself satisfied in this point. But do you in earnest think the real existence of sensible things consists in their being actually perceived? If so, how does it come that all mankind distinguishes between them? Ask the first man you meet, and he shall tell you, *to be perceived* is one thing and *to exist* is another.

Phil. I am content, Hylas, to appeal to the common sense of the world for the truth of my notion. Ask the gardener why he thinks the cherry tree over there exists in the garden, and he shall tell you because he sees and feels it—in a word, because he perceives it by his senses. Ask him why he thinks an orange tree is not there, and he shall tell you because he does not perceive it. What he perceives by sense, that he terms a real being and says it *is*, or *exists*; but that which is not perceivable, the same, he says, has no being.

Hyl. Yes, Philonous, I grant the existence of a sensible thing consists in being perceivable, but not in being actually perceived.

Phil. And what is perceivable but an idea? And can an idea exist without being actually perceived? These are points long since agreed between us.

Hyl. But be your opinion never so true, yet surely you will not deny it is shocking and contrary to the common sense of men. Ask the fellow whether tree over there has an existence out of his mind, what answer, do you think, he would make?

Phil. The same that I should myself, namely, that it does exist out of his mind. But then to a Christian it cannot surely be shocking to say the real tree existing without his mind is truly known and comprehended by (that is, *exists in*) the infinite mind of God. Probably he may not at first glance be aware of the direct and immediate proof there is of this, inasmuch as the very being of a tree or any other sensible thing implies a mind in which it is. But the point itself he cannot deny. The question between the materialists and me is not whether things have a real existence out of the mind of this or that person, but whether they have an absolute existence, distinct from being perceived by God and exterior to all minds. This, indeed, some heathens and philosophers have affirmed, but whoever entertains notions of the Deity suitable to the Holy Scriptures will be of another opinion.

Hyl. But, according to your notions, what difference is there between real things and chimeras formed by the imagination or the visions of a dream, since they are all equally in the mind?

Phil. The ideas formed by the imagination are faint and indistinct; they have, besides, an entire dependence on the will. But the ideas perceived by sense, that is, real things, are more vivid and clear, and, being imprinted on the mind by a spirit distinct from us, have not a like dependence on our will. There is, therefore, no danger of confounding these with the foregoing, and there is as little of confounding them with the visions of a dream, which are dim, irregular, and confused. And though they should happen to be never so lively and natural, yet, by their not being connected and of a piece with the preceding and subsequent transactions of our lives, they might easily be distinguished from realities. In short, by whatever method you distinguish *things* from *chimeras* on your own scheme, the same, it is evident, will hold also upon mine. For it must be, I presume, by some perceived difference, and

I am not for depriving you of any one thing that you perceive.

Hyl. But still, Philonous, you hold there is nothing in the world but spirits and ideas. And this, you must necessarily acknowledge, sounds very odd.

Phil. I admit the word *idea*, not being commonly used for *thing*, sounds something out of the way. My reason for using it was because a necessary relation to the mind is understood to be implied by that term and it is now commonly used by philosophers to denote the immediate objects of the understanding. But however odd the proposition may sound in words, yet it includes nothing so very strange or shocking in its sense, which in effect amounts to no more than this, namely, that there are only things perceiving and things perceived; or that every unthinking being is necessarily and from the very nature of its existence perceived by some mind, if not by any finite created mind, yet certainly by the infinite mind of God, in whom "we live, and move, and have our being" (Acts 17:28). Is this as strange as to say the sensible qualities are not in the objects or that we cannot be sure of the existence of things or know anything of their real natures, though we both see and feel them and perceive them by all our senses?

Hyl. And, in consequence of this, must we not think there are no such things as physical or corporeal causes, but that a spirit is the immediate cause of all the *phenomena* in nature? Can there be anything more extravagant than this?

Phil. Yes, it is infinitely more extravagant to say a thing which is inert operates on the mind and a thing which is unperceiving is the cause of our perceptions. Besides, that which to you, I do not know for what reason, seems so extravagant is no more than the Holy Scriptures assert in a hundred places. In them God is represented as the sole and immediate author of all those effects which some heathens and philosophers are accustomed to ascribe to nature, matter, fate, or the like unthinking principle. This is so much the constant language of Scripture that it would be needless to confirm it by citations.

Hyl. You are not aware, Philonous, that in making God the immediate author of all the motions in nature, you make him the author of murder, sacrilege, adultery, and the like heinous sins.

Phil. In answer to that I observe, first, that the imputation of guilt is the same whether a person commits an action with or without an instrument. In case, therefore, you suppose God to act by the mediation of an instrument or occasion called *matter*, you as truly make him the author of sin as I, who think him the immediate agent in all those operations vulgarly ascribed to nature. I further observe that sin or moral turpitude does not consist in the outward physical action or motion, but in the internal deviation of the will from the laws of reason and religion. This is plain, in that the killing an enemy in a battle or putting a criminal legally to death, is not thought sinful, though the outward acts are the very same with that in the case of murder. Since, therefore, sin does not consist in the physical action, making God an immediate cause of all such actions is not making him the author of sin. Lastly, I have nowhere said that God is the only agent who produces all the motions in bodies. It is true I have denied there are any other agents besides spirits, but this is very consistent with allowing to thinking, rational beings, in the production of motions, the use of limited powers ultimately indeed derived from God, but immediately under the direction of their own wills, which is sufficient to entitle them to all the guilt of their actions.

Hyl. But denying matter, Philonous, or corporeal substance—there is the point. You can never persuade me that this is not repugnant to the universal sense of mankind. Were our dispute to be determined by most voices, I am confident you would give up the point without gathering the votes.

Phil. I wish both our opinions were fairly stated and submitted to the judgment of men who had plain common sense without the prejudices of a learned education. Let me be represented as one who trusts his senses, who thinks he knows the things he sees and feels and entertains no doubts of their existence, and you fairly set forth with all your doubts, your paradoxes, and your skepticism about you, and I shall willingly acquiesce in the determination of any indifferent person. That there is no substance in which ideas can exist besides spirit is evident to me. And that the objects immediately perceived are ideas is agreed on all hands. And that sensible qualities are objects immediately perceived no one can deny. It is therefore evident there can be no *substratum* of those qualities but spirit, in which they exist, not by way of mode or property, but as a thing

perceived in that which perceives it. I deny, therefore, that there is any unthinking *substratum* of the objects of sense and, in that meaning, that there is any material substance. But if by *material substance* is meant only sensible body, that which is seen and felt (and the unphilosophical part of the world, I dare say, mean no more), then I am more certain of matter's existence than you or any other philosopher pretend to be. If there is anything which makes the generality of mankind averse from the notions I espouse, it is a misapprehension that I deny the reality of sensible things, but as it is you who are guilty of that and not I, it follows that in truth their aversion is against your notions and not mine. I do therefore assert that I am as certain of my own being as that there are bodies or corporeal substances (meaning the things I perceive by my senses), and that, granting this, the bulk of mankind will take no thought about, nor think themselves at all concerned in the fate of those unknown natures and philosophical quiddities which some men are so fond of.

Hyl. What do you say to this? Since, according to you, men judge of the reality of things by their senses, how can a man be mistaken in thinking the moon a plain lucid surface about a foot in diameter; or a square tower, seen at a distance, round; or an oar, with one end in the water, crooked?

Phil. He is not mistaken with regard to the ideas he actually perceives, but in the inferences he makes from his present perceptions. Thus, in the case of the oar, what he immediately perceives by sight is certainly crooked, and so far he is in the right. But if he then concludes that upon taking the oar out of the water he shall perceive the same crookedness, or that it would affect his touch as crooked things are accustomed to do, in that he is mistaken. In like manner, if he should conclude from what he perceives in one station, that, in case he advances toward the moon or tower, he should still be affected with the like ideas, he is mistaken. But his mistake does not lie in what he perceives immediately and at present (it being a manifest contradiction to suppose he should err in respect of that), but in the wrong judgment he makes concerning the ideas he apprehends to be connected with those immediately perceived, or concerning the ideas that, from what he perceives at present, he imagines would be perceived in other circumstances. The case is the same with regard to the Copernican system. We do not here perceive any motion of the earth, but it would be erroneous to conclude from this that, in case we were placed at as great a distance from that as we are now from the other planets, we should not then perceive its motion.

Hyl. I understand you and must necessarily admit you say things plausible enough, but give me leave to put you in mind of one thing. Pray, Philonous, were you not formerly as positive that matter existed as you are now that it does not?

Phil. I was. But here lies the difference. Before, my positiveness was founded without examination, upon prejudice; but now, after inquiry, upon evidence.

Hyl. After all, it seems our dispute is rather about words than things. We agree in the thing, but differ in the name. That we are affected with ideas from without is evident; and it is no less evident that there must be (I will not say archetypes, but) powers outside the mind corresponding to those ideas. And as these powers cannot subsist by themselves, there is some subject of them necessarily to be admitted, which I call *matter* and you call *spirit*. This is all the difference.

Phil. Pray, Hylas, is that powerful being, or subject of powers, extended?

Hyl. It has not extension; but it has the power to raise in you the idea of extension.

Phil. It is therefore itself unextended.

Hyl. I grant it.

Phil. Is it not also active?

Hyl. Without doubt; otherwise, how could we attribute powers to it?

Phil. Now let me ask you two questions: *First*, whether it is agreeable to the usage either of philosophers or others to give the name *matter* to an unextended active being? And *secondly*, whether it is not ridiculously absurd to misapply names contrary to the common use of language?

Hyl. Well then, let it not be called matter, since you will have it so, but some *third nature*, distinct from matter and spirit. For what reason is there why you should call it spirit? Does not the notion of spirit imply that it is thinking as well as active and unextended?

Phil. My reason is this: Because I have a mind to have some notion or meaning in what I say, but I have no notion of any action distinct from volition, neither can I conceive volition to be anywhere but in a spirit; therefore, when I speak of an active being, I am obliged to mean a spirit. Besides, what can be plainer than that a thing which has no ideas in itself cannot impart them to me; and if it has ideas, surely it must be a spirit. To make you comprehend the point still more clearly, if it is possible, I assert as well as you that since we are affected from without, we must allow powers to be without in a being distinct from ourselves. So far we are agreed. But then we differ as to the kind of this powerful being. I will have it to be spirit, you matter or I do not know what (I may add too, you do not know what) third nature. Thus I prove it to be spirit. From the effects I see produced, I conclude there are actions; and because actions, volitions; and because there are volitions, there must be a will. Again, the things I perceive must have an existence, they or their archetypes, out of my mind, but, being ideas, neither they nor their archetypes can exist otherwise than in an understanding; there is therefore an understanding. But will and understanding constitute in the strictest sense a mind or spirit. The powerful cause, therefore, of my ideas is in strict propriety of speech a *spirit*.

Hyl. And now, I warrant, you think you have made the point very clear, little suspecting that what you advance leads directly to a contradiction. Is it not an absurdity to imagine any imperfection in God?

Phil. Without doubt.

Hyl. To suffer pain is an imperfection.

Phil. It is.

Hyl. Are we not sometimes affected with pain and uneasiness by some other being?

Phil. We are.

Hyl. And have you not said that being is a spirit, and is not that spirit God?

Phil. I grant it.

Hyl. But you have asserted that whatever ideas we perceive from without are in the mind which affects us. The ideas, therefore, of pain and uneasiness are in God; or in other words, God suffers pain—that is to say, there is an imperfection in the divine nature, which you acknowledged was absurd. So you are caught in a plain contradiction.

Phil. That God knows or understands all things and that he knows among other things what pain is, even every sort of painful sensation, and what it is for his creatures to suffer pain, I make no question. But that God, though he knows and sometimes causes painful sensations in us, can himself suffer pain, I positively deny. We, who are limited and dependent spirits, are liable to impressions of sense, the effects of an external agent, which, being produced against our wills, are sometimes painful and uneasy. But God, whom no external being can affect, who perceives nothing by sense as we do, whose will is absolute and independent, causing all things and liable to be thwarted or resisted by nothing, it is evident such a being as this can suffer nothing, nor be affected with any painful sensation, or indeed any sensation at all. We are chained to a body, that is to say, our perceptions are connected with corporeal motions. By the law of our nature we are affected upon every alteration in the nervous parts of our sensible body—which sensible body rightly considered is nothing but a complexion of such qualities or ideas as have no existence distinct from being perceived by a mind—so that this connection of sensations with corporeal motions means no more than a correspondence in the order of nature between two sets of ideas or things immediately perceivable. But God is a pure spirit, disengaged from all such sympathy or natural ties. No corporeal motions are attended with the sensations of pain or pleasure in his mind. To know everything knowable is certainly a perfection; but to endure, or suffer, or feel anything by sense, is an imperfection. The former, I say, agrees to God, but not the latter. God knows or has ideas, but his ideas are not conveyed to him by sense as ours are. Your not distinguishing, where there is so manifest a difference, makes you fancy you see an absurdity where there is none.

Hyl. But all this while you have not considered that the quantity of matter has been demonstrated to be proportioned to the gravity of bodies. And what can withstand demonstration?

Phil. Let me see how you demonstrate that point.

Hyl. I lay it down for a principle that the moments or quantities of motion in bodies are in a direct compounded reason of the velocities and quantities of matter contained in them. Hence, where the velocities are equal, it follows the moments are directly as the quantity of matter in each. But it is found by experience that all bodies (bating the small inequalities arising from the resistance of the air) descend with an equal velocity,

the motion therefore of descending bodies, and consequently their gravity, which is the cause or principle of that motion, is proportional to the quantity of matter—which was to be demonstrated.

Phil. You lay it down as a self-evident principle that the quantity of motion in any body is proportional to the velocity and *matter* taken together; and this is made use of to prove a proposition from which the existence of *matter* is inferred. Pray is not this arguing in a circle?

Hyl. In the premise I only mean that the motion is proportional to the velocity, jointly with the extension and solidity.

Phil. But allowing this to be true, yet it will not then follow that gravity is proportional to *matter* in your philosophic sense of the word, except you take it for granted that unknown *substratum,* or whatever else you call it, is proportional to those sensible qualities—which to suppose is plainly begging the question. That there is magnitude and solidity, or resistance, perceived by sense, I readily grant, as likewise that gravity may be proportional to those qualities, I will not dispute. But that either these qualities as perceived by us or the powers producing them do exist in a *material substratum;* this is what I deny and you indeed affirm but, notwithstanding your demonstration, have not yet proved.

Hyl. I shall insist no longer on that point. Do you think, however, you shall persuade me that natural philosophers have been dreaming all this while? Pray what becomes of all their hypotheses and explications of the *phenomena* which suppose the existence of matter?

Phil. What do you mean, Hylas, by the *phenomena?*

Hyl. I mean the appearances which I perceive by my senses.

Phil. And the appearances perceived by sense, are they not ideas?

Hyl. I have told you so a hundred times.

Phil. Therefore, to explain the *phenomena* is to show how we come to be affected with ideas in that manner and order in which they are imprinted on our senses. Is it not?

Hyl. It is.

Phil. Now if you can prove that any philosopher has explained the production of any one idea in our minds by the help of *matter,* I shall forever acquiesce and look on all that has been said against it as nothing, but if you cannot, it is in vain to urge the explication of *phenomena*. That a being endowed with knowledge and will should produce or exhibit ideas is easily understood. But that a being which is utterly destitute of these faculties should be able to produce ideas, or in any sort to affect an intelligence, this I can never understand. This I say, though we had some positive conception of matter, though we knew its qualities and could comprehend its existence, would yet be so far from explaining things that it is itself the most inexplicable thing in the world. And yet for all this, it will not follow that philosophers have been doing nothing; for by observing and reasoning upon the connection of ideas, they discover the laws and methods of nature, which is a part of knowledge both useful and entertaining.

Hyl. After all, can it be supposed God would deceive all mankind? Do you imagine he would have induced the whole world to believe the being of matter if there was no such thing?

Phil. That every epidemic opinion arising from prejudice, or passion, or thoughtlessness, may be imputed to God, as the author of it, I believe you will not affirm. Whatever opinion we father on him, it must be either because he has discovered it to us by supernatural revelation or because it is so evident to our natural faculties, which were framed and given us by God, that it is impossible we should withhold our assent from it. But where is the revelation or where is the evidence that extorts the belief of matter? No, how does it appear that matter, taken for something distinct from what we perceive by our senses, is thought to exist by all mankind, or indeed by any except a few philosophers who do not know what they would be at? Your question supposes these points are clear; and when you have cleared them, I shall think myself obliged to give you another answer. In the meantime let it suffice that I tell you I do not suppose God has deceived mankind at all.

Hyl. But the novelty, Philonous, the novelty! There lies the danger. New notions should always be discountenanced; they unsettle men's minds and nobody knows where they will end.

Phil. Why rejecting a notion that has no foundation either in sense or in reason or in divine authority should be thought to unsettle the belief of such opinions as are grounded on all or any of these, I cannot imagine. That innovations in government and religion are dangerous and ought to be discountenanced, I freely admit. But is there the like reason why they should be discouraged in philosophy? Making anything known which was unknown before is an innovation in knowledge, and if all such innovations had been forbidden, men would [not] have made a notable progress in the arts and sciences. But it is none of my business to plead for novelties and paradoxes. That the qualities we perceive are not in the objects; that we must not believe our senses; that we know nothing of the real nature of things and can never be assured even of their existence; that real colors and sounds are nothing but certain unknown figures and motions; that motions are in themselves neither swift nor slow; that there are in bodies absolute extensions, without any particular magnitude or figure; that a thing stupid, thoughtless, and inactive operates on a spirit; that the least particle of a body contains innumerable extended parts. These are the novelties, these are the strange notions which shock the genuine uncorrupted judgment of all mankind, and, being once admitted, embarrass the mind with endless doubts and difficulties. And it is against these and the like innovations I endeavor to vindicate common sense. It is true, in doing this, I may perhaps be obliged to use some *ambages*[4] and ways of speech not common. But if my notions are once thoroughly understood, that which is most singular in them will in effect be found to amount to no more than this: that it is absolutely impossible and a plain contradiction to suppose that any unthinking being should exist without being perceived by a mind. And if this notion is singular, it is a shame it should be so at this time of day and in a Christian country.

Hyl. As for the difficulties other opinions may be liable to, those are out of the question. It is your business to defend your own opinion. Can anything be plainer than that you are for changing all things into ideas? You, I say, who are not ashamed to charge me with *skepticism*. This is so plain there is no denying it.

Phil. You mistake me. I am not for changing things into ideas, but rather ideas into things, since those immediate objects of perception, which, according to you, are only appearances of things, I take to be the real things themselves.

4. [Round-about ways of speech.]

Hyl. Things! You may pretend what you please, but it is certain you leave us nothing but the empty forms of things, the outside only which strikes the senses.

Phil. What you call the empty forms and outside of things seems to me the very things themselves. Nor are they empty or incomplete otherwise than upon your supposition that matter is an essential part of all corporeal things. We both, therefore, agree in this: that we perceive only sensible forms, but we differ in this: You will have them to be empty appearances; I, real beings. In short, you do not trust your senses; I do.

Hyl. You say you believe your senses and seem to applaud yourself that in this you agree with the vulgar. According to you, therefore, the true nature of a thing is discovered by the senses. If so, where does that disagreement come from? Why is not the same figure and other sensible qualities perceived all manner of ways? And why should we use a microscope, the better to discover the true nature of a body, if it were discoverable to the naked eye?

Phil. Strictly speaking, Hylas, we do not see the same object that we feel; neither is the same object perceived by the microscope which was by the naked eye. But in case every variation was thought sufficient to constitute a new kind or individual, the endless number or confusion of names would render language impracticable. Therefore, to avoid this as well as other inconveniences which are obvious upon a little thought, men combine together several ideas, apprehended by various senses, or by the same sense at different times, or in different circumstances, but observed, however, to have some connection in nature, either with respect to coexistence or succession; all which they refer to one name and consider as one thing. Hence it follows that, when I examine by my other senses a thing I have seen, it is not in order to understand better the same object which I had perceived by sight, the object of one sense not being perceived by the other senses. And when I look through a microscope, it is not that I may perceive more clearly what I perceived already with my bare eyes, the object perceived by the glass being quite different from the former. But in both cases my aim is only to know what ideas are connected together; and the more a man knows of the connection of ideas, the more he is said to know of the nature of things. What, therefore, if our ideas are variable? What if our senses are not in all cir-

cumstances affected with the same appearances? It will not then follow they are not to be trusted, or that they are inconsistent either with themselves or anything else, except with your preconceived notion of (I do not know what) one single, unchanged, unperceivable, real nature, marked by each name, which prejudice seems to have taken its rise from not rightly understanding the common language of men speaking of several distinct ideas as united into one thing by the mind. And, indeed, there is cause to suspect several erroneous conceits of the philosophers are owing to the same original: while they began to build their schemes, not so much on notions as words which were framed by the vulgar merely for convenience and dispatch in the common actions of life, without any regard to speculation.

Hyl. I think I apprehend your meaning.

Phil. It is your opinion the ideas we perceive by our senses are not real things, but images or copies of them. Our knowledge, therefore, is no further real than as our ideas are the true representations of those originals. But as these supposed originals are in themselves unknown, it is impossible to know how far our ideas resemble them or whether they resemble them at all. We cannot, therefore, be sure we have any real knowledge. Further, as our ideas are perpetually varied, without any change in the supposed real things, it necessarily follows they cannot all be true copies of them, or, if some are and others are not, it is impossible to distinguish the former from the latter. And this plunges us yet deeper in uncertainty. Again, when we consider the point, we cannot conceive how any idea, or anything like an idea, should have an absolute existence out of a mind, nor consequently, according to you, how there should be any real thing in nature. The result of all this is that we are thrown into the most hopeless and abandoned *skepticism*. Now give me leave to ask you, *first*, whether your referring ideas to certain absolutely existing unperceived substances, as their originals, is not the source of all this *skepticism? Secondly*, whether you are informed, either by sense or reason, of the existence of those unknown originals? And in case you are not, whether it is not absurd to suppose them? *Thirdly*, whether upon inquiry, you find there is anything distinctly conceived or meant by the *absolute or external existence of unperceiving substances? Lastly*, whether, the premises considered, it is not the wisest way to follow nature, trust your senses, and, laying aside all anxious thought about unknown natures or substances, admit with the vulgar those for real things which are perceived by the senses?

Hyl. For the present, I have no inclination to the answering part. I would much rather see how you can get over what follows. Pray, are not the objects perceived by the senses of one likewise perceivable to others present? If there were a hundred more here, they would all see the garden, the trees, and flowers as I see them. But they are not in the same manner affected with the ideas I frame in my imagination. Does not this make a difference between the former sort of objects and the latter?

Phil. I grant it does. Nor have I ever denied a difference between the objects of sense and those of imagination. But what would you infer from this? You cannot say that sensible objects exist unperceived because they are perceived by many.

Hyl. I admit I can make nothing of that objection, but it has led me into another. Is it not your opinion that by our senses we perceive only the ideas existing in our minds?

Phil. It is.

Hyl. But the same idea which is in my mind cannot be in yours or in any other mind. Does it not, therefore, follow from your principles that no two can see the same thing? And is not this highly absurd?

Phil. If the term *same* be taken in the vulgar meaning, it is certain (and not at all repugnant to the principles I maintain) that different persons may perceive the same thing, or the same thing or idea exist in different minds. Words are of arbitrary imposition; and since men are accustomed to apply the word *same* where no distinction or variety is perceived, and I do not pretend to alter their perceptions, it follows that, as men have said before, *several saw the same thing*, so they may upon like occasions, still continue to use the same phrase without any deviation either from propriety of language or the truth of things. But if the term *same* is used in the meaning of philosophers who pretend to an abstracted notion of identity, then, according to their sundry definitions of this notion (for it is not yet agreed in what that philosophic identity consists), it may or may not be possible for various persons to perceive the

same thing. But whether philosophers shall think fit to call a thing the *same* or not, is, I conceive, of small importance. Let us suppose several men together, all endowed with the same faculties, and consequently affected in like sort by their senses, and who had yet never known the use of language; they would without question agree in their perceptions. Though perhaps, when they came to the use of speech, some regarding the uniformity of what was perceived might call it the *same* thing; others, especially regarding the diversity of persons who perceived, might choose the denomination of different things. But who does not see that all the dispute is about a word — namely, whether what is perceived by different persons — may yet have the term *same* applied to it? Or suppose a house whose walls or outward shell remaining unaltered, the chambers are all pulled down and new ones built in their place, and that you should call this the *same*, and I should say it was not the *same* house — would we not for all this perfectly agree in our thoughts of the house considered in itself? And would not all the difference consist in a sound? If you should say we differ in our notions, for that you superadded to your idea of the house the simple abstracted idea of identity, whereas I did not; I would tell you I do not know what you mean by that *abstracted idea of identity*; and I should desire you to look into your own thoughts and be sure you understood yourself. — Why so silent, Hylas? Are you not yet satisfied that men may dispute about identity and diversity without any real difference in their thoughts and opinions abstracted from names? Take this further reflection with you, that whether matter be allowed to exist or not, the case is exactly the same as to the point in hand. For the materialists themselves acknowledge what we immediately perceive by our senses to be our own ideas. Your difficulty, therefore, that no two see the same thing makes equally against the materialists and me.

Hyl. But they suppose an external archetype to which, referring their several ideas, they may truly be said to perceive the same thing.

Phil. And (not to mention your having discarded those archetypes) so may you suppose an external archetype on my principles — *external*, I mean, to your own mind, though indeed it must be supposed to exist in that mind which comprehends all things; but then this serves all the ends of identity as well as if it existed out of a mind. And I am sure you yourself will not say it is less intelligible.

Hyl. You have indeed clearly satisfied me, either that there is no difficulty at bottom in this point or if there is, it counts equally against both opinions.

Phil. But that which counts equally against two contradictory opinions can be a proof against neither.

Hyl. I acknowledge it. But, after all, Philonous, when I consider the substance of what you advance against *skepticism*, it amounts to no more than this: We are sure that we really see, hear, feel—in a word, that we are affected with sensible impressions.

Phil. And how are we concerned any further? I see this *cherry*, I feel it, I taste it—and I am sure *nothing* cannot be seen or felt or tasted—it is therefore *real*. Take away the sensations of softness, moisture, redness, tartness, and you take away the *cherry*. Since it is not a being distinct from sensations, a *cherry*, I say, is nothing but a congeries of sensible impressions or ideas perceived by various senses, which ideas are united into one thing (or have one name given them) by the mind because they are observed to attend each other. Thus, when the palate is affected with such a particular taste, the sight is affected with a red color, the touch with roundness, softness, etc. Hence, when I see and feel and taste in sundry certain manners, I am sure the *cherry* exists or is real, its reality being, in my opinion, nothing abstracted from those sensations. But if by the word *cherry* you mean an unknown nature distinct from all those sensible qualities, and by its existence something distinct from its being perceived, then indeed I admit neither you nor I nor anyone else can be sure it exists.

Hyl. But what would you say, Philonous, if I should bring the very same reasons against the existence of sensible things in a mind which you have offered against their existing in a material *substratum?*

Phil. When I see your reasons, you shall hear what I have to say to them.

Hyl. Is the mind extended or unextended?

Phil. Unextended, without doubt.

Hyl. Do you say the things you perceive are in your mind?

Phil. They are.

Hyl. Again, have I not heard you speak of sensible impressions?

Phil. I believe you may.

Hyl. Explain to me now, O Philonous, how it is possible there should be room for all those trees and houses to exist in your mind. Can extended things be contained in that which is unextended? Or are we to imagine impressions made on a thing void of all solidity? You cannot say objects are in your mind as books in your study or that things are imprinted on it as the figure of a seal upon wax. In what sense, therefore, are we to understand those expressions? Explain this to me, if you can, and I shall then be able to answer all those queries you formerly put to me about my *substratum*.

Phil. Look you, Hylas, when I speak of objects as existing in the mind or imprinted on the senses, I would not be understood in the gross literal sense, as when bodies are said to exist in a place or a seal to make an impression upon wax. My meaning is only that the mind comprehends or perceives them and that it is affected from without or by some being distinct from itself. This is my explication of your difficulty, and how it can serve to make your tenet of an unperceiving material *substratum* intelligible, I would gladly know.

Hyl. No, if that be all, I confess I do not see what use can be made of it. But are you not guilty of some abuse of language in this?

Phil. None at all, it is no more than common custom, which you know is the rule of language, has authorized, nothing being more usual than for philosophers to speak of the immediate objects of the understanding as things existing in the mind. Nor is there anything in this, but what is conformable to the general analogy of language, most part of the mental operations being signified by words borrowed from sensible things—as is plain in the terms *comprehend, reflect, discourse,* etc., which being applied to the mind, must not be taken in their gross original sense.

Hyl. You have, I admit, satisfied me in this point. But there still remains one great difficulty which I do not know how you will get over. And, indeed, it is of such importance that if you could solve all others, without being able to find a solution for this, you must never expect to make me a proselyte to your principles.

Phil. Let me know this mighty difficulty.

Hyl. The Scripture account of the creation is what appears to me utterly irreconcilable with your notions. Moses tells us of a creation, a creation of what? Of ideas? No, certainly, but of things, of real things, solid corporeal substances. Bring your principles to agree with this and I shall perhaps agree with you.

Phil. Moses mentions the sun, moon, and stars, earth and sea, plants and animals—that all these do really exist and were in the beginning created by God, I make no question. If by *ideas* you mean fictions and fancies of the mind, then these are no ideas. If by *ideas* you mean immediate objects of the understanding, or sensible things which cannot exist unperceived, or out of a mind, then these things are ideas. But whether you do or do not call them *ideas*, it matters little. The difference is only about a name. And whether that name is retained or rejected, the sense, the truth, and reality of things continues the same. In common talk, the objects of our senses are not termed *ideas*, but *things*. Call them so still, provided you do not attribute to them any absolute external existence, and I shall never quarrel with you for a word. The creation, therefore, I allow to have been a creation of things, of *real* things. Neither is this in the least inconsistent with my principles, as is evident from what I have now said, and would have been evident to you without this, if you had not forgotten what had been so often said before. But as for solid corporeal substances, I desire you to show where Moses makes any mention of them, and if they should be mentioned by him or any other inspired writer, it would still be incumbent on you to show those words were not taken in the vulgar meaning, for things falling under our senses, but in the philosophic meaning, for matter, or an unknown quiddity, with an absolute existence. When you have proved these points, then (and not until then) may you bring the authority of Moses into our dispute.

Hyl. It is in vain to dispute about a point so clear. I am content to refer it to your own conscience. Are you not satisfied there is some peculiar repugnance between the Mosaic account of the creation and your notions?

Phil. If all possible sense which can be put on the first chapter of Genesis may be conceived as consistently with my principles as any other, then it has no peculiar repugnance with them. But there is no sense you may not as well conceive, believing as I do. Since, besides spirits, all you conceive are ideas, and the existence of these I do not deny. Neither do you pretend they exist without the mind.

Hyl. Pray, let me see any sense you can understand it in.

Phil. Why I imagine that if I had been present at the creation, I should have seen things produced into being, that is, become perceptible, in the order described by the sacred historian. I ever before believed the Mosaic account of the creation and now find no alteration in my manner of believing it. When things are said to begin or end their existence, we do not mean this with regard to God, but his creatures. All objects are eternally known by God, or, which is the same thing, have an eternal existence in his mind, but when things, before imperceptible to creatures, are by a decree of God made perceptible to them, then are they said to begin a relative existence with respect to created minds. Upon reading, therefore, the Mosaic account of the creation, I understand that the several parts of the world became gradually perceivable to finite spirits endowed with proper faculties, so that, whoever such were present, they were in truth perceived by them. This is the literal, obvious sense suggested to me by the words of the Holy Scripture, in which is included no mention or no thought, either of *substratum*, instrument, occasion, or absolute existence. And upon inquiry, I do not doubt it will be found that most plain, honest men, who believe the creation, never think of those things any more than I. What metaphysical sense you may understand it in, you only can tell.

Hyl. But, Philonous, you do not seem to be aware that you allow created things in the beginning only a relative and, consequently, hypothetical being—that is to say, upon supposition there were men to perceive them, without which they have no actuality of absolute existence in which creation might terminate. Is it not, therefore, according to you, plainly impossible that the creation of any inanimate creatures should precede that of man? And is not this directly contrary to the Mosaic account?

Phil. In answer to that, I say, *first*, created beings might begin to exist in the mind of other created intelligences besides men. You will not, therefore, be able to prove any contradiction between Moses and my notions unless you first show there was no other order of finite created spirits in being before man. I say further, in case we conceive the creation, as we should at this time, a parcel of plants or vegetables of all sorts produced by an invisible power in a desert where nobody was present—that this way of explaining or conceiving it is consistent with my principles, since they deprive you of nothing, either sensible or imaginable; that it exactly suits with the common, natural, undebauched notions of mankind; that it manifests the dependence of all things on God and, consequently, has all the good effect or influence which it is possible that important article of our faith should have in making men humble, thankful, and resigned to their Creator. I say, moreover, that in this naked conception of things, divested of words, there will not be found any notion of what you call the *actuality of absolute existence.* You may indeed raise a dust with those terms and so lengthen our dispute to no purpose. But I entreat you calmly to look into your own thoughts and then tell me if they are not a useless and unintelligible jargon.

Hyl. I admit I have no very clear notion annexed to them. But what do you say to this? Do you not make the existence of sensible things consist in their being in a mind? And were not all things eternally in the mind of God? Did they not therefore exist from all eternity, according to you? And how could that which was eternal be created in time? Can anything be clearer or better connected than this?

Phil. And are not you, too, of the opinion that God knew all things from eternity?

Hyl. I am.

Phil. Consequently, they always had a being in the divine intellect.

Hyl. This I acknowledge.

Phil. By your own confession, therefore, nothing is new, or begins to be, in respect of the mind of God. So we are agreed in that point.

Hyl. What shall we make then of the creation?

Phil. May we not understand it to have been entirely in respect of finite spirits, so that things with regard to us may properly be said to begin their existence, or be created, when God decreed they should become perceptible to intelligent creatures in that order and manner which he then established and we now call the laws of nature? You may call this a *relative,* or *hypothetical, existence* if you please. But so long as it supplies us with the most natural, obvious, and literal sense of the Mosaic history of the creation—so long as it answers all the religious ends of that great article—in a word, so long as you can assign no other sense or meaning in its stead, why should we reject this? Is it to comply with a ridiculous skeptical humor of making everything nonsense and unintelligible? I am sure you cannot say it is for the glory of God. For allowing it to be a thing possible and conceivable that the corporeal world should have an absolute subsistence extrinsic to the mind of God as well as to the minds of all created spirits yet how could this set forth either the immensity or omniscience of the Deity or the necessary and immediate dependence of all things on him? No, would it not rather seem to derogate from those attributes?

Hyl. Well, but as to this decree of God's for making things perceptible, what do you say, Philonous, is it not plain God did either execute that decree from all eternity or at some certain time began to will what he had not actually willed before, but only designed to will? If the former, then there could be no creation or beginning of existence in finite things. If the latter, then we must acknowledge something new to befall the Deity, which implies a sort of change; and all change argues imperfection.

Phil. Pray consider what you are doing. Is it not evident this objection concludes equally against a creation in any sense, no, against every other act of the Deity discoverable by the light of nature? None of which can we conceive otherwise than as performed in time and having a beginning. God is a being of transcendent and unlimited perfections; his nature, therefore, is incomprehensible to finite spirits. It is not, therefore, to be expected that any man, whether *materialist* or *immaterialist,* should have exactly just notions of the Deity, his attributes, and ways of operation. If then you would infer anything against me, your difficulty must not be drawn from the inadequateness of our conceptions of the divine nature, which is unavoidable on any scheme, but from the denial of matter, of which there is not one word directly or indirectly in what you have now objected.

Hyl. I must acknowledge the difficulties you are concerned to clear are such only as arise from the nonexistence of matter and are peculiar to that notion. So far you are in the right. But I cannot by any means bring myself to think there is no such peculiar repugnance between the creation and your opinion, though, indeed, where to fix it, I do not distinctly know.

Phil. What would you have? Do I not acknowledge a twofold state of things, the one ectypal,[5] or natural, the other archetypal and eternal? The former was created in time, the latter existed from everlasting in the mind of God. Is not this agreeable to the common notions of theologians? Or is any more than this necessary in order to conceive the creation? But you suspect some peculiar repugnance, though you do not know where it lies. To take away all possibility of scruple in the case, do but consider this one point. Either you are not able to conceive the creation on any hypothesis whatsoever and, if so, there is no ground for dislike or complaint against my particular opinion on that score, or you are able to conceive it and, if so, why not on my principles, since nothing conceivable is taken away by that means? You have all along been allowed the full scope of sense, imagination, and reason. Whatever, therefore, you could before apprehend, either immediately or mediately by your senses, or by ratiocination from your senses, whatever you could perceive, imagine, or understand remains still with you. If, therefore, the notion you have of the creation by other principles is intelligible, you have it still upon mine; if it is not intelligible, I conceive it to be no notion at all, and so there is no loss of it. And, indeed, it seems to me very plain that the supposition of matter, that is, a thing perfectly unknown and inconceivable, cannot serve to make us conceive anything. And I hope it does not need to be proved to you that if the existence of matter does not make the creation conceivable, the creation's being without it inconceivable can be no objection against its nonexistence.

Hyl. I confess, Philonous, you have almost satisfied me in this point of the creation.

Phil. I would gladly know why you are not quite satisfied. You tell me indeed of a repugnance between the Mosaic history and immaterialism, but you do not know where it lies. Is this reasonable, Hylas? Can you

expect I should solve a difficulty without knowing what it is? But, to pass by all that, would not a man think you were assured there is no repugnance between the received notions of materialists and the inspired writings?

Hyl. And so I am.

Phil. Ought the historical part of Scripture to be understood in a plain, obvious sense, or in a sense which is metaphysical and out of the way?

Hyl. In the plain sense, doubtless.

Phil. When Moses speaks of herbs, earth, water, etc., as having been created by God, do you not think the sensible things, commonly signified by those words, are suggested to every unphilosophical reader?

Hyl. I cannot help thinking so.

Phil. And are not all ideas, or things perceived by sense, to be denied a real existence by the doctrine of the materialists?

Hyl. This I have already acknowledged.

Phil. The creation, therefore, according to them, was not the creation of sensible things, which have only a relative being, but of certain unknown natures, which have an absolute being in which creation might terminate.

Hyl. True.

Phil. Is it not, therefore, evident the asserters of matter destroy the plain obvious sense of Moses, with which their notions are utterly inconsistent, and, instead of it, obtrude on us I do not know what, something equally unintelligible to themselves and me?

Hyl. I cannot contradict you.

Phil. Moses tells us of a creation. A creation of what? Of unknown quiddities, of occasions, or *substratums*? No, certainly; but of things obvious to the senses. You must first reconcile this with your notions if you expect I should be reconciled to them.

Hyl. I see you can assault me with my own weapons.

Phil. Then as to *absolute existence*, was there ever known a more jejune notion than that? Something it is, so abstracted and unintelligible, that you have frankly owned you could not conceive it, much less explain anything by it. But allowing matter to exist and the notion of absolute existence to be as clear as light, yet was this ever known to make the creation more credible? No, has it not furnished the *atheists* and *infidels* of all ages with the most plausible argument against a

5. [Copied from something else.]

creation? That a corporeal substance, which has an absolute existence without the minds of spirits, should be produced out of nothing by the mere will of a spirit has been looked upon as a thing so contrary to all reason, so impossible and absurd that not only the most celebrated among the ancients, but even various modern and Christian philosophers have thought matter coeternal with the Deity. Lay these things together and then judge whether materialism disposes men to believe the creation of things.

Hyl. I admit, Philonous, I think it does not. This of the *creation* is the last objection I can think of, and I must necessarily admit it has been sufficiently answered as well as the rest. Nothing now remains to be overcome but a sort of unaccountable backwardness that I find in myself toward your notions.

Phil. When a man is swayed to one side of a question, he does not know why; can this, do you think, be anything else but the effect of prejudice, which never fails to attend old and rooted notions? And indeed in this respect I cannot deny the belief of matter to have very much the advantage over the contrary opinion with men of a learned education.

Hyl. I confess it seems to be as you say.

Phil. As a balance, therefore, to this weight of prejudice, let us throw into the scale the great advantages that arise from the belief of immaterialism, in regard to both religion and human learning. The being of a God and incorruptibility of the soul, those great articles of religion, are they not proved with the clearest and most immediate evidence? When I say the being of a *God,* I do not mean an obscure, general cause of things, of which we have no conception, but *God* in the strict and proper sense of the word. A being whose spirituality, omnipresence, providence, omniscience, infinite power, and goodness are as conspicuous as the existence of sensible things, of which (notwithstanding the fallacious pretenses and affected scruples of *skeptics*) there is no more reason to doubt than of our own being. Then with relation to human sciences: In natural philosophy, what intricacies, what obscurities, what contradictions has the belief of matter led men into! To say nothing of the numberless disputes about its extent, continuity, homogeneity, gravity, divisibility, etc., do they not pretend to explain all things by bodies operating on bodies, according to the laws of motion? And

yet, are they able to comprehend how any one body should move another? No, admitting there was no difficulty in reconciling the notion of an inert being with a cause or in conceiving how an accident might pass from one body to another, yet by all their strained thoughts and extravagant suppositions, have they been able to reach the mechanical production of any one animal or vegetable body? Can they account, by the laws of motion, for sounds, tastes, smells, or colors, or for the regular course of things? Have they accounted, by physical principles, for the aptitude and contrivance even of the most inconsiderable parts of the universe? But laying aside matter and corporeal causes and admitting only the efficiency of an all-perfect mind, are not all the effects of nature easy and intelligible? If the *phenomena* are nothing else but *ideas,* God is a *spirit,* but matter an unintelligent, unperceiving being. If they demonstrate an unlimited power in their cause, God is active and omnipotent, but matter an inert mass. If the order, regularity, and usefulness of them can never be sufficiently admired, God is infinitely wise and provident, but matter destitute of all contrivance and design. These surely are great advantages in *physics.* Not to mention that the apprehension of a distant Deity naturally disposes men to a negligence in their *moral* actions, which they would be more cautious of in case they thought him immediately present and acting on their minds without the interposition of matter or unthinking second causes. Then in *metaphysics;* what difficulties concerning entity in abstract, substantial forms, hylarchic principles, plastic natures, substance and accident, principle of individuation, possibility of matter's thinking, origin of ideas, the manner how two independent substances so widely different as *spirit* and *matter* should mutually operate on each other! What difficulties, I say, and endless disquisitions concerning these and innumerable other the like points, do we escape by supposing only spirits and ideas? Even *mathematics* itself, if we take away the absolute existence of extended things, becomes much more clear and easy, the most shocking paradoxes and intricate speculations in those sciences depending on the infinite divisibility of finite extension, which depends on that supposition. But what need is there to insist on the particular sciences? Is not that opposition to all science whatsoever, that frenzy of the ancient and modern *skeptics*, built on the same foundation? Or can you produce so much as one argument against the reality of corporeal things, or in behalf of that avowed utter ignorance of their natures which does not suppose their reality to consist in an external absolute existence? Upon this supposition indeed the objections from the change of colors in a pigeon's neck or the appearances of a broken oar in the water must be allowed to have weight. But those and the like objections vanish if we do not maintain the being of absolute external originals, but place the reality of things in ideas, fleeting indeed, and changeable, however, not changed at random but according to the fixed order of nature. For in this consists that constancy and truth of things which secures all the concerns of life and distinguishes that which is *real* from the irregular visions of the fancy.

Hyl. I agree to all you have now said and must admit that nothing can incline me to embrace your opinion more than the advantages I see it is attended with. I am by nature lazy and this would be a mighty abridgment in knowledge. What doubts, what hypotheses, what labyrinths of amusement, what fields of disputation, what an ocean of false learning may be avoided by that single notion of *immaterialism?*

Phil. After all, is there anything further remaining to be done? You may remember, you promised to embrace that opinion which upon examination should appear most agreeable to common sense and remote from *skepticism*. This, by your own confession, is that which denies matter or the absolute existence of corporeal things. Nor is this all; the same notion has been proved several ways, viewed in different lights, pursued in its consequences, and all objections against it cleared. Can there be a greater evidence of its truth? Or is it possible it should have all the marks of a true opinion and yet be false?

Hyl. I admit myself entirely satisfied for the present in all respects. But what security can I have that I shall still continue the same full assent to your opinion and that no unthought-of objection or difficulty will occur hereafter?

Phil. Pray, Hylas, do you in other cases, when a point is once evidently proved, withhold your assent on account of objections or difficulties it may be liable to? Are the difficulties that attend the doctrine of incommensurable quantities, of the angle of contact, of the asymptotes to curves, or the like, sufficient to make you hold out against mathematical demonstration? Or will you disbelieve the providence of God because there may be some particular things which you do not know how to reconcile with it? If there are difficulties attending immaterialism, there are at the same time direct and evident proofs for it. But for the existence of matter there is not one proof, and far more numerous and insurmountable objections lie against it. But where are those mighty difficulties you insist on? Alas, you do not know where or what they are—something which may possibly occur later. If this is a sufficient pretense for withholding your full assent, you should never yield it to any proposition, however free from exceptions, however clearly and solidly demonstrated.

Hyl. You have satisfied me, Philonous.

Phil. But to arm you against all future objections, do but consider that what bears equally hard on two contradictory opinions can be a proof against neither. Whenever, therefore, any difficulty occurs, try if you can find a solution for it on the hypothesis of the *materialists*. Be not deceived by words, but sound your own thoughts. And in case you cannot conceive it easier by the help of *materialism*, it is plain it can be no objection against *immaterialism*. Had you proceeded all along by this rule, you would probably have spared yourself abundance of trouble in objecting, since of all your difficulties, I challenge you to show one that is explained by matter, no, which is not more unintelligible with than without that supposition and consequently makes rather *against* than *for* it. You should consider, in each particular, whether the difficulty arises from the *nonexistence of matter*. If it does not, you might as well argue from the infinite divisibility of extension against divine foreknowledge as from such a difficulty against *immaterialism*. And yet, upon recollection, I believe you will find this to have been often if not always the case. You should likewise take heed not to argue on a *petitio principii*. One is apt to say the unknown substances ought to be esteemed real things rather than the ideas in our minds; and who can tell but the unthinking external substance may concur as a cause or instrument in the production of our ideas? But is not this proceeding on a supposition that there are such external substances? And to suppose this, is it not begging the question? But, above all things, you should beware of imposing on yourself by that vulgar sophism, which is called *ignoratio elenchi*. You talked often as if you thought I maintained the nonexistence of sensible things, whereas in truth no one can be more thoroughly assured of their existence than I am, and it is you who doubt—I should have said, positively deny it. Everything that is seen, felt, heard, or any way perceived by the senses is, on the principles I embrace, a real being, but not on yours. Remember, the matter you contend for is an unknown somewhat (if indeed it may be termed *somewhat*) which is quite stripped of all sensible qualities and can be neither perceived by sense nor apprehended by the mind. Remember, I say that it is not any object which is hard or soft, hot or cold, blue or white, round or square, etc. For all these things I affirm do exist. Though, indeed, I deny they have existence distinct from being perceived or that they exist out of all minds whatsoever. Think on these points; let them be attentively considered and still kept in view. Otherwise you will not comprehend the state of the question—without which your objections will always be wide of the mark and, instead of mine, may possibly be directed (as more than once they have been) against your own notions.

Hyl. I must necessarily admit, Philonous, nothing seems to have kept me from agreeing with you more than this same *mistaking the question*. In denying matter, at first glimpse I am tempted to imagine you deny the things we see and feel, but, upon reflection, find there is no ground for it. What do you think, therefore, of retaining the name *matter* and applying it to sensible things? This may be done without any change in your sentiments, and, believe me, it would be a means of reconciling them to some persons who may be more shocked at an innovation in words than in opinion.

Phil. With all my heart, retain the word *matter* and apply it to the objects of sense, if you please, provided you do not attribute to them any subsistence distinct from their being perceived. I shall never quarrel with you for an expression. *Matter* or *material substance* are terms introduced by philosophers, and, as used by them, imply a sort of independence or a subsistence distinct from being perceived by a mind, but are never used by common people, or if ever, it is to signify the immediate objects of sense. One would think, therefore, so long as the names of all particular things, with

the terms *sensible, substance, body, stuff,* and the like, are retained, the word *matter* should be never missed in common talk. And in philosophical discourses it seems the best way to leave it quite out, since there is not perhaps any one thing that has more favored and strengthened the depraved bent of the mind toward atheism than the use of that general confused term.

Hyl. Well, but, Philonous, since I am content to give up the notion of an unthinking substance exterior to the mind, I think you ought not deny me the privilege of using the word *matter* as I please and annexing it to a collection of sensible qualities subsisting only in the mind. I freely admit there is no other substance in a strict sense than *spirit*. But I have been so long accustomed to the term *matter* that I do not know how to part with it. To say there is no *matter* in the world is still shocking to me. Whereas to say there is no *matter*, if by that term is meant an unthinking substance existing without the mind, but if by *matter* is meant some sensible thing whose existence consists in being perceived, then there is *matter*—this distinction gives it quite another turn—and men will come into your notions with small difficulty when they are proposed in that manner. For, after all, the controversy about *matter* in the strict meaning of it lies altogether between you and the philosophers whose principles, I acknowledge, are not near so natural or so agreeable to the common sense of mankind and Holy Scripture as yours. There is nothing we either desire or shun but as it makes or is apprehended to make some part of our happiness or misery. But what has happiness or misery, joy or grief, pleasure or pain to do with absolute existence or with unknown entities, abstracted from all relation to us? It is evident things regard us only as they are pleasing or displeasing, and they can please or displease only insofar as they perceived. Further, therefore, we are not concerned; and thus far you leave things as you found them. Yet still there is something new in this doctrine. It is plain I do not now think with the philosophers, nor yet altogether with the vulgar. I would like to know how the case stands in that respect, precisely what you have added to or altered in my former notions.

Phil. I do not pretend to be a setter-up of *new notions*. My endeavors tend only to unite and place in a clearer light that truth which was before shared between the vulgar and the philosophers—the former being of opinion that *those things they immediately perceive are the real things* and the latter that *the things immediately perceived are ideas which exist only in the mind* — which two notions put together do in effect constitute the substance of what I advance.

Hyl. I have been a long time distrusting my senses; I thought I saw things by a dim light and through false glasses. Now the glasses are removed and a new light breaks in upon my understanding. I am clearly convinced that I see things in their native forms and am no longer in pain about their unknown natures or absolute existence. This is the state I find myself in at present, though, indeed, the course that brought me to it I do not yet thoroughly comprehend. You set out upon the same principles that Academics, Cartesians, and the like sects usually do; and for a long time it looked as if you were advancing their philosophical *skepticism*; but, in the end, your conclusions are directly opposite to theirs.

Phil. You see, Hylas, the water of the fountain over there, how it is forced upwards in a round column to a certain height, at which it breaks and falls back into the basin from which it rose, its ascent as well as descent proceeding from the same uniform law or principle of *gravitation*. Just so, the same principles which, at first view, lead to *skepticism*, pursued to a certain point, bring men back to common sense.

George Berkeley, *On Motion* (1721)[1]

1. The most important thing in the pursuit of truth is to take care that ill-understood terms do not hinder us, a point which almost all philosophers warn of, but few attend to. Yet, this does not appear so difficult to observe, especially in the case of physics, where sensation, experience, and geometrical reasoning obtain. Laying aside then, as far as possible, every prejudice originating in the usual modes of speaking or in philosophical authority, we should diligently examine the very nature of things. Nor should the authority of anyone be set so high that his words and expressions be prized, unless they contain what is certain and clear.

2. The consideration of motion greatly disturbed the minds of the ancient philosophers, giving rise to various excessively difficult—not to say absurd—opinions, which, since they have now sunk into obscurity, do not deserve that we should give much attention to their discussion. But in works on motion by the more recent and sounder philosophers of our age, several words of too abstract and obscure signification occur, such as *solicitation of gravity, conatus, dead forces,* etc., terms which diffuse obscurity over writings that are in other respects very learned, and give rise to opinions not less at variance with truth than with common sense. It is necessary that these be discussed, not for the sake of proving others wrong, but on account of truth.

3. *Solicitation* and *effort* or *striving* are applicable properly to animate beings alone. When they are applied to others, they must be taken in a metaphorical sense. Philosophers, however, should abstain from metaphors. But if we reject affection of the mind and motion of the body, it will be clear to anyone giving attention to the matter that there is no clear and distinct meaning in those words.

4. As long as heavy bodies are sustained by us, we feel in ourselves effort, fatigue, and discomfort. We also perceive in heavy bodies, when falling, an accelerated motion toward the center of the earth, but nothing more, as far as our senses are concerned. However, reason proves that there is some cause or principle of these phenomena, and this is generally called *gravity*. Since, however, the cause of the fall of heavy bodies is dark and unknown, gravity in that sense cannot be called a sensible quality; consequently, it is an occult quality. But we can scarcely conceive—and indeed not even scarcely—what an occult quality is and how any quality can act or effect anything. It would be better then, if men would attend only to the sensible effects, putting the occult quality out of view. Abstract

1. [Translated from the Latin by G. N. Wright in *The Works of George Berkeley* (London, 1843), 2 vols., modified.]

words—however useful they are in discussion—should be discarded in meditation, and the mind should be fixed on particular and concrete things, that is, on the things themselves.

5. *Force* in the same way is attributed to bodies, but that word is used as if it signified a known quality, one distinct from figure, motion, and everything sensible, as also from every affection of animated life. But any person who accurately examines the subject will find that force is nothing else than an occult quality. Animal effort and corporeal motion are commonly regarded as symptoms and measures of this occult quality.

6. Thus it is plain that gravity or force is erroneously laid down as the principle of motion; for how can that principle be more clearly known by being called an occult quality? What is itself occult explains nothing—disregarding the view that the unknown acting cause can itself be better called a substance than a quality. Moreover, *force, gravity,* and words of that kind are employed more usually in the concrete—and not improperly—to denote the motion of bodies, the difficulty of resisting, etc. But when they are used by philosophers to signify natures distinct and abstracted from all these, which are neither objects of sense nor can be grasped by any force of intellect or the imagination, they are sure to produce error and confusion. [. . .]

26. Heavy bodies tend downwards, although affected by no apparent impulse, but we must not, therefore, suppose that the principle of motion is contained in them. Aristotle gives this account of the matter: "Heavy and light things are not moved of themselves; for that would be a characteristic of life, and they could stop themselves." All heavy bodies tend toward the center of the earth by a certain and constant law, and we do not perceive in them any principle or power of stopping or diminishing that motion, or of increasing it except by a fixed proportion, or of modifying it in any way; consequently, they behave quite passively. Moreover, the same should, strictly and accurately speaking, be said respecting percussive bodies. Those bodies, as long as they are moved, and also in the very moment of percussion, behave passively as when they are at rest. A body at

rest acts as much as a body in motion, as Newton admits when he says that the force of *inertia* is the same as *impetus*. But an inert body does nothing; so neither does a moved body.

27. In reality, a body equally persists in each state, either of motion or of rest. But its doing so can no more be called an action of the body than its existence can be called its action. Its persevering is nothing more than a continuation in the same mode of existing, which cannot properly be called action. But the resistance we experience in stopping a body in motion we imagine to be its action; but this is a delusion. For, in reality, that resistance we perceive is an impression in ourselves, and it does not prove that the body acts, but that we have an impression; it is certain that we should have the same impression whether that body were moved by itself or were impelled by some other principle.

28. Action and reaction are said to be in bodies, and such expressions are convenient for mechanical demonstrations. But we should be on our guard not to suppose for this reason that there is some real virtue in them which may be the cause or principle of motion. For those words are to be understood in the same way as the word *attraction*; and just as this is only a mathematical hypothesis, and not a physical quality, the same should be understood concerning those, and for the same reason. For as the truth and use of theorems concerning the mutual attraction of bodies remain unshaken in mechanical philosophy, as founded on the motion of bodies—whether that motion is supposed to be caused by the action of bodies mutually attracting each other or by the action of some agent different from body, impelling and stopping bodies—for the same reason, whatever has been laid down concerning the rules and laws of motions, and the theorems deduced from them, remain unquestionable, provided the sensible effects and the reasonings depending on them are granted, whether we suppose the action itself or the force causing these effects to be in body or in an incorporeal agent. [. . .]

35. These things not being sufficiently understood is the reason why some unjustly reject the mathematical principles of physics on the ground that they do

not assign efficient causes of things. When, in truth, it belongs to physics or mechanics to state only the rules of impulse and attraction, and not efficient causes—in a word, the laws of motions—and from these, when received, to assign the solution of particular phenomena but not their efficient cause.

36. It will be of great use to consider what a principle properly is and in what sense it must be taken among philosophers. Now the true, efficient, and preserving cause of all things is most properly called their source and principle. But the principles of experimental philosophy are properly called the grounds on which it rests or the sources from which is derived (I do not say the existence, but) the knowledge of corporeal things, these grounds being sensation and experience. In the same way, in mechanical philosophy, those are to be called principles in which the whole discipline is grounded and contained, being those primary laws of motions which, confirmed by experiments, are cultivated and rendered universal by reason. These laws of motion are appropriately called principles, since from them are derived both general theorems of mechanics and particular explanations of the phenomena.

37. Then truly something can be said to be explained mechanically when it is reduced to those most simple and universal principles and is shown by accurate reasoning to be suitable and connected with them. For once the laws of nature are found, then it remains for the philosopher to show that each thing necessarily follows in conformity with these laws, that is, that every phenomenon necessarily results from the principles. This is to explain and solve the phenomena, that is, to assign the reason why they take place.

38. The human mind delights in extending and enlarging its knowledge. But for this purpose, general notions and propositions must be formed in which particular propositions and knowledge are in some way contained and which then, and only then, are believed to be understood. This is well known to geometers. In mechanics also the course is first to lay down some notions, that is, definitions and elementary and general statements about motion, from which subsequently, in the mathematical style, more remote and less general conclusions are deduced. And, as

the magnitudes of particular bodies are measured by the application of geometrical theorems, so we ascertain and determine the motions of any parts of the mundane system and the phenomena depending on them by the application of the universal theorems of mechanics. And the physicist should exclusively aim at this.

39. And as geometers devise many things, for the sake of their discipline, which they themselves cannot describe nor find in the nature of things, for the same reason those who treat of mechanics employ certain abstract and general words and imagine in bodies force, action, attraction, solicitation, etc., which are exceedingly useful for theories, enunciations, and computations concerning motion, although in actual truth and in bodies actually existing, they are sought in vain, as much as are those things imagined by mathematical abstraction.

40. In reality, we perceive nothing by the use of our senses except effects or sensible qualities and entirely passive corporeal things, whether at rest or in motion; and reason and experience indicate nothing active except mind or soul. Whatever is imagined more than this must be regarded of the same sort as those mathematical hypotheses and abstractions; and we should thoroughly bear this in mind. Unless this takes place, we may easily relapse into the obscure subtlety of the Scholastics, which for so many ages infected philosophy like a dreadful plague.

41. The mechanical principles and universal laws of motions, or of nature, happily discovered in the last century, and treated of and applied by aid of geometry, have thrown a wonderful light on philosophy. But metaphysical principles and real efficient causes of the motion and existence of bodies or of corporeal attributes by no means belong to mechanics or experiment, nor can they throw light on them, except insofar as, by being previously known, they may serve to define the limits of physics, and thus to do away with difficulties and questions foreign to them. [. . .]

52. The Peripatetics distinguished various kinds of motion according to the variety of the changes which any body can undergo. Those who at present treat the subject take into account only local motion. But local motion cannot be understood unless we also

understand the meaning of *place*. This is defined by the moderns to be the part of space which body occupies, and therefore in reference to space it is divided into absolute and relative. For they distinguish between absolute or true space, and that which is apparent or relative. They maintain indeed that in every direction there exists an immense immovable space, not the object of sensation, but pervading and embracing all bodies; and this they call absolute space. But space comprehended or defined by body, and so subjected to our senses, is called relative, apparent, common space.

53. Let us imagine all bodies to be destroyed and annihilated. What remains they call absolute space, all relation resulting from the situation and distances of bodies, as well as the bodies themselves, being done away with. Now this space is infinite, immovable, indivisible, not the object of sensation, without relation and without distinction. That is, all its attributes are privative or negative; therefore, it seems to be a mere nothing. The only difficulty results from its being extended, for extension is a positive quality. But what sort of extension is that which can be neither divided nor measured, no part of which we can either perceive by our senses or picture in the imagination? For nothing can enter the imagination which from the nature of the thing cannot be perceived by sensation, since imagination is nothing else than a faculty representing the objects of sensation, either actually existing or at least being possible. It also evades pure intellect, since that faculty is concerned only with spiritual and unextended things, such as our minds, their habits, passions, virtues, and such things. Let us then take away mere words from absolute space, and nothing remains in sensation, imagination, or intellect. Nothing is therefore denoted by them but mere privation or negation, that is, mere nothing. [. . .]

66. From what has been said, it appears that, to ascertain the true nature of motion, it will be of great use: (1) to distinguish between mathematical hypotheses and the natures of things; (2) to beware of abstractions; (3) to consider motion as something, the object of sensation or at least of imagination; and [(4)] to be content with relative measures. If we do so, all the finest theorems of mechanical philosophy by means of which the recesses of nature are disclosed and the system of the world subjected to human calculation will remain untouched; and the consideration of motion will be freed from a thousand minute subtleties and abstract ideas. And let it suffice to say so much concerning the nature of motion.

67. It remains that we should treat the cause of the communication of motions. But most consider that force impressed on a movable body is the cause of motion in it. Nevertheless, it results from what has been laid down that they do not assign a known cause of motion, and one distinct from body and motion. It is further clear that force is not a certain and determinate thing, given that men of the greatest powers of mind advance different, and even contrary opinions, though retaining truth in their results. For Newton says that impressed force consists in action alone and is an action exercised on body to change its state and it does not continue after the action. Torricelli contends that a certain accumulation or aggregation of forces impressed by percussion is received into the moved body and remains there and constitutes the impetus. Borelli and some others maintain the same. But although Newton and Torricelli seem to differ, each advancing views consistent with themselves, the matter is sufficiently well explained by both. For forces attributed to bodies are as much mathematical hypotheses as attractive forces assigned to the planets and sun. Mathematical entities, however, have no stable essence in nature, but depend on the notion of the definer—hence the same thing can be differently explained. [. . .]

71. In physics, sensation and experience, which only reach apparent effects, are admitted; in mechanics, the abstract notions of mathematicians are admitted. In first philosophy or metaphysics, we treat of incorporeal things, causes, truth, and the existence of things. The physicist contemplates the series or successions of the objects of sense, by what laws they are connected, and in what order, observing what precedes as a cause, what follows as effect. And in this way we say that a moved body is the cause of motion in another or impresses motion on it; also it pulls or impels it. In this sense secondary corporeal causes should be understood, no account being taken of the actual places of the forces, or active powers, or of the real cause in which they are. Moreover,

beyond body, figure, and motion, the primary axioms of mechanical science can be called causes or mechanical principles, being regarded as the causes of the consequences.

72. The truly active causes can be extracted only by meditation and reasoning from the darkness in which they are involved, and thus at all become known. But it is the business of first philosophy or metaphysics to treat of them. And if each science were assigned its own province, its limits marked out, its principles and objects accurately distinguished, we could treat of what belongs to each with greater facility and perspicuity.

3. HUME'S *TREATISE,* INQUIRY, AND *DIALOGUES* AND ASSOCIATED TEXTS

David Hume was born in Edinburgh, Scotland, in 1711 and attended the University of Edinburgh for a few years in the 1720s, though he left without receiving a degree. After studying on his own for several years, he went to France in 1734 (to be more specific, to La Flèche, where Descartes had been educated) and wrote his first major work, *A Treatise of Human Nature,* published anonymously in 1739. Hume was quite disappointed with how it was received, remarking that it "fell dead-born from the press, without reaching such distinction as even to excite a murmur among the zealots." Over the next few decades, Hume reworked the content of the *Treatise* and published *Philosophical Essays Concerning Human Understanding* (later entitled *An Inquiry Concerning Human Understanding*) in 1748, *Dissertation on the Passions* in 1757, and *An Inquiry Concerning the Principles of Morals* in 1751. Hume also published *Essays, Moral and Political* in 1741–42, *Political Discourses* in 1752, and a six-volume *History of England* between 1754 and 1762. Hume's *Dialogues Concerning Natural Religion* was published posthumously in 1779. Unlike many of his philosophical predecessors and contemporaries, Hume never held an academic position. He was nominated for positions at Edinburgh (in 1744–45) and Glasgow (in 1751), but opposition from the clergy was decisive in both cases. Instead Hume was employed in a variety of ways, e.g., as a tutor to Marquess of Annandale, as a private secretary to General St. Clair (who was involved in plans to invade Canada) and to Lord Hertford (Ambassador to France), as a librarian for the Advocates Library in Edinburgh, and as Undersecretary of State (Northern Department).[1]

Hume's first major philosophical work, *A Treatise of Human Nature,* is a long and intricate work, divided into three books. Book One concerns the understanding and treats of traditional issues in epistemology

1. For more on Hume, see Barry Stroud, *Hume* (London: Routledge & Kegan Paul, 1978); David Fate Norton, *David Hume. Common Sense Moralist, Sceptical Metaphysician* (Princeton: Princeton University Press, 1982; and David Fate Norton, ed., *The Cambridge Companion to Hume* (Cambridge: Cambridge University Press, 1993).

and metaphysics. Book Two is on the passions and discusses emotions in detail. Book Three deals with morality in light of the discussion of the passions in Book Two. Thus, Hume's *Treatise* covers many traditional areas of philosophical inquiry.

Book One of the *Treatise* divides into four Parts. The bulk of Part One is devoted to laying out Hume's fundamental empiricist principles: All ideas are copies of impressions, All ideas are related to each other by means of resemblance, contiguity, and causality. In light of these principles, Hume then gives an account of our ideas of substances, modes, relations, and abstract ideas. Part Two discusses our ideas of space and time (in particular, whether they are infinitely divisible) and of existence. Part Three undertakes a detailed examination of a particularly important foundation of our knowledge, cause and effect relations. It also develops an account of belief that builds on the theory of ideas introduced in Part One. Part Four discusses a number of implications of Hume's theory of ideas and causality. In particular, Hume explains how his theories do and do not result in skepticism with respect to reason and the senses. In the latter case, Hume is especially concerned to provide an account of why we believe in the existence of bodies (given that there is no rational argument that can establish their existence). In Part Four Hume also discusses his account of the mind including personal identity, an issue he famously revisits in the Appendix to the *Treatise*.

Briefly, the situation Hume faces with respect to the self and self-consciousness is as follows. In light of his empiricist principle according to which all ideas must be derived from impressions, in Part One of Book One Hume looks for an impression of substance and discovers that he can find none. In Part Four of Book One Hume recognizes that this general point applies to the self as well. For when he considers his own mind, he discovers that he can find no impression of an enduring and identical self (or immaterial substance) that underlies all of his thoughts. As he puts it: "For my part, when I enter most intimately into what I call *myself*, I always stumble on some particular perception or other, of heat or cold, light or shade, love or hatred, pain or pleasure. I never can catch *myself* at any time without a perception and

never can observe anything but the perception." As a result, on Hume's account the self is nothing more than a collection or "bundle" of perceptions rather than an immaterial substance in which thoughts might inhere. However, in a famous passage from the Appendix, Hume expresses his dissatisfaction with this account, noting that it raises difficulties which, though not "absolutely insuperable," are "too hard for my understanding.".

Hume's *Inquiry Concerning Human Understanding* is a much abbreviated treatment of many of the issues discussed in detail in Book One of the *Treatise*. Its main focus (after briefly introducing his theory of ideas in §§1–3) is on causality and the implications his understanding of it has for a variety of issues such as liberty, miracles, and belief in the existence of God. Hume's main thesis is that the traditional notion of causality, which involves a necessary connection between cause and effect, is mistaken. For in any single instance of causality, we do not see anything that connects the cause and the effect with necessity. In line with his general empiricist stance, Hume notes that all one ever sees is one event followed by another, whether the events are the motions of bodies or thoughts in a mind. Nor is reason able to infer *a priori* any effect from the presence of any given cause; there would be no contradiction if the future did not resemble the past, and if we were presented with an object that we had never seen before, reason would not be able to determine its various effects. Accordingly, Hume revises our notion of causality and, as an empiricist, the only basis he can find for it is experience and habit. Thus, objectively, causality is simply the constant or customary conjunction of the cause and effect, whereas subjectively, it is our expectation, formed on the basis of repeated experience in the past rather than on reason, that one kind of event will follow another kind of event in the future.

Given this understanding of causality, Hume considers a variety of traditional philosophical issues in the *Inquiry*, at times coming to rather provocative conclusions. For example, in §8 he argues that liberty (which we now typically call free will) is not only compatible with, but is actually required by determinism. Determinism holds because we do find a constant conjunction between motives and actions and, moreover, we have come to expect this kind of correlation. If liberty is defined as a power of acting or not acting according to the determinations of the will, that is, as occurring when one's action is not constrained by external, non-volitional factors, then it is clear that everyone admits liberty. But obviously there is no conflict between the constant conjunction of motives and actions and the absence of external constraints. Rather, the absence of external constraints seems to require the connection between actions and motives, since moral judgments depend on the connection between motives and actions.

In §10 Hume presents his famous argument against miracles. Technically, the argument is not against miracles per se, but rather against the possibility that we could have enough evidence to accept miracles (especially those that are to be used to justify religious belief). If a miracle is defined as a violation of the laws of nature and the laws of nature have been overwhelmingly established by our vast experience, then the evidence in favor of a miracle will always be (and, as Hume argues, has always been) less than, or at least not greater than, our evidence for the laws of nature. Since one should proportion one's belief to the evidence (and since the evidence for them is less than the evidence against them, or at least the evidence against them cancels the evidence for them), one should not believe in miracles.

In §11 Hume argues that attempts to establish the existence of God on the basis of causality cannot succeed. Hume makes three main critical points.

First, it is illegitimate to infer from certain effects (e.g., what we see in the world) to a cause (e.g., God) and then to infer further, unobserved effects from that cause (e.g., that God will reward or punish humans for their past actions), since neither the first inference nor experience can justify the second inference. Second, one can never infer the infinite aspects of God's nature (e.g., omnipotence, omniscience, omnibenevolence, etc.) from the merely finite effects of the world. Third, if one has experienced a certain event only once, one might question whether one can infer that a cause is required at all. While these critical points could be taken to be hostile to Christianity (which might justify the clergy's opposition to Hume), one could also view Hume's position as neutral with respect to Christianity, for example by being congenial to fideism, the view that one's fundamental religious convictions are not subject to independent, rational evaluation. Bayle's discussion of Pyrrho provides a sense of the role of religious skepticism in this context. However, Hume's own views on religion are revealed in greater detail in his *Dialogues Concerning Natural Religion.* Though Hume does not take an official stand on the issue—by discussing proofs for the existence of God only indirectly by this work's three main figures (Demea, Cleanthes, and Philo)—it is plausible to suspect that Hume is using Philo, in particular, to express his own arguments, an interpretation consistent with the fact that Hume did not wish to publish this work during his lifetime.

Pierre Bayle, *Dictionary* (1697), "Pyrrho," Note B[1]

Pierre Bayle was a philosophical skeptic and religious writer born in 1647 to a Calvinist family in southern France. He became Professor of Philosophy at the Protestant Academy of Sedan, 1675–81. Upon its abolition, he moved to Rotterdam and became Professor of Philosophy at the Ecole Illustre; he died in Rotterdam in 1706. Bayle's main claim to fame is the five volume Historical and Critical Dictionary (1696), *which provides a full presentation of his skepticism. It went through numerous editions, including an English translation in 1710. As Bayle states in the* Dictionary, *Pyrrho was a Greek philosopher from the time of Alexander the Great. After examining all arguments pro and con for any given proposition, Pyrrho always found reasons for both affirming and denying it; thus he suspended judgment, concluding that the matter should be looked into further. Although he was not the inventor of this method of philosophizing, it goes by his name: Pyrrhonism. The article on Pyrrho provides Bayle with an opportunity to discuss early modern Pyrrhonism.[2]*

"Pyrrhonism is rightly detested in the divinity schools." Pyrrhonism is dangerous with respect to that divine science, but it is not very dangerous with respect to natural philosophy or the state. There is no harm in saying that the mind of man is too limited to discover anything in natural truths, in the causes which produce heat, cold, the tides, etc. It is enough for us to endeavor to find out some probable hypotheses and to collect experiments; and I am sure that there are very few good natural philosophers in our age who are not convinced that nature is an impenetrable abyss and that its springs are known to none but to the maker and director of them. So that all those philosophers are, in that respect, Academics and Pyrrhonists. Society does not need to be afraid of them, for skeptics do not deny that men should conform to the customs of their country, practice moral duties, and resolve upon those things from a probable reason without waiting for certainty. They might suspend their judgment on the question of whether such a duty is naturally and absolutely lawful, but they do not suspend it on the question of whether it is to be practiced on such and such an occasion. Thus, it follows that Pyrrhonism is only dangerous to

1. [Translated from the French in *The Dictionary Historical and Critical of Mr. Peter Bayle* (London, 1734–38), 5 vols., modified.]
2. [For more on Bayle, see Richard Popkin, *The High Road to Pyrrhonism* (2nd ed., Indianapolis: Hackett Publishing Company, 1989); or Elisabeth Labrousse, *Bayle* (Oxford: Oxford University Press, 1983).]

religion, for it ought to be grounded upon certainty; the design, the effects, and use of religion vanish as soon as the firm persuasion of its truth is blotted out of the mind. But, on the other hand, we do not need to be uneasy at it; there never was and there never will be but a small number of men capable of being deceived by the arguments of the skeptics. The grace which God bestows upon the faithful, the force of education in other men, and, if you will, ignorance, and the natural inclination men have to be peremptory are an impenetrable shield against the darts of the Pyrrhonists, although the sect fancies it is now more formidable than it was in former times. Let us see upon what grounds they build such a strange pretension.

About two months ago a learned man gave me a full account of a conference at which he had been present. Two abbots, one of whom had but common learning, the other was a good philosopher, grew so hot by degrees in their dispute that it almost became a full-fledged quarrel. The first had said, rather bluntly, that he forgave the pagan philosophers their floating in the uncertainty of their opinions, but that he could not understand how there could be any Pyrrhonists under the light of the Gospel. To which the other answered, "you are wrong to reason in such a manner. If Arcesilaus should return into the world and was to dispute with our theologians, he would be a thousand times more formidable than he was to the dogmatists of old Greece; Christian theology would afford him unanswerable arguments." All the company heard this with great surprise and begged the abbot to explain himself further, having no doubt that he had advanced a paradox which would only lead to his own confusion. He answered thus, addressing himself to the first abbot. "I will not make use of the advantages the new philosophy gives to the Pyrrhonists. The name of Sextus Empiricus was scarcely known in our schools; what he proposed with so great subtlety concerning suspending one's judgment was not less unknown than the Terra Australis, when Gassendi gave an abridgment of it, which opened our eyes. Cartesianism put the final touches to the work, and now no good philosopher any longer doubts that the skeptics were right to maintain that

the qualities of bodies which strike our senses are only appearances. Everyone of us may say, 'I feel heat before a fire,' but not 'I know that fire is in itself such as it appears to me.' Such was the style of the ancient Pyrrhonists. But now the new philosophy speaks more positively: Heat, smell, colors, etc. are not in the objects of our senses; they are only some modifications of my soul. I know that bodies are not at all as they appear to me. They were very willing to except extension and motion, but they could not do it; for if the objects of our senses appear to us colored, hot, cold, scented, though they are not so, why should they not appear extended and figured, at rest, and in motion, though they had no such thing. No, the objects of my senses cannot be the cause of my sensations; I might, therefore, feel cold and heat, see colors, figures, extension, and motion, though there was not one body in the world. I do not, therefore, have one good proof of the existence of bodies.[3] The only proof they give me for it is that God would deceive me if he imprinted in my soul the ideas I have of body without there being any. But that proof is very weak; it proves too much. Ever since the beginning of the world all mankind, except, perhaps, one in two hundred million, do firmly believe that bodies are colored, and yet it is a mistake. I ask whether God deceives men with respect to those colors. If he deceives them in that respect, what prevents him from doing so with respect to extension? This latter illusion will not be less innocent, nor less consistent, than the former with the most perfect being. If he does not deceive them with respect to colors, it is without doubt because he does not force them to say, 'those colors exist outside of my soul,' but only 'it appears to me there are some colors there.' The same may be said with respect to extension. God does not force you to say, 'it does exist,' but only to judge that you feel it and that it appears to you to exist. A Cartesian can as readily suspend his judgment about the existence of extension, as a peasant affirm that the sun

3. Father Malebranche shows in one of his *Elucidations* of the *Search after Truth*, "that it is very difficult to prove the existence of bodies and that nothing but faith can convince us that bodies do really exist."

shines, that snow is white, etc. And, therefore, if we are mistaken in affirming the existence of extension, God will not be the cause of it, since you acknowledge that he is not the cause of that peasant's error. Such are the advantages which the philosophers would procure to the Pyrrhonists, but I will not take advantage of them."

Immediately the same abbot, who was a philosopher, declared to the other that if he would have the better of a skeptic, he must, before all things, prove that the truth may certainly be known by certain marks. They are commonly called the criterion of truth [*criterium veritatis*]. You will rightly maintain against him that self-evidence is a certain characteristic of truth, for if self-evidence were not, we would have none. "Let it be so," he will say, "this is where I have you; I will show you several things as evident as can be, which you reject as false. 1. It is evident that things which do not differ from a third do not differ from each other. This is the basis of all our reasonings and all our syllogisms are grounded upon it; nevertheless, we are assured by the revelation of the mystery of the Trinity that it is a false axiom. You may invent as many distinctions as you please, but you will never be able to show that that maxim is not contradicted by this great mystery. 2. It is evident that there is no difference between individual, nature, and person. Nevertheless, the same mystery has convinced us that persons can be multiplied and that individuals and natures will not cease for all that to be one. 3. It is evident that for a man to be really and perfectly a person, it is enough to unite together a human body and a rational soul. But the mystery of the Incarnation has taught us that it is not sufficient. From this it follows that neither you nor I can be sure whether we are persons; for if it were essential that a human body and rational soul united together constitute a person, then God could never cause that they, thus united, did not constitute a person. We must therefore say that personality is merely accidental to them. But every accident may be separated from its subject in several ways; God, therefore, may prevent us from being persons in several ways, though we are made up of a body and a soul; and can anyone assure us that he does not make use of some such means to deprive us of our personality? Is he obliged to reveal

to us the several ways he disposes of us? 4. It is evident that a human body cannot be in several places at one time and that its head cannot be penetrated with all its other parts under an indivisible point; nevertheless, the mystery of the Eucharist teaches us that those two things happen every day. From this it follows that neither you nor I can be sure whether we are distinct from other men and whether we are not at this very moment in the seraglio of Constantinople, in Canada, in Japan, and in every town of the world, under different conditions in each place. Since God does nothing in vain, would he create several men when one man only, created in several places and clothed with several qualities, may suffice? This doctrine deprives us of the truth we find in numbers, for we no longer know what two or three are; we do not know what identity and diversity are. If we judge that John and Peter are two men, it is only because we see them in distinct places and because the one does not have the accidents of the other. But the basis for the distinction is destroyed by the doctrine of the Eucharist. It may be that there is only one creature in the world produced in several places with a diversity of qualities; we cast up long accounts in arithmetic, as if there were many distinct things;[4] but it is only a vain imagination. We are not only ignorant whether there are two bodies in the world, but we do not so much as know whether there is a body and a spirit; for if matter is penetrable, it is plain that extension is only an accident of the body, and so the body, according to its essence, is an unextended substance. It is, therefore, capable of all the attributes we conceive in a spirit, as the understanding, the will, the passions, and the sensations, so that we are left without any rule whereby we may discern whether a substance is spiritual by its nature or whether it is corporeal. 5. It is evident that the modes of a substance cannot subsist without the substance which they modify; but the mystery of transubstantiation has taught us that this is false. All our ideas are confounded by it; we can no longer define a substance; for if an accident can

4. Note that if a body may be produced in several places, any other being, spirit, place, accident, etc. may be multiplied the same way; and so there will not be a multitude of beings, but all things will be reduced to only one created being.

subsist without any subject, a substance may in its turn subsist dependently upon another substance, as accidents do; a mind may subsist after the manner of bodies, as in the Eucharist matter exists after the manner of minds; the latter may be impenetrable, as matter is penetrable in the Eucharist. Now, if by coming from the darkness of paganism to the light of the Gospel, we have learned the falsity of so many evident notions and of so many certain definitions, what will it be like when we shall come from the darkness of this life to the glory of heaven? Is it not very likely that we shall then learn the falsity of a thousand things which appear to us undeniable? Let us make a good use of the rashness of those who lived before the Gospel and who affirmed that some evident doctrines are true, the falsity of which has been revealed to us by the mysteries of our theology.

"I come now to morals. 1. It is evident that if it is possible, evil ought to be prevented, and that it is a sinful thing to permit it when it can be prevented. Nevertheless, our theology shows us that this is false; it teaches us that God does nothing unbecoming of his perfections when he permits all the disorders in the world which he might easily have prevented. 2. It is evident that a creature which does not exist cannot be an accomplice of an evil action. 3. And that it is unjust to punish that creature as an accomplice of that action. Nevertheless, our doctrine concerning original sin shows us the falsity of those evident truths. 4. It is evident that what is honest ought to be preferred to what is profitable, and that the more holy a being is, the less freedom it has to prefer what is profitable to what is honest. Nevertheless, our theologians tell us that since God chose between a world perfectly well regulated, adorned with all virtues, and a world like ours, where sin and disorder prevail, he preferred the latter to the former as being more consistent with the interest of his glory. If you should tell me that the duties of the Creator should not be measured by ours, you will fall into the net of your adversaries. They would have you there; the main thing they aim at is to prove that the absolute nature of things is unknown to us, and that we know only some relations they have one to another. We do not know, they say, whether sugar is sweet in itself; we only know that it seems sweet to us when we taste it. We do not know

whether a certain action is honest in itself and by its nature; we only believe that with respect to such a one, and by reason of certain circumstances, it has the appearance of honesty. But it is another thing in other respects and under other relations. See, therefore, how you expose yourself by telling them that the ideas we have of justice and honesty are liable to exception and are relative. Besides, I would have you observe that the more you raise the rights of God to the privilege of acting contrary to our ideas, the more you destroy the only means left to you to prove that there are bodies, namely, that God does not deceive us and that he would be doing so if the corporeal world did not exist. To show people a thing which does not exist outside their minds would be deceitful; but, they will answer you, *distinguo*—"I distinguish"; if a prince did so, *concedo*—"I grant it"; if God did it, *nego*—"I deny it"; for the rights of God are quite different from those of kings. Besides, if the exceptions you make to the principles of morality are based on the incomprehensible infinity of God, I can never be sure of anything; for I shall never be able to comprehend the whole extent of the rights of God. I conclude, therefore, that if truth were to be known by any mark, it would be by self-evidence; but self-evidence is no such mark, because it is compatible with falsities; therefore, etc."

The abbot, to whom this long discourse was directed, could hardly forbear interrupting it; he listened to it with great uneasiness, and when he perceived that everybody was silent, he fell into a rage against the Pyrrhonists and did not spare the abbot for having mentioned the objections which they take from the systems of divinity. This abbot replied modestly that he knew very well those objections were very inconsiderable and mere sophisms, but that it is reasonable that those who so much despise the Pyrrhonists should not be ignorant of the state of things. He went on and said, "you believed up to now that a Pyrrhonist could not puzzle you, answer me therefore; you are forty-five years of age, you do not doubt of it, and if there is anything that you are sure of, it is that you are the same person to whom the abbey of _____ was given two years ago. I am going to show you that you have no good reason to be sure of it; I argue from the principles of our theology. Your soul has been created; God must therefore at every moment renew its existence, for the conservation of creatures is a continued creation. How do you know that God did not permit this morning that your soul, which he had continued to create until then ever since the first moment of your life, to relapse into nothing? How do you know that he has not created another soul modified as yours was?[5] That new soul is that which you have now. Show me the contrary; let the company judge of my objection." A learned

5. That is to say, with the reminiscence which he would have reproduced if he had continued to create the soul of the Abbot.

theologian who was there answered and acknowledged that once creation was supposed, it was as easy for God to create a new soul at every moment as to reproduce the same, but that the ideas we have of his wisdom, and especially the light which his word affords us, are sufficient to assure us that we have the same numerical soul today which we had yesterday, the day before, etc. And he concluded that it was needless to dispute with the Pyrrhonists and that their sophisms could not easily be eluded by the mere force of reason, that they should be made sensible of the weakness of reason before all things, so that they may have recourse to a better guide, namely, faith.

David Hume, A *Treatise on Human Nature* (1739)[1]

Advertisement

My design in the present work is sufficiently explained in the Introduction. The reader must only observe that all the subjects I have there planned out to myself are not treated in these two volumes. The subjects of the understanding and passions make a complete chain of reasoning by themselves, and I was willing to take advantage of this natural division in order to try the taste of the public. If I have the good fortune to meet with success, I shall proceed to the examination of morals, politics, and criticism which will complete this *Treatise of Human Nature*. The approbation of the public I consider as the greatest reward of my labors, but am determined to regard its judgment, whatever it be, as my best instruction.

Introduction

Nothing is more usual and more natural for those who pretend to discover anything new to the world in philosophy and the sciences than to insinuate the praises of their own systems by decrying all those which have been advanced before them. And indeed were they content with lamenting that ignorance

1. [From *The Philosophical Works of David Hume*, T. H. Green and T. H. Grose, eds. (London: Longman's, Green, and Co., 1898), 4 vols., English, modified.]

which we still lie under in the most important questions that can come before the tribunal of human reason, there are few who have an acquaintance with the sciences that would not readily agree with them. It is easy for one of judgment and learning to perceive the weak foundation even of those systems which have obtained the greatest credit and have carried their pretensions highest to accurate and profound reasoning. Principles taken upon trust, consequences lamely deduced from them, want of coherence in the parts and of evidence in the whole, these are everywhere to be met with in the systems of the most eminent philosophers and seem to have drawn disgrace upon philosophy itself.

Nor is there required such profound knowledge to discover the present imperfect condition of the sciences, but even the rabble without doors may judge from the noise and clamor which they hear that all goes not well within. There is nothing which is not the subject of debate and in which men of learning are not of contrary opinions. The most trivial question does not escapes our controversy and in the most momentous we are not able to give any certain decision. Disputes are multiplied, as if everything was uncertain, and these disputes are managed with the greatest warmth, as if everything was certain. Amid all this bustle, it is not reason which carries the prize, but eloquence, and no man needs ever despair of gaining proselytes to the most extravagant hypothesis who has art enough to represent it in any favorable colors. The victory is not gained by the men at arms, who manage the pike and the sword, but by the trumpeters, drummers, and musicians of the army.

From hence, in my opinion, arises that common prejudice against metaphysical reasonings of all kinds, even among those who profess themselves scholars and have a just value for every other part of literature. By metaphysical reasonings, they do not understand those on any particular branch of science, but every kind of argument which is any way abstruse and requires some attention to be comprehended. We have so often lost our labor in such researches that we commonly reject them without hesitation and resolve, if we must forever be a prey to errors and delusions, that they shall at least be natural and entertaining. And, indeed, nothing but the most determined skepticism, along with a great degree of indolence, can justify this aversion to metaphysics. For, if truth be at all within the reach of human capacity, it is certain it must lie very deep and abstruse, and to hope we shall arrive at it without pains, while the greatest geniuses have failed with the utmost pains, must certainly be esteemed sufficiently vain and presumptuous. I pretend to no such advantage in the philosophy I am going to unfold and would esteem it a strong presumption against it, were it so very easy and obvious.

It is evident that all the sciences have a relation, greater or less, to human nature and that, however wide any of them may seem to run from it, they still return back by one passage or another. Even *mathematics, natural philosophy,* and *natural religion* are in some measure dependent on the science of MAN, since they lie under the cognizance of men and are judged of by their powers and faculties. It is impossible to tell what changes and improvements we might make in these sciences were we thoroughly acquainted with the extent and force of human understanding and could explain the nature of the ideas we employ and of the operations we perform in our reasonings. And these improvements are the more to be hoped for in natural religion, as it is not content with instructing us in the nature of superior powers but carries its views further, to their disposition to-

wards us and our duties towards them and, consequently, we ourselves are not only the beings that reason, but also one of the objects concerning which we reason.

If, therefore, the sciences of mathematics, natural philosophy, and natural religion have such a dependence on the knowledge of man, what may be expected in the other sciences, whose connection with human nature is more close and intimate? The sole end of logic is to explain the principles and operations of our reasoning faculty and the nature of our ideas; morals and criticism regard our tastes and sentiments; and politics consider men as united in society and dependent on each other. In these four sciences of *logic, morals, criticism,* and *politics* is comprehended almost everything which it can anyway import us to be acquainted with, or which can tend either to the improvement or ornament of the human mind.

Here, then, is the only expedient from which we can hope for success in our philosophical researches to leave the tedious lingering method which we have followed up to now and, instead of taking now and then a castle or village on the frontier, to march up directly to the capital or center of these sciences, to human nature itself, which, being once masters of, we may everywhere else hope for an easy victory. From this station we may extend our conquests over all those sciences which more intimately concern human life and may afterwards proceed at leisure to discover more fully those which are the objects of pure curiosity. There is no question of importance whose decision is not comprised in the science of man, and there is none which can be decided with any certainty before we become acquainted with that science. In pretending, therefore, to explain the principles of human nature, we in effect propose a complete system of the sciences, built on a foundation almost entirely new and the only one upon which they can stand with any security.

And as the science of man is the only solid foundation for the other sciences, so the only solid foundation we can give to this science itself must be laid on experience and observation. It is no astonishing reflection to consider that the application of experimental philosophy to moral subjects should come after that to natural [philosophy], at the distance of above a whole century, since we find in fact that there was about the same interval between the origins of these sciences, and that, reckoning from Thales to Socrates, the space of time is nearly equal to that between my Lord Bacon and some late philosophers[2] in England who have begun to put the science of man on a new footing and have engaged the attention and excited the curiosity of the public. So true it is that, however other nations may rival us in poetry and excel us in some other agreeable arts, the improvements in reason and philosophy can only be owing to a land of toleration and of liberty.

Nor ought we to think that this latter improvement in the science of man will do less honor to our native country than the former in natural philosophy, but ought rather to esteem it a greater glory upon account of the greater importance of that science as well as the necessity it lay under of such a reformation. For to me it seems evident that the essence of the mind being equally unknown to us with that of external bodies, it must be equally impossible to form any notion of its powers and qualities otherwise than from careful and exact experiments and the observation of those particular effects which result from its different circumstances and situations. And though we must endeavor to render all our principles as universal as possible by tracing up our experiments to the utmost and explaining all effects from the simplest and fewest causes, it is still certain we cannot go beyond experience, and any hypothesis that pretends to discover the ultimate original qualities of human nature ought at first to be rejected as presumptuous and chimerical.

I do not think a philosopher who would apply himself so earnestly to explaining the ultimate principles of the soul would show himself a great master in that very science of human nature which he pretends to explain or very knowing in what is naturally satisfactory to the mind of man. For nothing is more certain than that despair has almost the same effect upon us with enjoyment and that we are no sooner acquainted with the impossibility of satisfying any desire than the desire itself vanishes. When we see that we have arrived at the utmost extent of human

reason, we sit down contented, though we be perfectly satisfied in the main of our ignorance and perceive that we can give no reason for our most general and most refined principles, besides our experience of their reality, which is the reason of the mere vulgar and what it required no study at first to have discovered for the most particular and most extraordinary phenomenon. And as this impossibility of making any further progress is enough to satisfy the reader, so the writer may derive a more delicate satisfaction from the free confession of his ignorance and from his prudence in avoiding that error into which so many have fallen of imposing their conjectures and hypotheses on the world for the most certain principles. When this mutual contentment and satisfaction can be obtained between the master and scholar, I do not know what more we can require of our philosophy.

But if this impossibility of explaining ultimate principles should be esteemed a defect in the science of man, I will venture to affirm that it is a defect common to it with all the sciences and all the arts in which we can employ ourselves, whether they be such as are cultivated in the schools of the philosophers or practiced in the shops of the meanest artisans. None of them can go beyond experience or establish any principles which are not founded on that authority. Moral philosophy has, indeed, this peculiar disadvantage, which is not found in natural, that in collecting its experiments, it cannot make them purposely, with premeditation, and after such a manner as to satisfy itself concerning every particular difficulty which may arise. When I am at a loss to know the effects of one body upon another in any situation, I need only put them in that situation and observe what results from it. But should I endeavor to clear up, after the same manner, any doubt in moral philosophy by placing myself in the same case with that which I consider, it is evident this reflection and premeditation would so disturb the operation of my natural principles as must render it impossible to form any just conclusion from the phenomenon. We must, therefore, glean up our experiments in this science from a cautious observation of human life and take them as they appear in the common course of the world, by men's behavior in company, in affairs, and in their pleasures. Where experiments of this kind are judiciously

2. Mr. Locke, my Lord Shaftsbury, Dr. Mandeville, Mr. Hutchinson, Dr. Butler, etc.

collected and compared, we may hope to establish on them a science which will not be inferior in certainty, and will be much superior in utility, to any other of human comprehension.

Book I. Of the Understanding

Part I. Of Ideas, their Origin, Composition, Connection, Abstraction, etc.

Section 1: Of the Origin of Our Ideas

All the perceptions of the human mind resolve themselves into two distinct kinds, which I shall call *impressions* and *ideas*. The difference between these consists in the degrees of force and liveliness with which they strike upon the mind and make their way into our thought or consciousness. Those perceptions which enter with most force and violence we may name *impressions*, and under this name I comprehend all our sensations, passions, and emotions, as they make their first appearance in the soul. By *ideas* I mean the faint images of these in thinking and reasoning such as, for instance, are all the perceptions excited by the present discourse, excepting only those which arise from the sight and touch and excepting the immediate pleasure or uneasiness it may occasion. I believe it will not be very necessary to employ many words in explaining this distinction. Everyone of himself will readily perceive the difference between feeling and thinking. The common degrees of these are easily distinguished, though it is not impossible but, in particular instances, they may very nearly approach to each other. Thus, in sleep, in a fever, in madness, or in any very violent emotions of soul, our ideas may approach to our impressions—as, on the other hand, it sometimes happens that our impressions are so faint and low that we cannot distinguish them from our ideas. But, notwithstanding this near resemblance in a few instances, they are in general so very different that no one can make a scruple to rank them under distinct heads and assign to each a peculiar name to mark the difference.[3]

There is another division of our perceptions which it will be convenient to observe and which extends itself both to our impressions and ideas. This division is into *simple* and *complex*. Simple perceptions, or impressions and ideas, are such as admit of no distinction nor separation. The complex are the contrary to these and may be distinguished into parts. Though a particular color, taste, and smell are qualities all united together in this apple, it is easy to perceive they are not the same, but are at least distinguishable from each other.

Having by these divisions given an order and arrangement to our objects, we may now apply ourselves to consider with the more accuracy their qualities and relations. The first circumstance that strikes my eye is the great resemblance between our impressions and ideas in every other particular, except their degree of force and vivacity. The one seems to be, in a manner, the reflection of the other, so that all the perceptions of the mind are double and appear both as impressions and ideas. When I shut my eyes and think of my chamber, the ideas I form are exact representations of the impressions I felt; nor is there any circumstance of the one which is not to be found in the other. In running over my other perceptions, I find still the same resemblance and representation. Ideas and impressions appear always to correspond to each other. This circumstance seems to me remarkable and engages my attention for a moment.

Upon a more accurate survey I find I have been carried away too far by the first appearance, and that I must make use of the distinction of perceptions into *simple and complex*, to limit this general decision *that all our ideas and impressions are resembling*. I observe that many of our complex ideas never had impressions that corresponded to them, and that many of our complex impressions never are exactly copied in ideas. I can imagine to myself such a city as the

---

3. I here make use of these terms, *impression and idea*, in a sense different from what is usual, and I hope this liberty will be allowed me. Perhaps I rather restore the word *idea* to its original sense, from which Mr. Locke had perverted it in making it stand for all our perceptions. By the term of impression, I would not be understood to express the manner in which our lively perceptions are produced in the soul, but merely the perceptions themselves; for which there is no particular name either in the English or any other language that I know of.

New Jerusalem, whose pavement is gold and walls are rubies, though I never saw any such. I have seen *Paris*, but shall I affirm I can form such an idea of that city as will perfectly represent all its streets and houses in their real and just proportions?

I perceive, therefore, that though there is in general a great resemblance between our *complex* impressions and ideas, yet the rule is not universally true that they are exact copies of each other. We may next consider how the case stands with our *simple* perceptions. After the most accurate examination of which I am capable, I venture to affirm that the rule here holds without any exception, and that every simple idea has a simple impression which resembles it, and every simple impression a correspondent idea. That idea of red which we form in the dark and that impression which strikes our eyes in sunshine differ only in degree, not in nature. That the case is the same with all our simple impressions and ideas it is impossible to prove by a particular enumeration of them. Everyone may satisfy himself in this point by running over as many as he pleases. But if any one should deny this universal resemblance, I know no way of convincing him, but by desiring him to show a simple impression that has not a correspondent idea, or a simple idea that has not a correspondent impression. If he does not answer this challenge, as it is certain he cannot, we may, from his silence and our own observation, establish our conclusion.

Thus we find that all simple ideas and impressions resemble each other, and, as the complex are formed from them, we may affirm in general that these two species of perception are exactly correspondent. Having discovered this relation which requires no further examination, I am curious to find some other of their qualities. Let us consider how they stand with regard to their existence and which of the impressions and ideas are causes and which effects.

The *full* examination of this question is the subject of the present treatise, and therefore we shall here content ourselves with establishing one general proposition: *that all our simple ideas in their first appearance are derived from simple impressions, which are correspondent to them and which they exactly represent.*

In seeking for phenomena to prove this proposition, I find only those of two kinds, but in each kind the phenomena are obvious, numerous, and conclusive. I first make myself certain, by a new review of what I have already asserted, that every simple impression is attended with a correspondent idea and every simple idea with a correspondent impression. From this constant conjunction of resembling perceptions I immediately conclude that there is a great connection between our correspondent impressions and ideas and that the existence of the one has a considerable influence upon that of the other. Such a constant conjunction, in such an infinite number of instances, can never arise from chance, but clearly proves a dependence of the impressions on the ideas or of the ideas on the impressions. That I may know on which side this dependence lies, I consider the order of their *first appearance* and find, by constant experience, that the simple impressions always take the precedence of their correspondent ideas, but never appear in the contrary order. To give a child an idea of scarlet or orange, of sweet or bitter, I present the objects, or, in other words, convey to him these impressions, but proceed not so absurdly as to endeavor to produce the impressions by exciting the ideas. Our ideas, upon their appearance, produce not their correspondent impressions, nor do we perceive any color or feel any sensation merely upon thinking of them. On the other hand, we find that any impression, either of the mind or body, is constantly followed by an idea which resembles it and is only different in the degrees of force and liveliness. The constant conjunction of our resembling perceptions is a convincing proof that the one are the causes of the other, and this priority of the impressions is an equal proof that our impressions are the causes of our ideas, not our ideas of our impressions.

To confirm this, I consider another plain and convincing phenomenon, which is that wherever, by any accident, the faculties which give rise to any impressions are obstructed in their operations, as when one is born blind or deaf, not only the impressions are lost, but also their correspondent ideas, so that there never appear in the mind the least traces of either of them. Nor is this only true where the organs of sensation are entirely destroyed, but likewise where they have never been put in action to produce a particular impression. We cannot form to ourselves a just idea of the taste of a pineapple without having actually tasted it.

There is, however, one contradictory phenomenon which may prove that it is not absolutely impossible for ideas to go before their correspondent impressions. I believe it will readily be allowed that the several distinct ideas of colors which enter by the eyes, or those of sounds which are conveyed by the hearing, are really different from each other, though, at the same time, resembling. Now, if this is true of different colors, it must be no less so of the different shades of the same color, that each of them produces a distinct idea independent of the rest. For if this should be denied, it is possible, by the continual gradation of shades, to run a color insensibly into what is most remote from it; and if you will not allow any of the means to be different, you cannot, without absurdity, deny the extremes to be the same. Suppose, therefore, a person to have enjoyed his sight for thirty years and to have become perfectly well acquainted with colors of all kinds, excepting one particular shade of blue, for instance, which it never has been his fortune to meet with. Let all the different shades of that color, except that single one, be placed before him, descending gradually from the deepest to the lightest; it is plain that he will perceive a blank where that shade is wanting and will be sensible that there is a greater distance in that place between the contiguous colors than in any other. Now I ask whether it is possible for him, from his own imagination, to supply this deficiency and raise up to himself the idea of that particular shade, though it had never been conveyed to him by his senses? I believe there are few but will be of opinion that he can, and this may serve as a proof that the simple ideas are not always derived from the correspondent impressions, though the instance is so particular and singular that it is scarcely worth our observing and does not merit that we should alter our general maxim for it alone.

But, besides this exception, it may not be amiss to remark on this topic that the principle of the priority of impressions to ideas must be understood with another limitation, namely, that as our ideas are images of our impressions, so we can form secondary ideas which are images of the primary, as appears from this very reasoning concerning them. This is not, properly speaking, an exception to the rule so much as an explanation of it. Ideas produce the images of themselves in new ideas, but as the first ideas are supposed to be derived from impressions, it still remains true that all our simple ideas proceed, either mediately or immediately, from their correspondent impressions.

This, then, is the first principle I establish in the science of human nature, nor ought we to despise it because of the simplicity of its appearance. For it is remarkable that the present question concerning the precedence of our impressions or ideas is the same with what has made so much noise in other terms, when it has been disputed whether there are any *innate ideas* or whether all ideas are derived from sensation and reflection. We may observe that, in order to prove the ideas of extension and color not to be innate, philosophers do nothing but show that they are conveyed by our senses. To prove the ideas of passion and desire not to be innate, they observe that we have a preceding experience of these emotions in ourselves. Now, if we carefully examine these arguments, we shall find that they prove nothing but that ideas are preceded by other more lively perceptions, from which they are derived and which they represent. I hope this clear stating of the question will remove all disputes concerning it, and will render this principle of more use in our reasonings than it seems to have been up to now.

Section 2: Division of the Subject

Since it appears that our simple impressions are prior to their correspondent ideas and that the exceptions are very rare, method seems to require we should examine our impressions before we consider our ideas. Impressions may be divided into two kinds, those of *sensation* and those of *reflection*. The first kind arises in the soul originally from unknown causes. The second is derived in a great measure from our ideas, and that in the following order. An impression first strikes upon the senses and makes us perceive heat or cold, thirst or hunger, pleasure or pain of some kind or other. Of this impression there is a copy taken by the mind, which remains after the impression ceases, and this we call an idea. This idea of pleasure or pain, when it returns upon the soul, produces the new impressions of desire and aversion, hope and fear, which may properly be called impressions of reflection, because derived from it. These again are copied by the memory and imagination and become ideas—which, perhaps, in their turn, give rise to other impressions and ideas, so that the impressions of reflection are only antecedent to their correspondent ideas, but posterior to those of sensation and derived from them. The examination of our sensations belongs more to anatomists and natural philosophers than to moral, and, therefore, shall not at present be entered upon. And, as the impressions of reflection—namely, passions, desires, and emotions, which principally deserve our attention—arise mostly from ideas, it will be necessary to reverse that method which at first sight seems most natural and, in order to explain the nature and principles of the human mind, give a particular account of ideas, before we proceed to impressions. For this reason, I have here chosen to begin with ideas.

Section 3: Of the Ideas of the Memory and Imagination

We find by experience that when any impression has been present with the mind, it again makes its appearance there as an idea, and this it may do after two different ways: either when, in its new appearance, it retains a considerable degree of its first vivacity and is somewhat intermediate between an impression and an idea, or when it entirely loses that vivacity and is a perfect idea. The faculty by which we repeat our impressions in the first manner is called the *memory*, and the other the *imagination*. It is evident at first sight that the ideas of the memory are much more lively and strong than those of the imagination and that the former faculty paints its objects in more distinct colors than any which are employed by the latter. When we remember any past event, the idea of it flows in upon the mind in a forcible manner, whereas in the imagination the perception is faint and languid and cannot, without difficulty, be preserved by the mind steady and uniform for any consid-

erable time. Here, then, is a sensible difference between one species of ideas and another. But of this more fully hereafter.[4]

There is another difference between these two kinds of ideas, which is no less evident, namely, that though neither the ideas of the memory nor imagination, neither the lively nor faint ideas, can make their appearance in the mind unless their correspondent impressions have gone before to prepare the way for them, yet the imagination is not restrained to the same order and form with the original impressions, while the memory is in a manner tied down in that respect, without any power of variation.

It is evident that the memory preserves the original form in which its objects were presented and that wherever we depart from it in recollecting anything, it proceeds from some defect or imperfection in that faculty. An historian may, perhaps, for the more convenient carrying on of his narration, relate an event before another to which it was in fact posterior, but then he takes notice of this disorder, if he be exact, and, by that means, replaces the idea in its due position. It is the same case in our recollection of those places and persons with which we were formerly acquainted. The chief exercise of the memory is not to preserve the simple ideas, but their order and position. In short, this principle is supported by such a number of common and vulgar phenomena that we may spare ourselves the trouble of insisting on it any further.

The same evidence follows us in our second principle, *of the liberty of the imagination to transpose and change its ideas*. The fables we meet with in poems and romances put this entirely out of question. Nature there is totally confounded, and nothing mentioned but winged horses, fiery dragons, and monstrous giants. Nor will this liberty of the fancy appear strange when we consider that all our ideas are copied from our impressions and that there are not any two impressions which are perfectly inseparable. Not to mention that this is an evident consequence of the division of ideas into simple and complex. Wherever the imagination perceives a difference among ideas, it can easily produce a separation.

4. Part III, sec. 5.

Section 4: Of the Connection or Association of Ideas

As all simple ideas may be separated by the imagination and may be united again in what form it pleases, nothing would be more unaccountable than the operations of that faculty, were it not guided by some universal principles which render it in some measure uniform with itself in all times and places. Were ideas entirely loose and unconnected, chance alone would join them, and it is impossible the same simple ideas should fall regularly into complex ones (as they commonly do) without some bond of union among them, some associating quality, by which one idea naturally introduces another. This uniting principle among ideas is not to be considered as an inseparable connection, for that has been already excluded from the imagination—nor yet are we to conclude that without it the mind cannot join two ideas, for nothing is more free than that faculty—but we are only to regard it as a gentle force which commonly prevails and is the cause why, among other things, languages so nearly correspond to each other. Nature, in a manner, pointing out to everyone those simple ideas which are most proper to be united into a complex one. The qualities from which this association arises and by which the mind is, after this manner, conveyed from one idea to another are three, namely, *resemblance, contiguity* in time or place, and *cause* and *effect.*

I believe it will not be very necessary to prove that these qualities produce an association among ideas and, upon the appearance of one idea, naturally introduce another. It is plain that, in the course of our thinking and in the constant revolution of our ideas, our imagination runs easily from one idea to any other that *resembles* it and that this quality alone is, to the fancy, a sufficient bond and association. It is likewise evident that as the senses, in changing their objects, are necessitated to change them regularly and take them as they lie *contiguous* to each other, the imagination must, by long custom, acquire the same method of thinking and run along the parts of space and time in conceiving its objects. As to the connection that is made by the relation of *cause and effect*, we shall have occasion afterwards to examine it to the bottom and therefore shall not at present

insist upon it. It is sufficient to observe that there is no relation which produces a stronger connection in the fancy and makes one idea more readily recall another than the relation of cause and effect between their objects.

That we may understand the full extent of these relations, we must consider that two objects are connected together in the imagination not only when the one is immediately resembling, contiguous to, or the cause of the other but also when there is interposed between them a third object which bears to both of them any of these relations. This may be carried on to a great length, though at the same time we may observe that each remove considerably weakens the relation. Cousins in the fourth degree are connected by *causation,* if I may be allowed to use that term, but not so closely as brothers, much less as child and parent. In general, we may observe that all the relations of blood depend upon cause and effect and are esteemed near or remote according to the number of connecting causes interposed between the persons.

Of the three relations above mentioned, this of causation is the most extensive. Two objects may be considered as placed in this relation when one is the cause of any of the actions or motions of the other as well as when the former is the cause of the existence of the latter. For as that action or motion is nothing but the object itself, considered in a certain light, and as the object continues the same in all its different situations, it is easy to imagine how such an influence of objects upon one another may connect them in the imagination.

We may carry this further and remark not only that two objects are connected by the relation of cause and effect when the one produces a motion or any action in the other but also when it has a power of producing it. And this we may observe to be the source of all the relations of interest and duty by which men influence each other in society and are placed in the ties of government and subordination. A master is such a one as, by his situation, arising either from force or agreement, has a power of directing in certain particulars the actions of another whom we call servant. A judge is one who, in all disputed cases, can fix by his opinion the possession or property of anything between any members of the society. When a person is possessed of any power, there is no more required to convert it into action but the exertion of the will, and *that* in every case is considered as possible, and in many as probable, especially in the case of authority, where the obedience of the subject is a pleasure and advantage to the superior.

These are, therefore, the principles of union or cohesion among our simple ideas, and in the imagination [they] supply the place of that inseparable connection by which they are united in our memory. Here is a kind of *attraction* which in the mental world will be found to have as extraordinary effects as in the natural and to. show itself in as many and as various forms. Its effects are every where conspicuous, but as to its causes, they are mostly unknown and must be resolved into *original* qualities of human nature, which I pretend not to explain. Nothing is more requisite for a true philosopher than to restrain the intemperate desire of searching into causes and, having established any doctrine upon a sufficient number of experiments, rest contented with that, when he sees a further examination would lead him into obscure and uncertain speculations. In that case his inquiry would be much better employed in examining the effects than the causes of his principle.

Among the effects of this union or association of ideas, there are none more remarkable than those complex ideas which are the common subjects of our thoughts and reasoning and generally arise from some principle of union among our simple ideas. These complex ideas may be divided into *relations*, *modes*, and *substances*. We shall briefly examine each of these in order and shall subjoin some considerations concerning our *general* and *particular* ideas, before we leave the present subject, which may be considered as the elements of this philosophy.

Section 5: Of Relations

The word *relation* is commonly used in two senses considerably different from each other. Either for that quality by which two ideas are connected together in the imagination and the one naturally introduces the other, after the manner explained above; or for that particular circumstance in which, even upon the arbitrary union of two ideas in the fancy, we may think proper to compare them. In common language, the former is always the sense in which we use the word relation, and it is only in philosophy that we extend it to mean any particular subject of comparison, without a connecting principle. Thus, distance will be allowed by philosophers to be a true relation, because we acquire an idea of it by the comparing of objects: but in a common way we say *that nothing can be more distant than such or such things from each other, nothing can have less relation*, as if distance and relation were incompatible.

It may, perhaps, be esteemed an endless task to enumerate all those qualities which make objects admit of comparison and by which the ideas of *philosophical* relation are produced. But if we diligently consider them we shall find that without difficulty they may be comprised under seven general heads which may be considered as the sources of all *philosophical* relation.

1. The first is *resemblance:* And this is a relation without which no philosophical relation can exist, since no objects will admit of comparison but what have some degree of resemblance. But though resemblance be necessary to all philosophical relation, it does not follow that it always produces a connection or association of ideas. When a quality becomes very general and is common to a great many individuals, it leads not the mind directly to any one of them, but by presenting at once too great a choice does thereby prevent the imagination from fixing on any single object.

2. *Identity* may be esteemed a second species of relation. This relation I here consider as applied in its strictest sense to constant and unchangeable objects, without examining the nature and foundation of personal identity, which shall find its place afterwards. Of all relations the most universal is that of identity, being common to every being whose existence has any duration.

3. After identity the most universal and comprehensive relations are those of *space* and *time*, which are the sources of an infinite number of

comparisons, such as *distant, contiguous, above, below, before, after,* etc.

4. All those objects which admit of *quantity* or *number* may be compared in that particular, which is another very fertile source of relation.

5. When any two objects possess the same *quality* in common, the *degrees* in which they possess it form a fifth species of relation. Thus, of two objects which are both heavy, the one may be either of greater or less weight than the other. Two colors that are of the same kind may yet be of different shades and in that respect admit of comparison.

6. The relation of *contrariety* may at first sight be regarded as an exception to the rule that *no relation of any kind can subsist without some degree of resemblance.* But let us consider that no two ideas are in themselves contrary, except those of existence and non-existence, which are plainly resembling, as implying both of them an idea of the object, though the latter excludes the object from all times and places in which it is supposed not to exist.

7. All other objects, such as fire and water, heat and cold, are only found to be contrary from experience and from the contrariety of their *causes* or *effects,* which relation of cause and effect is a seventh philosophical relation as well as a natural one. The resemblance implied in this relation shall be explained afterwards.

It might naturally be expected that I should join *difference* to the other relations, but that I consider rather as a negation of relation than as anything real or positive. Difference is of two kinds, as opposed either to identity or resemblance. The first is called a difference of *number,* the other of *kind.*

Section 6: Of Modes and Substances

I would gladly ask those philosophers who found so much of their reasonings on the distinction of substance and accident and imagine we have clear ideas of each, whether the idea of *substance* be derived from the impressions of sensation or reflection? If it be conveyed to us by our senses, I ask, which of them, and after what manner? If it be perceived by the eyes, it must be a color; if by the ears, a sound; if by the palate, a taste; and so of the other senses. But I believe none will assert that substance is either a color, or sound, or a taste. The idea of substance must, therefore, be derived from an impression of reflection, if it really exist. But the impressions of reflection resolve themselves into our passions and emotions, none of which can possibly represent a substance. We have, therefore, no idea of substance distinct from that of a collection of particular qualities, nor have we any other meaning when we either talk or reason concerning it.

The idea of a substance, as well as that of a mode, is nothing but a collection of simple ideas that are united by the imagination and have a particular name assigned them by which we are able to recall, either to ourselves or others, that collection. But the difference between these ideas consists in this, that the particular qualities which form a substance are commonly referred to an unknown *something* in which they are supposed to inhere, or granting this fiction should not take place, are at least supposed to be closely and inseparably connected by the relations of contiguity and causation. The effect of this is that whatever new simple quality we discover to have the same connection with the rest, we immediately comprehend it among them, even though it did not enter into the first conception of the substance. Thus our idea of gold may at first be a yellow color, weight, malleableness, fusibility, but upon the discovery of its dissolubility in *aqua regia,* we join that to the other qualities and suppose it to belong to the substance as much as if its idea had from the beginning made a part of the compound one. The principle of union being regarded as the chief part of the complex idea gives entrance to whatever quality afterwards occurs and is equally comprehended by it, as are the others which first presented themselves.

That this cannot take place in modes is evident from considering their nature. The simple ideas of which modes are formed either represent qualities which are not united by contiguity and causation, but are dispersed in different subjects or, if they be all united together, the uniting principle is not regarded as the foundation of the complex idea. The idea of a dance is an instance of the first kind of modes, that of beauty of the second. The reason is obvious why such complex ideas cannot receive any new idea without changing the name which distinguishes the mode.

Section 7: Of Abstract Ideas

A very material question has been started concerning *abstract* or *general* ideas, *whether they be general or particular in the mind's conception of them*. A great philosopher[5] has disputed the received opinion in this particular and has asserted that all general ideas are nothing but particular ones annexed to a certain term which gives them a more extensive signification and makes them recall upon occasion other individuals which are similar to them. As I look upon this to be one of the greatest and most valuable discoveries that has been made of late years in the republic of letters, I shall here endeavor to confirm it by some arguments which I hope will put it beyond all doubt and controversy.

It is evident that, in forming most of our general ideas, if not all of them, we abstract from every particular degree of quantity and quality, and that an object does not cease to be of any particular species on account of every small alteration in its extension, duration, and other properties. It may, therefore, be thought that here is a plain dilemma that decides concerning the nature of those abstract ideas which have afforded so much speculation to philosophers. The abstract idea of a man represents men of all sizes and all qualities, which, it is concluded it cannot do but either by representing at once all possible sizes and all possible qualities or by representing no particular one at all. Now, it having been esteemed absurd to defend the former proposition as implying an infinite capacity in the mind, it has been commonly inferred in favor of the latter, and our abstract ideas have been supposed to represent no particular degree either of quantity or quality. But that this inference is erroneous, I shall endeavor to make appear, *first*,

5. Dr. Berkeley.

by proving that it is utterly impossible to conceive any quantity or quality without forming a precise notion of its degrees; and, *secondly*, by showing that though the capacity of the mind be not infinite, yet we can at once form a notion of all possible degrees of quantity and quality in such a manner at least as, however imperfect, may serve all the purposes of reflection and conversation.

To begin with the first proposition *that the mind cannot form any notion of quantity or quality without forming a precise notion of degrees of each*, we may prove this by the three following arguments. First, we have observed that whatever objects are different are distinguishable and that whatever objects are distinguishable are separable by the thought and imagination. And we may here add that these propositions are equally true in the *inverse*, and that whatever objects are separable are also distinguishable, and that whatever objects are distinguishable are also different. For how is it possible we can separate what is not distinguishable or distinguish what is not different? In order, therefore, to know whether abstraction implies a separation, we need only consider it in this view and examine whether all the circumstances which we abstract from in our general ideas be such as are distinguishable and different from those which we retain as essential parts of them. But it is evident at first sight that the precise length of a line is not different nor distinguishable from the line itself, nor the precise degree of any quality from the quality. These ideas, therefore, admit no more of separation than they do of distinction and difference. They are consequently conjoined with each other in the conception, and the general idea of a line, notwithstanding all our abstractions and refinements, has, in its appearance in the mind, a precise degree of quantity and quality, however it may be made to represent others which have different degrees of both.

Secondly, it is confessed that no object can appear to the senses, or in other words that no impression can become present to the mind, without being determined in its degrees both of quantity and quality. The confusion, in which impressions are sometimes involved, proceeds only from their faintness and unsteadiness, not from any capacity in the mind to receive any impression which in its real existence has no particular degree nor proportion. That is a contradiction in terms and even implies the flattest of all contradictions, namely, that it is possible for the same thing both to be and not to be.

Now, since all ideas are derived from impressions and are nothing but copies and representations of them, whatever is true of the one must be acknowledged concerning the other. Impressions and ideas differ only in their strength and vivacity. The foregoing conclusion is not founded on any particular degree of vivacity. It cannot, therefore, be affected by any variation in that particular. An idea is a weaker impression, and as a strong impression must necessarily have a determinate quantity and quality, the case must be the same with its copy or representative.

Thirdly, it is a principle generally received in philosophy that everything in nature is individual and that it is utterly absurd to suppose a triangle really existent which has no precise proportion of sides and angles. If this, therefore, be absurd *in fact and reality*, it must also be absurd *in idea*, since nothing of which we can form a clear and distinct idea is absurd and impossible. But to form the idea of an object and to form an idea simply is the same thing, the reference of the idea to an object being an extraneous denomination of which in itself it bears no mark or character. Now, as it is impossible to form an idea of an object that is possessed of quantity and quality and yet is possessed of no precise degree of either, it follows that there is an equal impossibility of forming an idea that is not limited and confined in both these particulars. Abstract ideas are, therefore, in themselves individual, however they may become general in their representation. The image in the mind is only that of a particular object, though the application of it in our reasoning be the same as if it were universal.

This application of ideas beyond their nature proceeds from our collecting all their possible degrees of quantity and quality in such an imperfect manner as may serve the purposes of life, which is the second proposition I proposed to explain. When we have found a resemblance among several objects that often occur to us, we apply the same name to all of them, whatever differences we may observe in the degrees of their quantity and quality and whatever other differences may appear among them. After we have acquired a custom of this kind, the hearing of that name revives the idea of one of these objects and makes the imagination conceive it with all its particular circumstances and proportions. But as the same word is supposed to have been frequently applied to other individuals that are different in many respects from that idea which is immediately present to the mind, the word not being able to revive the idea of all these individuals only touches the soul, if I may be allowed so to speak, and revives that custom which we have acquired by surveying them. They are not really and in fact present to the mind but only in power, nor do we draw them all out distinctly in the imagination, but keep ourselves in a readiness to survey any of them as we may be prompted by a present design or necessity. The word raises up an individual idea, along with a certain custom, and that custom produces any other individual one for which we may have occasion. But as the production of all the ideas to which the name may be applied is in most cases impossible, we abridge that work by a more partial consideration and find but few inconveniences to arise in our reasoning from that abridgment.

For this is one of the most extraordinary circumstances in the present affair, that after the mind has produced an individual idea upon which we reason, the attendant custom, revived by the general or abstract term, readily suggests any other individual, if by chance we form any reasoning that does not agree with it. Thus, should we mention the word triangle and form the idea of a particular equilateral one to correspond to it, and should we afterwards assert *that the three angles of a triangle are equal to each other,* the other individuals of a scalenum and isosceles, which we overlooked at first, immediately crowd in upon us and make us perceive the falsehood of this proposition, though it be true with relation to that idea which we had formed. If the mind does not suggest always these ideas upon occasion, it proceeds from some imperfection in its faculties, and such a one as is often the source of false reasoning and sophistry. But this is principally the case with those ideas which are abstruse and compounded. On other occasions the custom is more entire and it is seldom we run into such errors.

No, so entire is the custom that the very same idea

may be annexed to several different words and may be employed in different reasonings without any danger of mistake. Thus the idea of an equilateral triangle of an inch perpendicular may serve us in talking of a figure, of a rectilinear figure, of a regular figure, of a triangle, and of an equilateral triangle. All these terms, therefore, are in this case attended with the same idea, but as they are wont to be applied in a greater or lesser compass, they excite their particular habits and thereby keep the mind in a readiness to observe that no conclusion be formed contrary to any ideas which are usually comprised under them.

Before those habits have become entirely perfect, perhaps the mind may not be content with forming the idea of only one individual, but may run over several, in order to make itself comprehend its own meaning and the compass of that collection which it intends to express by the general term. That we may fix the meaning of the word *figure*, we may revolve in our mind the ideas of circles, squares, parallelograms, triangles of different sizes and proportions, and may not rest on one image or idea. However this may be, it is certain *that* we form the idea of individuals whenever we use any general term, *that* we seldom or never can exhaust these individuals, and *that* those which remain are only represented by means of that habit by which we recall them whenever any present occasion requires it. This, then, is the nature of our abstract ideas and general terms, and it is after this manner we account for the foregoing paradox *that some ideas are particular in their nature, but general in their representation*. A particular idea becomes general by being annexed to a general term, that is, to a term which, from a customary conjunction, has a relation to many other particular ideas and readily recalls them in the imagination.

The only difficulty that can remain on this subject must be with regard to that custom which so readily recalls every particular idea for which we may have occasion and is excited by any word or sound to which we commonly annex it. The most proper method, in my opinion, of giving a satisfactory explication of this act of the mind is by producing other instances which are analogous to it and other principles which facilitate its operation. To explain the ultimate causes of our mental actions is impossible. It is sufficient if we can give any satisfactory account of them from experience and analogy.

First, then, I observe that when we mention any great number, such as a thousand, the mind has generally no adequate idea of it, but only a power of producing such an idea by its adequate idea of the decimals under which the number is comprehended. This imperfection, however, in our ideas is never felt in our reasonings, which seems to be an instance parallel to the present one of universal ideas.

Secondly, we have several instances of habits which may be revived by one single word, as when a person who has, by rote, any periods of a discourse or any number of verses will be put in remembrance of the whole which he is at a loss to recollect by that single word or expression with which they begin.

Thirdly, I believe everyone who examines the situation of his mind in reasoning will agree with me that we do not annex distinct and complete ideas to every term we make use of and that in talking of *government, church, negotiation, conquest*, we seldom spread out in our minds all the simple ideas of which these complex ones are composed. It is, however, observable that notwithstanding this imperfection, we may avoid talking nonsense on these subjects and may perceive any repugnance among the ideas as well as if we had a full comprehension of them. Thus, if instead of saying *that in war the weaker have always recourse to negotiation*, we should say *that they have always recourse to conquest*, the custom which we have acquired of attributing certain relations to ideas still follows the words and makes us immediately perceive the absurdity of that proposition, in the same manner as one particular idea may serve us in reasoning concerning other ideas, however different from it in several circumstances.

Fourthly, as the individuals are collected together and placed under a general term with a view to that resemblance which they bear to each other, this relation must facilitate their entrance in the imagination and make them be suggested more readily upon occasion. And, indeed, if we consider the common progress of the thought, either in reflection or conversation, we shall find great reason to be satisfied in this particular. Nothing is more admirable than the readiness with which the imagination suggests its ideas and presents them at the very instant in which they become necessary or useful. The fancy runs from one end of the universe to the other in collecting those ideas which belong to any subject. One would think the whole intellectual world of ideas was at once subjected to our view and that we did nothing but pick out such as were most proper for our purpose. There may not, however, be any present besides those very ideas that are thus collected by a kind of magical faculty in the soul which, though it be always most perfect in the greatest geniuses and is properly what we call a genius, is, however, inexplicable by the utmost efforts of human understanding.

Perhaps these four reflections may help to remove all difficulties to the hypothesis I have proposed concerning abstract ideas so contrary to that which has prevailed in philosophy up to now. But to tell the truth, I place my chief confidence in what I have already proved concerning the impossibility of general ideas according to the common method of explaining them. We must certainly seek some new system on this head and there plainly is none besides what I have proposed. If ideas be particular in their nature and at the same time finite in their number, it is only by custom they can become general in their representation and contain an infinite number of other ideas under them.

Before I leave this subject, I shall employ the same principles to explain that *distinction of reason* which is so much talked of and is so little understood in the schools. Of this kind is the distinction between figure and the body figured, motion and the body moved. The difficulty of explaining this distinction arises from the principle above explained *that all ideas which are different are separable*. For it follows from thence that if the figure be different from the body, their ideas must be separable as well as distinguishable; if they be not different, their ideas can neither be separable nor distinguishable. What then is meant by a distinction of reason, since it implies neither a difference nor separation?

To remove this difficulty, we must have recourse to the foregoing explication of abstract ideas. It is certain that the mind would never have dreamed of distinguishing a figure from the body figured, as being in reality neither distinguishable, nor different, nor

separable, did it not observe that even in this simplicity there might be contained many different resemblances and relations. Thus, when a globe of white marble is presented, we receive only the impression of a white color disposed in a certain form, nor are we able to separate and distinguish the color from the form. But observing afterwards a globe of black marble and a cube of white and comparing them with our former object, we find two separate resemblances in what formerly seemed and really is perfectly inseparable. After a little more practice of this kind, we begin to distinguish the figure from the color by a *distinction of reason*, that is, we consider the figure and color together, since they are, in effect, the same and undistinguishable, but still view them in different aspects, according to the resemblances of which they are susceptible. When we would consider only the figure of the globe of white marble, we form in reality an idea both of the figure and color, but tacitly carry our eye to its resemblance with the globe of black marble and in the same manner, when we would consider its color only, we turn our view to its resemblance with the cube of white marble. By this means we accompany our ideas with a kind of reflection of which custom renders us, in a great measure, insensible. A person who desires us to consider the figure of a globe of white marble without thinking on its color, desires an impossibility, but his meaning is that we should consider the color and figure together, but still keep in our eye the resemblance to the globe of black marble or that to any other globe of whatever color or substance.

Part II. Of the Ideas of Space and Time

Section 6: Of the Ideas of Existence and of External Existence

It may not be amiss, before we leave this subject, to explain the ideas of *existence* and of *external existence*, which have their difficulties, as well as the ideas of space and time. By this means we shall be the better prepared for the examination of knowledge and probability, when we understand perfectly all those particular ideas which may enter into our reasoning.

There is no impression nor idea of any kind of which we have any consciousness or memory that is not conceived as existent, and it is evident that, from this consciousness, the most perfect idea and assurance of *being* is derived. From hence we may form a dilemma, the most clear and conclusive that can be imagined, namely, that since we never remember any idea or impression without attributing existence to it, the idea of existence must either be derived from a distinct impression conjoined with every perception or object of our thought, or must be the very same with the idea of the perception or object.

As this dilemma is an evident consequence of the principle that every idea arises from a similar impression, so our decision between the propositions of the dilemma is no more doubtful. So far from there being any distinct impression attending every impression and every idea that I do not think there are any two distinct impressions which are inseparably conjoined. Though certain sensations may at one time be united, we quickly find they admit of a separation and may be presented apart. And thus, though every impression and idea we remember be considered as existent, the idea of existence is not derived from any particular impression.

The idea of existence, then, is the very same with the idea of what we conceive to be existent. To reflect on anything simply and to reflect on it as existent are nothing different from each other. That idea, when conjoined with the idea of any object, makes no addition to it. Whatever we conceive, we conceive to be existent. Any idea we please to form is the idea of a being, and the idea of a being is any idea we please to form.

Whoever opposes this must necessarily point out that distinct impression from which the idea of entity is derived and must prove that this impression is inseparable from every perception we believe to be existent. This we may, without hesitation, conclude to be impossible.

Our foregoing reasoning[6] concerning the *distinction* of ideas, without any real *difference*, will not here serve us in any stead. That kind of distinction is founded on the different resemblances which the same simple idea may have to several different ideas. But no object can be presented resembling some object with respect to its existence and different from others in the same particular, since every object that is presented must necessarily be existent.

A like reasoning will account for the idea of *external existence*. We may observe that it is universally allowed by philosophers, and is besides pretty obvious of itself, that nothing is ever really present with the mind but its perceptions or impressions and ideas and that external objects become known to us only by those perceptions they occasion. To hate, to love, to think, to feel, to see; all this is nothing but to perceive.

Now since nothing is ever present to the mind but perceptions, and since all ideas are derived from something antecedently present to the mind, it follows that it is impossible for us so much as to conceive or form an idea of anything specifically different from ideas and impressions. Let us fix our attention out of ourselves as much as possible, let us chase our imagination to the heavens or to the utmost limits of the universe, we never really advance a step beyond ourselves, nor can conceive any kind of existence but those perceptions which have appeared in that narrow compass. This is the universe of the imagination, nor have we any idea but what is there produced.

The furthest we can go towards a conception of external objects, when supposed *specifically* different from our perceptions, is to form a relative idea of them without pretending to comprehend the related objects. Generally speaking, we do not suppose them specifically different, but only attribute to them different relations, connections, and durations. But of this more fully hereafter.[7]

Part III. Of Knowledge and Probability

Section 1: Of Knowledge

There are seven different kinds of philosophical relation,[8] namely, *resemblance, identity, relations of time and place, proportion in quantity or number, degrees in any quality, contrariety, and causation.* These relations may be divided into two classes: into such as depend entirely on the ideas which we compare together and such as may be changed without any

---

6. Part I, sec. 7.

7. Part IV, sec. 2.
8. Part I, sec. 5.

change in the ideas. It is from the idea of a triangle that we discover the relation of equality which its three angles bear to two right ones, and this relation is invariable as long as our idea remains the same. On the contrary, the relations of *contiguity* and *distance* between two objects may be changed merely by an alteration of their place, without any change on the objects themselves or on their ideas, and the place depends on a hundred different accidents which cannot be foreseen by the mind. It is the same case with *identity* and *causation*. Two objects, though perfectly resembling each other and even appearing in the same place at different times, may be numerically different and, as the power by which one object produces another is never discoverable merely from their idea, it is evident that *cause* and *effect* are relations of which we receive information from experience and not from any abstract reasoning or reflection. There is no single phenomenon, even the most simple, which can be accounted for from the qualities of the objects as they appear to us or which we could foresee without the help of our memory and experience.

It appears therefore that of these seven philosophical relations, there remain only four which, depending solely upon ideas, can be the objects of knowledge and certainty. These four are *resemblance, contrariety, degrees in quality, and proportions in quantity or number*. Three of these relations are discoverable at first sight and fall more properly under the province of intuition than demonstration. When any objects *resemble* each other, the resemblance will at first strike the eye, or rather the mind, and seldom requires a second examination. The case is the same with *contrariety* and with the *degrees* of any *quality*. No one can once doubt but existence and non-existence destroy each other and are perfectly incompatible and contrary. And though it be impossible to judge exactly of the degrees of any quality, such as color, taste, heat, cold, when the difference between them is very small, yet it is easy to decide that any of them is superior or inferior to another when their difference is considerable. And this decision we always pronounce at first sight, without any inquiry or reasoning.

We might proceed after the same manner in fixing the *proportions* of *quantity* or *number* and might at one view observe a superiority or inferiority between any numbers or figures, especially where the difference is very great and remarkable. As to equality or any exact proportion, we can only guess at it from a single consideration, except in very short numbers or very limited portions of extension which are comprehended in an instant and where we perceive an impossibility of falling into any considerable error. In all other cases we must settle the proportions with some liberty or proceed in a more *artificial* manner.

I have already observed that geometry, or the *art* by which we fix the proportions of figures, though it much excels the loose judgments of the senses and imagination both in universality and exactness, yet never attains a perfect precision and exactness. Its first principles are still drawn from the general appearance of the objects, and that appearance can never afford us any security when we examine the prodigious minuteness of which nature is susceptible. Our ideas seem to give a perfect assurance that no two right lines can have a common segment, but if we consider these ideas, we shall find that they always suppose a sensible inclination of the two lines and that where the angle they form is extremely small, we have no standard of a right line so precise as to assure us of the truth of this proposition. It is the same case with most of the primary decisions of the mathematics.

There remain, therefore, algebra and arithmetic as the only sciences in which we can carry on a chain of reasoning to any degree of intricacy and yet preserve a perfect exactness and certainty. We are possessed of a precise standard by which we can judge of the equality and proportion of numbers and, according as they correspond or not to that standard, we determine their relations without any possibility of error. When two numbers are so combined as that the one has always a unit answering to every unit of the other, we pronounce them equal, and it is for want of such a standard of equality in extension that geometry can scarcely be esteemed a perfect and infallible science.

But here it may not be amiss to obviate a difficulty which may arise from my asserting that though geometry falls short of that perfect precision and certainty which are peculiar to arithmetic and algebra, yet it excels the imperfect judgments of our senses and imagination. The reason why I impute any defect to geometry is because its original and fundamental principles are derived merely from appearances, and it may perhaps be imagined that this defect must always attend it and keep it from ever reaching a greater exactness in the comparison of objects or ideas than what our eye or imagination alone is able to attain. I admit that this defect attends it so far as to keep it from ever aspiring to a full certainty, but since these fundamental principles depend on the easiest and least deceitful appearances, they bestow on their consequences a degree of exactness of which these consequences are singly incapable. It is impossible for the eye to determine the angles of a chiliagon to be equal to 1,996 right angles or make any conjecture that approaches this proportion, but when it determines that right lines cannot concur, that we cannot draw more than one right line between two given points, its mistakes can never be of any consequence. And this is the nature and use of geometry, to run us up to such appearances as by reason of their simplicity cannot lead us into any considerable error.

I shall here take occasion to propose a second observation concerning our demonstrative reasonings which is suggested by the same object of the mathematics. It is usual with mathematicians to pretend that those ideas which are their objects are of so refined and spiritual a nature that they do not fall under the conception of the fancy, but must be comprehended by a pure and intellectual view of which the superior faculties of the soul are alone capable. The same notion runs through most parts of philosophy and is principally made use of to explain our abstract ideas and to show how we can form an idea of a triangle, for instance, which shall neither be an isosceles nor scalenum, nor be confined to any particular length and proportion of sides. It is easy to see why philosophers are so fond of this notion of some spiritual and refined perceptions, since by that means they cover many of their absurdities and may refuse to submit to the decisions of clear ideas by appealing to such as are obscure and uncertain. But to destroy this artifice, we need but reflect on that principle so oft insisted on *that all our ideas are copied from our impressions*. For from thence we may immediately conclude that since all impressions are clear and precise, the ideas which are copied from them

must be of the same nature and can never, but from our fault, contain anything so dark and intricate. An idea is by its very nature weaker and fainter than an impression, but, being in every other respect the same, cannot imply any very great mystery. If its weakness render it obscure, it is our business to remedy that defect as much as possible by keeping the idea steady and precise, and until we have done so, it is in vain to pretend to reasoning and philosophy.

Section 2: Of Probability, and of the Idea of Cause and Effect

This is all I think necessary to observe concerning those four relations which are the foundation of science, but as to the other three, which depend not upon the idea and may be absent or present even while *that* remains the same, it will be proper to explain them more particularly. These three relations are *identity, the situations in time and place, and causation*.

All kinds of reasoning consist in nothing but a comparison and a discovery of those relations, either constant or inconstant, which two or more objects bear to each other. This comparison we may make either when both the objects are present to the senses, or when neither of them is present, or when only one. When both the objects are present to the senses along with the relation, we call *this* perception rather than reasoning, nor is there in this case any exercise of the thought, or any action, properly speaking, but a mere passive admission of the impressions through the organs of sensation. According to this way of thinking, we ought not to receive as reasoning any of the observations we may make concerning *identity* and the *relations* of *time* and *place*, since in none of them can the mind go beyond what is immediately present to the senses, either to discover the real existence or the relations of objects. It is only *causation* which produces such a connection as to give us assurance from the existence or action of one object that it was followed or preceded by any other existence or action, nor can the other two relations be ever made use of in reasoning except so far as they either affect or are affected by it. There is nothing in any objects to persuade us that they are either always *remote* or always *contiguous*, and when from experience and observation we discover that their relation in this particular is invariable, we always conclude there is some secret *cause* which separates or unites them. The same reasoning extends to *identity*. We readily suppose an object may continue individually the same, though several times absent from and present to the senses, and ascribe to it an identity, notwithstanding the interruption of the perception, whenever we conclude that if we had kept our eye or hand constantly upon it, it would have conveyed an invariable and uninterrupted perception. But this conclusion beyond the impressions of our senses can be founded only on the connection of *cause and effect*, nor can we otherwise have any security that the object is not changed upon us, however much the new object may resemble that which was formerly present to the senses. Whenever we discover such a perfect resemblance, we consider whether it be common in that species of objects, whether possibly or probably any cause could operate in producing the change and resemblance and, according as we determine concerning these causes and effects, we form our judgment concerning the identity of the object.

Here then it appears that of those three relations which depend not upon the mere ideas, the only one that can be traced beyond our senses and informs us of existences and objects which we do not see or feel is *causation*. This relation, therefore, we shall endeavor to explain fully before we leave the subject of the understanding.

To begin regularly, we must consider the idea of *causation* and see from what origin it is derived. It is impossible to reason justly without understanding perfectly the idea concerning which we reason, and it is impossible perfectly to understand any idea without tracing it up to its origin and examining that primary impression from which it arises. The examination of the impression bestows a clearness on the idea and the examination of the idea bestows a like clearness on all our reasoning.

Let us therefore cast our eye on any two objects which we call cause and effect and turn them on all sides in order to find that impression which produces an idea of such prodigious consequence. At first sight I perceive that I must not search for it in any of the particular *qualities* of the objects, since, whichever of these qualities I pitch on, I find some object that is not possessed of it and yet falls under the denomination of cause or effect. And indeed there is nothing existent, either externally or internally, which is not to be considered either as a cause or an effect, though it is plain there is no one quality which universally belongs to all beings and gives them a title to that denomination.

The idea, then, of causation must be derived from some relation among objects and that *relation* we must now endeavor to discover. I find in the first place that whatever objects are considered as causes or effects are *contiguous*, and that nothing can operate in a time or place which is ever so little removed from those of its existence. Though distant objects may sometimes seem productive of each other, they are commonly found upon examination to be linked by a chain of causes which are contiguous among themselves and to the distant objects, and when in any particular instance we cannot discover this connection, we still presume it to exist. We may therefore consider the relation of *contiguity* as essential to that of causation — at least may suppose it such, according to the general opinion, until we can find a more proper occasion[9] to clear up this matter by examining what objects are or are not susceptible of juxtaposition and conjunction.

The second relation I shall observe as essential to causes and effects is not so universally acknowledged, but is liable to some controversy. It is that of *priority* of time in the cause before the effect. Some pretend that it is not absolutely necessary a cause should precede its effect, but that any object or action, in the very first moment of its existence, may exert its productive quality and give rise to another object or action, perfectly contemporary with itself. But beside that experience in most instances seems to contradict this opinion, we may establish the relation of priority by a kind of inference or reasoning. It is an established maxim, both in natural and moral philosophy that an object which exists for any time in its full perfection without producing another is not its sole cause, but is assisted by some other principle which pushes it

---

9. Part IV, sec. 5.

from its state of inactivity and makes it exert that energy of which it was secretly possessed. Now if any cause may be perfectly contemporary with its effect, it is certain, according to this maxim that they must all of them be so, since any one of them which retards its operation for a single moment does not exert itself at that very individual time in which it might have operated and therefore is no proper cause. The consequence of this would be no less than the destruction of that succession of causes which we observe in the world and indeed the utter annihilation of time. For if one cause were contemporary with its effect and this effect with *its* effect and so on, it is plain there would be no such thing as succession and all objects must be coexistent.

If this argument appear satisfactory, it is well. If not, I beg the reader to allow me the same liberty which I have used in the preceding case, of supposing it such. For he shall find that the affair is of no great importance.

Having thus discovered or supposed the two relations of *contiguity* and *succession* to be essential to causes and effects, I find I am stopped short and can proceed no further in considering any single instance of cause and effect. Motion in one body is regarded upon impulse as the cause of motion in another. When we consider these objects with the utmost attention, we find only that the one body approaches the other and that the motion of it precedes that of the other, but without any sensible interval. It is in vain to rack ourselves with *further* thought and reflection upon this subject. We can go no *further* in considering this particular instance.

Should any one leave this instance and pretend to define a cause by saying it is something productive of another, it is evident he would say nothing. For what does he mean by *production*? Can he give any definition of it that will not be the same with that of causation? If he can, I desire it may be produced. If he cannot, he here runs in a circle and gives a synonymous term instead of a definition.

Shall we then rest contented with these two relations of contiguity and succession as affording a complete idea of causation? By no means. An object may be contiguous and prior to another without being considered as its cause. There is a *necessary connec-*

tion to be taken into consideration and that relation is of much greater importance than any of the other two above mentioned.

Here again I turn the object on all sides in order to discover the nature of this necessary connection and find the impression or impressions from which its idea may be derived. When I cast my eye on the *known qualities* of objects, I immediately discover that the relation of cause and effect depends not in the least on *them*. When I consider their *relations*, I can find none but those of contiguity and succession, which I have already regarded as imperfect and unsatisfactory. Shall the despair of success make me assert that I am here possessed of an idea which is not preceded by any similar impression? This would be too strong a proof of levity and inconstancy, since the contrary principle has been already so firmly established as to admit of no further doubt, at least, until we have more fully examined the present difficulty.

We must therefore proceed like those who, being in search of anything that lies concealed from them and not finding it in the place they expected, beat about all the neighboring fields, without any certain view or design, in hopes their good fortune will at last guide them to what they search for. It is necessary for us to leave the direct survey of this question concerning the nature of that *necessary connection* which enters into our idea of cause and effect; and endeavor to find some other questions the examination of which will perhaps afford a hint that may serve to clear up the present difficulty. Of these questions there occur two, which I shall proceed to examine, namely,

First, for what reason we pronounce it *necessary* that everything whose existence has a beginning should also have a cause?

Secondly, why we conclude that such particular causes must *necessarily* have such particular effects, and what is the nature of that *inference* we draw from the one to the other and of the *belief* we repose in it?

I shall only observe, before I proceed any further, that though the ideas of cause and effect be derived from the impressions of reflection as well as from those of sensation, yet for brevity's sake, I commonly mention only the latter as the origin of these ideas, though I desire that whatever I say of them may also extend to the former. Passions are connected with their objects and with one another no less than external bodies are connected together. The same relation, then, of cause and effect which belongs to one must be common to all of them.

Section 3: Why a Cause Is Always Necessary

To begin with the first question concerning the necessity of a cause: It is a general maxim in philosophy that *whatever begins to exist, must have a cause of existence*. This is commonly taken for granted in all reasonings without any proof given or demanded. It is supposed to be founded on intuition and to be one of those maxims which, though they may be denied with the lips, it is impossible for men in their hearts really to doubt of. But if we examine this maxim by the idea of knowledge explained above, we shall discover in it no mark of any such intuitive certainty, but on the contrary shall find that it is of a nature quite foreign to that species of conviction.

All certainty arises from the comparison of ideas and from the discovery of such relations as are unalterable so long as the ideas continue the same. These relations are *resemblance, proportions in quantity and number, degrees of any quality, and contrariety,* none of which are implied in this proposition, *Whatever has a beginning has also a cause of existence.* That proposition therefore is not intuitively certain. At least anyone who would assert it to be intuitively certain must deny these to be the only infallible relations and must find some other relation of that kind to be implied in it, which it will then be time enough to examine.

But here is an argument which proves at once that the foregoing proposition is neither intuitively nor demonstrably certain. We can never demonstrate the necessity of a cause to every new existence, or new modification of existence, without showing at the same time the impossibility there is that anything can ever begin to exist without some productive principle; and where the latter proposition cannot be proved, we must despair of ever being able to prove the former. Now that the latter proposition is utterly incapable of a demonstrative proof, we may satisfy ourselves by considering that as all distinct ideas are separable from each other and as the ideas of cause and effect are evidently dis-

tinct, it will be easy for us to conceive any object to be non-existent this moment, and existent the next, without conjoining to it the distinct idea of a cause or productive principle. The separation, therefore, of the idea of a cause from that of a beginning of existence is plainly possible for the imagination, and consequently the actual separation of these objects is so far possible that it implies no contradiction nor absurdity and is therefore incapable of being refuted by any reasoning from mere ideas, without which it is impossible to demonstrate the necessity of a cause.

Accordingly, we shall find upon examination that every demonstration which has been produced for the necessity of a cause is fallacious and sophistical. All the points of time and place, say some philosophers,[10] in which we can suppose any object to begin to exist are in themselves equal, and unless there be some cause which is peculiar to one time and to one place and which by that means determines and fixes the existence, it must remain in eternal suspense and the object can never begin to be, for want of something to fix its beginning. But I ask: Is there any more difficulty in supposing the time and place to be fixed without a cause than to suppose the existence to be determined in that manner? The first question that occurs on this subject is always *whether* the object shall exist or not, the next, *when* and *where* it shall begin to exist. If the removal of a cause be intuitively absurd in the one case, it must be so in the other, and if that absurdity be not clear without a proof in the one case, it will equally require one in the other. The absurdity, then, of the one supposition can never be a proof of that of the other, since they are both upon the same footing and must stand or fall by the same reasoning.

The second argument,[11] which I find used on this head, labors under an equal difficulty. Everything, it is said, must have a cause. For if anything wanted a cause, *it* would produce *itself,* that is, exist before it existed, which is impossible. But this reasoning is plainly inconclusive, because it supposes that, in our denial of a cause, we still grant what we expressly deny, namely, that there must be a cause, which, therefore, is taken to be the object itself. And *that,*

10. Mr. Hobbes.
11. Dr. Clarke and others.

no doubt, is an evident contradiction. But to say that anything is produced or, to express myself more properly, comes into existence without a cause, is not to affirm that it is itself its own cause, but, on the contrary, in excluding all external causes, excludes *a fortiori* the thing itself which is created. An object that exists absolutely without any cause certainly is not its own cause, and when you assert that the one follows from the other, you suppose the very point in question, and take it for granted that it is utterly impossible anything can ever begin to exist without a cause, but that, upon the exclusion of one productive principle, we must still have recourse to another.

It is exactly the same case with the third argument,[12] which has been employed to demonstrate the necessity of a cause. Whatever is produced without any cause is produced by *nothing*, or, in other words, has nothing for its cause. But nothing can never be a cause, no more than it can be something, or equal to two right angles. By the same intuition that we perceive nothing not to be equal to two right angles, or not to be something, we perceive that it can never be a cause, and consequently must perceive that every object has a real cause of its existence.

I believe it will not be necessary to employ many words in showing the weakness of this argument after what I have said of the foregoing. They are all of them founded on the same fallacy and are derived from the same turn of thought. It is sufficient only to observe that when we exclude all causes, we really do exclude them and neither suppose nothing nor the object itself to be the causes of the existence and consequently can draw no argument from the absurdity of these suppositions to prove the absurdity of that exclusion. If everything must have a cause, it follows that, upon the exclusion of other causes, we must accept of the object itself or of nothing as causes. But it is the very point in question whether everything must have a cause or not and therefore, according to all just reasoning, it ought never to be taken for granted.

They are still more frivolous who say that every effect must have a cause, because it is implied in the very idea of effect. Every effect necessarily presupposes a cause, effect being a relative term of which

cause is the correlative. But this does not prove that every being must be preceded by a cause, no more than it follows, because every husband must have a wife that therefore every man must be married. The true state of the question is whether every object which begins to exist must owe its existence to a cause, and this I assert to be neither intuitively nor demonstratively certain and hope to have proved it sufficiently by the foregoing arguments.

Since it is not from knowledge or any scientific reasoning that we derive the opinion of the necessity of a cause to every new production, that opinion must necessarily arise from observation and experience. The next question, then, should naturally be: *How does experience give rise to such a principle?* But as I find it will be more convenient to sink this question in the following: *Why do we conclude that such particular causes must necessarily have such particular effects, and why do we form an inference from one to another?*, we shall make that the subject of our future inquiry. It will, perhaps, be found in the end that the same answer will serve for both questions.

Section 4: Of the Component Parts of Our Reasonings Concerning Cause and Effect

Though the mind in its reasonings from causes or effects carries its view beyond those objects which it sees or remembers, it must never lose sight of them entirely, nor reason merely upon its own ideas without some mixture of impressions, or at least of ideas of the memory, which are equivalent to impressions. When we infer effects from causes, we must establish the existence of these causes, which we have only two ways of doing, either by an immediate perception of our memory or senses, or by an inference from other causes; which causes again we must ascertain in the same manner, either by a present impression or by an inference from their causes, and so on, until we arrive at some object which we see or remember. It is impossible for us to carry on our inferences *in infinitum* and the only thing that can stop them is an impression of the memory or senses beyond which there is no room for doubt or inquiry.

To give an instance of this, we may choose any point of history and consider for what reason we either

12. Mr. Locke.

believe or reject it. Thus, we believe that Caesar was killed in the senate-house on the *ides* of *March*, and that, because this fact is established on the unanimous testimony of historians who agree to assign this precise time and place to that event. Here are certain characters and letters present either to our memory or senses; which characters we likewise remember to have been used as the signs of certain ideas; and these ideas were either in the minds of such as were immediately present at that action and received the ideas directly from its existence or they were derived from the testimony of others, and that again from another testimony, by a visible gradation, until we arrive at those who were eye-witnesses and spectators of the event. It is obvious that all this chain of argument or connection of causes and effects is at first founded on those characters or letters which are seen or remembered and that without the authority either of the memory or senses, our whole reasoning would be chimerical and without foundation. Every link of the chain would in that case hang upon another, but there would not be anything fixed to one end of it, capable of sustaining the whole, and consequently there would be no belief nor evidence. And this actually is the case with all *hypothetical* arguments, or reasonings upon a supposition, there being in them neither any present impression nor belief of a real existence.

I need not observe that it is no just objection to the present doctrine that we can reason upon our past conclusions or principles without having recourse to those impressions from which they first arose. For even supposing these impressions should be entirely effaced from the memory, the conviction they produced may still remain; and it is equally true that all reasonings concerning causes and effects are originally derived from some impression; in the same manner as the assurance of a demonstration proceeds always from a comparison of ideas, though it may continue after the comparison is forgotten.

Section 5: Of the Impressions of the Senses and Memory

In this kind of reasoning, then, from causation, we employ materials which are of a mixed and heterogeneous nature and which, however connected, are yet essentially different from each other. All our arguments concerning causes and effects consist both of an impression of the memory or senses and of the idea of that existence which produces the object of the impression or is produced by it. Here, therefore, we have three things to explain, namely, *first,* the original impression. *Secondly,* the transition to the idea of the connected cause or effect. *Thirdly,* the nature and qualities of that idea.

As to those *impressions* which arise from the *senses,* their ultimate cause is, in my opinion, perfectly inexplicable by human reason and it will always be impossible to decide with certainty whether they arise immediately from the object or are produced by the creative power of the mind or are derived from the Author of our being. Nor is such a question any way material to our present purpose. We may draw inferences from the coherence of our perceptions, whether they be true or false, whether they represent nature justly or be mere illusions of the senses.

When we search for the characteristic which distinguishes the *memory* from the imagination, we must immediately perceive that it cannot lie in the simple ideas it presents to us, since both these faculties borrow their simple ideas from the impressions and can never go beyond these original perceptions. These faculties are as little distinguished from each other by the arrangement of their complex ideas. For, though it be a peculiar property of the memory to preserve the original order and position of its ideas, while the imagination transposes and changes them as it pleases, yet this difference is not sufficient to distinguish them in their operation or make us know the one from the other, it being impossible to recall the past impressions in order to compare them with our present ideas and see whether their arrangement be exactly similar. Since, therefore, the memory is known neither by the order of its *complex* ideas nor the nature of its *simple* ones, it follows that the difference between it and the imagination lies in its superior force and vivacity. A man may indulge his fancy in feigning any past scene of adventures, nor would there be any possibility of distinguishing this from a remembrance of a like kind, were not the ideas of the imagination fainter and more obscure.

It frequently happens that when two men have

been engaged in any scene of action, the one shall remember it much better than the other and shall have all the difficulty in the world to make his companion recollect it. He runs over several circumstances in vain—mentions the time, the place, the company, what was said, what was done on all sides—until at last he hits on some lucky circumstance that revives the whole and gives his friend a perfect memory of everything. Here the person who forgets receives at first all the ideas from the discourse of the other, with the same circumstances of time and place, though he considers them as mere fictions of the imagination. But as soon as the circumstance is mentioned that touches the memory, the very same ideas now appear in a new light and have, in a manner, a different feeling from what they had before. Without any other alteration, besides that of the feeling, they become immediately ideas of the memory and are assented to.

Since, therefore, the imagination can represent all the same objects that the memory can offer to us and since those faculties are only distinguished by the different feeling of the ideas they present, it may be proper to consider what is the nature of that feeling. And here I believe everyone will readily agree with me that the ideas of the memory are more strong and lively than those of the fancy.

A painter who intended to represent a passion or emotion of any kind would endeavor to get a sight of a person actuated by a like emotion, in order to enliven his ideas and give them a force and vivacity superior to what is found in those which are mere fictions of the imagination. The more recent this memory is, the clearer is the idea, and when, after a long interval, he would return to the contemplation of his object, he always finds its idea to be much decayed, if not wholly obliterated. We are frequently in doubt concerning the ideas of the memory, as they become very weak and feeble, and are at a loss to determine whether any image proceeds from the fancy or the memory when it is not drawn in such lively colors as distinguish that latter faculty. I think I remember such an event, says one, but am not sure. A long tract of time has almost worn it out of my memory and leaves me uncertain whether or not it be the pure offspring of my fancy.

And as an idea of the memory, by losing its force and vivacity, may degenerate to such a degree as to be taken for an idea of the imagination, so, on the other hand, an idea of the imagination may acquire such a force and vivacity as to pass for an idea of the memory and counterfeit its effects on the belief and judgment. This is noted in the case of liars who, by the frequent repetition of their lies, come at last to believe and remember them as realities, custom and habit having, in this case as in many others, the same influence on the mind as nature and infixing the idea with equal force and vigor.

Thus it appears that the *belief* or *assent* which always attends the memory and senses is nothing but the vivacity of those perceptions they present, and that this alone distinguishes them from the imagination. To believe is, in this case, to feel an immediate impression of the senses or a repetition of that impression in the memory. It is merely the force and liveliness of the perception which constitutes the first act of the judgment and lays the foundation of that reasoning which we build upon it when we trace the relation of cause and effect.

Section 6: Of the Inference from the Impression to the Idea

It is easy to observe that, in tracing this relation, the inference we draw from cause to effect is not derived merely from a survey of these particular objects and from such a penetration into their essences as may discover the dependence of the one upon the other. There is no object which implies the existence of any other, if we consider these objects in themselves and never look beyond the ideas which we form of them. Such an inference would amount to knowledge and would imply the absolute contradiction and impossibility of conceiving anything different. But as all distinct ideas are separable, it is evident there can be no impossibility of that kind. When we pass from a present impression to the idea of any object, we might possibly have separated the idea from the impression and have substituted any other idea in its room.

It is therefore by *experience* only that we can infer the existence of one object from that of another. The nature of experience is this. We remember to have had frequent instances of the existence of one species of objects and also remember that the individuals of another species of objects have always attended them and have existed in a regular order of contiguity and succession with regard to them. Thus we remember to have seen that species of object we call *flame* and to have felt that species of sensation we call *heat.* We likewise call to mind their constant conjunction in all past instances. Without any further ceremony, we call the one *cause* and the other *effect,* and infer the existence of the one from that of the other. In all those instances from which we learn the conjunction of particular causes and effects, both the causes and effects have been perceived by the senses and are remembered, but in all cases wherein we reason concerning them, there is only one perceived or remembered and the other is supplied in conformity to our past experience.

Thus, in advancing, we have insensibly discovered a new relation between cause and effect when we least expected it and were entirely employed upon another subject. This relation is their *constant conjunction.* Contiguity and succession are not sufficient to make us pronounce any two objects to be cause and effect unless we perceive that these two relations are preserved in several instances. We may now see the advantage of quitting the direct survey of this relation in order to discover the nature of that *necessary connection* which makes so essential a part of it. There are hopes that by this means we may at last arrive at our proposed end, though, to tell the truth, this new-discovered relation of a constant conjunction seems to advance us but very little in our way. For it implies no more than this, that like objects have always been placed in like relations of contiguity and succession, and it seems evident, at least at first sight, that by this means we can never discover any new idea and can only multiply, but not enlarge, the objects of our mind. It may be thought that what we learn not from one object, we can never learn from a hundred which are all of the same kind and are perfectly resembling in every circumstance. As our senses show us in one instance two bodies, or motions, or qualities, in certain relations of succession and contiguity, so our memory presents us only with a multitude of instances wherein we always find like bodies, motions,

or qualities, in like relations. From the mere repetition of any past impression, even to infinity, there never will arise any new original idea, such as that of a necessary connection, and the number of impressions has in this case no more effect than if we confined ourselves to one only. But though this reasoning seems just and obvious, yet, as it would be folly to despair too soon, we shall continue the thread of our discourse and, having found that after the discovery of the constant conjunction of any objects, we always draw an inference from one object to another, we shall now examine the nature of that inference and of the transition from the impression to the idea. Perhaps it will appear in the end that the necessary connection depends on the inference, instead of the inference's depending on the necessary connection.

Since it appears that the transition from an impression present to the memory or senses to the idea of an object which we call cause or effect is founded on past *experience* and on our remembrance of their *constant conjunction,* the next question is whether experience produces the idea by means of the understanding or imagination, whether we are determined by reason to make the transition or by a certain association and relation of perceptions. If reason determined us, it would proceed upon that principle *that instances of which we have had no experience must resemble those of which we have had experience, and that the course of nature continues always uniformly the same.* In order, therefore, to clear up this matter, let us consider all the arguments upon which such a proposition may be supposed to be founded, and as these must be derived either from *knowledge* or *probability,* let us cast our eye on each of these degrees of evidence and see whether they afford any just conclusion of this nature.

Our foregoing method of reasoning will easily convince us that there can be no *demonstrative* arguments to prove *that those instances of which we have had no experience resemble those of which we have had experience.* We can at least conceive a change in the course of nature, which sufficiently proves that such a change is not absolutely impossible. To form a clear idea of anything is an undeniable argument for its possibility and is alone a refutation of any pretended demonstration against it.

Probability, as it discovers not the relations of ideas, considered as such, but only those of objects, must in some respects be founded on the impressions of our memory and senses and, in some respects, on our ideas. Were there no mixture of any impression in our probable reasonings, the conclusion would be entirely chimerical, and were there no mixture of ideas, the action of the mind, in observing the relation, would, properly speaking, be sensation, not reasoning. It is therefore necessary that in all probable reasonings there be something present to the mind, either seen or remembered, and that from this we infer something connected with it which is not seen nor remembered.

The only connection or relation of objects which can lead us beyond the immediate impressions of our memory and senses is that of cause and effect and that because it is the only one on which we can found a just inference from one object to another. The idea of cause and effect is derived from *experience*, which informs us that such particular objects, in all past instances, have been constantly conjoined with each other and, as an object similar to one of these is supposed to be immediately present in its impression, we thence presume on the existence of one similar to its usual attendant. According to this account of things, which is, I think, in every point unquestionable, probability is founded on the presumption of a resemblance between those objects of which we have had experience and those of which we have had none, and, therefore, it is impossible this presumption can arise from probability. The same principle cannot be both the cause and effect of another, and this is perhaps the only proposition concerning that relation which is either intuitively or demonstratively certain.

Should any one think to elude this argument and, without determining whether our reasoning on this subject be derived from demonstration or probability, pretend that all conclusions from causes and effects are built on solid reasoning, I can only desire that this reasoning may be produced in order to be exposed to our examination. It may perhaps be said that after experience of the constant conjunction of certain objects, we reason in the following manner. Such an object is always found to produce another. It is impossible it could have this effect if it was not en-dowed with a power of production. The power necessarily implies the effect and therefore there is a just foundation for drawing a conclusion from the existence of one object to that of its usual attendant. The past production implies a power, the power implies a new production, and the new production is what we infer from the power and the past production.

It were easy for me to show the weakness of this reasoning, were I willing to make use of those observations I have already made — that the idea of *production* is the same with that of *causation,* and that no existence certainly and demonstratively implies a power in any other object — or were it proper to anticipate what I shall have occasion to remark afterwards concerning the idea we form of *power* and *efficacy.* But as such a method of proceeding may seem either to weaken my system by resting one part of it on another or to breed a confusion in my reasoning, I shall endeavor to maintain my present assertion without any such assistance.

It shall therefore be allowed for a moment that the production of one object by another in any one instance implies a power and that this power is connected with its effect. But it having been already proved that the power lies not in the sensible qualities of the cause, and there being nothing but the sensible qualities present to us, I ask: Why in other instances you presume that the same power still exists, merely upon the appearance of these qualities? Your appeal to past experience decides nothing in the present case and at the utmost can only prove that that very object which produced any other was at that very instant endowed with such a power, but can never prove that the same power must continue in the same object or collection of sensible qualities, much less that a like power is always conjoined with like sensible qualities. Should it be said that we have experience that the same power continues united with the same object and that like objects are endowed with like powers, I would renew my question: *Why from this experience should we form any conclusion beyond those past instances of which we have had experience?* If you answer this question in the same manner as the preceding, your answer gives still occasion to a new question of the same kind, even *in infinitum,* which clearly proves that the foregoing reasoning had no just foundation.

Thus, not only our reason fails us in the discovery of the *ultimate connection* of causes and effects, but even after experience has informed us of their *constant conjunction*, it is impossible for us to satisfy ourselves by our reason why we should extend that experience beyond those particular instances which have fallen under our observation. We suppose, but are never able to prove that there must be a resemblance between those objects of which we have had experience and those which lie beyond the reach of our discovery.

We have already taken notice of certain relations which make us pass from one object to another, even though there be no reason to determine us to that transition; and this we may establish for a general rule, that wherever the mind constantly and uniformly makes a transition without any reason, it is influenced by these relations. Now, this is exactly the present case. Reason can never show us the connection of one object with another, though aided by experience and the observation of their constant conjunction in all past instances. When the mind therefore passes from the idea or impression of one object to the idea or belief of another, it is not determined by reason, but by certain principles which associate together the ideas of these objects and unite them in the imagination. Had ideas no more union in the fancy than objects seem to have to the understanding, we could never draw any inference from causes to effects, nor repose belief in any matter of fact. The inference therefore depends solely on the union of ideas.

The principles of union among ideas, I have reduced to three general ones and have asserted that the idea or impression of any object naturally introduces the idea of any other object that is resembling, contiguous to, or connected with it. These principles I allow to be neither the *infallible* nor the *sole* causes of a union among ideas. They are not the infallible causes. For one may fix his attention during some time on any one object without looking further. They are not the sole causes. For the thought has evidently a very irregular motion in running along its objects and may leap from the heavens to the earth, from one end of the creation to the other, without any certain method or order. But though I allow this

weakness in these three relations, and this irregularity in the imagination, yet I assert that the only *general* principles which associate ideas are resemblance, contiguity, and causation.

There is indeed a principle of union among ideas, which at first sight may be esteemed different from any of these, but will be found at the bottom to depend on the same origin. When every individual of any species of objects is found by experience to be constantly united with an individual of another species, the appearance of any new individual of either species naturally conveys the thought to its usual attendant. Thus, because such a particular idea is commonly annexed to such a particular word, nothing is required but the hearing of that word to produce the correspondent idea, and it will scarcely be possible for the mind, by its utmost efforts, to prevent that transition. In this case it is not absolutely necessary that upon hearing such a particular sound, we should reflect on any past experience and consider what idea has been usually connected with the sound. The imagination of itself supplies the place of this reflection and is so accustomed to pass from the word to the idea that it interposes not a moment's delay between the hearing of the one and the conception of the other.

But though I acknowledge this to be a true principle of association among ideas, I assert it to be the very same with that between the ideas of cause and effect and to be an essential part in all our reasonings from that relation. We have no other notion of cause and effect, but that of certain objects which have been *always conjoined* together and which in all past instances have been found inseparable. We cannot penetrate into the reason of the conjunction. We only observe the thing itself and always find that, from the constant conjunction, the objects acquire a union in the imagination. When the impression of one becomes present to us, we immediately form an idea of its usual attendant, and consequently we may establish this as one part of the definition of an opinion or belief that it is *an idea related to or associated with a present impression*.

Thus, though causation be a *philosophical* relation, as implying contiguity, succession, and constant conjunction, yet it is only so far as it is a natural relation and produces a union among our ideas that we are able to reason upon it or draw any inference from it.

Section 7: Of the Nature of Idea or Belief

The idea of an object is an essential part of the belief of it, but not the whole. We conceive many things which we do not believe. In order, then, to discover more fully the nature of belief or the qualities of those ideas we assent to, let us weigh the following considerations.

It is evident that all reasonings from causes or effects terminate in conclusions concerning matter of fact, that is, concerning the existence of objects or of their qualities. It is also evident that the idea of existence is nothing different from the idea of any object and that when, after the simple conception of anything, we would conceive it as existent, we in reality make no addition to or alteration on our first idea. Thus, when we affirm that God is existent, we simply form the idea of such a Being as he is represented to us, nor is the existence which we attribute to him conceived by a particular idea which we join to the idea of his other qualities and can again separate and distinguish from them. But I go further and, not content with asserting that the conception of the existence of any object is no addition to the simple conception of it, I likewise maintain that the belief of the existence joins no new ideas to those which compose the idea of the object. When I think of God, when I think of him as existent, and when I believe him to be existent, my idea of him neither increases nor diminishes. But as it is certain there is a great difference between the simple conception of the existence of an object and the belief of it, and as this difference does not lie in the parts or composition of the idea which we conceive, it follows that it must lie in the *manner* in which we conceive it.

Suppose a person present with me who advances propositions to which I do not assent, *that* Caesar *died in his bed, that silver is more fusible than lead, or mercury heavier than gold*; it is evident, that, notwithstanding my incredulity, I clearly understand his meaning and form all the same ideas which he forms. My imagination is endowed with the same powers as

his, nor is it possible for him to conceive any idea which I cannot conceive, or conjoin any which I cannot conjoin. I therefore ask: Wherein consists the difference between believing and disbelieving any proposition? The answer is easy with regard to propositions that are proved by intuition or demonstration. In that case, the person who assents not only conceives the ideas according to the proposition, but is necessarily determined to conceive them in that particular manner, either immediately or by the interposition of other ideas. Whatever is absurd is unintelligible, nor is it possible for the imagination to conceive anything contrary to a demonstration. But as, in reasonings from causation and concerning matters of fact, this absolute necessity cannot take place and the imagination is free to conceive both sides of the question, I still ask, *wherein consists the difference between incredulity and belief?*, since in both cases the conception of the idea is equally possible and requisite.

It will not be a satisfactory answer to say that a person who does not assent to a proposition you advance, after having conceived the object in the same manner with you, immediately conceives it in a different manner and has different ideas of it. This answer is unsatisfactory, not because it contains any falsehood, but because it does not discover all the truth. It is confessed that, in all cases wherein we dissent from any person, we conceive both sides of the question, but as we can believe only one, it evidently follows that the belief must make some difference between that conception to which we assent and that from which we dissent. We may mingle and unite and separate and confound and vary our ideas in a hundred different ways, but until there appears some principle which fixes one of these different situations, we have in reality no opinion, and this principle, as it plainly makes no addition to our precedent ideas, can only change the *manner* of our conceiving them.

All the perceptions of the mind are of two kinds, namely, impressions and ideas, which differ from each other only in their different degrees of force and vivacity. Our ideas are copied from our impressions and represent them in all their parts. When you would any way vary the idea of a particular object, you can only increase or diminish its force and vivacity. If you make any other change on it, it represents a different object or impression. The case is the same as in colors. A particular shade of any color may acquire a new degree of liveliness or brightness without any other variation. But when you produce any other variation, it is no longer the same shade or color, so that, as belief does nothing but vary the manner in which we conceive any object, it can only bestow on our ideas an additional force and vivacity. An opinion, therefore, or belief, may be most accurately defined as *a lively idea related to or associated with a present impression.*[13]

Here are the heads of those arguments which lead us to this conclusion. When we infer the existence

13. We may here take occasion to observe a very remarkable error which, being frequently inculcated in the schools, has become a kind of established maxim and is universally received by all logicians. This error consists in the vulgar division of the acts of the understanding into *conception, judgment,* and *reasoning,* and in the definitions we give of them. Conception is defined to be the simple survey of one or more ideas; judgment to be the separating or uniting of different ideas; reasoning to be the separating or uniting of different ideas by the interposition of others which show the relation they bear to each other. But these distinctions and definitions are faulty in very considerable articles. For, *first,* it is far from being true that in every judgment which we form we unite two different ideas, since in that proposition, *God* is, or indeed any other which regards existence, the idea of existence is no distinct idea which we unite with that of the object and which is capable of forming a compound idea by the union. *Secondly,* as we can thus form a proposition which contains only one idea, so we may exert our reason without employing more than two ideas and without having recourse to a third to serve as a medium between them. We infer a cause immediately from its effect, and this inference is not only a true species of reasoning, but the strongest of all others and more convincing than when we interpose another idea to connect the two extremes. What we may in general affirm concerning these three acts of the understanding is that taking them in a proper light, they all resolve themselves into the first and are nothing but particular ways of conceiving our objects. Whether we consider a single object or several; whether we dwell on these objects or run from them to others; and in whatever form or order we survey them, the act of the mind exceeds not a simple conception and the only remarkable difference which occurs on this occasion is when we join belief to the conception and are persuaded of the truth of what we conceive. This act of the mind has never yet been explained by any philosopher and therefore I am at liberty to propose my hypothesis concerning it, which is that it is only a strong and steady conception of any idea and such as approaches in some measure to an immediate impression.

of an object from that of others, some object must always be present either to the memory or senses in order to be the foundation of our reasoning; since the mind cannot run up with its inferences *in infinitum.* Reason can never satisfy us that the existence of any one object does ever imply that of another, so that when we pass from the impression of one to the idea or belief of another, we are not determined by reason, but by custom, or a principle of association. But belief is somewhat more than a simple idea. It is a particular manner of forming an idea and as the same idea can only be varied by a variation of its degrees of force and vivacity, it follows upon the whole that belief is a lively idea produced by a relation to a present impression, according to the foregoing definition.

This operation of the mind which forms the belief of any matter of fact, seems previously to have been one of the greatest mysteries of philosophy, though no one has so much as suspected that there was any difficulty in explaining it. For my part, I must admit that I find a considerable difficulty in the case, and that even when I think I understand the subject perfectly, I am at a loss for terms to express my meaning. I conclude, by an induction which seems to me very evident, that an opinion or belief is nothing but an idea that is different from a fiction, not in the nature or the order of its parts, but in the manner of its being conceived. But when I would explain this manner, I scarcely find any word that fully answers the case, but am obliged to have recourse to everyone's feeling in order to give him a perfect notion of this operation of the mind. An idea assented to feels different from a fictitious idea that the fancy alone presents to us and this different feeling I endeavor to explain by calling it a superior force or vivacity or solidity or firmness or steadiness. This variety of terms, which may seem so unphilosophical, is intended only to express that act of the mind which renders realities more present to us than fictions, causes them to weigh more in the thought, and gives them a superior influence on the passions and imagination. Provided we agree about the thing, it is needless to dispute about the terms. The imagination has the command over all its ideas and can join and mix and vary them in all the ways possible. It may conceive objects with all the circumstances of place and time. It may set them, in a manner, before our eyes in their true colors, just as they might have existed. But as it is impossible that that faculty can ever of itself reach belief, it is evident that belief consists not in the nature and order of our ideas, but in the manner of their conception and in their feeling to the mind. I confess that it is impossible to explain perfectly this feeling or manner of conception. We may make use of words that express something near it. But its true and proper name is belief, which is a term that everyone sufficiently understands in common life. And in philosophy we can go no further than assert that it is something felt by the mind which distinguishes the ideas of the judgment from the fictions of the imagination. It gives them more force and influence, makes them appear of greater importance, infixes them in the mind, and renders them the governing principles of all our actions.

This definition will also be found to be entirely conformable to everyone's feeling and experience. Nothing is more evident than that those ideas to which we assent are more strong, firm, and vivid than the loose reveries of a castle-builder. If one person sits down to read a book as a romance, and another as a true history, they plainly receive the same ideas and in the same order, nor does the incredulity of the one and the belief of the other hinder them from putting the very same sense upon their author. His words produce the same ideas in both, though his testimony has not the same influence on them. The latter has a more lively conception of all the incidents. He enters deeper into the concerns of the persons, represents to himself their actions and characters and friendships and enmities; he even goes so far as to form a notion of their features and air and person. While the former, who gives no credit to the testimony of the author, has a more faint and languid conception of all these particulars and, except on account of the style and ingenuity of the composition, can receive little entertainment from it.

Section 8: Of the Causes of Belief

Having thus explained the nature of belief and shown that it consists in a lively idea related to a present impression, let us now proceed to examine from what principles it is derived and what bestows the vivacity on the idea.

I would willingly establish it as a general maxim in the science of human nature *that when any impression becomes present to us, it not only transports the mind to such ideas as are related to it, but likewise communicates to them a share of its force and vivacity*. All the operations of the mind depend in a great measure on its disposition when it performs them; and according as the spirits are more or less elevated, and the attention more or less fixed, the action will always have more or less vigor and vivacity. When, therefore, any object is presented which elevates and enlivens the thought, every action to which the mind applies itself will be more strong and vivid as long as that disposition continues. Now, it is evident the continuance of the disposition depends entirely on the objects about which the mind is employed, and that any new object naturally gives a new direction to the spirits and changes the disposition, as on the contrary, when the mind fixes constantly on the same object or passes easily and insensibly along related objects, the disposition has a much longer duration. Hence it happens that when the mind is once enlivened by a present impression, it proceeds to form a more lively idea of the related objects by a natural transition of the disposition from the one to the other. The change of the objects is so easy that the mind is scarcely sensible of it, but applies itself to the conception of the related idea with all the force and vivacity it acquired from the present impression.

If, in considering the nature of relation and that facility of transition which is essential to it, we can satisfy ourselves concerning the reality of this phenomenon, it is well, but I must confess I place my chief confidence in experience to prove so material a principle. We may therefore observe, as the first experiment to our present purpose, that upon the appearance of the picture of an absent friend, our idea of him is evidently enlivened by the *resemblance*, and that every passion which that idea occasions, whether of joy or sorrow, acquires new force and vigor. In producing this effect there concur both a relation and a present impression. Where the picture bears him no resemblance, or at least was not intended for him, it never so much as conveys our thought to him, and where it is absent as well as the person, though the mind may pass from the thought of the one to that of the other, it feels its idea to be rather weakened than enlivened by that transition. We take a pleasure in viewing the picture of a friend when it is set before us, but when it is removed, choose to consider him directly rather than by reflection in an image which is equally distant and obscure.

The ceremonies of the *Roman Catholic* religion may be considered as experiments of the same nature. The devotees of that strange superstition usually plead, in excuse of the mummeries with which they are upbraided, that they feel the good effect of those external motions and postures and actions in enlivening their devotion and quickening their fervor, which otherwise would decay away if directed entirely to distant and immaterial objects. We shadow out the objects of our faith, say they, in sensible types and images and render them more present to us by the immediate presence of these types than it is possible for us to do merely by an intellectual view and contemplation. Sensible objects have always a greater influence on the fancy than any other, and this influence they readily convey to those ideas to which they are related and which they resemble. I shall only infer from these practices and this reasoning that the effect of resemblance in enlivening the idea is very common and as in every case a resemblance and a present impression must concur, we are abundantly supplied with experiments to prove the reality of the foregoing principle.

We may add force to these experiments by others of a different kind in considering the effects of *contiguity* as well as of *resemblance*. It is certain that distance diminishes the force of every idea and that, upon our approach to any object, though it does not discover itself to our senses, it operates upon the mind with an influence that imitates an immediate impression. The thinking on any object readily transports the mind to what is contiguous, but it is only the actual presence of an object that transports it with a superior vivacity. When I am a few miles from home, whatever relates to it touches me more nearly than when I am two hundred leagues distant, though even at that distance the reflecting on anything in the neighborhood of my friends and family naturally produces an

idea of them. But as in this latter case, both the objects of the mind are ideas; notwithstanding there is an easy transition between them; that transition alone is not able to give a superior vivacity to any of the ideas for want of some immediate impression.

No one can doubt but causation has the same influence as the other two relations of resemblance and contiguity. Superstitious people are fond of the relics of saints and holy men for the same reason that they seek after types and images, in order to enliven their devotion and give them a more intimate and strong conception of those exemplary lives which they desire to imitate. Now, it is evident one of the best relics a devotee could procure would be the handiwork of a saint, and if his clothes and furniture are ever to be considered in this light, it is because they were once at his disposal and were moved and affected by him, in which respect they are to be considered as imperfect effects and as connected with him by a shorter chain of consequences than any of those from which we learn the reality of his existence. This phenomenon clearly proves that a present impression with a relation of causation may enliven any idea and consequently produce belief or assent, according to the precedent definition of it.

But why need we seek for other arguments to prove that a present impression with a relation or transition of the fancy may enliven any idea, when this very instance of our reasonings from cause and effect will alone suffice to that purpose? It is certain we must have an idea of every matter of fact which we believe. It is certain that this idea arises only from a relation to a present impression. It is certain that the belief superadds nothing to the idea, but only changes our manner of conceiving it and renders it more strong and lively. The present conclusion concerning the influence of relation is the immediate consequence of all these steps, and every step appears to me sure and infallible. There enters nothing into this operation of the mind but a present impression, a lively idea, and a relation or association in the fancy between the impression and idea; so that there can be no suspicion of mistake.

In order to put this whole affair in a fuller light, let us consider it as a question in natural philosophy which we must determine by experience and observation. I suppose there is an object presented from which I draw a certain conclusion and form to myself ideas which I am said to believe or assent to. Here it is evident that however that object which is present to my senses and that other whose existence I infer by reasoning may be thought to influence each other by their particular powers or qualities, yet as the phenomenon of belief, which we at present examine, is merely internal, these powers and qualities, being entirely unknown, can have no hand in producing it. It is the present impression which is to be considered as the true and real cause of the idea and of the belief which attends it. We must therefore endeavor to discover by experiments the particular qualities by which it is enabled to produce so extraordinary an effect.

First, then, I observe that the present impression does not have this effect by its own proper power and efficacy and, when considered alone as a single perception, is limited to the present moment. I find that an impression from which, on its first appearance, I can draw no conclusion may afterwards become the foundation of belief, when I have had experience of its usual consequences. We must in every case have observed the same impression in past instances and have found it to be constantly conjoined with some other impression. This is confirmed by such a multitude of experiments that it does not admit of the smallest doubt.

From a second observation I conclude that the belief which attends the present impression and is produced by a number of past impressions and conjunctions, that this belief, I say, arises immediately without any new operation of the reason or imagination. Of this I can be certain, because I never am conscious of any such operation and find nothing in the subject on which it can be founded. Now, as we call everything *custom* which proceeds from a past repetition without any new reasoning or conclusion, we may establish it as a certain truth that all the belief which follows upon any present impression is derived solely from that origin. When we are accustomed to see two impressions conjoined together, the appearance or idea of the one immediately carries us to the idea of the other.

Being fully satisfied on this head, I make a third

set of experiments in order to know whether anything be requisite, besides the customary transition, towards the production of this phenomenon of belief. I therefore change the first impression into an idea and observe that though the customary transition to the correlative idea still remains, yet there is in reality no belief nor persuasion. A present impression, then, is absolutely requisite to this whole operation, and when after this I compare an impression with an idea and find that their only difference consists in their different degrees of force and vivacity, I conclude upon the whole that belief is a more vivid and intense conception of an idea, proceeding from its relation to a present impression.

Thus, all probable reasoning is nothing but a species of sensation. It is not solely in poetry and music we must follow our taste and sentiment, but likewise in philosophy. When I am convinced of any principle, it is only an idea which strikes more strongly upon me. When I give the preference to one set of arguments above another, I do nothing but decide from my feeling concerning the superiority of their influence. Objects have no discoverable connection together, nor is it from any other principle but custom operating upon the imagination that we can draw any inference from the appearance of one to the existence of another.

It will here be worth our observation that the past experience on which all our judgments concerning cause and effect depend may operate on our mind in such an insensible manner as never to be taken notice of and may even in some measure be unknown to us. A person who stops short in his journey upon meeting a river in his way foresees the consequences of his proceeding forward, and his knowledge of these consequences is conveyed to him by past experience, which informs him of such certain conjunctions of causes and effects. But can we think that on this occasion he reflects on any past experience and calls to remembrance instances that he has seen or heard of in order to discover the effects of water on animal bodies? No, surely, this is not the method in which he proceeds in his reasoning. The idea of sinking is so closely connected with that of water and the idea of suffocating with that of sinking that the mind makes the transition without the assistance of the memory.

The custom operates before we have time for reflection. The objects seem so inseparable that we interpose not a moment's delay in passing from the one to the other. But as this transition proceeds from experience and not from any primary connection between the ideas, we must necessarily acknowledge that experience may produce a belief and a judgment of causes and effects by a secret operation and without being once thought of. This removes all pretext, if there yet remains any, for asserting that the mind is convinced by reasoning of that principle *that instances of which we have no experience must necessarily resemble those of which we have.* For we here find that the understanding or imagination can draw inferences from past experience without reflecting on it, much more without forming any principle concerning it or reasoning upon that principle.

In general we may observe that in all the most established and uniform conjunctions of causes and effects, such as those of gravity, impulse, solidity, etc., the mind never carries its view expressly to consider any past experience, though in other associations of objects which are more rare and unusual it may assist the custom and transition of ideas by this reflection. No, we find in some cases that the reflection produces the belief without the custom or, more properly speaking, that the reflection produces the custom in an *oblique* and *artificial* manner. I explain myself. It is certain that not only in philosophy, but even in common life, we may attain the knowledge of a particular cause merely by one experiment, provided it be made with judgment and after a careful removal of all foreign and superfluous circumstances. Now, as after one experiment of this kind, the mind, upon the appearance either of the cause or the effect, can draw an inference concerning the existence of its correlative and as a habit can never be acquired merely by one instance, it may be thought that belief cannot in this case be esteemed the effect of custom. But this difficulty will vanish if we consider that, though we are here supposed to have had only one experiment of a particular effect, yet we have many millions to convince us of this principle *that like objects, placed in like circumstances, will always produce like effects*; and as this principle has established itself by a sufficient custom, it bestows an evidence and firmness on

any opinion to which it can be applied. The connection of the ideas is not habitual after one experiment, but this connection is comprehended under another principle that is habitual, which brings us back to our hypothesis. In all cases we transfer our experience to instances of which we have no experience, either *expressly* or *tacitly*, either *directly* or *indirectly*.

I must not conclude this subject without observing that it is very difficult to talk of the operations of the mind with perfect propriety and exactness, because common language has seldom made any very nice distinctions among them, but has generally called by the same term all such as nearly resemble each other. And as this is a source almost inevitable of obscurity and confusion in the author, so it may frequently give rise to doubts and objections in the reader which otherwise he would never have dreamed of. Thus, my general position that an opinion or belief is *nothing but a strong and lively idea derived from a present impression related to it,* may be liable to the following objection by reason of a little ambiguity in those words *strong* and *lively*. It may be said that not only an impression may give rise to reasoning, but that an idea may also have the same influence, especially upon my principle *that all our ideas are derived from correspondent impressions.* For, suppose I form at present an idea of which I have forgotten the correspondent impression, I am able to conclude from this idea that such an impression did once exist, and as this conclusion is attended with belief, it may be asked: From whence are the qualities of force and vivacity derived which constitute this belief? And to this I answer very readily: *from the present idea.* For as this idea is not here considered as the representation of any absent object, but as a real perception in the mind of which we are intimately conscious, it must be able to bestow on whatever is related to it the same quality, call it *firmness or solidity or force or vivacity,* with which the mind reflects upon it and is assured of its present existence. The idea here supplies the place of an impression and is entirely the same so far as regards our present purpose.

Upon the same principles we need not be surprised to hear of the remembrance of an idea, that is, of the idea of an idea and of its force and vivacity superior to the loose conceptions of the imagination. In thinking of our past thoughts we not only delineate out the objects of which we were thinking, but also conceive the action of the mind in the meditation that certain *je-ne-scai-quoi*, of which it is impossible to give any definition or description, but which every one sufficiently understands. When the memory offers an idea of this and represents it as past, it is easily conceived how that idea may have more vigor and firmness than when we think of a past thought of which we have no remembrance.

After this, anyone will understand how we may form the idea of an impression and of an idea and how we may believe the existence of an impression and of an idea.

Section 9: Of the Effects of Other Relations and Other Habits

However convincing the foregoing arguments may appear, we must not rest contented with them, but must turn the subject on every side in order to find some new points of view from which we may illustrate and confirm such extraordinary and such fundamental principles. A scrupulous hesitation to receive any new hypothesis is so laudable a disposition in philosophers and so necessary to the examination of truth that it deserves to be complied with and requires that every argument be produced which may tend to their satisfaction and every objection removed which may stop them in their reasoning.

I have often observed that, besides cause and effect, the two relations of resemblance and contiguity are to be considered as associating principles of thought and as capable of conveying the imagination from one idea to another. I have also observed that when of two objects connected together by any of these relations, one is immediately present to the memory or senses, not only the mind is conveyed to its correlative by means of the associating principle, but likewise conceives it with an additional force and vigor by the united operation of that principle and of the present impression. All this I have observed in order to confirm, by analogy, my explication of our judgments concerning cause and effect. But this very argument may perhaps be turned against me and, instead of a confirmation of my hypothesis, may be-

come an objection to it. For it may be said that if all the parts of that hypothesis be true, namely, *that* these three species of relation are derived from the same principles — *that* their effects in enforcing and enlivening our ideas are the same, and *that* belief is nothing but a more forcible and vivid conception of an idea — it should follow that that action of the mind may not only be derived from the relation of cause and effect, but also from those of contiguity and resemblance. But as we find by experience that belief arises only from causation and that we can draw no inference from one object to another, except they be connected by this relation, we may conclude that there is some error in that reasoning which leads us into such difficulties.

This is the objection: Let us now consider its solution. It is evident that whatever is present to the memory, striking upon the mind with a vivacity which resembles an immediate impression, must become of considerable moment in all the operations of the mind and must easily distinguish itself above the mere fictions of the imagination. Of these impressions or ideas of the memory we form a kind of system, comprehending whatever we remember to have been present, either to our internal perception or senses, and every particular of that system joined to the present impressions, we are pleased to call a *reality*. But the mind does not stop here. For finding that with this system of perceptions there is another connected by custom or, if you will, by the relation of cause or effect, it proceeds to the consideration of their ideas, and as it feels that it is in a manner necessarily determined to view these particular ideas and that the custom or relation by which it is determined does not admit of the least change, it forms them into a new system, which it likewise dignifies with the title of *realities*. The first of these systems is the object of the memory and senses, the second of the judgment.

It is this latter principle which peoples the world and brings us acquainted with such existences as, by their removal in time and place, lie beyond the reach of the senses and memory. By means of it I paint the universe in my imagination and fix my attention on any part of it I please. I form an idea of *Rome*, which I neither see nor remember, but which is connected with such impressions as I remember to have received from the conversation and books of travelers and historians. This idea of *Rome* I place in a certain situation on the idea of an object which I call the globe. I join to it the conception of a particular government and religion and manners. I look backward and consider its first foundation, its several revolutions, successes, and misfortunes. All this, and everything else which I believe, are nothing but ideas, though, by their force and settled order arising from custom and the relation of cause and effect, they distinguish themselves from the other ideas which are merely the offspring of the imagination.

As to the influence of contiguity and resemblance, we may observe that if the contiguous and resembling object be comprehended in this system of realities, there is no doubt but these two relations will assist that of cause and effect and infix the related idea with more force in the imagination. This I shall enlarge upon presently. Meanwhile I shall carry my observation a step further and assert that even where the related object is but feigned, the relation will serve to enliven the idea and increase its influence. A poet, no doubt, will be the better able to form a strong description of the *Elysian* fields that he prompts his imagination by the view of a beautiful meadow or garden, as at another time he may, by his fancy, place himself in the midst of these fabulous regions that by the feigned contiguity he may enliven his imagination.

But though I cannot altogether exclude the relations of resemblance and contiguity from operating on the fancy in this manner, it is observable that, when single, their influence is very feeble and uncertain. As the relation of cause and effect is requisite to persuade us of any real existence, so is this persuasion requisite to give force to these other relations. For where upon the appearance of an impression we not only feign another object, but likewise arbitrarily and of our mere good-will and pleasure give it a particular relation to the impression, this can have but a small effect upon the mind, nor is there any reason why, upon the return of the same impression, we should be determined to place the same object in the same relation to it. There is no manner of necessity for the mind to feign any resembling and contiguous objects, and if it feigns such, there is as little necessity for

it always to confine itself to the same without any difference or variation. And indeed such a fiction is founded on so little reason that nothing but pure *caprice* can determine the mind to form it and, that principle being fluctuating and uncertain, it is impossible it can ever operate with any considerable degree of force and constancy. The mind foresees and anticipates the change and even from the very first instant feels the looseness of its actions and the weak hold it has of its objects. And as this imperfection is very sensible in every single instance, it still increases by experience and observation when we compare the several instances we may remember and form a *general rule* against the reposing any assurance in those momentary glimpses of light which arise in the imagination from a feigned resemblance and contiguity.

The relation of cause and effect has all the opposite advantages. The objects it presents are fixed and unalterable. The impressions of the memory never change in any considerable degree, and each impression draws along with it a precise idea which takes its place in the imagination as something solid and real, certain and invariable. The thought is always determined to pass from the impression to the idea and from that particular impression to that particular idea without any choice or hesitation.

But not content with removing this objection, I shall endeavor to extract from it a proof of the present doctrine. Contiguity and resemblance have an effect much inferior to causation, but still have some effect and augment the conviction of any opinion and the vivacity of any conception. If this can be proved in several new instances besides what we have already observed, it will be allowed no inconsiderable argument that belief is nothing but a lively idea related to a present impression.

To begin with contiguity, it has been remarked among the *Mohametans* as well as *Christians* that those *pilgrims* who have seen *Mecca* or the *Holy Land* are ever after more faithful and zealous believers than those who have not had that advantage. A man whose memory presents him with a lively image of the *Red Sea, and the Desert, and Jerusalem, and Galilee* can never doubt of any miraculous events which are related either by *Moses or the Evangelists.* The lively idea of the places passes by an easy transition to the facts which are supposed to have been related to them by contiguity and increases the belief by increasing the vivacity of the conception. The remembrance of these fields and rivers has the same influence on the vulgar as a new argument, and from the same causes.

We may form a like observation concerning *resemblance*. We have remarked that the conclusion which we draw from a present object to its absent cause or effect is never founded on any qualities which we observe in that object, considered in itself, or, in other words, that it is impossible to determine otherwise than by experience what will result from any phenomenon or what has preceded it. But though this be so evident in itself that it seemed not to require any proof, yet some philosophers have imagined that there is an apparent cause for the communication of motion and that a reasonable man might immediately infer the motion of one body from the impulse of another without having recourse to any past observation. That this opinion is false will admit of an easy proof. For if such an inference may be drawn merely from the ideas of body, of motion, and of impulse, it must amount to a demonstration and must imply the absolute impossibility of any contrary supposition. Every effect, then, besides the communication of motion, implies a formal contradiction, and it is impossible not only that it can exist, but also that it can be conceived. But we may soon satisfy ourselves of the contrary by forming a clear and consistent idea of one body's moving upon another and of its rest immediately upon the contact; or of its returning back in the same line in which it came; or of its annihilation or circular or elliptical motion; and in short, of an infinite number of other changes which we may suppose it to undergo. These suppositions are all consistent and natural and the reason why we imagine the communication of motion to be more consistent and natural not only than those suppositions but also than any other natural effect, is founded on the relation of *resemblance* between the cause and effect which is here united to experience and binds the objects in the closest and most intimate manner to each other so as to make us imagine them to be absolutely inseparable. Resemblance, then, has the same or a parallel influence with experience and, as the only immediate effect of experience is to associate our ideas together,

it follows that all belief arises from the association of ideas, according to my hypothesis.

It is universally allowed by the writers on optics that the eye at all times sees an equal number of physical points and that a man on the top of a mountain has no larger an image presented to his senses than when he is cooped up in the narrowest court or chamber. It is only by experience that he infers the greatness of the object from some peculiar qualities of the image and this inference of the judgment he confounds with sensation, as is common on other occasions. Now it is evident that the inference of the judgment is here much more lively than what is usual in our common reasonings and that a man has a more vivid conception of the vast extent of the ocean from the image he receives by the eye when he stands on the top of the high promontory than merely from hearing the roaring of the waters. He feels a more sensible pleasure from its magnificence, which is a proof of a more lively idea, and he confounds his judgment with sensation, which is another proof of it. But as the inference is equally certain and immediate in both cases, this superior vivacity of our conception in one case can proceed from nothing but this, that in drawing an inference from the sight, besides the customary conjunction, there is also a resemblance between the image and the object we infer, which strengthens the relation and conveys the vivacity of the impression to the related idea with an easier and more natural movement.

No weakness of human nature is more universal and conspicuous than what we commonly call *credulity*, or a too easy faith in the testimony of others, and this weakness is also very naturally accounted for from the influence of resemblance. When we receive any matter of fact upon human testimony, our faith arises from the very same origin as our inferences from causes to effects and from effects to causes, nor is there anything but our *experience* of the governing principles of human nature which can give us any assurance of the veracity of men. But though experience be the true standard of this as well as of all other judgments, we seldom regulate ourselves entirely by it, but have a remarkable propensity to believe whatever is reported, even concerning apparitions, enchantments, and prodigies, however contrary to daily experience and observation. The words or discourses of others have an intimate connection with certain ideas in their mind and these ideas have also a connection with the facts or objects which they represent. This latter connection is generally much overrated and commands our assent beyond what experience will justify, which can proceed from nothing beside the resemblance between the ideas and the facts. Other effects only point out their causes in an oblique manner, but the testimony of men does it directly and is to be considered as an image as well as an effect. No wonder, therefore, we are so rash in drawing our inferences from it and are less guided by experience in our judgments concerning it than in those upon any other subject.

As resemblance, when conjoined with causation, fortifies our reasonings, so the want of it in any very great degree is able almost entirely to destroy them. Of this there is a remarkable instance in the universal carelessness and stupidity of men with regard to a future state, where they show as obstinate an incredulity as they do a blind credulity on other occasions. There is not indeed a more ample matter of wonder to the studious and of regret to the pious man than to observe the negligence of the bulk of mankind concerning their approaching condition, and it is with reason that many eminent theologians have not scrupled to affirm that though the vulgar have no formal principles of infidelity, yet they are really infidels in their hearts and have nothing like what we can call a belief of the eternal duration of their souls. For let us consider on the one hand what divines have displayed with such eloquence concerning the importance of eternity and at the same time reflect that though in matters of rhetoric we ought to lay our account with some exaggeration, we must in this case allow that the strongest figures are infinitely inferior to the subject. And after this, let us view on the other hand the prodigious security of men in this particular. I ask if these people really believe what is inculcated on them and what they pretend to affirm, and the answer is obviously in the negative. As belief is an act of the mind arising from custom, it is not strange the want of resemblance should overthrow what custom has established and diminish the force

of the idea as much as that latter principle increases it. A future state is so far removed from our comprehension and we have so obscure an idea of the manner in which we shall exist after the dissolution of the body that all the reasons we can invent, however strong in themselves and however much assisted by education, are never able with slow imaginations to surmount this difficulty or bestow a sufficient authority and force on the idea. I rather choose to ascribe this incredulity to the faint idea we form of our future condition, derived from its want of resemblance to the present life, than to that derived from its remoteness. For I observe that men are everywhere concerned about what may happen after their death, provided it regard this world, and that there are few to whom their name, their family, their friends, and their country are, in any period of time, entirely indifferent.

And indeed the want of resemblance in this case so entirely destroys belief that except those few who, upon cool reflection on the importance of the subject, have taken care by repeated meditation to imprint in their minds the arguments for a future state, there scarcely are any who believe the immortality of the soul with a true and established judgment such as is derived from the testimony of travelers and historians. This appears very conspicuously wherever men have occasion to compare the pleasures and pains, the rewards and punishments of this life with those of a future, even though the case does not concern themselves and there is no violent passion to disturb their judgment. The *Roman Catholics* are certainly the most zealous of any sect in the Christian world, and yet you will find few among the more sensible people of that communion who do not blame the *Gunpowder Treason* and the massacre of St. *Bartholomew* as cruel and barbarous, though projected or executed against those very people whom without any scruple they condemn to eternal and infinite punishments. All we can say in excuse for this inconsistency is that they really do not believe what they affirm concerning a future state, nor is there any better proof of it than the very inconsistency.

We may add to this a remark that in matters of religion men take a pleasure in being terrified and that no preachers are so popular as those who excite the most dismal and gloomy passions. In the common affairs of life, where we feel and are penetrated with the solidity of the subject, nothing can be more disagreeable than fear and terror, and it is only in dramatic performances and in religious discourses that they ever give pleasure. In these latter cases the imagination reposes itself indolently on the idea, and the passion, being softened by the want of belief in the subject, has no more than the agreeable effect of enlivening the mind and fixing the attention.

The present hypothesis will receive additional confirmation if we examine the effects of other kinds of custom as well as of other relations. To understand this, we must consider that custom, to which I attribute all belief and reasoning, may operate upon the mind in invigorating an idea after two several ways. For supposing that, in all past experience, we have found two objects to have been always conjoined together, it is evident that upon the appearance of one of these objects in an impression, we must, from custom, make an easy transition to the idea of that object which usually attends it and, by means of the present impression and easy transition, must conceive that idea in a stronger and more lively manner than we do any loose floating image of the fancy. But let us next suppose that a mere idea alone, without any of this curious and almost artificial preparation, should frequently make its appearance in the mind, this idea must, by degrees, acquire a facility and force, and, both by its firm hold and easy introduction, distinguish itself from any new and unusual idea. This is the only particular in which these two kinds of custom agree, and if it appear that their effects on the judgment are similar and proportional, we may certainly conclude that the foregoing explication of that faculty is satisfactory. But can we doubt of this agreement in their influence on the judgment when we consider the nature and effects of education?

All those opinions and notions of things to which we have been accustomed from our infancy take such deep root that it is impossible for us, by all the powers of reason and experience, to eradicate them, and this habit not only approaches in its influence, but even on many occasions prevails over that which arises from the constant and inseparable union of causes and effects. Here we must not be contented with saying that the vividness of the idea produces the belief; we must maintain that they are individually the same. The frequent repetition of any idea infixes it in the imagination, but could never possibly of itself produce belief, if that act of the mind was, by the original constitution of our natures, annexed only to a reasoning and comparison of ideas. Custom may lead us into some false comparison of ideas. This is the utmost effect we can conceive of it, but it is certain it could never supply the place of that comparison, nor produce any act of the mind which naturally belonged to that principle.

A person that has lost a leg or an arm by amputation endeavors for a long time afterwards to serve himself with them. After the death of anyone, it is a common remark of the whole family, but especially of the servants, that they can scarcely believe him to be dead but still imagine him to be in his chamber or in any other place where they were accustomed to find him. I have often heard in conversation, after talking of a person that is any way celebrated, that one who has no acquaintance with him will say, *I have never seen such a one, but almost fancy I have, so often have I heard talk of him.* All these are parallel instances.

If we consider this argument from *education* in a proper light, it will appear very convincing, and the more so that it is founded on one of the most common phenomena that is anywhere to be met with. I am persuaded that, upon examination, we shall find more than one half of those opinions that prevail among mankind to be owing to education and that the principles which are thus implicitly embraced over-balance those which are owing either to abstract reasoning or experience. As liars, by the frequent repetition of their lies, come at last to remember them, so the judgment, or rather the imagination, by the like means, may have ideas so strongly imprinted on it and conceive them in so full a light that they may operate upon the mind in the same manner with those which the senses, memory, or reason present to us. But as education is an artificial and not a natural cause and as its maxims are frequently contrary to reason and even to themselves in different times and places, it is never upon that account recognized by philosophers, though in reality it be built almost on the same foundation of custom and repetition as our reasonings from causes and effects.[14]

Section 12: Of the Probability of Causes

What I have said concerning the probability of chances can serve to no other purpose than to assist us in explaining the probability of causes, since it is commonly allowed by philosophers that what the vulgar call chance is nothing but a secret and concealed cause. That species of probability, therefore, is what we must chiefly examine.

The probabilities of causes are of several kinds, but are all derived from the same origin, namely, *the association of ideas to a present impression.* As the habit which produces the association arises from the frequent conjunction of objects, it must arrive at its perfection by degrees and must acquire new force from each instance that falls under our observation. The first instance has little or no force, the second makes some addition to it, the third becomes still more sensible, and it is by these slow steps that our judgment arrives at a full assurance. But before it attains this pitch of perfection, it passes through several inferior degrees and in all of them is only to be esteemed a presumption or probability. The gradation, therefore, from probabilities to proofs is in many cases insensible, and the difference between these kinds of evidence is more easily perceived in the remote degrees than in the near and contiguous.

It is worthy of remark on this occasion that though

the species of probability here explained be the first in order and naturally takes place before any entire proof can exist, yet no one who is arrived at the age of maturity can any longer be acquainted with it. It is true that nothing is more common than for people of the most advanced knowledge to have attained only an imperfect experience of many particular events, which naturally produces only an imperfect habit and transition, but then we must consider that the mind, having formed another observation concerning the connection of causes and effects, gives new force to its reasoning from that observation and by means of it can build an argument on one single experiment when duly prepared and examined. What we have found once to follow from any object, we conclude will forever follow from it, and if this maxim be not always built upon as certain, it is not for want of a sufficient number of experiments, but because we frequently meet with instances to the contrary, which leads us to the second species of probability, where there is a *contrariety* in our experience and observation.

It would be very happy for men in the conduct of their lives and actions, were the same objects always conjoined together and we had nothing to fear but the mistakes of our own judgment without having any reason to apprehend the uncertainty of nature. But as it is frequently found that one observation is contrary to another and that causes and effects follow not in the same order of which we have had experience, we are obliged to vary our reasoning on account of this uncertainty and take into consideration the contrariety of events. The first question that occurs on this head is concerning the nature and causes of the contrariety.

The vulgar, who take things according to their first appearance, attribute the uncertainty of events to such an uncertainty in the causes as makes them often fail of their usual influence, though they meet with no obstacle nor impediment in their operation. But philosophers, observing that almost in every part of nature there is contained a vast variety of springs and principles which are hidden by reason of their minuteness or remoteness, find that it is at least possible the contrariety of events may not proceed from any contingency in the cause, but from the secret operation

---

14. In general we may observe that as our assent to all probable reasonings is founded on the vivacity of ideas, it resembles many of those whimsies and prejudices which are rejected under the opprobrious character of being the offspring of the imagination. By this expression it appears that the word imagination is commonly used in two different senses, and though nothing be more contrary to true philosophy than this inaccuracy, yet, in the following reasonings, I have often been obliged to fall into it. When I oppose the imagination to the memory, I mean the faculty by which we form our fainter ideas. When I oppose it to reason, I mean the same faculty, excluding only our demonstrative and probable reasonings. When I oppose it to neither, it is indifferent whether it be taken in the larger or more limited sense, or at least the context will sufficiently explain the meaning.

of contrary causes. This possibility is converted into certainty by further observation, when they remark that upon an exact scrutiny, a contrariety of effects always betrays a contrariety of causes and proceeds from their mutual hindrance and opposition. A peasant can give no better reason for the stopping of any clock or watch than to say that commonly it does not go right, but an artisan easily perceives that the same force in the spring or pendulum has always the same influence on the wheels, but fails of its usual effect, perhaps by reason of a grain of dust, which puts a stop to the whole movement. From the observation of several parallel instances, philosophers form a maxim that the connection between all causes and effects is equally necessary and that its seeming uncertainty in some instances proceeds from the secret opposition of contrary causes.

But however philosophers and the vulgar may differ in their explication of the contrariety of events, their inferences from it are always of the same kind and founded on the same principles. A contrariety of events in the past may give us a kind of hesitating belief for the future after two several ways. *First*, by producing an imperfect habit and transition from the present impression to the related idea. When the conjunction of any two objects is frequent without being entirely constant, the mind is determined to pass from one object to the other, but not with so entire a habit as when the union is uninterrupted and all the instances we have ever met with are uniform and of a piece. We find from common experience, in our actions as well as reasonings, that a constant perseverance in any course of life produces a strong inclination and tendency to continue for the future, though there are habits of inferior degrees of force proportioned to the inferior degrees of steadiness and uniformity in our conduct.

There is no doubt but this principle sometimes takes place and produces those inferences we draw from contrary phenomena, though I am persuaded that, upon examination, we shall not find it to be the principle that most commonly influences the mind in this species of reasoning. When we follow only the habitual determination of the mind, we make the transition without any reflection and interpose not a moment's delay between the view of one object and the belief of that which is often found to attend it. As the custom depends not upon any deliberation, it operates immediately, without allowing any time for reflection. But this method of proceeding we have but few instances of in our probable reasonings and even fewer than in those which are derived from the uninterrupted conjunction of objects. In the former species of reasoning we commonly take knowingly into consideration the contrariety of past events, we compare the different sides of the contrariety and carefully weigh the experiments which we have on each side: whence we may conclude that our reasonings of this kind arise not *directly* from the habit, but in an *oblique* manner, which we must now endeavor to explain.

It is evident that when an object is attended with contrary effects, we judge of them only by our past experience and always consider those as possible which we have observed to follow from it. And as past experience regulates our judgment concerning the possibility of these effects, so it does that concerning their probability, and that effect which has been the most common we always esteem the most likely. Here, then, are two things to be considered, namely, the *reasons* which determine us to make the past a standard for the future and the *manner* how we extract a single judgment from a contrariety of past events.

First, we may observe that the supposition *that the future resembles the past* is not founded on arguments of any kind, but is derived entirely from habit by which we are determined to expect for the future the same train of objects to which we have been accustomed. This habit or determination to transfer the past to the future is full and perfect, and, consequently, the first impulse of the imagination in this species of reasoning is endowed with the same qualities.

But, *secondly*, when in considering past experiments we find them of a contrary nature, this determination, though full and perfect in itself, presents us with no steady object, but offers us a number of disagreeing images in a certain order and proportion. The first impulse therefore is here broke into pieces and diffuses itself over all those images of which each partakes an equal share of that force and vivacity that is derived from the impulse. Any of these past events may again happen, and we judge that when they do happen, they will be mixed in the same proportion as in the past.

If our intention, therefore, be to consider the proportions of contrary events in a great number of instances, the images presented by our past experience must remain in their *first form* and preserve their first proportions. Suppose, for instance, I have found, by long observation, that of twenty ships which go to sea, only nineteen return. Suppose I see at present twenty ships that leave the port. I transfer my past experience to the future and represent to myself nineteen of these ships as returning in safety and one as perishing. Concerning this there can be no difficulty. But as we frequently run over those several ideas of past events in order to form a judgment concerning one single event which appears uncertain, this consideration must change the *first form* of our ideas and draw together the divided images presented by experience, since it is to *it* we refer the determination of that particular event upon which we reason. Many of these images are supposed to concur and a superior number to concur on one side. These agreeing images unite together and render the idea more strong and lively, not only than a mere fiction of the imagination, but also than any idea which is supported by a lesser number of experiments. Each new experiment is as a new stroke of the pencil which bestows an additional vivacity on the colors without either multiplying or enlarging the figure. This operation of the mind has been so fully explained in treating of the probability of chance that I need not here endeavor to render it more intelligible. Every past experiment may be considered as a kind of chance, it being uncertain to us whether the object will exist conformable to one experiment or another. And for this reason everything that has been said on the one subject is applicable to both.

Thus, upon the whole, contrary experiments produce an imperfect belief, either by weakening the habit or by dividing and afterwards joining in different parts that *perfect* habit which makes us conclude, in general, that instances of which we have no experience must necessarily resemble those of which we have.

To justify still further this account of the second species of probability, where we reason with knowledge and reflection from a contrariety of past experiments, I shall propose the following considerations without fearing to give offence by that air of subtlety which attends them. Just reasoning ought still, perhaps, to retain its force, however subtle, in the same manner as matter preserves its solidity in the air and fire and animal spirits as well as in the grosser and more sensible forms.

First, we may observe that there is no probability so great as not to allow of a contrary possibility, because otherwise it would cease to be a probability and would become a certainty. That probability of causes which is most extensive and which we at present examine depends on a contrariety of experiments and it is evident that an experiment in the past proves at least a possibility for the future.

Secondly, the component parts of this possibility and probability are of the same nature and differ in number only, but not in kind. It has been observed that all single chances are entirely equal and that the only circumstance which can give any event that is contingent a superiority over another is a superior number of chances. In like manner, as the uncertainty of causes is discovered by experience which presents us with a view of contrary events, it is plain that when we transfer the past to the future, the known to the unknown, every past experiment has the same weight and that it is only a superior number of them which can throw the balance on any side. The possibility, therefore, which enters into every reasoning of this kind is composed of parts which are of the same nature both among themselves and with those that compose the opposite probability.

Thirdly, we may establish it as a certain maxim that in all moral as well as natural phenomena, wherever any cause consists of a number of parts and the effect increases or diminishes according to the variation of that number, the effect, properly speaking, is a compounded one and arises from the union of the several effects that proceed from each part of the cause. Thus, because the gravity of a body increases or diminishes by the increase or diminution of its parts, we conclude that each part contains this quality and contributes to the gravity of the whole. The absence or presence of a part of the cause is attended with that of a proportional part of the effect. This connection or constant conjunction sufficiently proves the one part to be the cause of the other. As the belief which we have of any event increases or diminishes according to the number of chances or past experiments, it is to be considered as a compounded effect of which each part arises from a proportional number of chances or experiments.

Let us now join these three observations and see what conclusion we can draw from them. To every probability there is an opposite possibility. This possibility is composed of parts that are entirely of the same nature with those of the probability and consequently have the same influence on the mind and understanding. The belief which attends the probability is a compounded effect and is formed by the concurrence of the several effects which proceed from each part of the probability. Since, therefore, each part of the probability contributes to the production of the belief, each part of the possibility must have the same influence on the opposite side, the nature of these parts being entirely the same. The contrary belief attending the possibility implies a view of a certain object as well as the probability does an opposite view. In this particular both these degrees of belief are alike. The only manner, then, in which the superior number of similar component parts in the one can exert its influence and prevail above the inferior in the other is by producing a stronger and more lively view of its object. Each part presents a particular view and all these views uniting together produce one general view, which is fuller and more distinct by the greater number of causes or principles from which it is derived.

The component parts of the probability and possibility, being alike in their nature, must produce like effects, and the likeness of their effects consists in this, that each of them presents a view of a particular object. But though these parts be alike in their nature, they are very different in their quantity and number, and this difference must appear in the effect as well as the similarity. Now, as the view they present is in both cases full and entire and comprehends the object in all its parts, it is impossible that, in this particular, there can be any difference, nor is there anything but a superior vivacity in the probability arising from the

concurrence of a superior number of views which can distinguish these effects.

Here is almost the same argument in a different light. All our reasonings concerning the probability of causes are founded on the transferring of past to future. The transferring of any past experiment to the future is sufficient to give us a view of the object, whether that experiment be single or combined with others of the same kind, whether it be entire or opposed by others of a contrary kind. Suppose then it acquires both these qualities of combination and opposition, it does not lose, upon that account, its former power of presenting a view of the object, but only concurs with and opposes other experiments that have a like influence. A question, therefore, may arise concerning the manner both of the concurrence and opposition. As to the *concurrence*, there is only the choice left between these two hypotheses. *First*, that the view of the object occasioned by the transference of each past experiment preserves itself entire and only multiplies the number of views. Or *secondly*, that it runs into the other similar and correspondent views and gives them a superior degree of force and vivacity. But that the first hypothesis is erroneous is evident from experience, which informs us that the belief attending any reasoning consists in one conclusion, not in a multitude of similar ones which would only distract the mind and, in many cases, would be too numerous to be comprehended distinctly by any finite capacity. It remains, therefore, as the only reasonable opinion that these similar views run into each other and unite their forces, so as to produce a stronger and clearer view than what arises from any one alone. This is the manner in which past experiments concur when they are transferred to any future event. As to the manner of their *opposition*, it is evident that, as the contrary views are incompatible with each other and it is impossible the object can at once exist conformable to both of them, their influence becomes mutually destructive and the mind is determined to the superior only with that force which remains after subtracting the inferior.

I am sensible how abstruse all this reasoning must appear to the generality of readers who, not being accustomed to such profound reflections on the intellectual faculties of the mind, will be apt to reject as chimerical whatever does not strike in with the common received notions and with the easiest and most obvious principles of philosophy. And, no doubt, there are some pains required to enter into these arguments, though perhaps very little are necessary to perceive the imperfection of every vulgar hypothesis on this subject and the little light which philosophy can yet afford us in such sublime and such curious speculations. Let men be once fully persuaded of these two principles, *that there is nothing in any object, considered in itself, which can afford us a reason for drawing a conclusion beyond it; and that even after the observation of the frequent or constant conjunction of objects, we have no reason to draw any inference concerning any object beyond those of which we have had experience*. I say: Let men be once fully convinced of these two principles, and this will throw them so loose from all common systems that they will make no difficulty of receiving any which may appear the most extraordinary. These principles we have found to be sufficiently convincing, even with regard to our most certain reasonings from causation, but I shall venture to affirm that with regard to these conjectural or probable reasonings they still acquire a new degree of evidence.

First, it is obvious that, in reasonings of this kind, it is not the object presented to us which, considered in itself, affords us any reason to draw a conclusion concerning any other object or event. For as this latter object is supposed uncertain and as the uncertainty is derived from a concealed contrariety of causes in the former, were any of the causes placed in the known qualities of that object, they would no longer be concealed, nor would our conclusion be uncertain.

But, *secondly,* it is equally obvious in this species of reasoning that if the transference of the past to the future were founded merely on a conclusion of the understanding, it could never occasion any belief or assurance. When we transfer contrary experiments to the future, we can only repeat these contrary experiments with their particular proportions, which could not produce assurance in any single event upon which we reason unless the fancy melted together all those images that concur and extracted from them one single idea or image which is intense and lively in proportion to the number of experiments from which it is derived and their superiority above their antagonists. Our past experience presents no determinate object, and as our belief, however faint, fixes itself on a determinate object, it is evident that the belief arises not merely from the transference of past to future, but from some operation of the *fancy* conjoined with it. This may lead us to conceive the manner in which that faculty enters into all our reasonings.

I shall conclude this subject with two reflections which may deserve our attention. The *first* may be explained after this manner. When the mind forms a reasoning concerning any matter of fact which is only probable, it casts its eye backward upon past experience and, transferring it to the future, is presented with so many contrary views of its object of which those that are of the same kind uniting together and running into one act of the mind, serve to fortify and enliven it. But suppose that this multitude of views or glimpses of an object proceeds not from experience, but from a voluntary act of the imagination; this effect does not follow, or, at least, follows not in the same degree. For though custom and education produce belief by such a repetition as is not derived from experience, yet this requires a long tract of time along with a very frequent and *undesigned* repetition. In general we may pronounce that a person who would *voluntarily* repeat any idea in his mind, though supported by one past experience, would be no more inclined to believe the existence of its object than if he had contented himself with one survey of it. Besides the effect of design, each act of the mind, being separate and independent, has a separate influence and does not join its force with that of its fellows. Not being united by any common object producing them, they have no relation to each other and consequently make no transition or union of forces. This phenomenon we shall understand better afterwards.

My *second* reflection is founded on those large probabilities which the mind can judge of and the minute differences it can observe between them. When the chances or experiments on one side amount to ten thousand and on the other to ten thousand and one, the judgment gives the preference to the latter upon account of that superiority, though it is plainly impossible for the mind to run over every particular view and distinguish the superior vivacity of the image arising from the superior number where the difference is so inconsiderable. We have a parallel instance in the affections. It is evident according to the principles above mentioned that when an object produces any passion in us which varies according to the different quantity of the object, I say, it is evident that the passion, properly speaking, is not a simple emotion, but a compounded one of a great number of weaker passions derived from a view of each part of the object, for otherwise it were impossible the passion should increase by the increase of these parts. Thus a man who desires a thousand pound has, in reality, a thousand or more desires which, uniting together, seem to make only one passion, though the composition evidently betrays itself upon every alteration of the object by the preference he gives to the larger number, if superior only by one unit. Yet nothing can be more certain than that so small a difference would not be discernible in the passions, nor could render them distinguishable from each other. The difference, therefore, of our conduct in preferring the greater number depends not upon our passions, but upon custom and *general rules*. We have found in a multitude of instances that the augmenting the numbers of any sum augments the passion, where the numbers are precise and the difference sensible. The mind can perceive from its immediate feeling that three guineas produce a greater passion than two, and *this* it transfers to larger numbers, because of the resemblance, and by a general rule assigns to a thousand guineas a stronger passion than to nine hundred and ninety-nine. These general rules we shall explain presently.

But besides these two species of probability, which are derived from an *imperfect* experience and from *contrary* causes, there is a third arising from *analogy*, which differs from them in some material circumstances. According to the hypothesis explained above, all kinds of reasoning from causes or effects are founded on two particulars, namely, the constant conjunction of any two objects in all past experience and the resemblance of a present object to any one of them. The effect of these two particulars is that the present object invigorates and enlivens the imagina-

tion, and the resemblance, along with the constant union, conveys this force and vivacity to the related idea, which we are therefore said to believe or assent to. If you weaken either the union or resemblance, you weaken the principle of transition and, of consequence, that belief which arises from it. The vivacity of the first impression cannot be fully conveyed to the related idea, either where the conjunction of their objects is not constant or where the present impression does not perfectly resemble any of those whose union we are accustomed to observe. In those probabilities of chance and causes explained above, it is the constancy of the union which is diminished, and in the probability derived from analogy, it is the resemblance only which is affected. Without some degree of resemblance as well as union, it is impossible there can be any reasoning. But as this resemblance admits of many different degrees, the reasoning becomes proportionally more or less firm and certain. An experiment loses of its force when transferred to instances which are not exactly resembling, though it is evident that it may still retain as much as may be the foundation of probability as long as there is any resemblance remaining.

Section 14: Of the Idea of Necessary Connection

Having thus explained the manner *in which we reason beyond our immediate impressions, and conclude that such particular causes must have such particular effects*, we must now return upon our footsteps to examine that question[15] which first occurred to us and which we dropped in our way, namely, *What is our idea of necessity when we say that two objects are necessarily connected together?* Upon this head I repeat what I have often had occasion to observe, namely, that as we have no idea that is not derived from an impression, we must find some impression that gives rise to this idea of necessity, if we assert we have really such an idea. In order to [determine] this, I consider in what objects necessity is commonly supposed to lie, and, finding that it is always ascribed to causes and effects, I turn my eye to two objects

15. Sec. 2.

supposed to be placed in that relation and examine them in all the situations of which they are susceptible. I immediately perceive that they are *contiguous* in time and place and that the object we call cause *precedes* the other we call effect. In no one instance can I go any further, nor is it possible for me to discover any third relation between these objects. I therefore enlarge my view to comprehend several instances where I find like objects always existing in like relations of contiguity and succession. At first sight, this seems to serve but little to my purpose. The reflection on several instances only repeats the same objects and therefore can never give rise to a new idea. But upon further inquiry I find that the repetition is not in every particular the same, but produces a new impression and, by that means, the idea which I at present examine. For, after a frequent repetition, I find that upon the appearance of one of the objects the mind is *determined* by custom to consider its usual attendant and to consider it in a stronger light upon account of its relation to the first object. It is this impression, then, or *determination*, which affords me the idea of necessity.

I doubt not but these consequences will at first sight be received without difficulty, as being evident deductions from principles which we have already established and which we have often employed in our reasonings. This evidence, both in the first principles and in the deductions, may seduce us unwarily into the conclusion and make us imagine it contains nothing extraordinary nor worthy of our curiosity. But though such an inadvertence may facilitate the reception of this reasoning, it will make it be the more easily forgotten, for which reason I think it proper to give warning that I have just now examined one of the most sublime questions in philosophy, namely, *that concerning the power and efficacy of causes,* where all the sciences seem so much interested. Such a warning will naturally rouse up the attention of the reader and make him desire a more full account of my doctrine as well as of the arguments on which it is founded. This request is so reasonable that I cannot refuse complying with it, especially as I am hopeful that these principles, the more they are examined, will acquire the more force and evidence.

There is no question which, on account of its im-

portance as well as difficulty, has caused more disputes both among ancient and modern philosophers than this concerning the efficacy of causes, or that quality which makes them be followed by their effects. But before they entered upon these disputes, I think it would not have been improper to have examined what idea we have of that efficacy which is the subject of the controversy. This is what I find principally wanting in their reasonings and what I shall here endeavor to supply.

I begin with observing that the terms of *efficacy, agency, power, force, energy, necessity, connection,* and *productive quality* are all nearly synonymous, and, therefore, it is an absurdity to employ any of them in defining the rest. By this observation we reject at once all the vulgar definitions which philosophers have given of power and efficacy and, instead of searching for the idea in these definitions, must look for it in the impressions from which it is originally derived. If it be a compound idea, it must arise from compound impressions. If simple, from simple impressions.

I believe the most general and most popular explication of this matter is to say[16] that finding from experience that there are several new productions in matter, such as the motions and variations of body, and concluding that there must somewhere be a power capable of producing them, we arrive at last by this reasoning at the idea of power and efficacy. But to be convinced that this explication is more popular than philosophical, we need but reflect on two very obvious principles. *First,* that reason alone can never give rise to any original idea and *secondly,* that reason, as distinguished from experience, can never make us conclude that a cause or productive quality is absolutely requisite to every beginning of existence. Both these considerations have been sufficiently explained and therefore shall not at present be any further insisted on.

I shall only infer from them that since reason can never give rise to the idea of efficacy, that idea must be derived from experience and from some particular instances of this efficacy which make their passage into the mind by the common channels of sensation

16. See Mr. Locke, chapter of Power.

or reflection. Ideas always represent their objects or impressions, and *vice versa*, there are some objects necessary to give rise to every idea. If we pretend, therefore, to have any just idea of this efficacy, we must produce some instance wherein the efficacy is plainly discoverable to the mind and its operations obvious to our consciousness or sensation. By the refusal of this, we acknowledge that the idea is impossible and imaginary, since the principle of innate ideas, which alone can save us from this dilemma, has been already refuted and is now almost universally rejected in the learned world. Our present business, then, must be to find some natural production where the operation and efficacy of a cause can be clearly conceived and comprehended by the mind without any danger of obscurity or mistake.

In this research we meet with very little encouragement from that prodigious diversity which is found in the opinions of those philosophers who have pretended to explain the secret force and energy of causes.[17] There are some who maintain that bodies operate by their substantial form; others, by their accidents or qualities; several, by their matter and form; some, by their form and accidents; others, by certain virtues and faculties distinct from all this. All these sentiments, again, are mixed and varied in a thousand different ways and form a strong presumption that none of them have any solidity or evidence and that the supposition of an efficacy in any of the known qualities of matter is entirely without foundation. This presumption must increase upon us when we consider that these principles of substantial forms and accidents and faculties are not in reality any of the known properties of bodies, but are perfectly unintelligible and inexplicable. For it is evident that philosophers would never have had recourse to such obscure and uncertain principles, had they met with any satisfaction in such as are clear and intelligible — especially in such an affair as this which must be an object of the simplest understanding, if not of the senses. Upon the whole, we may conclude that it is impossible, in any one instance, to show the principle in which the force and agency of a cause is placed and

that the most refined and most vulgar understandings are equally at a loss in this particular. If anyone think proper to refute this assertion, he need not put himself to the trouble of inventing any long reasonings, but may at once show us an instance of a cause where we discover the power or operating principle. This defiance we are obliged frequently to make use of, as being almost the only means of proving a negative in philosophy.

The small success which has been met with in all the attempts to fix this power has at last obliged philosophers to conclude that the ultimate force and efficacy of nature is perfectly unknown to us and that it is in vain we search for it in all the known qualities of matter. In this opinion they are almost unanimous, and it is only in the inference they draw from it that they discover any difference in their sentiments. For some of them, as the *Cartesians* in particular, having established it as a principle that we are perfectly acquainted with the essence of matter, have very naturally inferred that it is endowed with no efficacy and that it is impossible for it of itself to communicate motion or produce any of those effects which we ascribe to it. As the essence of matter consists in extension, and as extension implies not actual motion, but only mobility, they conclude that the energy which produces the motion cannot lie in the extension.

This conclusion leads them into another, which they regard as perfectly unavoidable. Matter, say they, is in itself entirely inactive and deprived of any power by which it may produce or continue or communicate motion, but since these effects are evident to our senses, and since the power that produces them must be placed somewhere, it must lie in the *Deity*, or that Divine Being who contains in his nature all excellency and perfection. It is the Deity, therefore, who is the prime mover of the universe and who not only first created matter and gave it its original impulse, but likewise, by a continued exertion of omnipotence, supports its existence and successively bestows on it all those motions and configurations and qualities with which it is endowed.

This opinion is certainly very curious and well worth our attention, but it will appear superfluous to examine it in this place if we reflect a moment on

17. See Father Malebranche, Book VI, Part II, chap. 3, and the illustrations upon it.

our present purpose in taking notice of it. We have established it as a principle that as all ideas are derived from impressions, or some precedent *perceptions*, it is impossible we can have any idea of power and efficacy, unless some instances can be produced wherein this power *is perceived* to exert itself. Now, as these instances can never be discovered in body, the *Cartesians*, proceeding upon their principle of innate ideas, have had recourse to a Supreme Spirit or Deity, whom they consider as the only active being in the universe and as the immediate cause of every alteration in matter. But the principle of innate ideas being allowed to be false, it follows that the supposition of a Deity can serve us in no stead in accounting for that idea of agency which we search for in vain in all the objects which are presented to our senses or which we are internally conscious of in our own minds. For if every idea be derived from an impression, the idea of a Deity proceeds from the same origin, and if no impression, either of sensation or reflection, implies any force or efficacy, it is equally impossible to discover or even imagine any such active principle in the Deity. Since these philosophers, therefore, have concluded that matter cannot be endowed with any efficacious principle, because it is impossible to discover in it such a principle, the same course of reasoning should determine them to exclude it from the Supreme Being. Or, if they esteem that opinion absurd and impious, as it really is, I shall tell them how they may avoid it, and that is by concluding from the very first that they have no adequate idea of power or efficacy in any object, since neither in body nor spirit, neither in superior nor inferior natures are they able to discover one single instance of it.

The same conclusion is unavoidable upon the hypothesis of those who maintain the efficacy of second causes and attribute a derivative, but a real, power and energy to matter. For as they confess that this energy does not lie in any of the known qualities of matter, the difficulty still remains concerning the origin of its idea. If we have really an idea of power, we may attribute power to an unknown quality, but as it is impossible that that idea can be derived from such a quality and as there is nothing in known qualities which can produce it, it follows that we deceive ourselves when we imagine we are possessed of any idea of this kind after the manner we commonly understand it. All ideas are derived from and represent impressions. We never have any impression that contains any power or efficacy. We never, therefore, have any idea of power.

Some have asserted that we feel an energy or power in our own mind and that, having in this manner acquired the idea of power, we transfer that quality to matter where we are not able immediately to discover it. The motions of our body and the thoughts and sentiments of our mind (say they) obey the will, nor do we seek any further to acquire a just notion of force or power. But to convince us how fallacious this reasoning is, we need only consider that the will being here considered as a cause has no more a discoverable connection with its effects than any material cause has with its proper effect. So far from perceiving the connection between an act of volition and a motion of the body, it is allowed that no effect is more inexplicable from the powers and essence of thought and matter. Nor is the empire of the will over our mind more intelligible. The effect is there distinguishable and separable from the cause and could be foreseen without the experience of their constant conjunction. We have command over our mind to a certain degree, but beyond that lose all empire over it. And it is evidently impossible to fix any precise bounds to our authority where we do not consult experience. In short, the actions of the mind are, in this respect, the same with those of matter. We perceive only their constant conjunction, nor can we ever reason beyond it. No internal impression has an apparent energy more than external objects have. Since, therefore, matter is confessed by philosophers to operate by an unknown force, we should in vain hope to attain an idea of force by consulting our own minds.[18]

---

18. The same imperfection attends our ideas of the Deity, but this can have no effect either on religion or morals. The order of the universe proves an omnipotent mind, that is, a mind whose will is constantly attended with the obedience of every creature and being. Nothing more is requisite to give a foundation to all the articles of religion, nor is it necessary we should form a distinct idea of the force and energy of the Supreme Being.

It has been established as a certain principle that general or abstract ideas are nothing but individual ones taken in a certain light and that, in reflecting on any object, it is as impossible to exclude from our thought all particular degrees of quantity and quality as from the real nature of things. If we be possessed, therefore, of any idea of power in general, we must also be able to conceive some particular species of it, and as power cannot subsist alone, but is always regarded as an attribute of some being or existence, we must be able to place this power in some particular being and conceive that being as endowed with a real force and energy by which such a particular effect necessarily results from its operation. We must distinctly and particularly conceive the connection between the cause and effect and be able to pronounce from a simple view of the one that it must be followed or preceded by the other. This is the true manner of conceiving a particular power in a particular body, and a general idea being impossible without an individual, where the latter is impossible, it is certain the former can never exist. Now nothing is more evident than that the human mind cannot form such an idea of two objects as to conceive any connection between them or comprehend distinctly that power or efficacy by which they are united. Such a connection would amount to a demonstration and would imply the absolute impossibility for the one object not to follow or to be conceived not to follow upon the other, which kind of connection has already been rejected in all cases. If anyone is of a contrary opinion and thinks he has attained a notion of power in any particular object, I desire he may point out to me that object. But until I meet with such a one, which I despair of, I cannot forbear concluding that since we can never distinctly conceive how any particular power can possibly reside in any particular object, we deceive ourselves in imagining we can form any such general idea.

Thus, upon the whole, we may infer that when we talk of any being, whether of a superior or inferior nature, as endowed with a power or force, proportioned to any effect; when we speak of a necessary connection between objects and suppose that this connection depends upon an efficacy or energy with which any of these objects are endowed; in all these

expressions, *so applied*, we have really no distinct meaning and make use only of common words without any clear and determinate ideas. But as it is more probable that these expressions do here lose their true meaning by being *wrongly applied* than that they never have any meaning, it will be proper to bestow another consideration on this subject to see if possibly we can discover the nature and origin of those ideas we annex to them.

Suppose two objects to be presented to us of which the one is the cause and the other the effect; it is plain that, from the simple consideration of one or both these objects, we never shall perceive the tie by which they are united or be able certainly to pronounce that there is a connection between them. It is not, therefore, from any one instance that we arrive at the idea of cause and effect, of a necessary connection of power, of force, of energy, and of efficacy. Did we never see any but particular conjunctions of objects, entirely different from each other, we should never be able to form any such ideas.

But, again, suppose we observe several instances in which the same objects are always conjoined together, we immediately conceive a connection between them and begin to draw an inference from one to another. This multiplicity of resembling instances, therefore, constitutes the very essence of power or connection and is the source from which the idea of it arises. In order, then, to understand the idea of power, we must consider that multiplicity, nor do I ask more to give a solution of that difficulty which has so long perplexed us. For thus I reason. The repetition of perfectly similar instances can never *alone* give rise to an original idea, different from what is to be found in any particular instance, as has been observed and as evidently follows from our fundamental principle *that all ideas are copied from impressions*. Since, therefore, the idea of power is a new original idea, not to be found in any one instance, and which yet arises from the repetition of several instances, it follows that the repetition *alone* does not have that effect, but must either *discover* or *produce* something new, which is the source of that idea. Did the repetition neither discover nor produce anything new, our ideas might be multiplied by it, but would not be enlarged above what they are upon the observation of one single instance. Every enlargement, therefore (such as the idea of power or connection) which arises from the multiplicity of similar instances is copied from some effects of the multiplicity and will be perfectly understood by understanding these effects. Wherever we find anything new to be discovered or produced by the repetition, there we must place the power and must never look for it in any other object.

But it is evident, in the first place, that the repetition of like objects in like relations of succession and contiguity *discovers* nothing new in any one of them, since we can draw no inference from it, nor make it a subject either of our demonstrative or probable reasonings, as has been already proved.[19] No, suppose we could draw an inference, it would be of no consequence in the present case, since no kind of reasoning can give rise to a new idea such as this of power is, but wherever we reason, we must antecedently be possessed of clear ideas which may be the objects of our reasoning. The conception always precedes the understanding, and where the one is obscure, the other is uncertain; where the one fails, the other must fail also.

Secondly, it is certain that this repetition of similar objects in similar situations *produces* nothing new either in these objects or in any external body. For it will readily be allowed that the several instances we have of the conjunction of resembling causes and effects are, in themselves, entirely independent and that the communication of motion, which I see result at present from the shock of two billiard balls, is totally distinct from that which I saw result from such an impulse a year ago. These impulses have no influence on each other. They are entirely divided by time and place and the one might have existed and communicated motion though the other never had been in being.

There is, then, nothing new either discovered or produced in any objects by their constant conjunction and by the uninterrupted resemblance of their relations of succession and contiguity. But it is from this resemblance that the ideas of necessity, of power, and of efficacy are derived. These ideas, therefore, represent not anything that does or can belong to the objects which are constantly conjoined. This is an argument which, in every view we can examine it, will be found perfectly unanswerable. Similar instances are still the first source of our idea of power or necessity, at the same time that they have no influence by their similarity either on each other or on any external object. We must, therefore, turn ourselves to some other quarter to seek the origin of that idea.

Though the several resembling instances which give rise to the idea of power have no influence on each other and can never produce any new quality *in the object,* which can be the model of that idea, yet the *observation* of this resemblance produces a new impression *in the mind,* which is its real model. For after we have observed the resemblance in a sufficient number of instances, we immediately feel a determination of the mind to pass from one object to its usual attendant and to conceive it in a stronger light upon account of that relation. This determination is the only effect of the resemblance and, therefore, must be the same with power or efficacy, whose idea is derived from the resemblance. The several instances of resembling conjunctions lead us into the notion of power and necessity. These instances are in themselves totally distinct from each other and have no union but in the mind which observes them and collects their ideas. Necessity, then, is the effect of this observation, and is nothing but an internal impression of the mind or a determination to carry our thoughts from one object to another. Without considering it in this view, we can never arrive at the most distant notion of it or be able to attribute it either to external or internal objects, to spirit or body, to causes or effects.

The necessary connection between causes and effects is the foundation of our inference from one to the other. The foundation of our inference is the transition arising from the accustomed union. These are, therefore, the same.

The idea of necessity arises from some impression. There is no impression conveyed by our senses which can give rise to that idea. It must, therefore, be derived from some internal impression, or impression of reflection. There is no internal impression which has any relation to the present business but that propensity which custom produces to pass from an object to the

19. Sec. 6.

idea of its usual attendant. This, therefore, is the essence of necessity. Upon the whole, necessity is something that exists in the mind, not in objects, nor is it possible for us ever to form the most distant idea of it, considered as a quality in bodies. Either we have no idea of necessity or necessity is nothing but that determination of the thought to pass from causes to effects and from effects to causes, according to their experienced union.

Thus, as the necessity which makes two times two equal to four, or three angles of a triangle equal to two right ones lies only in the act of the understanding by which we consider and compare these ideas, in like manner the necessity or power which unites causes and effects lies in the determination of the mind to pass from the one to the other. The efficacy or energy of causes is neither placed in the causes themselves, nor in the Deity, nor in the concurrence of these two principles, but belongs entirely to the soul, which considers the union of two or more objects in all past instances. It is here that the real power of causes is placed, along with their connection and necessity.

I am sensible that of all the paradoxes which I have had or shall hereafter have occasion to advance in the course of this Treatise, the present one is the most violent and that it is merely by dint of solid proof and reasoning I can ever hope it will have admission and overcome the inveterate prejudices of mankind. Before we are reconciled to this doctrine, how often must we repeat to ourselves *that* the simple view of any two objects or actions, however related, can never give us any idea of power or of a connection between them: *that* this idea arises from the repetition of their union: *that* the repetition neither discovers nor causes anything in the objects, but has an influence only on the mind by that customary transition it produces: *that* this customary transition is therefore the same with the power and necessity which are consequently qualities of perceptions, not of objects, and are internally felt by the soul and not perceived externally in bodies? There is commonly an astonishment attending everything extraordinary, and this astonishment changes immediately into the highest degree of esteem or contempt, according as we approve or disapprove of the subject. I am much afraid that though

the foregoing reasoning appears to me the shortest and most decisive imaginable, yet, with the generality of readers, the bias of the mind will prevail and give them a prejudice against the present doctrine.

This contrary bias is easily accounted for. It is a common observation that the mind has a great propensity to spread itself on external objects and to conjoin with them any internal impressions which they occasion and which always make their appearance at the same time that these objects discover themselves to the senses. Thus, as certain sounds and smells are always found to attend certain visible objects, we naturally imagine a conjunction, even in place, between the objects and qualities, though the qualities be of such a nature as to admit of no such conjunction and really exist nowhere. But of this more fully hereafter.[20] Meanwhile, it is sufficient to observe that the same propensity is the reason why we suppose necessity and power to lie in the objects we consider, not in our mind that considers them — notwithstanding it is not possible for us to form the most distant idea of that quality when it is not taken for the determination of the mind to pass from the idea of an object to that of its usual attendant.

But though this be the only reasonable account we can give of necessity, the contrary notion is so riveted in the mind from the principles mentioned above that I doubt not but my sentiments will be treated by many as extravagant and ridiculous. What! The efficacy of causes lie in the determination of the mind! As if causes did not operate entirely independent of the mind and would not continue their operation, even though there was no mind existent to contemplate them or reason concerning them. Thought may well depend on causes for its operation, but not causes on thought. This is to reverse the order of nature and make that secondary which is really primary. To every operation there is a power proportioned, and this power must be placed on the body that operates. If we remove the power from one cause, we must ascribe it to another, but to remove it from all causes and bestow it on a being that is noways related to the cause or effect but by perceiving them

20. Part IV, sec. 5.

is a gross absurdity and contrary to the most certain principles of human reason.

I can only reply to all these arguments that the case is here much the same as if a blind man should pretend to find a great many absurdities in the supposition that the color of scarlet is not the same with the sound of a trumpet, nor light the same with solidity. If we have really no idea of a power or efficacy in any object or of any real connection between causes and effects, it will be to little purpose to prove that an efficacy is necessary in all operations. We do not understand our own meaning in talking so, but ignorantly confound ideas which are entirely distinct from each other. I am, indeed, ready to allow that there may be several qualities, both in material and immaterial objects, with which we are utterly unacquainted, and if we please to call these *power* or *efficacy*, it will be of little consequence to the world. But when, instead of meaning these unknown qualities, we make the terms of power and efficacy signify something of which we have a clear idea and which is incompatible with those objects to which we apply it, obscurity and error begin then to take place and we are led astray by a false philosophy. This is the case when we transfer the determination of the thought to external objects and suppose any real intelligible connection between them, that being a quality which can only belong to the mind that considers them.

As to what may be said—that the operations of nature are independent of our thought and reasoning—I allow it and accordingly have observed that objects bear to each other the relations of contiguity and succession; that like objects may be observed, in several instances, to have like relations; and that all this is independent of and antecedent to the operations of the understanding. But if we go any further and ascribe a power or necessary connection to these objects, this is what we can never observe in them but must draw the idea of it from what we feel internally in contemplating them. And this I carry so far that I am ready to convert my present reasoning into an instance of it by a subtlety which it will not be difficult to comprehend.

When any object is presented to us, it immediately conveys to the mind a lively idea of that object which is usually found to attend it, and this determination

of the mind forms the necessary connection of these objects. But when we change the point of view from the objects to the perceptions, in that case the impression is to be considered as the cause and the lively idea as the effect, and their necessary connection is that new determination which we feel to pass from the idea of the one to that of the other. The uniting principle among our internal perceptions is as unintelligible as that among external objects and is not known to us any other way than by experience. Now, the nature and effects of experience have been already sufficiently examined and explained. It never gives us any insight into the internal structure or operating principle of objects, but only accustoms the mind to pass from one to another.

It is now time to collect all the different parts of this reasoning and, by joining them together, form an exact definition of the relation of cause and effect, which makes the subject of the present inquiry. This order would not have been excusable, of first examining our inference from the relation before we had explained the relation itself, had it been possible to proceed in a different method. But as the nature of the relation depends so much on that of the inference, we have been obliged to advance in this seemingly preposterous manner and make use of terms before we were able exactly to define them, or fix their meaning. We shall now correct this fault by giving a precise definition of cause and effect.

There may two definitions be given of this relation, which are only different by their presenting a different view of the same object and making us consider it either as a *philosophical* or as a *natural* relation, either as a comparison of two ideas or as an association between them. We may define a *cause* to be "An object precedent and contiguous to another and where all the objects resembling the former are placed in like relations of precedence and contiguity to those objects that resemble the latter." If this definition be esteemed defective, because drawn from objects foreign to the cause, we may substitute this other definition in its place, namely, "A cause is an object precedent and contiguous to another and so united with it that the idea of the one determines the mind to form the idea of the other and the impression of the one to form a more lively idea of the other."

Should this definition also be rejected for the same reason, I know no other remedy than that the persons who express this delicacy should substitute a more just definition in its place. But, for my part, I must admit my incapacity for such an undertaking. When I examine, with the utmost accuracy, those objects which are commonly denominated causes and effects, I find, in considering a single instance, that the one object is precedent and contiguous to the other, and in enlarging my view to consider several instances, I find only that like objects are constantly placed in like relations of succession and contiguity. Again, when I consider the influence of this constant conjunction, I perceive that such a relation can never be an object of reasoning and can never operate upon the mind but by means of custom, which determines the imagination to make a transition from the idea of one object to that of its usual attendant and from the impression of one to a more lively idea of the other. However extraordinary these sentiments may appear, I think it fruitless to trouble myself with any further inquiry or reasoning upon the subject, but shall repose myself on them as on established maxims.

It will only be proper, before we leave this subject, to draw some corollaries from it by which we may remove several prejudices and popular errors that have very much prevailed in philosophy. First, we may learn from the foregoing doctrine that all causes are of the same kind and that, in particular, there is no foundation for that distinction which we sometimes make between efficient causes and causes *sine qua non*, or between efficient causes and formal and material and exemplary and final causes. For as our idea of efficiency is derived from the constant conjunction of two objects, wherever this is observed, the cause is efficient, and where it is not, there can never be a cause of any kind. For the same reason we must reject the distinction between *cause* and *occasion*, when supposed to signify anything essentially different from each other. If constant conjunction be implied in what we call occasion, it is a real cause. If not, it is no relation at all and cannot give rise to any argument or reasoning.

Secondly, the same course of reasoning will make us conclude that there is but one kind of *necessity*, as there is but one kind of cause, and that the common distinction between *moral* and *physical* necessity is without any foundation in nature. This clearly appears from the precedent explication of necessity. It is the constant conjunction of objects, along with the determination of the mind, which constitutes a physical necessity, and the removal of these is the same thing with *chance*. As objects must either be conjoined or not, and as the mind must either be determined or not to pass from one object to another, it is impossible to admit of any medium between chance and an absolute necessity. In weakening this conjunction and determination you do not change the nature of the necessity, since even in the operation of bodies these have different degrees of constancy and force without producing a different species of that relation.

The distinction which we often make between *power* and the *exercise* of it is equally without foundation.

Thirdly, we may now be able fully to overcome all that repugnance which it is so natural for us to entertain against the foregoing reasoning by which we endeavored to prove that the necessity of a cause to every beginning of existence is not founded on any arguments either demonstrative or intuitive. Such an opinion will not appear strange after the foregoing definitions. If we define a cause to be *an object precedent and contiguous to another and where all the objects resembling the former are placed in a like relation of priority and contiguity to those objects that resemble the latter*, we may easily conceive that there is no absolute nor metaphysical necessity that every beginning of existence should be attended with such an object. If we define a cause to be *an object precedent and contiguous to another and so united with it in the imagination that the idea of the one determines the mind to form the idea of the other and the impression of the one to form a more lively idea of the other*, we shall make still less difficulty of assenting to this opinion. Such an influence on the mind is in itself perfectly extraordinary and incomprehensible, nor can we be certain of its reality but from experience and observation.

I shall add as a fourth corollary, that we can never have reason to believe that any object exists of which we cannot form an idea. For, as all our reasonings concerning existence are derived from causation, and as all our reasonings concerning causation are derived from the experienced conjunction of objects, not from any reasoning or reflection, the same experience must give us a notion of these objects and must remove all mystery from our conclusions. This is so evident that it would scarcely have merited our attention were it not to obviate certain objections of this kind which might arise against the following reasonings concerning *matter* and *substance*. I need not observe that a full knowledge of the object is not requisite, but only of those qualities of it which we believe to exist.

Section 15: Rules by Which to Judge of Causes and Effects

According to the precedent doctrine, there are no objects which, by the mere survey, without consulting experience, we can determine to be the causes of any other and no objects which we can certainly determine in the same manner not to be the causes. Anything may produce anything. Creation, annihilation, motion, reason, volition—all these may arise from one another or from any other object we can imagine. Nor will this appear strange if we compare two principles explained above *that the constant conjunction of objects determines their causation*[21] and *that, properly speaking, no objects are contrary to each other but existence and non-existence*. Where objects are not contrary, nothing hinders them from having that constant conjunction on which the relation of cause and effect totally depends.

Since, therefore, it is possible for all objects to become causes or effects to each other, it may be proper to fix some general rules by which we may know when they really are so.

1. The cause and effect must be contiguous in space and time.

2. The cause must be prior to the effect.

3. There must be a constant union between the cause and effect. It is chiefly this quality that constitutes the relation.

21. Part I, sec. 5.

4. The same cause always produces the same effect and the same effect never arises but from the same cause. This principle we derive from experience and is the source of most of our philosophical reasonings. For when by any clear experiment we have discovered the causes or effects of any phenomenon, we immediately extend our observation to every phenomenon of the same kind, without waiting for that constant repetition from which the first idea of this relation is derived.

5. There is another principle which hangs upon this, namely, that where several different objects produce the same effect, it must be by means of some quality which we discover to be common among them. For as like effects imply like causes, we must always ascribe the causation to the circumstance wherein we discover the resemblance.

6. The following principle is founded on the same reason. The difference in the effects of two resembling objects must proceed from that particular in which they differ. For as like causes always produce like effects, when in any instance we find our expectation to be disappointed, we must conclude that this irregularity proceeds from some difference in the causes.

7. When any object increases or diminishes with the increase or diminution of its cause, it is to be regarded as a compounded effect, derived from the union of the several different effects which arise from the several different parts of the cause. The absence or presence of one part of the cause is here supposed to be always attended with the absence or presence of a proportional part of the effect. This constant conjunction sufficiently proves that the one part is the cause of the other. We must, however, beware not to draw such a conclusion from a few experiments. A certain degree of heat gives pleasure; if you diminish that heat, the pleasure diminishes; but it does not follow that if you augment it beyond a certain degree, the pleasure will like-

wise augment, for we find that it degenerates into pain.

8. The eighth and last rule I shall take notice of is that an object which exists for any time in its full perfection without any effect is not the sole cause of that effect, but requires to be assisted by some other principle which may forward its influence and operation. For as like effects necessarily follow from like causes and in a contiguous time and place, their separation for a moment shows that these causes are not complete ones.

Here is all the logic I think proper to employ in my reasoning, and perhaps even this was not very necessary, but might have been supplied by the natural principles of our understanding. Our scholastic headpieces and logicians show no such superiority above the mere vulgar in their reason and ability as to give us any inclination to imitate them in delivering a long system of rules and precepts to direct our judgment in philosophy. All the rules of this nature are very easy in their invention but extremely difficult in their application, and even experimental philosophy, which seems the most natural and simple of any, requires the utmost stretch of human judgment. There is no phenomenon in nature but what is compounded and modified by so many different circumstances that in order to arrive at the decisive point we must carefully separate whatever is superfluous and inquire, by new experiments, if every particular circumstance of the first experiment was essential to it. These new experiments are liable to a discussion of the same kind, so that the utmost constancy is required to make us persevere in our inquiry and the utmost sagacity to choose the right way among so many that present themselves. If this be the case even in natural philosophy, how much more in moral, where there is a much greater complication of circumstances and where those views and sentiments which are essential to any action of the mind are so implicit and obscure that they often escape our strictest attention and are not only unaccountable in their causes, but even unknown in their existence? I am

much afraid lest the small success I meet with in my inquiries will make this observation bear the air of an apology rather than of boasting.

If anything can give me security in this particular, it will be the enlarging the sphere of my experiments as much as possible, for which reason it may be proper, in this place, to examine the reasoning faculty of brutes as well as that of human creatures.

Part IV. Of the Skeptical and Other Systems of Philosophy

Section 1: Of Skepticism with Regard to Reason

In all demonstrative sciences the rules are certain and infallible, but when we apply them, our fallible and uncertain faculties are very apt to depart from them and fall into error. We must, therefore, in every reasoning form a new judgment as a check or control on our first judgment or belief and must enlarge our view to comprehend a kind of history of all the instances wherein our understanding has deceived us compared with those wherein its testimony was just and true. Our reason must be considered as a kind of cause of which truth is the natural effect, but such a one as, by the irruption of other causes and by the inconstancy of our mental powers, may frequently be prevented. By this means all knowledge degenerates into probability, and this probability is greater or less, according to our experience of the veracity or deceitfulness of our understanding and according to the simplicity or intricacy of the question.

There is no algebraist nor mathematician so expert in his science as to place entire confidence in any truth immediately upon his discovery of it or regard it as anything but a mere probability. Every time he runs over his proofs, his confidence increases, but still more by the approbation of his friends and is raised to its utmost perfection by the universal assent and applauses of the learned world. Now, it is evident that this gradual increase of assurance is nothing but the addition of new probabilities and is derived from the constant union of causes and effects according to past experience and observation.

In accounts of any length or importance, merchants

seldom trust to the infallible certainty of numbers for their security, but, by the artificial structure of the accounts, produce a probability beyond what is derived from the skill and experience of the accountant. For that is plainly of itself some degree of probability, though uncertain and variable according to the degrees of his experience and length of the account. Now, as none will maintain that our assurance in a long numeration exceeds probability, I may safely affirm that there scarcely is any proposition concerning numbers of which we can have a fuller security. For it is easily possible, by gradually diminishing the numbers, to reduce the longest series of addition to the most simple question which can be formed, to an addition of two single numbers, and upon this supposition we shall find it impracticable to show the precise limits of knowledge and of probability or discover that particular number at which the one ends and the other begins. But knowledge and probability are of such contrary and disagreeing natures that they cannot well run insensibly into each other and that because they will not divide, but must be either entirely present or entirely absent. Besides, if any single addition were certain, every one would be so and consequently the whole or total sum, unless the whole can be different from all its parts. I had almost said that this was certain, but I reflect that it must reduce *itself* as well as every other reasoning and from knowledge degenerate into probability.

Since, therefore, all knowledge resolves itself into probability and becomes at last of the same nature with that evidence which we employ in common life, we must now examine this latter species of reasoning and see on what foundation it stands.

In every judgment which we can form concerning probability as well as concerning knowledge, we ought always to correct the first judgment, derived from the nature of the object, by another judgment, derived from the nature of the understanding. It is certain a man of solid sense and long experience ought to have and usually has a greater assurance in his opinions than one that is foolish and ignorant and that our sentiments have different degrees of authority, even with ourselves, in proportion to the degrees of our reason and experience. In the man of the best sense and longest experience, this authority

is never entire, since even such a one must be conscious of many errors in the past and must still dread the like for the future. Here then arises a new species of probability to correct and regulate the first and fix its just standard and proportion. As demonstration is subject to the control of probability, so is probability liable to a new correction by a reflex act of the mind, wherein the nature of our understanding and our reasoning from the first probability become our objects.

Having thus found in every probability, besides the original uncertainty inherent in the subject, a new uncertainty, derived from the weakness of that faculty which judges and, having adjusted these two together, we are obliged by our reason to add a new doubt, derived from the possibility of error in the estimation we make of the truth and fidelity of our faculties. This is a doubt which immediately occurs to us and of which, if we would closely pursue our reason, we cannot avoid giving a decision. But this decision, though it should be favorable to our preceding judgment, being founded only on probability, must weaken still further our first evidence and must itself be weakened by a fourth doubt of the same kind and so on *in infinitum,* until at last there remains nothing of the original probability, however great we may suppose it to have been and however small the diminution by every new uncertainty. No finite object can subsist under a decrease repeated *in infinitum,* and even the vastest quantity which can enter into human imagination must in this manner be reduced to nothing. Let our first belief be never so strong, it must infallibly perish by passing through so many new examinations of which each diminishes somewhat of its force and vigor. When I reflect on the natural fallibility of my judgment, I have less confidence in my opinions than when I only consider the objects concerning which I reason, and when I proceed still further, to turn the scrutiny against every successive estimation I make of my faculties, all the rules of logic require a continual diminution and at last a total extinction of belief and evidence.

Should it here be asked me, whether I sincerely assent to this argument which I seem to take such pains to inculcate and whether I be really one of those skeptics who hold that all is uncertain and that our judgment is not in anything possessed of *any* measures of truth and falsehood, I should reply that this question is entirely superfluous and that neither I nor any other person was ever sincerely and constantly of that opinion. Nature, by an absolute and uncontrollable necessity, has determined us to judge as well as to breathe and feel, nor can we any more forbear viewing certain objects in a stronger and fuller light upon account of their customary connection with a present impression than we can hinder ourselves from thinking as long as we are awake, or seeing the surrounding bodies when we turn our eyes towards them in broad sunshine. Whoever has taken the pains to refute the cavils of this *total* skepticism has really disputed without an antagonist and endeavored by arguments to establish a faculty which nature has antecedently implanted in the mind and rendered unavoidable.

My intention then in displaying so carefully the arguments of that fantastic sect is only to make the reader sensible of the truth of my hypothesis *that all our reasonings concerning causes and effects are derived from nothing but custom and that belief is more properly an act of the sensitive than of the cogitative part of our natures.* I have here proved that the very same principles which make us form a decision upon any subject and correct that decision by the consideration of our genius and capacity and of the situation of our mind, when we examined that subject—I say, I have proved that these same principles, when carried further and applied to every new reflex judgment, must, by continually diminishing the original evidence, at last reduce it to nothing and utterly subvert all belief and opinion. If belief, therefore, were a simple act of the thought, without any peculiar manner of conception or the addition of a force and vivacity, it must infallibly destroy itself and in every case terminate in a total suspense of judgment. But as experience will sufficiently convince anyone who thinks it worth while to try that though he can find no error in the foregoing arguments, yet he still continues to believe and think and reason as usual, he may safely conclude that his reasoning and belief is some sensation or peculiar manner of conception which it is impossible for mere ideas and reflections to destroy.

But here, perhaps, it may be demanded, how it happens, even upon my hypothesis, that these arguments explained above do not produce a total suspense of judgment and after what manner the mind ever retains a degree of assurance in any subject? For as these new probabilities, which, by their repetition, perpetually diminish the original evidence, are founded on the very same principles, whether of thought or sensation, as the primary judgment, it may seem unavoidable that in either case they must equally subvert it and by the opposition, either of contrary thoughts or sensations, reduce the mind to a total uncertainty. I suppose there is some question proposed to me and that, after revolving over the impressions of my memory and senses and carrying my thoughts from them to such objects as are commonly conjoined with them, I feel a stronger and more forcible conception on the one side than on the other. This strong conception forms my first decision. I suppose that afterwards I examine my judgment itself and, observing from experience that it is sometimes just and sometimes erroneous, I consider it as regulated by contrary principles or causes of which some lead to truth and some to error, and in balancing these contrary causes, I diminish, by a new probability, the assurance of my first decision. This new probability is liable to the same diminution as the foregoing and so on, *in infinitum*. It is therefore demanded *how it happens that, even after all, we retain a degree of belief which is sufficient for our purpose, either in philosophy or common life.*

I answer that after the first and second decision, as the action of the mind becomes forced and unnatural and the ideas faint and obscure, though the principles of judgment and the balancing of opposite causes be the same as at the very beginning, yet their influence on the imagination and the vigor they add to or diminish from the thought is by no means equal. Where the mind does not reach its objects with easiness and facility, the same principles do not have the same effect as in a more natural conception of the ideas, nor does the imagination feel a sensation which holds any proportion with that which arises from its common judgments and opinions. The attention is on the stretch, the posture of the mind is uneasy, and the spirits, being diverted from their natural course, are not governed in their movements by the same laws, at least not to the same degree, as when they flow in their usual channel.

If we desire similar instances, it will not be very difficult to find them. The present subject of metaphysics will supply us abundantly. The same argument which would have been esteemed convincing in a reasoning concerning history or politics has little or no influence in these more abstruse subjects, even though it be perfectly comprehended, and that because there is required a study and an effort of thought in order to its being comprehended, and this effort of thought disturbs the operation of our sentiments on which the belief depends. The case is the same in other subjects. The straining of the imagination always hinders the regular flowing of the passions and sentiments. A tragic poet that would represent his heroes as very ingenious and witty in their misfortunes would never touch the passions. As the emotions of the soul prevent any subtle reasoning and reflection, so these latter actions of the mind are equally prejudicial to the former. The mind as well as the body seems to be endowed with a certain precise degree of force and activity which it never employs in one action but at the expense of all the rest. This is more evidently true where the actions are of quite different natures, since in that case the force of the mind is not only diverted, but even the disposition changed so as to render us incapable of a sudden transition from one action to the other, and still more of performing both at once. No wonder, then, that the conviction which arises from a subtle reasoning diminishes in proportion to the efforts which the imagination makes to enter into the reasoning and to conceive it in all its parts. Belief, being a lively conception, can never be entire where it is not founded on something natural and easy.

This I take to be the true state of the question and cannot approve of that expeditious way which some take with the skeptics, to reject at once all their arguments without inquiry or examination. If the skeptical reasonings be strong, say they, it is a proof that reason may have some force and authority, if weak, they can never be sufficient to invalidate all the conclusions of our understanding. This argument is not just, be-

cause the skeptical reasonings, were it possible for them to exist and were they not destroyed by their subtlety, would be successively both strong and weak, according to the successive dispositions of the mind. Reason first appears in possession of the throne, prescribing laws and imposing maxims with an absolute sway and authority. Her enemy, therefore, is obliged to take shelter under her protection and, by making use of rational arguments to prove the fallaciousness and imbecility of reason, produces, in a manner, a patent under her hand and seal. This patent has at first an authority proportioned to the present and immediate authority of reason from which it is derived. But as it is supposed to be contradictory to reason, it gradually diminishes the force of that governing power and its own at the same time, until at last they both vanish away into nothing by a regular and just diminution. The skeptical and dogmatical reasons are of the same kind, though contrary in their operation and tendency, so that where the latter is strong, it has an enemy of equal force in the former to encounter, and as their forces were at first equal, they still continue so, as long as either of them subsists, nor does one of them lose any force in the contest without taking as much from its antagonist. It is happy, therefore, that nature breaks the force of all skeptical arguments in time and keeps them from having any considerable influence on the understanding. Were we to trust entirely to their self-destruction, that can never take place until they have first subverted all conviction and have totally destroyed human reason.

Section 2: Of Skepticism with Regard to the Senses

Thus the skeptic still continues to reason and believe, even though he asserts that he cannot defend his reason by reason, and by the same rule he must assent to the principle concerning the existence of body, though he cannot pretend, by any arguments of philosophy, to maintain its veracity. Nature has not left this to his choice and has doubtless esteemed it an affair of too great importance to be trusted to our uncertain reasonings and speculations. We may well ask: *What causes induce us to believe in the existence of body?* But it is in vain to ask: *Whether there be body or not?* That is a point which we must take for granted in all our reasonings.

The subject, then, of our present inquiry is concerning the *causes* which induce us to believe in the existence of body, and my reasonings on this head I shall begin with a distinction which at first sight may seem superfluous, but which will contribute very much to the perfect understanding of what follows. We ought to examine apart those two questions which are commonly confounded together, namely, why we attribute a *continued* existence to objects, even when they are not present to the senses, and why we suppose them to have an existence *distinct* from the mind and perception. Under this last head I comprehend their situation as well as relations, their *external* position as well as the *independence* of their existence and operation. These two questions concerning the continued and distinct existence of body are intimately connected together. For if the objects of our senses continue to exist even when they are not perceived, their existence is of course independent of and distinct from the perception, and *vice versa,* if their existence be independent of the perception and distinct from it, they must continue to exist even though they be not perceived. But though the decision of the one question decides the other, yet that we may the more easily discover the principles of human nature from whence the decision arises, we shall carry along with us this distinction and shall consider whether it be the *senses, reason,* or the *imagination* that produces the opinion of a *continued* or of a *distinct* existence. These are the only questions that are intelligible on the present subject. For as to the notion of external existence, when taken for something specifically different from our perceptions, we have already shown its absurdity.[22]

To begin with the *senses,* it is evident these faculties are incapable of giving rise to the notion of the *continued* existence of their objects after they no longer appear to the senses. For that is a contradiction in terms and supposes that the senses continue to operate even after they have ceased all manner of operation.

22. Part II, sec. 6.

These faculties, therefore, if they have any influence in the present case, must produce the opinion of a distinct, not of a continued existence and, in order to [do] that, must present their impressions either as images and representations or as these very distinct and external existences.

That our senses do not offer their impressions as the images of something *distinct* or *independent* and *external* is evident, because they convey to us nothing but a single perception and never give us the least intimation of anything beyond. A single perception can never produce the idea of a double existence but by some inference either of the reason or imagination. When the mind looks further than what immediately appears to it, its conclusions can never be put to the account of the senses, and it certainly looks further when from a single perception it infers a double existence and supposes the relations of resemblance and causation between them.

If our senses, therefore, suggest any idea of distinct existences, they must convey the impressions as those very existences by a kind of fallacy and illusion. Upon this head we may observe that all sensations are felt by the mind such as they really are and that, when we doubt whether they present themselves as distinct objects or as mere impressions, the difficulty is not concerning their nature, but concerning their relations and situation. Now, if the senses presented our impressions as external to and independent of ourselves, both the objects and ourselves must be obvious to our senses, otherwise they could not be compared by these faculties. The difficulty, then, is how far we are *ourselves* the objects of our senses.

It is certain there is no question in philosophy more abstruse than that concerning identity and the nature of the uniting principle which constitutes a person. So far from being able by our senses merely to determine this question, we must have recourse to the most profound metaphysics to give a satisfactory answer to it, and in common life it is evident these ideas of self and person are never very fixed nor determinate. It is absurd, therefore, to imagine the senses can ever distinguish between ourselves and external objects.

Add to this that every impression, external and internal, passions, affections, sensations, pains, and pleasures, are originally on the same footing and that whatever other differences we may observe among them, they appear, all of them, in their true colors as impressions or perceptions. And indeed, if we consider the matter aright, it is scarcely possible it should be otherwise, nor is it conceivable that our senses should be more capable of deceiving us in the situation and relations than in the nature of our impressions. For since all actions and sensations of the mind are known to us by consciousness, they must necessarily appear in every particular what they are and be what they appear. Everything that enters the mind, being in *reality* as the perception, it is impossible anything should to *feeling* appear different. This were to suppose that even where we are most intimately conscious, we might be mistaken.

But not to lose time in examining whether it is possible for our senses to deceive us and represent our perceptions as distinct from ourselves, that is, as *external* to and *independent* of us, let us consider whether they really do so, and whether this error proceeds from an immediate sensation or from some other causes.

To begin with the question concerning *external* existence, it may perhaps be said that setting aside the metaphysical question of the identity of a thinking substance, our own body evidently belongs to us, and as several impressions appear exterior to the body, we suppose them also exterior to ourselves. The paper on which I write at present is beyond my hand. The table is beyond the paper. The walls of the chamber beyond the table. And in casting my eye towards the window, I perceive a great extent of fields and buildings beyond my chamber. From all this it may be inferred that no other faculty is required besides the senses to convince us of the external existence of body. But to prevent this inference, we need only weigh the three following considerations. *First,* that, properly speaking, it is not our body we perceive when we regard our limbs and members, but certain impressions which enter by the senses, so that the ascribing a real and corporeal existence to these impressions or to their objects is an act of the mind as difficult to explain as that which we examine at present. *Secondly,* sounds and tastes and smells, though commonly regarded by the mind as continued inde-

pendent qualities, appear not to have any existence in extension and consequently cannot appear to the senses as situated externally to the body. The reason why we ascribe a place to them shall be considered afterwards.[23] *Thirdly,* even our sight does not inform us of distance or outness (so to speak) immediately and without a certain reasoning and experience, as is acknowledged by the most rational philosophers.

As to the *independence* of our perceptions on ourselves, this can never be an object of the senses, but any opinion we form concerning it must be derived from experience and observation, and we shall see afterwards that our conclusions from experience are far from being favorable to the doctrine of the independence of our perceptions. Meanwhile we may observe that when we talk of real distinct existences, we have commonly more in our eye their independence than external situation in place and think an object has a sufficient reality when its being is uninterrupted and independent of the incessant revolutions which we are conscious of in ourselves.

Thus, to resume what I have said concerning the senses, they give us no notion of continued existence, because they cannot operate beyond the extent in which they really operate. They as little produce the opinion of a distinct existence, because they neither can offer it to the mind as represented nor as original. To offer it as represented, they must present both an object and an image. To make it appear as original, they must convey a falsehood, and this falsehood must lie in the relations and situation in order to which they must be able to compare the object with ourselves, and even in that case they do not, nor is it possible they should, deceive us. We may therefore conclude with certainty that the opinion of a continued and of a distinct existence never arises from the senses.

To confirm this, we may observe that there are three different kinds of impressions conveyed by the senses. The first are those of the figure, bulk, motion, and solidity of bodies. The second, those of colors, tastes, smells, sounds, heat, and cold. The third are the pains and pleasures that arise from the application of objects to our bodies, as by the cutting of our flesh

23. Sec. 5.

with steel, and such like. Both philosophers and the vulgar suppose the first of these to have a distinct continued existence. The vulgar only regard the second as on the same footing. Both philosophers and the vulgar, again, esteem the third to be merely perceptions and, consequently, interrupted and dependent beings.

Now, it is evident that whatever may be our philosophical opinion, colors, sounds, heat, and cold, as far as appears to the senses, exist after the same manner with motion and solidity and that the difference we make between them in this respect arises not from the mere perception. So strong is the prejudice for the distinct continued existence of the former qualities that when the contrary opinion is advanced by modern philosophers, people imagine they can almost refute it from their feeling and experience and that their very senses contradict this philosophy. It is also evident that colors, sounds, etc., are originally on the same footing with the pain that arises from steel and pleasure that proceeds from a fire and that the difference between them is founded neither on perception nor reason, but on the imagination. For as they are confessed to be, both of them, nothing but perceptions arising from the particular configurations and motions of the parts of body, wherein possibly can their difference consist? Upon the whole, then, we may conclude that as far as the senses are judges, all perceptions are the same in the manner of their existence.

We may also observe in this instance of sounds and colors that we can attribute a distinct continued existence to objects without ever consulting *reason* or weighing our opinions by any philosophical principles. And, indeed, whatever convincing arguments philosophers may fancy they can produce to establish the belief of objects independent of the mind, it is obvious these arguments are known but to very few, and that it is not by them that children, peasants, and the greatest part of mankind are induced to attribute objects to some impressions and deny them to others. Accordingly, we find that all the conclusions which the vulgar form on this head are directly contrary to those which are confirmed by philosophy. For philosophy informs us that everything which appears to the mind is nothing but a perception and is inter-

rupted and dependent on the mind, whereas the vulgar confound perceptions and objects and attribute a distinct continued existence to the very things they feel or see. This sentiment, then, as it is entirely unreasonable, must proceed from some other faculty than the understanding. To which we may add that as long as we take our perceptions and objects to be the same, we can never infer the existence of the one from that of the other, nor form any argument from the relation of cause and effect, which is the only one that can assure us of matter of fact. Even after we distinguish our perceptions from our objects, it will appear presently that we are still incapable of reasoning from the existence of one to that of the other, so that, upon the whole, our reason neither does nor is it possible it ever should, upon any supposition, give us an assurance of the continued and distinct existence of body. That opinion must be entirely owing to the imagination, which must now be the subject of our inquiry.

Since all impressions are internal and perishing existences and appear as such, the notion of their distinct and continued existence must arise from a concurrence of some of their qualities with the qualities of the imagination, and since this notion does not extend to all of them, it must arise from certain qualities peculiar to some impressions. It will, therefore, be easy for us to discover these qualities by a comparison of the impressions to which we attribute a distinct and continued existence with those which we regard as internal and perishing.

We may observe, then, that it is neither upon account of the involuntariness of certain impressions, as is commonly supposed, nor of their superior force and violence that we attribute to them a reality and continued existence, which we refuse to others that are voluntary or feeble. For it is evident that our pains and pleasures, our passions and affections, which we never suppose to have any existence beyond our perception, operate with greater violence and are equally involuntary as the impressions of figure and extension, color and sound, which we suppose to be permanent beings. The heat of a fire, when moderate, is supposed to exist in the fire, but the pain which it causes upon a near approach is not taken to have any being except in the perception.

These vulgar opinions, then, being rejected, we must search for some other hypothesis by which we may discover those peculiar qualities in our impressions which makes us attribute to them a distinct and continued existence.

After a little examination, we shall find that all those objects to which we attribute a continued existence have a peculiar *constancy* which distinguishes them from the impressions whose existence depends upon our perception. Those mountains and houses and trees which lie at present under my eye have always appeared to me in the same order, and when I lose sight of them by shutting my eyes or turning my head, I soon after find them return upon me without the least alteration. My bed and table, my books and papers, present themselves in the same uniform manner and do not change upon account of any interruption in my seeing or perceiving them. This is the case with all the impressions whose objects are supposed to have an external existence and is the case with no other impressions, whether gentle or violent, voluntary or involuntary.

This constancy, however, is not so perfect as not to admit of very considerable exceptions. Bodies often change their position and qualities and, after a little absence or interruption, may become hardly knowable. But here it is observable that even in these changes they preserve a *coherence* and have a regular dependence on each other, which is the foundation of a kind of reasoning from causation and produces the opinion of their continued existence. When I return to my chamber after an hour's absence, I do not find my fire in the same situation in which I left it, but then I am accustomed in other instances to see a like alteration produced in a like time whether I am present or absent, near or remote. This coherence, therefore, in their changes is one of the characteristics of external objects as well as their constancy.

Having found that the opinion of the continued existence of body depends on the *coherence* and *constancy* of certain impressions, I now proceed to examine after what manner these qualities give rise to so extraordinary an opinion. To begin with the coherence, we may observe that though those internal impressions which we regard as fleeting and perishing have also a certain coherence or regularity in their

appearances, yet it is of somewhat a different nature from that which we discover in bodies. Our passions are found by experience to have a mutual connection with and dependence on each other, but on no occasion is it necessary to suppose that they have existed and operated when they were not perceived, in order to preserve the same dependence and connection of which we have had experience. The case is not the same with relation to external objects. Those require a continued existence, or otherwise lose, in a great measure, the regularity of their operation. I am here seated in my chamber with my face to the fire, and all the objects that strike my senses are contained in a few yards around me. My memory, indeed, informs me of the existence of many objects, but, then, this information does not extend beyond their past existence, nor do either my senses or memory give any testimony to the continuance of their being. When, therefore, I am thus seated and revolve over these thoughts, I hear on a sudden a noise as of a door turning upon its hinges and, a little after, see a porter who advances towards me. This gives occasion to many new reflections and reasonings. First, I never have observed that this noise could proceed from anything but the motion of a door and therefore conclude that the present phenomenon is a contradiction to all past experience unless the door, which I remember on the other side the chamber, be still in being. Again, I have always found that a human body was possessed of a quality which I call gravity and which hinders it from mounting in the air as this porter must have done to arrive at my chamber, unless the stairs I remember be not annihilated by my absence. But this is not all. I receive a letter which, upon opening it, I perceive by the handwriting and subscription to have come from a friend who says he is two hundred leagues distant. It is evident I can never account for this phenomenon, conformable to my experience in other instances, without spreading out in my mind the whole sea and continent between us and supposing the effects and continued existence of posts and ferries according to my memory and observation. To consider these phenomena of the porter and letter in a certain light, they are contradictions to common experience and may be regarded as objections to those maxims which we form concerning the connections of causes and effects. I am accustomed to hear such a sound and see such an object in motion at the same time. I have not received in this particular instance both these perceptions. These observations are contrary unless I suppose that the door still remains and that it was opened without my perceiving it, and this supposition, which was at first entirely arbitrary and hypothetical, acquires a force and evidence by its being the only one upon which I can reconcile these contradictions. There is scarcely a moment of my life wherein there is not a similar instance presented to me and I have not occasion to suppose the continued existence of objects in order to connect their past and present appearances and give them such a union with each other as I have found, by experience, to be suitable to their particular natures and circumstances. Here, then, I am naturally led to regard the world as something real and durable and as preserving its existence even when it is no longer present to my perception.

But, though this conclusion, from the coherence of appearances, may seem to be of the same nature with our reasonings concerning causes and effects, as being derived from custom and regulated by past experience, we shall find upon examination that they are at the bottom considerably different from each other and that this inference arises from the understanding and from custom in an indirect and oblique manner. For it will readily be allowed that since nothing is ever really present to the mind besides its own perceptions, it is not only impossible that any habit should ever be acquired otherwise than by the regular succession of these perceptions, but also that any habit should ever exceed that degree of regularity. Any degree, therefore, of regularity in our perceptions can never be a foundation for us to infer a greater degree of regularity in some objects which are not perceived, since this supposes a contradiction, namely, a habit acquired by what was never present to the mind. But it is evident that whenever we infer the continued existence of the objects of sense from their coherence and the frequency of their union, it is in order to bestow on the objects a greater regularity than what is observed in our mere perceptions. We remark a connection between two kinds of objects in their past appearance to the senses, but are not able

to observe this connection to be perfectly constant, since the turning about of our head or the shutting of our eyes is able to break it. What, then, do we suppose in this case but that these objects still continue their usual connection, notwithstanding their apparent interruption, and that the irregular appearances are joined by something of which we are insensible? But as all reasoning concerning matters of fact arises only from custom, and custom can only be the effect of repeated perceptions, the extending of custom and reasoning beyond the perceptions can never be the direct and natural effect of the constant repetition and connection, but must arise from the cooperation of some other principles.

I have already observed,[24] in examining the foundation of mathematics, that the imagination, when set into any train of thinking, is apt to continue even when its object fails it and, like a galley put in motion by the oars, carries on its course without any new impulse. This I have assigned for the reason why, after considering several loose standards of equality and correcting them by each other, we proceed to imagine so correct and exact a standard of that relation as is not liable to the least error or variation. The same principle makes us easily entertain this opinion of the continued existence of body. Objects have a certain coherence even as they appear to our senses, but this coherence is much greater and more uniform if we suppose the objects to have a continued existence, and as the mind is once in the train of observing a uniformity among objects, it naturally continues until it renders the uniformity as complete as possible. The simple supposition of their continued existence suffices for this purpose and gives us a notion of a much greater regularity among objects than what they have when we look no further than our senses.

But whatever force we may ascribe to this principle, I am afraid it is too weak to support alone so vast an edifice as is that of the continued existence of all external bodies and that we must join the *constancy* of their appearance to the *coherence*, in order to give a satisfactory account of that opinion. As the explication of this will lead me into a considerable compass of very profound reasoning, I think it proper, in order

24. Part II, sec. 4.

to avoid confusion, to give a short sketch or abridgment of my system and afterwards draw out all its parts in their full compass. This inference from the constancy of our perceptions, like the precedent from their coherence, gives rise to the opinion of the *continued* existence of body, which is prior to that of its *distinct* existence and produces that latter principle.

When we have been accustomed to observe a constancy in certain impressions and have found that the perception of the sun or ocean, for instance, returns upon us after an absence or annihilation with like parts and in a like order as at its first appearance, we are not apt to regard these interrupted perceptions as different (which they really are), but on the contrary consider them as individually the same upon account of their resemblance. But as this interruption of their existence is contrary to their perfect identity and makes us regard the first impression as annihilated and the second as newly created, we find ourselves somewhat at a loss and are involved in a kind of contradiction. In order to free ourselves from this difficulty, we disguise, as much as possible, the interruption, or rather remove it entirely by supposing that these interrupted perceptions are connected by a real existence of which we are insensible. This supposition, or idea of continued existence, acquires a force and vivacity from the memory of these broken impressions and from that propensity which they give us to suppose them the same, and, according to the precedent reasoning, the very essence of belief consists in the force and vivacity of the conception.

In order to justify this system, there are four things requisite. *First,* to explain the *principium individuationis,* or principle of identity. *Secondly,* give a reason why the resemblance of our broken and interrupted perceptions induces us to attribute an identity to them. *Thirdly,* account for that propensity which this illusion gives to unite these broken appearances by a continued existence. *Fourthly,* and lastly, explain that force and vivacity of conception which arises from the propensity.

First, as to the principle of individuation, we may observe that the view of any one object is not sufficient to convey the idea of identity. For in that proposition, *an object is the same with itself,* if the idea expressed by the word *object* were noways distinguished from that meant by *itself,* we really should mean nothing, nor would the proposition contain a predicate and a subject, which, however, are implied in this affirmation. One single object conveys the idea of unity, not that of identity.

On the other hand, a multiplicity of objects can never convey this idea, however resembling they may be supposed. The mind always pronounces the one not to be the other and considers them as forming two, three, or any determinate number of objects whose existences are entirely distinct and independent.

Since, then, both number and unity are incompatible with the relation of identity, it must lie in something that is neither of them. But to tell the truth, at first sight this seems utterly impossible. Between unity and number there can be no medium, no more than between existence and non-existence. After one object is supposed to exist, we must either suppose another also to exist, in which case we have the idea of number, or we must suppose it not to exist, in which case the first object remains at unity.

To remove this difficulty, let us have recourse to the idea of time or duration. I have already observed[25] that time, in a strict sense, implies succession and that when we apply its idea to any unchangeable object, it is only by a fiction of the imagination by which the unchangeable object is supposed to participate of the changes of the coexisting objects and, in particular, of that of our perceptions. This fiction of the imagination almost universally takes place, and it is by means of it that a single object placed before us and surveyed for any time without our discovering in it any interruption or variation is able to give us a notion of identity. For when we consider any two points of this time, we may place them in different lights: We may either survey them at the very same instant, in which case they give us the idea of number, both by themselves and by the object, which must be multiplied in order to be conceived at once as existent in these two different points of time. Or, on the other hand, we may trace the succession of time by a like succession of ideas and, conceiving first one moment along with the object then existent, imagine

25. Part II, sec. 5.

afterwards a change in the time without any *variation* or *interruption* in the object, in which case it gives us the idea of unity. Here then is an idea which is a medium between unity and number or, more properly speaking, is either of them, according to the view in which we take it, and this idea we call that of identity. We cannot, in any propriety of speech, say that an object is the same with itself unless we mean that the object existent at one time is the same with itself existent at another. By this means we make a difference between the idea meant by the word *object* and that meant by *itself*, without going the length of number and at the same time without restraining ourselves to a strict and absolute unity.

Thus the principle of individuation is nothing but the *invariableness* and *uninterruptedness* of any object through a supposed variation of time, by which the mind can trace it in the different periods of its existence without any break of the view and without being obliged to form the idea of multiplicity or number.

I now proceed to explain the *second* part of my system and show why the constancy of our perceptions makes us ascribe to them a perfect numerical identity, though there be very long intervals between their appearance and they have only one of the essential qualities of identity, namely, *invariableness*. That I may avoid all ambiguity and confusion on this head, I shall observe that I here account for the opinions and belief of the vulgar with regard to the existence of body and therefore must entirely conform myself to their manner of thinking and of expressing themselves. Now, we have already observed that however philosophers may distinguish between the objects and perceptions of the senses which they suppose coexistent and resembling, yet this is a distinction which is not comprehended by the generality of mankind, who, as they perceive only one being, can never assent to the opinion of a double existence and representation. Those very sensations which enter by the eye or ear are with them the true objects, nor can they readily conceive that this pen or paper, which is immediately perceived, represents another which is different from, but resembling it. In order, therefore, to accommodate myself to their notions, I shall at first suppose that there is only a single existence, which I shall call indifferently *object* or *perception*, according

as it shall seem best to suit my purpose, understanding by both of them what any common man means by a hat or shoe or stone or any other impression conveyed to him by his senses. I shall be sure to give warning when I return to a more philosophical way of speaking and thinking.

To enter therefore upon the question concerning the source of the error and deception with regard to identity when we attribute it to our resembling perceptions, notwithstanding their interruption, I must here recall an observation which I have already proved and explained.[26] Nothing is more apt to make us mistake one idea for another than any relation between them which associates them together in the imagination and makes it pass with facility from one to the other. Of all relations, that of resemblance is in this respect the most efficacious and that because it not only causes an association of ideas, but also of dispositions, and makes us conceive the one idea by an act or operation of the mind similar to that by which we conceive the other. This circumstance I have observed to be of great moment, and we may establish it for a general rule that whatever ideas place the mind in the same disposition or in similar ones are very apt to be confounded. The mind readily passes from one to the other and does not perceive the change without a strict attention of which, generally speaking, it is wholly incapable.

In order to apply this general maxim, we must first examine the disposition of the mind in viewing any object which preserves a perfect identity and then find some other object that is confounded with it by causing a similar disposition. When we fix our thought on any object and suppose it to continue the same for some time, it is evident we suppose the change to lie only in the time and never exert ourselves to produce any new image or idea of the object. The faculties of the mind repose themselves in a manner and take no more exercise than what is necessary to continue that idea of which we were formerly possessed and which subsists without variation or interruption. The passage from one moment to another is scarcely felt and does not distinguish itself by a different perception or idea, which may require a

26. Part II, sec. 5.

different direction of the spirits in order to [form] its conception.

Now, what other objects, besides identical ones, are capable of placing the mind in the same disposition when it considers them and of causing the same uninterrupted passage of the imagination from one idea to another? This question is of the last importance. For if we can find any such objects, we may certainly conclude from the foregoing principle that they are very naturally confounded with identical ones and are taken for them in most of our reasonings. But though this question be very important, it is not very difficult nor doubtful. For I immediately reply that a succession of related objects places the mind in this disposition and is considered with the same smooth and uninterrupted progress of the imagination as attends the view of the same invariable object. The very nature and essence of relation is to connect our ideas with each other and, upon the appearance of one, to facilitate the transition to its correlative. The passage between related ideas is therefore so smooth and easy that it produces little alteration on the mind and seems like the continuation of the same action, and as the continuation of the same action is an effect of the continued view of the same object, it is for this reason we attribute sameness to every succession of related objects. The thought slides along the succession with equal facility as if it considered only one object, and therefore confounds the succession with the identity.

We shall afterwards see many instances of this tendency of relation to make us ascribe an *identity* to *different* objects, but shall here confine ourselves to the present subject. We find by experience that there is such a *constancy* in almost all the impressions of the senses that their interruption produces no alteration on them and does not hinder them from returning the same in appearance and in situation as at their first existence. I survey the furniture of my chamber; I shut my eyes and afterwards open them and find the new perceptions to resemble perfectly those which formerly struck my senses. This resemblance is observed in a thousand instances and naturally connects together our ideas of these interrupted perceptions by the strongest relation and conveys the mind with an easy transition from one to another. An easy transi-

tion or passage of the imagination, along the ideas of these different and interrupted perceptions, is almost the same disposition of mind with that in which we consider one constant and uninterrupted perception. It is therefore very natural for us to mistake the one for the other.[27]

The persons who entertain this opinion concerning the identity of our resembling perceptions are, in general, all the unthinking and unphilosophical part of mankind (that is, all of us at one time or other,) and, consequently, such as suppose their perceptions to be their only objects and never think of a double existence internal and external, representing and represented. The very image which is present to the senses is with us the real body, and it is to these interrupted images we ascribe a perfect identity. But as the interruption of the appearance seems contrary to the identity and naturally leads us to regard these resembling perceptions as different from each other, we here find ourselves at a loss how to reconcile such opposite opinions. The smooth passage of the imagination along the ideas of the resembling perceptions makes us ascribe to them a perfect identity. The interrupted manner of their appearance makes us consider them as so many resembling, but still distinct beings which appear after certain intervals. The perplexity arising from this contradiction produces a propension to unite these broken appearances by the fiction of a continued existence, which is the *third* part of that hypothesis I proposed to explain.

Nothing is more certain from experience than that any contradiction either to the sentiments or passions gives a sensible uneasiness, whether it proceeds from without or from within, from the opposition of exter-

---

27. This reasoning, it must be confessed, is somewhat abstruse and difficult to be comprehended, but it is remarkable that this very difficulty may be converted into a proof of the reasoning. We may observe that there are two relations, and both of them resemblances, which contribute to our mistaking the succession of our interrupted perceptions for an identical object. The first is the resemblance of the perceptions; the second is the resemblance which the act of the mind, in surveying a succession of resembling objects, bears to that in surveying an identical object. Now these resemblances we are apt to confound with each other, and it is natural we should, according to this very reasoning. But let us keep them distinct and we shall find no difficulty in conceiving the precedent argument.

nal objects or from the combat of internal principles. On the contrary, whatever strikes in with the natural propensities and either externally forwards their satisfaction or internally concurs with their movements is sure to give a sensible pleasure. Now, there being here an opposition between the notion of the identity of resembling perceptions and the interruption of their appearance, the mind must be uneasy in that situation and will naturally seek relief from the uneasiness. Since the uneasiness arises from the opposition of two contrary principles, it must look for relief by sacrificing the one to the other. But as the smooth passage of our thought along our resembling perceptions makes us ascribe to them an identity, we can never, without reluctance, yield up that opinion. We must therefore turn to the other side and suppose that our perceptions are no longer interrupted, but preserve a continued as well as an invariable existence and are by that means entirely the same. But here the interruptions in the appearance of these perceptions are so long and frequent that it is impossible to overlook them, and as the appearance of a perception in the mind and its existence seem at first sight entirely the same, it may be doubted whether we can ever assent to so palpable a contradiction and suppose a perception to exist without being present to the mind. In order to clear up this matter and learn how the interruption in the *appearance* of a perception does not imply necessarily an interruption in its *existence*, it will be proper to touch upon some principles which we shall have occasion to explain more fully afterwards.[28]

We may begin with observing that the difficulty in the present case is not concerning the matter of fact, or whether the mind forms such a conclusion concerning the continued existence of its perceptions, but only concerning the manner in which the conclusion is formed and principles from which it is derived. It is certain that almost all mankind, and even philosophers themselves, for the greatest part of their lives take their perceptions to be their only objects and suppose that the very being which is intimately present to the mind is the real body or material existence. It is also certain that this very perception or object is

supposed to have a continued uninterrupted being and neither to be annihilated by our absence, nor to be brought into existence by our presence. When we are absent from it, we say it still exists, but that we do not feel, we do not see it. When we are present, we say we feel or see it. Here then may arise two questions: *First*, how we can satisfy ourselves in supposing a perception to be absent from the mind without being annihilated. *Secondly*, after what manner we conceive an object to become present to the mind without some new creation of a perception or image, and what we mean by this *seeing*, and *feeling*, and *perceiving*.

As to the first question, we may observe that what we call a *mind* is nothing but a heap or collection of different perceptions, united together by certain relations, and supposed, though falsely, to be endowed with a perfect simplicity and identity. Now, as every perception is distinguishable from another and may be considered as separately existent, it evidently follows that there is no absurdity in separating any particular perception from the mind, that is, in breaking off all its relations with that connected mass of perceptions which constitute a thinking being.

The same reasoning affords us an answer to the second question. If the name of *perception* does not render this separation from a mind absurd and contradictory, the name of *object*, standing for the very same thing, can never render their conjunction impossible. External objects are seen and felt and become present to the mind, that is, they acquire such a relation to a connected heap of perceptions as to influence them very considerably in augmenting their number by present reflections and passions and in storing the memory with ideas. The same continued and uninterrupted being may, therefore, be sometimes present to the mind and sometimes absent from it without any real or essential change in the being itself. An interrupted appearance to the senses does not imply necessarily an interruption in the existence. The supposition of the continued existence of sensible objects or perceptions involves no contradiction: We may easily indulge our inclination to that supposition. When the exact resemblance of our perceptions makes us ascribe to them an identity, we may remove the seeming interruption by feigning a continued

28. Sec. 6.

being which may fill those intervals and preserve a perfect and entire identity to our perceptions.

But as we here not only *feign* but *believe* this continued existence, the question is, *from whence arises such a belief?*, and this question leads us to the *fourth* member of this system. It has been proved already that belief, in general, consists in nothing but the vivacity of an idea and that an idea may acquire this vivacity by its relation to some present impression. Impressions are naturally the most vivid perceptions of the mind, and this quality is, in part, conveyed by the relation to every connected idea. The relation causes a smooth passage from the impression to the idea and even gives a propensity to that passage. The mind falls so easily from the one perception to the other that it scarcely perceives the change, but retains in the second a considerable share of the vivacity of the first. It is excited by the lively impression and this vivacity is conveyed to the related idea without any great diminution in the passage by reason of the smooth transition and the propensity of the imagination.

But suppose that this propensity arises from some other principle besides that of relation. It is evident it must still have the same effect and convey the vivacity from the impression to the idea. Now, this is exactly the present case. Our memory presents us with a vast number of instances of perceptions perfectly resembling each other that return at different distances of time and after considerable interruptions. This resemblance gives us a propension to consider these interrupted perceptions as the same and also a propension to connect them by a continued existence in order to justify this identity and avoid the contradiction in which the interrupted appearance of these perceptions seems necessarily to involve us. Here then we have a propensity to feign the continued existence of all sensible objects, and as this propensity arises from some lively impressions of the memory, it bestows a vivacity on that fiction or, in other words, makes us believe the continued existence of body. If sometimes we ascribe a continued existence to objects which are perfectly new to us and of whose constancy and coherence we have no experience, it is because the manner in which they present themselves to our senses resembles that of constant and coherent ob-

jects, and this resemblance is a source of reasoning and analogy and leads us to attribute the same qualities to the similar objects.

I believe an intelligent reader will find less difficulty to assent to this system than to comprehend it fully and distinctly and will allow, after a little reflection, that every part carries its own proof along with it. It is indeed evident that as the vulgar *suppose* their perceptions to be their only objects and at the same time *believe* the continued existence of matter, we must account for the origin of the belief upon that supposition. Now, upon that supposition, it is a false opinion that any of our objects, or perceptions, are identically the same after an interruption, and consequently the opinion of their identity can never arise from reason, but must arise from the imagination. The imagination is seduced into such an opinion only by means of the resemblance of certain perceptions, since we find they are only our resembling perceptions which we have a propension to suppose the same. This propension to bestow an identity on our resembling perceptions produces the fiction of a continued existence, since that fiction as well as the identity is really false, as is acknowledged by all philosophers, and has no other effect than to remedy the interruption of our perceptions, which is the only circumstance that is contrary to their identity. In the last place, this propension causes belief by means of the present impressions of the memory, since, without the remembrance of former sensations, it is plain we never should have any belief of the continued existence of body. Thus, in examining all these parts, we find that each of them is supported by the strongest proofs and that all of them together form a consistent system which is perfectly convincing. A strong propensity or inclination alone, without any present impression, will sometimes cause a belief or opinion. How much more when aided by that circumstance?

But though we are led after this manner, by the natural propensity of the imagination, to ascribe a continued existence to those sensible objects or perceptions which we find to resemble each other in their interrupted appearance, yet a very little reflection and philosophy is sufficient to make us perceive the fallacy of that opinion. I have already observed that there is an intimate connection between those two principles, of a *continued* and of a *distinct* or *independent* existence, and that we no sooner establish the one than the other follows as a necessary consequence. It is the opinion of a continued existence, which first takes place and without much study or reflection draws the other along with it wherever the mind follows its first and most natural tendency. But when we compare experiments and reason a little upon them, we quickly perceive that the doctrine of the independent existence of our sensible perceptions is contrary to the plainest experience. This leads us backward upon our footsteps to perceive our error in attributing a continued existence to our perceptions and is the origin of many very curious opinions, which we shall here endeavor to account for.

It will first be proper to observe a few of those experiments which convince us that our perceptions are not possessed of any independent existence. When we press one eye with a finger, we immediately perceive all the objects to become double and one half of them to be removed from their common and natural position. But as we do not attribute a continued existence to both these perceptions and as they are both of the same nature, we clearly perceive that all our perceptions are dependent on our organs and the disposition of our nerves and animal spirits. This opinion is confirmed by the seeming increase and diminution of objects according to their distance, by the apparent alterations in their figure, by the changes in their color and other qualities from our sickness and distempers, and by an infinite number of other experiments of the same kind from all of which we learn that our sensible perceptions are not possessed of any distinct or independent existence.

The natural consequence of this reasoning should be that our perceptions have no more a continued than an independent existence and, indeed, philosophers have so far run into this opinion that they change their system and distinguish (as we shall do for the future) between perceptions and objects, of which the former are supposed to be interrupted and perishing and different at every different return, the latter to be uninterrupted and to preserve a continued existence and identity. But however philosophical this new system may be esteemed, I assert that it is only a palliative remedy and that it contains all the difficulties of the vulgar system, with some others that are peculiar to itself. There are no principles either of the understanding or fancy which lead us directly to embrace this opinion of the double existence of perceptions and objects, nor can we arrive at it but by passing through the common hypothesis of the identity and continuance of our interrupted perceptions. Were we not first persuaded that our perceptions are our only objects and continue to exist even when they no longer make their appearance to the senses, we should never be led to think that our perceptions and objects are different and that our objects alone preserve a continued existence. "The latter hypothesis has no primary recommendation either to reason or the imagination, but acquires all its influence on the imagination from the former." This proposition contains two parts which we shall endeavor to prove as distinctly and clearly as such abstruse subjects will permit.

As to the first part of the proposition *that this philosophical hypothesis has no primary recommendation either to reason or the imagination*, we may soon satisfy ourselves with regard to reason by the following reflections. The only existences of which we are certain, are perceptions, which, being immediately present to us by consciousness, command our strongest assent and are the first foundation of all our conclusions. The only conclusion we can draw from the existence of one thing to that of another is by means of the relation of cause and effect, which shows that there is a connection between them and that the existence of one is dependent on that of the other. The idea of this relation is derived from past experience, by which we find that two beings are constantly conjoined together and are always present at once to the mind. But as no beings are ever present to the mind but perceptions, it follows that we may observe a conjunction or a relation of cause and effect between different perceptions, but can never observe it between perceptions and objects. It is impossible, therefore, that from the existence or any of the qualities of the former, we can ever form any conclusion concerning the existence of the latter or ever satisfy our reason in this particular.

It is no less certain that this philosophical system has no primary recommendation to the *imagination* and that that faculty would never, of itself and by its original tendency, have fallen upon such a principle. I confess it will be somewhat difficult to prove this to the full satisfaction of the reader, because it implies a negative, which in many cases will not admit of any positive proof. If anyone would take the pains to examine this question and would invent a system to account for the direct origin of this opinion from the imagination, we should be able, by the examination of that system, to pronounce a certain judgment in the present subject. Let it be taken for granted that our perceptions are broken and interrupted and, however like, are still different from each other, and let any one, upon this supposition, show why the fancy, directly and immediately, proceeds to the belief of another existence, resembling these perceptions in their nature, but yet continued and uninterrupted and identical, and after he has done this to my satisfaction, I promise to renounce my present opinion. Meanwhile I cannot forbear concluding from the very abstractedness and difficulty of the first supposition that it is an improper subject for the fancy to work upon. Whoever would explain the origin of the *common* opinion concerning the continued and distinct existence of body must take the mind in its *common* situation and must proceed upon the supposition that our perceptions are our only objects and continue to exist even when they are not perceived. Though this opinion be false, it is the most natural of any and has alone any primary recommendation to the fancy.

As to the second part of the proposition *that the philosophical system acquires all its influence on the imagination from the vulgar one,* we may observe that this is a natural and unavoidable consequence of the foregoing conclusion *that it has no primary recommendation to reason or the imagination.* For as the philosophical system is found by experience to take hold of many minds and, in particular, of all those who reflect ever so little on this subject, it must derive all its authority from the vulgar system, since it has no original authority of its own. The manner in which these two systems, though directly contrary, are connected together may be explained as follows.

The imagination naturally runs on in this train of thinking. Our perceptions are our only objects: resembling perceptions are the same, however broken or uninterrupted in their appearance: this appearing interruption is contrary to the identity: the interruption consequently does not extend beyond the appearance, and the perception or object really continues to exist, even when absent from us: our sensible perceptions have, therefore, a continued and uninterrupted existence. But as a little reflection destroys this conclusion that our perceptions have a continued existence by showing that they have a dependent one, it would naturally be expected that we must altogether reject the opinion that there is such a thing in nature as a continued existence, which is preserved even when it no longer appears to the senses. The case, however, is otherwise. Philosophers are so far from rejecting the opinion of a continued existence upon rejecting that of the independence and continuance of our sensible perceptions that though all sects agree in the latter sentiment, the former, which is in a manner its necessary consequence, has been peculiar to a few extravagant skeptics who, after all, maintained that opinion in words only and were never able to bring themselves sincerely to believe it.

There is a great difference between such opinions as we form after a calm and profound reflection and such as we embrace by a kind of instinct or natural impulse, on account of their suitableness and conformity to the mind. If these opinions become contrary, it is not difficult to foresee which of them will have the advantage. As long as our attention is bent upon the subject, the philosophical and studied principle may prevail, but the moment we relax our thoughts, nature will display herself and draw us back to our former opinion. No, she has sometimes such an influence that she can stop our progress, even in the midst of our most profound reflections, and keep us from running on with all the consequences of any philosophical opinion. Thus, though we clearly perceive the dependence and interruption of our perceptions, we stop short in our career and never, upon that account, reject the notion of an independent and continued existence. That opinion has taken such deep root in the imagination that it is impossible ever to eradicate it, nor will any strained metaphysical conviction of the dependence of our perceptions be sufficient for that purpose.

But though our natural and obvious principles here prevail above our studied reflections, it is certain there must be some struggle and opposition in the case, at least so long as these reflections retain any force or vivacity. In order to set ourselves at ease in this particular, we contrive a new hypothesis which seems to comprehend both these principles of reason and imagination. This hypothesis is the philosophical one of the double existence of perceptions and objects, which pleases our reason in allowing that our dependent perceptions are interrupted and different and at the same time is agreeable to the imagination in attributing a continued existence to something else which we call *objects*. This philosophical system, therefore, is the monstrous offspring of two principles which are contrary to each other, which are both at once embraced by the mind, and which are unable mutually to destroy each other. The imagination tells us that our resembling perceptions have a continued and uninterrupted existence and are not annihilated by their absence. Reflection tells us that even our resembling perceptions are interrupted in their existence and different from each other. The contradiction between these opinions we elude by a new fiction which is conformable to the hypotheses both of reflection and fancy, by ascribing these contrary qualities to different existences, the *interruption* to perceptions and the *continuance* to objects. Nature is obstinate and will not quit the field, however strongly attacked by reason, and at the same time reason is so clear in the point that there is no possibility of disguising her. Not being able to reconcile these two enemies, we endeavor to set ourselves at ease as much as possible by successively granting to each whatever it demands and by feigning a double existence where each may find something that has all the conditions it desires. Were we fully convinced that our resembling perceptions are continued and identical and independent, we should never run into this opinion of a double existence, since we should find satisfaction in our first supposition and would not look beyond. Again, were we fully convinced that our perceptions are dependent and interrupted and different, we should be as little inclined to embrace the opinion of a double existence, since in that case we should clearly perceive the error of our first supposition of

a continued existence and would never regard it any further. It is therefore from the intermediate situation of the mind that this opinion arises and from such an adherence to these two contrary principles as makes us seek some pretext to justify our receiving both, which happily at last is found in the system of a double existence.

Another advantage of this philosophical system is its similarity to the vulgar one, by which means we can humor our reason for a moment when it becomes troublesome and solicitous, and yet, upon its least negligence or inattention, can easily return to our vulgar and natural notions. Accordingly we find that philosophers do not neglect this advantage, but, immediately upon leaving their closets, mingle with the rest of mankind in those exploded opinions that our perceptions are our only objects and continue identically and uninterruptedly the same in all their interrupted appearances.

There are other particulars of this system wherein we may remark its dependence on the fancy in a very conspicuous manner. Of these, I shall observe the two following. *First*, we suppose external objects to resemble internal perceptions. I have already shown that the relation of cause and effect can never afford us any just conclusion from the existence or qualities of our perceptions to the existence of external continued objects, and I shall further add that even though they could afford such a conclusion, we should never have any reason to infer that our objects resemble our perceptions. That opinion, therefore, is derived from nothing but the quality of the fancy explained above *that it borrows all its ideas from some precedent perception*. We never can conceive anything but perceptions and therefore must make everything resemble them.

Secondly, as we suppose our objects in general to resemble our perceptions, so we take it for granted that every particular object resembles that perception which it causes. The relation of cause and effect determines us to join the other of resemblance, and, the ideas of these existences being already united together in the fancy by the former relation, we naturally add the latter to complete the union. We have a strong propensity to complete every union by joining new relations to those which we have before observed between any ideas, as we shall have occasion to observe presently.[29]

Having thus given an account of all the systems, both popular and philosophical, with regard to external existences, I cannot forbear giving vent to a certain sentiment which arises upon reviewing those systems. I began this subject by premising that we ought to have an implicit faith in our senses and that this would be the conclusion I should draw from the whole of my reasoning. But to be ingenuous, I feel myself *at present* of a quite contrary sentiment and am more inclined to repose no faith at all in my senses, or rather imagination, than to place in it such an implicit confidence. I cannot conceive how such trivial qualities of the fancy, conducted by such false suppositions, can ever lead to any solid and rational system. They are the coherence and constancy of our perceptions, which produce the opinion of their continued existence, though these qualities of perceptions have no perceivable connection with such an existence. The constancy of our perceptions has the most considerable effect and yet is attended with the greatest difficulties. It is a gross illusion to suppose that our resembling perceptions are numerically the same, and it is this illusion which leads us into the opinion that these perceptions are uninterrupted and are still existent even when they are not present to the senses. This is the case with our popular system. And as to our philosophical one, it is liable to the same difficulties and is, over and above, loaded with this absurdity, that it at once denies and establishes the vulgar supposition. Philosophers deny our resembling perceptions to be identically the same and uninterrupted, and yet have so great a propensity to believe them such that they arbitrarily invent a new set of perceptions to which they attribute these qualities. I say, a new set of perceptions. For we may well suppose in general, but it is impossible for us distinctly to conceive, objects to be in their nature anything but exactly the same with perceptions. What then can we look for from this confusion of groundless and extraordinary opinions but error and falsehood? And how can we justify to ourselves any belief we repose in them?

29. Sec. 5.

This skeptical doubt, both with respect to reason and the senses, is a malady which can never be radically cured, but must return upon us every moment, however we may chase it away, and sometimes may seem entirely free from it. It is impossible, upon any system, to defend either our understanding or senses, and we but expose them further when we endeavor to justify them in that manner. As the skeptical doubt arises naturally from a profound and intense reflection on those subjects, it always increases the further we carry our reflections, whether in opposition or conformity to it. Carelessness and inattention alone can afford us any remedy. For this reason I rely entirely upon them and take it for granted, whatever may be the reader's opinion at this present moment, that an hour hence he will be persuaded there is both an external and internal world and, going upon that supposition, I intend to examine some general systems, both ancient and modern, which have been proposed of both, before I proceed to a more particular inquiry concerning our impressions. This will not, perhaps, in the end, be found foreign to our present purpose.

Section 3: Of the Ancient Philosophy

Several moralists have recommended it as an excellent method of becoming acquainted with our own hearts and knowing our progress in virtue to recollect our dreams in a morning and examine them with the same rigor that we would our most serious and most deliberate actions. Our character is the same throughout, say they, and appears best where artifice, fear, and policy have no place and men can neither be hypocrites with themselves nor others. The generosity or baseness of our temper, our meekness or cruelty, our courage or pusillanimity, influence the fictions of the imagination with the most unbounded liberty and discover themselves in the most glaring colors. In like manner, I am persuaded that there might be several useful discoveries made from a criticism of the fictions of the ancient philosophy concerning *substances and substantial forms and accidents and occult qualities* which, however unreasonable and capricious, have a very intimate connection with the principles of human nature.

It is confessed by the most judicious philosophers that our ideas of bodies are nothing but collections formed by the mind of the ideas of the several distinct sensible qualities of which objects are composed and which we find to have a constant union with each other. But however these qualities may in themselves be entirely distinct, it is certain we commonly regard the compound which they form as one thing and as continuing the same under very considerable alterations. The acknowledged composition is evidently contrary to this supposed *simplicity* and the variation to the *identity*. It may therefore be worthwhile to consider the *causes* which make us almost universally fall into such evident contradictions as well as the means by which we endeavor to conceal them.

It is evident that as the ideas of the several distinct *successive* qualities of objects are united together by a very close relation, the mind, in looking along the succession, must be carried from one part of it to another by an easy transition and will no more perceive the change than if it contemplated the same unchangeable object. This easy transition is the effect, or rather essence, of relation, and as the imagination readily takes one idea for another where their influence on the mind is similar, hence it proceeds that any such succession of related qualities is readily considered as one continued object, existing without any variation. The smooth and uninterrupted progress of the thought, being alike in both cases, readily deceives the mind and makes us ascribe an identity to the changeable succession of connected qualities.

But when we alter our method of considering the succession and, instead of tracing it gradually through the successive points of time, survey at once any two distinct periods of its duration and compare the different conditions of the successive qualities, in that case the variations which were insensible when they arose gradually do now appear of consequence and seem entirely to destroy the identity. By this means there arises a kind of contrariety in our method of thinking from the different points of view in which we survey the object and from the nearness or remoteness of those instants of time which we compare together. When we gradually follow an object in its successive changes, the smooth progress of the thought makes us ascribe an identity to the succession, because it is by a similar act of the mind we consider an unchangeable object. When we compare its situation after a considerable change, the progress of the thought is broke, and consequently we are presented with the idea of diversity in order to reconcile which contradictions the imagination is apt to feign something unknown and invisible which it supposes to continue the same under all these variations, and this unintelligible something it calls a *substance, or original and first matter*.

We entertain a like notion with regard to the *simplicity* of substances and from like causes. Suppose an object perfectly simple and indivisible to be presented along with another object whose *coexistent* parts are connected together by a strong relation, it is evident the actions of the mind, in considering these two objects, are not very different. The imagination conceives the simple object at once, with facility, by a single effort of thought, without change or variation. The connection of parts in the compound object has almost the same effect and so unites the object within itself that the fancy does not feel the transition in passing from one part to another. Hence the color, taste, figure, solidity, and other qualities combined in a peach or melon are conceived to form *one thing*, and that on account of their close relation which makes them affect the thought in the same manner, as if perfectly uncompounded. But the mind does not rest here. Whenever it views the object in another light, it finds that all these qualities are different and distinguishable and separable from each other, which view of things being destructive of its primary and more natural notions obliges the imagination to feign an unknown something or *original* substance and matter as a principle of union or cohesion among these qualities and as what may give the compound object a title to be called one thing, notwithstanding its diversity and composition.

The Peripatetic philosophy asserts the *original* matter to be perfectly homogeneous in all bodies and considers fire, water, earth, and air as of the very same substance, on account of their gradual revolutions and changes into each other. At the same time it assigns to each of these species of objects a distinct *substantial form*, which it supposes to be the source of all those different qualities they possess and to be a new foundation of simplicity and identity to each particular species. All depends on our manner of viewing the objects. When we look along the insensible changes of bodies, we suppose all of them to be of the same substance or essence. When we consider their sensible differences, we attribute to each of them a substantial and essential difference. And in order to indulge ourselves in both these ways of considering our objects, we suppose all bodies to have at once a substance and a substantial form.

The notion of *accidents* is an unavoidable consequence of this method of thinking with regard to substances and substantial forms, nor can we forbear looking upon colors, sounds, tastes, figures, and other properties of bodies as existences which cannot subsist apart, but require a subject of inhesion to sustain and support them. For having never discovered any of these sensible qualities, where, for the reasons mentioned above, we did not likewise fancy a substance to exist, the same habit which makes us infer a connection between cause and effect makes us here infer a dependence of every quality on the unknown substance. The custom of imagining a dependence has the same effect as the custom of observing it would have. This conceit, however, is no more reasonable than any of the foregoing. Every quality being a distinct thing from another may be conceived to exist apart and may exist apart not only from every other quality, but from that unintelligible chimera of a substance.

But these philosophers carry their fictions still further in their sentiments concerning *occult qualities* and both suppose a substance supporting which they do not understand and an accident supported of which they have as imperfect an idea. The whole system, therefore, is entirely incomprehensible and yet is derived from principles as natural as any of these explained above.

In considering this subject, we may observe a gradation of three opinions that rise above each other, according as the persons who form them acquire new degrees of reason and knowledge. These opinions are that of the vulgar, that of a false philosophy, and that of the true, where we shall find upon inquiry that the true philosophy approaches nearer to the sentiments of the vulgar than to those of a mistaken knowledge. It is natural for men, in their common and careless way of thinking, to imagine they perceive a connection between such objects as they have constantly found united together, and because custom has rendered it difficult to separate the ideas, they are apt to fancy such a separation to be in itself impossible and absurd. But philosophers, who abstract from the effects of custom and compare the ideas of objects, immediately perceive the falsehood of these vulgar sentiments and discover that there is no known connection among objects. Every different object appears to them entirely distinct and separate, and they perceive that it is not from a view of the nature and qualities of objects we infer one from another, but only when in several instances we observe them to have been constantly conjoined. But these philosophers, instead of drawing a just inference from this observation and concluding that we have no idea of power or agency, separate from the mind and belonging to causes, I say, instead of drawing this conclusion, they frequently search for the qualities in which this agency consists and are displeased with every system which their reason suggests to them in order to explain it. They have sufficient force of genius to free them from the vulgar error that there is a natural and perceivable connection between the several sensible qualities and actions of matter, but not sufficient to keep them from ever seeking for this connection in matter or causes. Had they fallen upon the just conclusion, they would have returned back to the situation of the vulgar and would have regarded all these disquisitions with indolence and indifference. At present they seem to be in a very lamentable condition and such as the poets have given us but a faint notion of in their descriptions of the punishment of *Sisyphus* and *Tantillus.* For what can be imagined more tormenting than to seek with eagerness what forever flies [from] us and seek for it in a place where it is impossible it can ever exist?

But as Nature seems to have observed a kind of justice and compensation in everything, she has not neglected philosophers more than the rest of the creation, but has reserved them a consolation amid all their disappointments and afflictions. This consolation principally consists in their invention of the words *faculty* and *occult quality.* For it being usual, after the frequent use of terms which are really significant and intelligible, to omit the idea which we would express by them and to preserve only the custom by which we recall the idea at pleasure, so it naturally happens that after the frequent use of terms which are wholly insignificant and unintelligible, we fancy them to be on the same footing with the precedent and to have a secret meaning which we might discover by reflection. The resemblance of their appearance deceives the mind, as is usual, and makes us imagine a thorough resemblance and conformity. By this means these philosophers set themselves at ease and arrive at last, by an illusion, at the same indifference which the people attain by their stupidity and true philosophers by their moderate skepticism. They need only say that any phenomenon which puzzles them arises from a faculty or an occult quality and there is an end of all dispute and inquiry upon the matter.

But among all the instances wherein the Peripatetics have shown they were guided by every trivial propensity of the imagination, no one is more remarkable than their *sympathies, antipathies, and horrors of a vacuum*. There is a very remarkable inclination in human nature to bestow on external objects the same emotions which it observes in itself and to find everywhere those ideas which are most present to it. This inclination, it is true, is suppressed by a little reflection and only takes place in children, poets, and the ancient philosophers. It appears in children by their desire of beating the stones which hurt them, in poets by their readiness to personify everything, and in the ancient philosophers by these fictions of sympathy and antipathy. We must pardon children, because of their age, poets, because they profess to follow implicitly the suggestions of their fancy, but what excuse shall we find to justify our philosophers in so signal a weakness?

Section 4: Of the Modern Philosophy

But here it may be objected that the imagination, according to my own confession, being the ultimate judge of all systems of philosophy, I am unjust in blaming the ancient philosophers for making use of that faculty and allowing themselves to be entirely guided by it in their reasonings. In order to justify myself, I must distinguish in the imagination between the principles which are permanent, irresistible, and universal, such as the customary transition from causes to effects and from effects to causes, and the principles which are changeable, weak, and irregular, such as those I have just now taken notice of. The former are the foundation of all our thoughts and actions so that upon their removal, human nature must immediately perish and go to ruin. The latter are neither unavoidable to mankind nor necessary or so much as useful in the conduct of life, but, on the contrary, are observed only to take place in weak minds and, being opposite to the other principles of custom and reasoning, may easily be subverted by a due contrast and opposition. For this reason, the former are received by philosophy and the latter rejected. One who concludes somebody to be near him when he hears an articulate voice in the dark reasons justly and naturally, though that conclusion be derived from nothing but custom, which infixes and enlivens the idea of a human creature on account of his usual conjunction with the present impression. But one who is tormented, he knows not why, with the apprehension of specters in the dark, may perhaps be said to reason and to reason naturally, too, but then it must be in the same sense that a malady is said to be natural, as arising from natural causes, though it be contrary to health, the most agreeable and most natural situation of man.

The opinions of the ancient philosophers, their fictions of substance and accident, and their reasonings concerning substantial forms and occult qualities are like the specters in the dark and are derived from principles which, however common, are neither universal nor unavoidable in human nature. The *modern philosophy* pretends to be entirely free from this defect and to arise only from the solid, permanent, and consistent principles of the imagination. Upon what grounds this pretension is founded must now be the subject of our inquiry.

The fundamental principle of that philosophy is the opinion concerning colors, sounds, tastes, smells, heat, and cold, which it asserts to be nothing but impressions in the mind, derived from the operation of external objects and without any resemblance to the qualities of the objects. Upon examination, I find only one of the reasons commonly produced for this opinion to be satisfactory, namely, that derived from the variations of those impressions, even while the external object, to all appearance, continues the same. These variations depend upon several circumstances. Upon the different situations of our health, a man in a malady feels a disagreeable taste in meats, which before pleased him the most. Upon the different complexions and constitutions of men, that seems bitter to one which is sweet to another. Upon the difference of their external situation and position, colors reflected from the clouds change according to the distance of the clouds and according to the angle they make with the eye and luminous body. Fire also communicates the sensation of pleasure at one distance and that of pain at another. Instances of this kind are very numerous and frequent.

The conclusion drawn from them is likewise as satisfactory as can possibly be imagined. It is certain that when different impressions of the same sense arise from any object, every one of these impressions does not have a resembling quality existent in the object. For as the same object cannot, at the same time, be endowed with different qualities of the same sense and as the same quality cannot resemble impressions entirely different, it evidently follows that many of our impressions have no external model or archetype. Now, from like effects we presume like causes. Many of the impressions of color, sound, etc., are confessed to be nothing but internal existences and to arise from causes which noways resemble them. These impressions are in appearance nothing different from the other impressions of color, sound, etc. We conclude, therefore, that they are, all of them, derived from a like origin.

This principle being once admitted, all the other doctrines of that philosophy seem to follow by an easy consequence. For, upon the removal of sounds, colors, heat, cold, and other sensible qualities from the rank of continued independent existences, we are reduced merely to what are called primary qualities as the only *real* ones of which we have any adequate notion. These primary qualities are extension and solidity, with their different mixtures and modifications, figure, motion, gravity, and cohesion. The generation, increase, decay, and corruption of animals and vegetables are nothing but changes of figure and motion, as also the operations of all bodies on each other, of fire, of light, water, air, earth, and of all the elements and powers of nature. One figure and motion produces another figure and motion, nor does there remain in the material universe any other principle, either active or passive, of which we can form the most distant idea.

I believe many objections might be made to this system, but at present I shall confine myself to one which is, in my opinion, very decisive. I assert that instead of explaining the operations of external objects by its means, we utterly annihilate all these objects and reduce ourselves to the opinions of the most extravagant skepticism concerning them. If colors, sounds, tastes, and smells be merely perceptions, nothing we can conceive is possessed of a real, continued, and independent existence, not even motion, extension, and solidity, which are the primary qualities chiefly insisted on.

To begin with the examination of motion, it is evident this is a quality altogether inconceivable alone and without a reference to some other object. The idea of motion necessarily supposes that of a body moving. Now, what is our idea of the moving body, without which motion is incomprehensible? It must resolve itself into the idea of extension or of solidity and, consequently, the reality of motion depends upon that of these other qualities.

This opinion, which is universally acknowledged concerning motion, I have proved to be true with regard to extension and have shown that it is impossible to conceive extension but as composed of parts, endowed with color or solidity. The idea of extension is a compound idea, but as it is not compounded of an infinite number of parts or inferior ideas, it must at last resolve itself into such as are perfectly simple and indivisible. These simple and indivisible parts, not being ideas of extension, must be nonentities, unless conceived as colored or solid. Color is excluded from any real existence. The reality, therefore, of our idea of extension depends upon the reality of that of solidity, nor can the former be just while the latter is chimerical. Let us then lend our attention to the examination of the idea of solidity.

The idea of solidity is that of two objects which, being impelled by the utmost force, cannot penetrate each other, but still maintain a separate and distinct existence. Solidity, therefore, is perfectly incomprehensible alone and without the conception of some bodies which are solid and maintain this separate and distinct existence. Now, what idea do we have of these bodies? The ideas of colors, sounds, and other secondary qualities are excluded. The idea of motion depends on that of extension and the idea of extension on that of solidity. It is impossible, therefore, that the idea of solidity can depend on either of them. For that would be to run in a circle and make one idea depend on another, while, at the same time, the latter depends on the former. Our modern philosophy, therefore, leaves us no just nor satisfactory idea of solidity nor, consequently, of matter.

This argument will appear entirely conclusive to everyone who comprehends it, but because it may seem abstruse and intricate to the generality of readers, I hope to be excused if I endeavor to render it more obvious by some variation of the expression. In order to form an idea of solidity, we must conceive two bodies pressing on each other without any penetration, and it is impossible to arrive at this idea when we confine ourselves to one object, much more without conceiving any. Two nonentities cannot exclude each other from their places, because they never possess any place, nor can be endowed with any quality. Now I ask: What idea do we form of these bodies or objects to which we suppose solidity to belong? To say that we conceive them merely as solid is to run on *in infinitum*. To affirm that we paint them out to ourselves as extended either resolves all into a false idea or returns in a circle. Extension must necessarily be considered either as colored, which is a false idea, or as solid, which brings us back to the first question. We may make the same observation concerning mobility and figure and, upon the whole, must conclude that after the exclusion of color, sounds, heat, and cold, from the rank of external existences, there remains nothing which can afford us a just and consistent idea of body.

Add to this that, properly speaking, solidity or impenetrability is nothing but an impossibility of annihilation, as has been already observed,[30] for which reason it is the more necessary for us to form some distinct idea of that object whose annihilation we suppose impossible. An impossibility of being annihilated cannot exist and can never be conceived to exist by itself, but necessarily requires some object or real existence to which it may belong. Now, the difficulty still remains how to form an idea of this object or existence without having recourse to the secondary and sensible qualities.

Nor must we omit on this occasion our accustomed method of examining ideas by considering those impressions from which they are derived. The impressions which enter by the sight and hearing, the smell and taste, are affirmed by modern philosophy to be without any resembling objects, and consequently the idea of solidity, which is supposed to be real, can never be derived from any of these senses. There remains, therefore, the feeling as the only sense that can convey the impression which is original to the idea of solidity and, indeed, we naturally imagine that we feel the solidity of bodies and need but touch any object in order to perceive this quality. But this method of thinking is more popular than philosophical, as will appear from the following reflections.

First, it is easy to observe that though bodies are felt by means of their solidity, yet the feeling is a quite different thing from the solidity, and that they have not the least resemblance to each other. A man who has the palsy in one hand has as perfect an idea of impenetrability when he observes that hand to be supported by the table as when he feels the same table with the other hand. An object that presses upon any of our members meets with resistance, and that resistance, by the motion it gives to the nerves and animal spirits, conveys a certain sensation to the mind, but it does not follow that the sensation, motion, and resistance are any ways resembling.

Secondly, the impressions of touch are simple impressions, except when considered with regard to their extension, which makes nothing to the present

30. Part II, sec. 4.

purpose, and from this simplicity I infer that they neither represent solidity nor any real object. For let us put two cases, namely, that of a man who presses a stone or any solid body with his hand and that of two stones which press each other. It will readily be allowed that these two cases are not in every respect alike, but that in the former there is conjoined with the solidity a feeling or sensation of which there is no appearance in the latter. In order, therefore, to make these two cases alike, it is necessary to remove some part of the impression which the man feels by his hand, or organ of sensation, and, that being impossible in a simple impression, obliges us to remove the whole and proves that this whole impression has no archetype or model in external objects, to which we may add that solidity necessarily supposes two bodies along with contiguity and impulse, which, being a compound object, can never be represented by a simple impression. Not to mention that, though solidity continues always invariably the same, the impressions of touch change every moment upon us, which is a clear proof that the latter are not representations of the former.

Thus there is a direct and total opposition between our reason and our senses or, more properly speaking, between those conclusions we form from cause and effect and those that persuade us of the continued and independent existence of body. When we reason from cause and effect, we conclude that neither color, sound, taste nor smell have a continued and independent existence. When we exclude these sensible qualities, there remains nothing in the universe which has such an existence.

Section 5: Of the Immateriality of the Soul

Having found such contradictions and difficulties in every system concerning external objects and in the idea of matter which we fancy so clear and determinate, we shall naturally expect still greater difficulties and contradictions in every hypothesis concerning our internal perceptions and the nature of the mind which we are apt to imagine so much more obscure and uncertain. But in this we should deceive ourselves. The intellectual world, though involved in infinite obscurities, is not perplexed with any such

contradictions as those we have discovered in the natural. What is known concerning it agrees with itself, and what is unknown we must be contented to leave so.

It is true, would we listen to certain philosophers, they promise to diminish our ignorance, but I am afraid it is at the hazard of running us into contradictions from which the subject is of itself exempted. These philosophers are the curious reasoners concerning the material or immaterial substances in which they suppose our perceptions to inhere. In order to put a stop to these endless cavils on both sides, I know no better method than to ask these philosophers in a few words *what they mean by substance and inhesion?* And after they have answered this question, it will then be reasonable, and not until then, to enter seriously into the dispute.

This question we have found impossible to be answered with regard to matter and body, but, besides the fact that in the case of the mind it labors under all the same difficulties, it is burdened with some additional ones which are peculiar to that subject. As every idea is derived from a precedent impression, had we any idea of the substance of our minds, we must also have an impression of it, which is very difficult, if not impossible, to be conceived. For how can an impression represent a substance otherwise than by resembling it? And how can an impression resemble a substance, since, according to this philosophy, it is not a substance and has none of the peculiar qualities or characteristics of a substance?

But leaving the question *of what may or may not be* for that other *what actually is,* I desire those philosophers who pretend that we have an idea of the substance of our minds to point out the impression that produces it and tell distinctly after what manner that impression operates and from what object it is derived. Is it an impression of sensation or of reflection? Is it pleasant or painful or indifferent? Does it attend us at all times or does it only return at intervals? If at intervals, at what times principally does it return and by what causes is it produced?

If instead of answering these questions anyone should evade the difficulty by saying that the definition of a substance is *something which may exist by itself* and that this definition ought to satisfy us; should this be said, I should observe that this definition agrees to everything that can possibly be conceived and never will serve to distinguish substance from accident or the soul from its perceptions. For thus I reason. Whatever is clearly conceived may exist, and whatever is clearly conceived after any manner may exist after the same manner. This is one principle which has been already acknowledged. Again, everything which is different is distinguishable, and everything which is distinguishable is separable by the imagination. This is another principle. My conclusion from both is that since all our perceptions are different from each other and from everything else in the universe, they are also distinct and separable and may be considered as separately existent and may exist separately and have no need of anything else to support their existence. They are, therefore, substances, as far as this definition explains a substance.

Thus, neither by considering the first origin of ideas nor by means of a definition are we able to arrive at any satisfactory notion of substance, which seems to me a sufficient reason for abandoning utterly that dispute concerning the materiality and immateriality of the soul and makes me absolutely condemn even the question itself. We have no perfect idea of anything but of a perception. A substance is entirely different from a perception. We have, therefore, no idea of a substance. Inhesion in something is supposed to be requisite to support the existence of our perceptions. Nothing appears requisite to support the existence of a perception. We have, therefore, no idea of inhesion. What is the possibility then of answering that question *whether perceptions inhere in a material or immaterial substance*, when we do not so much as understand the meaning of the question?

There is one argument commonly employed for the immateriality of the soul which seems to me remarkable. Whatever is extended consists of parts, and whatever consists of parts is divisible, if not in reality, at least in the imagination. But it is impossible anything divisible can be *conjoined* to a thought or perception which is a being altogether inseparable and indivisible. For, supposing such a conjunction, would the indivisible thought exist on the left or on the right hand of this extended divisible body? On the surface or in the middle? On the back or foreside

of it? If it is conjoined with the extension, it must exist somewhere within its dimensions. If it exists within its dimensions, it must either exist in one particular part, and then that particular part is indivisible and the perception is conjoined only with it, not with the extension, or if the thought exists in every part, it must also be extended and separable and divisible as well as the body, which is utterly absurd and contradictory. For can anyone conceive a passion of a yard in length, a foot in breadth, and an inch in thickness? Thought, therefore, and extension are qualities wholly incompatible and never can incorporate together into one subject.

This argument does not affect the question concerning the *substance* of the soul, but only that concerning its *local conjunction* with matter, and, therefore, it may not be improper to consider in general what objects are or are not susceptible of a local conjunction. This is a curious question and may lead us to some discoveries of considerable moment.

The first notion of space and extension is derived solely from the senses of sight and feeling. Nor is there anything but what is colored or tangible that has parts disposed after such a manner as to convey that idea. When we diminish or increase a relish, it is not after the same manner that we diminish or increase any visible object, and when several sounds strike our hearing at once, custom and reflection alone make us form an idea of the degrees of the distance and contiguity of those bodies from which they are derived. Whatever marks the place of its existence either must be extended or must be a mathematical point without parts or composition. What is extended must have a particular figure, as square, round, triangular, none of which will agree to a desire or indeed to any impression or idea, except of these two senses above mentioned. Neither ought a desire, though indivisible, to be considered as a mathematical point. For in that case it would be possible by the addition of others to make two, three, four desires and these disposed and situated in such a manner as to have a determinate length, breadth, and thickness, which is evidently absurd.

It will not be surprising after this if I propose a maxim which is condemned by several metaphysicians and is esteemed contrary to the most certain principles of human reason. This maxim is *that an object may exist and yet be nowhere,* and I assert that this is not only possible but that the greatest part of beings do and must exist after this manner. An object may be said to be nowhere when its parts are not so situated with respect to each other as to form any figure or quantity, nor the whole with respect to other bodies so as to answer to our notions of contiguity or distance. Now this is evidently the case with all our perceptions and objects except those of the sight and feeling. A moral reflection cannot be placed on the right or on the left hand of a passion, nor can a smell or sound be either of a circular or a square figure. These objects and perceptions, so far from requiring any particular place, are absolutely incompatible with it and even the imagination cannot attribute it to them. And as to the absurdity of supposing them to be nowhere, we may consider that if the passions and sentiments appear to the perception to have any particular place, the idea of extension might be derived from them as well as from the sight and touch, contrary to what we have already established. If they *appear* not to have any particular place, they may possibly *exist* in the same manner, since whatever we conceive is possible.

It will not now be necessary to prove that those perceptions which are simple and exist nowhere are incapable of any conjunction in place with matter or body, which is extended and divisible, since it is impossible to found a relation but on some common quality. It may be better worth our while to remark that this question of the local conjunction of objects does not only occur in metaphysical disputes concerning the nature of the soul, but that even in common life we have every moment occasion to examine it. Thus, supposing we consider a fig at one end of the table and an olive at the other, it is evident that in forming the complex ideas of these substances one of the most obvious is that of their different relishes, and it is as evident that we incorporate and conjoin these qualities with such as are colored and tangible. The bitter taste of the one and sweet taste of the other are supposed to lie in the very visible body and to be separated from each other by the whole length of the table. This is so notable and so natural an illusion

that it may be proper to consider the principles from which it is derived.

Though an extended object is incapable of a conjunction in place with another that exists without any place or extension, yet they are still susceptible of many other relations. Thus the taste and smell of any fruit are inseparable from its other qualities of color and tangibility, and whichever of them is the cause or effect, it is certain they are always coexistent. Nor are they only coexistent in general, but also contemporary in their appearance in the mind, and it is upon the application of the extended body to our senses that we perceive its particular taste and smell. These relations, then, of *causation and contiguity in the time of their appearance* between the extended object and the quality which exists without any particular place must have such an effect on the mind that upon the appearance of one it will immediately turn its thought to the conception of the other. Nor is this all. We not only turn our thought from one to the other upon account of their relation, but likewise endeavor to give them a new relation, namely that of *a conjunction in place,* so that we may render the transition more easy and natural. For it is a quality which I shall often have occasion to remark in human nature and shall explain more fully in its proper place, that when objects are united by any relation, we have a strong propensity to add some new relation to them in order to complete the union. In our arrangement of bodies we never fail to place such as are resembling in contiguity to each other, or at least in correspondent points of view. Why? Because we feel a satisfaction in joining the relation of contiguity to that of resemblance or the resemblance of situation to that of qualities. The effects of this propensity have been already observed in that resemblance which we so readily suppose between particular impressions and their external causes. But we shall not find a more evident effect of it than in the present instance, where, from the relations of causation and contiguity in time between two objects, we feign likewise that of a conjunction in place in order to strengthen the connection.

But whatever confused notions we may form of a union in place between an extended body, as a fig, and its particular taste, it is certain that upon reflection we must observe in this union something altogether unintelligible and contradictory. For, should we ask ourselves one obvious question, namely, if the taste which we conceive to be contained in the circumference of the body is in every part of it or in one only, we must quickly find ourselves at a loss and perceive the impossibility of ever giving a satisfactory answer. We cannot reply that it is only in one part, for experience convinces us that every part has the same relish. We can as little reply that it exists in every part, for then we must suppose it figured and extended, which is absurd and incomprehensible. Here, then, we are influenced by two principles directly contrary to each other, namely that *inclination* of our fancy by which we are determined to incorporate the taste with the extended object and our *reason*, which shows us the impossibility of such a union. Being divided between these opposite principles, we renounce neither one nor the other, but involve the subject in such confusion and obscurity that we no longer perceive the opposition. We suppose that the taste exists within the circumference of the body, but in such a manner that it fills the whole without extension and exists entire in every part without separation. In short, we use in our most familiar way of thinking that scholastic principle which, when crudely proposed, appears so shocking, of *totum in toto, et totum in qualibet parte,*[31] which is much the same as if we should say that a thing is in a certain place and yet is not there.

All this absurdity proceeds from our endeavoring to bestow a place on what is utterly incapable of it, and that endeavor again arises from our inclination to complete a union which is founded on causation and a contiguity of time, by attributing to the objects a conjunction in place. But if ever reason is of sufficient force to overcome prejudice, it is certain that in the present case it must prevail. For we have only this choice left, either to suppose that some beings exist without any place or that they are figured and extended or that when they are incorporated with extended objects, the whole is in the whole and the whole is in every part. The absurdity of the two last suppositions proves sufficiently the veracity of the first. Nor is there any fourth opinion. For as to the supposition of their existence in the manner of mathematical points, it resolves itself into the second opinion and supposes that several passions may be placed in a circular figure, and that a certain number of smells, conjoined with a certain number of sounds, may make a body of twelve cubic inches, which appears ridiculous upon the bare mentioning of it.

But though in this view of things we cannot refuse to condemn the materialists who conjoin all thought with extension, yet a little reflection will show us equal reason for blaming their antagonists, who conjoin all thought with a simple and indivisible substance. The most vulgar philosophy informs us that no external object can make itself known to the mind immediately and without the interposition of an image or perception. That table which just now appears to me is only a perception and all its qualities are qualities of a perception. Now, the most obvious of all its qualities is extension. The perception consists of parts. These parts are so situated as to afford us the notion of distance and contiguity, of length, breadth, and thickness. The termination of these three dimensions is what we call figure. This figure is movable, separate, and divisible. Mobility and separability are the distinguishing properties of extended objects. And to cut short all disputes, the very idea of extension is copied from nothing but an impression and consequently must perfectly agree to it. To say the idea of extension agrees to anything is to say it is extended.

The freethinker may now triumph in his turn and, having found there are impressions and ideas really extended, may ask his antagonists how they can incorporate a simple and indivisible subject with an extended perception? All the arguments of theologians may here be retorted upon them. Is the indivisible subject, or immaterial substance, if you will, on the left or on the right hand of the perception? Is it in this particular part or in that other? Is it in every part without being extended? Or is it entire in any one part without deserting the rest? It is impossible to give any answer to these questions but what will both be absurd in itself and will account for the union of our indivisible perceptions with an extended substance.

This gives me an occasion to take anew into

---

31. [The whole is in the whole, and the whole is in every part.]

consideration the question concerning the substance of the soul, and though I have condemned that question as utterly unintelligible, yet I cannot forbear proposing some further reflections concerning it. I assert that the doctrine of the immateriality, simplicity, and indivisibility of a thinking substance is a true atheism and will serve to justify all those sentiments for which *Spinoza* is so universally infamous. From this topic I hope at least to reap one advantage—that my adversaries will not have any pretext to render the present doctrine odious by their declamations when they see that they can be so easily retorted on them.

The fundamental principle of the atheism of *Spinoza* is the doctrine of the simplicity of the universe and the unity of that substance in which he supposes both thought and matter to inhere. There is only one substance, he says, in the world, and that substance is perfectly simple and indivisible and exists everywhere without any local presence. Whatever we discover externally by sensation, whatever we feel internally by reflection, all these are nothing but modifications of that one simple and necessarily existent being and are not possessed of any separate or distinct existence. Every passion of the soul, every configuration of matter however different and various, inhere in the same substance and preserve in themselves their characters of distinction without communicating them to that subject in which they inhere. The same *substratum,* if I may so speak, supports the most different modifications without any difference in itself and varies them without any variation. Neither time, nor place, nor all the diversity of nature is able to produce any composition or change in its perfect simplicity and identity.

I believe this brief exposition of the principles of that famous atheist will be sufficient for the present purpose, and that, without entering further into these gloomy and obscure regions, I shall be able to show that this hideous hypothesis is almost the same with that of the immateriality of the soul, which has become so popular. To make this evident, let us remember that, as every idea is derived from a preceding perception, it is impossible our idea of a perception and that of an object or external existence can ever represent what are specifically different from each other. Whatever difference we may suppose between

them, it is still incomprehensible to us, and we are obliged either to conceive an external object merely as a relation without a relative or to make it the very same with a perception or impression.

The consequence I shall draw from this may, at first sight, appear a mere sophism, but upon the least examination will be found solid and satisfactory. I say then that since we may suppose, but never can conceive, a specific difference between an object and impression, any conclusion we form concerning the connection and repugnance of impressions will not be known certainly to be applicable to objects, but that, on the other hand, whatever conclusions of this kind we form concerning objects will most certainly be applicable to impressions. The reason is not difficult. As an object is supposed to be different from an impression, we cannot be sure that the circumstance upon which we found our reasoning is common to both, supposing we form the reasoning upon the impression. It is still possible that the object may differ from it in that particular. But when we first form our reasoning concerning the object, it is beyond doubt that the same reasoning must extend to the impression and that because the quality of the object upon which the argument is founded must at least be conceived by the mind and could not be conceived unless it were common to an impression, since we have no idea but what is derived from that origin. Thus we may establish it as a certain maxim that we can never, by any principle but by an irregular kind of reasoning from experience, discover a connection or repugnance between objects which extends not to impressions, though the inverse proposition may not be equally true, that all the discoverable relations of impressions are common to objects.

To apply this to the present case: There are two different systems of beings presented, to which I suppose myself under a necessity of assigning some substance or ground of inhesion. I observe first the universe of objects or of body: the sun, moon, and stars; the earth, seas, plants, animals, men, ships, houses, and other productions either of art or of nature. Here *Spinoza* appears and tells me that these are only modifications and that the subject in which they inhere is simple, uncompounded, and indivisible. After this I consider the other system of beings, namely, the universe of thought or my impressions and ideas. There I observe another sun, moon, and stars; an earth, and seas, covered and inhabited by plants and animals; towns, houses, mountains, rivers; and, in short, everything I can discover or conceive in the first system. Upon my inquiring concerning these, theologians present themselves and tell me that these also are modifications and modifications of one simple, uncompounded, and indivisible substance. Immediately upon which I am deafened with the noise of a hundred voices that treat the first hypothesis with detestation and scorn and the second with applause and veneration. I turn my attention to these hypotheses to see what may be the reason of so great a partiality and find that they have the same fault of being unintelligible and that, as far as we can understand them, they are so much alike that it is impossible to discover any absurdity in one which is not common to both of them. We have no idea of any quality in an object which does not agree to and may not represent a quality in an impression and that because all our ideas are derived from our impressions. We can never, therefore, find any repugnance between an extended object as a modification and a simple uncompounded essence as its substance, unless that repugnance takes place equally between the perception or impression of that extended object and the same uncompounded essence. Every idea of a quality in an object passes through an impression, and therefore every *perceivable* relation, whether of connection or repugnance, must be common both to objects and impressions.

But though this argument, considered in general, seems evident beyond all doubt and contradiction, yet to make it more clear and sensible, let us survey it in detail and see whether all the absurdities which have been found in the system of *Spinoza* may not likewise be discovered in that of theologians.

First, it has been said against *Spinoza*, according to the scholastic way of talking rather than thinking, that a mode, not being any distinct or separate existence, must be the very same with its substance, and consequently the extension of the universe must be in a manner identified with that simple, uncompounded essence in which the universe is supposed to inhere. But this, it may be pretended, is utterly impossible and inconceivable unless the indivisible substance expand itself so as to correspond to the extension or the extension contract itself so as to answer to the indivisible substance. This argument seems just, as far as we can understand it, and it is plain nothing is required but a change in the terms to apply the same argument to our extended perceptions and the simple essence of the soul, the ideas of objects and perceptions being in every respect the same, only attended with the supposition of a difference that is unknown and incomprehensible.

Secondly, it has been said that we have no idea of substance which is not applicable to matter, nor any idea of a distinct substance which is not applicable to every distinct portion of matter. Matter, therefore, is not a mode but a substance, and each part of matter is not a distinct mode but a distinct substance. I have already proved that we have no perfect idea of substance, but that taking it for *something that can exist by itself*, it is evident every perception is a substance and every distinct part of a perception a distinct substance; and, consequently, the one hypothesis labors under the same difficulties in this respect with the other.

Thirdly, it has been objected to the system of one simple substance in the universe that this substance, being the support or *substratum* of everything, must at the very same instant be modified into forms which are contrary and incompatible. The round and square figures are incompatible in the same substance at the same time. How, then, is it possible that the same substance can at once be modified into that square table and into this round one? I ask the same question concerning the impressions of these tables and find that the answer is no more satisfactory in one case than in the other.

It appears, then, that to whatever side we turn, the same difficulties follow us and that we cannot advance one step towards establishing the simplicity and immateriality of the soul without preparing the way for a dangerous and irrecoverable atheism. It is the same case if, instead of calling thought a modification of the soul, we should give it the more ancient and yet more fashionable name of an *action*. By an action we mean much the same thing as what is commonly called an abstract mode, that is, something which, properly speaking, is neither distinguishable nor separable from its substance and is only conceived by a distinction of reason or an abstraction. But nothing is gained by this change of the term of modification for that of action, nor do we free ourselves from one single difficulty by its means, as will appear from the two following reflections:

First, I observe that the word *action*, according to this explication of it, can never justly be applied to any perception, as derived from a mind or thinking substance. Our perceptions are all really different, and separable, and distinguishable from each other and from everything else which we can imagine, and therefore it is impossible to conceive how they can be the action or abstract mode of any substance. The instance of motion, which is commonly made use of to show after what manner perception depends as an action upon its substance, rather confounds than instructs us. Motion, to all appearance, induces no real nor essential change on the body, but only varies its relation to other objects. But between a person in the morning walking in a garden with company agreeable to him and a person in the afternoon enclosed in a dungeon and full of terror, despair, and resentment, there seems to be a radical difference and of quite another kind than what is produced on a body by the change of its situation. As we conclude, from the distinction and separability of their ideas, that external objects have a separate existence from each other, so, when we make these ideas themselves our objects, we must draw the same conclusion concerning *them* according to the precedent reasoning. At least it must be confessed that having no idea of the substance of the soul, it is impossible for us to tell how it can admit of such differences and even contrarieties of perception without any fundamental change and, consequently, can never tell in what sense perceptions are actions of that substance. The use, therefore, of the word *action*, unaccompanied with any meaning, instead of that of modification, makes no addition to our knowledge nor is of any advantage to the doctrine of the immateriality of the soul.

I add in the second place that if it brings any advantage to that cause, it must bring an equal to the cause of atheism. For do our theologians pretend to make a monopoly of the word *action*, and may not the atheists likewise take possession of it and affirm that plants, animals, men, etc., are nothing but particular actions of one simple universal substance, which exerts itself from a blind and absolute necessity? This, you will say, is utterly absurd. I admit it is unintelligible, but at the same time assert according to the principles above explained that it is impossible to discover any absurdity in the supposition that all the various objects in nature are actions of one simple substance, which absurdity will not be applicable to a like supposition concerning impressions and ideas.

From these hypotheses concerning the *substance* and *local conjunction* of our perceptions, we may pass to another which is more intelligible than the former and more important than the latter, namely concerning the *cause* of our perceptions. Matter and motion, it is commonly said in the schools, however varied, are still matter and motion and produce only a difference in the position and situation of objects. Divide a body as often as you please, it is still body. Place it in any figure, nothing ever results but figure or the relation of parts. Move it in any manner, you still find motion or a change of relation. It is absurd to imagine that motion in a circle, for instance, should be nothing but merely motion in a circle, while motion in another direction, as in an ellipse, should also be a passion or moral reflection—that the shocking of two globular particles should become a sensation of pain and that the meeting of two triangular ones should afford a pleasure. Now as these different shocks and variations and mixtures are the only changes of which matter is susceptible and as these never afford us any idea of thought or perception, it is concluded to be impossible that thought can ever be caused by matter.

Few have been able to withstand the seeming evidence of this argument, and yet nothing in the world is more easy than to refute it. We need only reflect on what has been proved at large, namely, that we are never sensible of any connection between causes and effects and that it is only by our experience of their constant conjunction we can arrive at any knowledge of this relation. Now, as all objects which are not contrary are susceptible of a constant conjunction and as no real objects are contrary, I have inferred from these principles that to consider the matter *a priori*, anything may produce anything and that we shall never discover a reason why any object may or may not be the cause of any other, however great or however little the resemblance may be between them. This evidently destroys the precedent reasoning concerning the cause of thought or perception. For though there appears no manner of connection between motion or thought, the case is the same with all other causes and effects. Place one body of a pound weight on one end of a lever and another body of the same weight on another end. You will never find in these bodies any principle of motion dependent on their distances from the center more than of thought and perception. If you pretend, therefore, to prove *a priori* that such a position of bodies can never cause thought, because, turn it which way you will, it is nothing but a position of bodies, you must, by the same course of reasoning, conclude that it can never produce motion, since there is no more apparent connection in the one case than in the other. But as this latter conclusion is contrary to evident experience and as it is possible we may have a like experience in the operations of the mind and may perceive a constant conjunction of thought and motion, you reason too hastily when, from the mere consideration of the ideas, you conclude that it is impossible motion can ever produce thought or a different position of parts give rise to a different passion or reflection. No, it is not only possible we may have such an experience, but it is certain we have it, since everyone may perceive that the different dispositions of his body change his thoughts and sentiments. And should it be said that this depends on the union of soul and body, I would answer that we must separate the question concerning the substance of the mind from that concerning the cause of its thought, and that, confining ourselves to the latter question, we find, by comparing their ideas, that thought and motion are different from each other, and, by experience, that they are constantly united. This being all the circumstances that enter into the idea of cause and effect, when applied to the operations of matter we may certainly conclude that motion may be, and actually is, the cause of thought and perception.

There seems only this dilemma left us in the present case: either to assert that nothing can be the cause of another but where the mind can perceive the connection in its idea of the objects, or to maintain that all objects which we find constantly conjoined are upon that account to be regarded as causes and effects. If we choose the first part of the dilemma, these are the consequences. *First*, we, in reality, affirm that there is no such thing in the universe as a cause or productive principle, not even the Deity himself, since our idea of that Supreme Being is derived from particular impressions, none of which contains any efficacy nor seems to have any connection with any other existence. As to what may be said that the connection between the idea of an infinitely powerful Being and that of any effect which he wills is necessary and unavoidable, I answer that we have no idea of a Being endowed with any power, much less of one endowed with infinite power. But if we will change expressions, we can only define power by connection, and then in saying that the idea of an infinitely powerful Being is connected with that of every effect which he wills, we really do no more than assert that a Being whose volition is connected with every effect is connected with every effect, which is an identical proposition and gives us no insight into the nature of this power or connection. But, *secondly*, supposing that the Deity were the great and efficacious principle which supplies the deficiency of all causes, this leads us into the grossest impieties and absurdities. For upon the same account that we have recourse to him in natural operations and assert that matter cannot of itself communicate motion or produce thought, namely because there is no apparent connection between these objects; I say, upon the very same account, we must acknowledge that the Deity is the author of all our volitions and perceptions, since they have no more apparent connection either with one another or with the supposed but unknown substance of the soul. This agency of the Supreme Being we know to have been asserted by several philosophers with relation to all the actions of the mind except volition, or rather an inconsiderable part of volition, though it is easy to perceive that this exception is a mere pretext to avoid the dangerous consequences of that doctrine. If nothing is active but what has an apparent power, thought is in no case any more active than matter, and if this inactivity must make us have recourse to a Deity, the Supreme Being is the real cause of all our actions, bad as well as good, vicious as well as virtuous.

Thus we are necessarily reduced to the other side of the dilemma, namely, that all objects which are found to be constantly conjoined are upon that account only to be regarded as causes and effects. Now, as all objects which are not contrary are susceptible of a constant conjunction, and as no real objects are contrary, it follows that, for all we can determine by the mere ideas, anything may be the cause or effect of anything, which evidently gives the advantage to the materialists above their antagonists.

To pronounce, then, the final decision upon the whole: The question concerning the substance of the soul is absolutely unintelligible; all our perceptions are not susceptible of a local union, either with what is extended or unextended, there being some of them of the one kind and some of the other; and as the constant conjunction of objects constitutes the very essence of cause and effect, matter and motion may often be regarded as the causes of thought as far as we have any notion of that relation.

It is certainly a kind of indignity to philosophy, whose sovereign authority ought everywhere to be acknowledged, to oblige her on every occasion to make apologies for her conclusions and justify herself to every particular art and science which may be offended at her. This puts one in mind of a king arraigned for high treason against his subjects. There is only one occasion when philosophy will think it necessary and even honorable to justify herself, and that is when religion may seem to be in the least offended, whose rights are as dear to her as her own and are indeed the same. If anyone, therefore, should imagine that the foregoing arguments are in any way dangerous to religion, I hope the following apology will remove his apprehensions.

There is no foundation for any conclusion *a priori,* either concerning the operations or duration of any object, of which it is possible for the human mind to form a conception. Any object may be imagined to become entirely inactive or to be annihilated in a moment, and it is an evident principle that *whatever we can imagine is possible.* Now this is no more true

of matter than of spirit—of an extended, compounded substance than of a simple and unextended. In both cases the metaphysical arguments for the immortality of the soul are equally inconclusive, and in both cases the moral arguments and those derived from the analogy of nature are equally strong and convincing. If my philosophy therefore makes no addition to the arguments for religion, I have at least the satisfaction to think it takes nothing from them, but that everything remains precisely as before.

Section 6: Of Personal Identity

There are some philosophers who imagine we are every moment intimately conscious of what we call our self, that we feel its existence and its continuance in existence, and are certain beyond the evidence of a demonstration both of its perfect identity and simplicity. The strongest sensation, the most violent passion, they say, instead of distracting us from this view, only fix it the more intensely and make us consider their influence on *self* either by their pain or pleasure. To attempt a further proof of this would be to weaken its evidence, since no proof can be derived from any fact of which we are so intimately conscious, nor is there anything of which we can be certain if we doubt of this.

Unluckily all these positive assertions are contrary to that very experience which is pleaded for them, nor have we any idea of *self* after the manner it is here explained. For from what impression could this idea be derived? This question it is impossible to answer without a manifest contradiction and absurdity, and yet it is a question which must necessarily be answered if we would have the idea of self pass for clear and intelligible. It must be some one impression that gives rise to every real idea. But self or person is not any one impression but that to which our several impressions and ideas are supposed to have a reference. If any impression gives rise to the idea of self, that impression must continue invariably the same through the whole course of our lives, since self is supposed to exist after that manner. But there is no impression constant and invariable. Pain and pleasure, grief and joy, passions and sensations succeed each other and never all exist at the same time. It cannot, therefore, be from any of these impressions or from any other that the idea of self is derived, and, consequently, there is no such idea.

But further, what must become of all our particular perceptions upon this hypothesis? All these are different, and distinguishable, and separable from each other, and may be separately considered, and may exist separately, and have no need of anything to support their existence. After what manner therefore do they belong to self, and how are they connected with it? For my part, when I enter most intimately into what I call *myself*, I always stumble on some particular perception or other, of heat or cold, light or shade, love or hatred, pain or pleasure. I never can catch *myself* at any time without a perception and never can observe anything but the perception. When my perceptions are removed for any time, as by sound sleep, so long am I insensible of myself and may truly be said not to exist. And were all my perceptions removed by death and could I neither think, nor feel, nor see, nor love, nor hate after the dissolution of my body, I should be entirely annihilated, nor do I conceive what is further requisite to make me a perfect nonentity. If anyone, upon serious and unprejudiced reflection, thinks he has a different notion of *himself*, I must confess I can reason no longer with him. All I can allow him is that he may be in the right as well as I and that we are essentially different in this particular. He may, perhaps, perceive something simple and continued which he calls *himself*, though I am certain there is no such principle in me.

But setting aside some metaphysicians of this kind, I may venture to affirm of the rest of mankind that they are nothing but a bundle or collection of different perceptions which succeed each other with an inconceivable rapidity and are in a perpetual flux and movement. Our eyes cannot turn in their sockets without varying our perceptions. Our thought is still more variable than our sight, and all our other senses and faculties contribute to this change; nor is there any single power of the soul which remains unalterably the same perhaps for one moment. The mind is a kind of theater where several perceptions successively make their appearance, pass, repass, glide away, and mingle in an infinite variety of postures and situations. There is properly no *simplicity* in it at one time nor *identity* in different, whatever natural propensity we may have to imagine that simplicity and identity. The comparison of the theater must not mislead us. They are the successive perceptions only that constitute the mind, nor have we the most distant notion of the place where these scenes are represented or of the materials of which it is composed.

What, then, gives us so great a propensity to ascribe an identity to these successive perceptions and to suppose ourselves possessed of an invariable and uninterrupted existence through the whole course of our lives? In order to answer this question we must distinguish between personal identity as it regards our thought or imagination and as it regards our passions or the concern we take in ourselves. The first is our present subject, and to explain it perfectly we must take the matter pretty deep and account for that identity which we attribute to plants and animals, there being a great analogy between it and the identity of a self or person.

We have a distinct idea of an object that remains invariable and uninterrupted through a supposed variation of time, and this idea we call that of *identity* or *sameness*. We have also a distinct idea of several different objects existing in succession and connected together by a close relation, and this, to an accurate view, affords as perfect a notion of *diversity* as if there was no manner of relation among the objects. But though these two ideas of identity and a succession of related objects be in themselves perfectly distinct and even contrary, yet it is certain that, in our common way of thinking, they are generally confounded with each other. That action of the imagination by which we consider the uninterrupted and invariable object and that by which we reflect on the succession of related objects are almost the same to the feeling, nor is there much more effort of thought required in the latter case than in the former. The relation facilitates the transition of the mind from one object to another and renders its passage as smooth as if it contemplated one continued object. This resemblance is the cause of the confusion and mistake and makes us substitute the notion of identity instead of that of related objects. However, at one instant we may consider the related succession as variable or interrupted, we are sure the next to ascribe to it a perfect identity and regard it as invariable and uninterrupted. Our propensity to this mistake is so great from the resemblance above mentioned that we fall into it before we are aware, and though we incessantly correct ourselves by reflection and return to a more accurate method of thinking, yet we cannot long sustain our philosophy or take off this bias from the imagination. Our last resource is to yield to it and boldly assert that these different related objects are in effect the same, however interrupted and variable. In order to justify to ourselves this absurdity, we often feign some new and unintelligible principle that connects the objects together and prevents their interruption or variation. Thus we feign the continued existence of the perceptions of our senses to remove the interruption and run into the notion of a *soul*, and *self*, and *substance* to disguise the variation. But we may further observe that where we do not give rise to such a fiction, our propensity to confound identity with relation is so great that we are apt to imagine something unknown and mysterious, connecting the parts, besides their relation, and this I take to be the case with regard to the identity we ascribe to plants and vegetables. And even when this does not take place, we still feel a propensity to confound these ideas, though we are not able fully to satisfy ourselves in that particular nor find anything invariable and uninterrupted to justify our notion of identity.

Thus the controversy concerning identity is not merely a dispute of words. For when we attribute identity, in an improper sense, to variable or interrupted objects, our mistake is not confined to the expression, but is commonly attended with a fiction, either of something invariable and uninterrupted, or of something mysterious and inexplicable, or at least with a propensity to such fictions. What will suffice to prove this hypothesis to the satisfaction of every fair inquirer is to show from daily experience and observation that the objects which are variable or interrupted, and yet are supposed to continue the same, are such only as consist of a succession of parts connected together by resemblance, contiguity, or causation. For as such a succession answers evidently to our notion of diversity, it can only be by mistake we ascribe to it an identity, and as the relation of parts, which leads us into this mistake, is really nothing but

a quality which produces an association of ideas and an easy transition of the imagination from one to another, it can only be from the resemblance which this act of the mind bears to that by which we contemplate one continued object that the error arises. Our chief business, then, must be to prove that all objects to which we ascribe identity without observing their invariableness and uninterruptedness are such as consist of a succession of related objects.

In order to [see] this, suppose any mass of matter of which the parts are contiguous and connected to be placed before us. It is plain we must attribute a perfect identity to this mass, provided all the parts continue uninterruptedly and invariably the same, whatever motion or change of place we may observe either in the whole or in any of the parts. But supposing some very *small* or *inconsiderable* part to be added to the mass or subtracted from it, though this absolutely destroys the identity of the whole, strictly speaking, yet as we seldom think so accurately, we scruple not to pronounce a mass of matter the same where we find so trivial an alteration. The passage of the thought from the object before the change to the object after it is so smooth and easy that we scarcely perceive the transition and are apt to imagine that it is nothing but a continued survey of the same object.

There is a very remarkable circumstance that attends this experiment, which is that though the change of any considerable part in a mass of matter destroys the identity of the whole, yet we must measure the greatness of the part, not absolutely, but by its *proportion* to the whole. The addition or diminution of a mountain would not be sufficient to produce a diversity in a planet, though the change of a very few inches would be able to destroy the identity of some bodies. It will be impossible to account for this but by reflecting that objects operate upon the mind and break or interrupt the continuity of its actions not according to their real greatness, but according to their proportion to each other, and therefore, since this interruption makes an object cease to appear the same, it must be the uninterrupted progress of the thought which constitutes the imperfect identity.

This may be confirmed by another phenomenon. A change in any considerable part of a body destroys its identity, but it is remarkable that where the change is produced *gradually* and *insensibly* we are less apt to ascribe to it the same effect. The reason can plainly be no other than that the mind, in following the successive changes of the body, feels an easy passage from surveying its condition in one moment to viewing of it in another and at no particular time perceives any interruption in its actions—from which continued perception it ascribes a continued existence and identity to the object.

But whatever precaution we may use in introducing the changes gradually and making them proportional to the whole, it is certain that where the changes are at last observed to become considerable, we make a scruple of ascribing identity to such different objects. There is, however, another artifice by which we may induce the imagination to advance a step further, and that is by producing a reference of the parts to each other and a combination to some *common end* or purpose. A ship of which a considerable part has been changed by frequent repairs is still considered as the same, nor does the difference of the materials hinder us from ascribing an identity to it. The common end in which the parts conspire is the same under all their variations and affords an easy transition of the imagination from one situation of the body to another.

But this is still more remarkable when we add a *sympathy* of parts to their *common end* and suppose that they bear to each other the reciprocal relation of cause and effect in all their actions and operations. This is the case with all animals and vegetables, where not only the several parts have a reference to some general purpose, but also a mutual dependence on and connection with each other. The effect of so strong a relation is that though everyone must allow that in a very few years both vegetables and animals endure a *total* change, yet we still attribute identity to them, while their form, size, and substance are entirely altered. An oak that grows from a small plant to a large tree is still the same oak, though there is not one particle of matter or figure of its parts the same. An infant becomes a man and is sometimes fat, sometimes lean without any change in his identity.

We may also consider the two following phenomena, which are remarkable in their kind. The first is that though we are commonly able to distinguish pretty exactly between numerical and specific iden-

tity, yet it sometimes happens that we confound them and in our thinking and reasoning employ the one for the other. Thus, a man who hears a noise that is frequently interrupted and renewed says it is still the same noise, though it is evident the sounds have only a specific identity or resemblance and there is nothing numerically the same but the cause which produced them. In like manner it may be said without breach of the propriety of language that such a church, which was formerly of brick, fell to ruin and that the parish rebuilt the same church of freestone and according to modern architecture. Here neither the form nor materials are the same, nor is there anything common to the two objects but their relation to the inhabitants of the parish. Yet this alone is sufficient to make us denominate them the same. But we must observe that in these cases the first object is in a manner annihilated before the second comes into existence, by which means we are never presented in any one point of time with the idea of difference and multiplicity and, for that reason, are less scrupulous in calling them the same.

Secondly, we may remark that though in a succession of related objects it is in a manner requisite that the change of parts are not sudden nor entire in order to preserve the identity, yet where the objects are in their nature changeable and inconstant, we admit of a more sudden transition than would otherwise be consistent with that relation. Thus, as the nature of a river consists in the motion and change of parts, though in less than twenty-four hours these are totally altered, this does not hinder the river from continuing the same during several ages. What is natural and essential to anything is, in a manner, expected, and what is expected makes less impression and appears of less moment than what is unusual and extraordinary. A considerable change of the former kind seems really less to the imagination than the most trivial alteration of the latter and, by breaking less the continuity of the thought, has less influence in destroying the identity.

We now proceed to explain the nature of *personal identity*, which has become so great a question in philosophy, especially of late years, in *England*, where all the more abstruse sciences are studied with a peculiar ardor and application. And here it is evident the same method of reasoning must be continued which has so successfully explained the identity of plants and animals, and ships, and houses, and of all the compounded and changeable productions either of art or nature. The identity which we ascribe to the mind of man is only a fictitious one and of a like kind with that which we ascribe to vegetables and animal bodies. It cannot, therefore, have a different origin, but must proceed from a like operation of the imagination upon like objects.

But lest this argument should not convince the reader, though in my opinion perfectly decisive, let him weigh the following reasoning, which is still closer and more immediate. It is evident that the identity which we attribute to the human mind, however perfect we may imagine it to be, is not able to run the several different perceptions into one and make them lose their characters of distinction and difference which are essential to them. It is still true that every distinct perception which enters into the composition of the mind is a distinct existence and is different, and distinguishable, and separable from every other perception, either contemporary or successive. But as, notwithstanding this distinction and separability, we suppose the whole train of perceptions to be united by identity, a question naturally arises concerning this relation of identity, whether it is something that really binds our several perceptions together or only associates their ideas in the imagination, that is, in other words, whether, in pronouncing concerning the identity of a person, we observe some real bond among his perceptions or only feel one among the ideas we form of them. This question we might easily decide if we would recollect what has been already proved at large, namely, that the understanding never observes any real connection among objects and that even the union of cause and effect, when strictly examined, resolves itself into a customary association of ideas. For from this it evidently follows that identity is nothing really belonging to these different perceptions and uniting them together but rather is merely a quality which we attribute to them because of the union of their ideas in the imagination when we reflect upon them. Now, the only qualities which can give ideas a union in the imagination are these three relations above mentioned. These

are the uniting principles in the ideal world and without them every distinct object is separable by the mind, and may be separately considered, and appears not to have any more connection with any other object than if disjoined by the greatest difference and remoteness. It is, therefore, on some of these three relations of resemblance, contiguity, and causation that identity depends, and as the very essence of these relations consists in their producing an easy transition of ideas, it follows that our notions of personal identity proceed entirely from the smooth and uninterrupted progress of the thought along a train of connected ideas, according to the principles above explained.

The only question, therefore, which remains is by what relations this uninterrupted progress of our thought is produced, when we consider the successive existence of a mind or thinking person. And here it is evident we must confine ourselves to resemblance and causation and must drop contiguity, which has little or no influence in the present case.

To begin with *resemblance*: Suppose we could see clearly into the breast of another and observe that succession of perceptions which constitutes his mind or thinking principle, and suppose that he always preserves the memory of a considerable part of past perceptions, it is evident that nothing could more contribute to bestowing a relation on this succession amid all its variations. For what is the memory but a faculty by which we raise up the images of past perceptions? And as an image necessarily resembles its object, must not the frequent placing of these resembling perceptions in the chain of thought convey the imagination more easily from one link to another and make the whole seem like the continuance of one object? In this particular, then, the memory not only discovers the identity, but also contributes to its production by producing the relation of resemblance among the perceptions. The case is the same whether we consider ourselves or others.

As to *causation*, we may observe that the true idea of the human mind is to consider it as a system of different perceptions or different existences which are linked together by the relation of cause and effect and mutually produce, destroy, influence, and modify each other. Our impressions give rise to their correspondent ideas, and these ideas, in their turn, produce other impressions. One thought chases another and draws after it a third by which it is expelled in its turn. In this respect, I cannot compare the soul more properly to anything than to a republic or commonwealth in which the several members are united by the reciprocal ties of government and subordination and give rise to other persons who propagate the same republic in the incessant changes of its parts. And as the same individual republic may not only change its members, but also its laws and constitutions, in like manner the same person may vary his character and disposition as well as his impressions and ideas without losing his identity. Whatever changes he endures, his several parts are still connected by the relation of causation. And in this view our identity with regard to the passions serves to corroborate that with regard to the imagination by making our distant perceptions influence each other and by giving us a present concern for our past or future pains or pleasures.

As memory alone acquaints us with the continuance and extent of this succession of perceptions, it is to be considered upon that account chiefly as the source of personal identity. Had we no memory, we never should have any notion of causation nor consequently of that chain of causes and effects which constitute our self or person. But having once acquired this notion of causation from the memory, we can extend the same chain of causes and, consequently, the identity of our persons beyond our memory and can comprehend times, circumstances, and actions which we have entirely forgotten, but suppose in general to have existed. For how few of our past actions are there of which we have any memory? Who can tell me, for instance, what were his thoughts and actions on the 1st of January 1715, the 11th of March 1719, and the 3rd of August 1733? Or will he affirm, because he has entirely forgotten the incidents of these days, that the present self is not the same person with the self of that time, and by that means overturn all the most established notions of personal identity? In this view, therefore, memory does not so much *produce* as *discover* personal identity by showing us the relation of cause and effect among our different perceptions. It will be incumbent on those who affirm that memory produces entirely our personal identity to give a reason why we can thus extend our identity beyond our memory.

The whole of this doctrine leads us to a conclusion which is of great importance in the present affair, namely that all the nice and subtle questions concerning personal identity can never possibly be decided and are to be regarded rather as grammatical than as philosophical difficulties. Identity depends on the relations of ideas, and these relations produce identity by means of that easy transition they occasion. But as the relations and the easiness of the transition may diminish by insensible degrees, we have no just standard by which we can decide any dispute concerning the time when they acquire or lose a title to the name of identity. All the disputes concerning the identity of connected objects are merely verbal, except so far as the relation of parts gives rise to some fiction or imaginary principle of union as we have already observed.

What I have said concerning the first origin and uncertainty of our notion of identity, as applied to the human mind, may be extended with little or no variation to that of *simplicity*. An object whose different coexistent parts are bound together by a close relation operates upon the imagination after much the same manner as one perfectly simple and indivisible and does not require a much greater stretch of thought in order to [form] its conception. From this similarity of operation we attribute a simplicity to it and feign a principle of union as the support of this simplicity and the center of all the different parts and qualities of the object.

Appendix

[. . .] I had entertained some hopes that however deficient our theory of the intellectual world might be, it would be free from those contradictions and absurdities which seem to attend every explication that human reason can give of the material world. But upon a more strict review of the section concerning *personal identity*, I find myself involved in such a labyrinth that, I must confess, I neither know how to correct my former opinions nor how to render them consistent. If this is not a good *general* reason for skepticism, it is at least a sufficient one (if I were not already abundantly supplied) for me to entertain a diffidence and modesty in all my decisions. I shall propose the arguments on both sides, beginning with those that induced me to deny the strict and proper identity and simplicity of a self or thinking being.

When we talk of *self* or *substance*, we must have an idea annexed to these terms; otherwise they are altogether unintelligible. Every idea is derived from preceding impressions and we have no impression of self or substance as something simple and individual. We have, therefore, no idea of them in that sense.

Whatever is distinct is distinguishable, and whatever is distinguishable is separable by the thought or imagination. All perceptions are distinct. They are, therefore, distinguishable and separable, and may be conceived as separately existent, and may exist separately without any contradiction or absurdity.

When I view this table and that chimney, nothing is present to me but particular perceptions, which are of a like nature with all the other perceptions. This is the doctrine of philosophers. But this table which is present to me, and that chimney, may and do exist separately. This is the doctrine of the vulgar and implies no contradiction. There is no contradiction, therefore, in extending the same doctrine to all the perceptions.

In general, the following reasoning seems satisfactory. All ideas are borrowed from preceding perceptions. Our ideas of objects, therefore, are derived from that source. Consequently, no proposition can be intelligible or consistent with regard to objects which is not so with regard to perceptions. But it is intelligible and consistent to say that objects exist distinct and independent without any common *simple* substance or subject of inhesion. This proposition, therefore, can never be absurd with regard to perceptions.

When I turn my reflection on *myself*, I never can perceive this *self* without some one or more perceptions, nor can I ever perceive anything but the perceptions. It is the composition of these, therefore, which forms the self.

We can conceive a thinking being to have either many or few perceptions. Suppose the mind to be reduced even below the life of an oyster. Suppose it to have only one perception, as of thirst or hunger. Consider it in that situation. Do you conceive any-thing but merely that perception? Do you have any notion of *self* or *substance*? If not, the addition of other perceptions can never give you that notion.

The annihilation which some people suppose to follow upon death and which entirely destroys this self is nothing but an extinction of all particular perceptions: love and hatred, pain and pleasure, thought and sensation. These, therefore, must be the same with self, since the one cannot survive the other.

Is *self* the same with *substance*? If it is, how can that question have place, concerning the subsistence of self, under a change of substance? If they are distinct, what is the difference between them? For my part, I have a notion of neither when conceived distinct from particular perceptions.

Philosophers begin to be reconciled to the principle that *we have no idea of external substance distinct from the ideas of particular qualities.* This must pave the way for a like principle with regard to the mind that *we have no notion of it distinct from the particular perceptions.*

So far I seem to be attended with sufficient evidence. But, having thus loosened all our particular perceptions, when I proceed to explain the principle of connection which binds them together and makes us attribute to them a real simplicity and identity, I am sensible that my account is very defective and that nothing but the seeming evidence of the precedent reasonings could have induced me to receive it. If perceptions are distinct existences, they form a whole only by being connected together. But no connections among distinct existences are ever discoverable by human understanding. We only *feel* a connection or determination of the thought to pass from one object to another. It follows, therefore, that the thought alone feels personal identity; when reflecting on the train of past perceptions that compose a mind, the ideas of them are felt to be connected together and naturally introduce each other. However extraordinary this conclusion may seem, it need not surprise us. Most philosophers seem inclined to think that personal identity *arises* from consciousness and consciousness is nothing but a reflected thought or perception. The present philosophy, therefore, has so far a promising aspect. But all my hopes vanish when I come to explain the principles that unite our successive perceptions in our thought or consciousness. I cannot discover any theory which gives me satisfaction on this head.

In short, there are two principles which I cannot render consistent, nor is it in my power to renounce either of them, namely, *that all our distinct perceptions are distinct existences* and *that the mind never perceives any real connection among distinct existences.* Did our perceptions either inhere in something simple and individual or did the mind perceive some real connection among them, there would be no difficulty in the case. For my part, I must plead the privilege of a skeptic and confess that this difficulty is too hard for my understanding. I do not pretend, however, to pronounce it absolutely insuperable. Others, perhaps, or myself, upon more mature reflections, may discover some hypothesis that will reconcile those contradictions. [. . .]

David Hume, *An Inquiry Concerning Human Understanding* (1748)[1]

Author's Advertisement.

Most of the principles and reasonings contained in this volume were published in a work in three volumes, called *A Treatise of Human Nature*, a work which the author had projected before he left college and which he wrote and published not long after. But not finding it successful, he was sensible of his error in going to the press too early, and he cast the whole anew in the following pieces, where some negligences in his former reasoning and more in the expression are, he hopes, corrected. Yet several writers who have honored the author's philosophy with answers have taken care to direct all their batteries against that juvenile work, which the author never acknowledged, and have affected to triumph in any advantages which, they imagined, they had obtained over it—a practice very contrary to all rules of candor and fair dealing and a strong instance of those polemical artifices which a bigoted zeal thinks itself authorized to employ. Henceforth, the author desires that the following pieces may alone be regarded as containing his philosophical sentiments and principles.

1. [From *The Philosophical Works of David Hume*, T. H. Green and T. H. Grose, eds. (London: Longman's, Green, and Co., 1898), 4 vols., English, modified, taking into account variations from numerous editions.]

Section I: *Of The Different Species of Philosophy.*

Moral philosophy, or the science of human nature, may be treated after two different manners, each of which has its peculiar merit and may contribute to the entertainment, instruction, and reformation of mankind. The one considers man chiefly as born for action and as influenced in his measures by taste and sentiment, pursuing one object and avoiding another according to the value which these objects seem to possess and according to the light in which they present themselves. As virtue, of all objects, is allowed to be the most valuable, this species of philosophers paint her in the most amiable colors, borrowing all help from poetry and eloquence and treating their subject in an easy and obvious manner, and such as is best fitted to please the imagination and engage the affections. They select the most striking observations and instances from common life, place opposite characters in a proper contrast, and, alluring us into the paths of virtue by the views of glory and happiness, direct our steps in these paths by the soundest precepts and most illustrious examples. They make us *feel* the difference between vice and virtue; they excite and regulate our sentiments; and so they can but bend our hearts to the love of probity and true honor, they think, that they have fully attained the end of all their labors.

The other species of philosophers consider man in the light of a reasonable rather than an active being and endeavor to form his understanding more than cultivate his manners. They regard human nature as a subject of speculation and, with a narrow scrutiny, examine it in order to find those principles which regulate our understanding, excite our sentiments, and make us approve or blame any particular object, action, or behavior. They think it a reproach to all literature that philosophy should not yet have fixed, beyond controversy, the foundation of morals, reasoning, and criticism, and should forever talk of truth and falsehood, vice and virtue, beauty and deformity, without being able to determine the source of these distinctions. While they attempt this arduous task, they are deterred by no difficulties; but proceeding from particular instances to general principles, they still push on their inquiries to principles more general and rest not satisfied until they arrive at those original principles by which, in every science, all human curiosity must be bounded. Though their speculations seem abstract and even unintelligible to common readers, they aim at the approbation of the learned and the wise and think themselves sufficiently compensated for the labor of their whole lives if they can discover some hidden truths which may contribute to the instruction of posterity.

It is certain that the easy and obvious philosophy will always, with the generality of mankind, have the preference above the accurate and abstruse, and by many will be recommended not only as more agreeable, but more useful than the other. It enters more into common life, molds the heart and affections, and, by touching those principles which actuate men, reforms their conduct and brings them nearer to that model of perfection which it describes. On the contrary, the abstruse philosophy, being founded on a turn of mind which cannot enter into business and action, vanishes when the philosopher leaves the shade and comes into open day, nor can its principles easily retain any influence over our conduct and behavior. The feelings of our heart, the agitation of our passions, the vehemence of our affections, dissipate

all its conclusions and reduce the profound philosopher to a mere plebeian.

This also must be confessed, that the most durable as well as most just fame has been acquired by the easy philosophy and that abstract reasoners seem, up to now, to have enjoyed only a momentary reputation from the caprice or ignorance of their own age, but have not been able to support their renown with more equitable posterity. It is easy for a profound philosopher to commit a mistake in his subtle reasonings; and one mistake is the necessary parent of another, while he pushes on his consequences and is not deterred from embracing any conclusion by its unusual appearance or its contradiction to popular opinion. But a philosopher whose only purpose is to represent the common sense of mankind in more beautiful and more engaging colors, if by accident he falls into error, goes no further, but, renewing his appeal to common sense and the natural sentiments of the mind, returns into the right path and secures himself from any dangerous illusions. The fame of Cicero flourishes at present, but that of Aristotle is utterly decayed. La Bruyère passes the seas and still maintains his reputation. But the glory of Malebranche is confined to his own nation and to his own age. And Addison, perhaps, will be read with pleasure when Locke shall be entirely forgotten.

The mere philosopher is a character which is commonly but little acceptable in the world, as being supposed to contribute nothing either to the advantage or pleasure of society, while he lives remote from communication with mankind and is wrapped up in principles and notions equally remote from their comprehension. On the other hand, the mere ignorant is still more despised, nor is anything deemed a surer sign of an illiberal genius in an age and nation where the sciences flourish than to be entirely destitute of all relish for those noble entertainments. The most perfect character is supposed to lie between those extremes: retaining an equal ability and taste for books, company, and business; preserving in conversation that discernment and delicacy which arise from polite letters, and in business that probity and accuracy which are the natural result of a just philosophy. In order to diffuse and cultivate so accomplished a character, nothing can be more useful than compositions of the easy style and manner which do not draw too much from life, require no deep application or retreat to be comprehended, and send back the student among mankind full of noble sentiments and wise precepts applicable to every exigency of human life. By means of such compositions virtue becomes amiable, science agreeable, company instructive, and retirement entertaining.

Man is a reasonable being and, as such, receives from science his proper food and nourishment. But so narrow are the bounds of human understanding that little satisfaction can be hoped for in this particular, either from the extent or security of his acquisitions. Man is a sociable no less than a reasonable being. But neither can he always enjoy company agreeable and amusing or preserve the proper relish for them. Man is also an active being and, from that disposition, as well as from the various necessities of human life, must submit to business and occupation. But the mind requires some relaxation and cannot always support its bent to care and industry. It seems, then, that nature has pointed out a mixed kind of life as most suitable to the human race and secretly admonished them to allow none of these biases to *draw* too much, so as to incapacitate them for other occupations and entertainments. Indulge your passion for science, she says, but let your science be human and such as may have a direct reference to action and society. Abstruse thought and profound researches I prohibit and will severely punish by the pensive melancholy which they introduce, by the endless uncertainty in which they involve you and by the cold reception which your pretended discoveries shall meet with, when communicated. Be a philosopher, but, amid all your philosophy, be still a man.

Were the generality of mankind contented to prefer the easy philosophy to the abstract and profound, without throwing any blame or contempt on the latter, it might not be improper, perhaps, to comply with this general opinion and allow every man to enjoy, without opposition, his own taste and sentiment. But as the matter is often carried further, even to the absolute rejecting of all profound reasonings, or what is commonly called *metaphysics*, we shall now proceed to consider what can reasonably be pleaded in their behalf.

We may begin with observing that one considerable advantage which results from the accurate and abstract philosophy is its subservience to the easy and humane, which, without the former, can never attain a sufficient degree of exactness in its sentiments, precepts, or reasonings. All polite letters are nothing but pictures of human life in various attitudes and situations, and inspire us with different sentiments of praise or blame, admiration or ridicule, according to the qualities of the object which they set before us. An artist must be better qualified to succeed in this undertaking who, besides a delicate taste and a quick apprehension, possesses an accurate knowledge of the internal fabric, the operations of the understanding, the workings of the passions, and the various species of sentiment which discriminate vice and virtue. However painful this inward search or inquiry may appear, it becomes in some measure requisite to those who would describe with success the obvious and outward appearances of life and manners. The anatomist presents to the eye the most hideous and disagreeable objects, but his science is useful to the painter in delineating even a Venus or a Helen. While the latter employs all the richest colors of his art and gives his figures the most graceful and engaging airs, he must still carry his attention to the inward structure of the human body, the position of the muscles, the fabric of the bones, and the use and figure of every part or organ. Accuracy is, in every case, advantageous to beauty, and just reasoning to delicate sentiment. In vain would we exalt the one by depreciating the other.

Besides, we may observe, in every art or profession, even those which most concern life or action, that a spirit of accuracy, however acquired, carries all of them nearer their perfection and renders them more subservient to the interests of society. And though a philosopher may live remote from business, the genius of philosophy, if carefully cultivated by several, must gradually diffuse itself throughout the whole society and bestow a similar correctness on every art and calling. The politician will acquire greater foresight and subtlety in the subdividing and balancing of power, the lawyer more method and finer principles in his reasonings, and the general more regularity in his discipline and more caution in his plans and operations. The stability of modern governments above the ancient and the accuracy of modern philosophy have improved, and probably will still improve, by similar gradations.

Were there no advantage to be reaped from these studies beyond the gratification of an innocent curiosity, yet ought not even this be despised as being one accession to those few safe and harmless pleasures which are bestowed on human race. The sweetest and most inoffensive path of life leads through the avenues of science and learning; and whoever can either remove any obstructions in this way or open up any new prospect ought so far to be esteemed a benefactor to mankind. And though these researches may appear painful and fatiguing, it is with some minds as with some bodies which, being endowed with vigorous and florid health, require severe exercise, and reap a pleasure from what, to the generality of mankind, may seem burdensome and laborious. Obscurity, indeed, is painful to the mind as well as to the eye, but to bring light from obscurity, by whatever labor, must necessarily be delightful and rejoicing.

But this obscurity in the profound and abstract philosophy is objected to, not only as painful and fatiguing, but as the inevitable source of uncertainty and error. Here indeed lies the most just and most plausible objection against a considerable part of metaphysics, that they are not properly a science, but arise either from the fruitless efforts of human vanity, which would penetrate into subjects utterly inaccessible to the understanding, or from the craft of popular superstitions, which, being unable to defend themselves on fair ground, raise these entangling brambles to cover and protect their weakness. Chased from the open country, these robbers fly into the forest and lie in wait to break in upon every unguarded avenue of the mind and overwhelm it with religious fears and prejudices. The stoutest antagonist, if he remits his watch a moment, is oppressed. And many, through cowardice and folly, open the gates to the enemies and willingly receive them with reverence and submission as their legal sovereigns.

But is this a sufficient reason why philosophers should desist from such researches and leave superstition still in possession of her retreat? Is it not proper to draw an opposite conclusion and perceive the necessity of carrying the war into the most secret recesses of the enemy? In vain do we hope that men, from frequent disappointment, will at last abandon such airy sciences and discover the proper province of human reason. For, besides the fact that many persons find too sensible an interest in perpetually recalling such topics—besides this, I say, the motive of blind despair can never reasonably have place in the sciences, since, however unsuccessful former attempts may have proved, there is still room to hope that the industry, good fortune, or improved sagacity of succeeding generations may reach discoveries unknown to former ages. Each adventurous genius will still leap at the arduous prize and find himself stimulated, rather than discouraged by the failures of his predecessors, while he hopes that the glory of achieving so hard an adventure is reserved for him alone. The only method of freeing learning at once from these abstruse questions is to inquire seriously into the nature of human understanding and show, from an exact analysis of its powers and capacity, that it is by no means fitted for such remote and abstruse subjects. We must submit to this fatigue in order to live at ease ever after and must cultivate true metaphysics with some care in order to destroy the false and adulterate. Indolence, which to some persons affords a safeguard against this deceitful philosophy, is, with others, overbalanced by curiosity; and despair, which at some moments prevails, may give place afterwards to sanguine hopes and expectations. Accurate and just reasoning is the only catholic remedy fitted for all persons and all dispositions and is alone able to subvert that abstruse philosophy and metaphysical jargon which, being mixed up with popular superstition, renders it in a manner impenetrable to careless reasoners and gives it the air of science and wisdom.

Besides this advantage of rejecting, after deliberate inquiry, the most uncertain and disagreeable part of learning, there are many positive advantages which result from an accurate scrutiny into the powers and faculties of human nature. It is remarkable concerning the operations of the mind that, though most intimately present to us, yet, whenever they become the object of reflection, they seem involved in obscurity, nor can the eye readily find those lines and boundaries which discriminate and distinguish them. The objects are too fine to remain long in the same aspect or situation and must be apprehended in an instant by a superior penetration derived from nature and improved by habit and reflection. It becomes, therefore, no inconsiderable part of science barely to know the different operations of the mind, to separate them from each other, to class them under their proper heads, and to correct all that seeming disorder in which they lie involved when made the object of reflection and inquiry. This task of ordering and distinguishing, which has no merit when performed with regard to external bodies, the objects of our senses, rises in its value when directed towards the operations of the mind in proportion to the difficulty and labor which we meet with in performing it. And if we can go no further than this mental geography or delineation of the distinct parts and powers of the mind, it is at least a satisfaction to go so far; and the more obvious this science may appear (and it is by no means obvious), the more contemptible still must the ignorance of it be esteemed in all pretenders to learning and philosophy.

Nor can there remain any suspicion that this science is uncertain and chimerical, unless we should entertain such a skepticism as is entirely subversive of all speculation and even action. It cannot be doubted that the mind is endowed with several powers and faculties, that these powers are distinct from each other, that what is really distinct to immediate perception may be distinguished by reflection, and consequently that there is a truth and falsehood in all propositions on this subject, and a truth and falsehood which does not lie beyond the compass of human understanding. There are many obvious distinctions of this kind, such as those between the will and understanding, the imagination and passions, which fall within the comprehension of every human creature; and the finer and more philosophical distinctions are no less real and certain, though more difficult to be comprehended. Some instances, especially late ones, of success in these inquiries may give us a more just notion of the certainty and solidity of this branch of

learning. And shall we esteem it worthy the labor of a philosopher to give us a true system of the planets and adjust the position and order of those remote bodies, while we affect to overlook those who, with so much success, delineate the parts of the mind in which we are so intimately concerned?[2]

But may we not hope that philosophy, if cultivated with care and encouraged by the attention of the public, may carry its researches still further and discover, at least in some degree, the secret springs and principles by which the human mind is actuated in its operations? Astronomers had long contented themselves with proving, from the phenomena, the true motions, order, and magnitude of the heavenly

---

2. That faculty by which we discern truth and falsehood and that by which we perceive vice and virtue had long been confounded with each other, and all morality was supposed to be built on eternal and immutable relations which, to every intelligent mind, were equally invariable as any proposition concerning quantity or number. But a late philosopher has taught us by the most convincing arguments that morality is nothing in the abstract nature of things, but is entirely relative to the sentiment or mental taste of each particular being in the same manner as the distinctions of sweet and bitter, hot and cold, arise from the particular feeling of each sense or organ. Moral perceptions, therefore, ought not be classed with the operations of the understanding, but with the tastes or sentiments.

It had been usual with philosophers to divide all the passions of the mind into two classes, the selfish and benevolent, which were supposed to stand in constant opposition and contrariety; nor was it thought that the latter could ever attain their proper object but at the expense of the former. Among the selfish passions were ranked avarice, ambition, revenge: Among the benevolent, natural affection, friendship, public spirit. Philosophers may now perceive the impropriety of this division. It has been proved, beyond all controversy, that even the passions commonly esteemed selfish carry the mind beyond self, directly to the object; that though the satisfaction of these passions gives us enjoyment, yet the prospect of this enjoyment is not the cause of the passion, but, on the contrary, the passion is antecedent to the enjoyment, and without the former, the latter could never possibly exist; that the case is precisely the same with the passions denominated benevolent, and consequently that a man is no more interested when he seeks his own glory than when the happiness of his friend is the object of his wishes; nor is he any more disinterested when he sacrifices his ease and quiet to public good than when he labors for the gratification of avarice or ambition. Here, therefore, is a considerable adjustment in the boundaries of the passions, which had been confounded by the negligence or inaccuracy of former philosophers. These two instances may suffice to show us the nature and importance of this species of philosophy.

bodies, until a philosopher at last arose who seems, from the happiest reasoning, to have also determined the laws and forces by which the revolutions of the planets are governed and directed. The like has been performed with regard to other parts of nature. And there is no reason to despair of equal success in our inquiries concerning the mental powers and economy, if prosecuted with equal capacity and caution. It is probable that one operation and principle of the mind depends on another, which again may be resolved into one more general and universal. And how far these researches may possibly be carried, it will be difficult for us, before or even after a careful trial, exactly to determine. This much is certain — that attempts of this kind are made every day even by those who philosophize the most negligently. And nothing can be more requisite than to enter upon the enterprise with thorough care and attention that, if it lies within the compass of human understanding, it may at last be happily achieved; if not, it may, however, be rejected with some confidence and security. This last conclusion, surely, is not desirable nor ought it be embraced too rashly. For how much must we diminish from the beauty and value of this species of philosophy upon such a supposition? Moralists have been accustomed up to now, when they considered the vast multitude and diversity of those actions that excite our approbation or dislike, to search for some common principle on which this variety of sentiments might depend. And though they have sometimes carried the matter too far, by their passion for some one general principle, it must, however, be confessed that they are excusable in expecting to find some general principles into which all the vices and virtues were justly to be resolved. The like has been the endeavor of critics, logicians, and even politicians; nor have their attempts been wholly unsuccessful, though perhaps longer time, greater accuracy, and more ardent application may bring these sciences still nearer their perfection. To throw up at once all pretensions of this kind may justly be deemed more rash, precipitate, and dogmatic than even the boldest and most affirmative philosophy that has ever attempted to impose its crude dictates and principles on mankind.

What? Though these reasonings concerning human nature seem abstract and of difficult comprehension, this affords no presumption of their falsehood. On the contrary, it seems impossible that what has escaped so many wise and profound philosophers up to now can be very obvious and easy. And whatever pains these researches may cost us, we may think ourselves sufficiently rewarded, not only in point of profit but of pleasure, if, by that means, we can make any addition to our stock of knowledge in subjects of such unspeakable importance.

But as, after all, the abstractedness of these speculations is no recommendation, but rather a disadvantage to them, and as this difficulty may perhaps be surmounted by care and art and the avoiding of all unnecessary detail, we have, in the following inquiry, attempted to throw some light upon subjects from which uncertainty has deterred the wise up to now, and obscurity the ignorant. Happy if we can unite the boundaries of the different species of philosophy by reconciling profound inquiry with clearness and truth with novelty! And still more happy if, reasoning in this easy manner, we can undermine the foundations of an abstruse philosophy which seems to have up to now served only as a shelter to superstition and a cover to absurdity and error!

Section II: *Of the Origin of Ideas.*

Everyone will readily allow that there is a considerable difference between the perceptions of the mind when a man feels the pain of excessive heat or the pleasure of moderate warmth and when he afterwards recalls to his memory this sensation or anticipates it by his imagination. These faculties may mimic or copy the perceptions of the senses, but they never can entirely reach the force and vivacity of the original sentiment. The utmost we say of them, even when they operate with greatest vigor, is that they represent their object in so lively a manner that we could *almost* say we feel or see it: But, unless the mind is disordered by disease or madness, they never can arrive at such a pitch of vivacity as to render these perceptions altogether indistinguishable. All the colors of poetry, however splendid, can never paint natural objects in such a manner as to make the description be taken for a real landscape. The most lively thought is still inferior to the dullest sensation.

We may observe a like distinction to run through all the other perceptions of the mind. A man in a fit of anger is actuated in a very different manner from one who only thinks of that emotion. If you tell me that any person is in love, I easily understand your meaning and form a just conception of his situation, but never can mistake that conception for the real disorders and agitations of the passion. When we reflect on our past sentiments and affections, our thought is a faithful mirror and copies its objects truly, but the colors which it employs are faint and dull in comparison of those in which our original perceptions were clothed. It requires no nice discernment or metaphysical head to mark the distinction between them.

Here, therefore, we may divide all the perceptions of the mind into two classes or species which are distinguished by their different degrees of force and vivacity. The less forcible and lively are commonly denominated thoughts or ideas. The other species want a name in our language and in most others, I suppose, because it was not requisite for any but philosophical purposes to rank them under a general term or appellation. Let us, therefore, use a little freedom and call them impressions, employing that word in a sense somewhat different from the usual. By the term *impression*, then, I mean all our more lively perceptions, when we hear, or see, or feel, or love, or hate, or desire, or will. And impressions are distinguished from ideas, which are the less lively perceptions of which we are conscious when we reflect on any of those sensations or movements above mentioned.

Nothing, at first view, may seem more unbounded than the thought of man, which not only escapes all human power and authority, but is not even restrained within the limits of nature and reality. To form monsters and join incongruous shapes and appearances costs the imagination no more trouble than to conceive the most natural and familiar objects. And while the body is confined to one planet, along which it creeps with pain and difficulty, the thought can in an instant transport us into the most distant regions of the universe or even beyond the universe into the unbounded chaos where nature is supposed to lie in total confusion. What never was seen or heard of, may yet be conceived, nor is anything beyond the power of thought except what implies an absolute contradiction.

But though our thought seems to possess this unbounded liberty, we shall find upon a nearer examination that it is really confined within very narrow limits and that all this creative power of the mind amounts to no more than the faculty of compounding, transposing, augmenting, or diminishing the materials afforded us by the senses and experience. When we think of a golden mountain, we only join two consistent ideas, *gold* and *mountain*, with which we were formerly acquainted. A virtuous horse we can conceive, because, from our own feeling, we can conceive virtue; and this we may unite to the figure and shape of a horse, which is an animal familiar to us. In short, all the materials of thinking are derived either from our outward or inward sentiment. The mixture and composition of these belongs alone to the mind and will. Or, to express myself in philosophical language, all our ideas or more feeble perceptions are copies of our impressions or more lively ones.

To prove this, the two following arguments will, I hope, be sufficient. *First,* when we analyze our thoughts or ideas, however compounded or sublime, we always find that they resolve themselves into such simple ideas as were copied from a precedent feeling or sentiment. Even those ideas which at first view seem the most wide of this origin are found, upon a nearer scrutiny, to be derived from it. The idea of God, as meaning an infinitely intelligent, wise, and good being, arises from reflecting on the operations of our own mind and augmenting, without limit, those qualities of goodness and wisdom. We may prosecute this inquiry to what length we please; where we shall always find that every idea which we examine is copied from a similar impression. Those who would assert that this position is not universally true, nor without exception, have only one method, and an easy one at that, of refuting it by producing that idea which, in their opinion, is not derived from this source. It will then be incumbent on us, if we would maintain our doctrine, to produce the impression or lively perception which corresponds to it.

Secondly, if it happens, from a defect of the organ,

that a man is not susceptible of any species of sensation, we always find that he is as little susceptible of the correspondent ideas. A blind man can form no notion of colors, a deaf man of sounds. Restore either of them that sense in which he is deficient by opening this new inlet for his sensations, you also open an inlet for the ideas and he finds no difficulty in conceiving these objects. The case is the same if the object proper for exciting any sensation has never been applied to the organ. A Laplander or Negro has no notion of the relish of wine. And though there are few or no instances of a like deficiency in the mind where a person has never felt or is wholly incapable of a sentiment or passion that belongs to his species, yet we find the same observation to take place in a less degree. A man of mild manners can form no idea of inveterate revenge or cruelty, nor can a selfish heart easily conceive the heights of friendship and generosity. It is readily allowed that other beings may possess many senses of which we can have no conception, because the ideas of them have never been introduced to us in the only manner by which an idea can have access to the mind, namely, by the actual feeling and sensation.

There is, however, one contradictory phenomenon which may prove that it is not absolutely impossible for ideas to arise independent of their correspondent impressions. I believe it will readily be allowed that the several distinct ideas of color which enter by the eye or those of sound which are conveyed by the ear are really different from each other, though at the same time resembling. Now if this is true of different colors, it must be no less so of the different shades of the same color; and each shade produces a distinct idea, independent of the rest. For if this should be denied, it is possible, by the continual gradation of shades, to run a color insensibly into what is most remote from it; and if you will not allow any of the means to be different, you cannot without absurdity deny the extremes to be the same. Suppose, therefore, a person to have enjoyed his sight for thirty years and to have become perfectly acquainted with colors of all kinds, except one particular shade of blue, for instance, which it never has been his fortune to meet with. Let all the different shades of that color, except that single one, be placed before him, descending

gradually from the deepest to the lightest, it is plain that he will perceive a blank where that shade is wanting, and will be sensible that there is a greater distance in that place between the contiguous colors than in any other. Now I ask whether it is possible for him, from his own imagination, to supply this deficiency and raise up to himself the idea of that particular shade, though it had never been conveyed to him by his senses? I believe there are few but will be of the opinion that he can. And this may serve as a proof that the simple ideas are not always, in every instance, derived from the correspondent impressions, though this instance is so singular that it is scarcely worth our observing and does not merit that for it alone we should alter our general maxim.

Here, therefore, is a proposition which not only seems in itself simple and intelligible, but, if a proper use were made of it, might render every dispute equally intelligible and banish all that jargon, which has so long taken possession of metaphysical reasonings and drawn disgrace upon them. All ideas, especially abstract ones, are naturally faint and obscure. The mind has but a slender hold of them. They are apt to be confounded with other resembling ideas; and when we have often employed any term, though without a distinct meaning, we are apt to imagine that it has a determinate idea annexed to it. On the contrary, all impressions, that is, all sensations either outward or inward, are strong and vivid. The limits between them are more exactly determined; nor is it easy to fall into any error or mistake with regard to them. When we entertain, therefore, any suspicion that a philosophical term is employed without any meaning or idea (as is but too frequent), we need but inquire *from what impression is that supposed idea derived?* And if it is impossible to assign any, this will serve to confirm our suspicion. By bringing ideas into so clear a light, we may reasonably hope to remove all dispute which may arise concerning their nature and reality.[3]

---

3. It is probable that no more was meant by those who denied innate ideas than that all ideas were copies of our impressions; though it must be confessed that the terms which they employed were not chosen with such caution, nor so exactly defined, as to prevent all mistakes about their doctrine. For what is meant by *innate?* If innate is equivalent to natural, then all the percep-

Section III: *Of the Association of Ideas.*

It is evident that there is a principle of connection between the different thoughts or ideas of the mind and that, in their appearance to the memory or imagination, they introduce each other with a certain degree of method and regularity. In our more serious thinking or discourse this is so observable that any particular thought which breaks in upon the regular tract or chain of ideas is immediately remarked and rejected. And even in our wildest and most wandering reveries, no, in our very dreams, we shall find, if we reflect, that the imagination did not run altogether at adventures, but that there was still a connection upheld among the different ideas which succeeded each other. Were the loosest and freest conversation to be transcribed, there would immediately be observed something which connected it in all its transitions. Or where this is wanting, the person who broke the thread of discourse might still inform you that there had secretly revolved in his mind a succession of thought which had gradually led him from the subject of conversation. Among different languages, even where we cannot suspect the least connection or communication, it is found that the words expressive of ideas the most compounded do yet nearly correspond to each other—certain proof that the simple ideas

---

tions and ideas of the mind must be allowed to be innate or natural, in whatever sense we take the latter word, whether in opposition to what is uncommon, artificial, or miraculous. If by innate is meant contemporary to our birth, the dispute seems to be frivolous; nor is it worthwhile to inquire at what time thinking begins, whether before, at, or after our birth. Again, the word *idea* seems to be commonly taken in a very loose sense by Locke and others as standing for any of our perceptions, our sensations and passions, as well as thoughts. Now in this sense, I should desire to know, what can be meant by asserting that self-love, or resentment of injuries, or the passion between the sexes is not innate?

But admitting these terms, *impressions* and *ideas*, in the sense above explained, and understanding by *innate* what is original or copied from no precedent perception, then may we assert that all our impressions are innate and our ideas not innate.

To be ingenuous, I must admit it to be my opinion that Mr. Locke was betrayed into this question by the schoolmen who, making use of undefined terms, draw out their disputes to a tedious length without ever touching the point in question. A like ambiguity and circumlocution seem to run through all that great philosopher's reasonings on this as well as most other subjects.

comprehended in the compound ones were bound together by some universal principle which had an equal influence on all mankind.

Though it is too obvious to escape observation that different ideas are connected together, I do not find that any philosopher has attempted to enumerate or class all the principles of association—a subject, however, that seems worthy of curiosity. To me there appear to be only three principles of connection among ideas, namely, *resemblance, contiguity* in time or place, and *cause* or *effect.*

That these principles serve to connect ideas will not, I believe, be much doubted. A picture naturally leads our thoughts to the original.[4] The mention of one apartment in a building naturally introduces an inquiry or discourse concerning the others;[5] and if we think of a wound, we can scarcely forbear reflecting on the pain which follows it.[6] But that this enumeration is complete, and that there are no other principles of association except these, may be difficult to prove to the satisfaction of the reader or even to a man's own satisfaction. All we can do, in such cases, is to run over several instances and examine carefully the principle which binds the different thoughts to each other, never stopping until we render the principle as general as possible.[7] The more instances we examine and the more care we employ, the more assurance shall we acquire that the enumeration, which we form from the whole, is complete and entire.

Section IV: *Skeptical Doubts Concerning the Operations of the Understanding.*

Part I.

All the objects of human reason or inquiry may naturally be divided into two kinds, namely, *relations of ideas* and *matters of fact.* Of the first kind are the

---

4. Resemblance.
5. Contiguity.
6. Cause and effect.
7. For instance, contrast or contrariety is also a connection among ideas, but it may perhaps be considered as a mixture of *causation* and *resemblance.* Where two objects are contrary, the one destroys the other—that is, the cause of its annihilation

sciences of geometry, algebra, and arithmetic, and, in short, every affirmation which is either intuitively or demonstratively certain. *That the square of the hypotenuse is equal to the squares of the two sides* is a proposition which expresses a relation between these figures. *That three times five is equal to the half of thirty* expresses a relation between these numbers. Propositions of this kind are discoverable by the mere operation of thought, without dependence on what is anywhere existent in the universe. Though there never were a circle or triangle in nature, the truths demonstrated by Euclid would forever retain their certainty and evidence.

Matters of fact, which are the second objects of human reason, are not ascertained in the same manner; nor is our evidence of their truth, however great, of a like nature with the foregoing. The contrary of every matter of fact is still possible, because it can never imply a contradiction and is conceived by the mind with the same facility and distinctness, as if ever so conformable to reality. *That the sun will not rise tomorrow* is no less intelligible a proposition and implies no more contradiction than the affirmation that *it will rise*. We should in vain, therefore, attempt to demonstrate its falsehood. Were it demonstratively false, it would imply a contradiction and could never be distinctly conceived by the mind.

It may, therefore, be a subject worthy of curiosity to inquire what is the nature of that evidence which assures us of any real existence and matter of fact beyond the present testimony of our senses or the records of our memory. This part of philosophy, it is observable, has been little cultivated either by the ancients or moderns, and, therefore, our doubts and errors in the prosecution of so important an inquiry may be the more excusable, while we march through such difficult paths without any guide or direction. They may even prove useful by exciting curiosity and destroying that implicit faith and security which is the bane of all reasoning and free inquiry. The discovery of defects in the common philosophy, if there are any, will not, I presume, be a discouragement, but rather an incitement, as is usual, to attempt something

more full and satisfactory than has yet been proposed to the public.

All reasonings concerning matter of fact seem to be founded on the relation of *cause and effect*. By means of that relation alone we can go beyond the evidence of our memory and senses. If you were to ask a man why he believes any matter of fact which is absent—for instance, that his friend is in the country or in France—he would give you a reason, and this reason would be some other fact: as a letter received from him or the knowledge of his former resolutions and promises. A man finding a watch or any other machine on a desert island would conclude that there had once been men on that island. All our reasonings concerning fact are of the same nature. And here it is constantly supposed that there is a connection between the present fact and that which is inferred from it. Were there nothing to bind them together, the inference would be entirely precarious. The hearing of an articulate voice and rational discourse in the dark assures us of the presence of some person. Why? Because these are the effects of the human make and fabric, and closely connected with it. If we anatomize all the other reasonings of this nature, we shall find that they are founded on the relation of cause and effect and that this relation is either near or remote, direct or collateral. Heat and light are collateral effects of fire, and the one effect may justly be inferred from the other.

If we would satisfy ourselves, therefore, concerning the nature of that evidence which assures us of matters of fact, we must inquire how we arrive at the knowledge of cause and effect.

I shall venture to affirm, as a general proposition which admits of no exception, that the knowledge of this relation is not, in any instance, attained by reasonings *a priori*, but arises entirely from experience when we find that any particular objects are constantly conjoined with each other. Let an object be presented to a man of ever so strong natural reason and abilities; if that object is entirely new to him, he will not be able, by the most accurate examination of its sensible qualities, to discover any of its causes or effects. Adam, though his rational faculties are supposed entirely perfect at the very first, could not have inferred from the fluidity and transparency of water that it would

and the idea of the annihilation of an object implies the idea of its former existence.

suffocate him, or from the light and warmth of fire that it would consume him. No object ever discovers, by the qualities which appear to the senses, either the causes which produced it or the effects which will arise from it; nor can our reason, unassisted by experience, ever draw any inference concerning real existence and matter of fact.

This proposition, *that causes and effects are discoverable, not by reason but by experience,* will readily be admitted with regard to such objects as we remember to have once been altogether unknown to us, since we must be conscious of the utter inability which we then lay under of foretelling what would arise from them. Present two smooth pieces of marble to a man who has no tincture of natural philosophy; he will never discover that they will adhere together in such a manner as to require great force to separate them in a direct line, while they make so small a resistance to a lateral pressure. Such events as bear little analogy to the common course of nature are also readily confessed to be known only by experience, nor does any man imagine that the explosion of gunpowder or the attraction of a lodestone could ever be discovered by *a priori* arguments. In like manner, when an effect is supposed to depend upon an intricate machinery or secret structure of parts, we make no difficulty in attributing all our knowledge of it to experience. Who will assert that he can give the ultimate reason why milk or bread is proper nourishment for a man, not for a lion or a tiger?

But the same truth may not appear at first sight to have the same evidence with regard to events which have become familiar to us from our first appearance in the world, which bear a close analogy to the whole course of nature, and which are supposed to depend on the simple qualities of objects without any secret structure of parts. We are apt to imagine that we could discover these effects by the mere operation of our reason without experience. We fancy that were we brought, all of the sudden, into this world, we could at first have inferred that one billiard ball would communicate motion to another upon impulse and that we did not need to have waited for the event in order to pronounce with certainty concerning it. Such is the influence of custom that where it is strongest it not only covers our natural ignorance, but even

conceals itself and seems not to take place, merely because it is found in the highest degree.

But to convince us that all the laws of nature and all the operations of bodies without exception are known only by experience, the following reflections may perhaps suffice. Were any object presented to us and were we required to pronounce concerning the effect which will result from it without consulting past observation, after what manner, I beseech you, must the mind proceed in this operation? It must invent or imagine some event which it ascribes to the object as its effect and it is plain that this invention must be entirely arbitrary. The mind can never possibly find the effect in the supposed cause by the most accurate scrutiny and examination. For the effect is totally different from the cause and consequently can never be discovered in it. Motion in the second billiard ball is a quite distinct event from motion in the first, nor is there anything in the one to suggest the smallest hint of the other. A stone or piece of metal raised into the air and left without any support immediately falls. But to consider the matter *a priori,* is there anything we discover in this situation which can beget the idea of a downward rather than an upward or any other motion in the stone or metal?

And as the first imagination or invention of a particular effect in all natural operations is arbitrary where we do not consult experience, so must we also esteem the supposed tie or connection between the cause and effect which binds them together and renders it impossible that any other effect could result from the operation of that cause. When I see, for instance, a billiard ball moving in a straight line towards another, even suppose motion in the second ball should by accident be suggested to me as the result of their contact or impulse, may I not conceive that a hundred different events might as well follow from that cause? May not both these balls remain at absolute rest? May not the first ball return in a straight line or leap off from the second in any line or direction? All these suppositions are consistent and conceivable. Why then should we give the preference to one which is no more consistent or conceivable than the rest? All our reasonings *a priori* will never be able to show us any foundation for this preference.

In a word, then, every effect is a distinct event from

its cause. It could not, therefore, be discovered in the cause and the first invention or conception of it, *a priori*, must be entirely arbitrary. And even after it is suggested, the conjunction of it with the cause must appear equally arbitrary, since there are always many other effects which, to reason, must seem fully as consistent and natural. In vain, therefore, should we pretend to determine any single event or infer any cause or effect without the assistance of observation and experience.

Hence we may discover the reason why no philosopher who is rational and modest has ever pretended to assign the ultimate cause of any natural operation or to show distinctly the action of that power which produces any single effect in the universe. It is confessed that the utmost effort of human reason is to reduce the principles productive of natural phenomena to a greater simplicity and to resolve the many particular effects into a few general causes by means of reasonings from analogy, experience, and observation. But as to the causes of these general causes, we should in vain attempt their discovery, nor shall we ever be able to satisfy ourselves by any particular explication of them. These ultimate springs and principles are totally shut up from human curiosity and inquiry. Elasticity, gravity, cohesion of parts, communication of motion by impulse—these are probably the ultimate causes and principles which we shall ever discover in nature; and we may esteem ourselves sufficiently happy if, by accurate inquiry and reasoning, we can trace up the particular phenomena to, or near to, these general principles. The most perfect philosophy of the natural kind only staves off our ignorance a little longer, as perhaps the most perfect philosophy of the moral or metaphysical kind serves only to discover larger portions of it. Thus the observation of human blindness and weakness is the result of all philosophy and meets us at every turn in spite of our endeavors to elude or avoid it.

Nor is geometry, when taken into the assistance of natural philosophy, ever able to remedy this defect or lead us into the knowledge of ultimate causes by all that accuracy of reasoning for which it is so justly celebrated. Every part of mixed mathematics proceeds upon the supposition that certain laws are established by nature in her operations and abstract reasonings

are employed either to assist experience in the discovery of these laws or to determine their influence in particular instances where it depends upon any precise degree of distance and quantity. Thus, it is a law of motion, discovered by experience, that the moment or force of any body in motion is in the compound ratio or proportion of its solid contents and its velocity, and consequently that a small force may remove the greatest obstacle or raise the greatest weight if, by any contrivance or machinery, we can increase the velocity of that force so as to make it an overmatch for its antagonist. Geometry assists us in the application of this law by giving us the just dimensions of all the parts and figures which can enter into any species of machine, but still the discovery of the law itself is owing merely to experience and all the abstract reasonings in the world could never lead us one step towards the knowledge of it. When we reason *a priori* and consider merely any object or cause as it appears to the mind, independent of all observation, it never could suggest to us the notion of any distinct object, such as its effect, much less show us the inseparable and inviolable connection between them. A man must be very sagacious who could discover by reasoning that crystal is the effect of heat, and ice of cold, without being previously acquainted with the operation of these qualities.

Part II.

But we have not yet attained any tolerable satisfaction with regard to the question first proposed. Each solution still gives rise to a new question as difficult as the foregoing and leads us on to further inquiries. When it is asked, *What is the nature of all our reasonings concerning matter of fact?* the proper answer seems to be that they are founded on the relation of cause and effect. When again it is asked, *What is the foundation of all our reasonings and conclusions concerning that relation?* it may be replied in one word, experience. But if we still carry on our sifting humor and ask, *What is the foundation of all conclusions from experience?* this implies a new question which may be of more difficult solution and explication. Philosophers who give themselves airs of superior wisdom and sufficiency have a hard task when they encounter persons of inquisitive dispositions, who push them from every corner to which they retreat, and who are sure at last to bring them to some dangerous dilemma. The best expedient to prevent this confusion is to be modest in our pretensions and even to discover the difficulty ourselves before it is objected to us. By this means we may make a kind of merit of our very ignorance.

I shall content myself in this section with an easy task and shall pretend only to give a negative answer to the question here proposed. I say, then, that even after we have experience of the operations of cause and effect, our conclusions from that experience are not founded on reasoning or any process of the understanding. This answer we must endeavor both to explain and to defend.

It must certainly be allowed that nature has kept us at a great distance from all her secrets and has afforded us only the knowledge of a few superficial qualities of objects, while she conceals from us those powers and principles on which the influence of these objects entirely depends. Our senses inform us of the color, weight, and consistency of bread, but neither sense nor reason can ever inform us of those qualities which fit it for the nourishment and support of a human body. Sight or feeling conveys an idea of the actual motion of bodies, but as to that wonderful force or power which would carry on a moving body forever in a continued change of place and which bodies never lose but by communicating it to others, of this we cannot form the most distant conception. But notwithstanding this ignorance of natural powers[8] and principles, we always presume when we see like sensible qualities that they have like secret powers and expect that effects similar to those which we have experienced will follow from them. If a body of like color and consistency with that bread which we have formerly eaten is presented to us, we make no scruple of repeating the experiment and foresee with certainty like nourishment and support. Now this is a process of the mind or thought of which I would willingly know the foundation. It is allowed on all hands that

there is no known connection between the sensible qualities and the secret powers, and consequently that the mind is not led to form such a conclusion concerning their constant and regular conjunction by anything which it knows of their nature. As to past *experience*, it can be allowed to give *direct* and *certain* information of those precise objects only and that precise period of time which fell under its cognizance. But why this experience should be extended to future times and to other objects which, for all we know, may be only similar in appearance; this is the main question on which I would insist. The bread which I formerly ate nourished me — that is, a body of such sensible qualities was, at that time, endowed with such secret powers. But does it follow that other bread must also nourish me at another time and that like sensible qualities must always be attended with like secret powers? The consequence seems in no way necessary. At least, it must be acknowledged that there is here a consequence drawn by the mind, that there is a certain step taken, a process of thought, and an inference which wants to be explained. These two propositions are far from being the same: *I have found that such an object has always been attended with such an effect*, and *I foresee that other objects which are similar in appearance will be attended with similar effects*. I shall allow, if you please, that the one proposition may justly be inferred from the other; I know in fact that it always is inferred. But if you insist that the inference is made by a chain of reasoning, I desire you to produce that reasoning. The connection between these propositions is not intuitive. There is required a medium which may enable the mind to draw such an inference, if indeed it is drawn by reasoning and argument. What that medium is, I must confess, passes my comprehension; and it is incumbent on those to produce it who assert that it really exists and is the origin of all our conclusions concerning matter of fact.

This negative argument must certainly, in process of time, become altogether convincing if many penetrating and able philosophers shall turn their inquiries this way and no one is ever able to discover any connecting proposition or intermediate step which supports the understanding in this conclusion. But as the question is yet new, every reader may not trust

---

8. The word *power* is here used in a loose and popular sense. The more accurate explication of it would give additional evidence to this argument. See Sec. VII.

so far to his own penetration as to conclude that, because an argument escapes his inquiry, therefore it does not really exist. For this reason it may be requisite to venture upon a more difficult task and, enumerating all the branches of human knowledge, endeavor to show that none of them can afford such an argument.

All reasonings may be divided into two kinds, namely, demonstrative reasoning, or that concerning relations of ideas, and moral reasoning, or that concerning matter of fact and existence. That there are no demonstrative arguments in the case seems evident, since it implies no contradiction that the course of nature may change and that an object, seemingly like those which we have experienced, may be attended with different or contrary effects. May I not clearly and distinctly conceive that a body, falling from the clouds and which in all other respects resembles snow, has yet the taste of salt or feeling of fire? Is there any more intelligible proposition than to affirm that all the trees will flourish in December and January and decay in May and June? Now, whatever is intelligible and can be distinctly conceived implies no contradiction and can never be proved false by any demonstrative argument or abstract reasoning *a priori*.

If we are, therefore, engaged by arguments to put trust in past experience and make it the standard of our future judgment, these arguments must be probable only, or such as regard matter of fact and real existence according to the division above mentioned. But that there is no argument of this kind must appear if our explication of that species of reasoning is admitted as solid and satisfactory. We have said that all arguments concerning existence are founded on the relation of cause and effect, that our knowledge of that relation is derived entirely from experience, and that all our experimental conclusions proceed upon the supposition that the future will be conformable to the past. To endeavor, therefore, the proof of this last supposition by probable arguments, or arguments regarding existence, must be evidently going in a circle and taking that which is the very point in question for granted.

In reality, all arguments from experience are founded on the similarity which we discover among natural objects and by which we are induced to expect effects similar to those which we have found to follow from such objects. And though none but a fool or madman will ever pretend to dispute the authority of experience or to reject that great guide of human life, it may surely be allowed a philosopher to have so much curiosity at least as to examine the principle of human nature which gives this mighty authority to experience and makes us draw advantage from that similarity which nature has placed among different objects. From causes which appear *similar*, we expect similar effects. This is the sum of all our experimental conclusions. Now it seems evident that, if this conclusion were formed by reason, it would be as perfect at first, and upon one instance, as after ever so long a course of experience. But the case is far otherwise. [There is] nothing so like as eggs, yet no one, on account of this appearing similarity, expects the same taste and relish in all of them. It is only after a long course of uniform experiments in any kind that we attain a firm reliance and security with regard to a particular event. Now where is that process of reasoning which, from one instance, draws a conclusion so different from that which it infers from a hundred instances that are in no way different from that single one? This question I propose as much for the sake of information as with an intention of raising difficulties. I cannot find, I cannot imagine any such reasoning. But I keep my mind still open to instruction, if anyone will vouchsafe to bestow it on me.

Should it be said that, from a number of uniform experiments, we *infer* a connection between the sensible qualities and the secret powers? This, I must confess, seems the same difficulty couched in different terms. The question still recurs: on what process of argument this *inference* is founded? Where is the medium, the interposing ideas which join propositions so very wide of each other? It is confessed that the color, consistency, and other sensible qualities of bread do not appear of themselves to have any connection with the secret powers of nourishment and support. For otherwise we could infer these secret powers from the first appearance of these sensible qualities without the aid of experience, contrary to the sentiment of all philosophers and contrary to plain matter of fact. Here, then, is our natural state of ignorance with regard to the powers and influence of all objects. How is this remedied by experience? It only shows us a number of uniform effects resulting from certain objects and teaches us that those particular objects, at that particular time, were endowed with such powers and forces. When a new object endowed with similar sensible qualities is produced, we expect similar powers and forces and look for a like effect. From a body of like color and consistency with bread, we expect like nourishment and support. But this surely is a step or progress of the mind which wants to be explained. When a man says, *I have found, in all past instances, such sensible qualities conjoined with such secret powers,* and when he says: *Similar sensible qualities will always be conjoined with similar secret powers*; he is not guilty of a tautology, nor are these propositions in any respect the same. You say that the one proposition is an inference from the other. But you must confess that the inference is not intuitive, neither is it demonstrative. Of what nature is it then? To say it is experimental is begging the question. For all inferences from experience suppose as their foundation that the future will resemble the past and that similar powers will be conjoined with similar sensible qualities. If there is any suspicion that the course of nature may change, and that the past may be no rule for the future, all experience becomes useless and can give rise to no inference or conclusion. It is impossible, therefore, that any arguments from experience can prove this resemblance of the past to the future, since all these arguments are founded on the supposition of that resemblance. Let the course of things be allowed up to now ever so regular, that alone, without some new argument or inference, does not prove that for the future it will continue so. In vain do you pretend to have learned the nature of bodies from your past experience. Their secret nature and, consequently, all their effects and influence may change without any change in their sensible qualities. This happens sometimes and with regard to some objects. Why may it not happen always and with regard to all objects? What logic, what process of argument secures you against this supposition? My practice, you say, refutes my doubts. But you mistake the purport of my question. As an agent, I am quite satisfied in the point; but as a philosopher who has some share of curiosity—I

will not say skepticism—I want to learn the foundation of this inference. No reading, no inquiry has yet been able to remove my difficulty or give me satisfaction in a matter of such importance. Can I do better than propose the difficulty to the public, even though, perhaps, I have small hopes of obtaining a solution? We shall at least, by this means, be sensible of our ignorance, if we do not augment our knowledge.

I must confess that a man is guilty of unpardonable arrogance who concludes, because an argument has escaped his own investigation, that therefore it does not really exist. I must also confess that, though all the learned for several ages should have employed themselves in fruitless search upon any subject, it may still, perhaps, be rash to conclude positively that the subject must therefore pass all human comprehension. Even though we examine all the sources of our knowledge and conclude them unfit for such a subject, there may still remain a suspicion that the enumeration is not complete or the examination not accurate. But with regard to the present subject, there are some considerations which seem to remove all this accusation of arrogance or suspicion of mistake.

It is certain that the most ignorant and stupid peasants—no, infants—no, even brute beasts—improves by experience and learn the qualities of natural objects by observing the effects which result from them. When a child has felt the sensation of pain from touching the flame of a candle, he will be careful not to put his hand near any candle, but will expect a similar effect from a cause which is similar in its sensible qualities and appearance. If you assert, therefore, that the understanding of the child is led into this conclusion by any process of argument or ratiocination, I may justly require you to produce that argument, nor have you any pretense to refuse so equitable a demand. You cannot say that the argument is abstruse and may possibly escape your inquiry, since you confess that it is obvious to the capacity of a mere infant. If you hesitate therefore a moment or if, after reflection, you produce any intricate or profound argument, you, in a manner, give up the question and confess that it is not reasoning which engages us to suppose the past resembling the future and to expect similar effects from causes which are similar to appearance. This is the proposition which I intended to enforce in the present section. If I am right, I pretend not to have made any mighty discovery. And if I am wrong, I must acknowledge myself to be indeed a very backward scholar, since I cannot now discover an argument which, it seems, was perfectly familiar to me long before I was out of my cradle.

Section V: *Skeptical Solution of These Doubts.*

Part I.

The passion for philosophy, like that for religion, seems liable to this inconvenience that, though it aims at the correction of our manners and extirpation of our vices, it may only serve, by imprudent management, to foster a predominant inclination and push the mind, with more determined resolution, towards that side which already *draws* too much by the bias and propensity of the natural temper. It is certain that, while we aspire to the magnanimous firmness of the philosophic sage and endeavor to confine our pleasures altogether within our own minds, we may, at last, render our philosophy like that of Epictetus and other *Stoics*, only a more refined system of selfishness, and reason ourselves out of all virtue as well as social enjoyment. While we study with attention the vanity of human life and turn all our thoughts towards the empty and transitory nature of riches and honors, we are, perhaps, all the while flattering our natural indolence which, hating the bustle of the world and drudgery of business, seeks a pretense of reason to give itself a full and uncontrolled indulgence. There is, however, one species of philosophy which seems little liable to this inconvenience, and that because it strikes in with no disorderly passion of the human mind, nor can mingle itself with any natural affection or propensity; and that is the Academic or skeptical philosophy. The Academics always talk of doubt and suspense of judgment, of danger in hasty determinations, of confining to very narrow bounds the inquiries of the understanding, and of renouncing all speculations which do not lie within the limits of common life and practice. Nothing, therefore, can be more contrary than such a philoso-

phy to the supine indolence of the mind, its rash arrogance, its lofty pretensions, and its superstitious credulity. Every passion is mortified by it except the love of truth; and that passion never is nor can be carried to too high a degree. It is surprising, therefore, that this philosophy, which in almost every instance must be harmless and innocent, should be the subject of so much groundless reproach and blame. But, perhaps, the very circumstance which renders it so innocent is what chiefly exposes it to the public hatred and resentment. By flattering no irregular passion, it gains few partisans. By opposing so many vices and follies, it raises to itself abundance of enemies who stigmatize it as libertine, profane, and irreligious.

Nor need we fear that this philosophy, while it endeavors to limit our inquiries to common life, should ever undermine the reasonings of common life and carry its doubts so far as to destroy all action as well as speculation. Nature will always maintain her rights and prevail in the end over any abstract reasoning whatsoever. Though we should conclude, for instance, as in the foregoing section that, in all reasonings from experience, there is a step taken by the mind which is not supported by any argument or process of the understanding, there is no danger that these reasonings, on which almost all knowledge depends, will ever be affected by such a discovery. If the mind is not engaged by argument to make this step, it must be induced by some other principle of equal weight and authority, and that principle will preserve its influence as long as human nature remains the same. What that principle is may well be worth the pains of inquiry.

Suppose a person, though endowed with the strongest faculties of reason and reflection, to be brought on a sudden into this world; he would, indeed, immediately observe a continual succession of objects and one event following another, but he would not be able to discover anything further. He would not at first, by any reasoning, be able to reach the idea of cause and effect, since the particular powers by which all natural operations are performed never appear to the senses; nor is it reasonable to conclude, merely because one event in one instance precedes another, that therefore the one is the cause, the other the effect. Their conjunction may be arbitrary and casual.

There may be no reason to infer the existence of one from the appearance of the other. And in a word, such a person without more experience could never employ his conjecture or reasoning concerning any matter of fact or be assured of anything beyond what was immediately present to his memory and senses.

Suppose again that he has acquired more experience and has lived so long in the world as to have observed similar objects or events to be constantly conjoined together—what is the consequence of this experience? He immediately infers the existence of one object from the appearance of the other. Yet he has not, by all his experience, acquired any idea or knowledge of the secret power by which the one object produces the other, nor is it by any process of reasoning he is engaged to draw this inference. But still he finds himself determined to draw it. And though he should be convinced that his understanding has no part in the operation, he would nevertheless continue in the same course of thinking. There is some other principle which determines him to form such a conclusion.

This principle is *custom* or *habit*. For wherever the repetition of any particular act or operation produces a propensity to renew the same act or operation without being impelled by any reasoning or process of the understanding, we always say that this propensity is the effect of *custom*. By employing that word we pretend not to have given the ultimate reason of such a propensity. We only point out a principle of human nature which is universally acknowledged and which is well known by its effects. Perhaps we can push our inquiries no further or pretend to give the cause of this cause, but must rest contented with it as the ultimate principle which we can assign of all our conclusions from experience. It is sufficient satisfaction that we can go so far without repining at the narrowness of our faculties because they will carry us no further. And it is certain we here advance a very intelligible proposition at least, if not a true one, when we assert that after the constant conjunction of two objects, heat and flame, for instance, or weight and solidity, we are determined by custom alone to expect the one from the appearance of the other. This hypothesis seems even the only one which explains the difficulty why we draw from a thousand instances an

inference which we are not able to draw from one instance that is in no respect different from them. Reason is incapable of any such variation. The conclusions which it draws from considering one circle are the same which it would form upon surveying all the circles in the universe. But no man, having seen only one body move after being impelled by another, could infer that every other body will move after a like impulse. All inferences from experience, therefore, are effects of custom, not of reasoning.[9]

9. Nothing is more usual than for writers, even on *moral, political,* or *physical* subjects, to distinguish between *reason* and *experience* and to suppose that these species of argumentation are entirely different from each other. The former are taken for the mere result of our intellectual faculties which, by considering *a priori* the nature of things and examining the effects that must follow from their operation, establish particular principles of science and philosophy. The latter are supposed to be derived entirely from sense and observation by which we learn what has actually resulted from the operation of particular objects and are able to infer from this what will result from them for the future. Thus, for instance, the limitations and restraints of civil government and a legal constitution may be defended, either from *reason,* which, reflecting on the great frailty and corruption of human nature, teaches that no man can safely be trusted with unlimited authority; or from *experience* and history, which inform us of the enormous abuses that ambition, in every age and country, has been found to make of so imprudent a confidence.

The same distinction between reason and experience is maintained in all our deliberations concerning the conduct of life, while the experienced statesman, general, physician, or merchant is trusted and followed and the unpracticed novice, with whatever natural talents endowed, neglected and despised. Though it is allowed that reason may form very plausible conjectures with regard to the consequences of such a particular conduct in such particular circumstances, it is still supposed imperfect without the assistance of experience, which is alone able to give stability and certainty to the maxims derived from study and reflection.

But notwithstanding that this distinction is thus universally received, both in the active and speculative scenes of life, I shall not scruple to pronounce that it is, at bottom, erroneous, at least, superficial.

If we examine those arguments which, in any of the sciences aforementioned, are supposed to be the mere effects of reasoning and reflection, they will be found to terminate, at last, in some general principle or conclusion for which we can assign no reason but observation and experience. The only difference between them and those maxims which are vulgarly esteemed the result of pure experience is that the former cannot be established without some process of thought and some reflection on what we have observed in order to distinguish its circumstances and trace its consequences. Whereas in the latter, the

Custom, then, is the great guide of human life. It is that principle alone which renders our experience useful to us and makes us expect, for the future, a similar train of events with those which have appeared in the past. Without the influence of custom we should be entirely ignorant of every matter of fact beyond what is immediately present to the memory and senses. We should never know how to adjust means to ends or to employ our natural powers in the production of any effect. There would be an end at once of all action as well as of the chief part of speculation.

But here it may be proper to remark that though our conclusions from experience carry us beyond our memory and senses and assure us of matters of fact which happened in the most distant places and most remote ages, yet some fact must always be present to the senses or memory from which we may first proceed in drawing these conclusions. A man who should find in a desert country the remains of pompous buildings would conclude that the country had, in

ancient times, been cultivated by civilized inhabitants, but did nothing of this nature occur to him, he could never form such an inference. We learn the events of former ages from history, but then we must peruse the volumes in which this instruction is contained and from this carry up our inferences from one testimony to another, until we arrive at the eyewitnesses and spectators of these distant events. In a word, if we proceed not upon some fact present to the memory or senses, our reasonings would be merely hypothetical; and however the particular links might be connected with each other, the whole chain of inferences would have nothing to support it, nor could we ever, by its means, arrive at the knowledge of any real existence. If I ask, why you believe any particular matter of fact which you relate, you must tell me some reason; and this reason will be some other fact connected with it. But as you cannot proceed after this manner *in infinitum*, you must at last terminate in some fact which is present to your memory or senses or must allow that your belief is entirely without foundation.

What then is the conclusion of the whole matter? A simple one, though it must be confessed, pretty remote from the common theories of philosophy. All belief of matter of fact or real existence is derived merely from some object present to the memory or senses and a customary conjunction between that and some other object. Or, in other words, having found in many instances that any two kinds of objects, flame and heat, snow and cold, have always been conjoined together, if flame or snow is presented anew to the senses, the mind is carried by custom to expect heat or cold and to *believe* that such a quality does exist and will discover itself upon a nearer approach. This belief is the necessary result of placing the mind in such circumstances. It is an operation of the soul when we are so situated, as unavoidable as feeling the passion of love, when we receive benefits — or hatred, when we meet with injuries. All these operations are a species of natural instincts which no reasoning or process of the thought and understanding is able either to produce or to prevent.

At this point, it would be very allowable for us to stop our philosophical researches. In most questions we can never make a single step further; and in all

---

experienced event is exactly and fully similar to that which we infer as the result of any particular situation. The history of a Tiberius or a Nero makes us dread a like tyranny, were our monarchs freed from the restraints of laws and senates. But the observation of any fraud or cruelty in private life is sufficient with the aid of a little thought to give us the same apprehension, while it serves as an instance of the general corruption of human nature and shows us the danger which we must incur by reposing an entire confidence in mankind. In both cases it is experience which is ultimately the foundation of our inference and conclusion.

There is no man so young and inexperienced as not to have formed from observation many general and just maxims concerning human affairs and the conduct of life; but it must be confessed that when a man comes to put these in practice, he will be extremely liable to error, until time and further experience both enlarge these maxims and teach him their proper use and application. In every situation or incident, there are many particular and seemingly minute circumstances which the man of greatest talents is, at first, apt to overlook, though on them the justness of his conclusions, and, consequently the prudence of his conduct, entirely depend. Not to mention that, to a young beginner, the general observations and maxims do not always occur on the proper occasions, nor can be immediately applied with due calmness and distinction. The truth is that an inexperienced reasoner could be no reasoner at all, were he absolutely inexperienced; and when we assign that character to anyone, we mean it only in a comparative sense and suppose him possessed of experience in a smaller and more imperfect degree.

questions, we must terminate here at last, after our most restless and curious inquiries. But still our curiosity will be pardonable, perhaps commendable, if it carry us on to still further researches and make us examine more accurately the nature of this *belief* and of the *customary conjunction* from which it is derived. By this means we may meet with some explications and analogies that will give satisfaction, at least to such as love the abstract sciences and can be entertained with speculations which, however accurate, may still retain a degree of doubt and uncertainty. As to readers of a different taste, the remaining part of this section is not calculated for them and the following inquiries may well be understood, though it is neglected.

Part II.

Nothing is more free than the imagination of man, and though it cannot exceed that original stock of ideas furnished by the internal and external senses, it has unlimited power of mixing, compounding, separating, and dividing these ideas, in all the varieties of fiction and vision. It can feign a train of events with all the appearance of reality, ascribe to them a particular time and place, conceive them as existent, and paint them out to itself with every circumstance that belongs to any historical fact which it believes with the greatest certainty. In what, therefore, consists the difference between such a fiction and belief? It lies not merely in any peculiar idea which is annexed to such a conception as commands our assent and which is wanting to every known fiction. For as the mind has authority over all its ideas, it could voluntarily annex this particular idea to any fiction and consequently be able to believe whatever it pleases; contrary to what we find by daily experience. We can, in our conception, join the head of a man to the body of a horse, but it is not in our power to believe that such an animal has ever really existed.

It follows, therefore, that the difference between *fiction* and *belief* lies in some sentiment or feeling which is annexed to the latter, not to the former, and which depends not on the will, nor can be commanded at pleasure. It must be excited by nature like all other sentiments and must arise from the particular situation in which the mind is placed at any particular juncture. Whenever any object is presented to the memory or senses, it immediately, by the force of custom, carries the imagination to conceive that object which is usually conjoined to it; and this conception is attended with a feeling or sentiment different from the loose reveries of the fancy. In this consists the whole nature of belief. For as there is no matter of fact which we believe so firmly that we cannot conceive the contrary, there would be no difference between the conception assented to and that which is rejected were it not for some sentiment which distinguishes the one from the other. If I see a billiard ball moving towards another on a smooth table, I can easily conceive it to stop upon contact. This conception implies no contradiction, but still it feels very differently from that conception by which I represent to myself the impulse and the communication of motion from one ball to another.

Were we to attempt a *definition* of this sentiment, we should, perhaps, find it a very difficult, if not an impossible task; in the same manner as if we should endeavor to define the feeling of cold, or passion of anger, to a creature who never had any experience of these sentiments. Belief is the true and proper name of this feeling, and no one is ever at a loss to know the meaning of that term, because every man is every moment conscious of the sentiment represented by it. It may not, however, be improper to attempt a *description* of this sentiment, in hopes we may by that means arrive at some analogies which may afford a more perfect explication of it. I say then that belief is nothing but a more vivid, lively, forcible, firm, steady conception of an object than what the imagination alone is ever able to attain. This variety of terms, which may seem so unphilosophical, is intended only to express that act of the mind which renders realities, or what is taken for such, more present to us than fictions, causes them to weigh more in the thought, and gives them a superior influence on the passions and imagination. Provided we agree about the thing, it is needless to dispute about the terms. The imagination has the command over all its ideas and can join and mix and vary them in all the ways possible. It may conceive fictitious objects with all the circumstances of place and time. It may set them in a manner before our eyes, in their true colors, just as they might have existed. But as it is impossible that this faculty of imagination can ever, of itself, reach belief, it is evident that belief consists not in the peculiar nature or order of ideas, but in the *manner* of their conception and in their *feeling* to the mind. I confess that it is impossible perfectly to explain this feeling or manner of conception. We may make use of words which express something near it. But its true and proper name, as we observed before, is *belief*, which is a term that everyone sufficiently understands in common life. And in philosophy we can go no further than assert that *belief* is something felt by the mind which distinguishes the ideas of the judgment from the fictions of the imagination. It gives them more weight and influence, makes them appear of greater importance, enforces them in the mind, and renders them the governing principle of our actions. I hear at present, for instance, a person's voice with whom I am acquainted, and the sound comes as from the next room. This impression of my senses immediately conveys my thought to the person, together with all the surrounding objects. I paint them out to myself as existing at present with the same qualities and relations of which I formerly knew them possessed. These ideas take faster hold of my mind than ideas of an enchanted castle. They are very different to the feeling and have a much greater influence of every kind, either to give pleasure or pain, joy or sorrow.

Let us, then, take in the whole compass of this doctrine and allow that the sentiment of belief is nothing but a conception more intense and steady than what attends the mere fictions of the imagination and that this *manner* of conception arises from a customary conjunction of the object with something present to the memory or senses. I believe that it will not be difficult, upon these suppositions, to find other operations of the mind analogous to it and to trace up these phenomena to principles still more general.

We have already observed that nature has established connections among particular ideas and that no sooner one idea occurs to our thoughts than it introduces its correlative and carries our attention towards it by a gentle and insensible movement. These principles of connection or association we have reduced to three, namely, *resemblance, contiguity,* and *causation*; these are the only bonds that unite our thoughts together and beget that regular train of reflection or discourse which, in a greater or less degree, takes place among all mankind. Now here arises a question on which the solution of the present difficulty will depend. Does it happen in all these relations that when one of the objects is presented to the senses or memory, the mind is not only carried to the conception of the correlative, but reaches a steadier and stronger conception of it than what otherwise it would have been able to attain? This seems to be the case with that belief which arises from the relation of cause and effect. And if the case is the same with the other relations or principles of association, this may be established as a general law which takes place in all the operations of the mind.

We may, therefore, observe, as the first experiment to our present purpose, that upon the appearance of the picture of an absent friend, our idea of him is evidently enlivened by the *resemblance*, and that every passion which that idea occasions, whether of joy or sorrow, acquires new force and vigor. In producing this effect there concur both a relation and a present impression. Where the picture bears him no resemblance, at least was not intended for him, it never so much as conveys our thought to him. And where it is absent, as well as the person, though the mind may pass from the thought of the one to that of the other, it feels its idea to be rather weakened than enlivened by that transition. We take a pleasure in viewing the picture of a friend when it is set before us; but when it is removed, rather choose to consider him directly than by reflection in an image which is equally distant and obscure.

The ceremonies of the Roman Catholic religion may be considered as instances of the same nature. The devotees of that superstition usually plead, in excuse for the mummeries[10] with which they are upbraided, that they feel the good effect of those external motions, and postures, and actions in enlivening their devotion and quickening their fervor, which otherwise would decay, if directed entirely to distant and immaterial objects. We shadow out the objects of our

10. [A pretentious or hypocritical show or ceremony.]

faith, they say, in sensible types and images, and render them more present to us by the immediate presence of these types than it is possible for us to do merely by an intellectual view and contemplation. Sensible objects have always a greater influence on the fancy than any other, and this influence they readily convey to those ideas to which they are related and which they resemble. I shall only infer from these practices and this reasoning that the effect of resemblance in enlivening the ideas is very common; and as in every case a resemblance and a present impression must concur, we are abundantly supplied with experiments to prove the reality of the foregoing principle.

We may add force to these experiments by others of a different kind, in considering the effects of *contiguity* as well as of *resemblance*. It is certain that distance diminishes the force of every idea and that, upon our approach to any object, though it does not discover itself to our senses, it operates upon the mind with an influence which imitates an immediate impression. The thinking on any object readily transports the mind to what is contiguous; but it is only the actual presence of an object that transports it with a superior vivacity. When I am a few miles from home, whatever relates to it touches me more nearly than when I am two hundred leagues distant, though even at that distance the reflecting on anything in the neighborhood of my friends or family naturally produces an idea of them. But, as in this latter case, both the objects of the mind are ideas, notwithstanding there is an easy transition between them; that transition alone is not able to give a superior vivacity to any of the ideas, for want of some immediate impression.[11]

No one can doubt but causation has the same influence as the other two relations of resemblance and contiguity. Superstitious people are fond of the relics of saints and holy men, for the same reason that they seek after types or images in order to enliven their devotion and give them a more intimate and strong conception of those exemplary lives which they desire to imitate. Now it is evident that one of the best relics which a devotee could procure would be the handiwork of a saint; and if his clothes and furniture are ever to be considered in this light, it is because they were once at his disposal and were moved and affected by him; in this respect they are to be considered as imperfect effects and as connected with him by a shorter chain of consequences than any of those by which we learn the reality of his existence.

Suppose that the son of a friend who had been long dead or absent were presented to us; it is evident that this object would instantly revive its correlative idea and recall to our thoughts all past intimacies and familiarities in more lively colors than they would otherwise have appeared to us. This is another phenomenon which seems to prove the principle above mentioned.

We may observe that in these phenomena the belief of the correlative object is always presupposed, with-

---

11. 'Naturane nobis, inquit, datum dicam, an errore quodam, ut, cum ea loca videamus, in quibus memoria dignos viros acceperimus multum esse versatos, magis moveamur, quam siquando eorum ipsorum aut facta audiamus aut scriptum aliquod legamus? Velut ego nunc moveor. Venit enim mihi Platonis in mentem, quem accepimus primum hic disputare solitum: Cujus etiam illi hortuli propinqui non memoriam solum mihi afferunt, sed ipsum videntur in conspectu meo hic ponere. Hic Speusippus, hic Xenocrates, hic ejus auditor Polemo; cujus ipsa illa sessio fuit, quam videamus. Equidem etiam curiam nostram Hostiliam dico, non hanc novam, quae mihi minor esse videtur postquam est major, solebam intuens, Scipionem, Catonem, Laelium, nostrum vero in primis avum cogitare. Tanta vis admonitionis est in locis; ut non sine causa ex his memoriae deducta sit disciplina.' Cicero de Finibus. Lib. v. 2. ["Whether it is a natural instinct or a mere illusion, I can't say; but one's emotions are more strongly aroused by seeing the places that tradition records to have been the resort of men of note in former days, than by hearing about their deeds or reading their writings. My own feelings at the present moment are a case in point. I am reminded of Plato, the first philosopher, so we are told, that made a practice of holding discussions in this place; and indeed the garden close at hand yonder not only recalls his memory but seems to bring the actual man before my eyes. This was the haunt of Speusippus, of Xenocrates, and of Xenocrates's pupil Polemo, who used to sit on the very seat we see over there. For my own part even the sight of our senate-house at home (I mean the Curia Hostilia, not the present new building, which looks to my eyes smaller since its enlargement) used to call up to me thoughts of Scipio, Cato, Laelius, and chief of all, my grandfather; such powers of suggestion do places possess. No wonder the scientific training of the memory is based upon locality." Cicero, *De Finibus Bonorum et Malorum*, translated by H. Rackham (Cambridge: Harvard University Press, 1914), pp. 391–3.]

out which the relation could have no effect. The influence of the picture supposes that we *believe* our friend to have once existed. Contiguity to home can never excite our ideas of home unless we *believe* that it really exists. Now I assert that this belief, where it reaches beyond the memory or senses, is of a similar nature and arises from similar causes with the transition of thought and vivacity of conception here explained. When I throw a piece of dry wood into a fire, my mind is immediately carried to conceive that it augments, not extinguishes, the flame. This transition of thought from the cause to the effect does not proceed from reason. It derives its origin altogether from custom and experience. And as it first begins from an object present to the senses, it renders the idea or conception of flame more strong and lively than any loose, floating reverie of the imagination. That idea arises immediately. The thought moves instantly towards it and conveys to it all that force of conception which is derived from the impression present to the senses. When a sword is leveled at my breast, does not the idea of wound and pain strike me more strongly than when a glass of wine is presented to me, even though by accident this idea should occur after the appearance of the latter object? But what is there in this whole matter to cause such a strong conception except only a present object and a customary transition to the idea of another object which we have been accustomed to conjoin with the former? This is the whole operation of the mind in all our conclusions concerning matter of fact and existence; and it is a satisfaction to find some analogies by which it may be explained. The transition from a present object does in all cases give strength and solidity to the related idea.

Here, then, is a kind of preestablished harmony between the course of nature and the succession of our ideas; and though the powers and forces by which the former is governed are wholly unknown to us, yet our thoughts and conceptions have still, we find, gone on in the same train with the other works of nature. Custom is that principle by which this correspondence has been effected, so necessary to the subsistence of our species and the regulation of our conduct in every circumstance and occurrence of human life. Had not the presence of an object instantly ex-

cited the idea of those objects commonly conjoined with it, all our knowledge must have been limited to the narrow sphere of our memory and senses and we should never have been able to adjust means to ends or employ our natural powers either to the producing of good or avoiding of evil. Those who delight in the discovery and contemplation of *final causes* have here ample subject to employ their wonder and admiration.

I shall add, for a further confirmation of the foregoing theory, that as this operation of the mind by which we infer like effects from like causes, and *vice versa*, is so essential to the subsistence of all human creatures, it is not probable that it could be trusted to the fallacious deductions of our reason, which is slow in its operations, does not appear, in any degree, during the first years of infancy, and, at best, is in every age and period of human life extremely liable to error and mistake. It is more conformable to the ordinary wisdom of nature to secure so necessary an act of the mind by some instinct or mechanical tendency which may be infallible in its operations, may discover itself at the first appearance of life and thought, and may be independent of all the labored deductions of the understanding. As nature has taught us the use of our limbs without giving us the knowledge of the muscles and nerves by which they are actuated, so has she implanted in us an instinct which carries forward the thought in a correspondent course to that which she has established among external objects, though we are ignorant of those powers and forces on which this regular course and succession of objects totally depends.

Section VI: *Of Probability.*[12]

Though there is no such thing as *chance* in the world, our ignorance of the real cause of any event has the same influence on the understanding and begets a like species of belief or opinion.

There is certainly a probability which arises from

12. Mr. Locke divides all arguments into demonstrative and probable. In this view, we must say that it is only probable all men must die or that the sun will rise tomorrow. But to conform our language more to common use, we ought to divide arguments into *demonstrations*, *proofs*, and *probabilities*—by proofs

a superiority of chances on any side and, according as this superiority increases and surpasses the opposite chances, the probability receives a proportional increase and begets still a higher degree of belief or assent to that side in which we discover the superiority. If a die were marked with one figure or number of spots on four sides, and with another figure or number of spots on the two remaining sides, it would be more probable that the former would turn up than the latter, though, if it had a thousand sides marked in the same manner and only one side different, the probability would be much higher and our belief or expectation of the event more steady and secure. This process of the thought or reasoning may seem trivial and obvious, but to those who consider it more narrowly, it may, perhaps, afford matter for curious speculation.

It seems evident that when the mind looks forward to discover the event which may result from the throw of such a die, it considers the turning up of each particular side as alike probable and it is the very nature of chance to render all the particular events comprehended in it entirely equal. But finding a greater number of sides concur in the one event than in the other, the mind is carried more frequently to that event and meets it more often in revolving the various possibilities or chances on which the ultimate result depends. This concurrence of several views in one particular event begets immediately, by an inexplicable contrivance of nature, the sentiment of belief and gives that event the advantage over its antagonist which is supported by a smaller number of views and recurs less frequently to the mind. If we allow that belief is nothing but a firmer and stronger conception of an object than what attends the mere fictions of the imagination, this operation may, perhaps, in some measure be accounted for. The concurrence of these several views or glimpses imprints the idea more strongly on the imagination, gives it superior force and vigor, renders its influence on the passions and affections more sensible, and, in a word, begets that reliance or security which constitutes the nature of belief and opinion.

The case is the same with the probability of causes as with that of chance. There are some causes which are entirely uniform and constant in producing a particular effect, and no instance has ever yet been found of any failure or irregularity in their operation. Fire has always burned, and water suffocated, every human creature. The production of motion by impulse and gravity is a universal law which has up to now admitted of no exception. But there are other causes which have been found more irregular and uncertain; nor has rhubarb always proved a purge, or opium a soporific, to everyone who has taken these medicines. It is true, when any cause fails of producing its usual effect, philosophers do not ascribe this to any irregularity in nature but suppose that some secret causes in the particular structure of parts have prevented the operation. Our reasonings, however, and conclusions concerning the event are the same as if this principle had no place. Being determined by custom to transfer the past to the future in all our inferences, where the past has been entirely regular and uniform, we expect the event with the greatest assurance and leave no room for any contrary supposition. But where different effects have been found to follow from causes which are to *appearance* exactly similar, all these various effects must occur to the mind in transferring the past to the future and enter into our consideration when we determine the probability of the event. Though we give the preference to that which has been found most usual and believe that this effect will exist, we must not overlook the other effects, but must assign to each of them a particular weight and authority in proportion as we have found it to be more or less frequent. It is more probable, in almost every country of Europe, that there will be frost sometime in January than that the weather will continue open throughout that whole month, though this probability varies according to the different climates and approaches to a certainty in the more northern kingdoms. Here, then, it seems evident that when we transfer the past to the future in order to determine the effect which will result from any cause, we transfer all the different events in the same proportion as they have appeared in the past and conceive one to have existed a hundred times, for instance, another, ten times, and another,

---

meaning such arguments from experience as leave no room for doubt or opposition.

once. As a great number of views do here concur in one event, they fortify and confirm it to the imagination, beget that sentiment which we call *belief*, and give its object the preference above the contrary event which is not supported by an equal number of experiments and does not recur so frequently to the thought in transferring the past to the future. Let anyone try to account for this operation of the mind upon any of the received systems of philosophy and he will be sensible of the difficulty. For my part, I shall think it sufficient if the present hints excite the curiosity of philosophers and make them sensible how defective all common theories are in treating of such curious and such sublime subjects.

Section VII: *Of the Idea of Necessary Connection.*

Part I.

The great advantage of the mathematical sciences above the moral consists in this, that the ideas of the former, being sensible, are always clear and determinate, the smallest distinction between them is immediately perceptible, and the same terms are still expressive of the same ideas without ambiguity or variation. An oval is never mistaken for a circle, nor an hyperbola for an ellipsis. The isosceles and scalene are distinguished by boundaries more exact than vice and virtue, right and wrong. If any term is defined in geometry, the mind readily, of itself, substitutes on all occasions the definition for the term defined. Or even when no definition is employed, the object itself may be presented to the senses and by that means be steadily and clearly apprehended. But the finer sentiments of the mind, the operations of the understanding, the various agitations of the passions, though really in themselves distinct, easily escape us when surveyed by reflection; nor is it in our power to recall the original object as often as we have occasion to contemplate it. Ambiguity, by this means, is gradually introduced into our reasonings. Similar objects are readily taken to be the same and the conclusion becomes at last very wide of the premises.

One may safely, however, affirm that if we consider these sciences in a proper light, their advantages and disadvantages nearly compensate each other and reduce both of them to a state of equality. If the mind, with greater facility, retains the ideas of geometry clear and determinate, it must carry on a much longer and more intricate chain of reasoning and compare ideas much wider of each other in order to reach the more abstruse truths of that science. And if moral ideas are apt, without extreme care, to fall into obscurity and confusion, the inferences are always much shorter in these disquisitions and the intermediate steps which lead to the conclusion much fewer than in the sciences which treat of quantity and number. In reality, there is scarcely a proposition in Euclid so simple as not to consist of more parts than are to be found in any moral reasoning which runs not into chimera and conceit. Where we trace the principles of the human mind through a few steps, we may be very well satisfied with our progress, considering how soon nature throws a bar to all our inquiries concerning causes and reduces us to an acknowledgment of our ignorance. The chief obstacle, therefore, to our improvement in the moral or metaphysical sciences is the obscurity of the ideas and ambiguity of the terms. The principal difficulty in mathematics is the length of inferences and compass of thought requisite to the forming of any conclusion. And, perhaps, our progress in natural philosophy is chiefly retarded by the want of proper experiments and phenomena which are often discovered by chance and cannot always be found when requisite, even by the most diligent and prudent inquiry. As moral philosophy seems up to now to have received less improvement than either geometry or physics, we may conclude that if there is any difference in this respect among these sciences, the difficulties which obstruct the progress of the former require superior care and capacity to be surmounted.

There are no ideas which occur in metaphysics more obscure and uncertain than those of *power, force, energy,* or *necessary connection,* of which it is every moment necessary for us to treat in all our disquisitions. We shall, therefore, endeavor in this section to fix, if possible, the precise meaning of these terms and thereby remove some part of that obscurity which is so much complained of in this species of philosophy.

It seems a proposition which will not admit of much dispute that all our ideas are nothing but copies of our impressions, or, in other words, that it is impossible for us to *think* of anything which we have not antecedently *felt* either by our external or internal senses. I have endeavored[13] to explain and prove this proposition and have expressed my hopes that by a proper application of it men may reach a greater clearness and precision in philosophical reasonings than what they have up to now been able to attain. Complex ideas may, perhaps, be well known by definition, which is nothing but an enumeration of those parts or simple ideas that compose them. But when we have pushed up definitions to the most simple ideas and find still some ambiguity and obscurity, what resource are we then possessed of? By what invention can we throw light upon these ideas and render them altogether precise and determinate to our intellectual view? Produce the impressions or original sentiments from which the ideas are copied. These impressions are all strong and sensible. They do not admit of ambiguity. They are not only placed in a full light themselves, but may throw light on their correspondent ideas, which lie in obscurity. And by this means we may, perhaps, attain a new microscope or species of optics by which, in the moral sciences, the most minute and most simple ideas may be so enlarged as to fall readily under our apprehension and be equally known with the grossest and most sensible ideas that can be the object of our inquiry.

To be fully acquainted, therefore, with the idea of power or necessary connection, let us examine its impression and, in order to find the impression with greater certainty, let us search for it in all the sources from which it may possibly be derived.

When we look about us towards external objects and consider the operation of causes, we are never able, in a single instance, to discover any power or necessary connection, any quality which binds the effect to the cause and renders the one an infallible consequence of the other. We only find that the one does actually in fact follow the other. The impulse of one billiard ball is attended with motion in the second. This is the whole that appears to the *outward*

senses. The mind feels no sentiment or *inward* impression from this succession of objects. Consequently, there is not, in any single particular instance of cause and effect, anything which can suggest the idea of power or necessary connection.

From the first appearance of an object we never can conjecture what effect will result from it. But were the power or energy of any cause discoverable by the mind, we could foresee the effect, even without experience, and might, at first, pronounce with certainty concerning it by the mere dint of thought and reasoning.

In reality, there is no part of matter that ever does, by its sensible qualities, discover any power or energy or give us ground to imagine that it could produce anything or be followed by any other object which we could denominate its effect. Solidity, extension, motion—these qualities are all complete in themselves and never point out any other event which may result from them. The scenes of the universe are continually shifting and one object follows another in an uninterrupted succession; but the power or force which actuates the whole machine is entirely concealed from us and never discovers itself in any of the sensible qualities of body. We know that, in fact, heat is a constant attendant of flame, but what is the connection between them, we have no room so much as to conjecture or imagine. It is impossible, therefore, that the idea of power can be derived from the contemplation of bodies in single instances of their operation, because no bodies ever discover any power which can be the original of this idea.[14]

Since, therefore, external objects as they appear to the senses give us no idea of power or necessary connection by their operation in particular instances, let us see whether this idea is derived from reflection on the operations of our own minds and is copied from any internal impression. It may be said that we are every moment conscious of internal power, while

---

13. Section II. Of the Origin of Ideas.

14. Mr. Locke, in his chapter on power, says that, finding from experience that there are several new productions in matter and concluding that there must somewhere be a power capable of producing them, we arrive at last by this reasoning at the idea of power. But no reasoning can ever give us a new, original simple idea—as this philosopher himself confesses. This, therefore, can never be the origin of that idea.

we feel that, by the simple command of our will, we can move the organs of our body or direct the faculties of our mind. An act of volition produces motion in our limbs or raises a new idea in our imagination. This influence of the will we know by consciousness. Hence we acquire the idea of power or energy and are certain that we ourselves and all other intelligent beings are possessed of power. This idea, then, is an idea of reflection, since it arises from reflecting on the operations of our own mind and on the command which is exercised by will, both over the organs of the body and faculties of the mind.

We shall proceed to examine this pretension and, first, with regard to the influence of volition over the organs of the body. This influence, we may observe, is a fact which, like all other natural events, can be known only by experience and can never be foreseen from any apparent energy or power in the cause which connects it with the effect and renders the one an infallible consequence of the other. The motion of our body follows upon the command of our will. Of this we are every moment conscious. But the means by which this is effected, the energy by which the will performs so extraordinary an operation, of this we are so far from being immediately conscious that it must forever escape our most diligent inquiry.

For *first*, is there any principle in all nature more mysterious than the union of soul with body, by which a supposed spiritual substance acquires such an influence over a material one that the most refined thought is able to actuate the grossest matter? Were we empowered by a secret wish to remove mountains or control the planets in their orbit, this extensive authority would not be more extraordinary, nor more beyond our comprehension. But if by consciousness we perceived any power or energy in the will, we must know this power; we must know its connection with the effect; we must know the secret union of soul and body, and the nature of both these substances by which the one is able to operate in so many instances upon the other.

Secondly, we are not able to move all the organs of the body with a like authority, though we cannot assign any reason besides experience for so remarkable a difference between one and the other. Why has the will an influence over the tongue and fingers,

not over the heart or liver? This question would never embarrass us were we conscious of a power in the former case, not in the latter. We should then perceive, independent of experience, why the authority of will over the organs of the body is circumscribed within such particular limits. Being in that case fully acquainted with the power or force by which it operates, we should also know why its influence reaches precisely to such boundaries, and no further.

A man suddenly struck with a palsy in the leg or arm or who had newly lost those members frequently endeavors, at first, to move them and employ them in their usual offices. Here he is as much conscious of power to command such limbs as a man in perfect health is conscious of power to actuate any member which remains in its natural state and condition. But consciousness never deceives. Consequently, neither in the one case nor in the other are we ever conscious of any power. We learn the influence of our will from experience alone. And experience only teaches us how one event constantly follows another, without instructing us in the secret connection which binds them together and renders them inseparable.

Thirdly, we learn from anatomy that the immediate object of power in voluntary motion is not the member itself which is moved, but certain muscles and nerves and animal spirits and, perhaps, something still more minute and more unknown through which the motion is successively propagated before it reaches the member itself whose motion is the immediate object of volition. Can there be a more certain proof that the power by which this whole operation is performed, so far from being directly and fully known by an inward sentiment or consciousness, is to the last degree mysterious and unintelligible? Here the mind wills a certain event. Immediately another event, unknown to ourselves and totally different from the one intended, is produced. This event produces another, equally unknown, until at last, through a long succession the desired event is produced. But if the original power was felt, it must be known. If it was known, its effect must also be known, since all power is relative to its effect. And *vice versa*, if the effect is not known, the power cannot be known nor felt. How indeed can we be conscious of a power to move our limbs when we have no such power, but only that to move certain animal spirits which, though they produce at last the motion of our limbs, yet operate in such a manner as is wholly beyond our comprehension?

We may, therefore, conclude from the whole, I hope, without any temerity, though with assurance, that our idea of power is not copied from any sentiment or consciousness of power within ourselves when we give rise to animal motion or apply our limbs to their proper use and office. That their motion follows the command of the will is a matter of common experience, like other natural events. But the power or energy by which this is effected, like that in other natural events, is unknown and inconceivable.[15]

Shall we then assert that we are conscious of a power or energy in our own minds when, by an act or command of our will, we raise up a new idea, fix the mind to the contemplation of it, turn it on all sides, and at last dismiss it for some other idea when we think that we have surveyed it with sufficient accuracy? I believe the same arguments will prove that even this command of the will gives us no real idea of force or energy.

First, it must be allowed that when we know a power, we know that very circumstance in the cause by which it is enabled to produce the effect, for these are supposed to be synonymous. We must, therefore, know both the cause and effect and the relation between them. But do we pretend to be acquainted with the nature of the human soul and the nature of an idea or the aptitude of the one to produce the other? This is a real creation, a production of something out of nothing, which implies a power so great that it may seem, at first sight, beyond the reach of any being less than infinite. At least it must be admitted that such a power is not felt, nor known, nor even conceivable by the mind. We only feel the event, namely, the existence of an idea consequent to a command of the will. But the manner in which this operation is performed, the power by which it is produced, is entirely beyond our comprehension.

Secondly, the command of the mind over itself is limited, as well as its command over the body; and these limits are not known by reason or any acquaintance with the nature of cause and effect, but only by experience and observation, as in all other natural events and in the operation of external objects. Our authority over our sentiments and passions is much weaker than that over our ideas; and even the latter authority is circumscribed within very narrow boundaries. Will anyone pretend to assign the ultimate reason of these boundaries or show why the power is deficient in one case, not in another?

Thirdly, this self-command is very different at different times. A man in health possesses more of it than one languishing with sickness. We are more master of our thoughts in the morning than in the evening—fasting, than after a full meal. Can we give any reason for these variations except experience? Where, then, is the power of which we pretend to be conscious? Is there not here, either in a spiritual or material substance or both, some secret mechanism or structure of parts upon which the effect depends and which, being entirely unknown to us, renders the power or energy of the will equally unknown and incomprehensible?

Volition is surely an act of the mind with which we are sufficiently acquainted. Reflect upon it. Consider it on all sides. Do you find anything in it like this creative power by which it raises from nothing a new idea and, with a kind of fiat, imitates the omnipotence of its Maker—if I may be allowed so to speak—who called forth into existence all the various scenes of nature? So far from being conscious of this energy in the will, it requires as certain experience

---

15. It may be pretended that the resistance which we meet with in bodies, obliging us frequently to exert our force and call up all our power, this gives us the idea of force and power. It is this *nisus* or strong endeavor of which we are conscious that is the original impression from which this idea is copied. But, first, we attribute power to a vast number of objects, where we never can suppose this resistance or exertion of force to take place; to the Supreme Being who never meets with any resistance; to the mind in its command over its ideas and limbs in common thinking and motion where the effect follows immediately upon the will without any exertion or summoning up of force; to inanimate matter which is not capable of this sentiment. *Secondly,* this sentiment of an endeavor to overcome resistance has no known connection with any event. What follows it, we know by experience, but could not know it *a priori.* It must, however, be confessed that the animal *nisus,* which we experience, though it can afford no accurate precise idea of power, enters very much into that vulgar, inaccurate idea which is formed of it.

as that of which we are possessed to convince us that such extraordinary effects do ever result from a simple act of volition.

The generality of mankind never find any difficulty in accounting for the more common and familiar operations of nature, such as the descent of heavy bodies, the growth of plants, the generation of animals, or the nourishment of bodies by food. But suppose that in all these cases they perceive the very force or energy of the cause by which it is connected with its effect and is forever infallible in its operation. They acquire, by long habit, such a turn of mind that upon the appearance of the cause they immediately expect with assurance its usual attendant and hardly conceive it possible that any other event could result from it. It is only on the discovery of extraordinary phenomena, such as earthquakes, pestilence, and prodigies of any kind, that they find themselves at a loss to assign a proper cause and to explain the manner in which the effect is produced by it. It is usual for men, in such difficulties, to have recourse to some invisible intelligent principle[16] as the immediate cause of that event which surprises them and which they think cannot be accounted for from the common powers of nature. But philosophers, who carry their scrutiny a little further, immediately perceive that, even in the most familiar events, the energy of the cause is as unintelligible as in the most unusual and that we only learn by experience the frequent conjunction of objects, without being ever able to comprehend anything like connection between them. Here, then, many philosophers think themselves obliged by reason to have recourse, on all occasions, to the same principle which the vulgar never appeal to but in cases that appear miraculous and supernatural. They acknowledge mind and intelligence to be not only the ultimate and original cause of all things, but the immediate and sole cause of every event which appears in nature. They pretend that those objects which are commonly denominated *causes* are in reality nothing but *occasions*; and that the true and direct principle of every effect is not any power or force in nature, but a volition of the Supreme Being, who wills that such particular objects should forever be

conjoined with each other. Instead of saying that one billiard ball moves another by a force which it has derived from the author of nature, it is the Deity himself, they say, who, by a particular volition, moves the second ball, being determined to this operation by the impulse of the first ball, in consequence of those general laws which he has laid down to himself in the government of the universe. But philosophers advancing still in their inquiries, discover that as we are totally ignorant of the power on which depends the mutual operation of bodies, we are no less ignorant of that power on which depends the operation of mind on body or of body on mind; nor are we able, either from our senses or consciousness, to assign the ultimate principle in one case more than in the other. The same ignorance, therefore, reduces them to the same conclusion. They assert that the Deity is the immediate cause of the union between soul and body and that they are not the organs of sense which, being agitated by external objects, produce sensations in the mind, but that it is a particular volition of our omnipotent Maker which excites such a sensation in consequence of such a motion in the organ. In like manner, it is not any energy in the will that produces local motion in our members. It is God himself, who is pleased to second our will, in itself impotent, and to command that motion which we erroneously attribute to our own power and efficacy. Nor do philosophers stop at this conclusion. They sometimes extend the same inference to the mind itself in its internal operations. Our mental vision or conception of ideas is nothing but a revelation made to us by our Maker. When we voluntarily turn our thoughts to any object and raise up its image in the fancy, it is not the will which creates that idea, it is the universal Creator who discovers it to the mind and renders it present to us.

Thus, according to these philosophers, every thing is full of God. Not content with the principle that nothing exists but by his will, that nothing possesses any power but by his concession, they rob nature and all created beings of every power in order to render their dependence on the Deity still more sensible and immediate. They do not consider that by this theory they diminish, instead of magnifying, the grandeur of those attributes which they affect so much to

---

16. *Quasi Deus ex machina.*

celebrate. It argues surely more power in the Deity to delegate a certain degree of power to inferior creatures than to produce everything by his own immediate volition. It argues more wisdom to contrive at first the fabric of the world with such perfect foresight that, of itself and by its proper operation, it may serve all the purposes of providence than if the great Creator were obliged every moment to adjust its parts and animate by his breath all the wheels of that stupendous machine.

But if we would have a more philosophical confutation of this theory, perhaps the two following reflections may suffice.

First, it seems to me that this theory of the universal energy and operation of the Supreme Being is too bold ever to carry conviction with it to a man sufficiently apprised of the weakness of human reason and the narrow limits to which it is confined in all its operations. Though the chain of arguments which conduct to it were ever so logical, there must arise a strong suspicion, if not an absolute assurance, that it has carried us quite beyond the reach of our faculties when it leads to conclusions so extraordinary and so remote from common life and experience. We arrived in fairyland long before we have reached the last steps of our theory; and *there* we have no reason to trust our common methods of argument or to think that our usual analogies and probabilities have any authority. Our line is too short to fathom such immense abysses. And however we may flatter ourselves that we are guided, in every step which we take, by a kind of verisimilitude and experience, we may be assured that this fancied experience has no authority when we thus apply it to subjects that lie entirely out of the sphere of experience. But on this we shall have occasion to touch afterwards.[17]

Secondly, I cannot perceive any force in the arguments on which this theory is founded. We are ignorant, it is true, of the manner in which bodies operate on each other. Their force or energy is entirely incomprehensible. But are we not equally ignorant of the manner or force by which a mind, even the supreme mind, operates either on itself or on body? From where, I beseech you, do we acquire any idea of it?

We have no sentiment or consciousness of this power in ourselves. We have no idea of the Supreme Being but what we learn from reflection on our own faculties. Were our ignorance, therefore, a good reason for rejecting anything, we should be led into that principle of denying all energy in the Supreme Being as much as in the grossest matter. We surely comprehend as little the operations of one as of the other. Is it more difficult to conceive that motion may arise from impulse than that it may arise from volition? All we know is our profound ignorance in both cases.[18]

Part II.

But to hasten to a conclusion of this argument, which is already drawn out to too great a length. We have sought in vain for an idea of power or necessary connection in all the sources from which we could suppose it to be derived. It appears that in single instances of the operation of bodies we never can, by our utmost scrutiny, discover anything but one event following another, without being able to comprehend any force or power by which the cause operates or any connection between it and its supposed effect. The same difficulty occurs in contemplating the oper-

---

17. Section XII.

18. I need not examine at length the *vis inertiae* which is so much talked of in the new philosophy and which is ascribed to matter. We find by experience that a body at rest or in motion continues forever in its present state until put from it by some new cause, and that a body impelled takes as much motion from the impelling body as it acquires itself. These are facts. When we call this a *vis inertiae*, we only mark these facts without pretending to have any idea of the inert power—in the same manner as, when we talk of gravity, we mean certain effects without comprehending that active power. It was never the meaning of Sir Isaac Newton to rob secondary causes of all force or energy, though some of his followers have endeavored to establish that theory upon his authority. On the contrary, that great philosopher had recourse to an ethereal active fluid to explain his universal attraction, though he was so cautious and modest as to allow that it was a mere hypothesis not to be insisted on without more experiments. I must confess that there is something in the fate of opinions a little extraordinary. Descartes insinuated that doctrine of the universal and sole efficacy of the Deity, without insisting on it. Malebranche and other Cartesians made it the foundation of all their philosophy. It had, however, no authority in England. Locke, Clarke, and Cudworth never so much as take notice of it, but suppose all along that matter has a real, though subordinate and derived, power. By what means has it become so prevalent among our modern metaphysicians?

ations of mind on body, where we observe the motion of the latter to follow upon the volition of the former, but are not able to observe or conceive the tie which binds together the motion and volition or the energy by which the mind produces this effect. The authority of the will over its own faculties and ideas is not a whit more comprehensible, so that, upon the whole, there does not appear, throughout all nature, any one instance of connection which is conceivable by us. All events seem entirely loose and separate. One event follows another, but we never can observe any tie between them. They seem *conjoined*, but never *connected*. And as we can have no idea of anything which never appeared to our outward sense or inward sentiment, the necessary conclusion *seems* to be that we have no idea of connection or power at all and that these words are absolutely without any meaning when employed either in philosophical reasonings or common life.

But there still remains one method of avoiding this conclusion and one source which we have not yet examined. When any natural object or event is presented, it is impossible for us, by any sagacity or penetration to discover, or even conjecture, without experience, what event will result from it or to carry our foresight beyond that object which is immediately present to the memory and senses. Even after one instance or experiment where we have observed a particular event to follow upon another, we are not entitled to form a general rule or foretell what will happen in like cases, it being justly esteemed an unpardonable temerity to judge of the whole course of nature from one single experiment, however accurate or certain. But when one particular species of event has always, in all instances, been conjoined with another, we make no longer any scruple of foretelling one upon the appearance of the other and of employing that reasoning which can alone assure us of any matter of fact or existence. We then call the one object *cause*, the other *effect*. We suppose that there is some connection between them, some power in the one by which it infallibly produces the other and operates with the greatest certainty and strongest necessity.

It appears, then, that this idea of a necessary connection among events arises from a number of similar instances which occur, of the constant conjunction of these events, nor can that idea ever be suggested by any one of these instances surveyed in all possible lights and positions. But there is nothing in a number of instances, different from every single instance, which is supposed to be exactly similar, except only that after a repetition of similar instances the mind is carried by habit, upon the appearance of one event, to expect its usual attendant and to believe that it will exist. This connection, therefore, which we *feel* in the mind, this customary transition of the imagination from one object to its usual attendant, is the sentiment or impression from which we form the idea of power or necessary connection. Nothing further is in the case. Contemplate the subject on all sides, you will never find any other origin of that idea. This is the sole difference between one instance, from which we can never receive the idea of connection, and a number of similar instances by which it is suggested. The first time a man saw the communication of motion by impulse, as by the shock of two billiard balls, he could not pronounce that the one event was *connected*, but only that it was *conjoined* with the other. After he has observed several instances of this nature, he then pronounces them to be *connected*. What alteration has happened to give rise to this new idea of *connection*? Nothing but that he now *feels* these events to be *connected* in his imagination and can readily foretell the existence of one from the appearance of the other. When we say, therefore, that one object is connected with another, we mean only that they have acquired a connection in our thought and give rise to this inference by which they become proofs of each other's existence—a conclusion which is somewhat extraordinary but which seems founded on sufficient evidence. Nor will its evidence be weakened by any general diffidence of the understanding or skeptical suspicion concerning every conclusion which is new and extraordinary. No conclusions can be more agreeable to skepticism than such as make discoveries concerning the weakness and narrow limits of human reason and capacity.

And what stronger instance can be produced of the surprising ignorance and weakness of the understanding than the present? For surely, if there is any relation among objects which it imports to us to know perfectly, it is that of cause and effect. On this are founded all our reasonings concerning matter of fact or existence. By means of it alone we attain any assurance concerning objects which are removed from the present testimony of our memory and senses. The only immediate utility of all sciences is to teach us how to control and regulate future events by their causes. Our thoughts and inquiries are, therefore, every moment employed about this relation; yet so imperfect are the ideas which we form concerning it that it is impossible to give any just definition of cause, except what is drawn from something extraneous and foreign to it. Similar objects are always conjoined with similar. Of this we have experience. Suitably to this experience, therefore, we may define a cause to be *an object followed by another and where all the objects similar to the first are followed by objects similar to the second.* Or, in other words, *where, if the first object had not been, the second never had existed.* The appearance of a cause always conveys the mind, by a customary transition, to the idea of the effect. Of this also we have experience. We may, therefore, suitably to this experience, form another definition of cause, and call it *an object followed by another and whose appearance always conveys the thought to that other.* But though both these definitions are drawn from circumstances foreign to the cause, we cannot remedy this inconvenience or attain any more perfect definition which may point out that circumstance in the cause which gives it a connection with its effect. We have no idea of this connection, nor even any distinct notion what it is we desire to know when we endeavor at a conception of it. We say, for instance, that the vibration of this string is the cause of this particular sound. But what do we mean by that affirmation? We either mean that *this vibration is followed by this sound, and that all similar vibrations have been followed by similar sounds*; or that *this vibration is followed by this sound and that upon the appearance of one, the mind anticipates the senses and forms immediately an idea of the other.* We may consider the relation of cause and effect in either of these two lights; but beyond these, we have no idea of it.[19]

19. According to these explications and definitions, the idea of *power* is relative as much as that of *cause*; and both have a

To recapitulate, therefore, the reasonings of this section: Every idea is copied from some preceding impression or sentiment; and where we cannot find any impression, we may be certain that there is no idea. In all single instances of the operation of bodies or minds, there is nothing that produces any impression, nor consequently can suggest any idea of power or necessary connection. But when many uniform instances appear and the same object is always followed by the same event, we then begin to entertain the notion of cause and connection. We then *feel* a new sentiment or impression, namely, a customary connection in the thought or imagination between one object and its usual attendant, and this sentiment is the original of that idea which we seek for. For as this idea arises from a number of similar instances and not from any single instance, it must arise from that circumstance in which the number of instances differ from every individual instance. But this customary connection or transition of the imagination is the

reference to an effect or some other event constantly conjoined with the former. When we consider the *unknown* circumstance of an object by which the degree or quantity of its effect is fixed and determined, we call that its power. And, accordingly, it is allowed by all philosophers that the effect is the measure of the power. But if they had any idea of power as it is in itself, why could not they measure it in itself? The dispute whether the force of a body in motion is as its velocity or the square of its velocity, this dispute I say, did not need to be decided by comparing its effects in equal or unequal times, but by a direct mensuration and comparison.

As to the frequent use of the words force, power, energy, etc., which everywhere occur in common conversation as well as in philosophy, that is no proof that we are acquainted in any instance with the connecting principle between cause and effect or can account ultimately for the production of one thing by another. These words as commonly used have very loose meanings annexed to them and their ideas are very uncertain and confused. No animal can put external bodies in motion without the sentiment of a *nisus*, or endeavor, and every animal has a sentiment or feeling from the stroke or blow of an external object in motion. These sensations, which are merely animal and from which we can *a priori* draw no inference, we are apt to transfer to inanimate objects and to suppose that they have some such feelings whenever they transfer or receive motion. With regard to energies which are exerted without our annexing to them any idea of communicated motion, we consider only the constant experienced conjunction of the events; and as we *feel* a customary connection between the ideas, we transfer that feeling to the objects—as nothing is more usual than to apply to external bodies every internal sensation which they occasion.

only circumstance in which they differ. In every other particular they are alike. The first instance which we saw of motion communicated by the shock of two billiard balls (to return to this obvious illustration) is exactly similar to any instance that may, at present, occur to us, except only that we could not at first *infer* one event from the other, which we are enabled to do at present, after so long a course of uniform experience. I do not know whether the reader will readily apprehend this reasoning. I am afraid that, should I multiply words about it or throw it into a greater variety of lights, it would only become more obscure and intricate. In all abstract reasonings, there is one point of view which, if we can happily hit, we shall go further towards illustrating the subject than by all the eloquence and copious expression in the world. This point of view we should endeavor to reach, and reserve the flowers of rhetoric for subjects which are more adapted to them.

Section VIII: *Of Liberty and Necessity.*

Part I.

It might reasonably be expected in questions which have been canvassed and disputed with great eagerness since the first origin of science and philosophy that the meaning of all the terms, at least, should have been agreed upon among the disputants, and our inquiries, in the course of two thousand years, been able to pass from words to the true and real subject of the controversy. For how easy may it seem to give exact definitions of the terms employed in reasoning and make these definitions, not the mere sound of words, the object of future scrutiny and examination? But if we consider the matter more narrowly, we shall be apt to draw a quite opposite conclusion. From this circumstance alone, that a controversy has been long kept on foot and remains still undecided, we may presume that there is some ambiguity in the expression and that the disputants affix different ideas to the terms employed in the controversy. For as the faculties of the mind are supposed to be naturally alike in every individual—otherwise nothing could be more fruitless than to reason or dispute together—it would be impossible, if men affix

the same ideas to their terms, that they could so long form different opinions of the same subject, especially when they communicate their views and each party turn themselves on all sides in search of arguments which may give them the victory over their antagonists. It is true that if men attempt the discussion of questions which lie entirely beyond the reach of human capacity, such as those concerning the origin of worlds or the economy of the intellectual system or region of spirits, they may long beat the air in their fruitless contests and never arrive at any determinate conclusion. But if the question regards any subject of common life and experience, nothing, one would think, could preserve the dispute so long undecided, but some ambiguous expressions which keep the antagonists still at a distance and hinder them from grappling with each other.

This has been the case in the long disputed question concerning liberty and necessity and to so remarkable a degree that, if I am not much mistaken, we shall find that all mankind, both learned and ignorant, have always been of the same opinion with regard to this subject and that a few intelligible definitions would immediately have put an end to the whole controversy. I admit that this dispute has been so much canvassed on all hands and has led philosophers into such a labyrinth of obscure sophistry that it is no wonder if a sensible reader indulge his ease so far as to turn a deaf ear to the proposal of such a question from which he can expect neither instruction nor entertainment. But the state of the argument here proposed may, perhaps, serve to renew his attention, as it has more novelty, promises at least some decision of the controversy, and will not much disturb his ease by any intricate or obscure reasoning.

I hope, therefore, to make it appear that all men have ever agreed in the doctrine both of necessity and of liberty, according to any reasonable sense which can be put on these terms, and that the whole controversy has up to now turned merely upon words. We shall begin with examining the doctrine of necessity.

It is universally allowed that matter, in all its operations, is actuated by a necessary force and that every natural effect is so precisely determined by the energy of its cause that no other effect, in such particular circumstances, could possibly have resulted from it. The degree and direction of every motion are, by the laws of nature, prescribed with such exactness that a living creature may as soon arise from the shock of two bodies as motion in any other degree or direction than what is actually produced by it. Would we, therefore, form a just and precise idea of *necessity*, we must consider from where that idea arises when we apply it to the operation of bodies.

It seems evident that, if all the scenes of nature were continually shifted in such a manner that no two events bore any resemblance to each other, but every object was entirely new, without any similitude to whatever had been seen before, we should never, in that case, have attained the least idea of necessity or of a connection among these objects. We might say, upon such a supposition, that one object or event has followed another, not that one was produced by the other. The relation of cause and effect must be utterly unknown to mankind. Inference and reasoning concerning the operations of nature would, from that moment, be at an end; and the memory and senses remain the only canals by which the knowledge of any real existence could possibly have access to the mind. Our idea, therefore, of necessity and causation arises entirely from the uniformity observable in the operations of nature, where similar objects are constantly conjoined together and the mind is determined by custom to infer the one from the appearance of the other. These two circumstances form the whole of that necessity which we ascribe to matter. Beyond the constant *conjunction* of similar objects and the consequent *inference* from one to the other, we have no notion of any necessity or connection.

If it appears, therefore, that all mankind have ever allowed, without any doubt or hesitation, that these two circumstances take place in the voluntary actions of men and in the operations of mind, it must follow that all mankind have ever agreed in the doctrine of necessity and that they have up to now disputed merely for not understanding each other.

As to the first circumstance, the constant and regular conjunction of similar events, we may possibly satisfy ourselves by the following considerations. It is universally acknowledged that there is a great uniformity among the actions of men in all nations and ages and that human nature remains still the same in its principles and operations. The same motives always produce the same actions. The same events follow from the same causes. Ambition, avarice, self-love, vanity, friendship, generosity, public spirit— these passions, mixed in various degrees and distributed through society, have been, from the beginning of the world, and still are the source of all the actions and enterprises which have ever been observed among mankind. Would you know the sentiments, inclinations, and course of life of the Greeks and Romans? Study well the temper and actions of the French and English. You cannot be much mistaken in transferring to the former *most* of the observations which you have made with regard to the latter. Mankind are so much the same, in all times and places, that history informs us of nothing new or strange in this particular. Its chief use is only to discover the constant and universal principles of human nature by showing men in all varieties of circumstances and situations and furnishing us with materials from which we may form our observations and become acquainted with the regular springs of human action and behavior. These records of wars, intrigues, factions, and revolutions are so many collections of experiments by which the politician or moral philosopher fixes the principles of his science, in the same manner as the physician or natural philosopher becomes acquainted with the nature of plants, minerals, and other external objects by the experiments which he forms concerning them. Nor are the earth, water, and other elements examined by Aristotle and Hippocrates more like to those which at present lie under our observation than the men described by Polybius and Tacitus are to those who now govern the world.

Should a traveler, returning from a far country, bring us an account of men wholly different from any with whom we were ever acquainted, men who were entirely divested of avarice, ambition, or revenge, who knew no pleasure but friendship, generosity, and public spirit, we should immediately, from these circumstances, detect the falsehood and prove him a liar with the same certainty as if he had stuffed his narration with stories of centaurs and dragons, miracles and prodigies. And if we would explode any forgery in history, we cannot make use of a more convincing argument than to prove that the actions ascribed to any person are directly contrary to the course of nature and that no human motives, in such circumstances, could ever induce him to such a conduct. The veracity of Quintus Curtius is as much to be suspected when he describes the supernatural courage of Alexander by which he was hurried on singly to attack multitudes, as when he describes his supernatural force and activity by which he was able to resist them. So readily and universally do we acknowledge a uniformity in human motives and actions as well as in the operations of body.

Hence, likewise, the benefit of that experience acquired by long life and a variety of business and company, in order to instruct us in the principles of human nature and regulate our future conduct as well as speculation. By means of this guide we mount up to the knowledge of men's inclinations and motives from their actions, expressions, and even gestures, and again descend to the interpretation of their actions from our knowledge of their motives and inclinations. The general observations, treasured up by a course of experience, give us the clue of human nature and teach us to unravel all its intricacies. Pretexts and appearances no longer deceive us. Public declarations pass for the specious coloring of a cause. And though virtue and honor are allowed their proper weight and authority, that perfect disinterestedness so often pretended to, is never expected in multitudes and parties, seldom in their leaders, and scarcely even in individuals of any rank or station. But were there no uniformity in human actions and were every experiment which we could form of this kind irregular and anomalous, it would be impossible to collect any general observations concerning mankind, and no experience, however accurately digested by reflection, would ever serve to any purpose. Why is the aged husband more skillful in his calling than the young beginner but because there is a certain uniformity in the operation of the sun, rain, and earth towards the production of vegetables, and experience teaches the old practitioner the rules by which this operation is governed and directed?

We must not, however, expect that this uniformity of human actions should be carried to such a length as that all men, in the same circumstances, will always act precisely in the same manner, without making any allowance for the diversity of characters, prejudices, and opinions. Such a uniformity in every particular is found in no part of nature. On the contrary, from observing the variety of conduct in different men, we are enabled to form a greater variety of maxims which still suppose a degree of uniformity and regularity.

Are the manners of men different in different ages and countries? We learn from this the great force of custom and education which mold the human mind from its infancy and form it into a fixed and established character. Is the behavior and conduct of the one sex very unlike that of the other? It is from this we become acquainted with the different characters which nature has impressed upon the sexes and which she preserves with constancy and regularity. Are the actions of the same person much diversified in the different periods of his life from infancy to old age? This affords room for many general observations concerning the gradual change of our sentiments and inclinations and the different maxims which prevail in the different ages of human creatures. Even the characters which are peculiar to each individual have a uniformity in their influence; otherwise our acquaintance with the persons and our observation of their conduct could never teach us their dispositions or serve to direct our behavior with regard to them.

I grant it possible to find some actions which seem to have no regular connection with any known motives and are exceptions to all the measures of conduct which have ever been established for the government of men. But if we would willingly know what judgment should be formed of such irregular and extraordinary actions, we may consider the sentiments commonly entertained with regard to those irregular events which appear in the course of nature and the operations of external objects. All causes are not conjoined to their usual effects with like uniformity. An artificer who handles only dead matter may be disappointed of his aim as well as the politician who directs the conduct of sensible and intelligent agents.

The vulgar, who take things according to their first appearance, attribute the uncertainty of events to such an uncertainty in the causes as makes the latter often fail of their usual influence, though they meet with no impediment in their operation. But philosophers, observing that almost in every part of nature there is contained a vast variety of springs and principles which are hid by reason of their minuteness or remoteness, find that it is at least possible the contrariety of events may not proceed from any contingency in the cause but from the secret operation of contrary causes. This possibility is converted into certainty by further observation when they remark that, upon an exact scrutiny, a contrariety of effects always betrays a contrariety of causes and proceeds from their mutual opposition. A peasant can give no better reason for the stopping of any clock or watch than to say that it does not commonly go right. But an artist easily perceives that the same force in the spring or pendulum always has the same influence on the wheels, but fails of its usual effect, perhaps by reason of a grain of dust which puts a stop to the whole movement. From the observation of several parallel instances, philosophers form a maxim that the connection between all causes and effects is equally necessary and that its seeming uncertainty in some instances proceeds from the secret opposition of contrary causes.

Thus, for instance, in the human body, when the usual symptoms of health or sickness disappoint our expectation, when medicines do not operate with their wonted powers, when irregular events follow from any particular cause, the philosopher and physician are not surprised at the matter, nor are ever tempted to deny, in general, the necessity and uniformity of those principles by which the animal economy is conducted. They know that a human body is a mighty complicated machine, that many secret powers lurk in it which are altogether beyond our comprehension, that to us it must often appear very uncertain in its operations, and that therefore the irregular events which outwardly discover themselves can be no proof that the laws of nature are not observed with the greatest regularity in its internal operations and government.

The philosopher, if he is consistent, must apply the same reasoning to the actions and volitions of intelligent agents. The most irregular and unexpected resolutions of men may frequently be accounted for

by those who know every particular circumstance of their character and situation. A person of an obliging disposition gives a peevish answer; but he has a toothache or has not dined. A stupid fellow discovers an uncommon alacrity in his carriage; but he has met with a sudden piece of good fortune. Or even when an action, as sometimes happens, cannot be particularly accounted for either by the person himself or by others, we know, in general, that the characters of men are to a certain degree inconstant and irregular. This is, in a manner, the constant character of human nature, though it is applicable in a more particular manner to some persons who have no fixed rule for their conduct, but proceed in a continued course of caprice and inconstancy. The internal principles and motives may operate in a uniform manner, notwithstanding these seeming irregularities—in the same manner as the winds, rain, clouds, and other variations of the weather are supposed to be governed by steady principles, though not easily discoverable by human sagacity and inquiry.

Thus, it appears not only that the conjunction between motives and voluntary actions is as regular and uniform as that between the cause and effect in any part of nature, but also that this regular conjunction has been universally acknowledged among mankind and has never been the subject of dispute either in philosophy or common life. Now, as it is from past experience that we draw all inferences concerning the future, and as we conclude that objects will always be conjoined together which we find to have always been conjoined, it may seem superfluous to prove that this experienced uniformity in human actions is a source from which we draw *inferences* concerning them. But in order to throw the argument into a greater variety of lights, we shall also insist, though briefly, on this latter topic.

The mutual dependence of men is so great in all societies that scarcely any human action is entirely complete in itself or is performed without some reference to the actions of others, which are requisite to make it answer fully the intention of the agent. The poorest artificer who labors alone expects at least the protection of the magistrate to ensure him the enjoyment of the fruits of his labor. He also expects that, when he carries his goods to market and offers them at a reasonable price, he shall find purchasers and shall be able, by the money he acquires, to engage others to supply him with those commodities which are requisite for his subsistence. In proportion as men extend their dealings and render their intercourse with others more complicated, they always comprehend in their schemes of life a greater variety of voluntary actions which they expect, from the proper motives, to cooperate with their own. In all these conclusions they take their measures from past experience in the same manner as in their reasonings concerning external objects and firmly believe that men as well as all the elements are to continue in their operations the same that they have ever found them. A manufacturer reckons upon the labor of his servants for the execution of any work as much as upon the tools which he employs and would be equally surprised were his expectations disappointed. In short, this experimental inference and reasoning concerning the actions of others enters so much into human life that no man, while awake, is ever a moment without employing it. Have we not reason, therefore, to affirm that all mankind have always agreed in the doctrine of necessity, according to the foregoing definition and explication of it?

Nor have philosophers ever entertained a different opinion from the people in this particular. For not to mention that almost every action of their life supposes that opinion, there are even few of the speculative parts of learning to which it is not essential. What would become of *history,* had we not a dependence on the veracity of the historian, according to the experience which we have had of mankind? How could *politics* be a science, if laws and forms of government had not a uniform influence upon society? Where would be the foundation of *morals,* if particular characters had no certain or determinate power to produce particular sentiments and if these sentiments had no constant operation on actions? And with what pretense could we employ our *criticism* upon any poet or polite author, if we could not pronounce the conduct and sentiments of his actors either natural or unnatural to such characters and in such circumstances? It seems almost impossible, therefore, to engage either in science or action of any kind without acknowledging the doctrine of necessity and this *inference* from motives to voluntary actions, from characters to conduct.

And indeed, when we consider how aptly *natural* and *moral* evidence link together and form only one chain of argument, we shall make no scruple to allow that they are of the same nature and derived from the same principles. A prisoner who has neither money nor interest discovers the impossibility of his escape as well when he considers the obstinacy of the jailer as the walls and bars with which he is surrounded and, in all attempts for his freedom, chooses to work upon the stone and iron of the one rather than upon the inflexible nature of the other. The same prisoner, when conducted to the scaffold, foresees his death as certainly from the constancy and fidelity of his guards as from the operation of the ax or wheel. His mind runs along a certain train of ideas: the refusal of the soldiers to consent to his escape; the action of the executioner; the separation of the head and body; bleeding, convulsive motions, and death. Here is a connected chain of natural causes and voluntary actions, but the mind feels no difference between them in passing from one link to another, nor is less certain of the future event than if it were connected with the objects present to the memory or senses by a train of causes cemented together by what we are pleased to call a *physical* necessity. The same experienced union has the same effect on the mind, whether the united objects are motives, volition, and actions, or figure and motion. We may change the names of things, but their nature and their operation on the understanding never change.

Were a man whom I know to be honest and opulent and with whom I live in intimate friendship to come into my house where I am surrounded with my servants, I rest assured that he is not to stab me before he leaves it in order to rob me of my silver standish;[20] and I no more suspect this event than the falling of the house itself which is new and solidly built and founded. — *But he may have been seized with a sudden*

---

20. [A stand containing ink, pens, and other writing materials and accessories, that is, an inkstand or an inkpot.]

and unknown frenzy.—So may a sudden earthquake arise, and shake and tumble my house about my ears. I shall therefore change the suppositions. I shall say that I know with certainty that he is not to put his hand into the fire and hold it there until it is consumed. And this event I think I can foretell with the same assurance as that, if he threw himself out at the window and met with no obstruction, he will not remain a moment suspended in the air. No suspicion of an unknown frenzy can give the least possibility to the former event which is so contrary to all the known principles of human nature. A man who at noon leaves his purse full of gold on the pavement at Charing Cross may as well expect that it will fly away like a feather as that he will find it untouched an hour after. Over one half of human reasonings contain inferences of a similar nature, attended with more or less degrees of certainty, proportioned to our experience of the usual conduct of mankind in such particular situations.

I have frequently considered what could possibly be the reason why all mankind, though they have ever, without hesitation, acknowledged the doctrine of necessity in their whole practice and reasoning, have yet discovered such a reluctance to acknowledge it in words and have rather shown a propensity, in all ages, to profess the contrary opinion. The matter, I think, may be accounted for after the following manner. If we examine the operations of body and the production of effects from their causes, we shall find that all our faculties can never carry us further in our knowledge of this relation than barely to observe that particular objects are *constantly conjoined* together and that the mind is carried, by a *customary transition,* from the appearance of one to the belief of the other. But though this conclusion concerning human ignorance is the result of the strictest scrutiny of this subject, men still entertain a strong propensity to believe that they penetrate further into the powers of nature and perceive something like a necessary connection between the cause and the effect. When again they turn their reflections towards the operations of their own minds and *feel* no such connection of the motive and the action, they are apt to suppose from this that there is a difference between the effects which result from material force and those which

arise from thought and intelligence. But being once convinced that we know nothing further of causation of any kind than merely the *constant conjunction* of objects and the consequent *inference* of the mind from one to another and finding that these two circumstances are universally allowed to have place in voluntary actions, we may be more easily led to admit the same necessity common to all causes. And though this reasoning may contradict the systems of many philosophers in ascribing necessity to the determinations of the will, we shall find, upon reflection, that they dissent from it in words only, not in their real sentiment. Necessity, according to the sense in which it is here taken, has never yet been rejected, nor can ever, I think, be rejected by any philosopher. It may only, perhaps, be pretended that the mind can perceive in the operations of matter some further connection between the cause and effect and a connection that has no place in the voluntary actions of intelligent beings. Now whether it is so or not can only appear upon examination, and it is incumbent on these philosophers to make good their assertion by defining or describing that necessity and pointing it out to us in the operations of material causes.

It would seem, indeed, that men begin at the wrong end of this question concerning liberty and necessity when they enter upon it by examining the faculties of the soul, the influence of the understanding, and the operations of the will. Let them first discuss a more simple question, namely, the operations of body and of brute unintelligent matter, and try whether they can there form any idea of causation and necessity except that of a constant conjunction of objects and subsequent inference of the mind from one to another. If these circumstances form, in reality, the whole of that necessity which we conceive in matter and if these circumstances are also universally acknowledged to take place in the operations of the mind, the dispute is at an end—at least must be admitted to be merely verbal thereafter. But as long as we will rashly suppose that we have some further idea of necessity and causation in the operations of external objects, at the same time that we can find nothing further in the voluntary actions of the mind, there is no possibility of bringing the question to any determinate issue while we proceed upon so erroneous a supposition. The only method of undeceiving us is to mount up higher, to examine the narrow extent of science when applied to material causes, and to convince ourselves that all we know of them is the constant conjunction and inference above mentioned. We may, perhaps, find that it is with difficulty we are induced to fix such narrow limits to human understanding. But we can afterwards find no difficulty when we come to apply this doctrine to the actions of the will. For as it is evident that these have a regular conjunction with motives and circumstances and characters and as we always draw inferences from one to the other, we must be obliged to acknowledge in words that necessity which we have already avowed in every deliberation of our lives and in every step of our conduct and behavior.[21]

21. The prevalence of the doctrine of liberty may be accounted for from another cause, namely, a false sensation or seeming experience which we have, or may have, of liberty or indifference in many of our actions. The necessity of any action, whether of matter or of mind, is not, properly speaking, a quality in the agent, but in any thinking or intelligent being who may consider the action; and it consists chiefly in the determination of his thoughts to infer the existence of that action from some preceding objects—as liberty, when opposed to necessity, is nothing but the want of that determination and a certain looseness or indifference which we feel in passing or not passing from the idea of one object to that of any succeeding one. Now we may observe that, though, in *reflecting* on human actions, we seldom feel such a looseness or indifference, but are commonly able to infer them with considerable certainty from their motives and from the dispositions of the agent, yet it frequently happens that, in *performing* the actions themselves, we are sensible of something like it. And as all resembling objects are readily taken for each other, this has been employed as a demonstrative and even intuitive proof of human liberty. We feel that our actions are subject to our will on most occasions and imagine we feel that the will itself is subject to nothing, because, when by a denial of it we are provoked to try, we feel that it moves easily every way and produces an image of itself (or a *Velleity*, as it is called in the schools), even on that side on which it did not settle. This image or faint motion, we persuade ourselves, could, at that time, have been completed into the thing itself, because, should that be denied, we find upon a second trial that, at present, it can. We do not consider that the fantastical desire of showing liberty is here the motive of our actions. And it seems certain that, however we may imagine we feel a liberty within ourselves, a spectator can commonly infer our actions from our motives and character and even where he cannot, he concludes in general that he might, were he perfectly acquainted with every circumstance of our situation and temper and the most secret springs of our

But to proceed in this reconciling project with regard to the question of liberty and necessity—the most contentious question of metaphysics, the most contentious science—it will not require many words to prove that all mankind have ever agreed in the doctrine of liberty as well as in that of necessity, and that the whole dispute, in this respect also, has been up to now merely verbal. For what is meant by liberty when applied to voluntary actions? We cannot surely mean that actions have so little connection with motives, inclinations, and circumstances that one does not follow with a certain degree of uniformity from the other and that one affords no inference by which we can conclude the existence of the other. For these are plain and acknowledged matters of fact. By liberty, then, we can only mean *a power of acting or not acting according to the determinations of the will*— that is, if we choose to remain at rest, we may; if we choose to move, we also may. Now this hypothetical liberty is universally allowed to belong to everyone who is not a prisoner and in chains. Here then is no subject of dispute.

Whatever definition we may give of liberty, we should be careful to observe two requisite circumstances: *first*, that it is consistent with plain matter of fact; *secondly*, that it is consistent with itself. If we observe these circumstances and render our definition intelligible, I am persuaded that all mankind will be found of one opinion with regard to it.

It is universally allowed that nothing exists without a cause of its existence and that chance, when strictly examined, is a mere negative word and does not mean any real power which has anywhere a being in nature. But it is pretended that some causes are necessary, some not necessary. Here then is the advantage of definitions. Let anyone *define* a cause without comprehending, as a part of the definition, a *necessary connection* with its effect, and let him show distinctly the origin of the idea expressed by the definition, and I shall readily give up the whole controversy. But if the foregoing explication of the matter is received, this must be absolutely impracticable. Had not objects a regular conjunction with each other, we should

complexion and disposition. Now this is the very essence of necessity according to the foregoing doctrine.

never have entertained any notion of cause and effect, and this regular conjunction produces that inference of the understanding which is the only connection that we can have any comprehension of. Whoever attempts a definition of cause exclusive of these circumstances will be obliged either to employ unintelligible terms or such as are synonymous to the term which he endeavors to define.[22] And if the definition above mentioned is admitted, liberty, when opposed to necessity, not to constraint, is the same thing with chance, which is universally allowed to have no existence.

Part II.

There is no method of reasoning more common, and yet none more blamable, than in philosophical disputes to endeavor the refutation of any hypothesis by a pretense of its dangerous consequences to religion and morality. When any opinion leads to absurdities, it is certainly false; but it is not certain that an opinion is false because it is of dangerous consequence. Such topics, therefore, ought entirely to be forborne as serving nothing to the discovery of truth but only to make the person of an antagonist odious. This I observe in general, without pretending to draw any advantage from it. I frankly submit to an examination of this kind and shall venture to affirm that the doctrines both of necessity and of liberty, as above explained, are not only consistent with morality, but are absolutely essential to its support.

Necessity may be defined two ways, conformably to the two definitions of cause of which it makes an essential part. It consists either in the constant conjunction of like objects or in the inference of the understanding from one object to another. Now necessity, in both these senses, (which, indeed, are at bottom the same) has universally, though tacitly,

22. Thus, if a cause is defined *that which produces anything,* it is easy to observe that producing is synonymous to causing. In like manner, if a cause is defined *that by which anything exists,* this is liable to the same objection. For what is meant by these words *by which?* Had it been said that a cause is *that* after which *anything constantly exists,* we should have understood the terms. For this is, indeed, all we know of the matter. And this constancy forms the very essence of necessity, nor have we any other idea of it.

in the schools, in the pulpit, and in common life been allowed to belong to the will of man, and no one has ever pretended to deny that we can draw inferences concerning human actions and that those inferences are founded on the experienced union of like actions with like motives, inclinations, and circumstances. The only particular in which anyone can differ is that either perhaps he will refuse to give the name of necessity to this property of human actions—but as long as the meaning is understood, I hope the word can do no harm—or that he will maintain it possible to discover something further in the operations of matter. But this, it must be acknowledged, can be of no consequence to morality or religion, whatever it may be to natural philosophy or metaphysics. We may here be mistaken in asserting that there is no idea of any other necessity or connection in the actions of body. But surely we ascribe nothing to the actions of the mind but what everyone does and must readily allow of. We change no circumstance in the received orthodox system with regard to the will, but only in that with regard to material objects and causes. Nothing, therefore, can be more innocent, at least, than this doctrine.

All laws being founded on rewards and punishments, it is supposed as a fundamental principle that these motives have a regular and uniform influence on the mind and both produce the good and prevent the evil actions. We may give to this influence what name we please; but, as it is usually conjoined with the action, it must be esteemed a *cause* and be looked upon as an instance of that necessity which we would here establish.

The only proper object of hatred or vengeance is a person or creature endowed with thought and consciousness, and when any criminal or injurious actions excite that passion, it is only by their relation to the person or connection with him. Actions are, by their very nature, temporary and perishing, and where they do not proceed from some cause in the character and disposition of the person who performed them, they can neither redound to his honor if good, nor infamy if evil. The actions themselves may be blamable; they may be contrary to all the rules of morality and religion. But the person is not answerable for them, and as they proceeded from nothing in him that is durable and constant and leave nothing of that nature behind them, it is impossible he can, upon their account, become the object of punishment or vengeance. According to the principle, therefore, which denies necessity and, consequently, causes, a man is as pure and untainted after having committed the most horrid crime as at the first moment of his birth, nor is his character any way concerned in his actions, since they are not derived from it, and the wickedness of the one can never be used as a proof of the depravity of the other.

Men are not blamed for such actions as they perform ignorantly and casually, whatever may be the consequences. Why? But because the principles of these actions are only momentary and terminate in them alone. Men are less blamed for such actions as they perform hastily and unpremeditatedly than for such as proceed from deliberation. For what reason? But because a hasty temper, though a constant cause or principle in the mind, operates only by intervals and does not infect the whole character. Again, repentance wipes off every crime, if attended with a reformation of life and manners. How is this to be accounted for? But by asserting that actions render a person criminal merely as they are proofs of criminal principles in the mind; and when, by an alteration of these principles, they cease to be just proofs, they likewise cease to be criminal. But, except upon the doctrine of necessity, they never were just proofs and consequently never were criminal.

It will be equally easy to prove, and from the same arguments, that *liberty*, according to that definition above mentioned, in which all men agree, is also essential to morality and that no human actions, where it is wanting, are susceptible of any moral qualities or can be the objects either of approbation or dislike. For as actions are objects of our moral sentiment only so far as they are indications of the internal character, passions, and affections, it is impossible that they can give rise either to praise or blame where they do not proceed from these principles, but are derived altogether from external violence.

I do not pretend to have obviated or removed all objections to this theory with regard to necessity and liberty. I can foresee other objections derived from topics which have not here been treated of. It may

be said, for instance, that if voluntary actions are subjected to the same laws of necessity with the operations of matter, there is a continued chain of necessary causes, pre-ordained and pre-determined, reaching from the original cause of all to every single volition of every human creature. No contingency anywhere in the universe, no indifference, no liberty. While we act, we are at the same time acted upon. The ultimate Author of all our volitions is the Creator of the world, who first bestowed motion on this immense machine and placed all beings in that particular position from which every subsequent event, by an inevitable necessity, must result. Human actions, therefore, either can have no moral turpitude at all, as proceeding from so good a cause, or if they have any turpitude, they must involve our Creator in the same guilt, while he is acknowledged to be their ultimate cause and author. For as a man who fired a mine is answerable for all the consequences, whether the train he employed is long or short, so wherever a continued chain of necessary causes is fixed, that Being, either finite or infinite, who produces the first is likewise the author of all the rest and must both bear the blame and acquire the praise which belong to them. Our clear and unalterable ideas of morality establish this rule upon unquestionable reasons when we examine the consequences of any human action, and these reasons must still have greater force when applied to the volitions and intentions of a Being infinitely wise and powerful. Ignorance or impotence may be pleaded for so limited a creature as man, but those imperfections have no place in our Creator. He foresaw, he ordained, he intended all those actions of men which we so rashly pronounce criminal. And we must therefore conclude either that they are not criminal or that the Deity, not man, is accountable for them. But as either of these positions is absurd and impious, it follows that the doctrine from which they are deduced cannot possibly be true, as being liable to all the same objections. An absurd consequence, if necessary, proves the original doctrine to be absurd in the same manner as criminal actions render criminal the original cause, if the connection between them is necessary and inevitable.

This objection consists of two parts, which we shall examine separately: *First*, that if human actions can be traced up, by a necessary chain, to the Deity, they can never be criminal, on account of the infinite perfection of that Being from whom they are derived and who can intend nothing but what is altogether good and laudable. Or, *secondly*, if they are criminal, we must retract the attribute of perfection which we ascribe to the Deity and must acknowledge him to be the ultimate author of guilt and moral turpitude in all his creatures.

The answer to the first objection seems obvious and convincing. There are many philosophers who, after an exact scrutiny of all the phenomena of nature, conclude that the whole, considered as one system, is, in every period of its existence, ordered with perfect benevolence and that the utmost possible happiness will, in the end, result to all created beings without any mixture of positive or absolute ill and misery. Every physical ill, they say, makes an essential part of this benevolent system and could not possibly be removed, even by the Deity himself, considered as a wise agent, without giving entrance to greater ill or excluding greater good which will result from it. From this theory some philosophers, and the ancient *Stoics* among the rest, derived a topic of consolation under all afflictions, while they taught their pupils that those ills under which they labored were in reality goods to the universe and that, to an enlarged view which could comprehend the whole system of nature, every event became an object of joy and exultation. But though this topic is specious and sublime, it was soon found in practice weak and ineffectual. You would surely more irritate than appease a man lying under the racking pains of gout, by preaching up to him the rectitude of those general laws which produced the malignant humors in his body and led them through the proper canals to the sinews and nerves, where they now excite such acute torments. These enlarged views may, for a moment, please the imagination of a speculative man who is placed in ease and security, but neither can they dwell with constancy on his mind, even though undisturbed by the emotions of pain or passion, much less can they maintain their ground when attacked by such powerful antagonists. The affections take a narrower and more natural survey of their object, and, by an economy more suitable to the infirmity of human minds, regard alone the beings around us, and are actuated by such events as appear good or ill to the private system.

The case is the same with *moral* as with *physical* ill. It cannot reasonably be supposed that those remote considerations which are found of so little efficacy with regard to one will have a more powerful influence with regard to the other. The mind of man is so formed by nature that, upon the appearance of certain characters, dispositions, and actions, it immediately feels the sentiment of approbation or blame; nor are there any emotions more essential to its frame and constitution. The characters which engage our approbation are chiefly such as contribute to the peace and security of human society, as the characters which excite blame are chiefly such as tend to public detriment and disturbance. From this it may reasonably be presumed that the moral sentiments arise, either mediately or immediately, from a reflection of these opposite interests. What though philosophical meditations establish a different opinion or conjecture that everything is right with regard to the whole, and that the qualities which disturb society are, in the main, as beneficial and are as suitable to the primary intention of nature as those which more directly promote its happiness and welfare? Are such remote and uncertain speculations able to counterbalance the sentiments which arise from the natural and immediate view of the objects? A man who is robbed of a considerable sum, does he find his vexation for the loss any way diminished by these sublime reflections? Why then should his moral resentment against the crime be supposed incompatible with them? Or why should not the acknowledgment of a real distinction between vice and virtue be reconcilable to all speculative systems of philosophy, as well as that of a real distinction between personal beauty and deformity? Both these distinctions are founded in the natural sentiments of the human mind. And these sentiments are not to be controlled or altered by any philosophical theory or speculation whatsoever.

The *second* objection does not admit of so easy and satisfactory an answer, nor is it possible to explain distinctly how the Deity can be the mediate cause of all the actions of men without being the author of sin and moral turpitude. These are mysteries which mere natural and unassisted reason is very unfit to handle; and whatever system she embraces, she must find herself involved in inextricable difficulties, and even contradictions, at every step which she takes with regard to such subjects. To reconcile the indifference and contingency of human actions with prescience, or to defend absolute decrees and yet free the Deity from being the author of sin, has been found up to now to exceed all the power of philosophy. Happy, if she is thence sensible of her temerity, when she pries into these sublime mysteries and, leaving a scene so full of obscurities and perplexities, return with suitable modesty to her true and proper province, the examination of common life, where she will find difficulties enough to employ her inquiries without launching into so boundless an ocean of doubt, uncertainty, and contradiction!

Section IX: *Of the Reason of Animals.*

All our reasonings concerning matter of fact are founded on a species of analogy which leads us to expect from any cause the same events which we have observed to result from similar causes. Where the causes are entirely similar, the analogy is perfect and the inference drawn from it is regarded as certain and conclusive. Nor does any man ever entertain a doubt where he sees a piece of iron that it will have weight and cohesion of parts, as in all other instances which have ever fallen under his observation. But where the objects do not have so exact a similarity, the analogy is less perfect and the inference is less conclusive, though still it has some force in proportion to the degree of similarity and resemblance. The anatomical observations formed upon one animal are, by this species of reasoning, extended to all animals; and it is certain that, when the circulation of the blood, for instance, is clearly proved to have place in one creature, as a frog, or fish, it forms a strong presumption that the same principle has place in all. These analogical observations may be carried further, even to this science of which we are now treating, and any theory by which we explain the operations of the understanding or the origin and connection of the passions in man will acquire additional authority if we find that the same theory is requisite to explain the same phenomena in all other animals. We shall

make trial of this with regard to the hypothesis by which we have, in the foregoing discourse, endeavored to account for all experimental reasoning, and it is hoped that this new point of view will serve to confirm all our former observations.

First, it seems evident that animals, as well as men, learn many things from experience and infer that the same events will always follow from the same causes. By this principle they become acquainted with the more obvious properties of external objects and gradually, from their birth, treasure up a knowledge of the nature of fire, water, earth, stones, heights, depths, etc., and of the effects which result from their operation. The ignorance and inexperience of the young are here plainly distinguishable from the cunning and sagacity of the old, who have learned, by long observation, to avoid what hurt them and to pursue what gave ease or pleasure. A horse that has been accustomed to the field becomes acquainted with the proper height which he can leap and will never attempt what exceeds his force and ability. An old greyhound will trust the more fatiguing part of the chase to the younger and will place himself so as to meet the hare in her doubles; nor are the conjectures which he forms on this occasion founded in anything but his observation and experience.

This is still more evident from the effects of discipline and education on animals who, by the proper application of rewards and punishments, may be taught any course of action the most contrary to their natural instincts and propensities. Is it not experience which renders a dog apprehensive of pain when you menace him or lift up the whip to beat him? Is it not even experience which makes him answer to his name and infer, from such an arbitrary sound, that you mean him rather than any of his fellows and intend to call him when you pronounce it in a certain manner and with a certain tone and accent?

In all these cases we may observe that the animal infers some fact beyond what immediately strikes his senses and that this inference is altogether founded on past experience, while the creature expects from the present object the same consequences which it has always found in its observation to result from similar objects.

Secondly, it is impossible that this inference of the

animal can be founded on any process of argument or reasoning by which he concludes that like events must follow like objects and that the course of nature will always be regular in its operations. For if there are in reality any arguments of this nature, they surely lie too abstruse for the observation of such imperfect understandings, since it may well employ the utmost care and attention of a philosophic genius to discover and observe them. Animals, therefore, are not guided in these inferences by reasoning. Neither are children. Neither are the generality of mankind in their ordinary actions and conclusions. Neither are philosophers themselves, who, in all the active parts of life, are in the main the same with the vulgar and are governed by the same maxims. Nature must have provided some other principle, of more ready and more general use and application; nor can an operation of such immense consequence in life as that of inferring effects from causes be trusted to the uncertain process of reasoning and argumentation. Were this doubtful with regard to men, it seems to admit of no question with regard to the brute creation; and the conclusion being once firmly established in the one, we have a strong presumption, from all the rules of analogy, that it ought to be universally admitted without any exception or reserve. It is custom alone which engages animals from every object that strikes their senses to infer its usual attendant and carries their imagination from the appearance of the one to conceive the other in that particular manner which we denominate *belief*. No other explication can be given of this operation, in all the higher as well as lower classes of sensitive beings which fall under our notice and observation.[23]

23. Since all reasoning concerning facts or causes is derived merely from custom, it may be asked how it happens that men so much surpass animals in reasoning and one man so much surpasses another? Does not the same custom have the same influence on all?

We shall here endeavor briefly to explain the great difference in human understandings. After this the reason of the difference between men and animals will easily be comprehended.

1. When we have lived any time and have been accustomed to the uniformity of nature, we acquire a general habit by which we always transfer the known to the unknown and conceive the latter to resemble the former. By means of this general habitual principle, we regard even one experiment as the foundation of reasoning and expect a similar event with some degree of certainty, where the experiment has been made accurately and free from all foreign circumstances. It is therefore considered as a matter of great importance to observe the consequences of things; and as one man may very much surpass another in attention and memory and observation, this will make a very great difference in their reasoning.

2. Where there is a complication of causes to produce any effect, one mind may be much larger than another and better able to comprehend the whole system of objects and to infer justly their consequences.

3. One man is able to carry on a chain of consequences to a greater length than another.

4. Few men can think long without running into a confusion of ideas and mistaking one for another; and there are various degrees of this infirmity.

5. The circumstance on which the effect depends is frequently involved in other circumstances which are foreign and extrinsic. The separation of it often requires great attention, accuracy, and subtlety.

6. The forming of general maxims from particular observation is a very nice operation; and nothing is more usual from haste or a narrowness of mind, which does not see on all sides, than to commit mistakes in this particular.

7. When we reason from analogies, the man who has the greater experience or the greater promptitude of suggesting analogies will be the better reasoner.

8. Biases from prejudice, education, passion, party, etc., hang more upon one mind than another.

9. After we have acquired a confidence in human testimony, books and conversation enlarge much more the sphere of one man's experience and thought than those of another.

It would be easy to discover many other circumstances that make a difference in the understandings of men.

But though animals learn many parts of their knowledge from observation, there are also many parts of it which they derive from the original hand of nature which much exceed the share of capacity they possess on ordinary occasions and in which they improve little or nothing by the longest practice and experience. These we denominate instincts and are so apt to admire as something very extraordinary and inexplicable by all the disquisitions of human understanding. But our wonder will perhaps cease or diminish when we consider that the experimental reasoning itself which we possess in common with beasts and on which the whole conduct of life depends is nothing but a species of instinct or mechanical power that acts in us unknown to ourselves and in its chief operations is not directed by any such relations or comparisons of ideas as are the proper objects of our intellectual faculties. Though the instinct is different, yet still it is an instinct which teaches a man to avoid the fire, as much as that which teaches a bird, with such exactness, the art of incubation and the whole economy and order of its nursery.

Section X: *Of Miracles.*

Part I.

There is, in Dr. Tillotson's writings, an argument against the *real presence*[24] which is as concise and elegant and strong as any argument can possibly be supposed against a doctrine so little worthy of a serious refutation. It is acknowledged on all hands, says that learned prelate, that the authority either of the Scripture or of tradition is founded merely in the testimony of the Apostles who were eyewitnesses to those miracles of our Savior by which he proved his divine mission. Our evidence, then, for the truth of the *Christian* religion is less than the evidence for the truth of our senses, because even in the first authors of our religion it was no greater; and it is evident it must diminish in passing from them to their disciples, nor can anyone rest such confidence in their testimony as in the immediate object of his senses. But a weaker evidence can never destroy a stronger; and, therefore, were the doctrine of the real presence ever so clearly revealed in Scripture, it would be directly contrary to the rules of just reasoning to give our assent to it. It contradicts sense, though both the Scripture and tradition, on which it is supposed to be built, do not carry such evidence with them as sense, when they are considered merely as external evidences and are not brought home to everyone's breast by the immediate operation of the Holy Spirit.

Nothing is so convenient as a decisive argument of this kind, which must at least *silence* the most arrogant bigotry and superstition and free us from their impertinent solicitations. I flatter myself that I have discovered an argument of a like nature which, if just, will, with the wise and learned, be an everlasting check to all kinds of superstitious delusion and consequently will be useful as long as the world endures. For so long, I presume, will the accounts of miracles and prodigies be found in all history, sacred and profane.

Though experience is our only guide in reasoning concerning matters of fact, it must be acknowledged that this guide is not altogether infallible, but in some cases is apt to lead us into errors. One who in our climate should expect better weather in any week of June than in one of December would reason justly and conformably to experience, but it is certain that he may happen, in the event, to find himself mistaken. However, we may observe that in such a case he would have no cause to complain of experience, because it commonly informs us beforehand of the uncertainty by that contrariety of events which we may learn from a diligent observation. All effects do not follow with like certainty from their supposed causes. Some events are found, in all countries and all ages, to have been constantly conjoined together. Others are found to have been more variable and sometimes to disappoint our expectations, so that in our reasonings concerning matter of fact there are all imaginable degrees of assurance, from the highest certainty to the lowest species of moral evidence.

A wise man, therefore, proportions his belief to the evidence. In such conclusions as are founded on an infallible experience, he expects the event with the last degree of assurance and regards his past experience as a full *proof* of the future existence of that event. In other cases he proceeds with more caution. He weighs the opposite experiments. He considers which side is supported by the greater number of experiments — to that side he inclines with doubt and hesitation; and when at last he fixes his judgment, the evidence does not exceed what we properly call *probability*. All probability, then, supposes an opposition of experiments and observations, where the one side is found to overbalance the other and to produce a degree of evidence proportioned to the superiority. A hundred instances or experiments on one side and fifty on another afford a doubtful expectation of any event, though a hundred uniform experiments with only one that is

24. [Of Christ in the sacrament of the Eucharist.]

contradictory reasonably beget a pretty strong degree of assurance. In all cases we must balance the opposite experiments where they are opposite and deduct the smaller number from the greater in order to know the exact force of the superior evidence.

To apply these principles to a particular instance, we may observe that there is no species of reasoning more common, more useful, and even necessary to human life than that which is derived from the testimony of men and the reports of eyewitnesses and spectators. This species of reasoning, perhaps, one may deny to be founded on the relation of cause and effect. I shall not dispute about a word. It will be sufficient to observe that our assurance in any argument of this kind is derived from no other principle than our observation of the veracity of human testimony and of the usual conformity of facts to the reports of witnesses. It being a general maxim that no objects have any discoverable connection together and that all the inferences which we can draw from one to another are founded merely on our experience of their constant and regular conjunction, it is evident that we ought not make an exception to this maxim in favor of human testimony whose connection with any event seems in itself as little necessary as any other. Were not the memory tenacious to a certain degree, had not men commonly an inclination to truth and a principle of probity, were they not sensible to shame when detected in a falsehood, were not these, I say, discovered by *experience* to be qualities inherent in human nature, we should never repose the least confidence in human testimony. A man delirious or noted for falsehood and villainy has no manner of authority with us.

And as the evidence derived from witnesses and human testimony is founded on past experience, so it varies with the experience and is regarded either as a *proof* or a *probability*, according as the conjunction between any particular kind of report and any kind of object has been found to be constant or variable. There are a number of circumstances to be taken into consideration in all judgments of this kind; and the ultimate standard by which we determine all disputes that may arise concerning them is always derived from experience and observation. Where this experience is not entirely uniform on any side, it is attended with an unavoidable contrariety in our judgments and with the same opposition and mutual destruction of argument as in every other kind of evidence. We frequently hesitate concerning the reports of others. We balance the opposite circumstances which cause any doubt or uncertainty; and when we discover a superiority on any side, we incline to it, but still with a diminution of assurance in proportion to the force of its antagonist.

This contrariety of evidence, in the present case, may be derived from several different causes: from the opposition of contrary testimony, from the character or number of the witnesses, from the manner of their delivering their testimony, or from the union of all these circumstances. We entertain a suspicion concerning any matter of fact when the witnesses contradict each other, when they are but few or of a doubtful character, when they have an interest in what they affirm, when they deliver their testimony with hesitation or, on the contrary, with too violent affirmations. There are many other particulars of the same kind which may diminish or destroy the force of any argument derived from human testimony.

Suppose, for instance, that the fact which the testimony endeavors to establish partakes of the extraordinary and the marvelous—in that case, the evidence resulting from the testimony admits of a diminution, greater or less in proportion as the fact is more or less unusual. The reason why we place any credit in witnesses and historians is not derived from any *connection* which we perceive *a priori* between testimony and reality, but because we are accustomed to find a conformity between them. But when the fact attested is such a one as has seldom fallen under our observation, here is a contest of two opposite experiences of which the one destroys the other as far as its force goes and the superior can only operate on the mind by the force which remains. The very same principle of experience which gives us a certain degree of assurance in the testimony of witnesses gives us also, in this case, another degree of assurance against the fact which they endeavor to establish—from which contradiction there necessarily arises a counterpoise and mutual destruction of belief and authority.

I should not believe such a story were it told me by Cato was a proverbial saying in Rome, even during the lifetime of that philosophical patriot. The incredibility of a fact, it was allowed, might invalidate so great an authority.

The Indian prince who refused to believe the first relations concerning the effects of frost reasoned justly, and it naturally required very strong testimony to engage his assent to facts that arose from a state of nature with which he was unacquainted and which bore so little analogy to those events of which he had had constant and uniform experience. Though they were not contrary to his experience, they were not conformable to it.[25]

But in order to increase the probability against the testimony of witnesses, let us suppose that the fact which they affirm, instead of being only marvelous, is really miraculous, and suppose also that the testimony, considered apart and in itself, amounts to an entire proof—in that case, there is proof against proof, of which the strongest must prevail, but still with a diminution of its force in proportion to that of its antagonist.

A miracle is a violation of the laws of nature; and as a firm and unalterable experience has established these laws, the proof against a miracle, from the very nature of the fact, is as entire as any argument from experience can possibly be imagined. Why is it more than probable that all men must die, that lead cannot of itself remain suspended in the air, that fire consumes wood and is extinguished by water, unless it is that these events are found agreeable to the laws of nature and there is required a violation of these laws or, in other words, a miracle, to prevent them? Nothing is esteemed a miracle if it ever happen in the common course of nature. It is no miracle that a man, seemingly in good health, should die all of a sudden, because such a kind of death, though more unusual than any other, has yet been frequently observed to happen. But it is a miracle that a dead man should come to life, because that has never been observed in any age or country. There must, therefore, be a uniform experience against every miraculous event; otherwise the event would not merit that appellation. And as a uniform experience amounts to a proof, there is here a direct and full *proof*, from the nature of the fact, against the existence of any miracle, nor can such a proof be destroyed or the miracle rendered credible but by an opposite proof which is superior.[26]

The plain consequence is (and it is a general maxim worthy of our attention): that no testimony is sufficient to establish a miracle, unless the testimony is of such a kind that its falsehood would be more miraculous than the fact which it endeavors to establish; and even in that case there is a mutual

---

25. No Indian, it is evident, could have experience that water did not freeze in cold climates. This is placing nature in a situation quite unknown to him; and it is impossible for him to tell *a priori* what will result from it. It is making a new experiment, the consequence of which is always uncertain. One may sometimes conjecture from analogy what will follow; but still this is but conjecture. And it must be confessed that, in the present case of freezing, the event follows contrary to the rules of analogy and is such as a rational Indian would not look for. The operations of cold upon water are not gradual, according to the degrees of cold; but whenever it comes to the freezing point, the water passes in a moment from the utmost liquidity to perfect hardness. Such an event, therefore, may be denominated *extraordinary* and requires a pretty strong testimony to render it credible to people in a warm climate. But still it is not *miraculous*, nor contrary to uniform experience of the course of nature in cases where all the circumstances are the same. The inhabitants of Sumatra have always seen water fluid in their own climate, and the freezing of their rivers ought to be deemed a prodigy: But they never saw water in Muscovy during the winter; and therefore they cannot reasonably be positive what would there be the consequence.

26. Sometimes an event may not, *in itself, seem* to be contrary to the laws of nature, and yet, if it were real, it might by reason of some circumstances be denominated a miracle, because, in *fact*, it is contrary to these laws. Thus, if a person claiming a divine authority should command a sick person to be well, a healthful man to fall down dead, the clouds to pour rain, the winds to blow, in short, should order many natural events, which immediately follow upon his command; these might justly be esteemed miracles because they are really, in this case, contrary to the laws of nature. For if any suspicion remain that the event and command concurred by accident, there is no miracle and no transgression of the laws of nature. If this suspicion is removed, there is evidently a miracle and a transgression of these laws, because nothing can be more contrary to nature than that the voice or command of a man should have such an influence. A miracle may be accurately defined *a transgression of a law of nature by a particular volition of the Deity or by the interposition of some invisible agent*. A miracle may either be discoverable by men or not. This does not alter its nature and essence. The raising of a house or ship into the air is a visible miracle. The raising of a feather when the wind wants ever so little of a force requisite for that purpose is as real a miracle, though not so sensible with regard to us.

destruction of arguments and the superior only gives us an assurance suitable to that degree of force which remains after deducting the inferior. When anyone tells me that he saw a dead man restored to life, I immediately consider with myself whether it is more probable that this person should either deceive or be deceived or that the fact which he relates should really have happened. I weigh the one miracle against the other and, according to the superiority which I discover, I pronounce my decision and always reject the greater miracle. If the falsehood of his testimony would be more miraculous than the event which he relates, then, and not until then, can he pretend to command my belief or opinion.

Part II.

In the foregoing reasoning we have supposed that the testimony upon which a miracle is founded may possibly amount to an entire proof and that the falsehood of that testimony would be a real prodigy. But it is easy to show that we have been a great deal too liberal in our concession and that there never was a miraculous event established on so full an evidence.

For *first,* there is not to be found, in all history, any miracle attested by a sufficient number of men of such unquestioned good sense, education, and learning, as to secure us against all delusion in themselves; of such undoubted integrity as to place them beyond all suspicion of any design to deceive others; of such credit and reputation in the eyes of mankind as to have a great deal to lose in case of their being detected in any falsehood, and at the same time attesting facts performed in such a public manner and in so celebrated a part of the world as to render the detection unavoidable — all which circumstances are requisite to give us a full assurance in the testimony of men.

Secondly, we may observe in human nature a principle which, if strictly examined, will be found to diminish extremely the assurance which we might, from human testimony, have in any kind of prodigy. The maxim by which we commonly conduct ourselves in our reasonings is that the objects of which we have no experience resemble those of which we have; that what we have found to be most usual is

always most probable; and that where there is an opposition of arguments, we ought to give the preference to such as are founded on the greatest number of past observations. But though, in proceeding by this rule, we readily reject any fact which is unusual and incredible in an ordinary degree, yet in advancing further, the mind does not observe always the same rule; but when anything is affirmed utterly absurd and miraculous, it rather the more readily admits of such a fact upon account of that very circumstance which ought to destroy all its authority. The passion of *surprise* and *wonder,* arising from miracles, being an agreeable emotion, gives a sensible tendency towards the belief of those events from which it is derived. And this goes so far that even those who cannot enjoy this pleasure immediately, nor can believe those miraculous events of which they are informed, yet love to partake of the satisfaction at secondhand or by rebound and place a pride and delight in exciting the admiration of others.

With what greediness are the miraculous accounts of travelers received, their descriptions of sea and land monsters, their relations of wonderful adventures, strange men, and uncouth manners? But if the spirit of religion joins itself to the love of wonder, there is an end of common sense, and human testimony in these circumstances loses all pretensions to authority. A religionist may be an enthusiast and imagine he sees what has no reality. He may know his narrative to be false and yet persevere in it with the best intentions in the world, for the sake of promoting so holy a cause. Or even where this delusion does not have place, vanity, excited by so strong a temptation, operates on him more powerfully than on the rest of mankind in any other circumstances, and self-interest with equal force. His auditors may not have and commonly do not have sufficient judgment to canvass his evidence. What judgment they have, they renounce by principle in these sublime and mysterious subjects. Or if they were ever so willing to employ it, passion and a heated imagination disturb the regularity of its operations. Their credulity increases his impudence, and his impudence overpowers their credulity.

Eloquence, when at its highest pitch, leaves little room for reason or reflection, but, addressing itself entirely to the fancy or the affections, captivates the willing hearers and subdues their understanding. Happily, this pitch it seldom attains. But what a Tully or a Demosthenes could scarcely effect over a Roman or Athenian audience, every Capuchin, every itinerant or stationary teacher can perform over the generality of mankind, and in a higher degree by touching such gross and vulgar passions.

The many instances of forged miracles and prophecies and supernatural events, which, in all ages, have either been detected by contrary evidence or which detect themselves by their absurdity, prove sufficiently the strong propensity of mankind to the extraordinary and the marvelous and ought reasonably to beget a suspicion against all relations of this kind. This is our natural way of thinking, even with regard to the most common and most credible events. For instance, there is no kind of report which rises so easily and spreads so quickly, especially in country places and provincial towns, as those concerning marriages, inasmuch that two young persons of equal condition never see each other twice but the whole neighborhood immediately join them together. The pleasure of telling a piece of news so interesting, of propagating it, and of being the first reporters of it, spreads the intelligence. And this is so well known that no man of sense gives attention to these reports until he finds them confirmed by some greater evidence. Do not the same passions, and others still stronger, incline the generality of mankind to believe and report with the greatest vehemence and assurance all religious miracles?

Thirdly, it forms a strong presumption against all supernatural and miraculous relations that they are observed chiefly to abound among ignorant and barbarous nations; or, if a civilized people has ever given admission to any of them, that people will be found to have received them from ignorant and barbarous ancestors, who transmitted them with that inviolable sanction and authority which always attend received opinions. When we peruse the first histories of all nations, we are apt to imagine ourselves transported into some new world where the whole frame of nature is disjointed and every element performs its operations in a different manner from what it does at present. Battles, revolutions, pestilence, famine, and death are never the effect of those natural causes which we

experience. Prodigies, omens, oracles, judgments, quite obscure the few natural events that are intermingled with them. But as the former grow thinner every page, in proportion as we advance nearer the enlightened ages, we soon learn that there is nothing mysterious or supernatural in the case, but that all proceeds from the usual propensity of mankind towards the marvelous, and that, though this inclination may at intervals receive a check from sense and learning, it can never be thoroughly extirpated from human nature.

It is strange, a judicious reader is apt to say upon the perusal of these wonderful historians, that *such prodigious events never happen in our days.* But it is nothing strange, I hope, that men should lie in all ages. You must surely have seen instances enough of that frailty. You have yourself heard many such marvelous relations started which, being treated with scorn by all the wise and judicious, have at last been abandoned even by the vulgar. Be assured that those renowned lies which have spread and flourished to such a monstrous height arose from like beginnings, but being sown in a more proper soil, shot up at last into prodigies almost equal to those which they relate.

It was a wise policy in that false prophet Alexander, who, though now forgotten, was once so famous, to lay the first scene of his impostures in Paphlagonia, where, as Lucian tells us, the people were extremely ignorant and stupid and ready to swallow even the grossest delusion. People at a distance, who are weak enough to think the matter at all worth inquiry, have no opportunity of receiving better information. The stories come magnified to them by a hundred circumstances. Fools are industrious in propagating the imposture, while the wise and learned are contented, in general, to deride its absurdity, without informing themselves of the particular facts by which it may be distinctly refuted. And thus the impostor above mentioned was enabled to proceed from his ignorant Paphlagonians to the enlisting of votaries, even among the Greek philosophers and men of the most eminent rank and distinction in Rome — no, could engage the attention of that sage emperor Marcus Aurelius so far as to make him trust the success of a military expedition to his delusive prophecies.

The advantages are so great of starting an imposture

among an ignorant people that, even though the delusion should be too gross to impose on the generality of them (*which, though seldom, is sometimes the case*), it has a much better chance for succeeding in remote countries than if the first scene had been laid in a city renowned for arts and knowledge. The most ignorant and barbarous of these barbarians carry the report abroad. None of their countrymen have a large correspondence or sufficient credit and authority to contradict and beat down the delusion. Men's inclination to the marvelous has full opportunity to display itself. And thus a story which is universally exploded in the place where it was first started shall pass for certain at a thousand miles distance. But had Alexander fixed his residence at Athens, the philosophers of that renowned mart of learning had immediately spread throughout the whole Roman empire their sense of the matter, which, being supported by so great authority and displayed by all the force of reason and eloquence, had entirely opened the eyes of mankind. It is true, Lucian, passing by chance through, had an opportunity of performing this good office. But, though much to be wished, it does not always happen that every Alexander meets with a Lucian, ready to expose and detect his impostures.

I may add, as a *fourth* reason which diminishes the authority of prodigies, that there is no testimony for any, even those which have not been expressly detected, that is not opposed by an infinite number of witnesses, so that not only the miracle destroys the credit of testimony, but the testimony destroys itself. To make this the better understood, let us consider that in matters of religion whatever is different is contrary and that it is impossible the religions of ancient Rome, of Turkey, of Siam, and of China should all of them be established on any solid foundation. Every miracle, therefore, pretended to have been wrought in any of these religions (and all of them abound in miracles), as its direct scope is to establish the particular system to which it is attributed, so it has the same force, though more indirectly, to overthrow every other system. In destroying a rival system, it likewise destroys the credit of those miracles on which that system was established, so that all the prodigies of different religions are to be regarded as contrary facts and the evidences of these prodigies, whether weak or strong, as opposite to each other. According to this method of reasoning, when we believe any miracle of Mahomet or his successors, we have for our warrant the testimony of a few barbarous Arabians. And, on the other hand, we are to regard the authority of Titus Livius, Plutarch, Tacitus, and, in short, of all the authors and witnesses, Greek, Chinese, and Roman Catholic, who have related any miracle in their particular religion—I say, we are to regard their testimony in the same light as if they had mentioned that Mahometan miracle and had in express terms contradicted it with the same certainty as they have for the miracle they relate. This argument may appear over subtle and refined, but is not in reality different from the reasoning of a judge who supposes that the credit of two witnesses maintaining a crime against anyone is destroyed by the testimony of two others who affirm him to have been two hundred leagues distant at the same instant when the crime is said to have been committed.

One of the best attested miracles in all profane history is that which Tacitus reports of Vespasian, who cured a blind man in Alexandria by means of his spittle and a lame man by the mere touch of his foot, in obedience to a vision of the god Serapis, who had enjoined them to have recourse to the Emperor for these miraculous cures. The story may be seen in that fine historian, where every circumstance seems to add weight to the testimony, and might be displayed at large with all the force of argument and eloquence if anyone were now concerned to enforce the evidence of that exploded and idolatrous superstition: the gravity, solidity, age, and probity of so great an emperor, who, through the whole course of his life, conversed in a familiar manner with his friends and courtiers and never affected those extraordinary airs of divinity assumed by Alexander and Demetrius; the historian, a contemporary writer noted for candor and veracity and, in addition, the greatest and most penetrating genius perhaps of all antiquity, and so free from any tendency to credulity that he even lies under the contrary imputation of atheism and profaneness; the persons from whose authority he related the miracle of established character for judgment and veracity, as we may well presume; eyewitnesses of the fact, and confirming their testimony after the Flavian family was despoiled of the empire and could no longer give any reward as the price of a lie. *Utrumque, qui interfuere, nunc quoque memorant, postquam nullum mendacio pretium.*[27] To which, if we add the public nature of the facts, as related, it will appear that no evidence can well be supposed stronger for so gross and so palpable a falsehood.

There is also a memorable story related by Cardinal de Retz, which may well deserve our consideration. When that intriguing politician fled into Spain to avoid the persecution of his enemies, he passed through Saragossa, the capital of Arragon, where he was shown, in the cathedral, a man who had served seven years as a doorkeeper and was well known to everybody in town who had ever paid his devotions at that church. He had been seen for so long a time wanting a leg, but recovered that limb by the rubbing of holy oil upon the stump; and when the Cardinal examined it, he found it to be a true natural leg like the other. This miracle was vouched by all the canons of the church; and the whole company in town were appealed to for a confirmation of the fact, whom the cardinal found, by their zealous devotion, to be thorough believers of the miracle. Here the relater was also contemporary to the supposed prodigy, of an incredulous and libertine character, as well as of great genius; the miracle of so *singular* a nature as could scarcely admit of a counterfeit, and the witnesses very numerous, and all of them, in a manner, spectators of the fact to which they gave their testimony. And what adds mightily to the force of the evidence and may double our surprise on this occasion is that the Cardinal himself, who relates the story, does not seem to give any credit to it and, consequently, cannot be suspected of any concurrence in the holy fraud. He considered justly that it was not requisite, in order to reject a fact of this nature, to be able accurately to disprove the testimony and to trace its falsehood through all the circumstances of knavery and credulity which produced it. He knew that, as this was commonly altogether impossible at any small distance of time and place, so was it extremely difficult, even where one was immediately

present, by reason of the bigotry, ignorance, cunning, and roguery of a great part of mankind. He therefore concluded, like a just reasoner, that such an evidence carried falsehood upon the very face of it and that a miracle supported by any human testimony was more properly a subject of derision than of argument.

There surely never was a greater number of miracles ascribed to one person than those which were lately said to have been wrought in France upon the tomb of Abbé Paris, the famous Jansenist, with whose sanctity the people were so long deluded. The curing of the sick, giving hearing to the deaf and sight to the blind, were everywhere talked of as the usual effects of that holy sepulcher. But what is more extraordinary, many of the miracles were immediately proved upon the spot, before judges of unquestioned integrity, attested by witnesses of credit and distinction, in a learned age, and on the most eminent theater that is now in the world. Nor is this all: A relation of them was published and dispersed everywhere, nor were the *Jesuits*, though a learned body supported by the civil magistrate and determined enemies to those opinions in whose favor the miracles were said to have been wrought, ever able distinctly to refute or detect them. Where shall we find such a number of circumstances agreeing to the corroboration of one fact? And what have we to oppose to such a cloud of witnesses but the absolute impossibility or miraculous nature of the events which they relate? And this, surely, in the eyes of all reasonable people, will alone be regarded as a sufficient refutation.

Is the consequence just, because some human testimony has the utmost force and authority in some cases, when it relates the battle of Philippi or Pharsalia, for instance, that therefore all kinds of testimony must in all cases have equal force and authority? Suppose that the Caesarean and Pompeian factions had, each of them, claimed the victory in these battles, and that the historians of each party had uniformly ascribed the advantage to their own side, how could mankind, at this distance, have been able to determine between them? The contrariety is equally strong between the miracles related by Herodotus or Plutarch and those delivered by Mariana, Bede, or any monkish historian.

The wise lend a very academic faith to every report

---

27. [Even now, those who were present speak of each event, though there is no reward for the lie.]

which favors the passion of the reporter, whether it magnifies his country, his family, or himself, or in any other way strikes in with his natural inclinations and propensities. But what greater temptation than to appear a missionary, a prophet, an ambassador from heaven? Who would not encounter many dangers and difficulties in order to attain so sublime a character? Or if, by the help of vanity and a heated imagination, a man has first made a convert of himself and entered seriously into the delusion, who ever scruples to make use of pious frauds in support of so holy and meritorious a cause?

The smallest spark may here kindle into the greatest flame, because the materials are always prepared for it. The *avidum genus auricularum*,[28] the gazing populace, receive greedily, without examination, whatever soothes superstition and promotes wonder.

How many stories of this nature have, in all ages, been detected and exploded in their infancy? How many more have been celebrated for a time and have afterwards sunk into neglect and oblivion? Where such reports, therefore, fly about, the solution of the phenomenon is obvious, and we judge in conformity to regular experience and observation when we account for it by the known and natural principles of credulity and delusion. And shall we, rather than have a recourse to so natural a solution, allow of a miraculous violation of the most established laws of nature?

I need not mention the difficulty of detecting a falsehood in any private or even public history at the place where it is said to happen, much more when the scene is removed to ever so small a distance. Even a court of judicature, with all the authority, accuracy, and judgment which they can employ, find themselves often at a loss to distinguish between truth and falsehood in the most recent actions. But the matter never comes to any issue, if trusted to the common method of altercation and debate and flying rumors, especially when men's passions have taken part on either side.

In the infancy of new religions, the wise and learned commonly esteem the matter too inconsiderable to deserve their attention or regard. And when

28. [Lucretius IV, 594. "A gossip-hungry race."]

afterwards they would willingly detect the cheat in order to undeceive the deluded multitude, the season is now past, and the records and witnesses which might clear up the matter have perished beyond recovery.

No means of detection remain but those which must be drawn from the very testimony itself of the reporters. And these, though always sufficient with the judicious and knowing, are commonly too fine to fall under the comprehension of the vulgar.

Upon the whole, then, it appears that no testimony for any kind of miracle has ever amounted to a probability, much less to a proof; and that, even supposing it amounted to a proof, it would be opposed by another proof derived from the very nature of the fact which it would endeavor to establish. It is experience only which gives authority to human testimony, and it is the same experience which assures us of the laws of nature. When, therefore, these two kinds of experience are contrary, we have nothing to do but subtract the one from the other and embrace an opinion either on one side or the other, with that assurance which arises from the remainder. But according to the principle here explained, this subtraction with regard to all popular religions amounts to an entire annihilation, and, therefore, we may establish it as a maxim that no human testimony can have such force as to prove a miracle and make it a just foundation for any such system of religion.

I beg the limitations here made may be remarked, when I say that a miracle can never be proved so as to be the foundation of a system of religion. For I admit that otherwise there may possibly be miracles or violations of the usual course of nature of such a kind as to admit of proof from human testimony; though perhaps it will be impossible to find any such in all the records of history. Thus, suppose all authors, in all languages, agree that from the first of January 1600 there was a total darkness over the whole earth for eight days; suppose that the tradition of this extraordinary event is still strong and lively among the people—that all travelers who return from foreign countries bring us accounts of the same tradition without the least variation or contradiction—it is evident that our present philosophers, instead of doubting the fact, ought to receive it as certain and ought to search for the causes from which it might be derived. The decay, corruption, and dissolution of nature is an event rendered probable by so many analogies that any phenomenon which seems to have a tendency towards that catastrophe comes within the reach of human testimony, if that testimony is very extensive and uniform.

But suppose that all the historians who treat of England should agree that on the first of January 1600, Queen Elizabeth died; that both before and after her death she was seen by her physicians and the whole court, as is usual with persons of her rank; that her successor was acknowledged and proclaimed by the parliament; and that, after being interred a month, she again appeared, resumed the throne, and governed England for three years—I must confess that I should be surprised at the concurrence of so many odd circumstances, but should not have the least inclination to believe so miraculous an event. I should not doubt of her pretended death and of those other public circumstances that followed it; I should only assert it to have been pretended, and that it neither was nor possibly could be real. You would in vain object to me the difficulty and almost impossibility of deceiving the world in an affair of such consequence; the wisdom and solid judgment of that renowned queen, with the little or no advantage which she could reap from so poor an artifice—all this might astonish me, but I would still reply that the knavery and folly of men are such common phenomena that I should rather believe the most extraordinary events to arise from their concurrence than admit of so signal a violation of the laws of nature.

But should this miracle be ascribed to any new system of religion, men in all ages have been so much imposed on by ridiculous stories of that kind that this very circumstance would be a full proof of a cheat, and sufficient, with all men of sense, not only to make them reject the fact, but even reject it without further examination. Though the Being to whom the miracle is ascribed is in this case Almighty, it does not, upon that account, become a whit more probable, since it is impossible for us to know the attributes or actions of such a Being otherwise than from the experience which we have of his productions in the usual course of nature. This still reduces us to past observation and

obliges us to compare the instances of the violation of truth in the testimony of men with those of the violation of the laws of nature by miracles, in order to judge which of them is most likely and probable. As the violations of truth are more common in the testimony concerning religious miracles than in that concerning any other matter of fact, this must diminish very much the authority of the former testimony and make us form a general resolution, never to lend any attention to it, with whatever specious pretense it may be covered.

Lord Bacon seems to have embraced the same principles of reasoning. "We ought," says he, "make a collection or particular history of all monsters and prodigious births or productions and, in a word, of everything new, rare, and extraordinary in nature. But this must be done with the most severe scrutiny, lest we depart from truth. Above all, every relation must be considered as suspicious which depends in any degree upon religion, as the prodigies of Livy. And no less so, everything that is to be found in the writers of natural magic or alchemy or such authors who seem, all of them, to have an unconquerable appetite for falsehood and fable."[29]

I am the better pleased with the method of reasoning here delivered, as I think it may serve to confound those dangerous friends or disguised enemies to the *Christian Religion* who have undertaken to defend it by the principles of human reason. Our most holy religion is founded on faith, not on reason; and it is a sure method of exposing it to put it to such a trial as it is by no means fitted to endure. To make this more evident, let us examine those miracles related in Scripture and, not to lose ourselves in too wide a field, let us confine ourselves to such as we find in the *Pentateuch*, which we shall examine according to the principles of these pretended Christians, not as the word or testimony of God himself, but as the production of a mere human writer and historian. Here then we are first to consider a book presented to us by a barbarous and ignorant people, written in an age when they were still more barbarous and, in all probability, long after the facts which it relates, corroborated by no concurring testimony, and

---

29. *New Organon* II, aphorism 29.

resembling those fabulous accounts which every nation gives of its origin. Upon reading this book we find it full of prodigies and miracles. It gives an account of a state of the world and of human nature entirely different from the present: of our fall from that state; of the age of man extended to near a thousand years; of the destruction of the world by a deluge; of the arbitrary choice of one people as the favorites of heaven, and that people the countrymen of the author; of their deliverance from bondage by prodigies the most astonishing imaginable; I desire anyone to lay his hand upon his heart and, after a serious consideration, declare whether he thinks that the falsehood of such a book, supported by such a testimony, would be more extraordinary and miraculous than all the miracles it relates—which is, however, necessary to make it be received according to the measures of probability above established.

What we have said of miracles may be applied without any variation to prophecies; and, indeed, all prophecies are real miracles and as such only can be admitted as proofs of any revelation. If it did not exceed the capacity of human nature to foretell future events, it would be absurd to employ any prophecy as an argument for a divine mission or authority from heaven. So that, upon the whole, we may conclude that the Christian religion not only was at first attended with miracles, but even at this day cannot be believed by any reasonable person without one. Mere reason is insufficient to convince us of its veracity. And whoever is moved by faith to assent to it is conscious of a continued miracle in his own person which subverts all the principles of his understanding and gives him a determination to believe what is most contrary to custom and experience.

Section XI: *Of a Particular Providence and of a Future State.*[30]

I was lately engaged in conversation with a friend who loves skeptical paradoxes, where, though he advanced many principles of which I can by no means approve, yet as they seem to be curious and to bear some

relation to the chain of reasoning carried on throughout this inquiry, I shall here copy them from my memory as accurately as I can in order to submit them to the judgment of the reader.

Our conversation began with my admiring the singular good fortune of philosophy, which, as it requires entire liberty above all other privileges and chiefly flourishes from the free opposition of sentiments and argumentation, received its first birth in an age and country of freedom and toleration, and was never cramped, even in its most extravagant principles, by any creeds, confessions, or penal statutes. For, except the banishment of Protagoras and the death of Socrates, which last event proceeded partly from other motives, there are scarcely any instances to be met with in ancient history of this bigoted jealousy with which the present age is so much infested. Epicurus lived at Athens to an advanced age in peace and tranquillity. Epicureans were even admitted to receive the sacerdotal character and to officiate at the altar in the most sacred rites of the established religion. And the public encouragement of pensions and salaries was afforded equally by the wisest of all the Roman emperors to the professors of every sect of philosophy. How requisite such kind of treatment was to philosophy, in her early youth, will easily be conceived, if we reflect that even at present, when she may be supposed more hardy and robust, she bears with much difficulty the inclemency of the seasons and those harsh winds of calumny and persecution which blow upon her.

You admire, says my friend, as the singular good fortune of philosophy what seems to result from the natural course of things and to be unavoidable in every age and nation. This pertinacious bigotry, of which you complain as so fatal to philosophy, is really her offspring who, after allying with superstition, separates himself entirely from the interest of his parent and becomes her most inveterate enemy and persecutor. Speculative dogmas of religion, the present occasions of such furious dispute, could not possibly be conceived or admitted in the early ages of the world, when mankind, being wholly illiterate, formed an idea of religion more suitable to their weak apprehension and composed their sacred tenets of such tales chiefly as were the objects of traditional belief more

---

30. [In another edition, this section is titled: Of the Practical Consequences of Natural Religion.]

than of argument or disputation. After the first alarm, therefore, was over, which arose from the new paradoxes and principles of the philosophers, these teachers seem ever after, during the ages of antiquity, to have lived in great harmony with the established superstition and to have made a fair partition of mankind between them—the former claiming all the learned and wise, the latter possessing all the vulgar and illiterate.

It seems then, I say, that you leave politics entirely out of the question and never suppose that a wise magistrate can justly be jealous of certain tenets of philosophy, such as those of Epicurus, which, denying a divine existence and, consequently, a providence and a future state, seem to loosen in a great measure the ties of morality and may be supposed, for that reason, pernicious to the peace of civil society.

I know, he replied, that in fact these persecutions never, in any age, proceeded from calm reason or from experience of the pernicious consequences of philosophy, but arose entirely from passion and prejudice. But what if I should advance further and assert that, if Epicurus had been accused before the people by any of the *sycophants* or informers of those days, he could easily have defended his cause and proved his principles of philosophy to be as salutary as those of his adversaries who endeavored with such zeal to expose him to the public hatred and jealousy?

I wish, I said, you would try your eloquence upon so extraordinary a topic and make a speech for Epicurus which might satisfy, not the mob of Athens, if you will allow that ancient and polite city to have contained any mob, but the more philosophical part of his audience, such as might be supposed capable of comprehending his arguments.

The matter would not be difficult upon such conditions, he replied; and if you please, I shall suppose myself Epicurus for a moment and make you stand for the Athenian people, and shall deliver you such an harangue as will fill all the urn with white beans and leave not a black one to gratify the malice of my adversaries.

Very well. Pray proceed upon these suppositions.

I come here, O you Athenians, to justify in your assembly what I maintained in my school, and I find myself impeached by furious antagonists, instead of reasoning with calm and dispassionate inquirers. Your deliberations, which of right should be directed to questions of public good and the interest of the commonwealth, are diverted to the disquisitions of speculative philosophy, and these magnificent, but perhaps fruitless inquiries take place of your more familiar, but more useful occupations. But so far as in me lies, I will prevent this abuse. We shall not here dispute concerning the origin and government of worlds. We shall only inquire how far such questions concern the public interest. And if I can persuade you that they are entirely indifferent to the peace of society and security of government, I hope that you will presently send us back to our schools, there to examine at leisure the question, the most sublime, but, at the same time, the most speculative of all philosophy.

The religious philosophers, not satisfied with the tradition of your forefathers and doctrine of your priests (in which I willingly acquiesce), indulge a rash curiosity in trying how far they can establish religion upon the principles of reason; and they thereby excite, instead of satisfying, the doubts which naturally arise from a diligent and scrutinous inquiry. They paint in the most magnificent colors the order, beauty, and wise arrangement of the universe and then ask if such a glorious display of intelligence could proceed from the fortuitous concourse of atoms or if chance could produce what the greatest genius can never sufficiently admire. I shall not examine the justness of this argument. I shall allow it to be as solid as my antagonists and accusers can desire. It is sufficient if I can prove, from this very reasoning, that the question is entirely speculative, and that, when, in my philosophical disquisitions, I deny a providence and a future state, I do not undermine the foundations of society, but advance principles which they themselves, upon their own topics, if they argue consistently, must allow to be solid and satisfactory.

You then, who are my accusers, have acknowledged that the chief or sole argument for a divine existence (which I never questioned) is derived from the order of nature, where there appear such marks of intelligence and design that you think it extravagant to assign for its cause either chance or the blind and unguided force of matter. You allow that this is an argument drawn from effects to causes. From the order of the work, you infer that there must have been project and forethought in the workman. If you cannot make out this point, you allow that your conclusion fails, and you do not pretend to establish the conclusion in a greater latitude than the phenomena of nature will justify. These are your concessions. I desire you to mark the consequences.

When we infer any particular cause from an effect, we must proportion the one to the other and can never be allowed to ascribe to the cause any qualities but what are exactly sufficient to produce the effect. A body of ten ounces raised in any scale may serve as a proof that the counterbalancing weight exceeds ten ounces, but can never afford a reason that it exceeds a hundred. If the cause assigned for any effect is not sufficient to produce it, we must either reject that cause or add to it such qualities as will give it a just proportion to the effect. But if we ascribe to it further qualities or affirm it capable of producing other effects, we can only indulge the license of conjecture and arbitrarily suppose the existence of qualities and energies without reason or authority.

The same rule holds whether the cause assigned is brute unconscious matter or a rational intelligent being. If the cause is known only by the effect, we never ought to ascribe to it any qualities beyond what are precisely requisite to produce the effect; nor can we, by any rules of just reasoning, return back from the cause and infer other effects from it, beyond those by which alone it is known to us. No one, merely from the sight of one of Zeuxis's pictures, could know that he was also a statuary or architect and was an artist no less skillful in stone and marble than in colors. The talents and taste displayed in the particular work before us—these we may safely conclude the workman to be possessed of. The cause must be proportioned to the effect; and if we exactly and precisely proportion it, we shall never find in it any qualities that point further or afford an inference concerning any other design or performance. Such qualities must be somewhat beyond what is merely requisite for producing the effect which we examine.

Allowing, therefore, the gods to be the authors of the existence or order of the universe, it follows that they possess that precise degree of power, intelligence, and benevolence which appears in their workman-

ship, but nothing further can ever be proved, except we call in the assistance of exaggeration and flattery to supply the defects of argument and reasoning. So far as the traces of any attributes at present appear, so far may we conclude these attributes to exist. The supposition of further attributes is mere hypothesis, much more the supposition that in distant regions of space or periods of time there has been or will be a more magnificent display of these attributes and a scheme of administration more suitable to such imaginary virtues. We can never be allowed to mount up from the universe, the effect, to Jupiter, the cause, and then descend downwards to infer any new effect from that cause, as if the present effects alone were not entirely worthy of the glorious attributes which we ascribe to that deity. The knowledge of the cause being derived solely from the effect, they must be exactly adjusted to each other and the one can never refer to anything further or be the foundation of any new inference and conclusion.

You find certain phenomena in nature. You seek a cause or author. You imagine that you have found him. You afterwards become so enamored of this offspring of your brain that you imagine it impossible but he must produce something greater and more perfect than the present scene of things, which is so full of ill and disorder. You forget that this superlative intelligence and benevolence are entirely imaginary, or, at least, without any foundation in reason, and that you have no ground to ascribe to him any qualities but what you see he has actually exerted and displayed in his productions. Let your gods, therefore, O philosophers, be suited to the present appearances of nature, and do not presume to alter these appearances by arbitrary suppositions in order to suit them to the attributes which you so fondly ascribe to your deities.

When priests and poets, supported by your authority, O Athenians, talk of a golden or silver age which preceded the present state of vice and misery, I hear them with attention and with reverence. But when philosophers who pretend to neglect authority and to cultivate reason hold the same discourse, I do not pay them, I admit, the same obsequious submission and pious deference. I ask: Who carried them into the celestial regions, who admitted them into the councils of the gods, who opened to them the book of fate that they thus rashly affirm that their deities have executed or will execute any purpose beyond what has actually appeared? If they tell me that they have mounted on the steps or by the gradual ascent of reason and by drawing inferences from effects to causes, I still insist that they have aided the ascent of reason by the wings of imagination; otherwise they could not thus change their manner of inference and argue from causes to effects, presuming that a more perfect production than the present world would be more suitable to such perfect beings as the gods and forgetting that they have no reason to ascribe to these celestial beings any perfection or any attribute but what can be found in the present world.

Hence all the fruitless industry to account for the ill appearances of nature and save the honor of the gods, while we must acknowledge the reality of that evil and disorder with which the world so much abounds. The obstinate and intractable qualities of matter, we are told, or the observance of general laws, or some such reason, is the sole cause which controlled the power and benevolence of Jupiter and obliged him to create mankind and every sensible creature so imperfect and so unhappy. These attributes, then, are, it seems, beforehand taken for granted in their greatest latitude. And upon that supposition, I admit that such conjectures may, perhaps, be admitted as plausible solutions of the ill phenomena. But still I ask: Why take these attributes for granted, or why ascribe to the cause any qualities but what actually appear in the effect? Why torture your brain to justify the course of nature upon suppositions which, for all you know, may be entirely imaginary and of which there are to be found no traces in the course of nature?

The religious hypothesis, therefore, must be considered only as a particular method of accounting for the visible phenomena of the universe. But no just reasoner will ever presume to infer from it any single fact and alter or add to the phenomena in any single particular. If you think that the appearances of things prove such causes, it is allowable for you to draw an inference concerning the existence of these causes. In such complicated and sublime subjects, everyone should be indulged in the liberty of conjecture and argument. But here you ought to rest. If you come

backward and, arguing from your inferred causes, conclude that any other fact has existed or will exist in the course of nature which may serve as a fuller display of particular attributes, I must admonish you that you have departed from the method of reasoning attached to the present subject and have certainly added something to the attributes of the cause beyond what appears in the effect; otherwise you could never, with tolerable sense or propriety, add anything to the effect in order to render it more worthy of the cause.

Where, then, is the odiousness of that doctrine which I teach in my school or, rather, which I examine in my gardens? Or what do you find in this whole question in which the security of good morals or the peace and order of society are in the least concerned?

I deny a providence, you say, and supreme governor of the world, who guides the course of events, and punishes the vicious with infamy and disappointment, and rewards the virtuous with honor and success in all their undertakings. But surely I do not deny the course itself of events, which lies open to everyone's inquiry and examination. I acknowledge that, in the present order of things, virtue is attended with more peace of mind than vice and meets with a more favorable reception from the world. I am sensible that, according to the past experience of mankind, friendship is the chief joy of human life and moderation the only source of tranquillity and happiness. I never balance between the virtuous and the vicious course of life, but am sensible that, to a well-disposed mind, every advantage is on the side of the former. And what can you say more, allowing all your suppositions and reasonings? You tell me, indeed, that this disposition of things proceeds from intelligence and design. But whatever it proceeds from, the disposition itself, on which depends our happiness or misery and consequently our conduct and deportment in life, is still the same. It is still open for me, as well as you, to regulate my behavior by my experience of past events. And if you affirm that, while a divine providence is allowed, and a supreme distributive justice in the universe, I ought to expect some more particular reward of the good and punishment of the bad beyond the ordinary course of events, I here find the same fallacy which I have before endeavored to detect. You persist in imagining that, if we grant that divine existence for which you so earnestly contend, you may safely infer consequences from it and add something to the experienced order of nature by arguing from the attributes which you ascribe to your gods. You do not seem to remember that all your reasonings on this subject can only be drawn from effects to causes and that every argument deduced from causes to effects must of necessity be a gross sophism, since it is impossible for you to know anything of the cause but what you have antecedently not inferred, but discovered to the full in the effect.

But what must a philosopher think of those vain reasoners who, instead of regarding the present scene of things as the sole object of their contemplation, so far reverse the whole course of nature as to render this life merely a passage to something further—a porch which leads to a greater and vastly different building, a prologue which serves only to introduce the piece and give it more grace and propriety? From where, do you think, can such philosophers derive their idea of the gods? From their own conceit and imagination surely. For if they derived it from the present phenomena, it would never point to anything further, but must be exactly adjusted to them. That the divinity may *possibly* be endowed with attributes which we have never seen exerted, may be governed by principles of action which we cannot discover to be satisfied. All this will freely be allowed. But still this is mere *possibility* and hypothesis. We never can have reason to *infer* any attributes or any principles of action in him, but so far as we know them to have been exerted and satisfied.

Are there any marks of a distributive justice in the world? If you answer in the affirmative, I conclude that, since justice here exerts itself, it is satisfied. If you reply in the negative, I conclude that you have then no reason to ascribe justice, in our sense of it, to the gods. If you hold a medium between affirmation and negation, by saying that the justice of the gods at present exerts itself in part, but not in its full extent, I answer that you have no reason to give it any particular extent, but only so far as you see it, *at present*, exert itself.

Thus I bring the dispute, O Athenians, to a short issue with my antagonists. The course of nature lies open to my contemplation as well as to theirs. The

experienced train of events is the great standard by which we all regulate our conduct. Nothing else can be appealed to in the field or in the senate. Nothing else ought ever to be heard of in the school or in the closet. In vain would our limited understanding break through those boundaries which are too narrow for our fond imagination. While we argue from the course of nature and infer a particular intelligent cause which first bestowed and still preserves order in the universe, we embrace a principle which is both uncertain and useless. It is uncertain because the subject lies entirely beyond the reach of human experience. It is useless because our knowledge of this cause being derived entirely from the course of nature, we can never, according to the rules of just reasoning, return back from the cause with any new inference or, making additions to the common and experienced course of nature, establish any new principles of conduct and behavior.

I observe (I said, finding he had finished his harangue) that you do not neglect the artifice of the demagogues of old, and as you were pleased to make me stand for the people, you insinuate yourself into my favor by embracing those principles to which, you know, I have always expressed a particular attachment. But allowing you to make experience (as indeed I think you ought) the only standard of our judgment concerning this and all other questions of fact, I do not doubt but, from the very same experience to which you appeal, it may be possible to refute this reasoning which you have put into the mouth of Epicurus. If you saw, for instance, a half-finished building surrounded with heaps of brick and stone and mortar and all the instruments of masonry, could you not *infer* from the effect that it was a work of design and contrivance? And could you not return again, from this inferred cause, to infer new additions to the effect and conclude that the building would soon be finished and receive all the further improvements which art could bestow upon it? If you saw upon the seashore the print of one human foot, you would conclude that a man had passed that way and that he had also left the traces of the other foot, though effaced by the rolling of the sands or inundation of the waters. Why then do you refuse to admit the same method of reasoning with regard to the order of nature? Consider the world and the present life only as an imperfect building from which you can infer a superior intelligence and, arguing from that superior intelligence which can leave nothing imperfect, why may you not infer a more finished scheme or plan which will receive its completion in some distant point of space or time? Are not these methods of reasoning exactly similar? And under what pretense can you embrace the one while you reject the other?

The infinite difference of the subjects, he replied, is a sufficient foundation for this difference in my conclusions. In works of human art and contrivance, it is allowable to advance from the effect to the cause, and, returning back from the cause, to form new inferences concerning the effect and examine the alterations which it has probably undergone or may still undergo. But what is the foundation of this method of reasoning? Plainly this: that man is a being whom we know by experience, whose motives and designs we are acquainted with, and whose projects and inclinations have a certain connection and coherence according to the laws which nature has established for the government of such a creature. When, therefore, we find that any work has proceeded from the skill and industry of man, as we are otherwise acquainted with the nature of the animal, we can draw a hundred inferences concerning what may be expected from him; and these inferences will all be founded in experience and observation. But did we know man only from the single work or production which we examine, it would be impossible for us to argue in this manner, because our knowledge of all the qualities which we ascribe to him, being in that case derived from the production, it is impossible they could point to anything further or be the foundation of any new inference. The print of a foot in the sand can only prove, when considered alone, that there was some figure adapted to it by which it was produced. But the print of a human foot proves likewise, from our other experience, that there was probably another foot which also left its impression, though effaced by time or other accidents. Here we mount from the effect to the cause, and, descending again from the cause, infer alterations in the effect; but this is not a continuation of the same simple chain of reasoning. We comprehend in this case a hundred

other experiences and observations concerning the *usual* figure and members of that species of animal without which this method of argument must be considered as fallacious and sophistical.

The case is not the same with our reasonings from the works of nature. The Deity is known to us only by his productions and is a single being in the universe, not comprehended under any species or genus from whose experienced attributes or qualities we can, by analogy, infer any attribute or quality in him. As the universe shows wisdom and goodness, we infer wisdom and goodness. As it shows a particular degree of these perfections, we infer a particular degree of them precisely adapted to the effect which we examine. But further attributes or further degrees of the same attributes we can never be authorized to infer or suppose by any rules of just reasoning. Now, without some such license of supposition, it is impossible for us to argue from the cause or infer any alteration in the effect beyond what has immediately fallen under our observation. Greater good produced by this Being must still prove a greater degree of goodness. A more impartial distribution of rewards and punishments must proceed from a greater regard to justice and equity. Every supposed addition to the works of nature makes an addition to the attributes of the Author of nature, and, consequently, being entirely unsupported by any reason or argument, can never be admitted but as mere conjecture and hypothesis.[31]

31. In general, it may, I think, be established as a maxim that where any cause is known only by its particular effects, it must be impossible to infer any new effects from that cause, since the qualities which are requisite to produce these new effects along with the former must either be different, or superior, or of more extensive operation than those which simply produced the effect, from which alone the cause is supposed to be known to us. We can never, therefore, have any reason to suppose the existence of these qualities. To say that the new effects proceed only from a continuation of the same energy, which is already known from the first effects, will not remove the difficulty. For even granting this to be the case (which can seldom be supposed), the very continuation and exertion of a like energy (for it is impossible it can be absolutely the same), I say, this exertion of a like energy, in a different period of space and time, is a very arbitrary supposition and what there cannot possibly be any traces of in the effects from which all our knowledge of the cause is originally derived. Let the *inferred* cause be exactly proportioned (as it should be) to the known effect; and it is

The great source of our mistake in this subject and of the unbounded license of conjecture which we indulge is that we tacitly consider ourselves as in the place of the Supreme Being and conclude that he will, on every occasion, observe the same conduct which we ourselves, in his situation, would have embraced as reasonable and eligible. But, besides that the ordinary course of nature may convince us that almost everything is regulated by principles and maxims very different from ours—besides this, I say, it must evidently appear contrary to all rules of analogy to reason from the intentions and projects of men to those of a Being so different and so much superior. In human nature there is a certain experienced coherence of designs and inclinations, so that when, from any fact, we have discovered one intention of any man, it may often be reasonable, from experience, to infer another and draw a long chain of conclusions concerning his past or future conduct. But this method of reasoning can never have place with regard to a Being so remote and incomprehensible, who bears much less analogy to any other being in the universe than the sun to a waxen taper, and who discovers himself only by some faint traces or outlines beyond which we have no authority to ascribe to him any attribute or perfection. What we imagine to be a superior perfection may really be a defect. Or were it ever so much a perfection, the ascribing of it to the Supreme Being, where it does not appear to have been really exerted to the full in his works, savors more of flattery and panegyric than of just reasoning and sound philosophy. All the philosophy, therefore, in the world and all the religion, which is nothing but a species of philosophy, will never be able to carry us beyond the usual course of experience or give us measures of conduct and behavior different from those which are furnished by reflections on common life. No new fact can ever be inferred from the religious hypothesis, no event foreseen or foretold, no reward or punishment expected or dreaded beyond what is already known by practice and observation. So that my apology for Epicurus will still appear solid and satisfactory, nor have the political interests of

society any connection with the philosophical disputes concerning metaphysics and religion.

There is still one circumstance, I replied, which you seem to have overlooked. Though I should allow your premises, I must deny your conclusion. You conclude that religious doctrines and reasonings *can* have no influence on life because they *ought* to have no influence, never considering that men reason not in the same manner you do, but draw many consequences from the belief of a divine Existence and suppose that the Deity will inflict punishments on vice and bestow rewards on virtue beyond what appear in the ordinary course of nature. Whether this reasoning of theirs is just or not is no matter. Its influence on their life and conduct must still be the same. And those who attempt to disabuse them of such prejudices may, for all I know, be good reasoners, but I cannot allow them to be good citizens and politicians, since they free men from one restraint upon their passions and make the infringement of the laws of society in one respect more easy and secure.

After all, I may perhaps agree to your general conclusion in favor of liberty, though upon different premises from those on which you endeavor to found it. I think that the state ought to tolerate every principle of philosophy, nor is there an instance that any government has suffered in its political interests by such indulgence. There is no enthusiasm among philosophers; their doctrines are not very alluring to the people, and no restraint can be put upon their reasonings but what must be of dangerous consequence to the sciences and even to the state, by paving the way for persecution and oppression in points where the generality of mankind are more deeply interested and concerned.

But there occurs to me (I continued) with regard to your main topic a difficulty which I shall just propose to you, without insisting on it, lest it lead into reasonings of too nice and delicate a nature. In a word, I much doubt whether it is possible for a cause to be known only by its effect (as you have all along supposed) or to be of so singular and particular a nature as to have no parallel and no similarity with any other cause or object that has ever fallen under our observation. It is only when two species of objects are found to be constantly conjoined that we can

---

impossible that it can possess any qualities from which new or different effects can be *inferred.*

infer the one from the other; and were an effect presented which was entirely singular and could not be comprehended under any known species, I do not see that we could form any conjecture or inference at all concerning its cause. If experience and observation and analogy are, indeed, the only guides which we can reasonably follow in inferences of this nature, both the effect and cause must bear a similarity and resemblance to other effects and causes which we know and which we have found in many instances to be conjoined with each other. I leave it to your own reflection to pursue the consequences of this principle. I shall just observe that, as the antagonists of Epicurus always suppose the universe, an effect quite singular and unparalleled, to be the proof of a Deity, a cause no less singular and unparalleled, your reasonings upon that supposition seem, at least, to merit our attention. There is, I admit, some difficulty how we can ever return from the cause to the effect and, reasoning from our ideas of the former, infer any alteration on the latter or any addition to it.

Section XII: *Of the Academic or Skeptical Philosophy.*

Part I.

There is not a greater number of philosophical reasonings displayed upon any subject than those which prove the existence of a Deity and refute the fallacies of *atheists*; and yet the most religious philosophers still dispute whether any man can be so blinded as to be a speculative atheist. How shall we reconcile these contradictions? The knights-errant who wandered about to clear the world of dragons and giants never entertained the least doubt with regard to the existence of these monsters.

The *skeptic* is another enemy of religion, who naturally provokes the indignation of all divines and graver philosophers, though it is certain that no man ever met with any such absurd creature or conversed with a man who had no opinion or principle concerning any subject, either of action or speculation. This begets a very natural question: What is meant by a skeptic? And how far it is possible to push these philosophical principles of doubt and uncertainty?

There is a species of skepticism, *antecedent* to all study and philosophy, which is much inculcated by Descartes and others as a sovereign preservative against error and precipitate judgment. It recommends a universal doubt not only of all our former opinions and principles, but also of our very faculties, of whose veracity, they say, we must assure ourselves by a chain of reasoning deduced from some original principle which cannot possibly be fallacious or deceitful. But neither is there any such original principle which has a prerogative above others that are self-evident and convincing. Or if there were, could we advance a step beyond it but by the use of those very faculties of which we are supposed to be already diffident. The Cartesian doubt, therefore, were it ever possible to be attained by any human creature (as it plainly is not) would be entirely incurable, and no reasoning could ever bring us to a state of assurance and conviction upon any subject.

It must, however, be confessed that this species of skepticism, when more moderate, may be understood in a very reasonable sense and is a necessary preparative to the study of philosophy by preserving a proper impartiality in our judgments and weaning our mind from all those prejudices which we may have imbibed from education or rash opinion. To begin with clear and self-evident principles, to advance by timorous and sure steps, to review frequently our conclusions and examine accurately all their consequences—though by these means we shall make both a slow and a short progress in our systems—are the only methods by which we can ever hope to reach truth and attain a proper stability and certainty in our determinations.

There is another species of skepticism, *consequent* to science and inquiry, when men are supposed to have discovered either the absolute fallaciousness of their mental faculties or their unfitness to reach any fixed determination in all those curious subjects of speculation about which they are commonly employed. Even our very senses are brought into dispute by a certain species of philosophers, and the maxims of common life are subjected to the same doubt as the most profound principles or conclusions of metaphysics and theology. As these paradoxical tenets (if they may be called tenets) are to be met with in some philosophers, and the refutation of them in several, they naturally excite our curiosity and make us inquire into the arguments on which they may be founded.

I need not insist upon the more trite topics employed by the skeptics in all ages against the evidence of *sense* such as those which are derived from the imperfection and fallaciousness of our organs on numberless occasions: the crooked appearance of an oar in water, the various aspects of objects according to their different distances, the double images which arise from the pressing one eye, with many other appearances of a like nature. These skeptical topics, indeed, are only sufficient to prove that the senses alone are not implicitly to be depended on, but that we must correct their evidence by reason and by considerations derived from the nature of the medium, the distance of the object, and the disposition of the organ, in order to render them, within their sphere, the proper *criteria* of truth and falsehood. There are other more profound arguments against the senses which do not admit of so easy a solution.

It seems evident that men are carried by a natural instinct or prepossession to repose faith in their senses, and that without any reasoning, or even almost before the use of reason, we always suppose an external universe which does not depend on our perception, but would exist though we and every sensible creature were absent or annihilated. Even the animal creation are governed by a like opinion and preserve this belief of external objects, in all their thoughts, designs, and actions.

It seems also evident that when men follow this blind and powerful instinct of nature they always suppose the very images presented by the senses to be the external objects and never entertain any suspicion that the one are nothing but representations of the other. This very table which we see white and which we feel hard is believed to exist independent of our perception and to be something external to our mind which perceives it. Our presence does not bestow being on it. Our absence does not annihilate it. It preserves its existence uniform and entire, independent of the situation of intelligent beings who perceive or contemplate it.

But this universal and primary opinion of all men is soon destroyed by the slightest philosophy which teaches us that nothing can ever be present to the mind but an image or perception, and that the senses are only the inlets through which these images are conveyed, without being able to produce any immediate intercourse between the mind and the object. The table which we see seems to diminish as we remove further from it. But the real table which exists independent of us suffers no alteration. It was, therefore, nothing but its image which was present to the mind. These are the obvious dictates of reason, and no man who reflects ever doubted that the existences which we consider when we say *this house* and *that tree* are nothing but perceptions in the mind and fleeting copies or representations of other existences which remain uniform and independent.

So far, then, are we necessitated by reasoning to contradict or depart from the primary instincts of nature and to embrace a new system with regard to the evidence of our senses. But here philosophy finds herself extremely embarrassed when she would justify this new system and obviate the cavils and objections of the skeptics. She can no longer plead the infallible and irresistible instinct of nature, for that led us to a quite different system which is acknowledged fallible and even erroneous. And to justify this pretended philosophical system by a chain of clear and convincing argument, or even any appearance of argument, exceeds the power of all human capacity.

By what argument can it be proved that the perceptions of the mind must be caused by external objects entirely different from them, though resembling them (if that is possible), and could not arise either from the energy of the mind itself, or from the suggestion of some invisible and unknown spirit, or from some other cause still more unknown to us? It is acknowledged that in fact many of these perceptions arise not from anything external, as in dreams, madness, and other diseases. And nothing can be more inexplicable than the manner in which body should so operate upon mind as ever to convey an image of itself to a substance supposed of so different and even contrary a nature.

It is a question of fact whether the perceptions of the senses are produced by external objects resembling them; how shall this question be determined? By experience, surely, as all other questions of a like nature. But here experience is and must be entirely silent. The mind never has anything present to it but the perceptions and cannot possibly reach any experience of their connection with objects. The supposition of such a connection is, therefore, without any foundation in reasoning.

To have recourse to the veracity of the supreme Being in order to prove the veracity of our senses is surely making a very unexpected circuit. If his veracity were at all concerned in this matter, our senses would be entirely infallible, because it is not possible that he can ever deceive. Not to mention that, if the external world is once called in question, we shall be at a loss to find arguments by which we may prove the existence of that Being or any of his attributes.

This is a topic, therefore, in which the profounder and more philosophical skeptics will always triumph when they endeavor to introduce a universal doubt into all subjects of human knowledge and inquiry. Do you follow the instincts and propensities of nature, may they say, in assenting to the veracity of sense? But these lead you to believe that the very perception or sensible image is the external object. Do you disclaim this principle in order to embrace a more rational opinion that the perceptions are only representations of something external? You here depart from your natural propensities and more obvious sentiments and yet are not able to satisfy your reason, which can never find any convincing argument from experience to prove that the perceptions are connected with any external objects.

There is another skeptical topic of a like nature, derived from the most profound philosophy, which might merit our attention were it requisite to dive so deep in order to discover arguments and reasonings which can so little serve to any serious purpose. It is universally allowed by modern inquirers that all the sensible qualities of objects, such as hard, soft, hot, cold, white, black, etc., are merely secondary and do not exist in the objects themselves, but are perceptions of the mind, without any external archetype or model which they represent. If this is allowed with regard to secondary qualities, it must also follow with regard to the supposed primary qualities of extension and solidity, nor can the latter be any more entitled to that denomination than the former. The idea of exten-

sion is entirely acquired from the senses of sight and feeling, and if all the qualities perceived by the senses are in the mind, not in the object, the same conclusion must reach the idea of extension which is wholly dependent on the sensible ideas or the ideas of secondary qualities. Nothing can save us from this conclusion but the asserting that the ideas of those primary qualities are attained by *abstraction*; an opinion which, if we examine it accurately, we shall find to be unintelligible and even absurd. An extension that is neither tangible nor visible cannot possibly be conceived; and a tangible or visible extension which is neither hard nor soft, black nor white, is equally beyond the reach of human conception. Let any man try to conceive a triangle in general which is neither *isosceles* nor *scalene*, nor has any particular length or proportion of sides, and he will soon perceive the absurdity of all the scholastic notions with regard to abstraction and general ideas.[32]

Thus the first philosophical objection to the evidence of sense or to the opinion of external existence consists in this, that such an opinion, if rested on natural instinct, is contrary to reason and, if referred to reason, is contrary to natural instinct and at the same time carries no rational evidence with it to convince an impartial inquirer. The second objection goes further and represents this opinion as contrary to reason, at least if it is a principle of reason that all sensible qualities are in the mind, not in the object. Deprive matter of all its intelligible qualities, both primary and secondary, you in a manner annihilate it and leave only a certain unknown, inexplicable *something* as the cause of our perceptions—a notion so imperfect that no skeptic will think it worthwhile to contend against it.

32. This argument is drawn from Dr. Berkeley; and indeed most of the writings of that very ingenious author form the best lessons of skepticism which are to be found either among the ancient or modern philosophers, Bayle not excepted. He professes, however, in his title-page (and undoubtedly with great truth) to have composed his book against the skeptics as well as against the atheists and freethinkers. But that all his arguments, though otherwise intended, are in reality merely skeptical, appears from this, *that they admit of no answer and produce no conviction.* Their only effect is to cause that momentary amazement and irresolution and confusion which is the result of skepticism.

Part II.

It may seem a very extravagant attempt of the skeptics to destroy *reason* by argument and ratiocination, yet is this the grand scope of all their inquiries and disputes. They endeavor to find objections both to our abstract reasonings and to those which regard matter of fact and existence.

The chief objection against all *abstract* reasonings is derived from the ideas of space and time—ideas which, in common life and to a careless view, are very clear and intelligible, but when they pass through the scrutiny of the profound sciences (and they are the chief object of these sciences) afford principles which seem full of absurdity and contradiction. No priestly *dogmas* invented on purpose to tame and subdue the rebellious reason of mankind ever shocked common sense more than the doctrine of the infinite divisibility of extension, with its consequences, as they are pompously displayed by all geometers and metaphysicians with a kind of triumph and exultation. A real quantity, infinitely less than any finite quantity, containing quantities infinitely less than itself, and so on *in infinitum*; this is an edifice so bold and prodigious that it is too weighty for any pretended demonstration to support because it shocks the clearest and most natural principles of human reason.[33] But what renders the matter more extraordinary is that these seemingly absurd opinions are supported by a chain of reasoning, the clearest and most natural, nor is it possible for us to allow the premises without admitting the consequences. Nothing can be more convincing and satisfactory than all the conclusions concerning the properties of circles and triangles, and yet, when these are once received, how can we deny that the angle of contact between a circle and its tangent is infinitely less than any rectilinear angle—that as you may increase the diameter of the circle *in infinitum*, this angle of contact becomes still less, even *in infinitum*, and that the angle of contact between other curves and their tangents may be infinitely less than those between any circle and its tangent, and so on, *in infinitum?* The demonstration of these principles seems as unexceptionable as that which proves the three angles of a triangle to be equal to two right ones, though the latter opinion is natural and easy and the former big with contradiction and absurdity. Reason here seems to be thrown into a kind of amazement and suspense which, without the suggestions of any skeptic, gives her a diffidence of herself and of the ground on which she treads. She sees a full light which illuminates certain places, but that light borders upon the most profound darkness. And between these she is so dazzled and confounded that she scarcely can pronounce with certainty and assurance concerning any one object.

The absurdity of these bold determinations of the abstract sciences seems to become, if possible, still more palpable with regard to time than extension. An infinite number of real parts of time, passing in succession and exhausted one after another, appears so evident a contradiction that no man, one should think, whose judgment is not corrupted, instead of being improved by the sciences, would ever be able to admit of it.

Yet still reason must remain restless and unquiet, even with regard to that skepticism to which she is driven by these seeming absurdities and contradictions. How any clear, distinct idea can contain circumstances contradictory to itself, or to any other clear, distinct idea, is absolutely incomprehensible and is, perhaps, as absurd as any proposition which can be formed—so that nothing can be more skeptical or more full of doubt and hesitation than this skepticism itself which arises from some of the paradoxical conclusions of geometry or the science of quantity.[34]

---

33. Whatever disputes there may be about mathematical points, we must allow that there are physical points—that is, parts of extension which cannot be divided or lessened, either by the eye or imagination. These images, then, which are present to the fancy or senses, are absolutely indivisible and consequently must be allowed by mathematicians to be infinitely less than any real part of extension; and yet nothing appears more certain to reason than that an infinite number of them composes an infinite extension. How much more an infinite number of those infinitely small parts of extension, which are still supposed infinitely divisible?

34. It seems to me not impossible to avoid these absurdities and contradictions, if it is admitted that there is no such thing as abstract or general ideas properly speaking; but that all general ideas are, in reality, particular ones attached to a general term, which recalls, upon occasion, other particular ones that resemble in certain circumstances the idea present to the mind. Thus,

The skeptical objections to *moral* evidence or to the reasonings concerning matter of fact are either *popular* or *philosophical*. The popular objections are derived from the natural weakness of human understanding: the contradictory opinions which have been entertained in different ages and nations; the variations of our judgment in sickness and health, youth and old age, prosperity and adversity; the perpetual contradiction of each particular man's opinions; and sentiments with many other topics of that kind. It is needless to insist further on this head. These objections are but weak. For as, in common life, we reason every moment concerning fact and existence and cannot possibly subsist without continually employing this species of argument, any popular objections derived from this must be insufficient to destroy that evidence. The great subverter of *Pyrrhonism*, or the excessive principles of skepticism, is action, and employment, and the occupations of common life. These principles may flourish and triumph in the schools, where it is indeed difficult, if not impossible, to refute them. But as soon as they leave the shade and by the presence of the real objects which actuate our passions and sentiments are put in opposition to the more powerful principles of our nature, they vanish like smoke and leave the most determined skeptic in the same condition as other mortals.

The skeptic, therefore, had better keep within his proper sphere and display those *philosophical* objections which arise from more profound researches. Here he seems to have ample matter of triumph, while he justly insists that all our evidence for any matter of fact which lies beyond the testimony of sense or memory is derived entirely from the relation of cause and effect; that we have no other idea of this relation than that of two objects which have been frequently *conjoined* together; that we have no argument to convince us that objects which have, in our experience, been frequently conjoined, will likewise, in other instances, be conjoined in the same manner; and that nothing leads us to this inference but custom or a certain instinct of our nature which it is indeed difficult to resist, but which, like other instincts, may be fallacious and deceitful. While the skeptic insists upon these topics, he shows his force, or rather, indeed, his own and our weakness, and seems, for the time at least, to destroy all assurance and conviction. These arguments might be displayed at greater length, if any durable good or benefit to society could ever be expected to result from them.

For here is the chief and most confounding objection to *excessive* skepticism, that no durable good can ever result from it while it remains in its full force and vigor. We need only ask such a skeptic *What his meaning is? And what he proposes by all these curious researches?* He is immediately at a loss and does not know what to answer. A Copernican or Ptolemaist who each supports his different system of astronomy may hope to produce a conviction which will remain constant and durable with his audience. A Stoic or Epicurean displays principles which may not only be durable, but which have an effect on conduct and behavior. But a Pyrrhonian cannot expect that his philosophy will have any constant influence on the mind, or, if it had, that its influence would be beneficial to society. On the contrary, he must acknowledge, if he will acknowledge anything, that all human life must perish were his principles universally and steadily to prevail. All discourse, all action would immediately cease and men would remain in a total lethargy until the necessities of nature, unsatisfied, put an end to their miserable existence. It is true—so fatal an event is very little to be dreaded. Nature is always too strong for principle. And though a Pyrrhonian may throw himself or others into a momentary amazement and confusion by his profound reasonings, the first and most trivial event in life will put to flight all his doubts and scruples and leave him the same, in every point of action and speculation, with the philosophers

---

when the term *horse* is pronounced, we immediately figure to ourselves the idea of a black or a white animal, of a particular size or figure. But as that term is also usually applied to animals of other colors, figures, and sizes, these ideas, though not actually present to the imagination, are easily recalled—and our reasoning and conclusion proceed in the same way as if they were actually present. If this is admitted (as seems reasonable), it follows that all the ideas of quanity upon which mathematicians reason are nothing but particular and such as are suggested by the senses and imagination and, consequently, cannot be infinitely divisible. It is sufficient to have dropped this hint at present without prosecuting it any further. It certainly concerns all lovers of science not to expose themselves to the ridicule and contempt of the ignorant by their conclusions; and this seems the readiest solution of these difficulties.

of every other sect or with those who never concerned themselves in any philosophical researches. When he awakes from his dream, he will be the first to join in the laugh against himself and to confess that all his objections are mere amusement and can have no other tendency than to show the whimsical condition of mankind, who must act and reason and believe, though they are not able, by their most diligent inquiry, to satisfy themselves concerning the foundation of these operations or to remove the objections which may be raised against them.

Part III.

There is, indeed, a more *mitigated* skepticism or *academic* philosophy which may be both durable and useful and which may, in part, be the result of this Pyrrhonism or *excessive* skepticism when its undistinguished doubts are in some measure corrected by common sense and reflection. The greater part of mankind are naturally apt to be affirmative and dogmatic in their opinions, and while they see objects only on one side and have no idea of any counterpoising argument, they throw themselves precipitately into the principles to which they are inclined, nor have they any indulgence for those who entertain opposite sentiments. To hesitate or balance perplexes their understanding, checks their passion, and suspends their action. They are, therefore, impatient, until they escape from a state which to them is so uneasy and they think that they can never remove themselves far enough from it by the violence of their affirmations and obstinacy of their belief. But could such dogmatic reasoners become sensible of the strange infirmities of human understanding, even in its most perfect state and when most accurate and cautious in its determinations, such a reflection would naturally inspire them with more modesty and reserve, and diminish their fond opinion of themselves and their prejudice against antagonists. The illiterate may reflect on the disposition of the learned who, amid all the advantages of study and reflection, are commonly still diffident in their determinations. And if any of the learned are inclined, from their natural temper, to haughtiness and obstinacy, a small tincture of Pyrrhonism might abate their pride by showing them that the few advantages which they may have attained over their fellows are but inconsiderable, if compared with the universal perplexity and confusion which is inherent in human nature. In general, there is a degree of doubt and caution and modesty which, in all kinds of scrutiny and decision, ought forever accompany a just reasoner.

Another species of *mitigated* skepticism which may be of advantage to mankind and which may be the natural result of the Pyrrhonian doubts and scruples is the limitation of our inquiries to such subjects as are best adapted to the narrow capacity of human understanding. The *imagination* of man is naturally sublime, delighted with whatever is remote and extraordinary, and running without control into the most distant parts of space and time in order to avoid the objects which custom has rendered too familiar to it. A correct *judgment* observes a contrary method and, avoiding all distant and high inquiries, confines itself to common life and to such subjects as fall under daily practice and experience, leaving the more sublime topics to the embellishment of poets and orators or to the arts of priests and politicians. To bring us to so salutary a determination, nothing can be more serviceable than to be once thoroughly convinced of the force of the Pyrrhonian doubt and of the impossibility that anything but the strong power of natural instinct could free us from it. Those who have a propensity to philosophy will still continue their researches, because they reflect that, besides the immediate pleasure attending such an occupation, philosophical decisions are nothing but the reflections of common life, methodized and corrected. But they will never be tempted to go beyond common life so long as they consider the imperfection of those faculties which they employ, their narrow reach, and their inaccurate operations. While we cannot give a satisfactory reason why we believe, after a thousand experiments, that a stone will fall or fire burn, can we ever satisfy ourselves concerning any determination which we may form with regard to the origin of worlds and the situation of nature from and to eternity?

This narrow limitation, indeed, of our inquiries is in every respect so reasonable that it suffices to make the slightest examination into the natural powers of the human mind and to compare them with their objects, in order to recommend it to us. We shall then find what are the proper subjects of science and inquiry.

It seems to me that the only objects of the abstract sciences or of demonstration are quantity and number and that all attempts to extend this more perfect species of knowledge beyond these bounds are mere sophistry and illusion. As the component parts of quantity and number are entirely similar, their relations become intricate and involved and nothing can be more curious, as well as useful, than to trace, by a variety of mediums, their equality or inequality through their different appearances. But as all other ideas are clearly distinct and different from each other, we can never advance further, by our utmost scrutiny, than to observe this diversity and, by an obvious reflection, pronounce one thing not to be another. Or if there is any difficulty in these decisions, it proceeds entirely from the indeterminate meaning of words, which is corrected by more just definitions. That *the square of the hypotenuse is equal to the squares of the other two sides* cannot be known, let the terms be ever so exactly defined, without a train of reasoning and inquiry. But to convince us of this proposition, *that where there is no property there can be no injustice*, it is only necessary to define the terms and explain injustice to be a violation of property. This proposition is, indeed, nothing but a more imperfect definition. It is the same case with all those pretended syllogistic reasonings which may be found in every other branch of learning except the sciences of quantity and number; and these may safely, I think, be pronounced the only proper objects of knowledge and demonstration.

All other inquiries of men regard only matter of fact and existence and these are evidently incapable of demonstration. Whatever *is* may *not be*. No negation of a fact can involve a contradiction. The nonexistence of any being, without exception, is as clear and distinct an idea as its existence. The proposition which affirms it not to be, however false, is no less conceivable and intelligible than that which affirms it to be. The case is different with the sciences, properly so called. Every proposition which is not true is there confused and unintelligible. That the cube root of 64 is equal to the half of 10 is a false proposition and

can never be distinctly conceived. But that Caesar, or the angel Gabriel, or any being, never existed may be a false proposition, but still is perfectly conceivable, and implies no contradiction.

The existence, therefore, of any being can only be proved by arguments from its cause or its effect and these arguments are founded entirely on experience. If we reason *a priori*, anything may appear able to produce anything. The falling of a pebble may, for all we know, extinguish the sun, or the wish of a man control the planets in their orbits. It is only experience which teaches us the nature and bounds of cause and effect and enables us to infer the existence of one object from that of another.[35] Such is the foundation of moral reasoning, which forms the greater part of human knowledge and is the source of all human action and behavior.

Moral reasonings are either concerning particular or general facts. All deliberations in life regard the former, as also all disquisitions in history, chronology, geography, and astronomy.

The sciences which treat of general facts are politics, natural philosophy, physics, chemistry, etc., where the qualities, causes, and effects of a whole species of objects are inquired into.

Divinity or theology, as it proves the existence of a Deity and the immortality of souls, is composed partly of reasonings concerning particular, partly concerning general facts. It has a foundation in *reason* so far as it is supported by experience. But its best and most solid foundation is *faith* and divine revelation.

Morals and criticism are not so properly objects of the understanding as of taste and sentiment. Beauty, whether moral or natural, is felt more properly than perceived. Or if we reason concerning it and endeavor to fix its standard, we regard a new fact, namely, the general taste of mankind or some such fact which may be the object of reasoning and inquiry.

When we run over libraries, persuaded of these

35. That impious maxim of the ancient philosophy, *Ex nihilo, nihil fit* [from nothing, comes nothing], by which the creation of matter was excluded, ceases to be a maxim according to this philosophy. Not only the will of the supreme Being may create matter, but, for all we know *a priori*, the will of any other being might create it or any other cause that the most whimsical imagination can assign.

principles, what havoc must we make? If we take in our hand any volume—of divinity or school metaphysics, for instance—let us ask: *Does it contain any abstract reasoning concerning quantity or number?* No. *Does it contain any experimental reasoning concerning matter of fact and existence?* No. Commit it then to the flames, for it can contain nothing but sophistry and illusion.

David Hume, *Dialogues Concerning Natural Religion* (1779)[1]

Pamphilus to Hermippus

It has been remarked, my *Hermippus*, that though the ancient Philosophers conveyed most of their instruction in the form of dialogue, this method of composition has been little practiced in later ages, and has seldom succeeded in the hands of those who have attempted it. Accurate and regular argument, indeed, such as is now expected of philosophical inquirers, naturally throws a man into the methodical and didactic manner, where he can immediately, without preparation, explain the point at which he aims, and thence proceed, without interruption, to deduce the proofs on which it is established. To deliver a *system* in conversation scarcely appears natural; and while the dialogue writer desires, by departing from the direct style of composition, to give a freer air to his performance and avoid the appearance of *author* and *reader*, he is apt to run into a worse inconvenience and convey the image of *pedagogue* and *pupil*. Or, if he carries on the dispute in the natural spirit of good company by throwing in a variety of topics and preserving a proper balance among the speakers, he often loses so much time in preparations and transitions that the reader will scarcely think

himself compensated by all the graces of dialogue for the order, brevity, and precision which are sacrificed to them.

There are some subjects, however, to which dialogue writing is peculiarly adapted and where it is still preferable to the direct and simple method of composition.

Any point of doctrine which is so *obvious* that it scarcely admits of dispute, but at the same time so *important* that it cannot be too often inculcated, seems to require some such method of handling it, where the novelty of the manner may compensate the triteness of the subject, where the vivacity of conversation may enforce the precept, and where the variety of lights presented by various personages and characters may appear neither tedious nor redundant.

Any question of philosophy, on the other hand, which is so *obscure* and *uncertain* that human reason can reach no fixed determination with regard to it — if it should be treated at all — seems to lead us naturally into the style of dialogue and conversation. Reasonable men may be allowed to differ where no one can reasonably be positive. Opposite sentiments, even without any decision, afford an agreeable amusement, and if the subject is curious and interesting, the book carries us, in a manner, into company, and unites the two greatest and purest pleasures of human life, study and society.

1. [From *The Philosophical Works of David Hume* (Boston: Little, Brown and Company, 1854), 4 vols., English, modified.]

Happily, these circumstances are all to be found in the subject of NATURAL RELIGION. What truth so obvious, so certain, as the *being* of a God, which the most ignorant ages have acknowledged, for which the most refined geniuses have ambitiously striven to produce new proofs and arguments? What truth so important as this, which is the ground of all our hopes, the surest foundation of morality, the firmest support of society, and the only principle which ought never to be a moment absent from our thoughts and meditations? But, in treating of this obvious and important truth, what obscure questions occur concerning the *nature* of that Divine Being, his attributes, his decrees, his plan of providence? These have been always subjected to the disputations of men; concerning these human reason has not reached any certain determination. But these are topics so interesting that we cannot restrain our restless inquiry with regard to them, though nothing but doubt, uncertainty, and contradiction have as yet been the result of our most accurate researches.

This I had lately occasion to observe, while I passed, as usual, part of the summer season with *Cleanthes,* and was present at those conversations of his with *Philo* and *Demea,* of which I gave you lately some imperfect account. Your curiosity, you then told me, was so excited that I must, of necessity, enter into a more exact detail of their reasonings and display those various systems which they advanced with regard to so delicate a subject as that of natural religion. The remarkable contrast in their characters still further raised your expectations, while you opposed the accurate philosophical turn of *Cleanthes* to the careless skepticism of *Philo,* or compared either of their dispositions with the rigid inflexible orthodoxy of *Demea.* My youth rendered me a mere auditor of their disputes, and that curiosity, natural to the early season of life, has so deeply imprinted in my memory the whole chain and connection of their arguments that I hope I shall not omit or confound any considerable part of them in the recital.

Part I

After I joined the company, whom I found sitting in *Cleanthes's* library, *Demea* paid *Cleanthes* some

compliments on the great care which he took of my education and on his unwearied perseverance and constancy in all his friendships. The father of *Pamphilus,* said he, was your intimate friend: The son is your pupil, and may indeed be regarded as your adopted son, were we to judge by the pains which you bestow in conveying to him every useful branch of literature and science. You are no more wanting, I am persuaded, in prudence than in industry. I shall, therefore, communicate to you a maxim which I have observed with regard to my own children, that I may learn how far it agrees with your practice. The method I follow in their education is founded on the saying of an ancient, *"That students of philosophy ought first to learn logic, then ethics, next physics, last of all the nature of the gods."*[2] This science of natural theology, according to him, being the most profound and abstruse of any, required the most mature judgment in its students, and none but a mind enriched with all the other sciences can safely be entrusted with it.

Are you so late, says *Philo,* in teaching your children the principles of religion? Is there no danger of their neglecting or rejecting altogether those opinions of which they have heard so little during the whole course of their education? It is only as a science, replied *Demea,* subjected to human reasoning and disputation, that I postpone the study of natural theology. To season their minds with early piety is my chief care; and by continual precept and instruction and I hope, too, by example, I imprint deeply on their tender minds an habitual reverence for all the principles of religion. While they pass through every other science, I still remark the uncertainty of each part; the eternal disputations of men; the obscurity of all philosophy; and the strange, ridiculous conclusions which some of the greatest geniuses have derived from the principles of mere human reason. Having thus tamed their mind to a proper submission and self-diffidence, I have no longer any scruple of opening to them the greatest mysteries of religion, nor apprehend any danger from that assuming arrogance of philosophy

2. Chrysippus according to Plutarch, *De Stoicorum repugnantis.*

which may lead them to reject the most established doctrines and opinions.

Your precaution, says *Philo*, of seasoning your children's minds early with piety is certainly very reasonable, and no more than is requisite in this profane and irreligious age. But what I chiefly admire in your plan of education is your method of drawing advantage from the very principles of philosophy and learning which, by inspiring pride and self-sufficiency, have commonly, in all ages, been found so destructive to the principles of religion. The vulgar, indeed, we may remark, who are unacquainted with science and profound inquiry, observing the endless disputes of the learned, have commonly a thorough contempt for philosophy and rivet themselves the faster, by that means, in the great points of theology which have been taught them. Those who enter a little into study and inquiry, finding many appearances of evidence in doctrines the newest and most extraordinary, think nothing too difficult for human reason and, presumptuously breaking through all fences, profane the inmost sanctuaries of the temple. But *Cleanthes* will, I hope, agree with me that after we have abandoned ignorance, the surest remedy, there is still one expedient left to prevent this profane liberty. Let *Demea's* principles be improved and cultivated: Let us become thoroughly sensible of the weakness, blindness, and narrow limits of human reason; let us duly consider its uncertainty and endless contrarieties, even in subjects of common life and practice; let the errors and deceits of our very senses be set before us, the insuperable difficulties which attend first principles in all systems, the contradictions which adhere to the very ideas of matter—cause and effect, extension, space, time, motion—and in a word, quantity of all kinds, the object of the only science that can fairly pretend to any certainty or evidence. When these topics are displayed in their full light, as they are by some philosophers and almost all divines, who can retain such confidence in this frail faculty of reason as to pay any regard to its determinations in points so sublime, so abstruse, so remote from common life and experience? When the coherence of the parts of a stone, or even that composition of parts which renders it extended, when these familiar objects, I say, are so inexplicable, and contain circumstances so repugnant

and contradictory, with what assurance can we decide concerning the origin of worlds or trace their history from eternity to eternity?

While *Philo* pronounced these words, I could observe a smile in the countenance both of *Demea* and *Cleanthes*. That of *Demea* seemed to imply an unreserved satisfaction in the doctrines delivered, but in *Cleanthes's* features I could distinguish an air of finesse, as if he perceived some raillery or artificial malice in the reasonings of *Philo*.

You propose then, *Philo*, said *Cleanthes*, to erect religious faith on philosophical skepticism, and you think that if certainty or evidence be expelled from every other subject of inquiry, it will all retire to these theological doctrines and there acquire a superior force and authority. Whether your skepticism be as absolute and sincere as you pretend, we shall learn by and by, when the company breaks up: We shall then see whether you go out at the door or the window and whether you really doubt if your body has gravity or can be injured by its fall, according to popular opinion, derived from our fallacious senses and more fallacious experience. And this consideration, *Demea*, may, I think, fairly serve to abate our ill-will to this humorous sect of the skeptics. If they be thoroughly in earnest, they will not long trouble the world with their doubts, cavils, and disputes; if they be only in jest, they are, perhaps, bad railers, but can never be very dangerous, either to the state, to philosophy, or to religion.

In reality, *Philo*, continued he, it seems certain that though a man, in a flush of humor, after intense reflection on the many contradictions and imperfections of human reason, may entirely renounce all belief and opinion, it is impossible for him to persevere in this total skepticism or make it appear in his conduct for a few hours. External objects press in upon him; passions solicit him; his philosophical melancholy dissipates; and even the utmost violence upon his own temper will not be able, during any time, to preserve the poor appearance of skepticism. And for what reason impose on himself such a violence? This is a point in which it will be impossible for him ever to satisfy himself, consistently with his skeptical principles. So that, upon the whole, nothing could be more ridiculous than the principles of the ancient *Pyrrhonians,* if in reality they endeavored, as is pretended, to extend, throughout, the same skepticism which they had learned from the declamations of their schools and which they ought to have confined to them.

In this view, there appears a great resemblance between the sects of the *Stoics* and *Pyrrhonians,* though perpetual antagonists; and both of them seem founded on this erroneous maxim that what a man can perform sometimes, and in some dispositions, he can perform always, and in every disposition. When the mind, by *Stoical* reflections, is elevated into a sublime enthusiasm of virtue and strongly smitten with any *species* of honor or public good, the utmost bodily pain and sufferings will not prevail over such a high sense of duty, and it is possible, perhaps, by its means, even to smile and exult in the midst of tortures. If this sometimes may be the case in fact and reality, much more may a philosopher, in his school or even in his closet, work himself up to such an enthusiasm, and support in imagination the most acute pain or most calamitous event which he can possibly conceive. But how shall he support this enthusiasm itself? The bent of his mind relaxes and cannot be recalled at pleasure; avocations lead him astray; misfortunes attack him unawares; and the *philosopher* sinks by degrees into the *plebeian.*

I allow of your comparison between the *Stoics* and *Skeptics,* replied *Philo.* But you may observe, at the same time, that though the mind cannot, in *Stoicism,* support the highest flights of philosophy, yet, even when it sinks lower, it still retains something of its former disposition; and the effects of the *Stoic's* reasoning will appear in his conduct in common life and through the whole tenor of his actions. The ancient schools, particularly that of *Zeno,* produced examples of virtue and constancy which seem astonishing to present times.

> Vain Wisdom all and false Philosophy.
> Yet with a pleasing sorcery could charm
> Pain, for a while, or anguish; and excite
> Fallacious Hope, or arm the obdurate breast
> With stubborn Patience, as with triple steel.[3]

3. [John Milton, *Paradise Lost,* Book II.]

In like manner, if a man has accustomed himself to skeptical considerations on the uncertainty and narrow limits of reason, he will not entirely forget them when he turns his reflection on other subjects, but in all his philosophical principles and reasoning, I dare not say in his common conduct, he will be found different from those who either never formed any opinions in the case or have entertained sentiments more favorable to human reason.

To whatever length anyone may push his speculative principles of skepticism, he must act, I admit, and live and converse like other men; and for this conduct he is not obliged to give any other reason than the absolute necessity he lies under of so doing. If he ever carries his speculations further than this necessity constrains him, and philosophizes either on natural or moral subjects, he is allured by a certain pleasure and satisfaction which he finds in employing himself after that manner. He considers, besides, that everyone, even in common life, is constrained to have more or less of this philosophy; that from our earliest infancy we make continual advances in forming more general principles of conduct and reasoning; that the larger experience we acquire and the stronger reason we are endued with, we always render our principles the more general and comprehensive; and that what we call *philosophy* is nothing but a more regular and methodical operation of the same kind. To philosophize on such subjects is nothing essentially different from reasoning on common life, and we may only expect greater stability, if not greater truth, from our philosophy on account of its more exact and more scrupulous method of proceeding.

But when we look beyond human affairs and the properties of the surrounding bodies—when we carry our speculations into the two eternities, before and after the present state of things; into the creation and formation of the universe; the existence and properties of spirits; the powers and operations of one universal Spirit existing without beginning and without end; omnipotent, omniscient, immutable, infinite, and incomprehensible—we must be far removed from the smallest tendency to skepticism not to be apprehensive that we have here got quite beyond the reach of our faculties. So long as we confine our speculations to trade, or morals, or politics, or criticism, we make appeals, every moment, to common sense and experience, which strengthen our philosophical conclusions, and remove, at least in part, the suspicion which we so justly entertain with regard to every reasoning that is very subtle and refined. But, in theological reasonings, we do not have this advantage; while, at the same time, we are employed upon objects which, we must be sensible, are too large for our grasp and, of all others, require most to be familiarized to our apprehension. We are like foreigners in a strange country, to whom everything must seem suspicious and who are in danger every moment of transgressing against the laws and customs of the people with whom they live and converse. We do not know how far we ought to trust our vulgar methods of reasoning in such a subject, since even in common life and in that province which is peculiarly appropriated to them, we cannot account for them and are entirely guided by a kind of instinct or necessity in employing them.

All skeptics pretend that if reason be considered in an abstract view, it furnishes invincible arguments against itself, and that we could never retain any conviction or assurance on any subject were not the skeptical reasonings so refined and subtle that they are not able to counterpoise the more solid and more natural arguments derived from the senses and experience. But it is evident, whenever our arguments lose this advantage and run wide of common life, that the most refined skepticism comes to be upon a footing with them and is able to oppose and counterbalance them. The one has no more weight than the other. The mind must remain in suspense between them, and it is that very suspense or balance which is the triumph of skepticism.

But I observe, says *Cleanthes*, with regard to you, *Philo*, and all speculative skeptics, that your doctrine and practice are as much at variance in the most abstruse points of theory as in the conduct of common life. Wherever evidence discovers itself, you adhere to it, notwithstanding your pretended skepticism, and I can observe, too, some of your sect to be as decisive as those who make greater professions of certainty and assurance. In reality, would not a man be ridiculous who pretended to reject Newton's explication of the wonderful phenomenon of the rainbow because that explication gives a minute anatomy of the rays of light, a subject, indeed, too refined for human comprehension? And what would you say to one, who, having nothing particular to object to the arguments of *Copernicus* and *Galileo* for the motion of the earth, should withhold his assent on that general principle that these subjects were too magnificent and remote to be explained by the narrow and fallacious reason of mankind?

There is indeed a kind of brutish and ignorant skepticism, as you well observed, which gives the vulgar a general prejudice against what they do not easily understand and makes them reject every principle which requires elaborate reasoning to prove and establish it. This species of skepticism is fatal to knowledge, not to religion, since we find that those who make greatest profession of it give often their assent not only to the great truths of theism and natural theology, but even to the most absurd tenets which a traditional superstition has recommended to them. They firmly believe in witches, though they will not believe nor attend to the most simple proposition of *Euclid*. But the refined and philosophical skeptics fall into an inconsistency of an opposite nature. They push their researches into the most abstruse corners of science, and their assent attends them in every step, proportioned to the evidence which they meet with. They are even obliged to acknowledge that the most abstruse and remote objects are those which are best explained by philosophy. Light is in reality anatomized. The true system of the heavenly bodies is discovered and ascertained. But the nourishment of bodies by food is still an inexplicable mystery. The cohesion of the parts of matter is still incomprehensible. These skeptics, therefore, are obliged, in every question, to consider each particular evidence apart and proportion their assent to the precise degree of evidence which occurs. This is their practice in all natural, mathematical, moral, and political science. And why not the same, I ask, in the theological and religious? Why must conclusions of this nature be alone rejected on the general presumption of the insufficiency of human reason without any particular discussion of the evidence? Is not such an unequal conduct a plain proof of prejudice and passion?

Our senses, you say, are fallacious; our understanding erroneous; our ideas, even of the most familiar objects—extension, duration, motion—full of absurdities and contradictions. You defy me to solve the difficulties or reconcile the repugnancies which you discover in them. I have not capacity for so great an undertaking; I have not leisure for it; I perceive it to be superfluous. Your own conduct, in every circumstance, refutes your principles and shows the firmest reliance on all the received maxims of science, morals, prudence, and behavior.

I shall never assent to so harsh an opinion as that of a celebrated writer who says that the *Skeptics* are not a sect of philosophers; they are only a sect of liars.[4] I may, however, affirm (I hope without offence) that they are a sect of jesters or railers. But for my part, whenever I find myself disposed to mirth and amusement, I shall certainly choose my entertainment of a less perplexing and abstruse nature. A comedy, a novel, or, at most, a history seems a more natural recreation than such metaphysical subtleties and abstractions.

In vain would the skeptic make a distinction between science and common life or between one science and another. The arguments employed in all, if just, are of a similar nature and contain the same force and evidence. Or if there be any difference among them, the advantage lies entirely on the side of theology and natural religion. Many principles of mechanics are founded on very abstruse reasoning, yet no man who has any pretensions to science, even no speculative skeptic, pretends to entertain the least doubt with regard to them. The *Copernican* system contains the most surprising paradox, and the most contrary to our natural conceptions, to appearances, and to our very senses; yet even monks and inquisitors are now constrained to withdraw their opposition to it. And shall *Philo*, a man of so liberal a genius and extensive knowledge, entertain any general undistinguished scruples with regard to the religious hypothesis, which is founded on the simplest and most obvious arguments and, unless it meets with artificial obstacles, has such easy access and admission into the mind of man?

And here we may observe, continued he, turning himself towards *Demea*, a pretty curious circumstance in the history of the sciences. After the union of philosophy with the popular religion, upon the first establishment of *Christianity*, nothing was more usual among all religious teachers than declamations against reason, against the senses, against every principle derived merely from human research and inquiry. All the topics of the ancient *Academics* were adopted by the fathers and thence propagated for several ages in every school and pulpit throughout *Christendom*. The Reformers embraced the same principles of reasoning, or rather declamation, and all panegyrics on the excellency of faith were sure to be interlarded with some severe strokes of satire against natural reason. A celebrated prelate too,[5] of the Romish communion, a man of the most extensive learning, who wrote a demonstration of Christianity, has also composed a treatise which contains all the cavils of the boldest and most determined *Pyrrhonism*. *Locke* seems to have been the first *Christian* who ventured openly to assert that *faith* was nothing but a species of *reason*; that religion was only a branch of philosophy; and that a chain of arguments, similar to that which established any truth in morals, politics, or physics, was always employed in discovering all the principles of theology, natural and revealed. The ill use which *Bayle* and other libertines made of the philosophical skepticism of the fathers and first reformers still further propagated the judicious sentiment of *Mr. Locke*, and it is now in a manner avowed by all pretenders to reasoning and philosophy that atheist and skeptic are almost synonymous. And as it is certain that no man is in earnest when he professes the latter principle, I would gladly hope that there are as few who seriously maintain the former.

Don't you remember, said *Philo*, the excellent saying of *Lord Bacon* on this head? That a little philosophy, replied *Cleanthes*, makes a man an atheist, a great deal converts him to religion. That is a very judicious remark too, said *Philo*. But what I have in my eye is another passage where, having mentioned

---

4. *L'art de penser.* [*The Art of Thinking,* commonly known as the *Port-Royal Logic,* written in 1662 by Antoine Arnauld and Pierre Nicole; see Discourse 1.]

5. Mons. Huet. [Pierre-Daniel Huet (1630–1721), Bishop of Avranches.]

David's fool, who said in his heart there is no God, this great philosopher observes that the atheists nowadays have a double share of folly; for they are not contented to say in their hearts there is no God, but they also utter that impiety with their lips and are thereby guilty of multiplied indiscretion and imprudence. Such people, though they were ever so much in earnest, cannot, I think, be very formidable.

But though you should rank me in this class of fools, I cannot forbear communicating a remark that occurs to me from the history of the religious and irreligious skepticism with which you have entertained us. It appears to me that there are strong symptoms of priestcraft in the whole progress of this affair. During ignorant ages, such as those which followed the dissolution of the ancient schools, the priests perceived that atheism, deism, or heresy of any kind could only proceed from the presumptuous questioning of received opinions and from a belief that human reason was equal to everything. Education had then a mighty influence over the minds of men and was almost equal in force to those suggestions of the senses and common understanding by which the most determined skeptic must allow himself to be governed. But at present, when the influence of education is much diminished and men, from a more open commerce of the world, have learned to compare the popular principles of different nations and ages, our sagacious divines have changed their whole system of philosophy, and talk the language of *Stoics*, *Platonists*, and *Peripatetics*, not that of *Pyrrhonians* and *Academics*. If we distrust human reason, we have now no other principle to lead us into religion. Thus, skeptics in one age, dogmatists in another; whichever system best suits the purpose of these reverend gentlemen in giving them an ascendant over mankind, they are sure to make it their favorite principle and established tenet.

It is very natural, said *Cleanthes*, for men to embrace those principles by which they find they can best defend their doctrines; nor need we have any recourse to priestcraft to account for so reasonable an expedient. And surely nothing can afford a stronger presumption that any set of principles are true and ought to be embraced than to observe that they tend

to the confirmation of true religion and serve to confound the cavils of atheists, libertines, and free thinkers of all denominations.

Part II

I must admit, *Cleanthes*, said *Demea*, that nothing can more surprise me than the light in which you have all along put this argument. By the whole tenor of your discourse, one would imagine that you were maintaining the being of a God against the cavils of atheists and infidels and were necessitated to become a champion for that fundamental principle of all religion. But this, I hope, is not by any means a question among us. No man, no man at least of common sense, I am persuaded, ever entertained a serious doubt with regard to a truth so certain and self-evident. The question is not concerning the *being*, but the *nature* of God. This, I affirm, from the infirmities of human understanding, to be altogether incomprehensible and unknown to us. The essence of that supreme mind, his attributes, the manner of his existence, the very nature of his duration; these, and every particular which regards so divine a being, are mysterious to men. Finite, weak, and blind creatures, we ought to humble ourselves in his august presence, and, conscious of our frailties, adore in silence his infinite perfections, which eye has not seen, ear has not heard, neither has it entered into the heart of man to conceive. They are covered in a deep cloud from human curiosity. It is profaneness to attempt penetrating through these sacred obscurities. And next to the impiety of denying his existence is the temerity of prying into his nature and essence, decrees, and attributes.

But lest you should think that my *piety* has here got the better of my *philosophy*, I shall support my opinion, if it needs any support, by a very great authority. I might cite all the divines, almost from the foundation of *Christianity*, who have ever treated of this or any other theological subject, but I shall confine myself, at present, to one equally celebrated for piety and philosophy. It is *Father Malebranche*, who, I remember, thus expresses himself. "One ought not so much," says he, "to call God a spirit, in order to express positively what he is, as in order to signify that he is not matter. He is a Being infinitely perfect, of this we cannot doubt. But in the same manner as we ought not to imagine, even supposing him corporeal, that he is clothed with a human body, as the *Anthropomorphites* asserted, under color that that figure was the most perfect of any, so neither ought we to imagine that the spirit of God has human ideas or bears any resemblance to our spirit, under color that we know nothing more perfect than a human mind. We ought rather to believe that as he comprehends the perfections of matter without being material . . . he comprehends also the perfections of created spirits without being spirit in the manner we conceive spirit; that his true name is, *He that is*; or, in other words, Being without restriction, All Being, the Being infinite and universal."[6]

After so great an authority, *Demea*, replied *Philo*, as that which you have produced, and a thousand more which you might produce, it would appear ridiculous in me to add my sentiment or express my approbation of your doctrine. But surely, where reasonable men treat these subjects, the question can never be concerning the *being*, but only the *nature* of the Deity. The former truth, as you well observe, is unquestionable and self-evident. Nothing exists without a cause, and the original cause of this universe (whatever it be) we call *God*, and piously ascribe to him every species of perfection. Whoever scruples this fundamental truth deserves every punishment which can be inflicted among philosophers, to wit, the greatest ridicule, contempt, and disapprobation. But as all perfection is entirely relative, we ought never to imagine that we comprehend the attributes of this divine Being or to suppose that his perfections have any analogy or likeness to the perfections of a human creature. Wisdom, thought, design, knowledge, these we justly ascribe to him, because these words are honorable among men and we have no other language or other conceptions by which we can express our adoration of him. But let us beware, lest we think that our ideas anywise correspond to his perfections or that his attributes have any resemblance to these qualities among men. He is infinitely superior

to our limited view and comprehension, and is more the object of worship in the temple than of disputation in the schools.

In reality, *Cleanthes*, continued he, there is no need of having recourse to that affected skepticism so displeasing to you in order to come at this determination. Our ideas reach no further than our experience. We have no experience of divine attributes and operations. I need not conclude my syllogism. You can draw the inference yourself. And it is a pleasure to me (and I hope to you too) that just reasoning and sound piety here concur in the same conclusion, and both of them establish the adorably mysterious and incomprehensible nature of the Supreme Being.

Not to lose any time in circumlocutions, said *Cleanthes*, addressing himself to *Demea*, much less in replying to the pious declamations of *Philo*, I shall briefly explain how I conceive this matter. Look round the world, contemplate the whole and every part of it, you will find it to be nothing but one great machine, subdivided into an infinite number of lesser machines which again admit of subdivisions to a degree beyond what human senses and faculties can trace and explain. All these various machines and even their most minute parts are adjusted to each other with an accuracy which ravishes into admiration all men who have ever contemplated them. The curious adapting of means to ends throughout all nature resembles exactly, though it much exceeds, the productions of human contrivance, of human designs, thought, wisdom, and intelligence. Since, therefore, the effects resemble each other, we are led to infer by all the rules of analogy that the causes also resemble, and that the Author of Nature is somewhat similar to the mind of man, though possessed of much larger faculties, proportioned to the grandeur of the work which he has executed. By this argument *a posteriori*, and by this argument alone, do we prove at once the existence of a Deity and his similarity to human mind and intelligence.

I shall be so free, *Cleanthes*, said *Demea*, as to tell you that from the beginning I could not approve of your conclusion concerning the similarity of the Deity to men; still less can I approve of the mediums by which you endeavor to establish it. What! No demonstration of the Being of God! No abstract argu-

---

6. *Recherche de la Verité*, Book III, chap. 9.

ments! No proofs *a priori!* Are these, which have been so much insisted on until now by philosophers, all fallacy, all sophism? Can we reach no further in this subject than experience and probability? I will not say that this is betraying the cause of a Deity, but surely, by this affected candor you give advantages to atheists, which they never could obtain by the mere dint of argument and reasoning.

What I chiefly scruple in this subject, said *Philo*, is not so much that all religious arguments are by *Cleanthes* reduced to experience, as that they appear not to be even the most certain and irrefragable of that inferior kind. That a stone will fall, that fire will burn, that the earth has solidity, we have observed a thousand and a thousand times, and when any new instance of this nature is presented, we draw without hesitation the accustomed inference. The exact similarity of the cases gives us a perfect assurance of a similar event, and a stronger evidence is never desired nor sought after. But wherever you depart in the least from the similarity of the cases, you diminish proportionally the evidence and may at last bring it to a very weak *analogy*, which is confessedly liable to error and uncertainty. After having experienced the circulation of the blood in human creatures, we make no doubt that it takes place in *Titius* and *Maevius*. But from its circulation in frogs and fishes, it is only a presumption, though a strong one, from analogy that it takes place in men and other animals. The analogical reasoning is much weaker when we infer the circulation of the sap in vegetables from our experience that the blood circulates in animals, and those who hastily followed that imperfect analogy are found by more accurate experiments to have been mistaken.

If we see a house, *Cleanthes*, we conclude with the greatest certainty that it had an architect or builder, because this is precisely that species of effect which we have experienced to proceed from that species of cause. But surely you will not affirm that the universe bears such a resemblance to a house that we can with the same certainty infer a similar cause or that the analogy is here entire and perfect. The dissimilitude is so striking that the utmost you can here pretend to is a guess, a conjecture, a presumption concerning a similar cause, and how that pretension will be received in the world, I leave you to consider.

It would surely be very ill received, replied *Cleanthes*, and I should be deservedly blamed and detested, did I allow that the proofs of a Deity amounted to no more than a guess or conjecture. But is the whole adjustment of means to ends in a house and in the universe so slight a resemblance? The economy of final causes? The order, proportion, and arrangement of every part? Steps of a stair are plainly contrived that human legs may use them in mounting, and this inference is certain and infallible. Human legs are also contrived for walking and mounting, and this inference, I allow, is not altogether so certain, because of the dissimilarity which you remark, but does it, therefore, deserve the name only of presumption or conjecture?

Good God! cried *Demea*, interrupting him, where are we? Zealous defenders of religion allow that the proofs of a Deity fall short of perfect evidence! And you, *Philo*, on whose assistance I depended in proving the adorable mysteriousness of the Divine Nature, do you assent to all these extravagant opinions of *Cleanthes*? For what other name can I give them? Or why spare my censure when such principles are advanced, supported by such an authority, before so young a man as *Pamphilus*?

You seem not to apprehend, replied *Philo*, that I argue with *Cleanthes* in his own way and, by showing him the dangerous consequences of his tenets, hope at last to reduce him to our opinion. But what sticks most with you, I observe, is the representation which *Cleanthes* has made of the argument *a posteriori*, and, finding that that argument is likely to escape your hold and vanish into air, you think it so disguised that you can scarcely believe it to be set in its true light. Now, however much I may dissent in other respects from the dangerous principles of *Cleanthes*, I must allow that he has fairly represented that argument, and I shall endeavor so to state the matter to you that you will entertain no further scruples with regard to it.

Were a man to abstract from everything which he knows or has seen, he would be altogether incapable, merely from his own ideas, to determine what kind of scene the universe must be or to give the preference to one state or situation of things above another. For, as nothing which he clearly conceives could be esteemed impossible or implying a contradiction, every chimera of his fancy would be upon an equal footing; nor could he assign any just reason why he adheres to one idea or system and rejects the others which are equally possible.

Again, after he opens his eyes and contemplates the world as it really is, it would be impossible for him at first to assign the cause of any one event, much less of the whole of things, or of the universe. He might set his fancy a-rambling, and she might bring him in an infinite variety of reports and representations. These would all be possible, but being all equally possible, he would never of himself give a satisfactory account for his preferring one of them to the rest. Experience alone can point out to him the true cause of any phenomenon.

Now according to this method of reasoning, *Demea*, it follows (and is, indeed, tacitly allowed by *Cleanthes* himself) that order, arrangement, or the adjustment of final causes is not of itself any proof of design, but only so far as it has been experienced to proceed from that principle. For all we can know *a priori*, matter may contain the source or spring of order originally within itself as well as mind does, and there is no more difficulty in conceiving that the several elements, from an internal unknown cause, may fall into the most exquisite arrangement than to conceive that their ideas, in the great universal mind, from a like internal unknown cause, fall into that arrangement. The equal possibility of both these suppositions is allowed. But, by experience, we find (according to *Cleanthes*) that there is a difference between them. Throw several pieces of steel together without shape or form; they will never arrange themselves so as to compose a watch. Stone, and mortar, and wood, without an architect, never erect a house. But the ideas in a human mind, we see, by an unknown, inexplicable economy, arrange themselves so as to form the plan of a watch or house. Experience, therefore, proves that there is an original principle of order in mind, not in matter. From similar effects we infer similar causes. The adjustment of means to ends is alike in the universe, as in a machine of human contrivance. The causes, therefore, must be resembling.

I was from the beginning scandalized, I must admit, with this resemblance which is asserted between the Deity and human creatures, and must conceive it to imply such a degradation of the Supreme Being as no sound theist could endure. With your assistance, therefore, *Demea*, I shall endeavor to defend what you justly call the adorable mysteriousness of the Divine Nature, and shall refute this reasoning of *Cleanthes*, provided he allows that I have made a fair representation of it.

When *Cleanthes* had assented, *Philo*, after a short pause, proceeded in the following manner.

That all inferences, *Cleanthes*, concerning fact are founded on experience and that all experimental reasonings are founded on the supposition that similar causes prove similar effects, and similar effects similar causes, I shall not at present much dispute with you. But observe, I entreat you, with what extreme caution all just reasoners proceed in the transferring of experiments to similar cases. Unless the cases be exactly similar, they repose no perfect confidence in applying their past observation to any particular phenomenon. Every alteration of circumstances occasions a doubt concerning the event, and it requires new experiments to prove certainly that the new circumstances are of no moment or importance. A change in bulk, situation, arrangement, age, disposition of the air, or surrounding bodies—any of these particulars may be attended with the most unexpected consequences, and unless the objects be quite familiar to us, it is the highest temerity to expect with assurance, after any of these changes, an event similar to that which before fell under our observation. The slow and deliberate steps of philosophers here, if anywhere, are distinguished from the precipitate march of the vulgar, who, hurried on by the smallest similitude, are incapable of all discernment or consideration.

But can you think, *Cleanthes*, that your usual phlegm and philosophy have been preserved in so wide a step as you have taken, when you compared to the universe houses, ships, furniture, machines, and, from their similarity in some circumstances, inferred a similarity in their causes? Thought, design, intelligence such as we discover in men and other animals is no more than one of the springs and principles of the universe, as well as heat or cold, attraction or repulsion, and a hundred others which fall under daily observation. It is an active cause by which some particular parts of nature, we find, produce alterations on other parts. But can a conclusion, with any propriety, be transferred from parts to the whole? Does not the great disproportion bar all comparison and inference? From observing the growth of a hair, can we learn anything concerning the generation of a man? Would the manner of a leaf's blowing, even though perfectly known, afford us any instruction concerning the vegetation of a tree?

But, allowing that we were to take the *operations* of one part of nature upon another for the foundation of our judgment concerning the *origin* of the whole (which never can be admitted), yet why select so minute, so weak, so bounded a principle as the reason and design of animals is found to be upon this planet? What peculiar privilege has this little agitation of the brain which we call thought, that we must thus make it the model of the whole universe? Our partiality in our own favor does indeed present it on all occasions, but sound philosophy ought carefully to guard against so natural an illusion.

So far from admitting, continued *Philo,* that the operations of a part can afford us any just conclusion concerning the origin of the whole, I will not allow any one part to form a rule for another part, if the latter be very remote from the former. Is there any reasonable ground to conclude that the inhabitants of other planets possess thought, intelligence, reason, or anything similar to these faculties in men? When nature has so extremely diversified her manner of operation in this small globe, can we imagine that she incessantly copies herself throughout so immense a universe? And if thought, as we may well suppose, be confined merely to this narrow corner, and has even there so limited a sphere of action, with what propriety can we assign it for the original cause of all things? The narrow views of a peasant who makes his domestic economy the rule for the government of kingdoms is, in comparison, a pardonable sophism.

But were we ever so much assured that a thought and reason resembling the human were to be found throughout the whole universe, and were its activity elsewhere vastly greater and more commanding than it appears in this globe; yet I cannot see why the operations of a world constituted, arranged, adjusted, can with any propriety be extended to a world which is in its embryo state and is advancing towards that constitution and arrangement. By observation we know something of the economy, action, and nourishment of a finished animal, but we must transfer with great caution that observation to the growth of a fetus in the womb, and still more in the formation of an animalcule in the loins of its male parent. Nature, we find, even from our limited experience, possesses an infinite number of springs and principles which incessantly discover themselves on every change of her position and situation. And what new and unknown principles would actuate her in so new and unknown a situation as that of the formation of a universe, we cannot, without the utmost temerity, pretend to determine.

A very small part of this great system, during a very short time, is very imperfectly discovered to us; and do we then pronounce decisively concerning the origin of the whole?

Admirable conclusion! Stone, wood, brick, iron, brass have not, at this time, in this minute globe of earth, an order or arrangement without human art and contrivance; therefore, the universe could not originally attain its order and arrangement without something similar to human art. But is a part of nature a rule for another part very wide of the former? Is it a rule for the whole? Is a very small part a rule for the universe? Is nature in one situation a certain rule for nature in another situation vastly different from the former?

And can you blame me, *Cleanthes,* if I here imitate the prudent reserve of *Simonides,* who, according to the noted story, being asked by *Hiero, What God was?* desired a day to think of it, and then two days more, and after that manner continually prolonged the term, without ever bringing in his definition or description? Could you even blame me if I answered at first that *I did not know,* and was sensible that this subject lay vastly beyond the reach of my faculties? You might cry out skeptic and raillier, as much as you pleased, but having found in so many other subjects, much more familiar, the imperfections and even contradictions of human reason, I never should expect any success from its feeble conjectures in a subject so sublime and so remote from the sphere of our observation. When two *species* of objects have always been observed to be conjoined together, I can *infer,* by custom, the existence of one wherever I see the existence of the other, and this I call an argument from experience. But how this argument can have place where the objects, as in the present case, are single, individual, without parallel or specific resemblance, may be difficult to explain. And will any man tell me with a serious countenance that an orderly universe must arise from some thought and art like the human, because we have experience of it? To ascertain this reasoning it were requisite that we had experience of the origin of worlds, and it is not sufficient, surely, that we have seen ships and cities arise from human art and contrivance.

Philo was proceeding in this vehement manner, somewhat between jest and earnest, as it appeared to me, when he observed some signs of impatience in *Cleanthes,* and then immediately stopped short. What I had to suggest, said *Cleanthes,* is only that you would not abuse terms or make use of popular expressions to subvert philosophical reasonings. You know that the vulgar often distinguish reason from experience, even where the question relates only to matter of fact and existence, though it is found, where that *reason* is properly analyzed, that it is nothing but a species of experience. To prove by experience the origin of the universe from mind is not more contrary to common speech than to prove the motion of the earth from the same principle. And a caviller might raise all the same objections to the *Copernican* system which you have urged against my reasonings. Have you other earths, might he say, which you have seen to move? Have . . .

Yes! cried *Philo,* interrupting him, we have other earths. Is not the moon another earth, which we see to turn round its center? Is not Venus another earth, where we observe the same phenomenon? Are not the revolutions of the sun also a confirmation, from analogy, of the same theory? All the planets, are they not earths which revolve about the sun? Are not the satellites moons which move round Jupiter and Saturn, and, along with these primary planets, round the sun? These analogies and resemblances, with others which I have not mentioned, are the sole proofs of the *Copernican* system, and to you it belongs to consider

whether you have any analogies of the same kind to support your theory.

In reality, *Cleanthes,* continued he, the modern system of astronomy is now so much received by all inquirers and has become so essential a part even of our earliest education that we are not commonly very scrupulous in examining the reasons upon which it is founded. It has now become a matter of mere curiosity to study the first writers on that subject who had the full force of prejudice to encounter and were obliged to turn their arguments on every side in order to render them popular and convincing. But if we peruse *Galileo's* famous *Dialogues* concerning the system of the world, we shall find that that great genius, one of the sublimest that ever existed, first bent all his endeavors to prove that there was no foundation for the distinction commonly made between elementary and celestial substances. The schools, proceeding from the illusions of sense, had carried this distinction very far and had established the latter substances to be ingenerable, incorruptible, unalterable, impassible and had assigned all the opposite qualities to the former. But Galileo, beginning with the moon, proved its similarity in every particular to the earth: its convex figure, its natural darkness when not illuminated, its density, its distinction into solid and liquid, the variations of its phases, the mutual illuminations of the earth and moon, their mutual eclipses, the inequalities of the lunar surface, etc. After many instances of this kind, with regard to all the planets, men plainly saw that these bodies became proper objects of experience and that the similarity of their nature enabled us to extend the same arguments and phenomena from one to the other.

In this cautious proceeding of the astronomers you may read your own condemnation, *Cleanthes* or, rather, may see that the subject in which you are engaged exceeds all human reason and inquiry. Can you pretend to show any such similarity between the fabric of a house and the generation of a universe? Have you ever seen nature in any such situation as resembles the first arrangement of the elements? Have worlds ever been formed under your eye, and have you had leisure to observe the whole progress of the phenomenon, from the first appearance of order to its final consummation? If you have, then cite your experience and deliver your theory.

Part III

How the most absurd argument, replied *Cleanthes*, in the hands of a man of ingenuity and invention may acquire an air of probability! Are you not aware, *Philo*, that it became necessary for *Copernicus* and his first disciples to prove the similarity of the terrestrial and celestial matter, because several philosophers, blinded by old systems and supported by some sensible appearances, had denied that similarity? But that it is by no means necessary that theists should prove the similarity of the works of nature to those of art, because this similarity is self-evident and undeniable? The same matter, a like form; what more is requisite to show an analogy between their causes and to ascertain the origin of all things from a divine purpose and intention? Your objections, I must freely tell you, are no better than the abstruse cavils of those philosophers who denied motion, and ought to be refuted in the same manner, by illustrations, examples, and instances rather than by serious argument and philosophy.

Suppose, therefore, that an articulate voice were heard in the clouds, much louder and more melodious than any which human art could ever reach; suppose that this voice were extended in the same instant over all nations and spoke to each nation in its own language and dialect; suppose that the words delivered not only contain a just sense and meaning, but convey some instruction altogether worthy of a benevolent Being, superior to mankind; could you possibly hesitate a moment concerning the cause of this voice, and must you not instantly ascribe it to some design or purpose? Yet I cannot see but all the same objections (if they merit that appellation) which lie against the system of theism may also be produced against this inference.

Might you not say that all conclusions concerning fact were founded on experience that, when we hear an articulate voice in the dark and thence infer a man, it is only the resemblance of the effects which leads us to conclude that there is a like resemblance in the cause; but that this extraordinary voice, by its loudness, extent, and flexibility to all languages, bears so little analogy to any human voice that we have no reason to suppose any analogy in their causes; and consequently that a rational, wise, coherent speech proceeded, you know not whence, from some accidental whistling of the winds, not from any divine reason or intelligence? You see clearly your own objections in these cavils, and I hope, too, you see clearly that they cannot possibly have more force in the one case than in the other.

But to bring the case still nearer the present one of the universe, I shall make two suppositions which imply not any absurdity or impossibility. Suppose that there is a natural, universal, invariable language, common to every individual of human race, and that books are natural productions, which perpetuate themselves in the same manner with animals and vegetables, by descent and propagation. Several expressions of our passions contain a universal language: All brute animals have a natural speech, which, however limited, is very intelligible to their own species. And as there are infinitely fewer parts and less contrivance in the finest composition of eloquence than in the coarsest organized body, the propagation of an *Iliad* or *Aeneid* is an easier supposition than that of any plant or animal.

Suppose, therefore, that you enter into your library, thus peopled by natural volumes, containing the most refined reason and most exquisite beauty, could you possibly open one of them and doubt that its original cause bore the strongest analogy to mind and intelligence? When it reasons and discourses; when it expostulates, argues, and enforces its views and topics; when it applies sometimes to the pure intellect, sometimes to the affections; when it collects, disposes, and adorns every consideration suited to the subject; could you persist in asserting that all this, at the bottom, had really no meaning and that the first formation of this volume in the loins of its original parent proceeded not from thought and design? Your obstinacy, I know, does not reach that degree of firmness; even your skeptical play and wantonness would be abashed at so glaring an absurdity.

But if there be any difference, *Philo*, between this supposed case and the real one of the universe, it is all to the advantage of the latter. The anatomy of an animal affords many stronger instances of design than the perusal of *Livy* or *Tacitus,* and any objection which you start in the former case, by carrying me back to so unusual and extraordinary a scene as the first formation of worlds, the same objection has place on the supposition of our vegetating library. Choose, then, your party, *Philo,* without ambiguity or evasion; assert either that a rational volume is no proof of a rational cause or admit of a similar cause to all the works of nature.

Let me here observe too, continued *Cleanthes,* that this religious argument, instead of being weakened by that skepticism so much affected by you, yet rather acquires force from it and becomes more firm and undisputed. To exclude all argument or reasoning of every kind is either affectation or madness. The declared profession of every reasonable skeptic is only to reject abstruse, remote, and refined arguments, to adhere to common sense and the plain instincts of nature, and to assent wherever any reasons strike him with so full a force that he cannot, without the greatest violence, prevent it. Now the arguments for natural religion are plainly of this kind, and nothing but the most perverse, obstinate metaphysics can reject them. Consider, anatomize the eye, survey its structure and contrivance, and tell me, from your own feeling, if the idea of a contriver does not immediately flow in upon you with a force like that of sensation. The most obvious conclusion, surely, is in favor of design, and it requires time, reflection, and study to summon up those frivolous, though abstruse, objections which can support infidelity. Who can behold the male and female of each species, the correspondence of their parts and instincts, their passions, and whole course of life before and after generation, but must be sensible that the propagation of the species is intended by nature? Millions and millions of such instances present themselves through every part of the universe, and no language can convey a more intelligible irresistible meaning than the curious adjustment of final causes. To what degree, therefore, of blind dogmatism must one have attained to reject such natural and such convincing arguments?

Some beauties in writing we may meet with which seem contrary to rules, and which gain the affections and animate the imagination in opposition to all the precepts of criticism and to the authority of the established masters of art. And if the argument for theism be, as you pretend, contradictory to the principles of logic, its universal, its irresistible influence proves clearly that there may be arguments of a like irregular nature. Whatever cavils may be urged, an orderly world as well as a coherent articulate speech will still be received as an incontestable proof of design and intention.

It sometimes happens, I admit, that the religious arguments do not have their due influence on an ignorant savage and barbarian, not because they are obscure and difficult, but because he never asks himself any question with regard to them. Whence arises the curious structure of an animal? From the copulation of its parents. And these whence? From *their* parents? A few removes set the objects at such a distance that to him they are lost in darkness and confusion; nor is he actuated by any curiosity to trace them further. But this is neither dogmatism nor skepticism, but stupidity: a state of mind very different from your sifting, inquisitive disposition, my ingenious friend. You can trace causes from effects, you can compare the most distant and remote objects, and your greatest errors proceed not from barrenness of thought and invention, but from too luxuriant a fertility, which suppresses your natural good sense by a profusion of unnecessary scruples and objections.

Here I could observe, *Hermippus,* that *Philo* was a little embarrassed and confounded. But while he hesitated in delivering an answer, luckily for him, *Demea* broke in upon the discourse and saved his countenance.

Your instance, *Cleanthes,* said he, drawn from books and language, being familiar, has, I confess, so much more force on that account, but is there not some danger, too, in this very circumstance, and may it not render us presumptuous by making us imagine we comprehend the Deity and have some adequate idea of his nature and attributes? When I read a volume, I enter into the mind and intention of the author: I become him, in a manner, for the instant, and have an immediate feeling and conception of those ideas which revolved in his imagination while employed in that composition. But so near an approach we never surely can make to the Deity. His ways are not our ways. His attributes are perfect but incomprehensible. And this volume of nature contains a great and inexplicable riddle, more than any intelligible discourse or reasoning.

The ancient *Platonists*, you know, were the most religious and devout of all the Pagan philosophers, yet many of them, particularly *Plotinus*, expressly declare that intellect or understanding is not to be ascribed to the Deity and that our most perfect worship of him consists not in acts of veneration, reverence, gratitude, or love, but in a certain mysterious self-annihilation, or total extinction of all our faculties. These ideas are, perhaps, too far stretched, but still it must be acknowledged that, by representing the Deity as so intelligible and comprehensible and so similar to a human mind, we are guilty of the grossest and most narrow partiality and make ourselves the model of the whole universe.

All the *sentiments* of the human mind, gratitude, resentment, love, friendship, approbation, blame, pity, emulation, envy, have a plain reference to the state and situation of man and are calculated for preserving the existence and promoting the activity of such a being in such circumstances. It seems, therefore, unreasonable to transfer such sentiments to a supreme existence or to suppose him actuated by them, and the phenomena, besides, of the universe will not support us in such a theory. All our *ideas* derived from the senses are confusedly false and illusive and cannot therefore be supposed to have place in a supreme intelligence, and as the ideas of internal sentiment, added to those of the external senses, compose the whole furniture of human understanding, we may conclude that none of the *materials* of thought are in any respect similar in the human and in the divine intelligence. Now, as to the *manner* of thinking how can we make any comparison between them or suppose them anywise resembling? Our thought is fluctuating, uncertain, fleeting, successive, and compounded; and were we to remove these circumstances, we absolutely annihilate its essence, and it would in such a case be an abuse of terms to apply to it the name of thought or reason. At least if it appeared more pious and respectful (as it really is) still to retain these terms when we mention the Supreme Being, we ought to acknowledge that their meaning,

in that case, is totally incomprehensible and that the infirmities of our nature do not permit us to reach any ideas which in the least correspond to the ineffable sublimity of the Divine attributes.

Part IV

It seems strange to me, said *Cleanthes*, that you, *Demea*, who are so sincere in the cause of religion, should still maintain the mysterious, incomprehensible nature of the Deity, and should insist so strenuously that he has no manner of likeness or resemblance to human creatures. The Deity, I can readily allow, possesses many powers and attributes of which we can have no comprehension, but if our ideas, so far as they go, be not just and adequate and correspondent to his real nature, I know not what there is in this subject worth insisting on. Is the name, without any meaning, of such mighty importance? Or how do you *mystics*, who maintain the absolute incomprehensibility of the Deity, differ from skeptics or atheists, who assert that the first cause of all is unknown and unintelligible? Their temerity must be very great, if, after rejecting the production by a mind, I mean a mind resembling the human (for I know of no other), they pretend to assign, with certainty, any other specific intelligible cause; and their conscience must be very scrupulous indeed, if they refuse to call the universal unknown cause a God or Deity and to bestow on him as many sublime eulogies and unmeaning epithets as you shall please to require of them.

Who could imagine, replied *Demea*, that *Cleanthes*, the calm philosophical *Cleanthes*, would attempt to refute his antagonists by affixing a nickname to them and, like the common bigots and inquisitors of the age, have recourse to invective and declamation instead of reasoning? Or does he not perceive that these topics are easily retorted and that *anthropomorphite* is an appellation as invidious, and implies as dangerous consequences, as the epithet of *mystic* with which he has honored us? In reality, *Cleanthes*, consider what it is you assert when you represent the Deity as similar to a human mind and understanding. What is the soul of man? A composition of various faculties, passions, sentiments, ideas, united, indeed, into one self or person, but still distinct from each other. When it reasons, the ideas which are the parts of its discourse arrange themselves in a certain form or order, which is not preserved entire for a moment, but immediately gives place to another arrangement. New opinions, new passions, new affections, new feelings arise which continually diversify the mental scene and produce in it the greatest variety and most rapid succession imaginable. How is this compatible with that perfect immutability and simplicity which all true theists ascribe to the Deity? By the same act, say they, he sees past, present, and future; his love and hatred, his mercy and justice, are one individual operation; he is entire in every point of space and complete in every instant of duration. No succession, no change, no acquisition, no diminution. What he is implies not in it any shadow of distinction or diversity. And what he is this moment he ever has been and ever will be, without any new judgment, sentiment, or operation. He stands fixed in one simple, perfect state; nor can you ever say with any propriety that this act of his is different from that other or that this judgment or idea has been lately formed and will give place, by succession, to any different judgment or idea.

I can readily allow, said *Cleanthes,* that those who maintain the perfect simplicity of the Supreme Being, to the extent in which you have explained it, are complete *mystics* and chargeable with all the consequences which I have drawn from their opinion. They are, in a word, *atheists* without knowing it. For though it be allowed that the Deity possesses attributes of which we have no comprehension, yet ought we never to ascribe to him any attributes which are absolutely incompatible with that intelligent nature essential to him. A mind whose acts and sentiments and ideas are not distinct and successive, one that is wholly simple and totally immutable, is a mind which has no thought, no reason, no will, no sentiment, no love, no hatred, or, in a word, is no mind at all. It is an abuse of terms to give it that appellation, and we may as well speak of limited extension without figure, or of number without composition.

Pray consider, said *Philo,* whom you are at present inveighing against. You are honoring with the appellation of *atheist* all the sound, orthodox divines, almost, who have treated of this subject; and you will at last be, yourself, found, according to your reckoning, the only sound theist in the world. But if idolaters be atheists, as, I think, may justly be asserted, and *Christian* theologians the same, what becomes of the argument, so much celebrated, derived from the universal consent of mankind?

But because I know you are not much swayed by names and authorities, I shall endeavor to show you a little more distinctly the inconveniences of that anthropomorphism which you have embraced and shall prove that there is no ground to suppose a plan of the world to be formed in the divine mind, consisting of distinct ideas, differently arranged, in the same manner as an architect forms in his head the plan of a house which he intends to execute.

It is not easy, I admit, to see what is gained by this supposition, whether we judge of the matter by *reason* or by *experience.* We are still obliged to mount higher in order to find the cause of this cause which you had assigned as satisfactory and conclusive.

If *reason* (I mean abstract reason derived from inquiries *a priori*) be not alike mute with regard to all questions concerning cause and effect, this sentence at least it will venture to pronounce: that a mental world, or universe of ideas, requires a cause as much as does a material world, or universe of objects, and if similar in its arrangement, must require a similar cause. For what is there in this subject which should occasion a different conclusion or inference? In an abstract view, they are entirely alike, and no difficulty attends the one supposition which is not common to both of them.

Again, when we will necessarily need *experience* to pronounce some sentence, even on these subjects which lie beyond her sphere, neither can she perceive any material difference in this particular between these two kinds of worlds, but finds them to be governed by similar principles and to depend upon an equal variety of causes in their operations. We have specimens in miniature of both of them. Our own mind resembles the one, a vegetable or animal body the other. Let experience, therefore, judge from these samples. Nothing seems more delicate with regard to its causes than thought, and, as these causes never operate in two persons after the same manner, so we never find two persons who think exactly alike. Nor indeed does the same person think exactly alike at any two different periods of time. A difference of age, of the disposition of his body, of weather, of food, of company, of books, of passions; any of these particulars or others more minute are sufficient to alter the curious machinery of thought and communicate to it very different movements and operations. As far as we can judge, vegetables and animal bodies are not more delicate in their motions nor depend upon a greater variety or more curious adjustment of springs and principles.

How, therefore, shall we satisfy ourselves concerning the cause of that Being whom you suppose the Author of Nature, or, according to your system of anthropomorphism, the ideal world into which you trace the material? Have we not the same reason to trace that ideal world into another ideal world or new intelligent principle? But if we stop and go no further, why go so far? Why not stop at the material world? How can we satisfy ourselves without going on *in infinitum*? And, after all, what satisfaction is there in that infinite progression? Let us remember the story of the Indian philosopher and his elephant.[7] It was never more applicable than to the present subject. If the material world rests upon a similar ideal world, this ideal world must rest upon some other, and so on without end. It were better, therefore, never to look beyond the present material world. By supposing it to contain the principle of its order within itself, we really assert it to be God, and the sooner we arrive at that Divine Being, so much the better. When you go one step beyond the mundane system, you only excite an inquisitive humor which it is impossible ever to satisfy.

To say that the different ideas which compose the reason of the Supreme Being fall into order of themselves and by their own nature is really to talk without any precise meaning. If it has a meaning, I would gladly know why it is not as good sense to say that the parts of the material world fall into order of themselves and by their own nature. Can the one opinion be intelligible, while the other is not so?

We have, indeed, experience of ideas which fall into order of themselves and without any *known*

cause. But, I am sure, we have a much larger experience of matter which does the same, as in all instances of generation and vegetation where the accurate analysis of the cause exceeds all human comprehension. We have also experience of particular systems of thought and of matter which have no order: of the first in madness, of the second in corruption. Why, then, should we think that order is more essential to one than the other? And if it requires a cause in both, what do we gain by your system in tracing the universe of objects into a similar universe of ideas? The first step which we make leads us on forever. It were, therefore, wise in us to limit all our inquiries to the present world without looking further. No satisfaction can ever be attained by these speculations which so far exceed the narrow bounds of human understanding.

It was usual with the *Peripatetics*, you know, *Cleanthes*, when the cause of any phenomenon was demanded, to have recourse to their *faculties* or *occult qualities* and to say, for instance, that bread nourished by its nutritive faculty, and senna purged by its purgative. But it has been discovered that this subterfuge was nothing but the disguise of ignorance and that these philosophers, though less ingenuous, really said the same thing with the skeptics or the vulgar, who fairly confessed that they did not know the cause of these phenomena. In like manner, when it is asked what cause produces order in the ideas of the Supreme Being, can any other reason be assigned by you, anthropomorphites, than that it is a rational faculty and that such is the nature of the Deity? But why a similar answer will not be equally satisfactory in accounting for the order of the world without having recourse to any such intelligent creator as you insist on may be difficult to determine. It is only to say that *such* is the nature of material objects and that they are all originally possessed of a *faculty* of order and proportion. These are only more learned and elaborate ways of confessing our ignorance, nor has the one hypothesis any real advantage above the other except in its greater conformity to vulgar prejudices.

You have displayed this argument with great emphasis, replied *Cleanthes*. You seem not sensible how easy it is to answer it. Even in common life, if I assign a cause for any event, is it any objection, *Philo*, that

7. [See above, Locke's *Essay* Book II, chap. 13, sec. 19, and chap. 23, sec. 2.]

I cannot assign the cause of that cause and answer every new question which may incessantly be started? And what philosophers could possibly submit to so rigid a rule? Philosophers who confess ultimate causes to be totally unknown and are sensible that the most refined principles into which they trace the phenomena are still to them as inexplicable as these phenomena themselves are to the vulgar. The order and arrangement of nature, the curious adjustment of final causes, the plain use and intention of every part and organ; all these bespeak in the clearest language an intelligent cause or author. The heavens and the earth join in the same testimony, the whole chorus of Nature raises one hymn to the praises of its Creator. You alone, or almost alone, disturb this general harmony. You start abstruse doubts, cavils, and objections. You ask me what is the cause of this cause? I know not; I care not; that does not concern me. I have found a Deity, and here I stop my inquiry. Let those go further who are wiser or more enterprising.

I pretend to be neither, replied *Philo,* and for that very reason I should never perhaps have attempted to go so far, especially when I am sensible that I must at last be contented to sit down with the same answer which, without further trouble, might have satisfied me from the beginning. If I am still to remain in utter ignorance of causes and can absolutely give an explication of nothing, I shall never esteem it any advantage to shove off for a moment a difficulty which, you acknowledge, must immediately, in its full force, recur upon me. Naturalists, indeed, very justly explain particular effects by more general causes, though these general causes themselves should remain, in the end totally, inexplicable, but they never surely thought it satisfactory to explain a particular effect by a particular cause which was no more to be accounted for than the effect itself. An ideal system, arranged of itself, without a precedent design, is not a whit more explicable than a material one which attains its order in a like manner; nor is there any more difficulty in the latter supposition than in the former.

Part V

But to show you still more inconveniences, continued *Philo,* in your anthropomorphism, please take a new survey of your principles. *Like effects prove like causes.* This is the experimental argument, and this, you say, too, is the sole theological argument. Now, it is certain that the more alike the effects are which are seen and the more alike causes which are inferred, the stronger is the argument. Every departure on either side diminishes the probability and renders the experiment less conclusive. You cannot doubt of the principle, neither ought you to reject its consequences.

All the new discoveries in astronomy which prove the immense grandeur and magnificence of the works of Nature are so many additional arguments for a Deity, according to the true system of Theism, but, according to your hypothesis of experimental Theism, they become so many objections by removing the effect still further from all resemblance to the effects of human art and contrivance. For if *Lucretius,* even following the old system of the world, could exclaim, "Who is strong enough to rule the sum, who to hold in hand and control the mighty bridle of the unfathomable deep? Who to turn about all the heavens at one time, and warm the fruitful worlds with ethereal ires, or to be present in all places and at all times?"[8]

If Tully esteemed this reasoning so natural as to put it into the mouth of his Epicurean: "What mental vision enabled your master Plato to descry the vast and elaborate architectural process which, as he makes out, the deity adopted in building the structure of the universe? What method of engineering was employed? What tools and levers and derricks? What agents carried out so vast an understanding? And how were air, fire, water, and earth enabled to obey and execute the will of the architect?"[9] If this argument, I say, had any force in former ages, how much greater must it have at present, when the bounds of Nature are so infinitely enlarged and such a magnificent scene is opened to us? It is still more unreasonable to form our idea of so unlimited a cause from our experience of the narrow productions of human design and invention.

The discoveries by microscopes, as they open a new universe in miniature, are still objections according to you, arguments according to me. The further we push

8. Book I, 1094 [trans. W. D. Rouse].
9. *De Natura Deorum,* Book I [trans. H. Rackham].

our researches of this kind, we are still led to infer the universal cause of all to be vastly different from mankind or from any object of human experience and observation.

And what do you say to the discoveries in anatomy, chemistry, botany? . . . These surely are no objections, replied *Cleanthes*. They only discover new instances of art and contrivance. It is still the image of mind reflected on us from innumerable objects. Add a mind *like the human*, said *Philo*. I know of no other, replied *Cleanthes*. And the more alike, the better, insisted *Philo*. To be sure, said *Cleanthes*.

Now, *Cleanthes*, said *Philo*, with an air of alacrity and triumph, mark the consequences. *First*, by this method of reasoning, you renounce all claim to infinity in any of the attributes of the Deity. For, as the cause ought only to be proportioned to the effect, and the effect, so far as it falls under our cognizance, is not infinite, what pretensions have we, upon your suppositions, to ascribe that attribute to the Divine Being? You will still insist that, by removing him so much from all similarity to human creatures, we give in to the most arbitrary hypothesis and at the same time weaken all proofs of his existence.

Secondly, you have no reason, on your theory, for ascribing perfection to the Deity, even in his finite capacity or for supposing him free from every error, mistake, or incoherence in his undertakings. There are many inexplicable difficulties in the works of Nature which, if we allow a perfect author to be proved *a priori*, are easily solved and become only seeming difficulties from the narrow capacity of man who cannot trace infinite relations. But according to your method of reasoning, these difficulties become all real and perhaps will be insisted on as new instances of likeness to human art and contrivance. At least, you must acknowledge that it is impossible for us to tell from our limited views whether this system contains any great faults or deserves any considerable praise, if compared to other possible and even real systems. Could a peasant, if the *Aeneid* were read to him, pronounce that poem to be absolutely faultless or even assign to it its proper rank among the productions of human wit, he, who had never seen any other production?

But were this world ever so perfect a production,

it must still remain uncertain whether all the excellences of the work can justly be ascribed to the workman. If we survey a ship, what an exalted idea must we form of the ingenuity of the carpenter who framed so complicated, useful, and beautiful a machine? And what surprise must we feel when we find him a stupid mechanic who imitated others and copied an art which, through a long succession of ages, after multiplied trials, mistakes, corrections, deliberations, and controversies, had been gradually improving? Many worlds might have been botched and bungled, throughout an eternity, before this system was struck out; much labor lost, many fruitless trials made; and a slow, but continued improvement carried on during infinite ages in the art of world-making. In such subjects, who can determine where the truth, nay, who can conjecture where the probability lies, amidst a great number of hypotheses which may be proposed and a still greater which may be imagined?

And what shadow of an argument, continued *Philo*, can you produce from your hypothesis to prove the unity of the Deity? A great number of men join in building a house or ship, in rearing a city, in framing a commonwealth. Why may not several deities combine in contriving and framing a world? This is only so much greater similarity to human affairs. By sharing the work among several, we may so much further limit the attributes of each and get rid of that extensive power and knowledge which must be supposed in one deity and which, according to you, can only serve to weaken the proof of his existence. And if such foolish, such vicious creatures as man can yet often unite in framing and executing one plan, how much more those deities or demons whom we may suppose several degrees more perfect!

To multiply causes without necessity is indeed contrary to true philosophy. But this principle does not apply to the present case. Were one deity antecedently proved by your theory who was possessed of every attribute requisite to the production of the universe, it would be needless, I admit, (though not absurd) to suppose any other deity existent. But while it is still a question whether all these attributes are united in one subject or dispersed among several independent beings, by what phenomena in nature can we pretend to decide the controversy? Where we see a body raised in a scale, we are sure that there is in the opposite scale, however concealed from sight, some counterpoising weight equal to it, but it is still allowed to doubt whether that weight be an aggregate of several distinct bodies or one uniform united mass. And if the weight requisite very much exceeds anything which we have ever seen conjoined in any single body, the former supposition becomes still more probable and natural. An intelligent being of such vast power and capacity as is necessary to produce the universe or, to speak in the language of ancient philosophy, so prodigious an animal exceeds all analogy and even comprehension.

But further, *Cleanthes,* men are mortal and renew their species by generation, and this is common to all living creatures. The two great sexes of male and female, says *Milton,* animate the world. Why must this circumstance, so universal, so essential, be excluded from those numerous and limited deities? Behold, then, the theogony of ancient times brought back upon us.

And why not become a perfect anthropomorphite? Why not assert the deity or deities to be corporeal and to have eyes, a nose, mouth, ears, etc.? *Epicurus* maintained that no man had ever seen reason but in a human figure. Therefore, the gods must have a human figure. And this argument, which is deservedly so much ridiculed by *Cicero,* becomes, according to you, solid and philosophical.

In a word, *Cleanthes,* a man who follows your hypothesis is able perhaps to assert or conjecture that the universe sometime arose from something like design, but beyond that position he cannot ascertain one single circumstance and is left afterwards to fix every point of his theology by the utmost license of fancy and hypothesis. This world, for all he knows, is very faulty and imperfect compared to a superior standard and was only the first rude essay of some infant deity who afterwards abandoned it, ashamed of his lame performance: It is the work only of some dependent, inferior deity and is the object of derision to his superiors: It is the production of old age and dotage in some superannuated deity and, ever since his death, has run on at adventures from the first impulse and active force which it received from him. You justly give signs of horror, *Demea,* at these strange

suppositions. But these, and a thousand more of the same kind, are *Cleanthes's* suppositions, not mine. From the moment the attributes of the Deity are supposed finite, all these have place. And I cannot, for my part, think that so wild and unsettled a system of theology is in any respect preferable to none at all.

These suppositions I absolutely disown, cried *Cleanthes.* They strike me, however, with no horror, especially when proposed in that rambling way in which they drop from you. On the contrary, they give me pleasure when I see that, by the utmost indulgence of your imagination, you never get rid of the hypothesis of design in the universe, but are obliged at every turn to have recourse to it. To this concession I adhere steadily and this I regard as a sufficient foundation for religion. [. . .]

Part IX

But if so many difficulties attend the argument *a posteriori,* said *Demea,* had we not better adhere to that simple and sublime argument *a priori* which, by offering to us infallible demonstration, cuts off at once all doubt and difficulty? By this argument, too, we may prove the *infinity* of the Divine attributes which, I am afraid, can never be ascertained with certainty from any other topic. For how can an effect which either is finite or, for all we know, may be so; how can such an effect, I say, prove an infinite cause? The unity, too, of the Divine Nature it is very difficult, if not absolutely impossible, to deduce merely from contemplating the works of nature; nor will the uniformity alone of the plan, even were it allowed, give us any assurance of that attribute. Whereas the argument *a priori* . . .

You seem to reason, *Demea,* interposed *Cleanthes,* as if those advantages and conveniences in the abstract argument were full proofs of its solidity. But it is first proper, in my opinion, to determine what argument of this nature you choose to insist on, and we shall afterwards, from itself, better than from its *useful* consequences, endeavor to determine what value we ought to put upon it.

The argument, replied *Demea,* which I would insist on is the common one. Whatever exists must have a cause or reason of its existence, it being absolutely impossible for anything to produce itself or be the cause of its own existence. In mounting up, therefore, from effects to causes, we must either go on in tracing an infinite succession without any ultimate cause at all or must at last have recourse to some ultimate cause that is *necessarily* existent. Now, that the first supposition is absurd may be thus proved. In the infinite chain or succession of causes and effects, each single effect is determined to exist by the power and efficacy of that cause which immediately preceded; but the whole eternal chain or succession, taken together, is not determined or caused by anything; and yet it is evident that it requires a cause or reason as much as any particular object which begins to exist in time. The question is still reasonable why this particular succession of causes existed from eternity and not any other succession or no succession at all. If there be no necessarily existent being, any supposition which can be formed is equally possible; nor is there any more absurdity in nothing's having existed from eternity than there is in that succession of causes which constitutes the universe. What was it, then, which determined something to exist rather than nothing, and bestowed being on a particular possibility, exclusive of the rest? *External causes*, there are supposed to be none. *Chance* is a word without a meaning. Was it *nothing*? But that can never produce anything. We must, therefore, have recourse to a necessarily existent Being who carries the *reason* of his existence in himself and who cannot be supposed not to exist without an express contradiction. There is, consequently, such a Being, that is, there is a Deity.

I shall not leave it to *Philo*, said *Cleanthes*, though I know that starting objections is his chief delight, to point out the weakness of this metaphysical reasoning. It seems to me so obviously ill-grounded and at the same time of so little consequence to the cause of true piety and religion that I shall myself venture to show the fallacy of it.

I shall begin with observing that there is an evident absurdity in pretending to demonstrate a matter of fact or to prove it by any arguments *a priori*. Nothing is demonstrable unless the contrary implies a contradiction. Nothing that is distinctly conceivable implies a contradiction. Whatever we conceive as existent, we can also conceive as non-existent. There is no

being, therefore, whose non-existence implies a contradiction. Consequently there is no being whose existence is demonstrable. I propose this argument as entirely decisive and am willing to rest the whole controversy upon it.

It is pretended that the Deity is a necessarily existent being and this necessity of his existence is attempted to be explained by asserting that if we knew his whole essence or nature, we should perceive it to be as impossible for him not to exist as for twice 2 not to be 4. But it is evident that this can never happen while our faculties remain the same as at present. It will still be possible for us at any time to conceive the non-existence of what we formerly conceived to exist; nor can the mind ever lie under a necessity of supposing any object to remain always in being in the same manner as we lie under a necessity of always conceiving twice two to be four. The words, therefore, *necessary existence* have no meaning or, which is the same thing, none that is consistent.

But further, why may not the material universe be the necessarily existent being, according to this pretended explication of necessity? We dare not affirm that we know all the qualities of matter, and, for all we can determine, it may contain some qualities which, were they known, would make its non-existence appear as great a contradiction as that twice two is five. I find only one argument employed to prove that the material world is not the necessarily existent Being, and this argument is derived from the contingency both of the matter and the form of the world. "Any particle of matter," it is said,[10] "may be *conceived* to be annihilated, and any form may be *conceived* to be altered. Such an annihilation or alteration, therefore, is not impossible." But it seems a great partiality not to perceive that the same argument extends equally to the Deity so far as we have any conception of him, and that the mind can at least imagine him to be non-existent or his attributes to be altered. It must be some unknown, inconceivable qualities which can make his non-existence appear impossible or his attributes unalterable, and no reason can be assigned why these qualities may not belong

10. Dr. Clarke. [Samuel Clarke (1675–1729), an English theologian and follower of Newton.]

to matter. As they are altogether unknown and inconceivable, they can never be proved incompatible with it.

Add to this that in tracing an eternal succession of objects it seems absurd to inquire for a general cause or first author. How can anything that exists from eternity have a cause, since that relation implies a priority in time and a beginning of existence?

In such a chain, too, or succession of objects, each part is caused by that which preceded it and causes that which succeeds it. Where then is the difficulty? But the *whole*, you say, wants a cause. I answer that the uniting of these parts into a whole, like the uniting of several distinct countries into one kingdom or several distinct members into one body, is performed merely by an arbitrary act of the mind and has no influence on the nature of things. Did I show you the particular causes of each individual in a collection of twenty particles of matter, I should think it very unreasonable should you afterwards ask me what was the cause of the whole twenty. This is sufficiently explained in explaining the cause of the parts.

Though the reasonings which you have urged, *Cleanthes*, may well excuse me, said *Philo*, from starting any further difficulties, yet I cannot forbear insisting still upon another topic. It is observed by arithmeticians that the products of 9 compose always either 9 or some lesser product of 9, if you add together all the characters of which any of the former products is composed. Thus, of 18, 27, 36, which are products of 9, you make 9 by adding 1 to 8, 2 to 7, 3 to 6. Thus, 369 is a product also of 9; and if you add 3, 6, and 9, you make 18, a lesser product of 9.[11] To a superficial observer, so wonderful a regularity may be admired as the effect either of chance or design, but a skillful algebraist immediately concludes it to be the work of necessity and demonstrates that it must forever result from the nature of these numbers. Is it not probable, I ask, that the whole economy of the universe is conducted by a like necessity, though no human algebra can furnish a key which solves the difficulty? And instead of admiring the order of natural beings, may it not happen that, could we penetrate into the intimate nature of bodies, we should clearly

see why it was absolutely impossible they could ever admit of any other disposition? So dangerous is it to introduce this idea of necessity into the present question! And so naturally does it afford an inference directly opposite to the religious hypothesis!

But dropping all these abstractions, continued *Philo*, and confining ourselves to more familiar topics, I shall venture to add an observation that the argument *a priori* has seldom been found very convincing, except to people of a metaphysical head who have accustomed themselves to abstract reasoning and who, finding from mathematics that the understanding frequently leads to truth through obscurity and contrary to first appearances, have transferred the same habit of thinking to subjects where it ought not to have place. Other people, even of good sense and the best inclined to religion, feel always some deficiency in such arguments, though they are not perhaps able to explain distinctly where it lies, a certain proof that men ever did and ever will derive their religion from other sources than from this species of reasoning.

Part X

It is my opinion, I admit, replied *Demea*, that each man feels, in a manner, the truth of religion within his own breast and, from a consciousness of his imbecility and misery rather than from any reasoning, is led to seek protection from that Being on whom he and all nature is dependent. So anxious or so tedious are even the best scenes of life that futurity is still the object of all our hopes and fears. We incessantly look forward and endeavor, by prayers, adoration, and sacrifice to appease those unknown powers whom we find, by experience, so able to afflict and oppress us. Wretched creatures that we are! What resource for us amidst the innumerable ills of life, did not religion suggest some methods of atonement and appease those terrors with which we are incessantly agitated and tormented?

I am indeed persuaded, said *Philo*, that the best and indeed the only method of bringing everyone to a due sense of religion is by just representations of the misery and wickedness of men. And for that purpose a talent of eloquence and strong imagery is more requi-

11. *Republique des Lettres,* August 1685.

site than that of reasoning and argument. For is it necessary to prove what everyone feels within himself? It is only necessary to make us feel it, if possible, more intimately and sensibly.

The people, indeed, replied *Demea*, are sufficiently convinced of this great and melancholy truth. The miseries of life; the unhappiness of man; the general corruptions of our nature; the unsatisfactory enjoyment of pleasures, riches, honors; these phrases have become almost proverbial in all languages. And who can doubt of what all men declare from their own immediate feeling and experience?

In this point, said *Philo*, the learned are perfectly agreed with the vulgar, and in all letters, *sacred* and *profane*, the topic of human misery has been insisted on with the most pathetic eloquence that sorrow and melancholy could inspire. The poets, who speak from sentiment, without a system, and whose testimony has therefore the more authority, abound in images of this nature. From *Homer* down to *Dr. Young*,[12] the whole inspired tribe have ever been sensible that no other representation of things would suit the feeling and observation of each individual.

As to authorities, replied *Demea*, you need not seek them. Look round this library of *Cleanthes*. I shall venture to affirm that, except authors of particular sciences such as chemistry or botany who have no occasion to treat of human life, there is scarce one of those innumerable writers from whom the sense of human misery has not, in some passage or other, extorted a complaint and confession of it. At least, the chance is entirely on that side, and no one author has ever, so far as I can recollect, been so extravagant as to deny it.

There you must excuse me, said *Philo*. *Leibniz* has denied it and is perhaps the first[13] who ventured upon so bold and paradoxical an opinion; at least, the first who made it essential to his philosophical system.

And by being the first, replied *Demea*, might he not have been sensible of his error? For is this a subject in which philosophers can propose to make discoveries, especially in so late an age? And can any man hope by a simple denial (for the subject scarcely admits of reasoning) to bear down the united testimony of mankind founded on sense and consciousness?

And why should man, added he, pretend to an exemption from the lot of all other animals? The whole earth, believe me, *Philo*, is cursed and polluted. A perpetual war is kindled amongst all living creatures. Necessity, hunger, want stimulate the strong and courageous; fear, anxiety, terror agitate the weak and infirm. The first entrance into life gives anguish to the new-born infant and to its wretched parent; weakness, impotence, distress attend each stage of that life; and it is at last finished in agony and horror.

Observe, too, says *Philo*, the curious artifices of Nature in order to embitter the life of every living being. The stronger prey upon the weaker and keep them in perpetual terror and anxiety. The weaker, too, in their turn, often prey upon the stronger and vex and molest them without relaxation. Consider that innumerable race of insects which either are bred on the body of each animal or, flying about, infix their stings in him. These insects have others still less than themselves which torment them. And thus on each hand, before and behind, above and below, every animal is surrounded with enemies which incessantly seek his misery and destruction.

Man alone, said *Demea*, seems to be, in part, an exception to this rule. For by combination in society, he can easily master lions, tigers, and bears, whose greater strength and agility naturally enable them to prey upon him.

On the contrary, it is here chiefly, cried *Philo*, that the uniform and equal maxims of nature are most apparent. Man, it is true, can, by combination, surmount all his real enemies and become master of the whole animal creation, but does he not immediately raise up to himself *imaginary* enemies, the demons of his fancy, who haunt him with superstitious terrors and blast every enjoyment of life? His pleasure, as he imagines, becomes, in their eyes, a crime: His food and repose give them umbrage and offence, his very sleep and dreams furnish new materials to anxious fear, and even death, his refuge from every other ill,

12. [Edward Young (1683–1765), poet.]
13. That sentiment had been maintained by Dr. King [Dr. William King (1650–1729) archbishop of Dublin] and some few others before Leibniz, though by none of so great fame as that German philosopher.

presents only the dread of endless and innumerable woes. Nor does the wolf molest the timid flock more than superstition does the anxious breast of wretched mortals.

Besides, consider, *Demea,* this very society by which we surmount those wild beasts, our natural enemies. What new enemies does it not raise to us? What woe and misery does it not occasion? Man is the greatest enemy of man. Oppression, injustice, contempt, contumely, violence, sedition, war, calumny, treachery, fraud; by these they mutually torment each other and they would soon dissolve that society which they had formed, were it not for the dread of still greater ills which must attend their separation.

But though these external insults, said *Demea,* from animals, from men, from all the elements which assault us, form a frightful catalogue of woes, they are nothing in comparison of those which arise within ourselves from the distempered condition of our mind and body. How many lie under the lingering torment of diseases? Hear the pathetic enumeration of the great poet.

> Intestine stone and ulcer, colic-pangs,
> Demoniac frenzy, moping melancholy,
> And moon-struck madness, pining atrophy,
> Marasmus, and wide-wasting pestilence.
> Dire was the tossing, deep the groans: *despair*
> Tended the sick, busiest from couch to couch.
> And over them triumphant *death* his dart
> Shook: but delayed to strike, though oft invoked
> With vows, as their chief good and final hope.[14]

The disorders of the mind, continued *Demea,* though more secret, are not perhaps less dismal and vexatious. Remorse, shame, anguish, rage, disappointment, anxiety, fear, dejection, despair; who has ever passed through life without cruel inroads from these tormentors? How many have scarcely ever felt any better sensations? Labor and poverty, so abhorred by everyone, are the certain lot of the far greater number, and those few privileged persons who enjoy ease and opulence never reach contentment or true felicity. All the goods of life united would not make a very

14. [John Milton, *Paradise Lost,* Book XI.]

happy man, but all the ills united would make a wretch indeed, and any one of them almost (and who can be free from every one?), nay, often the absence of one good (and who can possess all?) is sufficient to render life ineligible.

Were a stranger to drop on a sudden into this world, I would show him, as a specimen of its ills, a hospital full of diseases, a prison crowded with malefactors and debtors, a field of battle strewed with carcasses, a fleet foundering in the ocean, a nation languishing under tyranny, famine, or pestilence. To turn the gay side of life to him and give him a notion of its pleasures, where should I conduct him? To a ball, to an opera, to court? He might justly think that I was only showing him a diversity of distress and sorrow.

There is no evading such striking instances, said *Philo,* but by apologies, which still further aggravate the charge. Why have all men, I ask, in all ages, complained incessantly of the miseries of life? . . . They have no just reason, says one: These complaints proceed only from their discontented, repining, anxious disposition . . . And can there possibly, I reply, be a more certain foundation of misery than such a wretched temper?

But if they were really as unhappy as they pretend, says my antagonist, why do they remain in life? . . .

Not satisfied with life, afraid of death.

This is the secret chain, say I, that holds us. We are terrified, not bribed to the continuance of our existence.

It is only a false delicacy, he may insist, which a few refined spirits indulge and which has spread these complaints among the whole race of mankind . . . And what is this delicacy, I ask, which you blame? Is it anything but a greater sensibility to all the pleasures and pains of life? And if the man of a delicate, refined temper, by being so much more alive than the rest of the world, is only so much more unhappy, what judgment must we form in general of human life?

Let men remain at rest, says our adversary, and they will be easy. They are willing artificers of their own misery . . . No! reply I, an anxious languor follows their repose; disappointment, vexation, trouble, their activity and ambition.

I can observe something like what you mention in

some others, replied *Cleanthes*, but I confess I feel little or nothing of it in myself and hope that it is not so common as you represent it.

If you do not feel human misery yourself, cried *Demea*, I congratulate you on so happy a singularity. Others, seemingly the most prosperous, have not been ashamed to vent their complaints in the most melancholy strains. Let us attend to the great, the fortunate emperor, *Charles V*, when, tired with human grandeur, he resigned all his extensive dominions into the hands of his son. In the last harangue which he made on that memorable occasion, he publicly avowed *that the greatest prosperities which he had ever enjoyed had been mixed with so many adversities that he might truly say he had never enjoyed any satisfaction or contentment.* But did the retired life in which he sought for shelter afford him any greater happiness? If we may credit his son's account, his repentance commenced the very day of his resignation.

Cicero's fortune, from small beginnings, rose to the greatest luster and renown, yet what pathetic complaints of the ills of life do his familiar letters as well as philosophical discourses contain? And suitably to his own experience, he introduces Cato, the great, the fortunate Cato, protesting in his old age that had he a new life in his offer, he would reject the present.

Ask yourself, ask any of your acquaintances, whether they would live over again the last ten or twenty years of their lives. No! But the next twenty, they say, will be better:

And from the dregs of life, hope to receive
What the first sprightly running could not give.[15]

Thus, at last, they find (such is the greatness of human misery, it reconciles even contradictions) that they complain at once of the shortness of life and of its vanity and sorrow.

And is it possible, *Cleanthes*, said *Philo*, that after all these reflections and infinitely more which might be suggested, you can still persevere in your anthropomorphism and assert the moral attributes of the Deity, his justice, benevolence, mercy, and rectitude, to be of the same nature with these virtues in human crea-

tures? His power, we allow, is infinite. Whatever he wills is executed. But neither man nor any other animal is happy. Therefore, he does not will their happiness. His wisdom is infinite; he is never mistaken in choosing the means to any end; but the course of Nature tends not to human or animal felicity; therefore, it is not established for that purpose. Through the whole compass of human knowledge, there are no inferences more certain and infallible than these. In what respect, then, do his benevolence and mercy resemble the benevolence and mercy of men?

Epicurus's old questions are yet unanswered.

Is he willing to prevent evil, but not able? Then is he impotent. Is he able, but not willing? Then is he malevolent. Is he both able and willing? Whence then is evil?

You ascribe, *Cleanthes*, (and I believe justly) a purpose and intention to nature. But what, I beseech you, is the object of that curious artifice and machinery which she has displayed in all animals? The preservation alone of individuals and propagation of the species. It seems enough for her purpose, if such a rank be barely upheld in the universe without any care or concern for the happiness of the members that compose it. No resource for this purpose: no machinery in order merely to give pleasure or ease, no fund of pure joy and contentment, no indulgence without some want or necessity accompanying it. At least the few phenomena of this nature are overbalanced by opposite phenomena of still greater importance.

Our sense of music, harmony, and, indeed, beauty of all kinds gives satisfaction without being absolutely necessary to the preservation and propagation of the species. But what racking pains, on the other hand, arise from gouts, gravels, migraines, toothaches, rheumatisms, where the injury to the animal machinery is either small or incurable? Mirth, laughter, play, frolic seem gratuitous satisfactions which have no further tendency: spleen, melancholy, discontent, superstition are pains of the same nature. How, then, does the Divine benevolence display itself in the sense of you anthropomorphites? None but we mystics, as you were pleased to call us, can account for this strange mixture of phenomena by deriving it from attributes, infinitely perfect, but incomprehensible.

15. [John Dryden, *Aurengzebe*, Act IV, scene 1.]

And have you at last, said *Cleanthes* smiling, betrayed your intentions, *Philo*? Your long agreement with *Demea* did indeed a little surprise me, but I find you were all the while erecting a concealed battery against me. And I must confess that you have now fallen upon a subject worthy of your noble spirit of opposition and controversy. If you can make out the present point and prove mankind to be unhappy or corrupted, there is an end at once of all religion. For to what purpose establish the natural attributes of the Deity, while the moral are still doubtful and uncertain?

You take umbrage very easily, replied *Demea*, at opinions the most innocent and the most generally received, even amongst the religious and devout themselves. And nothing can be more surprising than to find a topic like this, concerning the wickedness and misery of man, charged with no less than atheism and profaneness. Have not all pious divines and preachers who have indulged their rhetoric on so fertile a subject; have they not easily, I say, given a solution of any difficulties which may attend it? This world is but a point in comparison of the universe, this life but a moment in comparison of eternity. The present evil phenomena, therefore, are rectified in other regions and in some future period of existence. And the eyes of men, being then opened to larger views of things, see the whole connection of general laws and trace with adoration the benevolence and rectitude of the Deity through all the mazes and intricacies of his providence.

No! replied *Cleanthes*. No! These arbitrary suppositions can never be admitted, contrary to matter of fact, visible and uncontroverted. Whence can any cause be known but from its known effects? Whence can any hypothesis be proved but from the apparent phenomena? To establish one hypothesis upon another is building entirely in the air, and the utmost we ever attain by these conjectures and fictions is to ascertain the bare possibility of our opinion. But never can we, upon such terms, establish its reality.

The only method of supporting Divine benevolence, and it is what I willingly embrace, is to deny absolutely the misery and wickedness of man. Your representations are exaggerated; your melancholy views mostly fictitious; your inferences contrary to fact and experience. Health is more common than sickness; pleasure than pain; happiness than misery. And for one vexation which we meet with, we attain, upon computation, a hundred enjoyments.

Admitting your position, replied *Philo*, which yet is extremely doubtful, you must at the same time allow that if pain be less frequent than pleasure, it is infinitely more violent and durable. One hour of it is often able to outweigh a day, a week, a month of our common insipid enjoyments. And how many days, weeks, and months are passed by several in the most acute torments? Pleasure, scarcely in one instance, is ever able to reach ecstasy and rapture, and in no one instance can it continue for any time at its highest pitch and altitude. The spirits evaporate, the nerves relax, the fabric is disordered, and the enjoyment quickly degenerates into fatigue and uneasiness. But pain often—good God, how often!—rises to torture and agony, and the longer it continues, it becomes still more genuine agony and torture. Patience is exhausted, courage languishes, melancholy seizes us, and nothing terminates our misery but the removal of its cause or another event which is the sole cure of all evil, but which, from our natural folly, we regard with still greater horror and consternation.

But not to insist upon these topics, continued *Philo*, though most obvious, certain, and important, I must use the freedom to admonish you, *Cleanthes*, that you have put the controversy upon a most dangerous issue and are unawares introducing a total skepticism into the most essential articles of natural and revealed theology. What! No method of fixing a just foundation for religion unless we allow the happiness of human life and maintain a continued existence even in this world, with all our present pains, infirmities, vexations, and follies, to be eligible and desirable! But this is contrary to everyone's feeling and experience; it is contrary to an authority so established as nothing can subvert. No decisive proofs can ever be produced against this authority; nor is it possible for you to compute, estimate, and compare all the pains and all the pleasures in the lives of all men and of all animals: and thus, by your resting the whole system of religion on a point which, from its very nature, must forever be uncertain, you tacitly confess that that system is equally uncertain.

But allowing you what never will be believed, at least what you never possibly can prove, that animal or, at least, human happiness in this life exceeds its misery, you have yet done nothing. For this is not, by any means, what we expect from infinite power, infinite wisdom, and infinite goodness. Why is there any misery at all in the world? Not by chance surely. From some cause then. Is it from the intention of the Deity? But he is perfectly benevolent. Is it contrary to his intention? But he is almighty. Nothing can shake the solidity of this reasoning, so short, so clear, so decisive, unless we assert that these subjects exceed all human capacity and that our common measures of truth and falsehood are not applicable to them, a topic which I have all along insisted on, but which you have, from the beginning, rejected with scorn and indignation.

But I will be contented to retire still from this entrenchment, for I deny that you can ever force me in it. I will allow that pain or misery in man is *compatible* with infinite power and goodness in the Deity, even in your sense of these attributes. What are you advanced by all these concessions? A mere possible compatibility is not sufficient. You must *prove* these pure, unmixed, and uncontrollable attributes from the present mixed and confused phenomena and from these alone. A hopeful undertaking! Were the phenomena ever so pure and unmixed, yet being finite, they would be insufficient for that purpose. How much more, where they are also so jarring and discordant!

Here, *Cleanthes*, I find myself at ease in my argument. Here I triumph. Formerly, when we argued concerning the natural attributes of intelligence and design, I needed all my skeptical and metaphysical subtlety to elude your grasp. In many views of the universe and of its parts, particularly the latter, the beauty and fitness of final causes strike us with such irresistible force that all objections appear (what I believe they really are) mere cavils and sophisms; nor can we then imagine how it was ever possible for us to repose any weight on them. But there is no view of human life or of the condition of mankind from which, without the greatest violence, we can infer the moral attributes or learn that infinite benevolence, conjoined with infinite power and infinite wisdom,

which we must discover by the eyes of faith alone. It is your turn now to tug the laboring oar and to support your philosophical subtleties against the dictates of plain reason and experience.

Part XI

I scruple not to allow, said *Cleanthes*, that I have been apt to suspect the frequent repetition of the word *infinite* which we meet with in all theological writers, to savor more of panegyric than of philosophy, and that any purposes of reasoning, and even of religion, would be better served, were we to rest contented with more accurate and more moderate expressions. The terms *admirable, excellent, superlatively great, wise, and holy*—these sufficiently fill the imaginations of men, and anything beyond, besides that it leads into absurdities, has no influence on the affections or sentiments. Thus, in the present subject, if we abandon all human analogy, as seems your intention, *Demea*, I am afraid we abandon all religion and retain no conception of the great object of our adoration. If we preserve human analogy, we must forever find it impossible to reconcile any mixture of evil in the universe with infinite attributes, much less can we ever prove the latter from the former. But supposing the Author of Nature to be finitely perfect, though far exceeding mankind, a satisfactory account may then be given of natural and moral evil and every untoward phenomenon be explained and adjusted. A lesser evil may then be chosen in order to avoid a greater, inconveniences be submitted to in order to reach a desirable end, and, in a word, benevolence regulated by wisdom and limited by necessity may produce just such a world as the present. You, *Philo*, who are so prompt at starting views and reflections and analogies, I would gladly hear, at length, without interruption, your opinion of this new theory, and if it deserve our attention, we may afterwards, at more leisure, reduce it into form.

My sentiments, replied *Philo*, are not worth being made a mystery of. And therefore, without any ceremony, I shall deliver what occurs to me with regard to the present subject. It must, I think, be allowed that if a very limited intelligence whom we shall suppose utterly unacquainted with the universe were assured that it were the production of a very good, wise, and powerful Being, however finite, he would, from his conjectures, form *beforehand* a different notion of it from what we find it to be by experience; nor would he ever imagine, merely from these attributes of the cause of which he is informed, that the effect could be so full of vice and misery and disorder as it appears in this life. Supposing now that this person were brought into the world, still assured that it was the workmanship of such a sublime and benevolent Being; he might, perhaps, be surprised at the disappointment, but would never retract his former belief, if founded on any very solid argument, since such a limited intelligence must be sensible of his own blindness and ignorance and must allow that there may be many solutions of those phenomena which will forever escape his comprehension. But supposing, which is the real case with regard to man, that this creature is not antecedently convinced of a supreme intelligence, benevolent and powerful, but is left to gather such a belief from the appearances of things; this entirely alters the case, nor will he ever find any reason for such a conclusion. He may be fully convinced of the narrow limits of his understanding, but this will not help him in forming an inference concerning the goodness of superior powers, since he must form that inference from what he knows, not from what he is ignorant of. The more you exaggerate his weakness and ignorance, the more diffident you render him and give him the greater suspicion that such subjects are beyond the reach of his faculties. You are obliged, therefore, to reason with him merely from the known phenomena and to drop every arbitrary supposition or conjecture.

Did I show you a house or palace where there was not one apartment convenient or agreeable; where the windows, doors, fires, passages, stairs, and the whole economy of the building were the source of noise, confusion, fatigue, darkness, and the extremes of heat and cold; you would certainly blame the contrivance without any further examination. The architect would in vain display his subtlety and prove to you that if this door or that window were altered, greater ills would ensue. What he says may be strictly true: The alteration of one particular, while the other parts of the building remain, may only augment the inconveniences. But still you would assert in general that, if the architect had had skill and good intentions, he might have formed such a plan of the whole and might have adjusted the parts in such a manner as would have remedied all or most of these inconveniences. His ignorance, or even your own ignorance of such a plan, will never convince you of the impossibility of it. If you find any inconveniences and deformities in the building, you will always, without entering into any detail, condemn the architect.

In short, I repeat the question: Is the world, considered in general and as it appears to us in this life, different from what a man or such a limited being would *beforehand* expect from a very powerful, wise, and benevolent Deity? It must be strange prejudice to assert the contrary. And from thence I conclude that however consistent the world may be, allowing certain suppositions and conjectures, with the idea of such a Deity, it can never afford us an inference concerning his existence. The consistency is not absolutely denied, only the inference. Conjectures, especially where infinity is excluded from the Divine attributes, may perhaps be sufficient to prove a consistency, but can never be foundations for any inference.

There seems to be *four* circumstances on which depend all or the greatest part of the ills that molest sensible creatures, and it is not impossible but all these circumstances may be necessary and unavoidable. We know so little beyond common life or even of common life that, with regard to the economy of a universe, there is no conjecture, however wild, which may not be just; nor any one, however plausible, which may not be erroneous. All that belongs to human understanding in this deep ignorance and obscurity is to be skeptical or at least cautious and not to admit of any hypothesis whatever, much less of any which is supported by no appearance of probability. Now, this I assert to be the case with regard to all the causes of evil and the circumstances on which it depends: None of them appear to human reason in the least degree necessary or unavoidable, nor can we suppose them such without the utmost license of imagination.

The *first* circumstance which introduces evil is that contrivance or economy of the animal creation by which pains as well as pleasures are employed to excite all creatures to action and make them vigilant in the great work of self-preservation. Now pleasure alone, in its various degrees, seems to human understanding sufficient for this purpose. All animals might be constantly in a state of enjoyment, but when urged by any of the necessities of nature—such as thirst, hunger, weariness—instead of pain, they might feel a diminution of pleasure by which they might be prompted to seek that object which is necessary to their subsistence. Men pursue pleasure as eagerly as they avoid pain; at least they might have been so constituted. It seems, therefore, plainly possible to carry on the business of life without any pain. Why then is any animal ever rendered susceptible of such a sensation? If animals can be free from it an hour, they might enjoy a perpetual exemption from it, and it required as particular a contrivance of their organs to produce that feeling as to endow them with sight, hearing, or any of the senses. Shall we conjecture that such a contrivance was necessary without any appearance of reason? And shall we build on that conjecture as on the most certain truth?

But a capacity of pain would not alone produce pain, were it not for the *second* circumstance, namely, the conducting of the world by general laws, and this seems nowise necessary to a very perfect Being. It is true, if everything were conducted by particular volitions, the course of nature would be perpetually broken, and no man could employ his reason in the conduct of life. But might not other particular volitions remedy this inconvenience? In short, might not the Deity exterminate all ill, wherever it were to be found, and produce all good, without any preparation or long progress of causes and effects?

Besides, we must consider that, according to the present economy of the world, the course of nature, though supposed exactly regular, yet to us appears not so, and many events are uncertain, and many disappoint our expectations. Health and sickness, calm and tempest, with an infinite number of other accidents whose causes are unknown and variable, have a great influence both on the fortunes of particular persons and on the prosperity of public societies; and indeed all human life, in a manner, depends on such accidents. A being, therefore, who knows the secret springs of the universe might easily, by particular volitions, turn all these accidents to the good of mankind and render the whole world happy without discovering himself in any operation. A fleet whose purposes were salutary to society might always meet with a fair wind; good princes enjoy sound health and long life; persons born to power and authority be framed with good tempers and virtuous dispositions. A few such events as these, regularly and wisely conducted, would change the face of the world, and yet would no more seem to disturb the course of nature or confound human conduct than the present economy of things, where the causes are secret and variable and compounded. Some small touches given to *Caligula's* brain in his infancy might have converted him into a *Trajan*. One wave, a little higher than the rest, by burying *Caesar* and his fortune in the bottom of the ocean, might have restored liberty to a considerable part of mankind. There may, for all we know, be good reasons why Providence does not interpose in this manner, but they are unknown to us, and though the mere supposition that such reasons exist may be sufficient to save the conclusion concerning the Divine attributes, yet surely it can never be sufficient to establish that conclusion.

If everything in the universe be conducted by general laws and if animals be rendered susceptible of pain, it scarcely seems possible but some ill must arise in the various shocks of matter and the various concurrence and opposition of general laws, but this ill would be very rare were it not for the *third* circumstance which I proposed to mention, namely, the great frugality with which all powers and faculties are distributed to every particular being. So well adjusted are the organs and capacities of all animals and so well fitted to their preservation that, as far as history or tradition reaches, there appears not to be any single species which has yet been extinguished in the universe. Every animal has the requisite endowments, but these endowments are bestowed with so scrupulous an economy that any considerable diminution must entirely destroy the creature. Wherever one power is increased, there is a proportional abatement in the others. Animals which excel in swiftness are commonly defective in force. Those which possess both are either imperfect in some of their senses or are oppressed with the most craving wants. The human species, whose chief excellency is reason and sagacity, is of all others the most necessitous and the most deficient in bodily advantages; without clothes, without arms, without food, without lodging, without any convenience of life, except what they owe to their own skill and industry. In short, nature seems to have formed an exact calculation of the necessities of her creatures, and, like a *rigid master,* has afforded them little more powers or endowments than what are strictly sufficient to supply those necessities. An *indulgent parent* would have bestowed a large stock in order to guard against accidents and secure the happiness and welfare of the creature in the most unfortunate concurrence of circumstances. Every course of life would not have been so surrounded with precipices that the least departure from the true path, by mistake or necessity, must involve us in misery and ruin. Some reserve, some fund, would have been provided to insure happiness; nor would the powers and the necessities have been adjusted with so rigid an economy. The Author of Nature is inconceivably powerful: His force is supposed great, if not altogether inexhaustible, nor is there any reason, as far as we can judge, to make him observe this strict frugality in his dealings with his creatures. It would have been better, were his power extremely limited, to have created fewer animals and to have endowed these with more faculties for their happiness and preservation. A builder is never esteemed prudent who undertakes a plan beyond what his stock will enable him to finish.

In order to cure most of the ills of human life, I do not require that man should have the wings of the eagle, the swiftness of the stag, the force of the ox, the arms of the lion, the scales of the crocodile or rhinoceros; much less do I demand the sagacity of an angel or cherubim. I am contented to take an increase in one single power or faculty of his soul. Let him be endowed with a greater propensity to industry and labor, a more vigorous spring and activity of mind, a more constant bent to business and application. Let the whole species possess naturally an equal diligence with that which many individuals are able to attain by habit and reflection, and the most beneficial consequences, without any alloy of ill, is the immediate and necessary result of this endowment. Almost all the moral as well as natural evils of human life arise from idleness; and were our species, by the original constitution of their frame, exempt from this vice or infirmity, the perfect cultivation of land, the improvement of arts and manufactures, the exact execution of every office and duty immediately follow, and men at once may fully reach that state of society which is so imperfectly attained by the best regulated government. But as industry is a power, and the most valuable of any, Nature seems determined, suitably to her usual maxims, to bestow it on men with a very sparing hand and rather to punish him severely for his deficiency in it than to reward him for his attainments. She has so contrived his frame that nothing but the most violent necessity can oblige him to labor, and she employs all his other wants to overcome, at least in part, the want of diligence and to endow him with some share of a faculty of which she has thought fit naturally to bereave him. Here our demands may be allowed very humble and therefore the more reasonable. If we required the endowments of superior penetration and judgment, of a more delicate taste of beauty, of a nicer sensibility to benevolence and friendship, we might be told that we impiously pretend to break the order of Nature; that we want to exalt ourselves into a higher rank of being; that the presents which we require, not being suitable to our state and condition, would only be pernicious to us. But it is hard—I dare to repeat it—it is hard that, being placed in a world so full of wants and necessities, where almost every being and element is either our foe or refuses its assistance, we should also have our own temper to struggle with and should be deprived of that faculty which can alone fence against these multiplied evils.

The *fourth* circumstance whence arises the misery and ill of the universe is the inaccurate workmanship of all the springs and principles of the great machine of Nature. It must be acknowledged that there are few parts of the universe which seem not to serve some purpose and whose removal would not produce a visible defect and disorder in the whole. The parts hang all together; nor can one be touched without affecting the rest in a greater or less degree. But at the same time, it must be observed that none of these parts or principles, however useful, are so accurately adjusted as to keep precisely within those bounds in which their utility consists; but they are, all of them, apt on every occasion to run into the one extreme or the other. One would imagine that this grand production had not received the last hand of the maker, so little finished is every part and so coarse are the strokes with which it is executed. Thus, the winds are requisite to convey the vapors along the surface of the globe and to assist men in navigation, but how often, rising up to tempests and hurricanes, do they become pernicious? Rains are necessary to nourish all the plants and animals of the earth, but how often are they defective? How often excessive? Heat is requisite to all life and vegetation, but is not always found in the due proportion. On the mixture and secretion of the humors and juices of the body depend the health and prosperity of the animal, but the parts perform not regularly their proper function. What more useful than all the passions of the mind, ambition, vanity, love, anger? But how often do they break their bounds and cause the greatest convulsions in society? There is nothing so advantageous in the universe but what frequently becomes pernicious by its excess or defect; nor has Nature guarded with the requisite accuracy against all disorder or confusion. The irregularity is never perhaps so great as to destroy any species, but is often sufficient to involve the individuals in ruin and misery.

On the concurrence, then, of these *four* circumstances does all or the greatest part of natural evil depend. Were all living creatures incapable of pain or were the world administered by particular volitions, evil never could have found access into the universe, and were animals endowed with a large stock of powers and faculties beyond what strict necessity requires, or were the several springs and principles of the universe so accurately framed as to preserve always the just temperament and medium, there must have been very little ill in comparison of what we feel at present. What, then, shall we pronounce on this occasion? Shall we say that these circumstances are not necessary and that they might easily have been altered in the contrivance of the universe? This decision seems too presumptuous for creatures so blind and ignorant. Let us be more modest in our conclusions. Let us allow that, if the goodness of the Deity (I mean a

goodness like the human) could be established on any tolerable reasons *a priori*, these phenomena, however untoward, would not be sufficient to subvert that principle, but might easily, in some unknown manner, be reconcilable to it. But let us still assert that as this goodness is not antecedently established, but must be inferred from the phenomena, there can be no grounds for such an inference while there are so many ills in the universe and while these ills might so easily have been remedied as far as human understanding can be allowed to judge on such a subject. I am skeptic enough to allow that the bad appearances, notwithstanding all my reasonings, may be compatible with such attributes as you suppose, but surely they can never prove these attributes. Such a conclusion cannot result from skepticism, but must arise from the phenomena and from our confidence in the reasonings which we deduce from these phenomena.

Look round this universe. What an immense profusion of beings, animated and organized, sensible and active! You admire this prodigious variety and fecundity. But inspect a little more narrowly these living existences, the only beings worth regarding. How hostile and destructive to each other! How insufficient all of them for their own happiness! How contemptible or odious to the spectator! The whole presents nothing but the idea of a blind Nature, impregnated by a great vivifying principle, and, pouring forth from her lap, without discernment or parental care, her maimed and abortive children!

Here the Manichaean system occurs as a proper hypothesis to solve the difficulty and, no doubt, in some respects it is very specious and has more probability than the common hypothesis by giving a plausible account of the strange mixture of good and ill which appears in life. But if we consider, on the other hand, the perfect uniformity and agreement of the parts of the universe, we shall not discover in it any marks of the combat of a malevolent with a benevolent being. There is indeed an opposition of pains and pleasures in the feelings of sensible creatures. But are not all the operations of Nature carried on by an opposition of principles, of hot and cold, moist and dry, light and heavy? The true conclusion is that the original source of all things is entirely indifferent to all these principles and has no more regard to good above ill than to heat above cold or to drought above moisture or to light above heavy.

Four hypotheses may be framed concerning the first causes of the universe: *that* they are endowed with perfect goodness, *that* they have perfect malice, *that* they are opposite and have both goodness and malice, *that* they have neither goodness nor malice. Mixed phenomena can never prove the two former unmixed principles, and the uniformity and steadiness of general laws seem to oppose the third. The fourth, therefore, seems by far the most probable.

What I have said concerning natural evil will apply to moral with little or no variation; and we have no more reason to infer that the rectitude of the Supreme Being resembles human rectitude than that his benevolence resembles the human. Nay, it will be thought that we have still greater cause to exclude from him moral sentiments such as we feel them, since moral evil, in the opinion of many, is much more predominant above moral good than natural evil above natural good.

But even though this should not be allowed and though the virtue which is in mankind should be acknowledged much superior to the vice, yet so long as there is any vice at all in the universe, it will very much puzzle you anthropomorphites how to account for it. You must assign a cause for it without having recourse to the first cause. But as every effect must have a cause and that cause another, you must either carry on the progression *in infinitum* or rest on that original principle who is the ultimate cause of all things . . .

Hold! hold! cried *Demea:* Whither does your imagination hurry you? I joined in alliance with you in order to prove the incomprehensible nature of the Divine Being and refute the principles of *Cleanthes,* who would measure everything by human rule and standard. But I now find you running into all the topics of the greatest libertines and infidels and betraying that holy cause which you seemingly espoused. Are you secretly, then, a more dangerous enemy than *Cleanthes* himself?

And are you so late in perceiving it? replied *Cleanthes.* Believe me, *Demea,* your friend *Philo,* from the beginning, has been amusing himself at both our expense, and it must be confessed that the injudicious

reasoning of our vulgar theology has given him but too just a handle of ridicule. The total infirmity of human reason, the absolute incomprehensibility of the Divine Nature, the great and universal misery, and still greater wickedness of men; these are strange topics, surely, to be so fondly cherished by orthodox divines and doctors. In ages of stupidity and ignorance, indeed, these principles may safely be espoused, and perhaps no views of things are more proper to promote superstition than such as encourage the blind amazement, the diffidence, and melancholy of mankind. But at present . . .

Blame not so much, interposed *Philo,* the ignorance of these reverend gentlemen. They know how to change their style with the times. Formerly, it was a most popular theological topic to maintain that human life was vanity and misery and to exaggerate all the ills and pains which are incident to men. But of late years, divines, we find, begin to retract this position and maintain, though still with some hesitation, that there are more goods than evils, more pleasures than pains, even in this life. When religion stood entirely upon temper and education, it was thought proper to encourage melancholy, as indeed mankind never have recourse to superior powers so readily as in that disposition. But as men have now learned to form principles and to draw consequences, it is necessary to change the batteries and to make use of such arguments as will endure at least some scrutiny and examination. This variation is the same (and from the same causes) with that which I formerly remarked with regard to skepticism.

Thus *Philo* continued to the last his spirit of opposition and his censure of established opinions. But I could observe that *Demea* did not at all relish the latter part of the discourse, and he took occasion soon after, on some pretence or other, to leave the company.

Part XII

After *Demea's* departure, *Cleanthes* and *Philo* continued the conversation in the following manner. Our friend, I am afraid, said *Cleanthes,* will have little inclination to revive this topic of discourse while you are in company, and to tell the truth, *Philo,* I should rather wish to reason with either of you apart on a subject so sublime and interesting. Your spirit of controversy, joined to your abhorrence of vulgar superstition, carries you strange lengths when engaged in an argument, and there is nothing so sacred and venerable, even in your own eyes, which you spare on that occasion.

I must confess, replied *Philo*, that I am less cautious on the subject of natural religion than on any other, both because I know that I can never, on that head, corrupt the principles of any man of common sense and because no one, I am confident, in whose eyes I appear a man of common sense will ever mistake my intentions. You, in particular, *Cleanthes*, with whom I live in unreserved intimacy, you are sensible that, notwithstanding the freedom of my conversation and my love of singular arguments, no one has a deeper sense of religion impressed on his mind or pays more profound adoration to the Divine Being as he discovers himself to reason in the inexplicable contrivance and artifice of nature. A purpose, an intention, a design, strikes everywhere the most careless, the most stupid thinker, and no man can be so hardened in absurd systems as at all times to reject it. *That Nature does nothing in vain* is a maxim established in all the schools merely from the contemplation of the works of Nature, without any religious purpose, and, from a firm conviction of its truth, an anatomist who had observed a new organ or canal would never be satisfied until he had also discovered its use and intention. One great foundation of the *Copernican* system is the maxim that *Nature acts by the simplest methods and chooses the most proper means to any end*, and astronomers often, without thinking of it, lay this strong foundation of piety and religion. The same thing is observable in other parts of philosophy and thus all the sciences almost lead us insensibly to acknowledge a first intelligent Author and their authority is often so much the greater as they do not directly profess that intention.

It is with pleasure I hear *Galen* reason concerning the structure of the human body. The anatomy of a man, says he,[16] discovers above six hundred different muscles, and whoever duly considers these will find

16. *De Formatione Fetus*.

that, in each of them, Nature must have adjusted at least ten different circumstances in order to attain the end which she proposed: proper figure, just magnitude, right disposition of the several ends, upper and lower position of the whole, the due insertion of the several nerves, veins, and arteries; so that, in the muscles alone, above six thousand several views and intentions must have been formed and executed. The bones he calculates to be two hundred and eighty-four; the distinct purposes aimed at in the structure of each, above forty. What a prodigious display of artifice, even in these simple and homogeneous parts! But if we consider the skin, ligaments, vessels, glandules, humors, the several limbs and members of the body, how must our astonishment rise upon us in proportion to the number and intricacy of the parts so artificially adjusted! The further we advance in these researches, we discover new scenes of art and wisdom, but descry still, at a distance, further scenes beyond our reach: in the fine internal structure of the parts, in the economy of the brain, in the fabric of the seminal vessels. All these artifices are repeated in every different species of animal, with wonderful variety and with exact propriety, suited to the different intentions of Nature in framing each species. And if the infidelity of *Galen*, even when these natural sciences were still imperfect, could not withstand such striking appearances, to what pitch of pertinacious obstinacy must a philosopher in this age have attained who can now doubt of a Supreme Intelligence!

Could I meet with one of this species (who, I thank God, are very rare), I would ask him: Supposing there were a God who did not discover himself immediately to our senses, were it possible for him to give stronger proofs of his existence than what appear on the whole face of Nature? What indeed could such a Divine Being do, but copy the present economy of things; render many of his artifices so plain that no stupidity could mistake them; afford glimpses of still greater artifices which demonstrate his prodigious superiority above our narrow apprehensions; and conceal altogether a great many from such imperfect creatures? Now, according to all rules of just reasoning, every fact must pass for undisputed when it is supported by all the arguments which its nature admits of, even though these arguments be not in themselves very numerous or forcible. How much more, in the present case, where no human imagination can compute their number and no understanding estimate their cogency!

I shall further add, said *Cleanthes,* to what you have so well urged, that one great advantage of the principle of theism is that it is the only system of cosmogony which can be rendered intelligible and complete and yet can throughout preserve a strong analogy to what we every day see and experience in the world. The comparison of the universe to a machine of human contrivance is so obvious and natural and is justified by so many instances of order and design in nature that it must immediately strike all unprejudiced apprehensions and procure universal approbation. Whoever attempts to weaken this theory cannot pretend to succeed by establishing in its place any other that is precise and determinate; it is sufficient for him if he start doubts and difficulties and, by remote and abstract views of things, reach that suspense of judgment which is here the utmost boundary of his wishes. But, besides that this state of mind is in itself unsatisfactory, it can never be steadily maintained against such striking appearances as continually engage us into the religious hypothesis. A false, absurd system, human nature, from the force of prejudice, is capable of adhering to with obstinacy and perseverance, but no system at all, in opposition to theory supported by strong and obvious reason, by natural propensity, and by early education, I think it absolutely impossible to maintain or defend.

So little, replied *Philo,* do I esteem this suspense of judgment in the present case to be possible that I am apt to suspect there enters somewhat of a dispute of words into this controversy, more than is usually imagined. That the works of nature bear a great analogy to the productions of art is evident, and according to all the rules of good reasoning, we ought to infer, if we argue at all concerning them, that their causes have a proportional analogy. But as there are also considerable differences, we have reason to suppose a proportional difference in the causes and, in particular, ought to attribute a much higher degree of power and energy to the supreme cause than any we have ever observed in mankind. Here, then, the existence

of a DEITY is plainly ascertained by reason, and if we make it a question whether, on account of these analogies, we can properly call him a *mind* or *intelligence,* notwithstanding the vast difference which may reasonably be supposed between him and human minds, what is this but a mere verbal controversy? No man can deny the analogies between the effects; to restrain ourselves from inquiring concerning the causes is scarcely possible. From this inquiry, the legitimate conclusion is that the causes have also an analogy, and if we are not contented with calling the first and supreme cause a GOD or DEITY, but desire to vary the expression, what can we call him but MIND or THOUGHT, to which he is justly supposed to bear a considerable resemblance?

All men of sound reason are disgusted with verbal disputes, which abound so much in philosophical and theological inquiries, and it is found that the only remedy for this abuse must arise from clear definitions, from the precision of those ideas which enter into any argument, and from the strict and uniform use of those terms which are employed. But there is a species of controversy which, from the very nature of language and of human ideas, is involved in perpetual ambiguity and can never, by any precaution or any definitions, be able to reach a reasonable certainty or precision. These are the controversies concerning the degrees of any quality or circumstance. Men may argue to all eternity whether *Hannibal* be a great, or a very great, or a superlatively great man, what degree of beauty *Cleopatra* possessed, what epithet of praise *Livy* or *Thucydides* is entitled to, without bringing the controversy to any determination. The disputants may here agree in their sense and differ in the terms, or *vice versa,* yet never be able to define their terms so as to enter into each other's meaning, because the degrees of these qualities are not, like quantity or number, susceptible of any exact mensuration, which may be the standard in the controversy. That the dispute concerning theism is of this nature and, consequently, is merely verbal or perhaps, if possible, still more incurably ambiguous will appear upon the slightest inquiry. I ask the theist if he does not allow that there is a great and immeasurable, because incomprehensible, difference between the *human* and the *divine* mind.

The more pious he is, the more readily will he assent to the affirmative and the more will he be disposed to magnify the difference. He will even assert that the difference is of a nature which cannot be too much magnified. I next turn to the atheist, who, I assert, is only nominally so and can never possibly be in earnest and I ask him whether, from the coherence and apparent sympathy in all the parts of this world, there be not a certain degree of analogy among all the operations of Nature, in every situation and in every age; whether the rotting of a turnip, the generation of an animal, and the structure of human thought be not energies that probably bear some remote analogy to each other. It is impossible he can deny it; he will readily acknowledge it. Having obtained this concession, I push him still further in his retreat, and I ask him if it be not probable that the principle which first arranged and still maintains order in this universe bears not also some remote inconceivable analogy to the other operations of nature and, among the rest, to the economy of human mind and thought. However reluctant, he must give his assent. Where then, cry I to both these antagonists, is the subject of your dispute? The theist allows that the original intelligence is very different from human reason. The atheist allows that the original principle of order bears some remote analogy to it. Will you quarrel, gentlemen, about the degrees and enter into a controversy which admits not of any precise meaning, nor consequently of any determination? If you should be so obstinate, I should not be surprised to find you insensibly change sides; while the theist, on the one hand, exaggerates the dissimilarity between the Supreme Being and frail, imperfect, variable, fleeting, and mortal creatures, and the atheist, on the other, magnifies the analogy among all the operations of nature, in every period, every situation, and every position. Consider, then, where the real point of controversy lies, and if you cannot lay aside your disputes, endeavor, at least, to cure yourselves of your animosity.

And here I must also acknowledge, *Cleanthes*, that as the works of Nature have a much greater analogy to the effects of *our* art and contrivance than to those of our benevolence and justice, we have reason to infer that the natural attributes of the Deity have a greater resemblance to those of men than his moral have to human virtues. But what is the consequence? Nothing but this: that the moral qualities of man are more defective in their kind than his natural abilities. For, as the Supreme Being is allowed to be absolutely and entirely perfect, whatever differs most from him departs the furthest from the supreme standard of rectitude and perfection.[17]

These, *Cleanthes*, are my unfeigned sentiments on this subject, and these sentiments, you know, I have ever cherished and maintained. But in proportion to my veneration for true religion is my abhorrence of vulgar superstitions, and I indulge a peculiar pleasure, I confess, in pushing such principles, sometimes into absurdity, sometimes into impiety. And you are sensible that all bigots, notwithstanding their great aversion to the latter above the former, are commonly equally guilty of both.

My inclination, replied *Cleanthes*, lies, I admit, a contrary way. Religion, however corrupted, is still better than no religion at all. The doctrine of a future state is so strong and necessary a security to morals that we never ought to abandon or neglect it. For if finite and temporary rewards and punishments have so great an effect, as we daily find, how much greater must be expected from such as are infinite and eternal?

How does it happen then, said *Philo*, if vulgar superstition be so salutary to society, that all history abounds so much with accounts of its pernicious consequences on public affairs? Factions, civil wars, persecutions, subversions of government, oppression,

---

17. It seems evident that the dispute between the skeptics and dogmatists is entirely verbal, or at least regards only the degrees of doubt and assurance which we ought to indulge with regard to all reasoning, and such disputes are commonly, at the bottom, verbal and do not admit of any precise determination. No philosophical dogmatist denies that there are difficulties both with regard to the senses and to all science and that these difficulties are in a regular, logical method absolutely insolvable. No skeptic denies that we lie under an absolute necessity, notwithstanding these difficulties, of thinking and believing and reasoning with regard to all kinds of subjects, and even of frequently assenting with confidence and security. The only difference, then, between these sects, if they merit that name, is that the skeptic, from habit, caprice, or inclination, insists most on the difficulties; the dogmatist, for like reasons, on the necessity.

slavery; these are the dismal consequences which always attend its prevalence over the minds of men. If the religious spirit be ever mentioned in any historical narration, we are sure to meet afterwards with a detail of the miseries which attend it. And no period of time can be happier or more prosperous than those in which it is never regarded or heard of.

The reason of this observation, replied *Cleanthes*, is obvious. The proper office of religion is to regulate the heart of men, humanize their conduct, infuse the spirit of temperance, order, and obedience, and as its operation is silent and only enforces the motives of morality and justice, it is in danger of being overlooked and confounded with these other motives. When it distinguishes itself and acts as a separate principle over men, it has departed from its proper sphere and has become only a cover to faction and ambition.

And so will all religion, said *Philo*, except the philosophical and rational kind. Your reasonings are more easily eluded than my facts. The inference is not just, because finite and temporary rewards and punishments have so great influence that therefore such as are infinite and eternal must have so much greater. Consider, I beseech you, the attachment which we have to present things and the little concern which we discover for objects so remote and uncertain. When divines are declaiming against the common behavior and conduct of the world, they always represent this principle as the strongest imaginable (which indeed it is) and describe almost all human kind as lying under the influence of it and sunk into the deepest lethargy and unconcern about their religious interests. Yet these same divines, when they refute their speculative antagonists, suppose the motives of religion to be so powerful that, without them, it were impossible for civil society to subsist. Nor are they ashamed of so palpable a contradiction. It is certain from experience that the smallest grain of natural honesty and benevolence has more effect on men's conduct than the most pompous views suggested by theological theories and systems. A man's natural inclination works incessantly upon him; it is forever present to the mind and mingles itself with every view and consideration, whereas religious motives, where they act at all, operate only by starts and bounds, and it is scarcely possible

for them to become altogether habitual to the mind. The force of the greatest gravity, say the philosophers, is infinitely small in comparison of that of the least impulse, yet it is certain that the smallest gravity will, in the end, prevail above a great impulse, because no strokes or blows can be repeated with such constancy as attraction and gravitation.

Another advantage of inclination: It engages on its side all the wit and ingenuity of the mind and, when set in opposition to religious principles, seeks every method and art of eluding them, in which it is almost always successful. Who can explain the heart of man or account for those strange salvos and excuses with which people satisfy themselves when they follow their inclinations in opposition to their religious duty? This is well understood in the world, and none but fools ever repose less trust in a man because they hear that from study and philosophy he has entertained some speculative doubts with regard to theological subjects. And when we have to do with a man who makes a great profession of religion and devotion, has this any other effect upon several who pass for prudent than to put them on their guard, lest they be cheated and deceived by him?

We must further consider that philosophers, who cultivate reason and reflection, stand less in need of such motives to keep them under the restraint of morals, and that the vulgar, who alone may need them, are utterly incapable of so pure a religion as represents the Deity to be pleased with nothing but virtue in human behavior. The recommendations to the Divinity are generally supposed to be either frivolous observances, or rapturous ecstasies, or a bigoted credulity. We need not run back into antiquity or wander into remote regions to find instances of this degeneracy. Amongst ourselves, some have been guilty of that atrociousness, unknown to the Egyptian and Grecian superstitions, of declaiming in express terms against morality and representing it as a sure forfeiture of the Divine favor if the least trust or reliance be laid upon it.

But even though superstition or enthusiasm should not put itself in direct opposition to morality, the very diverting of the attention, the raising up a new and frivolous species of merit, the preposterous distribution which it makes of praise and blame, must have the most pernicious consequences and weaken extremely men's attachment to the natural motives of justice and humanity.

Such a principle of action likewise, not being any of the familiar motives of human conduct, acts only by intervals on the temper and must be roused by continual efforts in order to render the pious zealot satisfied with his own conduct and make him fulfil his devotional task. Many religious exercises are entered into with seeming fervor, where the heart, at the time, feels cold and languid: A habit of dissimulation is by degrees contracted, and fraud and falsehood become the predominant principle. Hence the reason of that vulgar observation that the highest zeal in religion and the deepest hypocrisy, so far from being inconsistent, are often or commonly united in the same individual character.

The bad effects of such habits, even in common life, are easily imagined, but where the interests of religion are concerned, no morality can be forcible enough to bind the enthusiastic zealot. The sacredness of the cause sanctifies every measure which can be made use of to promote it.

The steady attention alone to so important an interest as that of eternal salvation is apt to extinguish the benevolent affections and beget a narrow, contracted selfishness. And when such a temper is encouraged, it easily eludes all the general precepts of charity and benevolence.

Thus, the motives of vulgar superstition have no great influence on general conduct; nor is their operation favorable to morality in the instances where they predominate.

Is there any maxim in politics more certain and infallible than that both the number and authority of priests should be confined within very narrow limits and that the civil magistrate ought, forever, to keep his *fasces* and *axes* from such dangerous hands? But if the spirit of popular religion were so salutary to society, a contrary maxim ought to prevail. The greater number of priests and their greater authority and riches will always augment the religious spirit. And though the priests have the guidance of this spirit, why may we not expect a superior sanctity of life and greater benevolence and moderation from persons who are set apart for religion, who are contin-

ually inculcating it upon others, and who must themselves imbibe a greater share of it? Whence comes it then that, in fact, the utmost a wise magistrate can propose with regard to popular religions is, as far as possible, to make a saving game of it and to prevent their pernicious consequences with regard to society? Every expedient which he tries for so humble a purpose is surrounded with inconveniences. If he admits only one religion among his subjects, he must sacrifice to an uncertain prospect of tranquillity every consideration of public liberty, science, reason, industry, and even his own independence. If he gives indulgence to several sects, which is the wiser maxim, he must preserve a very philosophical indifference to all of them and carefully restrain the pretensions of the prevailing sect; otherwise he can expect nothing but endless disputes, quarrels, factions, persecutions, and civil commotions.

True religion, I allow, has no such pernicious consequences, but we must treat of religion as it has commonly been found in the world; nor have I anything to do with that speculative tenet of theism which, as it is a species of philosophy, must partake of the beneficial influence of that principle and at the same time must lie under a like inconvenience of being always confined to very few persons.

Oaths are requisite in all courts of judicature, but it is a question whether their authority arises from any popular religion. It is the solemnity and importance of the occasion, the regard to reputation, and the reflecting on the general interests of society which are the chief restraints upon mankind. Custom-house oaths and political oaths are but little regarded even by some who pretend to principles of honesty and religion, and a *Quaker's* asseveration is with us justly put upon the same footing with the oath of any other person. I know that *Polybius*[18] ascribes the infamy of Greek faith to the prevalence of the *Epicurean* Philosophy, but I know also that Punic faith had as bad a reputation in ancient times as Irish evidence has in modern, though we cannot account for these vulgar observations by the same reason. Not to mention that Greek faith was infamous before the rise of

18. *Histories*, Book VI, chap. 54.

the *Epicurean* philosophy, and *Euripides*,[19] in a passage which I shall point out to you, has glanced a remarkable stroke of satire against his nation with regard to this circumstance.

Take care, *Philo*, replied *Cleanthes*, take care, push not matters too far, allow not your zeal against false religion to undermine your veneration for the true. Forfeit not this principle, the chief, the only great comfort in life, and our principal support amidst all the attacks of adverse fortune. The most agreeable reflection which it is possible for human imagination to suggest is that of genuine theism, which represents us as the workmanship of a Being perfectly good, wise, and powerful, who created us for happiness, and who, having implanted in us immeasurable desires of good, will prolong our existence to all eternity and will transfer us into an infinite variety of scenes in order to satisfy those desires and render our felicity complete and durable. Next to such a Being himself (if the comparison be allowed), the happiest lot which we can imagine is that of being under his guardianship and protection.

These appearances, said *Philo*, are most engaging and alluring and with regard to the true Philosopher, they are more than appearances. But it happens here, as in the former case, that, with regard to the greater part of mankind, the appearances are deceitful and that the terrors of religion commonly prevail above its comforts.

It is allowed that men never have recourse to devotion so readily as when dejected with grief or depressed with sickness. Is not this a proof that the religious spirit is not so nearly allied to joy as to sorrow?

But men, when afflicted, find consolation in religion, replied *Cleanthes*. Sometimes, said *Philo*, but it is natural to imagine that they will form a notion of those unknown beings, suitable to the present gloom and melancholy of their temper, when they betake themselves to the contemplation of them. Accordingly, we find the tremendous images to predominate in all religions, and we ourselves, after having employed the most exalted expression in our descriptions of the Deity, fall into the flattest contradiction

19. *Iphigenia in Tauride.*

in affirming that the damned are infinitely superior in number to the elect.

I shall venture to affirm that there never was a popular religion which represented the state of departed souls in such a light as would render it eligible for human kind that there should be such a state. These fine models of religion are the mere product of philosophy. For as death lies between the eye and the prospect of futurity, that event is so shocking to Nature that it must throw a gloom on all the regions which lie beyond it and suggest to the generality of mankind the idea of *Cerberus* and *Furies*, devils, and torrents of fire and brimstone.

It is true that both fear and hope enter into religion because both these passions, at different times, agitate the human mind, and each of them forms a species of divinity suitable to itself. But when a man is in a cheerful disposition, he is fit for business or company or entertainment of any kind, and he naturally applies himself to these and thinks not of religion. When melancholy and dejected, he has nothing to do but brood upon the terrors of the invisible world and to plunge himself still deeper in affliction. It may indeed happen that after he has, in this manner, engraved the religious opinions deep into his thought and imagination, there may arrive a change of health or circumstances which may restore his good-humor and, raising cheerful prospects of futurity, make him run into the other extreme of joy and triumph. But still it must be acknowledged that, as terror is the primary principle of religion, it is the passion which always predominates in it and admits but of short intervals of pleasure.

Not to mention that these fits of excessive, enthusiastic joy, by exhausting the spirits, always prepare the way for equal fits of superstitious terror and dejection; nor is there any state of mind so happy as the calm and equable. But this state it is impossible to support, where a man thinks that he lies in such profound darkness and uncertainty, between an eternity of happiness and an eternity of misery. No wonder that such an opinion disjoints the ordinary frame of the mind and throws it into the utmost confusion. And though that opinion is seldom so steady in its operation as to influence all the actions, yet it is apt to make a considerable breach in the temper and to produce that gloom and melancholy so remarkable in all devout people.

It is contrary to common sense to entertain apprehensions or terrors upon account of any opinion whatsoever or to imagine that we run any risk hereafter by the freest use of our reason. Such a sentiment implies both an *absurdity* and an *inconsistency*. It is an absurdity to believe that the Deity has human passions, and one of the lowest of human passions, a restless appetite for applause. It is an inconsistency to believe that, since the Deity has this human passion, he has not others also and, in particular, a disregard to the opinions of creatures so much inferior.

To know God, says Seneca, *is to worship him*. All other worship is indeed absurd, superstitious, and even impious. It degrades him to the low condition of mankind, who are delighted with entreaty, solicitation, presents, and flattery. Yet is this impiety the smallest of which superstition is guilty? Commonly, it depresses the Deity far below the condition of mankind and represents him as a capricious demon who exercises his power without reason and without humanity! And were that Divine Being disposed to be offended at the vices and follies of silly mortals, who are his own workmanship, ill would it surely fare with the votaries of most popular superstitions. Nor would any of human race merit his *favor*, but a very few, the philosophical theists, who entertain, or rather indeed endeavor to entertain, suitable notions of his Divine perfections. As the only persons entitled to his *compassion* and *indulgence* would be the philosophical skeptics, a sect almost equally rare, who, from a natural diffidence of their own capacity, suspend or endeavor to suspend all judgment with regard to such sublime and such extraordinary subjects.

If the whole of natural theology, as some people seem to maintain, resolves itself into one simple, though somewhat ambiguous, at least undefined, proposition, that *the cause or causes of order in the universe probably bear some remote analogy to human intelligence*; if this proposition be not capable of extension, variation, or more particular explication; if it

affords no inference that affects human life or can be the source of any action or forbearance; and if the analogy, imperfect as it is, can be carried no further than to the human intelligence and cannot be transferred, with any appearance of probability, to the qualities of the mind; if this really be the case, what can the most inquisitive, contemplative, and religious man do more than give a plain, philosophical assent to the proposition as often as it occurs and believe that the arguments on which it is established exceed the objections which lie against it? Some astonishment, indeed, will naturally arise from the greatness of the object; some melancholy from its obscurity; some contempt of human reason that it can give no solution more satisfactory with regard to so extraordinary and magnificent a question. But believe me, *Cleanthes*, the most natural sentiment which a well-disposed mind will feel on this occasion is a longing desire and expectation that heaven would be pleased to dissipate, at least alleviate, this profound ignorance by affording some particular revelation to mankind and making discoveries of the nature, attributes, and operations of the divine object of our faith. A person seasoned with a just sense of the imperfections of natural reason will fly to revealed truth with the greatest avidity, while the haughty dogmatist, persuaded that he can erect a complete system of theology by the mere help of philosophy, disdains any further aid and rejects this adventitious instructor. To be a philosophical skeptic is, in a man of letters, the first and most essential step towards being a sound, believing *Christian*, a proposition which I would willingly recommend to the attention of *Pamphilus*, and I hope *Cleanthes* will forgive me for interposing so far in the education and instruction of his pupil.

Pamphilus: *Cleanthes* and *Philo* did not pursue this conversation much further, and, as nothing ever made greater impression on me than all the reasonings of that day, so I confess that, upon a serious review of the whole, I cannot but think that *Philo's* principles are more probable than *Demea's*, but that those of *Cleanthes* approach still nearer to the truth.

Thomas Reid, *Inquiry into the Human Mind* (1764), Conclusion; and *Essays on the Intellectual Powers of Man* (1785), Essay VI, "Of Judgment," chap. 2, Of Common Sense[1]

Thomas Reid (1710–1796) was born at Strachan in Kincardinshire, Scotland. After being educated in a local parish school and at the University of Aberdeen, he first became a university librarian and then, in 1737, entered the ministry, as was traditional for the paternal side of his family. In 1752, he was appointed professor of philosophy at King's College in Aberdeen, where he would found the Aberdeen Philosophical Society. In 1764, Reid succeeded Adam Smith as professor of moral philosophy in Glasgow. He resigned this position in 1781 in order to devote more time to his writing. Reid first published "An Essay on Quantity" in 1748, which was followed by An Inquiry into the Human Mind on the Principles of Common Sense *in 1764,* Essays on the Intellectual Powers of Man *in 1785, and finally* Essays on the Active Powers of Man *in 1788. Reid is best known for two doctrines in particular: i) his criticism of "the way of ideas" as espoused by many modern philosophers, but especially David Hume, and ii) his endorsement and explanation of common sense as a fundamental philosophical principle. According to Reid, what human beings directly perceive are not ideas (as Descartes had famously maintained in his Second Meditation and as Locke had explained in Book II of his* Essay concerning Human Understanding*) but rather the external objects themselves. In the "Conclusion" to* An Inquiry *Reid distinguishes two different approaches to understanding the mind: the way of analogy and the way of reflection. This distinction, Reid believes, will allow him to illustrate what is mistaken about the way of analogy which leads to the way of ideas and how this mistake can be corrected by means of accurate reflection. In the chapter "Of Common Sense" from the* Essays on the Intellectual Powers of Man, *Reid explains that common sense is not simply what anyone off the street would immediately assent to, but rather an ability to judge what is self-evident.*[2]

---

1. ["Conclusion" selected from *Philosophical Works of Thomas Reid*, ed. W. Hamilton (Edinburgh, 1895); and "Of Judgment" selected from *The Works of Thomas Reid*, published by Samuel Etheridge Jr. (Charlestown, MA, 1813–15), modified.]

2. [For more on Reid, see Roger Gallie, *Thomas Reid and "The Way of Ideas"* (Kluwer: Dordrecht, 1989); or Keith Lehrer, *Thomas Reid* (Routledge: New York, 1991).]

An Inquiry into the Human Mind, Conclusion

Containing Reflections upon the Opinions of Philosophers on this Subject

There are two ways in which men may form their notions and opinions concerning the mind and concerning its powers and operations. The first is the only way that leads to truth, but it is narrow and rugged and few have entered upon it. The second is broad and smooth and has been much beaten, not only by the vulgar, but even by philosophers; it is sufficient for common life and is well adapted to the purposes of the poet and orator, but in philosophical disquisitions concerning the mind, it leads to error and delusion.

We may call the first of these ways *the way of reflection*. When the operations of the mind are exerted, we are conscious of them, and it is in our power to attend to them and to reflect upon them until they become familiar objects of thought. This is the only way in which we can form just and accurate notions of those operations. But this attention and reflection is so difficult to man, surrounded on all hands by external objects which constantly solicit his attention, that it has been very little practiced, even by philosophers. In the course of this *Inquiry*, we have had many occasions to show how little attention has been given to the most familiar operations of the senses.

The second and the most common way in which men form their opinions concerning the mind and its operations we may call *the way of analogy*. There is nothing in the course of nature so singular but we can find some resemblance, or at least some analogy, between it and other things with which we are acquainted. The mind naturally delights in hunting after such analogies and attends to them with pleasure. From them, poetry and wit derive a great part of their charms, and eloquence not a little of its persuasive force.

Besides the pleasure we receive from analogies, they are of very considerable use, both to facilitate the conception of things, when they are not easily apprehended without such a handle, and to lead us to probable conjectures about their nature and qualities, when we want the means of more direct and immediate knowledge. When I consider that the planet Jupiter, in like manner as the earth, rolls round his own axis and revolves round the sun and that it is enlightened by several secondary planets, as the earth is enlightened by the moon, I am apt to conjecture from analogy that as the earth by these means is fitted to be the habitation of various orders of animals, so the planet Jupiter is by the like means fitted for the same purpose; and having no argument more direct and conclusive to determine me in this point, I yield to this analogical reasoning a degree of assent proportioned to its strength. When I observe that the potato plant very much resembles the *solanum* in its flower and fructification and am informed that the last is poisonous, I am apt from analogy to have some suspicion of the former; but, in this case, I have access to more direct and certain evidence and therefore ought not to trust to analogy, which would lead me into an error.

Arguments from analogy are always at hand and grow up spontaneously in a fruitful imagination, while arguments that are more direct and more conclusive, often require painful attention and application; and, therefore, mankind in general has been very much disposed to trust to the former. If one attentively examines the systems of the ancient philosophers, either concerning the material world or concerning the mind, he will find them to be built solely upon the foundation of analogy. Lord Bacon first delineated the strict and severe method of induction; since his time it has been applied with very happy success in some parts of natural philosophy, and hardly in anything else. But there is no subject in which mankind is so much disposed to trust to the analogical way of thinking and reasoning as in what concerns the mind and its operations, because to form clear and distinct notions of those operations in the direct and proper way and to reason about them requires a habit of attentive reflection, of which few are capable, and which, even by those few, cannot be attained without much pains and labor.

Every man is apt to form his notions of things difficult to be apprehended, or less familiar, from their analogy to things which are more familiar. Thus, if a man bred to the seafaring life, and accustomed to think and talk only of matters relating to navigation, enters into discourse upon any other subject, it is well known that the language and the notions proper to his own profession are infused into every subject, and all things are measured by the rules of navigation; and if he should take it into his head to philosophize concerning the faculties of the mind, it cannot be doubted but he would draw his notions from the fabric of his ship and would find in the mind, sails, masts, rudder, and compass.

Sensible objects of one kind or other do no less occupy and engross the rest of mankind than things relating to navigation occupy the seafaring man. For a considerable part of life, we can think of nothing but the objects of sense; and to attend to objects of another nature so as to form clear and distinct notions of them is no easy matter, even after we come to years of reflection. The condition of mankind, therefore, affords good reason to apprehend that their language and their common notions concerning the mind and its operations will be analogical, and derived from the objects of sense; and that these analogies will be apt to impose upon philosophers as well as upon the vulgar and to lead them to materialize the mind and its faculties; and experience abundantly confirms the truth of this.

How generally men of all nations and in all ages of the world have conceived the soul, or thinking principle in man, to be some subtle matter, like breath or wind, the names given to it almost in all languages sufficiently testify. We have words which are proper, and not analogical, to express the various ways in which we perceive external objects by the senses — such as *feeling, sight, taste* — but we are often obliged to use these words analogically to express other powers of the mind which are of a very different nature. And the powers which imply some degree of reflection have generally no names but such as are analogical. The objects of thought are said to be *in the mind,* to be *apprehended, comprehended, conceived, imagined, retained, weighed, ruminated.*

It does not appear that the notions of the ancient philosophers with regard to the nature of the soul were much more refined than those of the vulgar or that they were formed in any other way. We shall distinguish the philosophy that regards our subject into the *old* and the *new.* The old reached down to Descartes, who gave it a fatal blow, of which it has been gradually expiring ever since, and is now almost extinct. Descartes is the father of the new philosophy that relates to this subject, but it has been gradually improving since his time, upon the principles laid down by him. The old philosophy seems to have been purely analogical; the new is more derived from reflection, but still with a very considerable mixture of the old analogical notions.

Because the objects of sense consist of *matter* and *form,* the ancient philosophers conceived everything to belong to one of these, or to be made up of both. Some therefore thought that the soul is a particular kind of subtle matter, separable from our gross bodies; others thought that it is only a particular form of the body, and inseparable from it. For there seem to have been some among the ancients, as well as among the moderns, who conceived that a certain structure or organization of the body is all that is necessary to render it sensible and intelligent. The different powers of the mind were, accordingly, by the last sect of philosophers, conceived to belong to different parts of the body, as the heart, the brain, the liver, the stomach, the blood.

They who thought that the soul is a subtle matter separable from the body disputed to which of the four elements it belongs, whether to earth, water, air, or fire. Of the three last, each had its particular advocates. But some were of the opinion that it partakes of all the elements; that it must have something in its composition similar to everything we perceive; and that we perceive earth by the earthly part, water by the watery part, and fire by the fiery part of the soul. Some philosophers, not satisfied with determining of what kind of matter the soul is made, inquired likewise into its figure, which they determined to be spherical, that it might be the more fit for motion. The most spiritual and sublime notion concerning the nature of the soul to be met with among the ancient philosophers, I conceive to be that of the Platonists, who held that it is made of that celestial and incorruptible matter of which the fixed stars were made, and therefore has a natural tendency to rejoin its proper element. I am at a loss to say in which of these classes of philosophers Aristotle ought to be placed. He defines the soul to be the first εντελεχεια of a natural body which has potential life. I beg to be excused from translating the Greek word, because I do not know the meaning of it.

The notions of the ancient philosophers with regard to the operations of the mind, particularly with regard to perceptions and ideas, seem likewise to have been formed by the same kind of analogy.

Plato, of the writers that are extant, first introduced the word *idea* into philosophy, but his doctrine on this subject was somewhat peculiar. He agreed with the rest of the ancient philosophers in this, that all things consist of matter and form, and that the matter of which all things were made existed from eternity, without form; but he likewise believed that there are eternal forms of all possible things which exist without matter; and to these eternal and immaterial forms he gave the name of *ideas*, maintaining that they are the only object of true knowledge. It is of no great moment to us whether he borrowed these notions from Parmenides or whether they were the issue of his own creative imagination. The later Platonists seem to have improved upon them in conceiving those ideas, or eternal forms of things, to exist, not of themselves, but in the Divine Mind, and to be the models and patterns according to which all things were made. [. . .]

To these Platonic notions, that of Malebranche is very nearly allied. This author seems more than any other, to have been aware of the difficulties attending the common hypothesis concerning ideas, namely, that ideas of all objects of thought are in the human mind; and, therefore, in order to avoid those difficulties, makes the ideas, which are the immediate objects of human thought, to be the ideas of things in the Divine Mind, who, being intimately present to every human mind, may discover his ideas to it as far as pleases him.

The Platonists and Malebranche excepted, all other philosophers, as far as I know, have conceived that there are ideas or images of every object of thought in the human mind, or at least in some part

of the brain, where the mind is supposed to have its residence.

Aristotle had no good affection for the word *idea* and seldom or never uses it but in refuting Plato's notions about ideas. He thought that matter may exist without form, but that forms cannot exist without matter. But at the same time he taught that there can be no sensation, no imagination, nor intellection, without forms, phantasms, or species in the mind and that things sensible are perceived by sensible species and things intelligible by intelligible species. His followers taught, more explicitly, that those sensible and intelligible species are sent forth by the objects and make their impressions upon the passive intellect and that the active intellect perceives them in the passive intellect. And this seems to have been the common opinion while the Peripatetic philosophy retained its authority.

The Epicurean doctrine, as explained by Lucretius, though widely different from the Peripatetic in many things, is almost the same in this. He affirms that slender films or ghosts — *tenuia rerum simulacra* — are still going off from all things and flying about and that these, being extremely subtle, easily penetrate our gross bodies and, striking upon the mind, cause thought and imagination.

After the Peripatetic system had reigned above a thousand years in the schools of Europe almost without a rival, it sunk before that of Descartes, the perspicuity of whose writings and notions, contrasted with the obscurity of Aristotle and his commentators, created a strong prejudice in favor of this new philosophy. The characteristic of Plato's genius was sublimity, that of Aristotle's, subtlety; but Descartes far excelled both in perspicuity and bequeathed this spirit to his successors. The system which is now generally received with regard to the mind and its operations derives not only its spirit from Descartes, but its fundamental principles and, after all the improvements made by Malebranche, Locke, Berkeley, and Hume, may still be called the Cartesian system; we shall therefore make some remarks upon its spirit and tendency in general, and upon its doctrine concerning ideas in particular.

1. It may be observed that the method which Descartes pursued naturally led him to attend more to

the operations of the mind by accurate reflection and to trust less to analogical reasoning upon this subject than any philosopher had done before him. Intending to build a system upon a new foundation, he began with a resolution to admit nothing but what was absolutely certain and evident. He supposed that his senses, his memory, his reason, and every other faculty to which we trust in common life, might be fallacious, and resolved to disbelieve everything until he was compelled by irresistible evidence to yield assent.

In this method of proceeding, what appeared to him, first of all, certain and evident was that he thought, that he doubted, that he deliberated. In a word, the operations of his own mind, of which he was conscious, must be real and no delusion; and though all his other faculties should deceive him, his consciousness could not. This, therefore, he looked upon as the first of all truths. This was the first firm ground upon which he set his foot, after being tossed in the ocean of skepticism; and he resolved to build all knowledge upon it without seeking after any more first principles.

As every other truth, therefore, and particularly the existence of the objects of sense, was to be deduced by a train of strict argumentation from what he knew by consciousness, he was naturally led to give attention to the operations of which he was conscious without borrowing his notions of them from external things.

It was not in the way of analogy, but of attentive reflection, that he was led to observe that thought, volition, remembrance, and the other attributes of the mind, are altogether unlike extension, figure, and all the attributes of body; that we have no reason, therefore, to conceive thinking substances to have any resemblance to extended substances; and that as the attributes of the thinking substance are things of which we are conscious, we may have a more certain and immediate knowledge of them by reflection than we can have of external objects by our senses.

These observations, as far as I know, were first made by Descartes. And they are of more importance and throw more light upon the subject than all that had been said upon it before. They ought to make us diffident and jealous of every notion concerning the mind and its operations which is drawn from sensible

objects in the way of analogy, and to make us rely only upon accurate reflection as the source of all real knowledge upon this subject.

2. I observe that as the Peripatetic system has a tendency to materialize the mind and its operations, so the Cartesian has a tendency to spiritualize body and its qualities. One error common to both systems leads to the first of these extremes in the way of analogy and to the last in the way of reflection. The error I mean is that we can know nothing about body or its qualities but as far as we have sensations which resemble those qualities. Both systems agreed in this, but, according to their different methods of reasoning, they drew very different conclusions from it: the Peripatetic drawing his notions of sensation from the qualities of body; the Cartesian, on the contrary, drawing his notions of the qualities of body from his sensations.

The Peripatetic, taking it for granted that bodies and their qualities do really exist and are such as we commonly take them to be, inferred from them the nature of his sensations and reasoned in this manner: Our sensations are the impressions which sensible objects make upon the mind and may be compared to the impression of a seal upon wax; the impression is the image or form of the seal, without the matter of it; in like manner, every sensation is the image or form of some sensible quality of the object. This is the reasoning of Aristotle, and it has an evident tendency to materialize the mind and its sensations.

The Cartesian, on the contrary, thinks that the existence of the body, or of any of its qualities, is not to be taken as a first principle; and that we ought to admit nothing concerning it but what, by just reasoning, can be deduced from our sensations; and he knows that by reflection we can form clear and distinct notions of our sensations without borrowing our notions of them by analogy from the objects of sense. The Cartesians, therefore, beginning to give attention to their sensations, first discovered that the sensations corresponding to secondary qualities cannot resemble any quality of body. Hence, Descartes and Locke inferred that sound, taste, smell, color, heat, and cold, which the vulgar took to be qualities of body, were not qualities of body, but mere sensations of the mind. Afterward the ingenious Berkeley, considering more attentively the nature of sensation in general, discovered and demonstrated that no sensation whatever could possibly resemble any quality of an insentient being, such as body is supposed to be; and hence he inferred very justly that there is the same reason to hold extension, figure, and all the primary qualities to be mere sensations as there is to hold the secondary qualities to be mere sensations. Thus, by just reasoning upon the Cartesian principles, matter was stripped of all its qualities; the new system, by a kind of metaphysical sublimation, converted all the qualities of matter into sensations, and spiritualized body as the old had materialized spirit.

The way to avoid both these extremes is to admit the existence of what we see and feel as a first principle, as well as the existence of things of which we are conscious; and to take our notions of the qualities of body from the testimony of our senses, with the Peripatetics; and our notions of our sensations from the testimony of consciousness, with the Cartesians.

3. I observe that the modern skepticism is the natural issue of the new system; and that, although it did not bring forth this monster until the year 1739, it may be said to have carried it in its womb from the beginning.

The old system admitted all the principles of common sense as first principles without requiring any proof of them; and, therefore, though its reasoning was commonly vague, analogical, and dark, yet it was built upon a broad foundation and had no tendency to skepticism. We do not find that any Peripatetic thought it incumbent upon him to prove the existence of a material world; but every writer upon the Cartesian system attempted this, until Berkeley clearly demonstrated the futility of their arguments, and thence concluded that there was no such thing as a material world and that the belief of it ought to be rejected as a vulgar error.

The new system admits only one of the principles of common sense as a first principle and pretends, by strict argumentation, to deduce all the rest from it. That our thoughts, our sensations, and everything of which we are conscious has a real existence, is admitted in this system as a first principle, but everything else must be made evident by the light of reason. Reason must rear the whole fabric of knowledge upon this single principle of consciousness.

There is a disposition in human nature to reduce things to as few principles as possible; and this, without doubt, adds to the beauty of a system, if the principles are able to support what rests upon them. The mathematicians glory, very justly, in having raised so noble and magnificent a system of science upon the foundation of a few axioms and definitions. This love of simplicity, of reducing things to few principles, has produced many a false system; but there never was any system in which it appears so remarkably as that of Descartes. His whole system concerning matter and spirit is built upon one axiom, expressed in one word, *cogito*. Upon the foundation of conscious thought, with ideas for his materials, he builds his system of the human understanding and attempts to account for all its phenomena; and having, as he imagined, from his consciousness, proved the existence of matter and of a certain quantity of motion originally impressed upon it, he builds his system of the material world and attempts to account for all its phenomena.

These principles, with regard to the material system, have been found insufficient; and it has been made evident that, besides matter and motion, we must admit gravitation, cohesion, and corpuscular attraction, magnetism, and other centripetal and centrifugal forces, by which the particles of matter attract and repel each other. Newton, having discovered this and demonstrated that these principles cannot be resolved into matter and motion, was led by analogy and the love of simplicity to conjecture, but with a modesty and caution peculiar to him, that all the phenomena of the material world depended upon attracting and repelling forces in the particles of matter. But we may now venture to say that this conjecture fell short of the mark. For, even in the unorganized kingdom, the powers by which salts, crystals, spars, and many other bodies concrete into regular forms can never be accounted for by attracting and repelling forces in the particles of matter. And in the vegetable and animal kingdoms, there are strong indications of powers of a different nature from all the powers of unorganized bodies. We see, then, that although in the structure of the material world there is, without doubt, all the beautiful simplicity consistent with the purposes for which it was made, it is not so simple as the great Descartes determined it to be; no, it is not so simple as the greater Newton modestly conjectured it to be. Both were misled by analogy and the love of simplicity. One had been much conversant about extension, figure, and motion; the other had enlarged his views to attracting and repelling forces; and both formed their notions of the unknown parts of nature from those with which they were acquainted. [. . .] This is a just picture of the analogical way of thinking.

But to come to the system of Descartes concerning the human understanding, it was built, as we have observed, upon consciousness as its sole foundation and with ideas as its materials; and all his followers have built upon the same foundation and with the same materials. They acknowledge that nature has given us various simple ideas. These are analogous to the matter of Descartes's physical system. They acknowledge, likewise, a natural power by which ideas are compounded, disjoined, associated, compared. This is analogous to the original quantity of motion in Descartes's physical system. From these principles they attempt to explain the phenomena of the human understanding just as in the physical system the phenomena of nature were to be explained by matter and motion. It must indeed be acknowledged that there is great simplicity in this system as well as in the other. There is such a similitude between the two as may be expected between children of the same father; but as the one has been found to be the child of Descartes, and not of nature, there is ground to think that the other is so likewise.

That the natural issue of this system is skepticism with regard to everything except the existence of our ideas and of their necessary relations which appear upon comparing them, is evident, for ideas being the only objects of thought and having no existence but when we are conscious of them, it necessarily follows that there is no object of our thought which can have a continued and permanent existence. Body and spirit, cause and effect, time and space, to which we were wont to ascribe an existence independent of our thought, are all turned out of existence by this short dilemma: Either these things are ideas of sensation or reflection or they are not; if they are ideas of sensation or reflection, they can have no existence but when we are conscious of them; if they are not ideas of sensation or reflection, they are words without any meaning.

Neither Descartes nor Locke perceived this consequence of their system concerning ideas. Bishop Berkeley was the first who discovered it. And what followed upon this discovery? Why, with regard to the material world and with regard to space and time, he admits the consequence that these things are mere ideas and have no existence but in our minds, but with regard to the existence of spirits or minds, he does not admit the consequence; and if he had admitted it, he must have been an absolute skeptic. But how does he evade this consequence with regard to the existence of spirits? The expedient which the good bishop uses on this occasion is very remarkable and shows his great aversion to skepticism. He maintains that we have no ideas of spirits; and that we can think, and speak, and reason about them, and about their attributes, without having any ideas of them. If this is so, my lord, what should hinder us from thinking and reasoning about bodies and their qualities without having ideas of them? The bishop either did not think of this question or did not think fit to give any answer to it. However, we may observe that, in order to avoid skepticism, he fairly starts out of the Cartesian system, without giving any reason why he did so in this instance and in no other. This, indeed, is the only instance of a deviation from Cartesian principles which I have met with in the successors of Descartes, and it seems to have been only a sudden start, occasioned by the terror of skepticism; for in all other things Berkeley's system is founded upon Cartesian principles.

Thus we see that Descartes and Locke take the road that leads to skepticism without knowing the end of it; but they stop short for want of light to carry them farther. Berkeley, frightened at the appearance of the dreadful abyss, starts aside and avoids it. But the author of the *Treatise of Human Nature,* more daring and intrepid, without turning aside to the right hand or to the left, like Virgil's *Alecto,* shoots directly into the gulf. [. . .]

4. We may observe that the account given by the new system of that furniture of the human understanding which is the gift of nature, and not the

acquisition of our own reasoning faculty, is extremely lame and imperfect.

The natural furniture of the human understanding is of two kinds: first, the *notions* or simple apprehensions which we have of things; and, secondly, the *judgments* or the belief which we have concerning them. As to our notions, the new system reduces them to two classes—*ideas of sensation* and *ideas of reflection*—the first are conceived to be copies of our sensations, retained in the memory or imagination; the second to be copies of the operations of our minds whereof we are conscious, in like manner retained in the memory or imagination; and we are taught that these two comprehend all the materials about which the human understanding is or can be employed. As to our judgment of things, or the belief which we have concerning them, the new system allows no part of it to be the gift of nature, but holds it to be the acquisition of reason and to be gotten by comparing our ideas and perceiving their agreements or disagreements. Now I take this account, both of our notions and of our judgments or belief, to be extremely imperfect; and I shall briefly point out some of its capital defects.

The division of our notions into ideas of sensation and ideas of reflection is contrary to all rules of logic, because the second member of the division includes the first. For, can we form clear and just notions of our sensations any other way than by reflection? Surely we cannot. Sensation is an operation of the mind of which we are conscious; and we get the notion of sensation by reflecting upon that which we are conscious of. In like manner, doubting and believing are operations of the mind whereof we are conscious; and we get the notion of them by reflecting upon what we are conscious of. The ideas of sensation, therefore, are ideas of reflection as much as the ideas of doubting, or believing, or any other ideas whatsoever.

But to pass over the inaccuracy of this division, it is extremely incomplete. For, since sensation is an operation of the mind as well as all the other things of which we form our notions by reflection, when it is asserted that all our notions are either ideas of sensation or ideas of reflection, the plain English of this is that mankind neither do nor can think of

anything but of the operations of their own minds. Nothing can be more contrary to truth or more contrary to the experience of mankind. I know that Locke, while he maintained this doctrine, believed the notions which we have of body and of its qualities and the notions which we have of motion and of space to be ideas of sensation. But why did he believe this? Because he believed those notions to be nothing else but images of our sensations. If, therefore, the notions of body and its qualities, of motion and space, are not images of our sensations, will it not follow that those notions are not ideas of sensation? Most certainly.

There is no doctrine in the new system which more directly leads to skepticism than this. And the author of the *Treatise of Human Nature* knew very well how to use it for that purpose: For if you maintain that there is any such existence as body or spirit, time or place, cause or effect, he immediately catches you between the horns of this dilemma; your notions of these existences are either ideas of sensation or ideas of reflection: If of sensation, from what sensation are they copied? If of reflection, from what operations of the mind are they copied?

It is indeed to be wished that those who have written much about sensation and about the other operations of the mind had likewise thought and reflected much, and with great care, upon those operations; but is it not very strange that they will not allow it to be possible for mankind to think of anything else?

The account which this system gives of our judgment and belief concerning things is as far from the truth as the account it gives of our notions or simple apprehensions. It represents our senses as having no other office but that of furnishing the mind with notions or simple apprehensions of things and makes our judgment and belief concerning those things to be acquired by comparing our notions together and perceiving their agreements or disagreements.

We have shown, on the contrary, that every operation of the senses, in its very nature, implies judgment or belief as well as simple apprehension. Thus, when I feel the pain of the gout in my toe, I have not only a notion of pain, but a belief of its existence and a belief of some disorder in my toe which occasions it; and this belief is not produced by comparing ideas and perceiving their agreements and disagreements; it is included in the very nature of the sensation. When I perceive a tree before me, my faculty of seeing gives me not only a notion or simple apprehension of the tree, but a belief of its existence, and of its figure, distance, and magnitude; and this judgment or belief is not gotten by comparing ideas; it is included in the very nature of the perception. We have taken notice of several original principles of belief in the course of this *Inquiry*; and when other faculties of the mind are examined, we shall find more which have not occurred in the examination of the five senses.

Such original and natural judgments are therefore a part of that furniture which nature has given to the human understanding. They are the inspiration of the Almighty, no less than our notions of simple apprehensions. They serve to direct us in the common affairs of life, where our reasoning faculty would leave us in the dark. They are a part of our constitution, and all the discoveries of our reason are grounded upon them. They make up what is called *the common sense of mankind*; and what is manifestly contrary to any of those first principles is what we call *absurd*. The strength of them is *good sense*, which is often found in those who are not acute in reasoning. A remarkable deviation from them, arising from a disorder in the constitution, is what we call *lunacy*—as when a man believes that he is made of glass. When a man suffers himself to be reasoned out of the principles of common sense by *metaphysical arguments*, we may call this *metaphysical lunacy*, which differs from the other species of the distemper in this, that it is not continued, but intermittent—it is apt to seize the patient in solitary and speculative moments; but when he enters into society, common sense recovers her authority. A clear explication and enumeration of the principles of common sense is one of the chief *desiderata* in logic. We have only considered such of them as occurred in the examination of the five senses.

5. The last observation that I shall make upon the new system is that, although it professes to set out in the way of reflection and not of analogy, it has retained some of the old analogical notions concerning the operations of the mind, particularly, that things which do not now exist in the mind itself can only be perceived, remembered, or imagined by means of ideas or images of them in the mind, which are the immediate objects of perception, remembrance, and imagination. This doctrine appears evidently to be borrowed from the old system, which taught that external things make impressions upon the mind like the impressions of a seal upon wax; that it is by means of those impressions that we perceive, remember, or imagine them; and that those impressions must resemble the things from which they are taken. When we form our notions of the operations of the mind by analogy, this way of conceiving them seems to be very natural and offers itself to our thoughts, for, as everything which is felt must make some impression upon the body, we are apt to think that everything which is understood must make some impression upon the mind.

From such analogical reasoning this opinion of the existence of ideas or images of things in the mind seems to have taken its rise and to have been so universally received among philosophers. It was observed already that Berkeley, in one instance, apostatizes from this principle of the new system by affirming that we have no ideas of spirits and that we can think of them immediately without ideas. But I do not know whether in this he has had any followers. There is some difference likewise among modern philosophers with regard to the ideas or images by which we perceive, remember, or imagine sensible things. For though all agree in the existence of such images, they differ about their place, some placing them in a particular part of the brain where the soul is thought to have her residence and others placing them in the mind itself. Descartes held the first of these opinions, to which Newton seems likewise to have inclined. [. . .] But Locke seems to place the ideas of sensible things in the mind, and that Berkeley and the author of the *Treatise of Human Nature* were of the same opinion is evident. The last makes a very curious application of this doctrine by endeavoring to prove from it that the mind either is no substance or that it is an extended and divisible substance, because the ideas of extension cannot be in a subject which is indivisible and unextended.

I confess I think his reasoning in this, as in most cases, is clear and strong. For whether the idea of extension is only another name for extension itself, as Berkeley and this author assert, or whether the idea of extension is an image and resemblance of extension, as Locke conceived, I appeal to any man of common sense whether extension, or any image of extension, can be in an unextended and indivisible subject. But while I agree with him in his reasoning, I would make a different application of it. He takes it for granted that there are ideas of extension in the mind and thence infers that if it is at all a substance, it must be an extended and divisible substance. On the contrary, I take it for granted, upon the testimony of common sense, that my mind is a substance, that is, a permanent subject of thought, and my reason convinces me that it is an unextended and indivisible substance; and hence I infer that there cannot be in it anything that resembles extension. If this reasoning had occurred to Berkeley, it would probably have led him to acknowledge that we may think and reason concerning bodies without having ideas of them in the mind, as well as concerning spirits.

I intended to have examined more particularly and fully this doctrine of the existence of ideas or images of things in the mind; and likewise another doctrine, which is founded upon it, namely, that judgment or belief is nothing but a perception of the agreement or disagreement of our ideas, but having already shown, through the course of this inquiry, that the operations of the mind which we have examined give no countenance to either of these doctrines and in many things contradict them, I have thought it proper to drop this part of my design. It may be executed with more advantage, if it is at all necessary, after inquiring into some other powers of the human understanding.

Although we have examined only the five senses and the principles of the human mind which are employed about them, or such as have fallen in our way in the course of this examination, we shall leave the further prosecution of this inquiry to future deliberation. The powers of memory, of imagination, of taste, of reasoning, of moral perception, the will, the passions, the affections, and all the active powers of the soul present a vast and boundless field of philosophical disquisition, which the author of this inquiry is far from thinking himself able to survey with accuracy. Many authors of ingenuity, ancient and modern, have made excursions into this vast territory and have communicated useful observations, but there is reason to believe that those who have pretended to give us a map of the whole have satisfied themselves with a very inaccurate and incomplete survey. If Galileo had attempted a complete system of natural philosophy, he had, probably, done little service to mankind, but by confining himself to what was within his comprehension, he laid the foundation of a system of knowledge which rises by degrees and does honor to the human understanding. Newton, building upon this foundation and, in like manner, confining his inquiries to the law of gravitation and the properties of light, performed wonders. If he had attempted a great deal more, he would have done a great deal less, and perhaps nothing at all. Ambitious of following such great examples, with unequal steps—alas!— and unequal force, we have attempted an inquiry only into one little corner of the human mind, that corner which seems to be most exposed to vulgar observation and to be most easily comprehended; and yet, if we have delineated it justly, it must be acknowledged that the accounts previously given of it were very lame and wide of the truth.

Essays on the Intellectual Powers of Man, "Of Judgment," chap. 2, Of Common Sense.

The word *sense*, in common language, seems to have a different meaning from that which it has in the writings of philosophers; and those different meanings are apt to be confounded and to occasion embarrassment and error.

Not to go back to ancient philosophy upon this point, modern philosophers consider sense as a power that has nothing to do with judgment—as the power by which we compare those ideas and perceive their necessary agreements and disagreements.

The external senses give us the idea of color, figure, sound, and other qualities of body, primary or secondary. Mr. Locke gave the name of an internal sense to consciousness, because by it we have the idea of thought, memory, reasoning, and other operations of our own minds. Dr. Hutcheson of Glasgow, conceiving that we have simple and original ideas which cannot be imputed either to the external senses or to consciousness, introduced other internal senses such as the sense of harmony, the sense of beauty, and the moral sense. Ancient philosophers also spoke of internal senses, of which memory was accounted one.

But all these senses, whether external or internal, have been represented by philosophers as the means of furnishing our minds with ideas, without including any kind of judgment. Dr. Hutcheson defines a sense to be a determination of the mind to receive any idea from the presence of an object independent on our will.

"By this term, sense, philosophers in general have denominated those faculties, in consequence of which we are liable to feelings relative to ourselves only, and from which they have not pretended to draw any conclusions concerning the nature of things; whereas truth is not relative, but absolute, and real." *Dr. Priestly's Examination of Dr. Reid . . .,* p. 123.

On the contrary, in common language, sense always implies judgment. A man of sense is a man of judgment. Good sense is good judgment which is common to men with whom we can converse and transact business.

Seeing and hearing, by philosophers are called senses because we have ideas by them; by the vulgar they are called senses because we judge by them. We judge of colors by the eye; of sounds by the ear; of beauty and deformity by taste; of right and wrong in conduct by our moral sense, or conscience.

Sometimes philosophers, who represent it as the sole province of sense to furnish us with ideas, fall unawares into the popular opinion that they are judging faculties. Thus Locke, book 4. chap. 11: "And of this, that the quality or accident of color does really exist, and has a being without me, the greatest assurance I can possibly have and to which my faculties can attain is the testimony of my eyes, which are the proper and sole judge of this thing."

This popular meaning of the word *sense* is not peculiar to the English language. The corresponding words in Greek, Latin, and I believe in all the European languages have the same latitude. The Latin words *sentire, sententia, sensa, sensus,* from the last of which the English word *sense* is borrowed, express judgment or opinion and are applied indifferently to objects of external sense, of taste, of morals, and of the understanding.

I cannot pretend to assign the reason why a word which is no term of art, which is familiar in common conversation, should have so different a meaning in philosophical writings. I shall only observe that the philosophical meaning corresponds perfectly with the account which Mr. Locke and other modern philosophers give of judgment. For if the sole province of the senses, external and internal, is to furnish the mind with the ideas about which we judge and reason, it seems to be a natural consequence that the sole province of judgment should be to compare those ideas and to perceive their necessary relations.

These two opinions seem to be so connected that one may have been the cause of the other. I apprehend, however, that if both are true, there is no room left for any knowledge or judgment, either of the real existence of contingent things or of their contingent relations.

To return to the poplar meaning of the word *sense,* I believe it would be much more difficult to find good authors who never use it in that meaning, than to find such as do.

We may take Mr. Pope as good authority for the meaning of an English word. He uses it often and, in his epistle to the Earl of Burlington, has made a little descant upon it.

Oft have you hinted to your brother Peers
A certain truth, which many buy too dear;
Something there is more needful than expense,
And something previous ev'n to taste,—'tis sense,
Good sense, which only is the gift of Heaven;
And though no science, fairly worth the seven;
A light, which in yourself you must perceive,
Jones and Le Notre have it not to give.

This inward light or sense is given by Heaven to different persons in different degrees. There is a certain degree of it which is necessary to our being subjects of law and government, capable of managing our own affairs and answerable for our conduct toward others. This is called common sense, because it is common to all men with whom we can transact business or call to account for their conduct.

The laws of all civilized nations distinguish those

who have this gift of Heaven from those who have it not. The last may have rights which ought not to be violated, but having no understanding in themselves to direct their actions, the laws appoint them to be guided by the understanding of others. It is easily discerned by its effects in men's actions, in their speeches, and even in their looks; and when it is made a question, whether a man has this natural gift or not, a judge or a jury, upon a short conversation with him, can for the most part determine the question with great assurance.

The same degree of understanding which makes a man capable of acting with common prudence in the conduct of life makes him capable of discovering what is true and what is false in matters that are self-evident and which he distinctly apprehends.

All knowledge and all science must be built upon principles that are self-evident; and of such principles every man who has common sense is a competent judge when he conceives them distinctly. Hence it is that disputes very often terminate in an appeal to common sense.

While the parties agree in the first principles on which their arguments are grounded, there is room for reasoning; but when one denies what to the other appears too evident to need, or to admit of proof, reasoning seems to be at an end; and appeal is made to common sense, and each party is left to enjoy his own opinion.

There seems to be no remedy for this nor any way left to discuss such appeals, unless the decisions of common sense can be brought into a code in which all reasonable men shall acquiesce. This indeed, if it is possible, would be very desirable and would supply a desideratum in logic; and why should it be thought impossible that reasonable men should agree in things that are self-evident?

All that is intended in this chapter is to explain the meaning of common sense, that it may not be treated, as it has been by some, as a new principle or as a word without any meaning. I have endeavored to show that sense, in its most common and therefore its most proper meaning, signifies judgment, though philosophers often use it in another meaning. From this it is natural to think that common sense should mean common *judgment*; and so it really does.

What the precise limits are which divide common judgment from what is beyond it, on the one hand, and from what falls short of it, on the other, may be difficult to determine; and men may agree in the meaning of the word who have different opinions about those limits, or who even never thought of fixing them. This is as intelligible as that all Englishmen should mean the same thing by the county of York, though perhaps not a hundredth part of them can point out its precise limits.

Indeed, it seems to me that *common sense* is as unambiguous a word, and as well understood, as the *county of York*. We find it in innumerable places in good writers; we hear it on innumerable occasions in conversation, and, as far as I am able to judge, always in the same meaning. And this is probably the reason why it is so seldom defined or explained. [. . .]

From the account I have given of the meaning of this term, it is easy to judge both of the proper use and of the abuse of it.

It is absurd to conceive that there can be any opposition between reason and common sense. It is, indeed, the first born of reason, and, as they are commonly joined together in speech and in writing, they are inseparable in their nature.

We ascribe to reason two offices, or two degrees. The first is to judge of things self-evident; the second, to draw conclusions that are not self-evident from those that are. The first of these is the province, and the sole province, of common sense; and therefore it coincides with reason in its whole extent and is only another name for one branch or one degree of reason. Perhaps it may be said, Why then should you give it a particular name, since it is acknowledged to be only a degree of reason? It would be sufficient answer to this, Why do you abolish a name which is to be found in the language of all civilized nations and has acquired a right by prescription? Such an attempt is equally foolish and ineffectual. Every wise man will be apt to think that a name which is found in all languages as far back as we can trace them is not without some use.

But there is an obvious reason why this degree of reason should have a name appropriated to it; and that is, that in the greatest part of mankind no other degree of reason is to be found. It is this degree that entitles them to the denomination of reasonable creatures. It is this degree of reason, and this only, that makes a man capable of managing his own affairs and answerable for his conduct toward others. There is, therefore, the best reason why it should have a name appropriated to it.

These two degrees of reason differ in other respects, which would be sufficient to entitle them to distinct names.

The first is purely the gift of Heaven. And where Heaven has not given it, no education can supply the lack. The second is learned by practice and rules, when the first is not wanting. A man who has common sense may be taught to reason. But if he has not that gift, no teaching will make him able either to judge of first principles or to reason from them.

I have only this further to observe, that the province of common sense is more extensive in refutation than in confirmation. A conclusion drawn by a train of just reasoning from true principles cannot possibly contradict any decision of common sense, because truth will always be consistent with itself. Neither can such a conclusion receive any confirmation from common sense, because it is not within its jurisdiction.

But it is possible that by setting out from false principles or by an error in reasoning, a man may be led to a conclusion that contradicts the decision of common sense. In this case, the conclusion is within the jurisdiction of common sense, though the reasoning on which it was grounded is not; and a man of common sense may fairly reject the conclusion without being able to show the error of the reasoning that led to it.

Thus, if a mathematician, by a process of intricate demonstration in which some false step was made, should be brought to this conclusion, that two quantities which are both equal to a third are not equal to each other, a man of common sense, without pretending to be a judge of the demonstration, is well entitled to reject the conclusion and to pronounce it absurd.